An Interdisciplinary Approach to Computer Science and Technology

An Interdisciplinary Approach to Computer Science and Technology

Edited by Tom Halt

CLANRYE
INTERNATIONAL
www.clanryeinternational.com

Clanrye International,
750 Third Avenue, 9th Floor,
New York, NY 10017, USA

ISBN: 978-1-63240-700-9

Cataloging-in-Publication Data

An interdisciplinary approach to computer science and technology / edited by Tom Halt.
    p. cm.
Includes bibliographical references and index.
ISBN 978-1-63240-700-9
1. Computer science. 2. Information technology. 3. Interdisciplinary approach to knowledge. I. Halt, Tom.
QA76 .I58 2018
004--dc23

For information on all Clanrye International publications
visit our website at www.clanryeinternational.com

Contents

Permissions

List of Contributors

Index

Preface

The main aim of this book is to educate learners and enhance their research focus by presenting diverse topics covering this vast field. This is an advanced book which compiles significant studies by distinguished experts in the area of analysis. This book addresses successive solutions to the challenges arising in the area of application, along with it; the book provides scope for future developments.

Computer science is a fast growing field and has occupied an important place in today's time. The subject of computer science studies the theories and experiments used in building new designs of computers. The two main areas of computer science are theoretical computer science and applied computer science. This book studies, analyses and upholds the pillars of computer science and related technology. A number of latest researches have been included to keep the readers up-to-date with the global concepts in this area of study.

It was a great honour to edit this book, though there were challenges, as it involved a lot of communication and networking between me and the editorial team. However, the end result was this all-inclusive book covering diverse themes in the field.

Finally, it is important to acknowledge the efforts of the contributors for their excellent chapters, through which a wide variety of issues have been addressed. I would also like to thank my colleagues for their valuable feedback during the making of this book.

Editor

Identification of Different Varieties of Sesame Oil Using Near-Infrared Hyperspectral Imaging and Chemometrics Algorithms

Chuanqi Xie, Qiaonan Wang, Yong He*

College of Biosystems Engineering and Food Science, Zhejiang University, Hangzhou, China

Abstract

This study investigated the feasibility of using near infrared hyperspectral imaging (NIR-HSI) technique for non-destructive identification of sesame oil. Hyperspectral images of four varieties of sesame oil were obtained in the spectral region of 874–1734 nm. Reflectance values were extracted from each region of interest (ROI) of each sample. Competitive adaptive reweighted sampling (CARS), successive projections algorithm (SPA) and x-loading weights (x-LW) were carried out to identify the most significant wavelengths. Based on the sixty-four, seven and five wavelengths suggested by CARS, SPA and x-LW, respectively, two classified models (least squares-support vector machine, LS-SVM and linear discriminant analysis,LDA) were established. Among the established models, CARS-LS-SVM and CARS-LDA models performed well with the highest classification rate (100%) in both calibration and prediction sets. SPA-LS-SVM and SPA-LDA models obtained better results (95.59% and 98.53% of classification rate in prediction set) with only seven wavelengths (938, 1160, 1214, 1406, 1656, 1659 and 1663 nm). The x-LW-LS-SVM and x-LW-LDA models also obtained satisfactory results (>80% of classification rate in prediction set) with the only five wavelengths (921, 925, 995, 1453 and 1663 nm). The results showed that NIR-HSI technique could be used to identify the varieties of sesame oil rapidly and non-destructively, and CARS, SPA and x-LW were effective wavelengths selection methods.

Editor: Xi-Nian Zuo, Institute of Psychology, Chinese Academy of Sciences, China

Funding: This work was supported by 863 National High-Tech Research and Development Plan (Project No: 2012AA101903), Ningbo Department of Science and Technology (2011C11024) and the Fundamental Research Funds for the Central Universities of China (2012FZA6005, 2013QNA6011). The funders had no role in study design, data collection and analysis, decision to publish, or preparation of the manuscript.

Competing Interests: The authors have declared that no competing interests exist.

* E-mail: yhe@zju.edu.cn

Introduction

Sesame oil, which contains high nutrient value such as unsaturated fatty acid and vitamin E, is welcome by many people [1]. It includes 43% oleic and linoleic each, 9% palmitic and 4% stearic fatty acids [2]. Eating sesame oil can control blood cholesterol level [3], prevent atherosclerosis [4] and reduce the risks of heart attack, arteriosclerosis and cancer [5]. The variety is one of the most important factors that strongly associated with the quality features of sesame oil. Different varieties own different levels of nutrient values. Because of the great economic benefit of sesame oil, some unscrupulous traders used low value of sesame oil or illegal cooking oil to pretend to be high value of edible oil in recent years. The counterfeit sesame oil has not only harmed the consumers' economy interests but also throw a threat to the people's health. Therefore, in order to guarantee and promote high quality sesame oil produced, the identification of the variety of sesame oil is extremely essential.

The most conventional method to discriminate varieties of oil is the physical-chemical technique. Although the obtained result by using this technique is accurate, it must be pointed out that there were limitations for the method. For example, it is time-consuming, inefficient and destructive, and it requires a professional highly trained and qualified. Moreover, it cannot be used in

on-line identification, in the industry. Thus, an advanced method to identify the varieties of sesame oil is in urgent need.

At present, spectral technique has been used for identification the oil [6], [7], [8]. Compared to the physical-chemical method mentioned above, spectral technique has many advantages such as fast, nondestructive, low cost and accurate. However, to identify the varieties of sesame oil is not usually found, especially using hyperspectral imaging technique. Near infrared hyperspectral imaging (NIR-HSI) integrates both spectral and imaging techniques together. NIR-HIS technique has already been widely studied in many fields due to its advantages [9], [10], [11]. By hyperspectral imaging system, one pixel of each hyperspectral image has a wavelength covering the whole spectral range. Finally, a spatial map (hyperspectral cube), which is composed of a series of images at each wavelength, is generated (Figure 1).

The aim of this study was carried out to develop a method to identify the varieties of sesame oil by using NIR-HSI technique based on spectral information. The objectives of this work were: (1) to find the quantitative relationships between the spectral information and the varieties of sesame oil; (2) to select effective wavelengths that are useful for the identification of varieties of sesame oil by CARS, SPA and x-LW, respectively; (3) to compare the performance of different identification models; (4) to identify the optimal calibration model for the identification of the varieties of sesame oil.

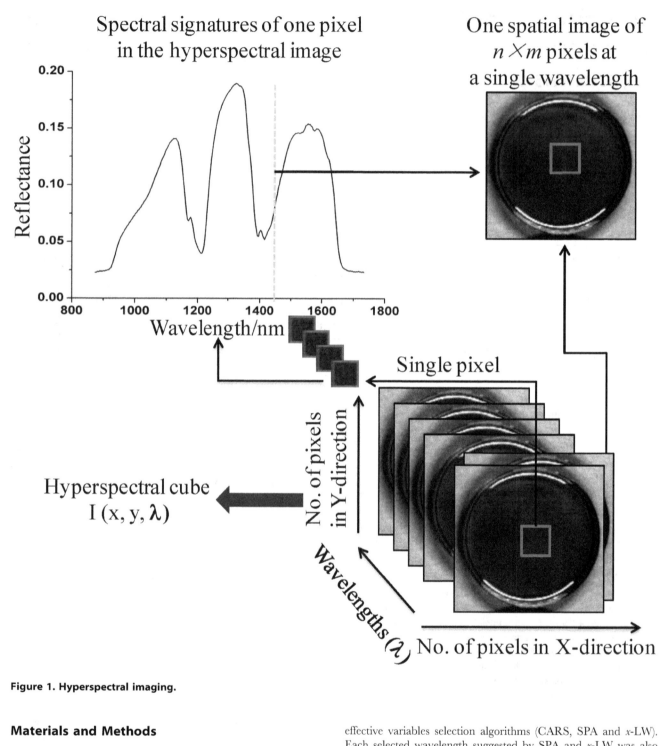

Figure 1. Hyperspectral imaging.

Materials and Methods

Flow of the study

The main steps of the whole procedures can be described as follows. Raw hyperspectral images of the four varieties of sesame oil were obtained by the NIR-HSI system across the wavelength region of 874–1734 nm in the first step. The raw hyperspectral images were corrected by equation (1), and the reflectance information of ROI of the corrected hyperspectral images was extracted to be treated as X variables. The samples were divided into calibration set and prediction set with the ratio of 2:1. Identification models were then established based on full spectral wavelengths and selected wavelengths recommended by several effective variables selection algorithms (CARS, SPA and x-LW). Each selected wavelength suggested by SPA and x-LW was also used to establish identification model. Optimal identification model was selected by comparison in terms of the identification power (correct classification rate, CCR). Finally, identification of different varieties of sesame oil was achieved by the model.

Hyperspectral imaging system and software

A near infrared hyperspectral imaging (NIR-HSI) system in the spectral range of 874–1734 nm was used as shown in Figure 2. The system contains a lens, an imaging spectrograph (N17E, Specim, Finland), a light source (Oriel Instruments, Irvine, Cal.) that included two 150 W quartz tungsten halogen lamps, a conveyor belt operated by a stepper motor (IRCP0076, Isuzu Optics Corp, Taiwan, China) and a computer. The area CCD array detector of the camera has 320×256 (spatial ×spectral) pixels, and the spectral resolution is 5 nm. The NIR-HSI system scans the sample line by line, and the reflected light was dispersed by the spectrograph and captured by the area CCD array detector in spatial-spectral($x\times\lambda$) axes. The ENVI 4.7 software (Research system Inc, Boulder, Co.USA), Unscrambler 9.7 software (Camo, Process, As, Oslo, Norway) and MATLAB R2009a (The Math Works, Natick, USA) software were used to preprocess the raw spectral information and establish identification models in this study.

Samples

Four varieties of sesame oil including Huiyi, Liuyanghe, Taitaile and Xiaomo which been usually found in China, were purchased in the local market. Then, a volume of 60 ml of each variety of the sesame oil was evenly distributed in glass dishes of the same size (d = 90 mm). Each dish was then imaged individually by the NIR-HSI system. There were a total of 50 samples (50 glass dishes) of each variety.

Image acquisition and correction

Each glass dish was placed on the conveyor belt to be scanned line by line by using the NIR-HSI system. The moving speed was set as 25 mm/sec and exposure time was 5 ms. Each hyperspectral image was obtained by using the imaging spectrograph of N17E across the wavelength region of 874–1734 nm. A raw hyperspectral image (hyperspectral cube) with a dimension of (x, y, λ) was created as the sample was scanned along the direction of the ydimension. The dimension of the hyperspectral cube was 320 pixels in ydimension and 256 bands in λ dimension. When the raw hyperspectral image was generated, it should be corrected into the reference hyperspectral image with black and white reference images based on the equation (1). The black reference image with the reflectance factor of 0% was obtained by turning off the light and keeping the lens being covered of its cap. The white one was obtained from a white Teflon board (CAL-tile200, 200 mm×25 mm×10 mm) with the reflectance factor of about 99%.

$$R = \frac{I - B}{W - B} \quad (1)$$

Where R is the corrected hyperspectral image, I is the raw hyperspectral image, B is the black reference image, W is the white reference image.

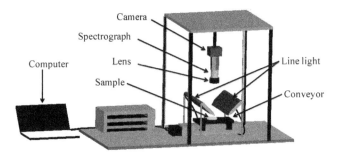

Figure 2. Schematic diagram of the NIR hyperspectral imaging system.

Data acquisition

An area with 25×25 pixels which was treated as the ROI (region of interest) was cropped from the center of each corrected hyperspectral image (each sample), resulting in a total of 200 samples of the four varieties of sesame oil. Reflectance values of all pixels of ROI were acquired by ENVI4.7 software. These spectral features were calculated via MATLAB R2009a software for establishing calibration model to identify different varieties of sesame oil.

A total of 33 samples were randomly picked out from each variety, which resulted in 132 samples of calibration set and 68 ones of prediction set [12]. The statistical information of each set was shown in Table 1.

Calibration models

Least squares-support vector machine (LS-SVM), which has been widely used in many aspects [13], [14], can deal with both linear and nonlinear multivariate calibration problems [15]. A set of linear equations instead of a quadratic programming (QP) problem was applied in order to obtain the support vectors (SV) [16]. The radial basis function (RBF) was used in this study due to its excellent performance compared with other kernels. The LS-SVM algorithm could be described as follows:

$$y(x) = \sum_{k=1}^{N} \alpha_k K(x,x_k) + b \quad (2)$$

Where α_i are Lagrange multipliers, $K(x,x_i)$ is the kernel function, b is the bias value.

The regularization parameter *gam (γ)* was used to determine the tradeoff between minimizing the training error and minimizing model complexity, and the width parameter *sig2 (σ^2)* was used to defined the nonlinear mapping from input space to high-dimensional feature space [17]. The optimal parameter values of (γ, σ^2) were calculated by grid search in this study. They were calculated by the free LS-SVM toolbox (LS-SVM v1.5, Suykens, Leuven, Belgium) in MATLAB R2009a.

Linear discriminant analysis (LDA) is a supervised recognition method used in statistics, pattern recognition and machine learning in order to find a linear combination of features that separate two or more classes of objects [18]. The principle of LDA for selection of latent variables is the maximum differentiation between the varieties and minimizes the variance within varieties. This algorithm produces a number of orthogonal linear discriminant functions, which allow the samples to be classified in one or another category [19].

Effective wavelengths selection

The spectral information, which was acquired in the spectral region of 874 to 1734 nm, was characterized by high dimensionality with redundancy among contiguous wavelengths [20]. Therefore, the selection of effective wavelengths is a significant step in spectral studies [21]. The goal of effective wavelengths selection is to identify a subset of spectral features as smaller as possible to replace the full wavelengths for identification of different samples. The selected wavelengths can be equally or more efficient than the full spectral wavelengths [22]. Moreover, they cannot only reduce the dimensionality of raw data but also be used to develop the multispectral imaging identification system.

Competitive adaptive reweighted sampling (CARS) is an effective wavelengths selection algorithm. It selects effective wavelengths on the basis of the "survival of the fittest" principle.

Table 1. Statistical information of calibration and prediction sets.

Data sets	Huiyi	Liuyanghe	Taitaile	Xiaomo	Total
Calibration set	33	33	33	33	132
Prediction set	17	17	17	17	68
Total	50	50	50	50	200

Firstly, it removes the wavelengths that are of small regression coefficients by exponentially decreasing function (EDF). Then, the ratio of wavelengths is calculated by an EDF equation [23]. The steps of each sampling run can be described as follows [24], [25]: (a) model sampling using Monte Carlo (MC) principle; (b) wavelengths selection based on EDF; (c) competitive wavelength selection by using adaptive reweighted sampling (ARS); (d) evaluation of the subset using cross validation. Finally, wavelengths that are of little or no effective information are eliminated while effective wavelengths are retained.

Successive projections algorithm (SPA), which aims to solve the collinear problems by selecting optimal variables with minimal redundancy, has been widely used in many fields [26], [27]. It uses a projection operation in a vector space for selecting key wavelengths with small collinearity [28].

In this study, x-loading weights (x-LW) were also used to select the most effective wavelengths for identification of varieties of sesame oil. It represents how much of each wavelength contributes to the variety variation in the data. The x-loading weights show how much of each wavelength contributes to explaining the response variation. Wavelengths with high loading weight values are significant for the varieties classification, and wavelengths with low loading weight values are not important [29]. Thus, the wavelengths with high absolute values of loading weight were considered as the key wavelengths while the low absolute values were rejected [30].

Results and Discussion

Spectral feature of tested samples

The spectral reflectance curves of the four varieties of sesame oil were shown in Figure 3. Specifically, general trends of spectral curves of the four varieties of samples were similar with some spectral noise at the beginning and ending of the wavelengths. To eliminate noises and establish robust models, wavelengths at beginning and ending were rejected, resulting in spectral wavelengths from 921 to 1663 nm (bands 15 to 235) were used for further studies. Additionally, there were some strong absorption peaks, which were assigned to the functional groups such as C-H, C-C, C-N, C=O and O-H. However, there were no obvious differences among the spectral curves of the four varieties, which indicated that sesame oil could not be identified from spectral curves directly. In order to identify the varieties effectively, classification models based on chemometrics should be established.

Identification model based on full wavelengths

In this study, identification model (LS-SVM) was first established based on full spectral wavelengths (821–1663 nm). The reflectance values extracted from ROI of hyperspectral image were treated as X variables, and the varieties were treated as Y variables (Huiyi-1, Liuyanghe-2, Taitaile-3, Xiaomo-4). The LS-SVM model obtained a satisfying result with the classification rate of 100% in the calibration set and 98.53% in prediction set.

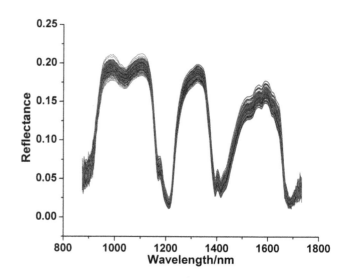

Figure 3. Spectral reflectance curves of the four different varieties of sesame oil.

However, the input variables were too much, which will affect the robust and accurate of the discriminated model, increase the calculation time and could not be used in practical industry. Thus, several effective wavelengths selection methods were used to select key wavelengths for establishing simplified models.

Effective wavelengths

Effective wavelengths recommended by CARS. In order to improve the performance of the identified ability and simplify the calibration model, CARS was firstly carried out to select effective wavelengths from the whole spectral wavelengths. It can be found in Figure 4 that the changing trend of the number of sampled variables (a), 10-fold *RMSECV* values (b) and the regression coefficient of each variable (c) with the increasing of sampling runs. In Figure 4 (a), it could be seen that the number of sampled variables decreased fast in the first step and slowly in the second step. In Figure 4 (b), the value of *RMSECV* firstly decreased which indicates the uninformative variables were eliminated, and then changed slightly which means variables do not change obviously, finally increased which is caused by the elimination of some key variables. In Figure 4 (c), each line represents the coefficient of each variable at different sampling runs. Some variables were extracted in each sampling run, and the optimal variables with the lowest value of *RMSECV* were marked by the vertical asterisk line. After the asterisk line, the value of *RMSECV* increased which owes to the removing of some effective wavelengths. The value of *RMSECV* sharply rose up to a higher stage at the point of dot line L1 because one variable (P1) dropped

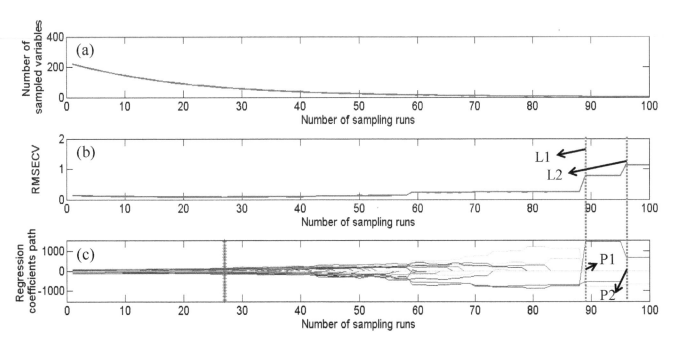

Figure 4. The changing trend of the number of sampled variables (a), 10-fold RMSECV values (b) and regression coefficients of each variable (c) with the increasing of sampling runs. The line (marked by asterisk).

to zero. A same case is that a sharp rising of the value of *RMSECV* (L2) which was caused by another variable (P2) dropping to zero. In the CARS calculation, some variables were eliminated while some key variables were retained. As a result, sixty-four wavelengths were identified as the optimal wavelengths which were shown in Table 2. The number of selected variables was only 28.96% of that of the whole wavebands (Band15-Band235). These wavelengths were then used to replace the full wavelengths for identification of sesame oil. They were extremely relevant for the identification of sesame oil. The spectral data set was reduced to a matrix with a dimension of $m \times x$, where m was the number of samples and x was the number of selected wavelengths.

Key wavelengths selected by SPA. SPA algorithm was also carried out to select effective wavelengths from full wavelengths in this study. As a result, seven wavelengths (938, 1160, 1214, 1406, 1656, 1659 and 1663 nm) were identified as the optimal wavelengths which were shown in Figure 5. The selected wavelengths were used to replace the full wavelengths for identification of different varieties. The spectral dataset was reduced to a matrix with a dimension of 200×7 (200 was the number of samples and 7 was the number of selected wavelengths). Then, LS-SVM and LDA models based on the seven selected wavelengths was established.

Key wavelengths selected by x-LW. Effective wavelengths for varieties classification were conducted based on x-loading weights. It can be seen in Figure 6 that the loading weights and

explanation of X and Y variations. The number of loading weights was automatically determined by Unscrambler 9.7 software based on the minimum value of the predicted residual error sum of squares (PRESS) by full cross validation. The first six loading weights explained 99% of spectral variances and 97% of

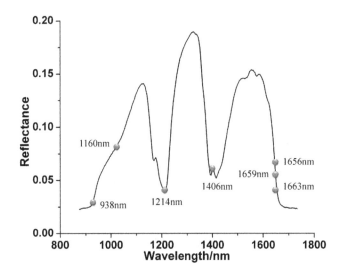

Figure 5. Effective wavelengths selected by SPA.

Table 2. Effective wavelengths suggested by CARS.

Algorithm	Number	Selected wavelengths/nm
CARS	64	962, 975, 985, 999, 1012, 1046, 1049, 1052, 1056, 1076, 1109, 1113, 1130, 1143, 1167, 1170, 1193, 1197, 1200, 1207, 1214, 1220, 1230, 1234, 1274, 1288, 1291, 1301, 1311, 1321, 1325, 1342, 1345, 1352, 1359, 1375, 1382, 1396, 1399, 1402, 1406, 1413, 1419, 1429, 1433, 1500, 1507, 1517, 1521, 1541, 1544, 1551, 1554, 1565, 1588, 1601, 1605, 1632, 1639, 1642, 1649, 1652, 1656, 1659

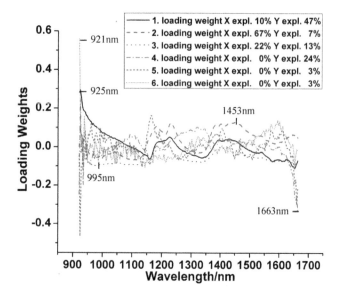

Figure 6. Effective wavelengths selected by *x*-LW.

concentration variances, respectively. It suggested that the six loadings could be used to represent the full spectral wavelengths. Thus, wavelengths corresponding to the highest absolute values were selected as key wavelengths. The first and fifth loading obtained the same result (925 nm). Finally, a total of five wavelengths (921, 925, 995, 1453, and 1663 nm) were obtained. These wavelengths were then used to establish identification models.

Identification models based on selected wavelengths

Identification models based on CARS. The LS-SVM and LDA models, which were established based on selected wavelengths suggested by CARS, obtained outstanding results with the CCR of 100% in both calibration and prediction sets. Compared with LS-SVM model, which were established based on full spectral wavelengths, there was a little increasing of the classification rate

in CARS-LS-SVM model. The number of input variables of CARS-LS-SVM and CARS-LDA models was only 28.96% of that of the full spectral wavelengths. From the analysis, it could be found that CARS algorithm was an effective wavelengths selection method, and NIR-HIS could be used in the identification of varieties of sesame oil effectively. However, the number of input variables of CARS-LS-SVM and CARS-LDA models was a little more. Thus, other effective wavelengths selection methods should be used in the following analysis.

Identification model based on SPA. In this study, SPA was carried out to select effective variables. Then, SPA-LS-SVA and SPA-LDA models were established based on the selected wavelengths. The SPA-LS-SVM model obtained a satisfying result with the CCR of 100% in the calibration set and 95.59% in prediction set. The SPA-LDA model obtained an excellent result with the CCR of 100% in the calibration set and 98.53% in prediction set. Although, the CCR of SPA-LS-SVM model was a little decreasing compared with LS-SVM and CARS-LS-SVM models in prediction set, the number of its input variables was only seven, which was only account for 3.17% of that of LS-SVM model and 10.94% of that of CARS-LS-SVM model, respectively. Compared with CARS-LDA model, the CCR of SPA-LDA model was also a little decreasing in despite, while the number of its input variables was only seven. It was 3.17% of that of CARS-LDA model. The less variables suggested by SPA could not only simplify the model and speed up the calculated efficiency but also be used in practical industry. Thus, SPA was also an effective method to select key wavelengths.

Identification model based on *x*-LW. In this study, *x*-LW was also carried out to select effective variables. Then, *x*-LW-LS-SVM and *x*-LW-LDA models were established based on the selected wavelengths. Both of the two models performed well with the CCR greater than 80% in both calibration and prediction sets. Though the results obtained by *x*-LW-LS-SVM and *x*-LW-LDA models were a little worse than those obtained by the models established based on full spectral wavelengths, CARS and SPA, the results were acceptable and promising. However, the number of the input variables was only five, which was an account for 2.26% and 7.81% of those of full spectral wavelengths and

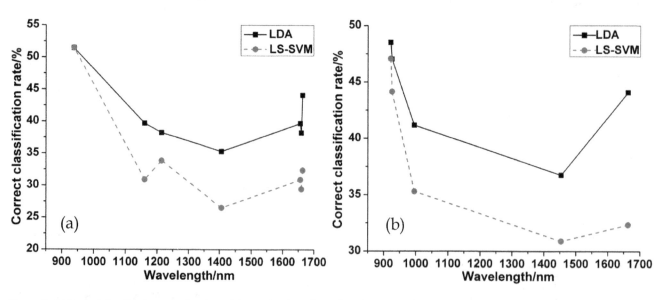

Figure 7. (a) Correct classification rate of each model at each selected wavelength suggested by SPA, (b) Correct classification rate of each model at each selected wavelength suggested by *x*-LW.

Identification of Different Varieties of Sesame Oil Using Near-Infrared Hyperspectral Imaging...   7

Table 3. Correct classification rate of different models based on different wavelengths selection methods.

Number	Classification model	Number of wavelengths	Calibration			Prediction		
			No.	Missed	CCR*/%	No.	Missed	CCR*/%
1	LS-SVM	221	132	0	100	68	1	98.53
2	CARS-LS-SVM	64	132	0	100	68	0	100
3	CARS-LDA	64	132	0	100	68	0	100
4	SPA-LS-SVM	7	132	0	100	68	3	95.59
5	SPA-LDA	7	132	0	100	68	1	98.53
6	x-LW-LS-SVM	5	132	13	90.15	68	12	82.35
7	x-LW-LDA	5	132	18	86.36	68	9	86.76

CCR* Correct Classification Rate.

wavelengths suggested by CARS. It demonstrated that x-LW was also an effective method to select key wavelengths.

Classified result at each selected wavelength

Each key wavelength, which was selected by SPA and x-LW algorithms, was also used to establish classification model. The results at each selected wavelength can be seen in Figure 7 (a) (b). It could be found that the classified results were different at different wavelengths. LDA model performed better than LS-SVM model at any wavelength. The general trend of CCRs firstly decreased and then increased in no matter LDA or LS-SVM models. In Figure 7 (a), the wavelength of 938 nm performed best with the CCR of 51.47% in both LDA and LS-SVM models. The wavelength of 1406 nm performed relatively worse with the CCR of 35.29% in LDA and 26.47% in LS-SVM models, respectively. In Figure 7 (b), the wavelength of 921 nm performed best with the CCR of 48.53% in LDA and 47.06% in LS-SVM models, respectively. The wavelength of 1453 nm performed relatively worse with the CCR of 36.76% in LDA and 30.88% in LS-SVM models, respectively. From above analysis, it can be seen that some wavelengths played prominent roles in the classification of varieties while some other wavelengths did not.

Comparison of different models based on full wavelengths and selected wavelengths

The results of the seven identification models established based on full spectral wavelengths, and selected wavelengths (suggested by CARS, SPA and x-LW) were shown in Table 3. Different classification results, ranging from 82.35% to 100%, were shown in Table 3. From Table 3, it could be found that each model obtained an outstanding result. However, the number of full spectral wavebands was too much though the result was excellent (100% in the calibration set and 98.53% in prediction set). CARS-LS-SVM and CARS-LDA models performed better than LS-SVM model with a little increasing of CCR in prediction set and less input variables. It may because that the redundant information, which existed in the large number of input variables, affected the robust and ability of the model. The selected wavelengths contained most of the effective information and little redundant information. The number of input variables of SPA-LS-SVM and SPA-LDA models was only seven. It decreased largely compared to the full spectral wavelengths and wavelengths suggested by CARS. The obtained results were 95.59% and 98.53% in prediction sets of SPA-LS-SVM and SPA-LDA models, respectively. Though the CCRs obtained by x-LW-LS-SVM and x-LW-LDA models were lower than those obtained by other models, the results were acceptable. Both of the two models obtained the CCRs greater than 80%. More, the number of the input variables was only account for 2.26% of that of full spectral wavelengths. The results obtained by selected wavelengths were acceptable and encouraged for further study. The less input variables greatly accelerate the calculated speed and simplify the model. It demonstrates again that NIR-HSI technique could be used to identify the varieties of sesame oil, and CARS, SPA and x-LW were effective wavelengths selection methods.

Conclusion

This study was carried out to evaluate the feasibility of using NIR-HSI system, which covers the spectral range of 874 to1734 nm, to identify the varieties of sesame oil. The overall results in this study indicated that NIR-HSI technique had the potential to be used to discriminate different varieties of sesame oil. CARS, SPA and x-LW were conducted to select effective wavelengths for establish identification model. Each model obtained an outstanding result with the CCR greater than 80%. CARS-LS-SVM and CARS-LDA models obtained the highest value of CCR of 100% with 64 input variables. The SPA-LS-SVM and SPA-LDA models obtained better results (95.59% and 98.53%) with only seven wavelengths. The x-LW-LS-SVM and x-LW-LDA models also obtained excellent results (>80% of CCR) with only five wavelengths. Among the wavelengths selected by SPA (38, 1160, 1214, 1406, 1656, 1659 and 1663 nm), wavelength of 938 nm performed best. The wavelength of 921 nm played the most prominent role among the wavelengths selected by x-LW (921, 925, 995, 1453 and 1663 nm). From the results, it could be seen that NIR-HSI technique could be used to identify the varieties of sesame oil rapidly and non-destructively, and CARS, SPA and x-LW were effective wavelengths selection methods.

However, this study was only a preliminary work. In future study, more samples with different varieties and more different spectral parameters should be used for establishing more robust and accurate model which could be used in practical industry.

Author Contributions

Conceived and designed the experiments: CQX QNW YH. Performed the experiments: CQX QNW YH. Analyzed the data: CQX QNW YH. Contributed reagents/materials/analysis tools: CQX QNW YH. Wrote the paper: CQX.

References

1. Azeez MA, Morakinyo JA (2011) Genetic diversity of fatty acids in sesame and its relatives in Nigeria. Eur J Lipid Sci Tech 113: 238–244.
2. Sowmya M, Jeyarani T, Jyotsna R, Indrani D (2009) Effect of replacement of fat with sesame oil and additives on rheological, microstructural, quality characteristics and fatty acid profile of cakes. Food Hydrocolloid 23: 1827–1836.
3. Sharmila V, Ganesh SK, Gunasekaran M (2007) Generation mean analysis for quantitative traits in sesame (Sesamum indicum L.) crosses. Genet Mol Biol 30: 80–84.
4. Mondal N, Bhat KV, Srivastava PS (2010) Variation in fatty acid composition in Indian germplasm of sesame. J AmOil Chem Soc 87: 1263–1269.
5. Criado M, Otero C (2010) Optiization of the synthesis of lower glycerides rich in unsaturated fatty acid residues obtained via enzymatic ethanolysis of sesame oil. Eur J Lipid Sci Tech 112: 246–258.
6. Lin P, Chen YM, He Y (2012) Identification of geographical origin of olive oil using visible and near-infrared spectroscopy technique combined with chemometrics. Food Bioprocess Tech 5: 235–242.
7. Luna AS, Silva AP, Pinho JSA, Ferré J, Boqué R (2013) Rapid characterization of transgenic and non-transgenic soybean oils by chemometric methods using NIR spectroscopy. Spectrochimica Acta A 100: 115–119.
8. Pizarro C, Rodríguez-Tecedor S, Pérez-del-Notario N, Esteban-Díez I, Gonzáiz JM (2013) Classification of Spanish extra virgin olive oils by data fusion of visible spectroscopic fingerprints and chemical descriptors. Food Chem 138: 915–922.
9. ElMasry G, Iqbal A, Sun DW, Allen P, Ward P (2011) Quality classification of cooked, sliced turkey hams using NIR hyperspctral imaging system. J Food Eng 103: 333–344.
10. Wu D, Wang SJ, Wang NF, Nie PC, He Y, et al. (2013) Application of time series hyperspectral imaging (TS-HSI) for determining water distribution within beef and spectral kinetics analysis during dehydration. Food Bioprocess Tech 6: 2943–2958.
11. Xie CQ, He Y, Li XL, Liu F, Du PP, et al. (2012) Study of detection of SPAD value in tomato leaves stressed by grey mold based on hyperspectral technique. Spectrosc Spect Anal 32: 3324–3328.
12. Li XL, Xie CQ, He Y, Qiu ZJ, Zhang YC (2012) Characterizing the moisture content of tea with diffuse reflectance spectroscopy using wavelet transform and multivariate analysis. Sensors 12: 9847–9861.
13. Chen XJ, Wu D, He Y, Liu S (2011) Nondestructive differentiation of panax species using visible and shortwave near-infrared spectroscopy. Food Bioprocess Tech 4: 753–761.
14. Zhang XL, Liu F, He Y, Li XL (2012) Application of hyperspectral imaging and chemometric calibration for variety discrimination of maize seeds. Sensors 12: 17234–17246.
15. Suykens JAK, Vandewalle J (1999) Least squares support vector machine classifiers. Neural Process Lett 9: 293–300.
16. Wu D, Chen JY, Lu BY, Xiong LN, He Y, et al. (2012) Application of near infrared spectroscopy for the rapid determination of antioxidant activity of bamboo leaf extract. Food Chem 135: 2147–2156.
17. Liu F, Jiang YH, He Y (2009) Variable selection in visible/near infrared spectra for linear and nonlinear calibration: A case study to determine soluble solids content of beer. Anal Chim Acta 635: 45–52.
18. Wei X, Liu F, Qiu ZJ, Shao YN, He Y (2014) Ripeness classification of astringent persimmon using hyperspectral imaging technique. Food Bioprocess Tech 7: 1371–1380.
19. Riovanto R, Cynkar WU, Berzaghi P, Cozzolino D (2011) Discrimination between Shiraz wines from different Australian regions: The role of spectroscopy and chemometrics. J Agr Food Chem 59: 10356–10360.
20. ElMasry G, Sun DW, Allen P (2012) Near-infrared hyperspectral imaging for predicting colour, pH and tenderness of fresh beef. J Food Eng 110: 127–140.
21. Barbin DF, ElMasry G, Sun DW, Allen P (2012) Predicting quality and sensory attributes of pork using near-infrared hyperspectral imaging. Anal Chim Acta 719: 30–42.
22. Kamruzzaman M, Elmasry G, Sun DW, Allen P (2011) Application of NIR hyperspectral imaging for discrimination of lamb muscles. J Food Eng 104: 332–340.
23. Li HD, Liang YZ, Xu QS, Cao DS (2009) Key wavelength screening using competitive adaptive reweighted sampling method for multivariate calibration. Anal Chim Acta 648: 77–84.
24. Wu D, Sun DW (2013) Potential of time series-hyperspectral imaging (TS-HIS) for non-invasive determination of microbial spoilage of salmon flesh. Talanta 111: 39–46.
25. Wei X, Xu N, Wu D, He Y (2014) Determination of branched-amino acid content in fermented cordyces sinensis mycelium by using FT-NIR spectroscopy technique. Food Bioprocess Tech 7: 184–190.
26. Araújo MCU, Saldanha TCB, Galvão RKH, Yoneyama T, Chame HC, et al. (2001) The successive projections algorithm for variable selection in spectroscopy, ulticomponent analysis. Chemometr Intell Lab 57: 65–73.
27. Wu D, He Y, Shi JH, Feng SJ (2009) Exploring near and midinfrared spectroscopy to predict trace iron and zinc contents in powdered milk. J Agr Food Chem 57: 1697–1704.
28. Galvão RKH, Araújo MCU, Fragoso WD, Silva EC, José GE, et al. (2008) A variable elimination method to improve the parsimony of MLR models using successive projections algorithm. Chemom. Intell. Lab. Syst 92: 83–91.
29. Liu F, He Y (2008) Classification of brands of instant noodles using Vis/NIR spectroscopy and chemometrics. Food Res Int 41: 562–567.
30. Zhang XL, He Y (2013) Rapid estimation of seed yield using hyperspectral images of oilseed rape leaves. Ind Crop Prod 42: 416–420.

2

Statistically Validated Networks in Bipartite Complex Systems

Michele Tumminello[1,2], Salvatore Miccichè[2], Fabrizio Lillo[2,3,4], Jyrki Piilo[5], Rosario N. Mantegna[2]*

1 Department of Social and Decision Sciences, Carnegie Mellon University, Pittsburgh, Pennsylvania, United States of America, **2** Dipartimento di Fisica, Università di Palermo, Palermo, Italy, **3** Santa Fe Institute, Santa Fe, New Mexico, United States of America, **4** Scuola Normale Superiore di Pisa, Pisa, Italy, **5** Department of Physics and Astronomy, Turku Centre for Quantum Physics, University of Turku, Turun yliopisto, Finland

Abstract

Many complex systems present an intrinsic bipartite structure where elements of one set link to elements of the second set. In these complex systems, such as the system of actors and movies, elements of one set are qualitatively different than elements of the other set. The properties of these complex systems are typically investigated by constructing and analyzing a projected network on one of the two sets (for example the actor network or the movie network). Complex systems are often very heterogeneous in the number of relationships that the elements of one set establish with the elements of the other set, and this heterogeneity makes it very difficult to discriminate links of the projected network that are just reflecting system's heterogeneity from links relevant to unveil the properties of the system. Here we introduce an unsupervised method to statistically validate each link of a projected network against a null hypothesis that takes into account system heterogeneity. We apply the method to a biological, an economic and a social complex system. The method we propose is able to detect network structures which are very informative about the organization and specialization of the investigated systems, and identifies those relationships between elements of the projected network that cannot be explained simply by system heterogeneity. We also show that our method applies to bipartite systems in which different relationships might have different qualitative nature, generating statistically validated networks in which such difference is preserved.

Editor: Eshel Ben-Jacob, Tel Aviv University, Israel

Funding: J.P. acknowledges financial support by the Magnus Ehrnrooth Foundation and the Vilho, Yrjo, and Kalle Väisälä Foundation. F.L., S.M. and R.N.M. acknowledge partial support from the Complex World Network funded by EUROCONTROL under the SESAR Work Package E framework, Contract Ref. 10-220210-C3. The funders had no role in study design, data collection and analysis, decision to publish, or preparation of the manuscript.

Competing Interests: The authors have declared that no competing interests exist.

* E-mail: rn.mantegna@gmail.com

Introduction

In recent years, many complex systems have been described and modeled in terms of bipartite networks [1–5]. Examples include movies and actors [1,2,4], authors and scientific papers [6–9], email accounts and emails [10], mobile phones and phone calls [11], plants and animals that pollinate them [12,13]. One ubiquitous property of bipartite complex systems is their heterogeneity. For example, in a given period of time, some actors play in many movies, whereas others play in a few, some authors write a few papers, whereas others write many. Movies are also heterogeneous because of the size of cast, as well as papers because of the number of authors. Heterogeneity is also a common feature of biological complex systems. The genome of some organisms might contain a small set of proteins performing a given class of biological functions whereas the corresponding set of proteins is large for other organisms. Bipartite networks are composed by two different sets of nodes such that every link connects a node of the first set with a node of the second set. The properties of bipartite complex systems are often investigated by considering the one-mode projection of the bipartite network. One creates a network of nodes belonging to one of the two sets and two nodes are connected when they have at least one common neighboring node of the other set. In this paper we deal with the problem of identifying preferential links in the projected network.

Specifically we use the term *preferential link* to indicate a link whose presence in the projected network cannot be explained in terms of random co-occurrence of neighbors in the bipartite system. We argue that these preferential links carry relevant information about the structure and organization of the system. When one constructs a projected network with nodes from only one set, the system heterogeneity makes it very difficult to discriminate preferential links from links which are consistent with a random null hypothesis taking into account the heterogeneity of the system. It is therefore of great importance to devise a method allowing to statistically validate whether a given link in the projected network is consistent or not with a null hypothesis of random connectivity between elements of the bipartite network.

The paper is organized as follows. In the Section Methods, we introduce our method to obtain a statistically validated network. In the Section Results and Discussion we first consider a *network of organisms*. Specifically, we obtain and discuss the statistically validated network of organisms used to define the clusters of orthologous genes database. We then study the *network of stocks* of the system of 500 stocks traded in the US equity markets and we point out that the statistically validated network of this section presents links describing a set of different relationships among the elements of the considered complex system. The last set of results concerns the *network of movies* where we consider the social bipartite system of movies and actors and we obtain statistically validated networks of movies. These networks are investigated with respect to their community structure and community characterization in the Text S1, where a few illustrative case studies of the informativeness of movies communities detected in statistically validated networks are provided. Finally, we draw some conclusions.

Methods

Here we introduce an unsupervised method to statistically validate each link of the projected network. A schematic summary of our method is provided in Fig. 1. The key ingredients of our method are (i) the selection of a null hypothesis of random connectivity between elements in the bipartite network consistent with the degree of heterogeneity of both sets of elements, (ii) the identification of an analytical or computationally feasible procedure to associate a p-value with each link of the projected network,

in order to test the presence of the link against the selected null hypothesis, and (iii) the appropriate correction of the statistical significance level in the presence of multiple hypothesis testing [14,15] of links across the network.

Statistically validated networks

The method works as follows. Let us consider a bipartite system **S** in which links connect the N_A elements of set A to the N_B elements of set B. In the present discussion, we focus on the projected network on set A but the same approach is also valid when considering the projected network on set B. The adjacency projected network is obtained by linking together those vertices of A which share at least a common first neighbor element of B in the bipartite system. We aim to statistically validate each link of the projected network against a null hypothesis of random co-occurrence of common

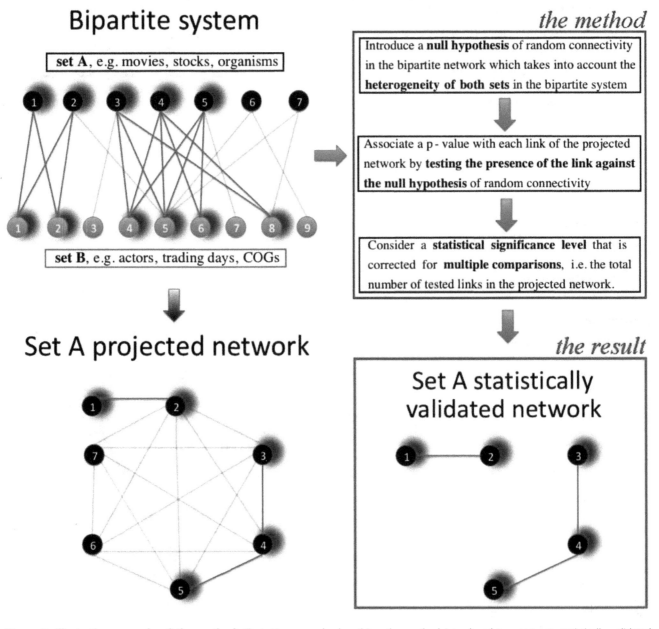

Figure 1. Illustrative example of the method. Illustrative example describing the method introduced to construct statistically validated networks in bipartite complex system.

neighbors that takes into account the degree heterogeneity of elements of both set A and set B. In order to accomplish this goal we first decompose the bipartite system in subsystems. Fig. 2 shows an illustration of the link validation procedure in a specific subsystem. Each subsystem $\mathbf{S}_k$ consists of all the N_B^k elements of set B with a given degree k and of all the elements from set A linked to them. By construction, a subsystem $\mathbf{S}_k$ is homogeneous with respect to the degree of elements belonging to set B, because they all have the same degree k. We indicate the set of elements of B with a certain degree k as set B_k. In the bipartite subsystem $\mathbf{S}_k$ we are therefore left just with heterogeneity of elements of set A. Let us consider now two elements i and j of set A, and assume they have $N_{i,j}^k$ common neighbors in set B_k. We denote the degree of elements i and j in the subsystem $\mathbf{S}_k$ as N_i^k and N_j^k, respectively. Under the hypothesis that elements i and j randomly connect to the elements of set B_k, the probability that elements i and j share X neighbors in set B_k is given by the hypergeometric distribution [16], i.e.

$$H\left(X|N_B^k,N_i^k,N_j^k\right) = \frac{\binom{N_i^k}{X}\binom{N_B^k-N_i^k}{N_j^k-X}}{\binom{N_B^k}{N_j^k}}. \qquad (1)$$

It is worth to mention that this distribution is symmetric with respect to exchange of elements i and j, i.e. $H(X|N_B^k,N_i^k,N_j^k) = H(X|N_B^k,N_j^k,N_i^k)$. The distribution given in Eq. (1) allows one to associate a p-value $p(N_{i,j}^k)$ with the actual number $N_{i,j}^k$ of neighbors that elements i and j share:

$$p(N_{i,j}^k) = 1 - \sum_{X=0}^{N_{i,j}^k-1} H(X|N_B^k,N_i^k,N_j^k). \qquad (2)$$

This way we have shown how to associate a p-value with the link between each pair of elements i and j of the projected network for each subsystem $\mathbf{S}_k$. The next step of the method is to set a level of statistical significance s, which takes into account the fact that we are performing multiple hypothesis testing - specifically a test for each pair of elements of A for each subsystem $\mathbf{S}_k$. If we consider that the degree of elements of set B in the bipartite system ranges between k_{min}^B and k_{max}^B then the total number of tests that we perform will be $N_t \leq (k_{max}^B - k_{min}^B + 1) \times N_A \times (N_A-1)/2$. In the following examples, we will use a statistical level of significance of 0.01 corrected for the N_t multiple comparisons in two different ways. Specifically we will use the very conservative Bonferroni correction [14], i.e. $s = 0.01/N_t$ for multiple hypothesis testing and the less restrictive False Discovery Rate (FDR) [15]. For the moment, let us just assume that a value of statistical significance s has been set, and proceed in the construction of the statistically validated network. We compare each p-value $p(N_{i,j}^k)$ with s. If $p(N_{i,j}^k) < s$ then we validate the link between elements i and j for the specific subsystem $\mathbf{S}_k$. We then summarize all validations obtained in the projected adjacency network and associate with the link between i and j a weight equal to the total number of subsystems $\mathbf{S}_k$s in which the relationship between i and j has been statistically validated. If the weight of a link turns out to be zero then the link is removed. The resulting weighted network is the aimed statistically validated network. Of course the obtained statistically validated network depends on the way we set the statistical threshold s. We name the statistically validated network

obtained by setting s according to the Bonferroni correction as *Bonferroni network*. A less stringent correction for multiple hypothesis testing is the False Discovery Rate (FDR) [15]. The FDR correction for multiple hypothesis testing is defined as follows. Specifically, p-values of different tests are first arranged in increasing order $(p_1 < p_2 < \ldots < p_{N_t})$, and the FDR threshold is obtained by finding the largest t_{max} such that $p_{t_{max}} < t_{max}0.01/N_t$. It is worth noting that by construction, the Bonferroni network is always a subnetwork of the FDR network. The advantage of using the FDR network is the fact that it allows one to include more interactions in the network, because the FDR correction is less restrictive than the Bonferroni correction. On the other hand, interactions included in the Bonferroni network are on average statistically more robust than interactions included in the FDR network. In this paper, we also consider the FDR correction and we refer to the network obtained by using it as the *FDR network*.

We apply our method to three different systems, namely the set of clusters of orthologous genes (COG) detected in completely sequenced genomes [17,18], a set of daily returns of 500 US financial stocks, and the set of world movies of the IMDb database (http://www.imdb.com/). In the first set of COGs we can fully take into account both sources of heterogeneity of COGs and organisms. In the second set of excess returns of 500 US financial stocks the second source of heterogeneity is quite limited and therefore it is neglected. The last example presents a very large system with a high degree of heterogeneity of set B (actors) that cannot be efficiently taken into account with our method. However the second source of heterogeneity, although very large in absolute terms it is quite limited in relative terms with respect to the full size of the system. For this reason, although the statistically validated networks we obtain by neglecting the second source of heterogeneity are approximated, we show that they are fully informative about this large heterogeneous complex system. Moreover, we also show that the role of actors heterogeneity can be heuristically taken into account in the analysis of movies communities detected in the statistically validated networks. We choose to analyze these three systems because they are of interest in three different areas of science and they are different in size and level of heterogeneity, giving us the opportunity to show the power of our method under quite different conditions.

Results and Discussion

Network of organisms

The COG database [17,18] provides the relationship between organisms and clusters of orthologous proteins present in their genome. Orthologous proteins have evolved from an ancestral protein and are likely to perform similar biological tasks in different genomes. By monitoring COGs across organisms one can therefore track the presence of different proteins involved in similar biological processes in different organisms. A projected network of organisms based on the co-occurrence of specific COGs might therefore highlight the degree of similarity of two organisms based on the functional characteristics of proteins present in their genome. Set A of the database is composed by 66 organisms (13 Archaea, 50 Bacteria and 3 unicellular Eukaryota) and set B by 4,873 COGs present in their genomes. The number of COGs in a genome is heterogeneous, ranging from 362 to 2,243. Similarly, COGs can be present in a different number of genomes. We call any COG that is present in k different genomes a k-COG. In the present system, k ranges between 3 and 66. We consider the projected network of organisms, in which we set a link between two organisms if at least one COG is present in the genome of both organisms. In the following we will refer to this

Bipartite subsystem S_2

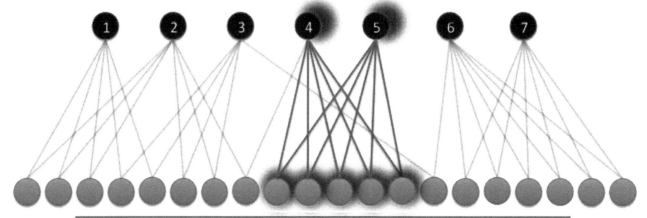

set **A**, e.g. organisms, is composed by $N = 7$ elements

set **B_2**, e.g. COG - 2, is composed by $N_B^2 = 20$ elements

(set B_2 is homogeneous : all elements have the same degree $k = 2$)

Set A projected subnetwork

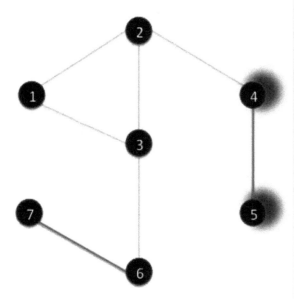

dimension of **set A** : $N = 7$;

dimension of **set B_2** : $N_B^2 = 20$;

link validation :

Assume the level of statistical significance is $s = 0.0005$;

validation of link 4 - 5 : $N_4^2 = 6$; $N_5^2 = 5$; $N_{4,5}^2 = 5$;

$$p(N_{4,5}^2) = 1 - \sum_{X=0}^{N_{4,5}^2-1} H(X \mid N_B^2, N_4^2, N_5^2) \cong 0.0004;$$

$p(N_{4,5}^2) < s \Rightarrow$ **link 4 - 5 is statistically validated.**

(also link 6 - 7 turns out to be statistically validated)

Figure 2. Illustrative example of the link validation procedure. Illustrative example describing the procedure introduced to validate the link between node 4 and 5 in the projected network of set A associated with the subsystem S_2 of a bipartite complex system. From the bipartite subsystem we note that the degree of elements 4 and 5 is $N_4^2 = 6$ and $N_5^2 = 5$ respectively. The number of elements of set B common to this pair of elements is $N_{4,5}^2 = 5$. The computation of the p-*value* and his comparison with the chosen multiple hypothesis testing correction ($s = 0.0005$ in the example) is given in the box of the figure. For the illustrated subsystem and for the chosen multiple hypothesis testing correction the link 6–7 is also statistically validated.

network as the adjacency network of organisms, which turns out to be a complete network. The statistically validated networks are obtained by performing the procedure described in the previous Section. First we divide the bipartite system into COG_k subsystems. Each COG_k ($k = 3, \ldots, 66$) bipartite subsystem is characterized by the fact that all the COGs involved in it are k-COGs. In each COG_k subsystem we are therefore left only with the heterogeneity of organisms. We test the existence of a preferential relationship between each pair of organisms separately for each COG_k subsystem. Specifically, given two organisms i and j, let N_i^k be the number of k-COGs in organism i, N_j^k the number of k-COGs in organism j and $N_{i,j}^k$ the number of k-COGs belonging to both i and j. Under the null hypothesis of random co-occurrence, the probability of observing X co-occurrences is given by $H(X|N_k, N_i^k, N_j^k)$ where N_k is the total number of k-COGs in the system. We can therefore associate a p-value to the observed $N_{i,j}^k$ as described in Eq. 2. The described link validation procedure involves multiple hypothesis testing and therefore the statistical threshold must be corrected for multiple hypothesis testing. In our case the number of organisms is $N_o = 66$ and we test $N_t = 64N_o(N_o-1)/2$ hypotheses, equal to the number of pairs of organisms times the number of COG_k subsystems. Thus our Bonferroni threshold is $p_b = 0.01 \cdot 2/(64N_o(N_o-1)) \simeq 7.3 \times 10^{-8}$. Each validated link has a weight equal to the total number of subsystems COG_ks in which the relationship between i and j has been statistically validated.

Let us now analyze the statistically validated networks obtained for this biological system. The Bonferroni network of organisms includes 58 non isolated nodes connected by 216 weighted links (Fig. 3A) and it shows seven connected components, each one having a clear biological interpretation in terms of organisms' lineage. The FDR network of organisms includes all the 66 organisms and the number of weighted links in this network is 369 (Fig. 3B). Thus the entire set is covered and the additional preferential links provide relations among the groups already observed in the Bonferroni network. The Bonferroni network (Fig. 3A) presents 7 connected components and 8 isolated nodes (isolated nodes are not shown in the figure). The largest connected component of the network, which is on the left in Fig. 3A, is composed by bacteria belonging to the phylum of Proteobacteria. Subgroups belonging to different classes can also be recognized. In fact, Eco, Ecz, Ecs, Ype, Hin, Pmu, Vch, Pae and Sty belong to the class of Gammaproteobacteria, whereas Atu, Sme, Bme, Ccr, Rpr, Rco and Mlo are Alphaproteobacteria and NmA, Nme and Rso are Betaproteobacteria. The second connected component is composed by Archaea genomes belonging to the two phyla of Euryarchaeota (Mth, Mja, Hbs, Tac, Tvo, Pho, Pab, Afu, Mka, and Mac) and Crenarchaeota (Pya, Sso and Ape). Archaea are also linked to the three unicellular eukaryotes present in the set, namely Ecu, Sce and Spo, although the weight of links between eukaryotes and Archaea is markedly smaller than the weight of links among Archaea genomes [19]. The FDR network (Fig. 3B) is connected. However the group including Archaea and Eukaryota is clearly distinct from the network region of Bacteria. It is worth noting that both the Bonferroni and the FDR network display a clear clustered structure. Indeed the application of community detection algorithms [20,21], such as Infomap [22], to the statistically validated networks reveal clusters of organisms with a direct biological interpretation in terms of lineage (see Fig. 3). This is not true for the adjacency network, and shows that the statistically validated networks are able to identify the many preferential links inside communities and the few preferential links bridging different communities of organisms.

Network of financial stocks

As a second example we consider the collective dynamics of the daily returns of $N_s = 500$ highly capitalized US financial stocks in the period 2001–2003 ($T = 748$ trading days). Many studies investigating correlation based networks have shown that the information about the different economic sectors of the quoted companies is incorporated into their price dynamics [23]. In this case, the two sets of the bipartite system are the stocks (with categorical information on their returns) and the trading days. Here we focus on the projected network of stocks. The interest in this example is that we (i) generalize our procedure to complex systems where the elements are monitored by continuous variables, (ii) show how to simplify the above procedure when the second source of heterogeneity (in the previous example the COG frequency in different organisms) is small, and (iii) show how to classify links according to the type of relation between the two nodes.

Since we want to identify similarities and differences among stock returns not due to the global market behavior, we investigate the excess return of each stock i with respect to the average daily return of all the stocks in our set. The excess return of each stock i at day t is then converted into a categorical variable with 3 states: *up*, *down*, and *null*. For each stock we introduce a daily varying threshold $\sigma_i(t)$ as the average of the absolute excess return (a proxy of volatility) of stock i over the previous 20 days. State *up* (*down*) is assigned when the excess return of stock i at day t is larger (smaller) than $\sigma_i(t)$ (-$\sigma_i(t)$). The state *null* is assigned to the remaining days. We study the co-occurrence of states *up* and *down* for each pair of stocks. In this case we can neglect the heterogeneity of state occurrence in different trading days because the number of *up* (*down*) states is only moderately fluctuating across different days and it has a bell shaped distribution with a range of fluctuations smaller than one decade for each stock. With this approximation we can statistically validate the co-occurrence of state P (either *up* or *down*) of stock i and state Q (either *up* or *down*) of stock j with the following procedure (illustrated in Fig. 4). Let us call N_P (N_Q) the number of days in which stock i (j) is in the state P (Q). Let us call $N_{P,Q}$ the number of days when we observe the co-occurrence of state P for stock i and state Q for stock j. Under the null hypothesis of random co-occurrence of state P for stock i and state Q for stock j, the probability of observing X co-occurrences of the investigated states of the two stocks in T observations is again described by the hypergeometric distribution, $H(X|T, N_P, N_Q)$. As before we can associate a p-value with each pair of stocks for each combination of the investigated states. We indicate the state *up* (*down*) of stock i as i_u (i_d). The possible combinations are (i_u, j_u), (i_u, j_d), (i_d, j_u), and (i_d, j_d). As before the statistical test is a multiple hypothesis test and therefore either the Bonferroni or FDR correction is necessary. The Bonferroni threshold is $p_b = p_t/(2N_s(N_s-1))$ where the denominator of the threshold is the number of considered stock pairs ($N_s(N_s-1)/2$) times 4, which is the number of different co-occurrences investigated. Each pair of stocks is characterized by the set of the above four combinations which are statistically validated. There are $2^4 - 1 = 15$ possible cases with at least one co-occurrence validation, but we observe only 5 kinds of preferential links: L1 in which the co-occurrences (i_u, j_u) and (i_d, j_d) are both validated; L2 in which only the co-occurrence (i_d, j_d) is validated, L3 in which only the co-occurrence (i_u, j_u) is validated, L4 in which either only (i_u, j_d) or only (i_d, j_u) is validated; and L5 when both the co-occurrence (i_u, j_d) and (i_d, j_u) are validated. Note that we put in the same relationship L4 two cases which are different only for the order in which the two nodes are considered. The set of relationships $L1$, $L2$, and $L3$ and the associated links describe a

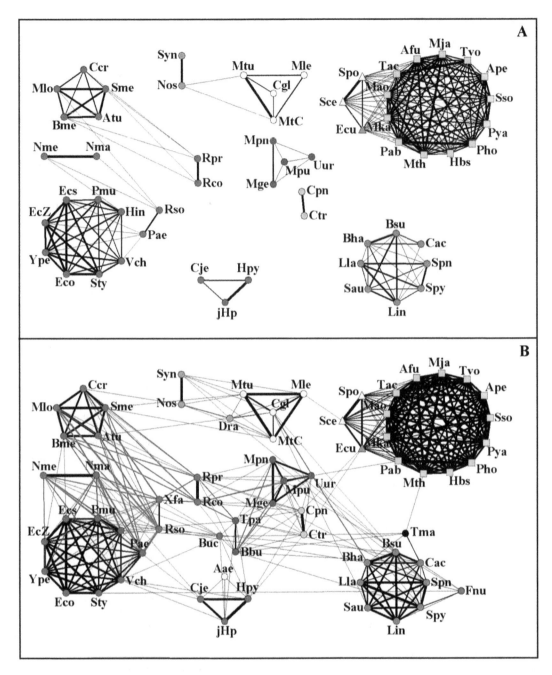

Figure 3. Statistically validated networks of organisms. Bonferroni (Panel A) and FDR (Panel B) networks of the organisms investigated in the COG database. The shape of the node indicates the super kingdom of the organism: Archaea (squares), Bacteria (circles), and Eukaryota (triangles). The color of the node indicates the phylum of the organism. The thickness of the link is related to its weight and it is proportional to the logarithm of the number of COG_k validations between the two connected nodes. Red links bridge different communities of organisms, as revealed by applying Infomap [22] to the statistically validated networks.

coherent movement of the price of the two stocks, while the set of relationships $L4$ and $L5$ describes opposite deviation from the average market behavior. We can therefore construct networks where the statistically validated links are associated with a label that specifies the type of relationship between the two connected nodes. This structure is richer than a simple unweighted network, but it is also different from a weighted network because it describes relationships which cannot be described by a numerical value only. We address the set of different relationships present between two nodes of the statistically validated network with the term *multi-link*.

The Bonferroni network of the system is composed by 349 stocks connected by 2,230 multi-links. The multi-links are of different nature. Specifically, we observe 1,158 $L1$-links, 494 $L2$-links, 354 $L3$-links, 196 $L4$-links, and 28 $L5$-links. The largest connected component of the network includes 273 stocks. There are also 19 smaller connected components of size ranging from 2 to 15. In Fig. 5A we show the largest connected component of the Bonferroni network. It presents several regions in which stocks are strongly connected by $L1$, $L2$, and $L3$ multi-links. These regions are very homogeneous with respect to the economic sector of the stocks. The connection between different regions is in some cases

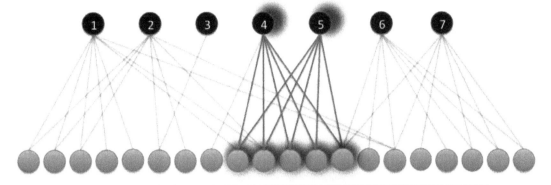

Bipartite system

set A, e.g. movies, stock/states, is composed of N = 7 elements

set B, e.g. actors, trading days, is composed of T = 20 elements

Set A projected network

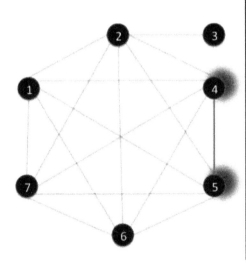

dimension of **set A** : $N = 7$;

dimension of **set B** : $T = 20$;

validation of link 4 - 5 :

$N_4 = 6$; $N_5 = 5$; $N_{4,5} = 5$;

$p(N_{4,5}) = 1 - \sum_{X=0}^{N_{4,5}-1} H(X \mid T, N_4, N_5) \cong 0.0004$;

$p_B = \dfrac{0.01}{N(N-1)/2} \cong 0.0005$; $0.0004 < p_B$;

link 4 - 5 is statistically validated.

Figure 4. Illustrative example of the link validation procedure. Illustrative example describing the procedure introduced to validate a link in the projected network when the degree heterogeneity of Set B is negligible or cannot properly be taken into account. The example explicitly worked out in the box of the figure considers the validation of the link 4–5 of the projected network of set A. For these nodes the degree of elements 4 and 5 is $N_4^2 = 6$ and $N_5^2 = 5$ respectively. The number of elements of set B common to this pair of elements is $N_{4,5}^2 = 5$. The computation of the p-*value* and his comparison with the Bonferroni multiple hypothesis testing correction (s = 0.0005 in the example) is given in the box of the figure.

provided by a large number of L4 and L5 multi-links. This is especially evident for the group of technology stocks (red circles). All except one of the multi-links outgoing from the group are L4 and L5 multi-links, indicating moderate or strong anti-correlation of technology stocks with the other groups. The strongest anti-correlation is detected between technology and services stocks (cyan circles).

The multi-link statistically validated network of 500 stocks is a new kind of network presenting qualitatively and quantitatively different classes of links. For this reason, there are no established

methods specifically devised to detect communities of nodes in this kind of network. Here we propose a minimalist approach in which we just distinguish between co-occurrences of correlated evolution from co-occurrences of anti-correlated evolutions. Our procedure works as follows: first we remove all the links describing anti-correlated evolutions (L4 and L5) from the multi-link statistically validated network (see Fig. 5B). Then we weight the remaining links by taking into account whether the statistical validation of the link is single or twofold. With this choice, the twofold link L1 has a weight equal to 2, whereas single links L2 and L3 have a weight

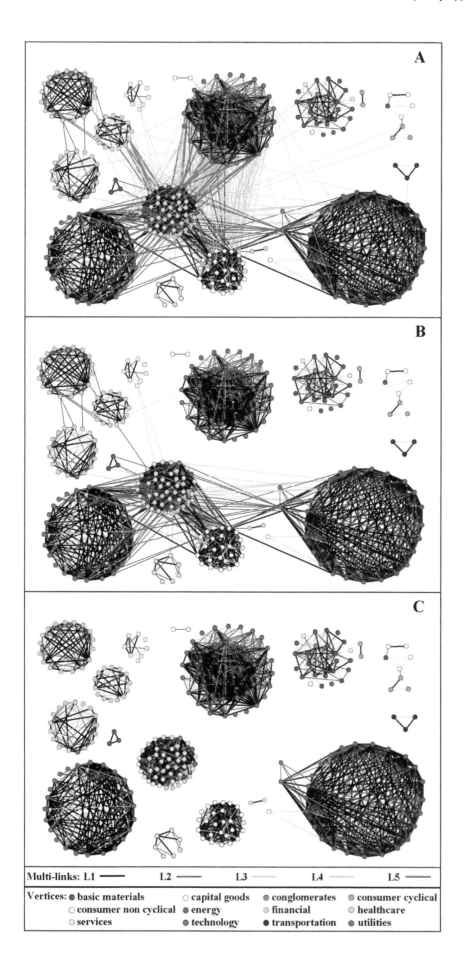

Multi-links: L1 ——— L2 ——— L3 ——— L4 ——— L5 ———

Vertices: ● basic materials   ○ capital goods   ● conglomerates   ● consumer cyclical
          ○ consumer non cyclical   ● energy   ● financial   ● healthcare
          ● services   ● technology   ● transportation   ● utilities

Figure 5. Bonferroni network of stocks. The largest connected component of the Bonferroni network associated with the system of 500 stocks. The nodes represent stocks and links connecting different stocks correspond to the statistically validated relationships. The node color identifies the economic sector of the corresponding stock. The economic sector classification is done according to Yahoo Finance. The color of a multi-link identifies the corresponding validated relationship. In panel A we report the largest connected component of the Bonferroni network. In panel B we remove links corresponding to anti-correlated evolution of stock returns, i.e. links L4 and L5. In panel C we also remove links bridging different clusters detected by the Infomap method.

equal to 1. We then perform community detection on the resulting "standard" weighted network of Fig. 5B, by using the Infomap method [22]. While our approach is pragmatic and heuristic, we are aware that a more theoretically grounded approach to partitioning multi-link networks would certainly be useful in the study of networks where links of different nature can be naturally defined, as in the present case.

We analyze the clusters of stocks detected in the weighted Bonferroni network by using the information about the economic sectors and subsectors of stocks in each cluster. Economic sectors according to Yahoo Finance classification of stocks are Basic Materials, Capital Good, Conglomerates, Consumer Cyclical, Consumer Non Cyclical, Energy, Financial, Healthcare, Services, Technology, Transportation, Utilities. A statistical method to perform this analysis is given in Ref. [24]. The total number of economic sectors is 12, and they are detailed in Fig. 5. Economic subsectors represent a more detailed classification of stocks. There are 81 different subsectors characterizing the $N = 349$ non isolated stocks in the Bonferroni network. The Infomap method detects 37 clusters of stocks with size ranging from 2 to 48 in the Bonferroni network. In Fig. 5C, we show the clusters of stocks obtained for the largest connected component of the Bonferroni network. It is evident from Fig. 5C that most of the clusters are very homogeneous in terms of the economic sector of stocks. However some clusters are better characterized in terms of subsectors. Let us for instance focus on the 3 clusters of financial stocks (green vertices in Fig. 5) at the top left corner in Fig. 5C. From top to bottom, these three clusters are composed by stocks belonging to the sub-sectors of insurance (life, and property and casualty), of investment services, and of regional banks. Another example is the cluster at the center of Fig. 5C, which is mostly composed by stocks of the services sector (cyan in the figure). These stocks belong to the sub-sector of services – real estate. It is to notice that this cluster is strongly anti-correlated (links L4 and L5 in Fig. 5A) with a large cluster of stocks belonging to the sector of technology (red vertices in Fig. 5).

We have also computed the FDR network of the system. As expected, it includes more stocks (494) and more multi-links (11,281) than the Bonferroni network, since the requirement on the statistical validation is less restrictive. The FDR network has a single connected component and the fraction of L4 and L5 multi-links is higher (35.9%) than in the case of the Bonferroni network (10.0%).

As before the adjacency network of stocks is a complete graph. On the contrary both the Bonferroni and the FDR networks display a highly clustered structure with clusters having a clear economic meaning. The use of Infomap on these statistically validated networks gives a partition in communities, which are extremely homogeneous in terms of economic sector. Therefore our method allows to construct networks where (i) links are statistically validated, (ii) multi-links describe qualitatively different relationships between pairs of stocks, e.g. both co-movements and opposite movements occurring between pairs of stocks, and (iii) a very accurate identification of communities of stocks is possible. To the best of our knowledge the presence of all these features is pretty unique and it is not shared by other

similarity networks [23] based on topological constraints [25–27], correlation threshold [28,29], or validated with bootstrap [30].

Network of movies

The last system we investigate is the bipartite system of movies and actors of the Internet Movie Database (IMDb), which is the largest web repository of world movies. We consider here the bipartite relationship between movies and actors produced in the period 1990–2008 all over the world. The set includes movies realized in 169 countries. We choose this system because (i) it is a large system (89,605 movies and 412,143 actors), (ii) it has a large heterogeneity both in movies and in actors, and (iii) it allows a sophisticated cluster characterization analysis based on the characteristics of the movie, namely genre, language, country, and filming locations.

The actors degree heterogeneity ranges between 1 and 247 and it is so pronounced that we did not find a practical solution to take it into account when constructing statistically validated networks of movies. The approach of the k-subsets is not feasible in this case due to lack of sufficient statistics. Therefore, we perform a statistical validation of links against a null hypothesis fully taking into account the movies heterogeneity but not describing the heterogeneity of actors. In spite of this limitation, the results obtained for the statistically validated networks are very informative about several aspects of the movie industry as it will be shown in the following. We conjecture that this is due to the fact that although the degree heterogeneity of actors is remarkable in absolute terms, making it unfeasible to use the k-subset approach, it is small as compared with the total number of movies. Indeed the fraction between the maximum number of movies performed by a single actor in the database and the total number of movies is $247/89,605 = 0.003$. This fact indicates that no actors contribute systematically to increase the co-occurrence between all movies pairs, or even a relevant fraction of them. This situation is significantly different than the one observed for the system of organisms and COGs, where the maximum degree of COGs was 66, i.e. the same as the total number of organisms in the database.

We construct the statistically validated networks of movies by testing the co-occurrence of actors in the cast of each movie pair. A schematic representation of the procedure used to validate links is provided in Fig. 4. The null hypothesis of random co-coccurecence is again described by the hypergeometric distribution, which naturally takes into account the heterogeneity of the system due

Table 1. Basic properties of movie networks.

	Movies	Links	Number of conn. comp.s	Largest conn. comp.
Adjacency	78,686	2,902,060	647	77,193
FDR	37,429	205,553	2,443	30,934
Bonferroni	12,850	29,281	2,456	1,627

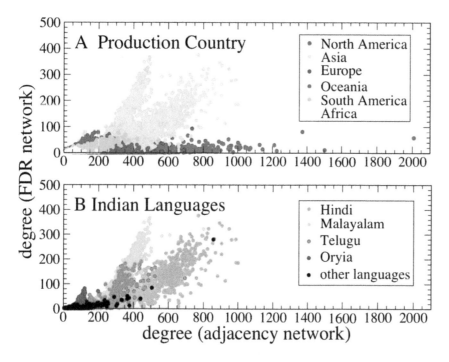

Figure 6. Comparison between adjacency and FDR networks of movies. Scatter plots of the degree of movies in the adjacency and FDR networks. Each circle represents a movie. We do not report movies with vanishing degree in at least one of the two networks. The panel A shows movies produced all over the world. The color of each symbol identifies the continent of the production country. Only movies with a single production country are shown. The panel B shows the data for the Indian movies and the color indicates the movie language. Only movies with a single language are shown.

to the different size of the cast of movies. Table 1 shows the severe filtering of nodes and links that is obtained in the validated networks of movies with respect to the adjacency network. Only 16% (47%) of the nodes and 1% (7%) of the links of the adjacency network are statistically validated in the Bonferroni (FDR) network. Also the size of the largest connected component varies significantly across the three networks. Specifically the largest connected component (i) is covering almost completely the adjacency network, (ii) comprises the largest fraction of movies in the FDR network (83%), but (iii) contains only 13% of the movies of the Bonferroni network. This shows that the Bonferroni network already provides a natural partition of the movies included in it.

A comparison of the degree of movies in the adjacency and FDR networks allows to clearly distinguish the Asian movie industry from the rest of the world movie industry, and different languages within single countries like India (see Fig. 6). The North American movie industry shows typically a high degree of movies in the adjacency network and a relatively low degree in the FDR network (see Fig. 6A), probably indicating a tendency to avoid a similar cast in different movies. A different behavior is observed in Asia, while Europe is an intermediate case. The analysis of indian movies (see Fig. 6B) shows the existence of groups of movies characterized by a common language. According to the present state of the IMDb database, the comparison between the degree of adjacency network and the degree of FDR network suggests that the Asian movie industry, and the Indian movie industry in particular, presents a level of variety in the cast formation that is lower than the variety observed in the western movie industry. In the Text S1, we analyze the movie communities detected when the Infomap method is applied to different movie networks. Specifically we investigate and compare the community structure of adjacency, FDR and Bonferroni networks. Different aspects of the

comparison are summarized in Figure S1, and Tables S1, S2, and S3. In the community detection of adjacency and statistically validated networks we weight links according to Ref. [31] to heuristically take into account actors' heterogeneity in the number of performed movies. In the Text S1, we show that the clusters of movies obtained from the Bonferroni and FDR networks have a higher homogeneity in terms of production country, language, genre, and filming location than the clusters of movies detected from the adjacency network.

Conclusions

In summary, our method allows to validate links describing preferential relationships among the heterogeneous elements of bipartite complex systems. Our method is very robust with respect to the presence of false positive links, i.e. links that might be just due to statistical fluctuations. In fact, we verified for all the investigated systems that the Bonferroni network associated with a random rewiring of the bipartite network turns out to be empty. By applying the method to three different systems, we showed that it is extremely flexible, since it can be applied to systems with different degree of heterogeneity and described by binary relationships and categorical variables.

Supporting Information

Figure S1 Rank plot of the size of clusters in the adjacency, Bonferroni and FDR networks. Rank plot of the size of clusters obtained with the Infomap algorithm for the adjacency movie network, the FDR network and the Bonferroni network both for the unweighted and weighted links. The difference between the partitions decreases for the statistically validated networks (see text for a measure of the mutual information between unweighted and weighted partitions). In the legend, the number in parenthesis is the number of detected clusters in the corresponding network.

Table S1 Cluster over-expression analysis of production country, language, genre and filming location. Clusters are obtained by performing the Infomap partitioning of the adjacency weighted movie network (ADJ-W), FDR weighted movie network (FDR-W) and the Bonferroni weighted movie network (BONF-W). For each of the four considered classifications, we report the total number of observed over-expressions for each network. The number in parenthesis is the number of distinct clusters where at least one over-expression has been observed.

Table S2 Over-expression of production country (C), language (L), genre (G) and filming locations (F) for seven large clusters of the FDR weighted network. Here we consider only those movies that are also present in cluster 1 of the adjacency weighted network (ADJ-W). In fact, the number in parenthesis indicates the number of movies in a specific FDR-W cluster that are also present in cluster 1 of the adjacency weighted movie network.

Table S3 Over-expression of production country (C), language (L), genre (G) and filming locations (F) for two large clusters of FDR weighted network and five large clusters of Bonferroni weighted networks. Here we consider the movies that are also present in cluster 24 of the adjacency weighted movie network. In fact, the number in parenthesis indicate the number of movies in a specific FDR-W or BONF-W cluster that are also present in cluster 24 of the adjacency weighted movie network.

Text S1 Community detection and characterization.

Acknowledgments

We thank S. Fortunato and J. Kertész for fruitful discussions.

Author Contributions

Conceived and designed the experiments: MT SM FL JP RNM. Analyzed the data: MT SM RNM. Wrote the paper: MT SM FL JP RNM. Conceived the idea of the method: MT.

References

1. Watts DJ, Strogatz SH (1998) Collective dynamics of small-world networks. Nature 393: 440–442.
2. Barabási AL, Albert R (1999) Emergence of scaling in random networks. Science 286: 509–512.
3. Newman MEJ, Watts DJ, Strogatz SH (2002) Random graph models of social networks. Proc Natl Acad Sci USA 99: 2566–2572.
4. Song CM, Havlin S, Makse HA (2005) Self-similarity of complex networks. Nature 433: 392–395.
5. Schweitzer F, Fagiolo G, Sornette D, Vega-Redondo F, Vespignani A, et al. (2009) Economic networks: The new challenges. Science 325: 422–425.
6. Newman MEJ (2001) The structure of scientific collaboration networks. Proc Natl Acad Sci USA 98: 404–409.
7. Barabási AL, Jeong H, Neda Z, Ravasz E, Schubert A, et al. (2002) Evolution of the social network of scientific collaborations. Physica A 311: 590–614.
8. Guimera R, Uzzi B, Spiro J, Amaral LAN (2005) Team assembly mechanisms determine collaboration network structure and team performance. Science 308: 697–702.
9. Colizza V, Flammini A, Serrano MA, Vespignani A (2006) Detecting rich-club ordering in complex networks. Nat Phys 2: 110–115.
10. McCallum A, Wang XR, Corrada-Emmanuel A (2007) Topic and role discovery in social networks with experiments on enron and academic email. J Artif Intell Res 30: 249–272.
11. Onnela JP, Saramaki J, Hyvonen J, Szabo G, de Menezes MA, et al. (2007) Analysis of a large-scale weighted network of one-to-one human communication. New J Phys 9: 179.
12. Bascompte J, Jordano P, Melián CJ, Olesen JE (2003) The nested assembly of plant-animal mutualistic networks. Proc Natl Acad Sci USA 100: 9383–9387.
13. Reed-Tsochas F, Uzzi B (2009) A simple model of bipartite cooperation for ecological and organizational networks. Nature 457: 463–466.
14. Miller RG (1981) Simultaneous Statistical Inference. New York: Springer-Verlag, second edition.
15. Benjamini Y, Hochberg Y (1995) Controlling the false discovery rate: a practical and powerful approach to multiple testing. J R Statist Soc B 57: 289–300.
16. Feller W (1968) An Introduction to Probability Theory and Its Applications, volume 1. New York: Wiley, third edition.
17. Tatusov RL, Koonin EK, Lipman DJ (1997) A genomic perspective of protein families. Science 278: 631–637.
18. Tatusov RL, Fedorova ND, Jackson JD, Jacobs AR, Kiryutin B, et al. (2003) The cog database: an updated version includes eukaryotes. BMC Bioinformatics 4: 41.
19. Ciccarelli FD, Doerks T, von Mering C, Creevey CJ, Snel B, et al. (2006) Toward automatic reconstruction of a highly resolved tree of life. Science 311: 1283–1287.
20. Girvan M, Newman MEJ (2002) Community structure in social and biological networks. Proc Natl Acad Sci USA 99: 7821–7826.
21. Fortunato S (2010) Community detection in graphs. Physics Reports 486: 75–174.
22. Rosvall M, Bergstrom CT (2008) Maps of random walks on complex networks reveal community structure. Proc Natl Acad Sci USA 105: 1118–1123.
23. Tumminello M, Lillo F, Mantegna RN (2010) Correlation, hierarchies, and networks in financial markets. J Econ Behav Organ 75: 40–58.
24. Tumminello M, Micciché S, Lillo F, Varho J, Piilo J, et al. (2011) Community characterization of heterogeneous complex systems. J Stat Mech-Theory Exp. pp P01019.
25. Mantegna RN (1999) Hierarchical structure in financial markets. Eur Phys J B 11: 193–197.
26. Bonanno G, Caldarelli G, Lillo F, Mantegna RN (2003) Topology of correlation-based minimal spanning trees in real and model markets. Phys Rev E 68: 046130.
27. Tumminello M, Aste T, Matteo TD, Mantegna RN (2005) A tool for filtering information in complex systems. Proc Natl Acad Sci USA 102: 10421–10426.
28. Onnela JP, Chakraborti A, Kaski K, Kertész J, Kanto A (2003) Dynamics of market correlations: Taxonomy and portfolio analysis. Phys Rev E 68: 056110.
29. Kenett DY, Tumminello M, Madi A, Gur-Gershgoren G, Mantegna RN, et al. (2010) Dominating clasp of the financial sector revealed by partial correlation analysis of the stock market. PLoS ONE 5: 15032.
30. Tumminello M, Coronnello C, Lillo F, Micciché S, Mantegna RN (2007) Spanning trees and bootstrap reliability estimation in correlation based networks. Int J Bifurcation Chaos 17: 2319–2329.
31. Newman MEJ (2001) Scientific collaboration networks. ii. shortest paths, weighted networks, and centrality. Phys Rev E 64: 016132.

3

Noise Properties in the Ideal Kirchhoff-Law-Johnson-Noise Secure Communication System

Zoltan Gingl*, Robert Mingesz

Department of Technical Informatics, University of Szeged, Szeged, Hungary

Abstract

In this paper we determine the noise properties needed for unconditional security for the ideal Kirchhoff-Law-Johnson-Noise (KLJN) secure key distribution system using simple statistical analysis. It has already been shown using physical laws that resistors and Johnson-like noise sources provide unconditional security. However real implementations use artificial noise generators, therefore it is a question if other kind of noise sources and resistor values could be used as well. We answer this question and in the same time we provide a theoretical basis to analyze real systems as well.

Editor: James P. Brody, University of California, Irvine, United States of America

Funding: The publication/presentation is supported by the European Union and co-funded by the European Social Fund. Project title: "Telemedicine-focused research activities on the field of Matematics, Informatics and Medical sciences." Project number: TÁMOP-4.2.2.A-11/1/KONV-2012-0073. The funders had no role in study design, data collection and analysis, decision to publish, or preparation of the manuscript.

Competing Interests: The authors have declared that no competing interests exist.

* E-mail: gingl@inf.u-szeged.hu

Introduction

Communication security is getting more and more important in many different applications including electronic banking, protecting personal data, securing intellectual property of companies, transmission of medical data and many more. The Kirchhoff-Law-Johnson-Noise (KLJN) protocol was introduced as a low cost unconditionally secure key exchange protocol using only passive components: four resistors, two switches and interconnecting wires [1]. The protocol is based only on the laws of classical physics and has been introduced as an inexpensive alternative to quantum communicators. The first real implementation has been shown a few years after its discovery [2,3] and it has inspired the development of another secret key exchanged method [4]. There are many potential applications including securing computers, algorithms and hardware (memories, processors, keyboards, mass storage media) [5], key distribution over the Smart Grid [6], ethernet cables [7], uncloneable hardware keys [8]. Several attack methods has been discussed [9–14], however the ideal KLJN system is found to be secure. Debates are still going on [15,16] and recent papers discuss practical considerations for the applications [17,18].

The KLJN key exchange protocol is rather simple. During the communication a secret key is generated and shared between the two communicating parties, Alice and Bob. The system consists of two communicators and a transmission wire, see Fig. 1. Each communicator includes two resistors R_L and R_H and two series voltage noise sources $V_{LA}(t)$, $V_{HA}(t)$ and $V_{LB}(t)$, $V_{HB}(t)$ representing the thermal noise of the resistors at Alice and Bob, respectively:

$$S_L(f) = 4kTR_L \qquad (1)$$

$$S_H(f) = 4kTR_H \qquad (2)$$

where $S_L(f)$ is the power spectral density of the voltage noise sources $V_{LA}(t)$, $V_{LB}(t)$ and $S_H(f)$ is the power spectral density of the voltage noise sources $V_{HA}(t)$, $V_{HB}(t)$; k is the Boltzmann constant and T is the temperature.

A switch is used to select one of the resistors to be connected to the wire connecting the two communicators, see Fig. 1. At the beginning of each bit exchange, both Alice and Bob connect a resistor (R_H or R_L) to the wire. If both, Alice and Bob connect the higher value resistor, the voltage noise level will be high in the wire. If they both connect the low value resistor, the voltage noise will be low. If they connect different value resistors, the noise level will be intermediate and this is invariant if the resistors are swapped. [1,13]. This level can also be identified by the eavesdropper, Eve, however she cannot determine who has chosen the low value resistor. For this reason, this is the secure state that can be used for key exchange.

Note that in real applications the noise would be too small, therefore artificial noise generators are used to provide large enough signals in a given frequency band. In this case, the noise equivalent temperature is above 10^9 K [1]. On the other hand generators can enhance the security and offer new schemes with higher practical security in the non-ideal situations [17].

Results

According to the papers about the KLJN communication method the artificial noise generators are only used to emulate high temperatures, so they must generate Johnson-like noise. Therefore the security proof based on physical laws remains valid [1]. Our approach is in some sense opposite to the previous ones, when security has been proven for the given noise properties. Here we determine what the requirements of noise properties for unconditional security are. On the other hand, our analysis is based on statistical methods instead of physical laws of thermodynamics, therefore it can be more easily understandable for computer engineers and software engineers.

Let us assume that the system is operated in the LH situation, when Alice has switched on the lower value resistor and noise, while Bob uses the higher value resistor and noise as shown in Fig. 1.

In this case Eve measures the following voltage $V_E(t)$ and current $I_E(t)$ (flowing from Bob's side towards Alice) in the wire:

$$V_E(t) = \frac{V_{LA}(t) \cdot R_H + V_{HB}(t) \cdot R_L}{R_L + R_H} \tag{3}$$

and

$$I_E(t) = \frac{V_{HB}(t) - V_{LA}(t)}{R_L + R_H} \tag{4}$$

where $V_{LA}(t)$ and $V_{HB}(t)$ are the voltage noise signals at Alice and Bob, respectively. She can have two hypotheses: the correct one and the opposite. She can calculate the statistics of Alice's voltage noise for both cases. Since she knows the resistor values and the used voltage noise statistics, it is clear, that she will know that her assumption is wrong, if she gets invalid values during her calculations. For the correct assumption she must get correct results of course. Let us see what happens in the case of the wrong hypothesis. In this case Eve assumes that the high value resistor has been chosen by Alice. Therefore she calculates Alice's noise voltage $V_A(t)$ as:

$$
\begin{aligned}
V_A(t) &= V_E(t) - I_E(t) \cdot R_H \\
&= \frac{V_{LA}(t) \cdot R_H + V_{HB}(t) \cdot R_L}{R_L + R_H} + \frac{V_{HB}(t) - V_{LA}(t)}{R_L + R_H} R_H
\end{aligned} \tag{5}
$$

$$V_A(t) = \frac{V_{LA}(t) \cdot 2 \cdot R_H + V_{HB}(t) \cdot (R_H - R_L)}{R_L + R_H} \tag{6}$$

$$V_A(t) = V_{LA}(t) \cdot \frac{2 \cdot R_H}{R_L + R_H} + V_{HB}(t) \cdot \frac{R_H - R_L}{R_L + R_H} \tag{7}$$

The variance is given by the sum of variances:

$$\sigma_A^2 = \sigma_L^2 \cdot \left(\frac{2 \cdot R_H}{R_L + R_H} \right)^2 + \sigma_H^2 \cdot \left(\frac{R_H - R_L}{R_L + R_H} \right)^2 \tag{8}$$

where σ_A^2 is the variance of $V_A(t)$ and σ_L^2 and σ_H^2 are the variances of the voltage noise $V_{LA}(t)$ and $V_{HB}(t)$, respectively.

The communication can only be secure if $\sigma_A = \sigma_H$, otherwise Eve will know that Alice connected the low value resistor and voltage generator to the wire. Substituting this into Eq. (8) yields:

$$\frac{\sigma_H^2}{\sigma_L^2} \left(1 - \left(\frac{R_H - R_L}{R_L + R_H} \right)^2 \right) = \left(\frac{2 \cdot R_H}{R_L + R_H} \right)^2 \tag{9}$$

$$
\begin{aligned}
\frac{\sigma_H^2}{\sigma_L^2} &= \frac{(2 \cdot R_H)^2}{(R_L + R_H)^2 - (R_H - R_L)^2} \\
&= \frac{4 \cdot R_H^2}{R_L^2 + 2 \cdot R_L \cdot R_H + R_H^2 - (R_H^2 - 2 \cdot R_L \cdot R_H + R_L^2)}
\end{aligned} \tag{10}
$$

$$\frac{\sigma_H^2}{\sigma_L^2} = \frac{R_H}{R_L} \tag{11}$$

or in other form

$$\frac{\sigma_H}{\sigma_L} = \sqrt{\frac{R_H}{R_L}} \tag{12}$$

Therefore the noise amplitude must depend on the resistance as in the case of thermal noise; it must be proportional to the square root of the resistance. Otherwise the communication is certainly unsecure.

In the following we check how the security depends on the probability distribution of the noise. When the eavesdropper makes the correct assumption, she can calculate the noise signal that Alice is using exactly; therefore she gets the correct probability distribution of course. When she makes the wrong assumption then she obtains:

$$V_A(t) = V_L(t) \cdot \frac{2 \cdot R_H}{R_L + R_H} + V_H(t) \cdot \frac{R_H - R_L}{R_L + R_H} \tag{13}$$

The probability density $p_A(x)$ of $V_A(t)$ is given by the convolution of the probability densities of the two independent terms in Eq. (13). If $p(x)$ is the probability density function with unity variance,

$$\alpha = \sigma_L \cdot \frac{2 \cdot R_H}{R_L + R_H} \tag{14}$$

and

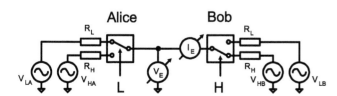

Figure 1. The KLJN secure communication system.

$$\beta = \sigma_H \cdot \frac{R_H - R_L}{R_L + R_H} \qquad (15)$$

then

$$\sigma_A^2 = \alpha^2 + \beta^2 \qquad (16)$$

where σA^2 is the variance of $V_A(t)$, and

$$p_A(x) = \int_{-\infty}^{\infty} \frac{1}{\alpha} p\left(\frac{x'}{\alpha}\right) \cdot \frac{1}{\beta} p\left(\frac{x - x'}{\beta}\right) dx' \qquad (17)$$

If Eq. (12) is satisfied, then $\sigma_A = \sigma_H$, that is needed for secure communication. Furthermore $p_A(x)$ measured by Eve must also be identical to the probability density function $p_H(x)$ of the noise voltages $V_{HA}(t)$ and $V_{HB}(t)$, otherwise Eve can detect that her assumption is wrong. Therefore using Eqs. (16) and (17) $p_A(x)$ can be expressed as.

$$p_A(x) = p_H(x) = \frac{1}{\sigma_H} p\left(\frac{x}{\sigma_H}\right) = \frac{1}{\sqrt{\alpha^2 + \beta^2}} p\left(\frac{x}{\sqrt{\alpha^2 + \beta^2}}\right) \qquad (18)$$

and finally we get

$$\frac{1}{\sqrt{\alpha^2 + \beta^2}} p\left(\frac{x}{\sqrt{\alpha^2 + \beta^2}}\right) = \int_{-\infty}^{\infty} \frac{1}{\alpha} p\left(\frac{x'}{\alpha}\right) \cdot \frac{1}{\beta} p\left(\frac{x - x'}{\beta}\right) dx'. \qquad (19)$$

Discussion

Eq. (19) is valid for normal distribution only [19], therefore we can conclude that the noise sources $V_{LA}(t)$, $V_{LB}(t)$ and $V_{HA}(t)$, $V_{HB}(t)$ must have normal distribution and the ratio of their amplitude must be equal to the square root of the ratio of the corresponding resistor values. In other words, Johnson-like noise must be used for the secure key exchange in the KLJN system. Note that although several other distributions – for example Cauchy-distribution – satisfy the condition that the convolution in Eq. (19) does not change the type of distribution, however the finite variance required by energetic considerations is only provided by normal distribution.

It is easy to see that for example random numbers with uniform distribution can't be used for secure communication. In this case Eq. (17) gives a trapezoidal probability density function for $p_A(x)$ as shown on Fig. 2, therefore its deviation from $p_H(x)$ can be very easily detected. We have developed a simple software application written in LabVIEW that can be used to simulate the KLJN protocol [20]. Normal or uniform distribution can be selected and the values of R_L, R_H, amplitude of $V_{LA}(t)$ and $V_{HA}(t)$, $V_{HB}(t)$ can be arbitrarily chosen. The application performs Eve's calculation of $V_A(t)$ for both hypotheses, and plots the corresponding measured amplitudes and probability densities.

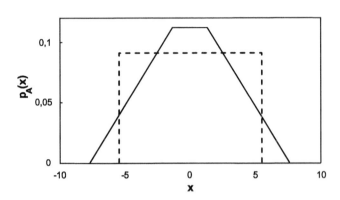

Figure 2. The probability density function $p_A(x)$ in the case of uniform distribution (solid line) strongly differs from $p_H(x)$ (dashed line).

Limitations and Open Questions

We have presented a mathematical statistical approach to determine the noise properties and resistor values required for secure communication and the results are in agreement with the original physical approach [1]. On the other hand our work does not address the question of complete security.

Considerable additional work could be carried out to investigate several attack types with similar approach. For example, in practical applications the effect of resistor inaccuracies, wire resistances can also be analyzed using our method; Eq. (8) can be applied to find the difference between the observed and expected variances, σ_A^2 and σ_H^2, respectively. This means that the information leak due to these inaccuracies can be estimated. On the other hand, if the desired security level is given, the required resistor values and accuracy of the components can be obtained.

Furthermore one can consider correlation properties, bandwidth of the noise sources that is important in practical applications and discussed in several publications.

Conclusions

In this paper we have shown a mathematical statistical approach to find out what kind of noise sources are required for secure communications in the Kirchhoff-Loop-Johnson-Noise unconditionally secure key exchange system. In agreement with the results can be found in the literature we found that the noise amplitude must scale with the square root of the corresponding resistor value and Gaussian noise sources must be used.

Note that our approach can serve as a starting point to quantitatively analyze several attack types in practical applications.

Acknowledgments

Zoltan Gingl thanks Béla Szentpáli for drawing his attention to the problem. Discussions with Gyula Pap about probability distributions are greatly appreciated.

Author Contributions

Wrote the paper: ZG. Contributed to the analysis: ZG RM.

References

1. Kish LB (2006) Totally secure classical communication utilizing Johnson(-like) noise and Kirchhoff's law. Phys. Lett. A 352: 178–182. doi: 10.1016/j.physleta.2005.11.062.
2. Mingesz R, Gingl Z, Kish LB (2008) Johnson(-like)-noise-Kirchhoff-loop based secure classical communicator characteristics, for ranges of two to two thousand kilometers, via model-line, Phys Lett A 372: 978–984. doi: 10.1016/j.physleta.2007.07.086.
3. Mingesz R, Kish LB, Gingl Z, Granqvist CG, Wen H, et al. (2013) Unconditional security by the laws of classical physics. Metrology & Measurement Systems XX: 3–16 DOI:10.2478/mms-2013-0001. Available:

http://www.degruyter.com/view/j/mms.2013.20.issue-1/mms-2013-0001/mms-2013-0001.xml.

4. Liu PL (2009) A key agreement protocol using band-limited random signals and feedback. IEEE J Lightwave Technol 27: 5230–5234. doi: 10.1109/jlt.2009.2031421.

5. Kish LB, Saidi O (2008) Unconditionally secure computers, algorithms and hardware. Fluct Noise Lett 8: L95–L98. doi: 10.1142/s0219477508004362.

6. Gonzalez E, Kish LB, Balog RS, Enjeti P (2013) Information theoretically secure, enhanced Johnson noise based key distribution over the smart grid with switched filters. PLOS ONE 8(7): e70206. doi: 10.1371/journal.pone.0070206.

7. Lin PK, Ivanov A, Johnson B, Khatri SP (2011) "A novel cryptographic key exchange scheme using resistors." In Computer Design (ICCD), 2011 IEEE 29th International Conference on, 451–452. IEEE, doi: 10.1109/ICCD.2011.6081445.

8. Kish LB, Kwan C (2013) Physical uncloneable function hardware keys utilizing Kirchhoff-Law-Johnson-Noise secure key exchange and noise-based logic, Fluctuation and Noise Letters, 12, 1350018 http://dx.doi.org/10.1142/S0219477513500181, Available: http://vixra.org/abs/1305.0068.

9. Hao F (2006) Kish's key exchange scheme is insecure. IEE Proc. Inform. Soc. 153: 141–142. doi: 10.1049/ip-ifs:20060068.

10. Kish LB (2006) Response to Feng Hao's paper "Kish's key exchange scheme is insecure". Fluct. Noise Lett. 6: C37–C41. doi: 10.1142/s0219477750600363x.

11. Scheuer J, Yariv A (2006) A classical key-distribution system based on Johnson (like) noise – How secure? Phys. Lett. A 359: 737–740. doi: 10.1016/j.physleta.2006.07.013.

12. Kish LB (2006) Response to Scheuer-Yariv: "A classical key-distribution system based on Johnson (like) noise – How secure?". Phys. Lett. A 359: 741–744. doi: 10.1016/j.physleta.2006.07.037.

13. Kish LB, Horvath T (2009) Notes on recent approaches concerning the Kirchhoff-law-Johnson-noise-based secure key exchange. Phys. Lett. A 373: 901–904. doi: 10.1016/j.physleta.2009.05.077.

14. Kish LB, Scheuer J (2010) Noise in the wire: The real impact of wire resistance for the Johnson(-like) noise based secure communicator. Phys. Lett. A 374: 2140–2142. doi: 10.1016/j.physleta.2010.03.021.

15. Bennett CH, Riedel CJ (2013) On the security of key distribution based on Johnson-Nyquist noise. Available: http://arxiv.org/abs/1303.7435.

16. Kish LB, Abbott D, Granqvist CG (2013) Critical analysis of the Bennett–Riedel attack on secure cryptographic key distributions via the Kirchhoff-Law-Johnson-Noise scheme. PLOS ONE 8(12): e81810. doi:10.1371/journal.pone.0081810.

17. Kish LB (2013) Enhanced secure key exchange systems based on the Johnson-noise scheme. Metrology & Measurement Systems XX: 191–204 Available: http://www.degruyter.com/view/j/mms.2013.20.issue-2/mms-2013-0017/mms-2013-0017.xml?format=INT.

18. Saez Y, Kish LB (2013) Errors and their mitigation at the Kirchhoff-Law-Johnson-Noise secure key exchange. PLOS ONE 8(11): e81103. doi:10.1371/journal.pone.0081103.

19. Feller W (1968, 1971), An introduction to probability theory and its applications, Vol. 1 and Vol. 2, John Wiley & Sons, ISBN 0 471 25708-7 and 0 471 25709-5.

20. Kirchhoff's-Law-Johnson-Noise secure key distribution simulation software. Available: http://www.noise.inf.u-szeged.hu/Research/kljn.

4

A Review of Evaluations of Electronic Event-Based Biosurveillance Systems

Kimberly N. Gajewski[1], Amy E. Peterson[2], Rohit A. Chitale[2], Julie A. Pavlin[3], Kevin L. Russell[3], Jean-Paul Chretien[2]*

1 Response Directorate, Federal Emergency Management Agency, Washington, DC, United States of America, 2 Division of Integrated Biosurveillance, Armed Forces Health Surveillance Center, Silver Spring, MD, United States of America, 3 Headquarters, Armed Forces Health Surveillance Center, Silver Spring, MD, United States of America

Abstract

Electronic event-based biosurveillance systems (EEBS's) that use near real-time information from the internet are an increasingly important source of epidemiologic intelligence. However, there has not been a systematic assessment of EEBS evaluations, which could identify key uncertainties about current systems and guide EEBS development to most effectively exploit web-based information for biosurveillance. To conduct this assessment, we searched PubMed and Google Scholar to identify peer-reviewed evaluations of EEBS's. We included EEBS's that use publicly available internet information sources, cover events that are relevant to human health, and have global scope. To assess the publications using a common framework, we constructed a list of 17 EEBS attributes from published guidelines for evaluating health surveillance systems. We identified 11 EEBS's and 20 evaluations of these EEBS's. The number of published evaluations per EEBS ranged from 1 (Gen-Db, GODsN, MiTAP) to 8 (GPHIN, HealthMap). The median number of evaluation variables assessed per EEBS was 8 (range, 3–15). Ten published evaluations contained quantitative assessments of at least one key variable. No evaluations examined usefulness by identifying specific public health decisions, actions, or outcomes resulting from EEBS outputs. Future EEBS assessments should identify and discuss critical indicators of public health utility, especially the impact of EEBS's on public health response.

Editor: Joel M. Montgomery, Global Disease Detection-Kenya, United States of America

Funding: This project was funded using internal operational funds of the Armed Forces Health Surveillance Center. The funders had no role in study design, data collection and analysis, decision to publish, or preparation of the manuscript.

Competing Interests: The authors have declared that no competing interests exist.

* Email: jean.chretien.mil@mail.mil

Introduction

Approximately 65% of the world's first news about infectious disease events comes from informal sources, such as the internet, and almost all major outbreaks investigated by the World Health Organization (WHO) are first identified through these informal sources [1–3]. Electronic event-based biosurveillance uses information on events impacting human health or the economy from internet sources, simultaneously incorporating diverse streams of data [4]. Electronic event-based biosurveillance systems (EEBS's) are an increasingly important source of epidemiologic intelligence [1–2].

Rapidly expanding worldwide access to the internet has fueled an increase in the number, and popularity, of EEBS's. There are several benefits to these new forms of surveillance. Many EEBS's allow citizens to report public health events via social media platforms or electronic communication channels independently of governments. Governments are no longer in sole control of their public health information, making it substantially harder to hide or delay outbreak or event reports [3]. Additionally, since protocols and confirmatory testing requirements do not delay the reports, they are considerably timelier than traditional surveillance sources [3]. Another beneficial aspect of EEBS's is that many are publicly

accessible. All subscribers have equally timely access to breaking reports regardless of their public health affiliations.

However, the same aspects of EEBS's that make them important new surveillance tools also may make them less reliable tools. Because many sources of data are not verified by public health professionals, these systems are prone to noise and false alarms [2]. Several researchers have commented that EEBS's especially tend to lack specificity in their alerts and reports [4–6]. Many EEBS's also face challenges in interoperability, scalability, population coverage, and interface customizability [4].

There have been evaluations of individual EEBS's, but there have not been structured evaluations of multiple EEBS's, or a comprehensive assessment of all EEBS evaluations. Our objective was to assess evaluations of EEBS's, and to recommend criteria for future evaluations. Our findings may help guide future EEBS development to most effectively exploit web-based information for biosurveillance.

Methods

We consulted an EEBS inventory [7] and biosurveillance experts (via informal queries to staff within our organization) to identify EEBS's that use publicly available internet information sources, include events that impact human health, and have global scope. We excluded systems that did not include infectious disease events.

To construct an evaluation framework for EEBS's, we reviewed the Centers for Disease Control and Prevention (CDC) surveillance system evaluation guidelines [8] and CDC evaluation guidelines for outbreak detection systems [9]. From those guidelines we selected evaluation variables highlighted as of primary importance in one of the guidelines, or mentioned as of secondary importance in both guidelines. We combined variables that are highly similar, narrowing the list to 17 variables: acceptability, accessibility, cost, data quality, flexibility, population coverage, predictive value positive, purpose, portability, representativeness, resources needed, sensitivity, simplicity, stability, timeliness, usefulness, and validity.

We searched PubMed and Google Scholar for publications with the name of one or more of the included EEBS's in any search field. We included structured evaluations of the systems as well as system descriptions if they discussed the system's performance with respect to one of the evaluation variables, even if that discussion was not a structured evaluation. For each evaluation, we recorded the evaluation variables discussed for each EEBS, and determined whether the evaluation assessed the variable quantitatively or qualitatively.

Results

We identified 11 EEBS's meeting the inclusion criteria (Table 1) [1–2,4–6,10–22]. The oldest system was ProMed, founded in 1994 and the newest system was Geni-Db, founded in 2012. The systems used automation to varying degrees in extracting information from the internet, processing it, and producing reports or alerts. For example, some EEBS's relied heavily on subject matter experts to assess reports from various sources (e.g., ProMED) or on manual translation by linguists with regional expertise (e.g., Argus); others used automated procedures for posting and mapping (e.g., HealthMap) or translation (e.g., GPHIN).

Older systems had more evaluations than the newer systems, with the exception of HealthMap, which ranked second for the most evaluations despite being founded in 2006. The median number of key variables assessed per EEBS was 8 (range, 3–15), with 6 evaluations assessing 7 or more key variables. Older systems were more likely to be reviewed in parallel with each other. There were two or fewer published evaluations on the GODsN, EpiSpider, MiTAP and Geni-Db systems.

Ten of 20 published evaluations contained quantitative assessments of at least one key variable, while the others mentioned evaluation variables but did not provide results reflective of a systematic assessment of those variables. Timeliness and purpose were assessed for 10 of 11 EEBS's, while data quality and validity were assessed for 4 of 11 EEBS's (Figure 1).

Nine evaluations assessed usefulness for 7 EEBS's by citing instances where the EEBS detected an outbreak earlier than other surveillance systems, or by eliciting user feedback, but none identified specific public health decisions, actions, or outcomes resulting from EEBS outputs. No evaluations examined system stability, and only two systems were evaluated on cost.

Table 1. Number of published evaluations and variables on identified EEBS's.

EEBS*	Year started	Description	No. evaluations	No. key variables assessed
Argus	2005	Manual translation of news reports by linguists with regional expertise	5 [2,4,10–12]	7
BioCaster (http://born.nii.ac.jp)	2006	Automated text mining of RSS newsfeeds	5 [2,12–15]	9
EpiSpider	2006	Automated conversion of topic and location data for online event reports (e.g., ProMED) to RSS feeds	2 [2,15]	4
Geni-Db (http://born.nii.ac.jp/_dev/static/genidb)	2012	Extracts event data from Biocaster and provides in searchable tables	1 [16]	4
GODSn	2006	Natural language processing and mapping for RSS news feeds	1 [11]	3
GPHIN (http://www.who.int/csr/alertresponse/epidemicintelligence/en)	1997	Automated translation and classification of reports from news feed aggregators with analyst decision to alert	7 [1–2,4,6,10,17,18]	10
HealthMap (http://www.healthmap.org/en)	2006	Automated processing and mapping of reports from RSS feeds and other online sources (e.g., official reports)	7 [2,4–5,15,18–20]	12
MedISys (http://medusa.jrc.it/medisys/homeedition/en/home.html)	2006	Automated processing of news source reports with email alerting	2 [4,21]	4
MiTAP	2001	Automated translation and processing of online reports	1 [22]	5
ProMed (http://www.promedmail.org)	1994	Manual screening/posting of reports from various sources (e.g., media, official reports, local observations)	5 [4–6,17–18]	12
PULS (http://puls.cs.helsinki.fi/static/index.html)	2006	Extracts event data from MedISys and provides in searchable tables	2 [4,21]	5

*Not all EEBS's were operational at the time of this report. URL provided when one could be identified.

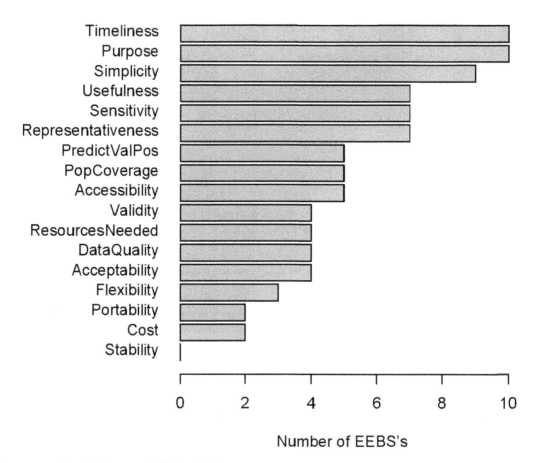

Number of EEBS's

Figure 1. Assessment of variables across EEBS evaluations.

Because of the lack of detail provided for evaluations on key variables, it was not possible to determine which EEBS's have been most useful or which EEBS approaches are most promising.

Discussion

We found a paucity of evaluation results for EEBS's on key evaluation variables, with only half of published evaluations reporting quantitative assessments of at least one key variable. Many evaluations mentioned key variables only in passing, and did not present results suggesting that a systematic quantitative or qualitative assessment was performed.

Timeliness, a possible advantage of EEBS's compared to traditional surveillance systems, was assessed for 10 of 11 EEBS's, but data quality and validity, for which EEBS's may face more challenges, were infrequently assessed (4 out of the 11 EEBS's). Perhaps most importantly, no evaluations cited specific examples of public health decisions, actions, or outcomes resulting from EEBS alerts. To our knowledge, this is the first comprehensive assessment of the evaluation literature for EEBS's, and provides a snapshot of the current knowledge of EEBS performance characteristics and overall usefulness.

We note two important limitations of this study. First, we focused on global-scale EEBS's. While these may be of broad interest to the public health community, we cannot comment on the extent of local or regional-scale EEBS evaluation. Evaluations of these systems may provide useful lessons for global-scale EEBS's. Second, we limited the assessment to peer-reviewed, published evaluations. This approach likely does not capture all EEBS evaluations, though some excluded evaluations may be difficult to access or of less-certain quality.

Future EEBS evaluations should identify and discuss critical indicators of public health utility, using quantitative or qualitative approaches to assess the usefulness of EEBS's in guiding public health action. They should also assess the novel aspects of EEBS's compared to traditional surveillance approaches, and include variables of special interest to potential EEBS users such as policy readiness, number and geographic profiles of users, number of sources, system redundancy, and input/output geography [23]; explore benefits of participatory biosurveillance and analytical tools, which some systems offer [24]; and consider ways of integrating outputs of various EEBS's to combine their respective strengths. Initial investigations into the effects of combining systems by Barboza et al. [25] have concluded that significant value can be added and synergistic effects can be observed. Further investigations into the value added by combining systems need to be explored, particularly any improvements in sensitivity, predictive value positive and usefulness.

We urge developers and users to conduct and publish evaluations of EEBS's. While they clearly offer powerful biosurveillance capabilities complementing traditional surveillance approaches, further indications of how and under what circumstances they are most useful, based on real-world experience, could advance EEBS development and effective integration into public health programs.

Acknowledgments

Disclaimer: The views are those of the authors, and do not necessarily reflect those of the Department of Defense or the Federal Emergency Management Agency.

References

1. Heymann DL, Rodier GR (2001) Hot spots in a wired world: WHO surveillance of emerging and re-emerging infectious diseases. Lancet Infect Dis 1: 345.
2. Keller M, Blench M, Tolentino H, Freifeld CC, Mandl KD, et al. (2009) Use of unstructured event-based reports for global infectious disease surveillance. Emerg Infect Dis 5: 689.
3. Tsai FJ, Tseng E, Chan CC, Tamashiro H, Motamed S, et al. (2013) Is the reporting timeliness gap for avian flu and H1N1 outbreaks in global health surveillance systems associated with country transparency? Global Health 9: 14.
4. Hartley D, Nelson N, Walters R, Arthur R, Yangarber R, et al. (2010) Landscape of international event-based biosurveillance. Emerg Health Threats J 3: 19.
5. Chan EH, Keller M, Sonricker AL, Freifeld CC, Brownstein JS (2011) Large-Scale Evaluation of Informal Online Reporting for Outbreak Detection. Children's Hospital Informatics Program, Children's Hospital Boston, Boston, United States.
6. Woodall JP (2001) Global surveillance of emerging diseases: the ProMED-mail perspective. Cad Saude Publica 17: 1037.
7. Deshpande A, Brown MG, Castro LA, Daniel WB, Generous EN, et al. (2013) A systematic evaluation of traditional and non-traditional data systems for integrated global biosurveillance – final report. Los Alamos National Laboratory.
8. German RR, Lee LM, Horan JM, Milstein RL, Pertowski CA, et al. (2001) Updated guidelines for evaluating public health surveillance systems: Recommendations from the Guidelines Working Group. MMWR Recomm Rep 50 (RR-13): 1.
9. Buehler JW, Hopkins RS, Overhage JM, Sosin DM, Tong V (2004) Framework for evaluating public health surveillance systems for early detection of outbreaks: Recommendations from the CDC working group. MMWR Recomm Rep 53 (RR-5): 1.
10. Morse SS (2012) Public health surveillance and infectious disease detection. Biosecur Bioterror 10: 6.
11. Khan SA, Patel CO, Kukafka R (2006) GODSN: Global News Driven Disease Outbreak and Surveillance. AMIA Annu Symp Proc 2006: 983.
12. Torii M, Yin L, Nguyen T, Mazumdar CT, Liu H, et al. (2011) An exploratory study of a text classification framework for Internet-based surveillance of emerging epidemics. Int J Med Inform 80: 56.
13. Collier N (2012) Uncovering text mining: a survey of current work on web-based epidemic intelligence. Glob Public Health 7: 731.
14. Collier N, Doan S, Kawazoe A, Goodwin RM, Conway M, et al. (2008) BioCaster: detecting public health rumors with a Web-based text mining system. Bioinformatics 24: 2940.
15. Lyon A, Nunn M, Grossel G, Burgman M (2012) Comparison of web-based biosecurity intelligence systems: BioCaster, EpiSpider and HealthMap. Transbound Emerg Dis 59: 223.
16. Collier N, Doan S (2012) GENI-DB: a database of global events for epidemic intelligence. Bioinformatics 28: 1186.
17. Mykhalovskiy E, Weir L (2006) The Global Public Health Intelligence Network and early warning outbreak detection: a Canadian contribution to global public health. Can J Public Health 97: 42.
18. Wilson K, Brownstein JS (2009) Early detection of disease outbreaks using the Internet. CMAJ 180: 829.
19. Brownstein JS, Freifeld CC, Reis BY, Mandl KD (2008) Surveillance Sans Frontieres: Internet-based emerging infectious disease intelligence and the HealthMap project. PLoS Med 5: e151.
20. Freifeld CC, Mandl KD, Reis BY, Brownstein JS (2008) HealthMap: global infectious disease monitoring through automated classification and visualization of Internet media reports. J Am Med Inform Assoc 15: 150.
21. Yangarber R, Steinberger R (2009) Automatic epidemiological surveillance from on-line news in MedISys and PULS. Proceedings of IMED-2009: International Meeting on Emerging Diseases and Surveillance.
22. Damianos L, Ponte J, Wohlever S, Reeder F, Day D, et al. (2002) MiTAP for biosecurity: a case study. AI Magazine 23: 13.
23. Corley CD, Lancaster MJ, Brigantic RT, Chung JS, Walters RA, et al. (2012) Assessing the continuum of event-based biosurveillance through an operational lens. Biosecur Bioterror 10: 131.
24. Hartley DM, Nelson NP, Arthur RR, Barboza P, Collier N, et al. (2013) An overview of internet biosurveillance. Clin Microbiol Infect 19: 1006.
25. Barboza P, Vaillant L, Mawudeku A, Nelson NP, Hartley DM, et al. (2013) Evaluation of epidemic intelligence systems integrated in the early alerting and reporting project for the detection of A/H5N1 influenza events. PLoS ONE 8: e57252.

Author Contributions

Conceived and designed the experiments: KNG AEP JPC. Performed the experiments: KNG JPC. Analyzed the data: KNG JAP JPC. Contributed reagents/materials/analysis tools: RAC JAP KLR. Wrote the paper: KNG AEP RAC JAP KLR JPC.

5

Ensemble-Based Network Aggregation Improves the Accuracy of Gene Network Reconstruction

Rui Zhong[1,**◕**], **Jeffrey D. Allen**[1,2,**◕**], **Guanghua Xiao**[1], **Yang Xie**[1,2]*

1 Quantitative Biomedical Research Center, Department of Clinical Sciences, University of Texas Southwestern Medical Center, Dallas, Texas, United States of America, **2** Harold C. Simmons Comprehensive Cancer Center, University of Texas Southwestern Medical Center, Dallas, Texas, United States of America

Abstract

Reverse engineering approaches to constructing gene regulatory networks (GRNs) based on genome-wide mRNA expression data have led to significant biological findings, such as the discovery of novel drug targets. However, the reliability of the reconstructed GRNs needs to be improved. Here, we propose an ensemble-based network aggregation approach to improving the accuracy of network topologies constructed from mRNA expression data. To evaluate the performances of different approaches, we created dozens of simulated networks from combinations of gene-set sizes and sample sizes and also tested our methods on three *Escherichia coli* datasets. We demonstrate that the ensemble-based network aggregation approach can be used to effectively integrate GRNs constructed from different studies – producing more accurate networks. We also apply this approach to building a network from epithelial mesenchymal transition (EMT) signature microarray data and identify hub genes that might be potential drug targets. The R code used to perform all of the analyses is available in an R package entitled "ENA", accessible on CRAN (http://cran.r-project.org/web/packages/ENA/).

Editor: Alberto de la Fuente, Leibniz-Institute for Farm Animal Biology (FBN), Germany

Funding: This work was supported by NIH grants 5R01CA152301 and 1R01CA172211, and Cancer Prevention Research Institute of Texas award RP101251. The funders had no role in study design, data collection and analysis, decision to publish, or preparation of the manuscript.

Competing Interests: The authors have declared that no competing interests exist.

* Email: Yang.Xie@utsouthwestern.edu

◕ These authors contributed equally to this work.

Introduction

With the advent of high-throughput technologies such as microarrays, next generation sequencing, and other state-of-the-art techniques, huge datasets have been generated in a variety of contexts (*e.g.*, cancer and aging) in order to identify novel biomarkers and drug targets [1]. However, the utility and interpretation of those collected data remains challenging and needs to be improved. Recently, reconstructions of gene regulatory networks (GRNs) from high-throughput data have been widely used to identify novel drug targets or therapeutic compounds [1–4]. GRNs provide new information regarding gene-gene interactions and how they work in networks to regulate cellular functions, allowing for a systematic understanding of the molecular and cellular mechanisms underlying specific biological functions and processes [5–10]. For GRNs in particular, genes that have many interactions with other genes (called "hub genes") are likely to be "drivers" of disease status, based on their GRN regulatory roles. An analysis of hub genes is thus a promising approach for identifying key tumorigenic genes for both basic and clinical research [11–15].

Although accurate reconstruction of GRNs has proven valuable to a myriad of areas throughout biomedical research, the method remains only moderately satisfactory [7–10]. Researchers have previously used approaches such as Bayesian Network- [16,17], Correlation- [18], and Partial-Correlation-based approaches [19,20], all of which have demonstrated various strengths and weaknesses under different biological/simulation settings, with no one method excelling under all conditions [21]. Additionally, leveraging gene expression data from multiple datasets to construct gene networks is often difficult, due to discrepancies in microarray platform selection as well as in normalization and data processing techniques [22–24]. In this study, we propose an Ensemble-based Network Aggregation (ENA) approach to integrate gene networks derived from different methods and datasets, to improve the accuracy of network inference.

For the construction of our ENA, we used a non-parametric, inverse-rank-product method to combine networks reconstructed from the same set of genes. The rank-product method, introduced by Breitling et al [21,25,26], is effective for detecting differentially expressed genes in microarray studies. Because the rank-product method is both powerful and computationally efficient, it has now been extended for use in other fields, such as RNAi screening [27] and proteomics [28]. Additionally, this method can be directly related to linear rank statistics [29]. In this study, we show three ways to leverage this approach to generate ensemble-based networks: 1) samples in a dataset can be "bootstrapped" to reconstruct multiple networks out of a single original dataset using a single reconstruction method, which can then be aggregated into a more accurate and reproducible network; 2) networks produced by various reconstruction methods can be aggregated into a single network that is more accurate than the network provided by any individual method; and 3) networks reconstructed from different studies that contain the same genes can be combined into a single, more accurate network, despite differences in platforms or normalization techniques. Because this approach requires few resources, it can be applied efficiently to dozens or hundreds of networks reconstructed on the same set of genes. We show here that this approach has the ability to improve the accuracy of GRN reconstruction in all three of the above-described applications, based on simulated gene expression data as well as on *Escherichia coli* (*E. coli*) datasets [30–33].

An important application of network reconstruction is to identify hub genes in a network that might be biologically and pharmaceutically interesting. When we applied ENA to micro-array data that was previously used to delineate an epithelial-mesenchymal transition (EMT) signature [34], we built a network for the identification of hub genes that had been experimentally validated to be EMT-relevant, thus representing potential drug targets. Though our demonstration is focused on microarray data for consistency purposes, ENA should be easily implemented in the analysis pipeline of next-generation sequencing (NGS) data, such as RNA-Seq. Cutting-edge technology enables the simulta-neous measurement of millions of cellular data points and sheds light on a brand-new pattern in drug discovery, where medication is viewed in the context of pathways and networks rather than individual proteins or genes [1]. In the near future, in combination with patient-specific genomic profile and drug-target interaction knowledge, GRNs could be used to facilitate both the prediction and treatment of personalized therapy [2].

Materials and Methods

Overview of the inverse-rank-product network aggregation approach

Reconstructed gene networks are often returned as a weighted undirected graph $G = (N, \Omega)$, where G is a reconstructed graph, $N = \{1,...,n\}$ is the set of vertices (genes) in the graph, and $\Omega - [\omega_{ij}]_{i,j \in N}$ is referred to as the adjacency matrix, in which ω_{ij} represents the confidence score of the interaction between genes i and j. A larger (absolute) value of ω_{ij} indicates a stronger interaction or higher confidence in the edge between genes i and j, while $\omega_{ij} = 0$ indicates no interaction or conditional independence between genes i and j. Some techniques, such as Sparse PArtial Correlation Estimation (SPACE) [19], return a sparse matrix in which many of the possible interactions are 0; other techniques return complete graphs in which all edges are assigned non-zero weightings. Additionally, the distribution of ω_i can vary drastically among reconstruction techniques. For this reason, aggregating networks that were reconstructed using different techniques or different datasets is challenging. However, the rank-based method offers a non-parametric approach that does not depend on the actual distribution of scores of edges derived from different methods [35]. In this study, we used a rank-product method to combine networks to overcome the problem of different distribu-tions observed in this approach.

Specifically, suppose $G = \{G^k\}$ is a set of networks constructed on the same set of genes N, where $k = \{1,...,K\}$ is the index of a particular network. For each single network $G^k = (N, \Omega^k)$, we calculate r_{ij}^k, the rank of ω_{ij}^k for $\{i, j \in N$ and $i < j\}$. Since the adjacency matrix Ω of an undirected graph is symmetric, we only need to calculate the rank of the $N * (N-1)/2$ elements in ω_{ij}, constituting the lower triangle (i<j) of Ω. In this study, we assign the lower rank to the higher confidence interaction. For example, the interaction with the highest confidence will have rank 1. This operation is performed on each individual graph G^k independently. After the rank of r_{ij}^k has been computed for each network G^k, we calculate the rank of a particular edge between genes i and j in the aggregated network by taking the product of the ranks of

the same edge across all networks in G, according to: $\tilde{r}_{ij} = \prod_{k=1}^{K} r_{ij}^k$. This function is iterated over all possible edges to construct the aggregated network $\tilde{G} = (N, \tilde{r}_{ij})$, in which the confidence scores of the edges in the new network are based on the aforementioned rank-product calculation.

This algorithm can be efficiently applied to large networks with many reconstructed networks in G. The complexity of the algorithm is that $O(K \cdot |N| \log(|N|))$, as $\frac{|N|^2 - |N|}{2} = O(N^2)$ elements must be sorted for each network in G^k.

Three applications of our ENA approach

The initial application was to leverage the rank-product method to "bootstrap" samples. Each time, we constructed the gene network using a randomly selected subset of the available samples. By repeating this process B times, we created a set G consisting of B graphs, each reconstructed using only randomly selected bootstrap samples in the dataset. For example, here is the procedure to generate the bootstrapping network from a microarray dataset designated MD:

$$MD \xrightarrow{Bootstrap} \begin{cases} MD^1 \to G^1 = \{N, \Omega^1\} \to r_{ij}^1 \text{ (for } 1 \leq i < j \leq n) \searrow \\ \vdots \qquad \vdots \qquad \vdots \qquad \to \text{RankProduct} \to \tilde{G} \\ MD^B \to G^B = \{N, \Omega^B\} \to r_{ij}^B \text{ (for } 1 \leq i < j \leq n) \nearrow \end{cases}$$

Of course, this bootstrapping procedure inflates the computa-tional complexity of GRN reconstruction by several orders of magnitude, as GRNs must be reconstructed B times rather than just once. Because each graph in G can be reconstructed independently, it is possible to take advantage of the "paralleliz-ability" of these simulations by utilizing multiple cores or computers, as we discuss below. Note also that the complexity of GRN reconstruction does scale on the order of samples included, so that each permuted GRN can be constructed slightly more quickly than a single global GRN. For the reconstruction techniques employed in this study, however, the performance did not vary greatly based on the number of samples included.

The second application of the rank-product network merging method was to reconstruct an aggregated GRN, based on the output of multiple different reconstruction techniques. We have observed that reconstruction techniques perform differently based on different simulation settings [21], with no one method outperforming the others on all metrics. Thus, we were interested to see whether or not merging these GRNs would improve performance. In this application, the set of graphs G consist of one graph per network reconstruction technique employed. In our analysis, we leveraged GeneNet [20], Weighted Correlation Network Analysis (WGCNA) [18], and SPACE, creating a set of three graphs which could then be aggregated. GeneNet and SPACE are partial-correlation-based inference algorithms. Gene-Net uses the Moore-Penrose pseudoinverse [36] and bootstrapping to estimate the concentration matrix. The SPACE algorithm creates a regression problem when trying to estimate the concentration matrix and then optimizes the results with a symmetric constraint and an L1 penalization, while WGCNA is a correlation-based approach that can identify sub-networks using hierarchical clustering. Conceptually, the aggregated graph should place higher confidence on those edges that consistently rank highly across the three methods and lower confidence on those edges that ranked highly in only one graph. The following procedure is used to derive the ensemble network, based on M different methods within the same dataset MD:

$$MD \begin{cases} \xrightarrow{\text{method} 1} G^1 = \{N, \Omega^1\} \rightarrow r_{ij}^1 \text{ (for } 1 \le i < j \le n) \\ \vdots \quad\quad \vdots \quad\quad \vdots \quad\quad \rightarrow \text{RankProduct} \rightarrow \tilde{G} \\ \xrightarrow{\text{method} M} G^M = \{N, \Omega^M\} \rightarrow r_{ij}^M \text{ (for } 1 \le i < j \le n) \end{cases}$$

The final application evaluated in this study was in the merging of networks constructed from different datasets. Historically, gene expression datasets have been collected from various sites on different microarray platforms with different procedures for tissue collection, which creates incompatibilities and difficulties when performing analyses on data from different datasets simultaneously. Because the rank-product method makes no assumptions about the distribution of the data at any point, we employ it to combine GRNs produced from different datasets, yielding a single aggregated GRN which aims to capture the consistencies in network topology from the GRNs produced on different datasets. We thus derive the aggregated network from datasets MD^1, $MD^2 \dots MD^D$ as follows:

$$\begin{aligned} MD^1 &\rightarrow G^1 = \{N, \Omega^1\} \rightarrow r_{ij}^1 \text{ (for } 1 \le i < j \le n) \\ \vdots \quad &\quad \vdots \quad\quad\quad \vdots \quad\quad \rightarrow \text{RankProduct} \rightarrow \tilde{G} \\ MD^D &\rightarrow G^D = \{N, \Omega^D\} \rightarrow r_{ij}^D \text{ (for } 1 \le i < j \le n) \end{aligned}$$

Software

The code used to bootstrap samples and aggregate the resultant networks was written in the R programming language. We created an R Package entitled "ENA" and made it available on CRAN (http://cran.r-project.org/web/packages/ENA/index.html), from which the compiled binaries, as well as all original source code, are also available for download.

Because of the parallelization opportunities in this algorithm, we ensured that our software would be able to distribute the bootstrapping process across multiple cores and multiple nodes using MPI [37]. Thus, if 150 CPU cores were available simultaneously, a bootstrapping of 150 samples could run in approximately the same amount of wall-clock time as a single reconstruction using all the samples. The ENA package includes robust documentation and (optionally) leverages the RMPI package to allow for parallel execution of the bootstrapping simulations, where such a computational infrastructure is available.

Additionally, we leveraged the Git revision control system via GitHub (http://github.com) to control not only the R code developed for the ENA package, but also all code, reports, and data used in the aforementioned simulations and reconstruction techniques; all of this code is freely available at https://github.com/QBRC/ENA-Research. All the data analysis code used to generate the results in this study was compiled into a single report and can be reproduced easily using the knitr R package [38,39]. Due to the computational complexity involved in reconstructing this quantity of gene regulatory networks, the execution may take some time to analyze larger networks if the process is not distributed across a large computing cluster.

Reproducibility

Our analysis code and results were structured in reproducible reports, which are publicly available at https://github.com/QBRC/ENA-Research. The results in this study can be regenerated by a simple mouse click to make everything transparent to researchers.

Results

Simulation

We first tested the ENA methods on a wide array of simulated datasets. We simulated the gene expression datasets based on previously observed protein-protein interaction networks [40,41] from the human protein reference database (HPRD), while the expression data were simulated from conditional normal distributions [42]. We extracted five different network sizes in an approximately scale-free topology: 17 genes with 20 connections, 44 genes with 57 connections, 83 genes with 114 connections, 231 genes with 311 connections, or 612 genes with 911 connections by varying the number of publications required for each connection. For example, if we required each connection to be supported by at least 7 publications (the most reliable connections), it resulted in a very small network with 17 connections; while if we required each connection to be supported by at least 3 publications, it led to a very large network with 911 connections. For each network size, we simulated datasets with differing numbers of samples (microarrays): 20, 50, 100, 200, 500, and 1,000. Finally, we varied the noise by setting the standard deviation of the expression values to 0.25, 0.5, 1.0, or 1.5. In total, we generated 120 datasets to cover all possible arrangements of the above variables.

To test the effect of integrating networks derived from different datasets, we generated three different datasets of 200 samples each from the 231-gene networks with noise values (standard deviation of the distribution of gene expression) of 0.25, 1, and 2. We used the methods described above to reconstruct three networks (one from each dataset) and then aggregated those networks. For comparison, we also combined all three datasets into a single dataset containing these 600 samples and then reconstructed a single network from this larger dataset.

The performance of methods in this setting can be represented by a Receiver Operating Characteristic (ROC) Curve, which plots the True Positive Rate against the False Positive Rate, demonstrating the performance of the method at all relevant edge confidence score thresholds. The performance of a method can be quantified by calculating the Area Under the ROC Curve (AUC). The greater the AUC, the better the performance of the method represented. A perfect reconstruction would have an AUC of 1, while a random guess would obtain an AUC of 0.5. An alternative approach to evaluating gene regulatory network reconstruction is the Area Under the Precision Recall curve (AUPR). In a precision recall curve, recall (also known as sensitivity) is plotted against precision (positive predictive value).

ENA of bootstrapping samples

We found that bootstrapping samples can increase the accuracy of network inference. In our study, we randomly selected 70% of all samples and rebuilt networks and repeated the abovementioned process more than 100 times for each dataset to get the bootstrapping results. For example, the networks reconstructed from the dataset on the 231-gene network with a noise value of 0.25 can be compared to demonstrate variations in performance (Figures 1 and 2).

Figure 1 (left) shows that by bootstrapping samples using the SPACE algorithm, the AUC of the reconstructed network can improve from 0.748 to 0.816. In order to evaluate the precision of ENA, we also plotted the Precision-Recall Curve (Figure 1, right); the area under the precision-recall curve improved from 0.249 to

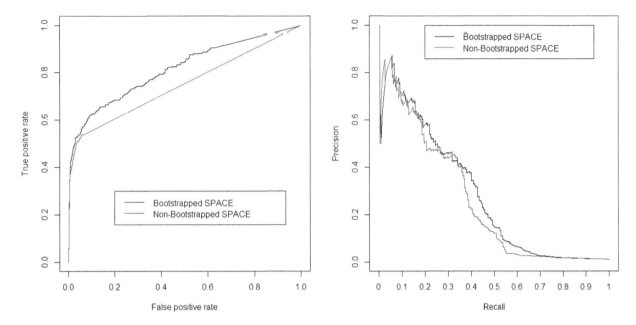

Figure 1. Receiver Operating Characteristic (ROC) curves and the Precision Recall Curve both demonstrate the performance of the SPACE algorithm on the 231-gene network with 20 samples and a noise value of 0.25 when performing a single iteration (*i.e.,* "non-bootstrapped") or bootstrapping the dataset using the Ensemble Network Aggregation approach. In this case, the Area Under the ROC Curve (AUC) of the non-bootstrapped SPACE method was 0.748, while that of the bootstrapped SPACE method was 0.816. The Area Under the Precision-Recall (AUPR) curve also improves from 0.249 (SPACE) to 0.273 (bootstrapping).

0.273. Figure 2 shows the degree of AUC improvement with each iteration of bootstrapping in SPACE, WGCNA and GeneNet with sample sizes of 20, 50 and 100 (left, middle and right panels). As shown in this figure, the bootstrapping method increases the performance of SPACE substantially, improves GeneNet slightly (when the number of microarrays is small), but does not noticeably improve the performance of WGCNA. The AUC improvements for different sample sizes and different network sizes are plotted in Figures S1–S4 in File S1. From these figures, we can see that SPACE benefits from bootstrapping in 80% of all simulated networks and in 89% of "large" network simulations. Figure 3 shows the average performance increase achieved by bootstrapping SPACE on different network sizes. The improvement increases as the network size increases. Based on this evidence, we suggest employing the bootstrapping approach when using the SPACE algorithm, but not when using the others evaluated in this study.

ENA of different methods

Aside from optimizing individual reconstruction techniques, we found that combining different network reconstruction techniques that were executed on the same dataset also has the power to significantly improve the accuracy of the reconstructed networks. Using the dataset from the 83-gene network with 200 samples and a noise value of 0.25, we evaluated the comparative performance of each reconstruction technique, as well as that of the aggregated network. Figure 4 shows that the aggregated network outperformed all of the individual constituent reconstruction techniques.

We also observed this trend to hold true across most of the datasets (Figure S5 and Figure S6 in File S1) that we tested: the aggregated method typically outperformed any single reconstruction technique. This is especially beneficial in scenarios in which the top-performing individual network reconstruction technique

may vary based on the context, *e.g.,* some methods perform well on larger networks, while others excel in datasets containing few samples. Thus, to have an aggregation technique that consistently outperforms or matches the best performing individual method eliminates the need to choose a single reconstruction technique based on the context.

In addition, we compared our method with the method used in Marbach et al. The result (Figure S8 in File S1) indicates the proposed ENA method performs better in the simulation settings.

ENA of different datasets

Finally, we found the ENA approach to work very well when attempting to integrate various datasets, especially among heterogeneous datasets containing different distributions of expression data. After generating three datasets from the 231-gene network, each with 200 samples and noise values of 0.25, 1, and 2, we reconstructed each network using bootstrapped SPACE, GeneNet, and WGCNA, and then aggregated the resultant networks into a single network for each of the three datasets. We then used the ENA approach to consolidate these three networks into a single network representing the underlying network behind the three distinct datasets. We also compared this approach to the alternative of simply merging all three datasets into a single 600-sample dataset and using the same approach to reconstruct a single network. As shown in Figure 5, the proposed ENA approach outperformed the alternative approach of simply combining the expression data into a single dataset. Reconstructing on each dataset independently produced AUCs of 0.96, 0.96, and 0.89 from noise values of 0.25, 1, and 2, respectively. "Naïvely" merging the datasets by combining them into one large dataset yielded an AUC of 0.96. The network aggregation approach, however, yielded the best performance, with an AUC of 0.98.

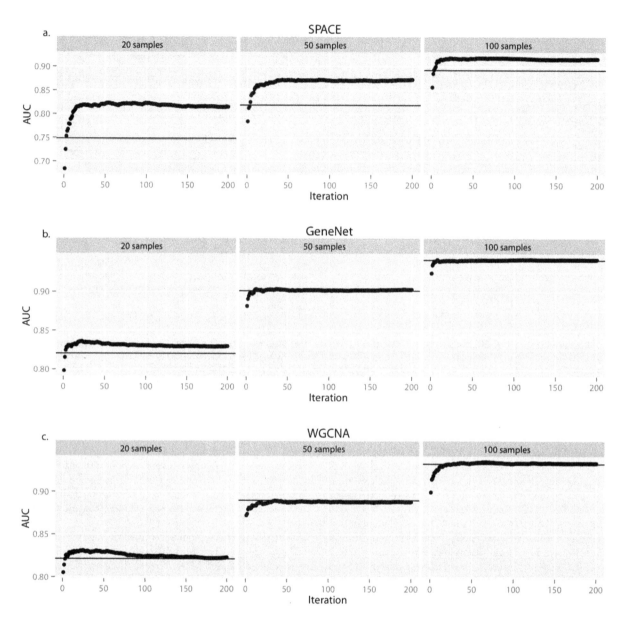

Figure 2. Comparison of the Area Under the Curves (AUCs) of the re-constructed networks from the 231-gene network with a noise value of 0.25 and different sample sizes (20, 50 or 100) for SPACE (a.), GeneNet (b.), and WGCNA (c.). In these plots, the y-axis shows the performance of the reconstructed network, measured by the AUCs; a horizontal line is drawn to represent the AUC of the non-bootstrapped reconstruction (a single reconstruction using all available samples). The x-axis represents the number of iterations in the bootstrapping process. Points below the horizontal line represent a loss in accuracy of the reconstructed networks, and points above the horizontal line represent a gain of AUC (*i.e.,* an increase in model performance).

Evaluating ENA approach in *E. coli* datasets

We then tested the ENA approach on three *Escherichia coli* (*E. coli*) datasets: 1) the Many Microbe Microarrays Database ("M3D") [30] containing 907 microarrays measured under 466 experimental conditions using Affymetrix GeneChip *E. coli* Genome arrays; 2) the second dataset ("Str") of expression data from laboratory evolution of *E. coli* on lactate or glycerol (GSE33147) [31], which contains 96 microarrays measured under laboratory adaptive evolution experiments using Affymetrix E. coli Antisense Genome Arrays; and 3) the third dataset [32,33] ("BC") containing 217 arrays measuring the transcriptional response of *E. coli* to different perturbations and stresses, such as drug treatments, UV treatments and heat shock. The RegulonDB database [43,44],

which contains the largest and best-known information on transcriptional regulation in *E. coli*, was thus used as a "gold standard" to evaluate the accuracy of the variously constructed networks.

We were able to obtain similarly positive results by employing these approaches on the *E. coli* data (Figure 6). Bootstrapping and aggregating the three methods on each dataset independently produced AUCs of 0.574, 0.616, and 0.599 for the BC, Str, and MD3 datasets respectively. By merging the three networks produced on each dataset using ENA, we were able to produce a network with an AUC of 0.655, larger than the AUC of any network produced by any of the datasets independently. Because the performance of ENA in the real dataset was evaluated based on our current biological knowledge, which may only be a partial

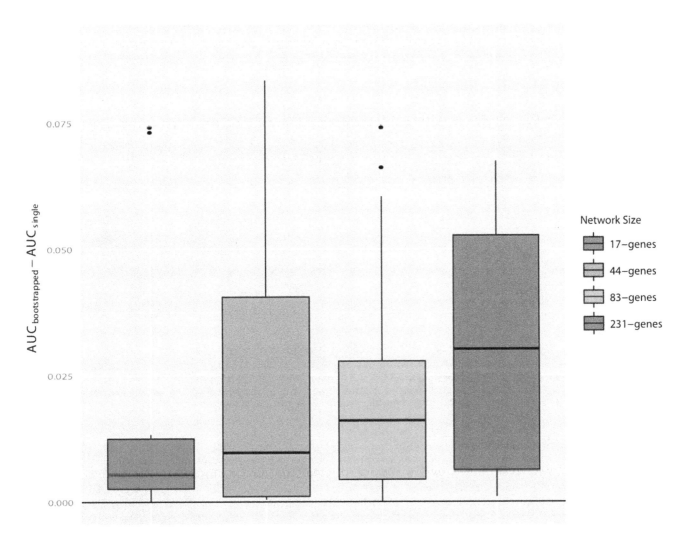

Figure 3. The effect of network size on ENA performance. The y-axis represents the improvement in AUC of the bootstrapped SPACE networks vs. the non-bootstrapped SPACE networks. Different bars represent different sizes of networks in the simulation study.

truth, the overall network reconstruction accuracy observed in the real dataset was much lower than those in the simulated datasets, where the full truth was known. On the other hand, simulated data might also partially reflect the true situation by simplifying aspects of an over-complicated biological process. However, the ENA approach consistently improved the network reconstruction accuracy in both simulated and real datasets.

Network reconstruction via ENA to identify potential drug targets

Network reconstruction of gene expression data helps identify hub genes that might be novel drug targets because of their role in engaging multiple molecules, a process that has been used to identify gene sets predictive of benefit for adjuvant chemotherapy in non-small-cell lung cancer [13]. Here we applied ENA to a dataset consisting of 76 genes from 54 non-small-cell lung cancer (NSCLC) cell lines that were previously identified to comprise an epithelial-mesenchymal transition (EMT) "signature" for NSCLC [34]. This signature consisted of genes whose expressions were either positively or negatively correlated with at least 1 of 4 putative EMT markers, including E-cadherin (*CDH1*), vimentin

(*VIM*), N-cadherin (*CDH2*) and/or fibronectin 1 (*FN1*), and followed a bimodal distribution pattern across the cell lines [34].

Overall, we attempted to identify hub genes clinically interesting for NSCLC treatment. We thus employed multiple methods to build GRN networks and combined them via ENA. As shown in Figure 7, we identified three major nodes. Of these, *ZEB1*, which had the highest degree in the resulting ENA network, is a well-known EMT activator and tumor promoter that represses stemness-inhibiting microRNAs [45] and mediates the loss of E-cadherin expression to allow cell detachment [46]. *MARVELD3* is known as a tight junction molecule and has been shown to be downregulated during Snail-induced EMT [47]. Finally, *EPHA1*, the first member of the erythropoietin-producing hepatocellular (Eph) family of receptor tyrosine kinases, was recently shown to potentially play a role in carcinogenesis and the progression of several cancer types [48]. *EPHA1* is also frequently mutated in NSCLC patients, along with other known "driver" mutations [49].

Discussion

The ability to aggregate networks using the rank-product merging approach has proven to be a valuable contribution in

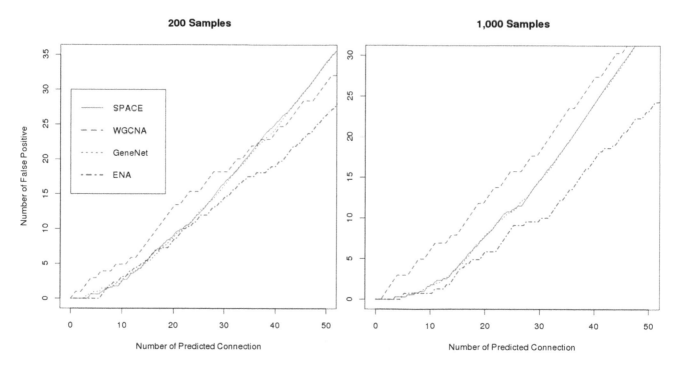

Figure 4. The performance in aggregating different methods. A comparison of the accuracy of the reconstructed networks using the datasets containing 200 samples (left) and 1,000 samples (right) from the 83-gene network with a noise value of 0.25. As can be seen here, the ensemble network aggregation approach performs better than any of the other individual techniques on these two networks.

reconstructing gene regulatory networks – and likely in other fields, as well. By bootstrapping a single dataset using a single approach such as SPACE, we were able to significantly improve the performance of the algorithm. By aggregating the networks produced by different reconstruction techniques on a single dataset, we were able to consistently match or outperform the

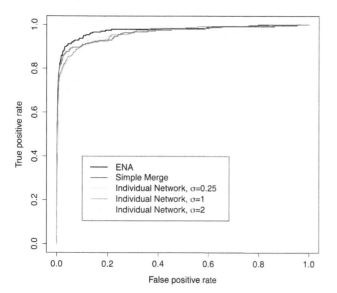

Figure 5. The ROC curves of different approaches to reconstruct the gene network based on three simulated datasets. The ENA approach outperformed the alternative approach of simply combining the expression into a single dataset and individual network with increasing noise of 0.25, 1, and 2. AUCs of all five approaches are 0.98, 0.96, 0.96, 0.96, and 0.89 respectively.

best-performing technique for that dataset, regardless of fluctuations in the performance of any one algorithm. By aggregating networks constructed independently on different datasets capturing similar biological environments, we were able to reconstruct the network more accurately than would be possible using any one dataset alone. So far, the study of integration of gene regulatory networks has been continuously advancing. Both Marbach D. et al. 2012 [50] and Hase T. et al. 2013 [51] have devised methods for integrating gene regulatory networks. The former is based on integration through rescoring gene-gene interaction according to average ranks across multiple methods, while the latter is focused on combining the confidence of each gene-gene interaction by multiple algorithms through leveraging the diversity of the different techniques. ENA is able to integrate networks from multiple algorithms. In addition, ENA performs bootstrapping within single dataset and also takes advantage of integrating multiple datasets to improve the performance. In this study, we showed that when integrating bootstrapped samples, different algorithms and data sets could achieve the best performance (Figure 6).

It is likely that SPACE was the only method to show consistent and significant improvement from bootstrapping because the SPACE algorithm models gene regulation using linear regression; as a result, the network construction problem is converted to a straightforward variable selection problem. In SPACE, the variable selection problem is solved by sparse regression techniques with a symmetric constraint. By solving all the regression models simultaneously, SPACE attempts to accrue the globally optimized results. However, due to the instability in variable selection [52] caused by collinearity in the data, the networks constructed by SPACE are sensitive to sampling. A small change in the samples selected may lead to a relatively large

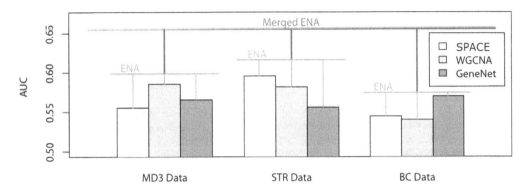

Figure 6. The AUCs of the generated networks when executed on the E. coli datasets. Note that the aggregating ENA networks from SPACE, WGCNA and GeneNet increase the accuracy within each individual dataset, and aggregating results from three datasets further increases the accuracy beyond that of any one dataset.

change in the network structure. As a result, the networks constructed from bootstrapping samples are relatively "independent", which leads to greater accuracy in the aggregated network.

As a sample application, we applied our approach to an EMT signature data set, successfully building a gene regulatory network and identifying hub genes with interesting therapeutic and

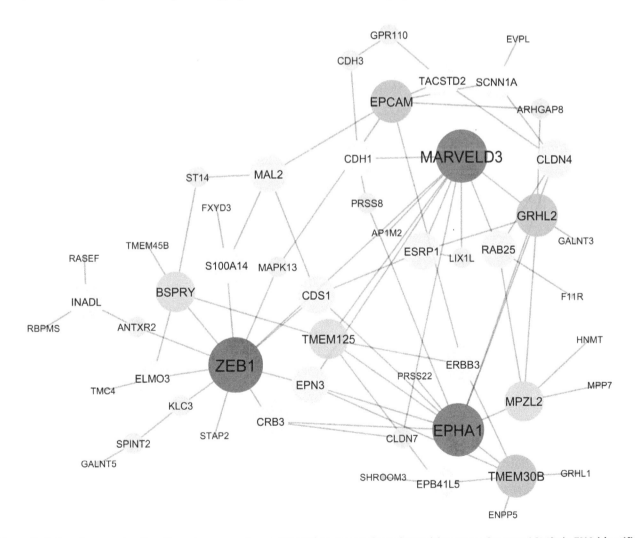

Figure 7. Network reconstruction (based on a previous epithelial-to-mesenchymal transition gene signature) [34] via ENA identifies potential drug targets for non-small-cell lung cancer (NSCLC). Microarray data from 54 NSCLC cell lines were analyzed using four different methods and the results integrated via ENA. Identified hub genes *ZEB1*, *MARVELD3* and *EPHA1* have interesting clinical implications as novel drug targets. Node color and size are proportional to the degree of connectivity (*i.e.*, the number of edges connecting each node).

pharmacological implications (Figure 7). Our discovery has also been experimentally validated in previous literature. Ingenuity Pathway Analysis (IPA) (http://www.ingenuity.com/products/ipa) is a pathway and network database based on curated literatures. When we used IPA to analyze our data, ZEB1 was identified as a hub gene, which confirmed our discovery using the ENA approach. Additionally, predicted interactions such as the CDH1–CDH3 interaction and the CLDN4-GRHL2 interaction were also confirmed (Figure S7 in File S1). While here we showed results only from microarray data analyses, ENA can also be conveniently applied to next-generation sequencing techniques such as RNA-Seq. Thus, combining individualized genomic profiles with the reconstruction of gene regulatory networks might facilitate personalized therapy (possibly using "hub genes" as therapeutic targets).

To make ENA implementation user-friendly for the biological research community, we provide a publically available R package to allow others to use these techniques on their own datasets. By leveraging the MPI framework, we were able to run the bootstrapping process in parallel across many cores and nodes, drastically reducing the amount of time it takes to run such analyses. We include in this package a function that can permute random networks and perform ENA in order to better estimate the significance of any particular connection observed in a network.

This function can be used to reduce a continuous, complete graph to an unweighted graph that includes only statistically significant edges.

Finally, we went to great lengths to ensure that all of our analysis would be as reproducible as possible by collating our analysis code into reproducible reports – most of which can be regenerated at the click of a button – and making all of these freely available online at https://github.com/QBRC/ENA-Research. We feel that this transparency is an important but uncommon step in the scientific process and hope that other researchers may begin incorporating such practices into their own investigations to foster more open, collaborative research.

Author Contributions

Conceived and designed the experiments: JA RZ GX YX. Performed the experiments: RZ JA GX YX. Analyzed the data: RZ JA GX YX. Contributed reagents/materials/analysis tools: JA RZ GX YX. Wrote the paper: RZ JA GX YX.

References

1. Sun X, Vilar S, Tatonetti NP (2013) High-throughput methods for combinatorial drug discovery. Sci Transl Med 5: 205rv201.
2. Rix U, Colinge J, Blatt K, Gridling M, Remsing Rix LL, et al. (2013) A Target-Disease Network Model of Second-Generation BCR-ABL Inhibitor Action in Ph+ ALL. PLoS One 8: e77155.
3. Zhao H, Jin G, Cui K, Ren D, Liu T, et al. (2013) Novel modeling of cancer cell signaling pathways enables systematic drug repositioning for distinct breast cancer metastases. Cancer Res 73: 6149–6163.
4. Wang XS, Simon R (2013) Identification of potential synthetic lethal genes to p53 using a computational biology approach. Bmc Medical Genomics 6.
5. Friedman N (2004) Inferring cellular networks using probabilistic graphical models. Science 303: 799–805.
6. Ihmels J, Friedlander G, Bergmann S, Sarig O, Ziv Y, et al. (2002) Revealing modular organization in the yeast transcriptional network. Nature Genetics 31: 370–377.
7. Lee I, Date SV, Adai AT, Marcotte EM (2004) A probabilistic functional network of yeast genes. Science 306: 1555–1558.
8. Sachs K, Perez O, Pe'er D, Lauffenburger DA, Nolan GP (2005) Causal protein-signaling networks derived from multiparameter single-cell data. Science 308: 523–529.
9. Segal E, Shapira M, Regev A, Pe'er D, Botstein D, et al. (2003) Module networks: identifying regulatory modules and their condition-specific regulators from gene expression data. Nat Genet 34: 166–176.
10. Stuart JM, Segal E, Koller D, Kim SK (2003) A gene-coexpression network for global discovery of conserved genetic modules. Science 302: 249–255.
11. Kendall SD, Linardic CM, Adam SJ, Counter CM (2005) A network of genetic events sufficient to convert normal human cells to a tumorigenic state. Cancer Research 65: 9824–9828.
12. Mani KM, Lefebvre C, Wang K, Lim WK, Basso K, et al. (2008) A systems biology approach to prediction of oncogenes and molecular perturbation targets in B-cell lymphomas. Molecular Systems Biology 4.
13. Tang H, Xiao G, Behrens C, Schiller J, Allen J, et al. (2013) A 12-gene set predicts survival benefits from adjuvant chemotherapy in non-small cell lung cancer patients. Clin Cancer Res 19: 1577–1586.
14. Nibbe RK, Koyuturk M, Chance MR (2010) An Integrative -omics Approach to Identify Functional Sub-Networks in Human Colorectal Cancer. Plos Computational Biology 6.
15. Slavov N, Dawson KA (2009) Correlation signature of the macroscopic states of the gene regulatory network in cancer. Proceedings of the National Academy of Sciences of the United States of America 106: 4079–4084.
16. Friedman N, Linial M, Nachman I, Pe'er D (2000) Using Bayesian networks to analyze expression data. J Comput Biol 7: 601–620.
17. Liang F (2009) Learning Bayesian Networks for Gene Expression Data. In: Dey D, Ghosh S, Mallick B, editors. Bayesian Modeling in Bioinformatics: Chapman & Hall/CRC Biostatistics Series.
18. Langfelder P, Horvath S (2008) WGCNA: an R package for weighted correlation network analysis. BMC Bioinformatics 9: 559–559.
19. Peng J, Wang P, Zhou N, Zhu J (2009) Partial Correlation Estimation by Joint Sparse Regression Models. J Am Stat Assoc 104: 735–746.
20. Schäfer J, Strimmer K (2005) An empirical Bayes approach to inferring large-scale gene association networks. Bioinformatics 21: 754–764.
21. Allen JD, Xie Y, Chen M, Girard L, Xiao G (2012) Comparing statistical methods for constructing large scale gene networks. PLoS One 7: e29348.
22. Allen JD, Wang S, Chen M, Girard L, Minna JD, et al. (2012) Probe mapping across multiple microarray platforms. Brief Bioinform 13: 547–554.
23. Liu J, Huang J, Ma S (2013) Incorporating network structure in integrative analysis of cancer prognosis data. Genet Epidemiol 37: 173–183.
24. Ma S, Huang J, Song X (2011) Integrative analysis and variable selection with multiple high-dimensional data sets. Biostatistics 12: 763–775.
25. Breitling R, Armengaud P, Amtmann A, Herzyk P (2004) Rank products: a simple, yet powerful, new method to detect differentially regulated genes in replicated microarray experiments. FEBS Lett 573: 83–92.
26. Breitling R, Herzyk P (2005) Rank-based methods as a non-parametric alternative of the T-statistic for the analysis of biological microarray data. J Bioinform Comput Biol 3: 1171–1189.
27. Birmingham A, Selfors LM, Forster T, Wrobel D, Kennedy CJ, et al. (2009) Statistical methods for analysis of high-throughput RNA interference screens. Nat Methods 6: 569–575.
28. Wiederhold E, Gandhi T, Permentier HP, Breitling R, Poolman B, et al. (2009) The yeast vacuolar membrane proteome. Mol Cell Proteomics 8: 380–392.
29. Koziol JA (2010) Comments on the rank product method for analyzing replicated experiments. FEBS Lett 584: 941–944.
30. Faith JJ, Driscoll ME, Fusaro VA, Cosgrove EJ, Hayete B, et al. (2008) Many Microbe Microarrays Database: uniformly normalized Affymetrix compendia with structured experimental metadata. Nucleic Acids Res 36: 866–870.
31. Fong SS, Joyce AR, Palsson BØ (2005) Parallel adaptive evolution cultures of Escherichia coli lead to convergent growth phenotypes with different gene expression states. Genome Res 15: 1365–1372.
32. Sangurdekar DP, Srienc F, Khodursky AB (2006) A classification based framework for quantitative description of large-scale microarray data. Genome Biol 7.
33. Xiao G, Wang X, Khodursky AB (2011) Modeling Three-Dimensional Chromosome Structures Using Gene Expression Data. J Am Stat Assoc 106: 61–72.
34. Byers LA, Diao L, Wang J, Saintigny P, Girard L, et al. (2013) An epithelial-mesenchymal transition gene signature predicts resistance to EGFR and PI3K inhibitors and identifies Axl as a therapeutic target for overcoming EGFR inhibitor resistance. Clin Cancer Res 19: 279–290.
35. Lim J, Lee S, Choi H (2006) Information loss from censoring in rank-based procedures. Statistics & Probability Letters 76: 1705–1713.
36. Penrose R (1954) A Generalized Inverse for Matrices; 1954. pp. 406–413.
37. Gabriel E, Fagg GE, Bosilca G, Angskun T, Dongarra JJ, et al. (2004) Open MPI: Goals, Concept, and Design of a Next Generation MPI Implementation. Proceedings, 11th European PVM/MPI Users' Group Meeting. Budapest, Hungary. pp. 97–104.
38. Xie Y (2013) knitr: A Comprehensive Tool for Reproducible Research in R. In: Stodden V, Leisch F, Peng D, editors. Implementing Reproducible Computational Research: Chapman and Hall/CRC.

39. Xie Y (2013) Dynamic Documents with R and knitr: Chapman and Hall/CRC.
40. Mishra GR, Suresh M, Kumaran K, Kannabiran N, Suresh S, et al. (2006) Human protein reference database—2006 update. Nucleic Acids Res 34: 411–414.
41. Peri S, Navarro JD, Kristiansen TZ, Amanchy R, Surendranath V, et al. (2004) Human protein reference database as a discovery resource for proteomics. Nucleic Acids Research 32: D497–D501.
42. Pan W, Lin J, Le CT (2002) How many replicates of arrays are required to detect gene expression changes in microarray experiments? A mixture model approach. Genome Biol 3.
43. Gama-Castro S, Salgado H, Peralta-Gil M, Santos-Zavaleta A, Muñiz-Rascado L, et al. (2011) RegulonDB version 7.0: transcriptional regulation of Escherichia coli K-12 integrated within genetic sensory response units (Gensor Units). Nucleic Acids Res 39: 98–9105.
44. Salgado H, Martinez-Flores I, Lopez-Fuentes A, Garcia-Sotelo JS, Porron-Sotelo L, et al. (2012) Extracting regulatory networks of Escherichia coli from RegulonDB. Methods Mol Biol 804: 179–195.
45. Wellner U, Schubert J, Burk UC, Schmalhofer O, Zhu F, et al. (2009) The EMT-activator ZEB1 promotes tumorigenicity by repressing stemness-inhibiting microRNAs. Nat Cell Biol 11: 1487–1495.
46. Schmalhofer O, Brabletz S, Brabletz T (2009) E-cadherin, beta-catenin, and ZEB1 in malignant progression of cancer. Cancer Metastasis Rev 28: 151–166.
47. Kojima T, Sawada N (2012) Regulation of tight junctions in human normal pancreatic duct epithelial cells and cancer cells. Ann N Y Acad Sci 1257: 85–92.
48. Peng L, Wang H, Dong Y, Ma J, Wen J, et al. (2013) Increased expression of EphA1 protein in prostate cancers correlates with high Gleason score. Int J Clin Exp Pathol 6: 1854–1860.
49. Maki-Nevala S, Kaur Sarhadi V, Tuononen K, Lagstrom S, Ellonen P, et al. (2013) Mutated Ephrin Receptor Genes in Non-Small Cell Lung Carcinoma and Their Occurrence with Driver Mutations-Targeted Resequencing Study on Formalin-Fixed, Paraffin-Embedded Tumor Material of 81 Patients. Genes Chromosomes Cancer.
50. Marbach D, Costello JC, Kuffner R, Vega NM, Prill RJ, et al. (2012) Wisdom of crowds for robust gene network inference. Nat Methods 9: 796–804.
51. Hase T, Ghosh S, Yamanaka R, Kitano H (2013) Harnessing diversity towards the reconstructing of large scale gene regulatory networks. PLoS Comput Biol 9: e1003361.
52. Breiman L (1996) Heuristics of Instability and Stabilization in Model Selection. The Annals of Statistics 24: 2350–2383.

6

Effect of the Internet Commerce on Dispersal Modes of Invasive Alien Species

Magdalena Lenda[1]*, **Piotr Skórka**[2], **Johannes M. H. Knops**[3], **Dawid Moroń**[4], **William J. Sutherland**[5], **Karolina Kuszewska**[1], **Michał Woyciechowski**[1]

1 Institute of Environmental Sciences, Jagiellonian University, Krakow, Poland, 2 Institute of Zoology, Poznan University of Life Sciences, Poznan, Poland, 3 School of Biological Sciences, University of Nebraska, Lincoln, Nebraska, United States of America, 4 Institute of Systematics and Evolution of Animals, Polish Academy of Sciences, Kraków, Poland, 5 Conservation Science Group, Department of Zoology, University of Cambridge, Cambridge, United Kingdom

Abstract

The spread of invasive alien plants has considerable environmental and economic consequences, and is one of the most challenging ecological problems. The spread of invasive alien plant species depends largely on long-distance dispersal, which is typically linked with human activity. The increasing domination of the internet will have impacts upon almost all components of our lives, including potential consequences for the spread of invasive species. To determine whether the rise of Internet commerce has any consequences for the spread of invasive alien plant species, we studied the sale of thirteen of some of the most harmful Europe invasive alien plant species sold as decorative plants from twenty-eight large, well known gardening shops in Poland that sold both via the Internet and through traditional customer sales. We also analyzed temporal changes in the number of invasive plants sold in the largest Polish internet auction portal. When sold through the Internet invasive alien plant species were transported considerably longer distances than for traditional sales. For internet sales, seeds of invasive alien plant species were transported further than were live plants saplings; this was not the case for traditional sales. Also, with e-commerce the shape of distance distribution were flattened with low skewness comparing with traditional sale where the distributions were peaked and right-skewed. Thus, e-commerce created novel modes of long-distance dispersal, while traditional sale resembled more natural dispersal modes. Moreover, analysis of sale in the biggest Polish internet auction portal showed that the number of alien specimens sold via the internet has increased markedly over recent years. Therefore internet commerce is likely to increase the rate at which ecological communities become homogenized and increase spread of invasive species by increasing the rate of long distance dispersal.

Editor: Mari Moora, University of Tartu, Estonia

Funding: Funding for this project was partially provided by the Jagiellonian University, DS/BiNoZ/INoŚ/756, and Polish National Science Centre UMO-2011/01/N/NZ8/03211. WJS is funded by Arcadia. ML and KK were beneficiaries of the Grant for Young Scientists "Start" of the Foundation for Polish Science. The funders had no role in study design, data collection and analysis, decision to publish, or preparation of the manuscript.

Competing Interests: The authors have declared that no competing interests exist.

* Email: lenda.m@vp.pl

Introduction

Species invasions are both a result and cause of global ecological changes. Numerous studies have shown that invasive alien plant species can often establish and change edaphic conditions in new habitats, change their structure or even create novel invasive-dominated ecosystems [1–8]. However, a key factor is invasive species dispersal; species can only become successful invaders if they can disperse to suitable habitats.

Most plant dispersal is over a short range and it has a right skewed leptokurtic distribution, with a tail of few individuals travelling very long distances [9], [10]. These few long distance dispersers are important in colonization of new areas and in determining the rate of geographical range spread [10], [11]. This tail is the most important factor shaping the invasion mechanisms of alien plant species. The long tail of extreme movements by invasive species is often attributable to various forms of human transportation, which allows alien species to cross geographical barriers and to colonize new localities as well as escape from lag phase of colonization [5], [12–15].

Just as some alien species benefitted from the development of the train network in the UK, such as Oxford Ragwort, whose seeds were carried along the tracks after the trains [16], alien species currently benefit from the worldwide development of vehicle, navy and aerial transportation [12–15]. In recent years much of the trade has been through internet sales, with an associated transportation network [17], [18]. However, we barely understand how the relatively new global phenomenon of internet commerce may affect the dispersal modes of invasive alien plants at landscape or regional scales.

Currently, many alien plant species, including invasive ones, are available for sale in many garden shops [19], [20]. The traditional commercial model in shops or floral markets comprises sales to visiting customers, which limits the type of transportation, and distances on which alien plant species are transported. However, the recent rise in internet sales have included the development of trade in animals and plants to customers who may not even know where the shop is located [21], [22]. Thus, the internet trade is much less constrained in transportation type and distance by which alien invasive species may travel from shop to customer. Consequently, the distribution of distances that are travelled by alien species from a shop to a customer should be less peaked and much less skewed (be more Gaussian-like distribution) than in case of traditional sale, assuming that buyers in the internet are located at random distances from the shop. There are currently few studies that show how internet commerce enhances purchase of invasive species, and so increases propagule pressure of invasive species [22]. There is thus a need to determine how internet commerce affects dispersal modes and the functioning of populations in the environment on landscape or regional scales and how this compares with the traditional shop trade.

The aim of this study was to characterize the role of the internet sale in the long distance dispersal and spread of invasive species. The study was carried out in Poland, where the internet and traditional commerce of garden flowering plants are both relatively well developed. The following hypotheses were tested:

1. Internet trade results in larger movement distances of invasive plant species than does traditional trading, where much of the trade will be to local people.

2. Internet trade is less constrained by the distance and generates distribution of dispersal distances that are less peaked and less skewed than in more limited traditional trading.

3. Seeds are transported on longer distances than seedlings. Seedlings are known to be more fragile and more likely to be collected in person than sent by post.

4. Supply and demand of invasive alien species sold via internet auctions is growing over time indicating increased interest in alien invasive species, what suggests also higher propagule pressure of exotic species.

Materials and Methods

We chose 13 invasive species that are widespread in Poland, some of which are amongst the most harmful invasive plant species in Europe [23], and which were easily available through garden shops and internet auctions. The following species were studied: *Acer negundo, Buddleia davidii, Echinocystis lobata, Elodea canadensis, Impatiens glandulifera, Prunus serotina, Quercus rubra, Rhus typhina, Robinia pseudoacacia, Rosa rugosa*. We also examined the following genera that are rarely distinguishing at the species level so can be sold under the same name (for example whether *Solidago gigantea* or *Solidago canadensis*): *Reynoutria* sp., *Rudbeckia* sp., *Solidago* sp. However, in all cases the species within a genus are similar in biology and habitats they occupy.

Data collection

Comparison of distances that alien invasive plants travelled according to whether sold on-line and by traditional shops

To compare distances on which invasive alien species were transported when sold via internet and in traditional shops, we chose 50 large shops in Poland in different regions of Poland that carried both internet and traditional sale of alien species listed above, and we asked owners to collect data about customers postal codes, sale objects and volume for both internet and traditional commerce. To find suitable shops we searched Google using the phrase: "sklep ogrodniczy"(garden shop) then Yellow Pages portals (www.yellowpages.pl) and Panorama firm (www. panoramafirm.pl, only in polish), the latter is the oldest and best known source for locating all kinds of business including shops. We also selected shops in such a manner that they were dispersed across the entire country. Twenty eight of the owners of these shops agreed to collect the data. We collected data in 2011 for each species on the geographic location of both the shops and customers, number of purchasers, number of plants sold, their life form (whether seedlings or seeds). Shop keepers were aware that data about plant commerce collected by them would be used for further analyses, PhD dissertation, writing scientific papers and publishing. However, they did not know the specific hypotheses that we planned to test. The shop owners were informed about results and ensured that the database will be de-identified, and that they could withdraw the date they had already donated as well as being assured that their personal data (name of the shop and its location etc.) will not be published anywhere. The goal of collected data was to study plant commerce not the human behaviour, and the research possessed no risk to the participants, meaning that the probability and magnitude of harm or discomfort anticipated in the research are not greater in and of themselves than those ordinarily encountered in daily life or during the performance of routine physical or psychological examinations or tests. The data were de-identified. Moreover this research did not involve vulnerable populations and possessed no risk to the participants and, as such, this research did not require Institutional Review Board approval in Poland.

Data provided by the shop owners allowed us to map and visualize the geographical location of the source and destination of each species. Collecting zip codes and location name is a common sales practice as it allows sellers to target subsequent promotions [24]. We also used location name and zip codes to calculate distances between shops and buyers for both internet and traditional sales. We used centroids of the area of a destination location and zip code to calculate the distance transported. We used Quantum 1.7 Wroclaw GIS system.

Temporal changes in the number of invasive species sold on the internet auction portal

In order to check if internet commerce of invasive species has increased during last 6 years, we used data from the public available archive of Allegro (see http://allegro.pl), the largest on-line auction portal in Poland, to collect data on the number of auctions of the selected invasive alien species. We were able to retrieve data from years 2006–2011. We preferred Allegro as a database instead of the previously chosen sample of shops, because we were interested in (i) estimating the number of all cases of the selected alien invasive species for sale in the entire Poland and (ii) number of purchases made by as many as possible customers in the same period. Moreover, the garden shops had no accurate data on the amount of the two types of sale from past 6 years (or had not recorded it) and some of shops had existed for short period of time. The data were public, thus collecting it did not require Institutional Review Board approval.

Data processing and analysis

Distances travelled by alien plants through the different purchasing routes were compared using a general linear mixed model; plant species and shop identity were assigned as random factors. A general linear mixed model is an extension to the general linear model in which the linear predictor contains random effects in addition to the usual fixed effects. They are particularly useful in settings where repeated measurements are made on the same statistical units (for example species in our study), or where measurements are made on clusters of related statistical units (shops in this study). Because of their advantages in dealing with data dependency, mixed effects models are often preferred over more traditional approaches, such as repeated measures ANOVA [25]. Random factors in our analyses account for differences between unspecified traits of species and shops that have not been measured during the study.

We also compared features (skewness and kurtosis) of the distance distribution in both sale types for each plant species. Then, we used paired t-student tests to analyse differences between internet and traditional sales in shops. Skewness is a measure of the degree of asymmetry of a distribution around a mean with zeros indicating symmetrical, positive values for right skewed distributions and negative values for left skewed. Kurtosis measures the degree of peakedness of a distribution. Kurtosis higher and lower than 0 indicate leptokurtic (peaked) distribution and platykurtic (flattened) distribution, respectively.

To compare the distances at which seeds and seedlings were transported in the internet and traditional sale we used general linear mixed model. Sale type (internet vs. traditional), life stage (seeds vs. seedling) and interaction between them were introduced as fixed factors. Species identity and shop identity were random effects. In this model only species with both seeds and seedlings in shops' offer were included.

We used correlation analysis to assess the statistical significance of the temporal trend in the number of internet auctions and number of purchasers in Allegro portal. All statistical analyses were done in SPSS 19.

Results

Comparison of distances that alien invasive plants travelled according to whether sold on-line and from traditional shops

For all species the mean distance from a shop to a purchaser was significantly greater when alien invasive plants were sold through the internet than from traditional trade in shops (GLMM $F_{1,\ 4048} = 42.58$, $P<0.001$, Fig. 1). The effect was consistent among species (Fig. 1). Figure 2 maps, for three species, the distances plants were transported according to whether sold on the internet or in traditional sales; maps for the other species, together with distance distributions, are in Figures S1–S23 in File S1. Also shapes of distributions of distances covered by plants differed between internet and traditional sales. Mean skewness of distance distribution of plants sold via internet was lower than for plants sold in traditional shops (paired t-tests: $t_{12} = 5.40$, $P<0.001$, Fig. 3). The kurtosis coefficient for distance distribution of species sold via internet was lower than in plants sold in a traditional manner (paired t-tests: $t_{12} = 3.71$, $P=0.003$, Fig. 3).

The total number of records of purchases from the 28 analyzed shops was 4,050. The number of records involving purchasing seeds was 811 and 3,239 for seedlings. The total number of seeds sold was at least 62,646, and 6,894 for seedlings (in several transactions the number of the plants sold was not specified). For internet commerce the mean transportation distances of seeds were significantly higher (interaction term in GLMM $F_{1,\ 1990} = 13.85$, $P<0.001$ with Tukey post hoc test $P<0.010$) than for seedlings (Fig. 4) but this was not the case for traditional sales (Fig. 4).

Temporal changes in the number of invasive species sold on the internet auction portal

The total sale of 13 selected invasive alien species in the largest Polish internet portal increased over time whether measured as total number of purchasers (r = 0.98; $P<0.001$) or auctions (r = 0.99; $P<0.001$) (Fig. 5). Both the number of purchasers and the number of auctions increased for most species studied (Figures S24–S36 in File S1).

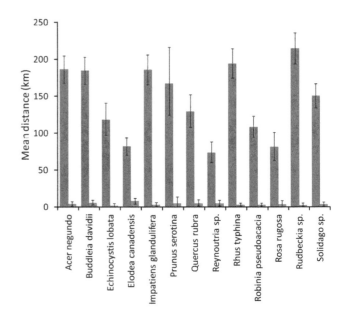

Figure 1. Mean transportation distances for all 13 species traded online (red bars) and in traditional sales (green bars). Whiskers are 95% confidence intervals.

Discussion

Only 40 years of the internet persistence was necessary for it to become the fastest and the most effective way of communication, but also a very popular means of purchasing goods. Our study shows that socioeconomical changes, especially e-commerce and accessible transport for long distances, modifies dispersal patterns of invasive alien plant species.

Our results clearly show that the distances that invasive species were transported were several times larger if they were ordered by internet than for traditional sales. This result has important ramifications for the understanding invasion processes and indicates that the internet sale generates frequent long-distance dispersal events. Although such long-distance dispersal plays prominent role in invasion ecology and biology of plants [10], [26], natural vectors rarely achieve comparable distances in terrestrial landscapes as the dispersal pattern generated by the internet sale. Therefore such innovative means of species purchasing may play a unique role in alien species invasions. It is believed that the increasing number of the invasions of many groups of organisms is tied to the frequent migration or movements of humans and facilitated long-distance transport [15], [27–30]. Also, frequent long distance dispersal is one of the most important factors triggering alien species from the lag phase into population expansion [31–33]. The role of distant transport in vehicles and plains has been already recognized, however such cases are rare and incidental and usually represents only tail of the longest dispersal distances. The transport and long-distance dispersal events caused by internet sale are regular and become increasingly frequent. Moreover, the shape of distribution of the distances covered by plants sold via internet were flatten and less skewed than in plant sold in a traditional way. The latter was similar to natural dispersal distance distributions, which are highly right skewed and leptokurtic. The distribution of the distances in the internet sale did not resemble any natural (long) distance distribution of dispersing propagules as it was flatten and only little skewed. Thus it is clear that the internet trade generates novel dispersal modes of invasive species.

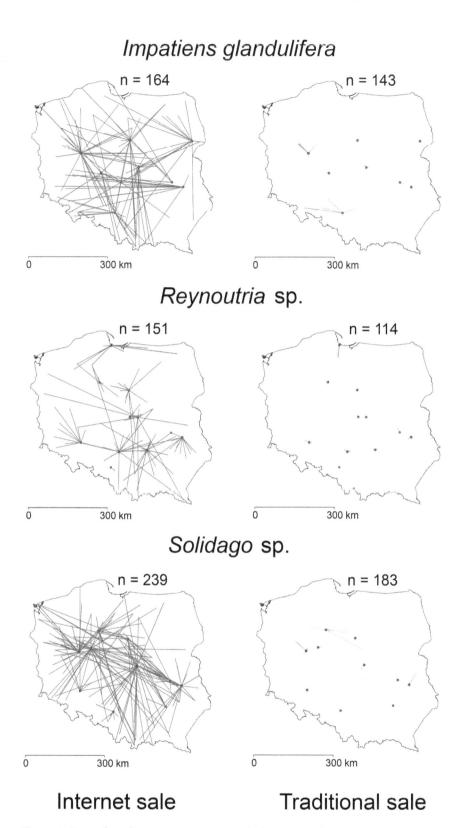

Impatiens glandulifera

n = 164   n = 143

Reynoutria sp.

n = 151   n = 114

Solidago sp.

n = 239   n = 183

Internet sale   Traditional sale

Figure 2. Examples of movement patterns of plants according to the sale type. *Impatiens glandulifera* (a, b), *Reynoutria sp.* (c, d) and *Solidago sp.* (e, f). Red lines indicate distances in the internet trade and green lines in traditional trade. Red dots denote shops locations.

Obviously, natural vectors are, and probably will continue to be, important in the spread of alien species. Wind, native dispersers and floods may enhance dispersal of alien species [34–37], especially in more traditional landscapes and regions or countries where internet sale is still not well developed. However, if the development of internet web progress these regions will be threaten by invasions of alien species. One of the gaps in understanding consequences of plant long distance dispersal, in

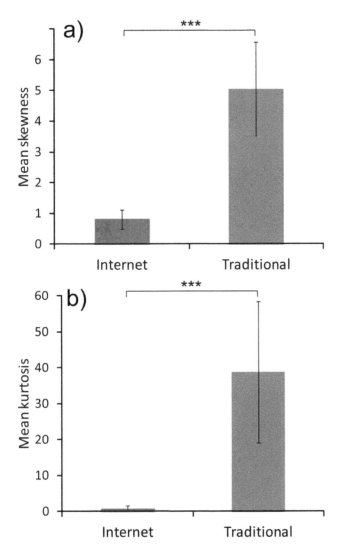

Figure 3. Mean skewness (a) and kurtosis coefficient (b) of distance distribution of invasive plant species traded on-line (red bars) and in a traditional manner (green bars). Explanations: *** - P<0.001. Whiskers are 95% confidence intervals.

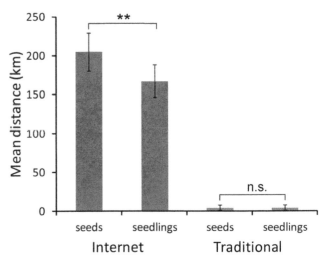

Figure 4. Mean transportation distances of seeds and seedling traded on-line (red bars) and in a traditional manner (green bars). Explanations: ** - P = 0.010; n.s. – statistically non-significant difference. Whiskers are 95% confidence intervals.

the success of dispersion, colonization and subsequent invasion [40–42]. Such human related long distance dispersal and increasing propagule pressure enhance genetic variation in populations and help overcome Allee effects and genetic drift that may otherwise reduce invasion success or keeping the invasion process in a very early stage, in a lag phase [43], [44].

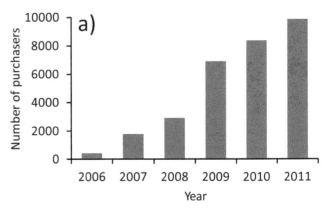

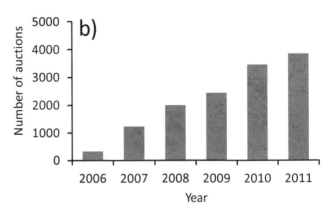

Figure 5. Number of purchasers (a) and number of auctions (b) of 13 invasive alien species in different years in the largest polish internet auctioning portal.

general, is that different life stages (seeds, seedlings, adults) may disperse, but documented examples are scarce [10], [38]. This phenomenon was apparent even in the internet sale. In our study seeds were transported on longer distances than seedlings in the internet and this pattern was not shown in traditional sales, probably because purchasers considered seedlings less suitable for long distance postal trade. These differences are likely to have implications for the pattern of use and the probability of establishment. Although seedlings covered slightly shorter distances than seeds the probability of their survival and growth is possibly higher because they are already developed young plants. Usually, only certain proportion of seeds germinate and grow (in a commercial sale it is usually no less than 80%). However, the amount of seeds sold was nine times larger than seedlings indicating that this life form of alien species may be responsible for colonization of new areas and spread. Moreover, seeds may be sometimes lost during transportation adding to occasional spread of alien species outside the gardens (e.g. at road verges) [39].

The frequency with which alien species are transported along a route and delivered to a specific location is strongly associated with

Education of potential human vectors is believed to be main factor that can slow down invasions and prevent new ones. However, the example of 13 chosen invasive species, some of the most harmful ones in Europe, shows that they were commonly sold via internet and the number of purchases on the most popular internet portal increased hugely, over one hundred-fold over last few year's (2006–2011). Thus, the internet commerce clearly enhances not only distance of transport but also potentially increase propagule pressure of invasive alien species because customers buying these species usually plant them in gardens so allowing their escape into natural habitats. This growth in sale of aliens seems to reflect general trend in number of internet users that increased globally by 566% between 2000 and 2012 (see http://www.internetworldstats.com) as a result of convenience and time saving provided by the internet communication and internet transactions. The development of the internet sale included numerous alien plant that are not recognized currently as invasive but may become harmful in future. For example, our survey on the internet portals indicated that there are over 300 decorative alien plant species (with different varieties) that have not been recognized as invasive but have being introducing into Poland (Lenda et al. unpublished). This also indicates that ever increasing number of scientific research on invasive species [45] seems not to be effective in preventing invasions and the reason can be poor reflection of professional reports on society education and effectiveness in preventing invasions.

Alien species sold in the internet may become efficient vectors of alien parasites or pathogens also those harmful for native organisms. Much of the spread to the United Kingdom of ash dieback disease *Hymenoscyphus pseudoalbidus* or the sudden oak death **Phytophthora ramorum** in USA was attributed to the movement of saplings for forestry [46], [47]. Therefore, the increased number of alien plants being sold, and large distances they are transported via internet sale, amplifies an environmental hazard and creates invasion debt associated with unrecognized pathogens for which aliens species may be just dispersal vectors [48].

Studies in New Zealand show that alien snails, reptile species and alien established frogs were for sale on the internet [22], [48] and that GMO species, forbidden in that country, were also available and were purchased from internet auctions [22], [48]. Finally, internet sales may be a threat for native fauna and flora not only due to commerce of alien invasive species but also by offering many endangered red listed species [21].

E-commerce contractions and practical recommendation

Countries from European Union, Australia, New Zealand passed legal restrictions (in Poland since 2012) aimed to limit e-commerce of alien and invasive species [22], [48]. However, in all cases sales via the internet still exists, and is even increasing, as sellers may avoid regulations by, for example, changing names of invasive species (like misspelling) or by using very traditional names that are not on police lists (Lenda et al. unpublished).

Solutions to this invasion problem can include increased restrictions, controlling trade, greater enforcement of existing regulations and applying reliable financial fines not only for customers but also for sellers. Further restrictions should limit selling of new alien species or species that are regarded as invasive in other regions of the world. The list of invasive species should be easily accessible for all people and their harmful effects for economy should be estimated in order to caution society about real losses to economy and environment when invasions occur.

Sold plants should include information for buyers whether this is an alien or native plant in a given country. More effective reflection of scientific results on invasive species and possible invasion debts on education of society and encouragement for gardeners to grow more benign rather than environmentally damaging plants is desirable.

The growing number of introduced alien species for gardening and agriculture often comes from fashion and follows some recommendations and news in popular media [49]. The society may become much more nature-oriented and aware about environment after watching some nature programs in television or on the internet, or when society follows life-style of some well known, charismatic persons [50–53]. Therefore creating a new fashion of planting native plants might be equally important as legal restrictions.

Conclusions

Our results shed new light on understanding the effects of trade and transportation on spread of alien species by incorporating the increasingly dominating manner of communication between people and societies– the internet. The internet commerce made long distance dispersal very common, which contradicts existing results indicating it is a rare phenomenon. Moreover, internet trade generated shapes of distance distribution that differs from that shown by all other known dispersal vectors. As the number of invasive alien species sold via internet increased over years with the development of e-commerce that may play prominent role for success of alien plants in rapidly changing world.

Thus, a social component of dispersal needs to be included in future dispersal models of alien species. Specifically, further research needs to examine if internet sales affects the spatial pattern of local invasions risks. Buyers' locations may occur in clusters and an examination of socioeconomical factors related to the buyers (such as income, local population size, gross domestic product, education) may provide insights in what drives plant buyers behavior. Ultimately, a better understanding of what drives the buyers of invasive nonnative species may lead to insights in how to manage and limit invasive alien species spread.

Supporting Information

File S1 Detailed data on distances on which invasive alien were transported when sold on-line and in traditional way in studied garden shops (Figures S1–S23), and the rate of ecommerce for these species in popular Polish auctioning internet portal (Figures S24–S36).

Acknowledgments

We are grateful to prof. Yvonne Buckley for helpful comments on the manuscript. Three anonymous referees provided valuable criticism on earlier versions of this manuscript.

Author Contributions

Conceived and designed the experiments: ML. Performed the experiments: ML PS KK WJS DM JMHK MW. Analyzed the data: ML PS. Contributed reagents/materials/analysis tools: ML PS KK WJS DM JMHK MW. Wrote the paper: ML PS. Edited and improved the paper: ML PS JMHK WJS MW KK DM.

References

1. Elton CS (1958) The Ecology of Invasions of Animals and Plants. London: Methuen.
2. White PCL, Ford AES, Clout MN, Engeman RM, Roy S, et al. (2008) Alien invasive vertebrates in ecosystems pattern, process and the social dimension. Wildlife Res 35: 171–179.
3. Davis MA (2009) Invasion Biology. Oxford: Oxford University Press.
4. Moroń D, Lenda M, Skórka P, Szentgyorgyi H, Settele J, et al. (2009) Wild pollinator communities are negatively affected by invasion of alien goldenrods in grassland landscape. Biol Conserv 142: 1322–1332.
5. Lenda M, Skórka P, Knops JMH, Moroń D, Tworek S, et al. (2012) Plant establishment and invasions: an increase in a seed disperser combined with land abandonment cause an invasion of the non-native walnut in Europe. Proc R Soc B 279: 1491–1497.
6. Pyšek P, Jarošík V, Hulme PE, Pergl J, Hejda M, et al. (2012) A global assessment of invasive plant impacts on resident species, communities and ecosystems: the interaction of impact measures, invading species' traits and environment. Global Change Biol 18: 1725–1737.
7. Rieseberg LH, Kim S-C, Randell R, Whitney K, Gross B, et al. (2007) Hybridization and the colonization of novel habitats by annual sunflowers. Genetica 129: 149–165.
8. Hobbs RJ, Higgs E, Harris JA (2009) Novel ecosystems: implications for conservation and restoration. Trends Ecol Evol 24: 599–605.
9. Bullock JM, Clarke RT (2000) Long distance seed dispersal by wind: measuring and modelling the tail of the curve. Oecologia 124: 506–521.
10. Nathan R, Schurr FM, Spiegel O, Steinitz O, Trakhtenbrot A, et al. (2008) Mechanisms of long-distance seed dispersal. Trends Ecol Evol 23: 638–647.
11. Bartoń KA, Hovestadt T, Phillips BL, Travis JMJ (2012) Risky movement increases the rate of range expansion. Proc R Soc B 279: 1194–1202.
12. Chittka L, Schürkens S (2001) Successful invasion of a floral market. Nature 411: 653–653.
13. Margolis M, Shogren J, Fischer C (2005) How trade politics affect invasive species control. Ecol Econ 52: 305–313.
14. Ward DF, Beggs JR, Clout MN, Harris RJ, O'connor S (2006) The diversity and origin of exotic ants arriving in New Zealand via human-mediated dispersal. Divers Distrib 12: 601–609.
15. Tatem AJ (2009) The worldwide airline network and the dispersal of exotic species: 2007-2010. Ecography 32: 94–102.
16. Abbott RJ, Brennan AC, James JK, Forbes DF, Hegarty MJ, et al. (2009) Recent hybrid origin and invasion in the British Isles by a self-incompatible species, Oxford ragwort (Senecio squalidus L, Asteraceae). Biol Inv 11: 1145–1158.
17. Bauer C, Colgan J (2002) The internet as a driver for unbundling: a transaction perspective from the stockbroking industry. Electron Markets 12: 130–134.
18. Freund C, Weinhold D (2004) The effect of the Internet on international trade. J Int Econ 62: 171–189.
19. Rixon CAM, Duggan IC, Bergeron NMN, Ricciardi A, Macisaac HJ (2005) Invasion risks posed by the aquarium trade and live fish markets on the Laurentian Great Lakes. Biodivers Conserv 14: 1365–1381.
20. Dehnen-Schmutz K, Touza J, Perrings C, Williamson M (2007) The horticultural trade and ornamental plant invasions in Britain. Conserv Biol 21: 224–231.
21. Lipinska AM, Golab MJ (2009) Internet trade on Polish endangered species of butterflies, beetles and molluscs. Nat Conserv 65: 79–87.
22. Kikillus KH, Hare KM, Hartley S (2012) Online trading tools as a method of estimating propagule pressure via the pet-release pathway. Biol Inv 14: 2657–2664.
23. DAISIE (2009) Handbook of Alien Species in Europe. Dordrecht: Springer.
24. Longley PA, Goodchild MF, Maguire DJ, Rhind DW (2010) Geographical Information Systems and Science (Third Edition). Hoboken NJ: Willey.
25. Quinn GP, Keough MJ (2002) Experimental Design and Data Analysis for Biologists. Cambridge: Cambridge University Press.
26. Nathan R (2006) Long-distance dispersal of plants. Science 313: 786–788.
27. Forman RTT, Sperling D, Bissonette JA, Clevenger AP, Cutshall CD, et al. (2002) Road Ecology: Science and Solution. Washington DC: Island Press.
28. McCullough DG, Work TT, Cavey JF, Liebhold AM, Marshall D (2006) Interceptions of nonindigenous plant pests at US ports of entry and border crossings over a 17-year period. Biol Inv 8: 611–630.
29. Lines J (2007) Chikungunya in Italy. Brit Med J 335: 576.
30. Hulme PE (2009) Trade, transport and trouble: managing invasive species pathways in an era of globalization. J Appl Ecol 46: 10–18.
31. Crooks JA (2005) Lag times and exotic species: the ecology and management of biological invasions in slow motion. Ecoscience 12: 316–329.
32. Essl F, Dullinger S, Rabitsch W, Hulme PE, Hülber K, et al. (2011) Socioeconomic legacy yields an invasion debt. Proc Natl Acad Sci USA 108: 203–207.
33. Essl F, Mang T, Moser D (2012) Ancient and recent alien species in temperate forests: steady state and time lags. Biol Inv 14: 1331–1342.
34. Saura-Mas S, Lloret F (2005) Wind effects on dispersal patterns of the invasive alien Cortaderia selloana in Mediterranean wetlands. Acta Oecol 27: 129–133.
35. Pyšek P, Prach K (1994) How important are rivers for supporting plant invasions? In: De Waal LC, Child EL, Wade PM, Brock JH, (eds) Ecology and Management of Invasive Riverside Plants, pp. 19–26. Chichester, UK: Wiley.
36. Richardson DM, Allsopp N, D'Antonio C, Milton SJ, Rejmanek M (2000) Plant invasions — the role of mutualisms. Biol Rev 75: 65–93.
37. Czarnecka J, Orłowski G, Karg J (2012) Endozoochorous dispersal of alien and native plants by two palearctic avian frugivores with special emphasis on invasive American Goldenrod Solidago gigantea. Cent Eur J Biol 7: 895–901.
38. Gillespie RG, Baldwin BC, Waters JM, Fraser CI, Nikula R, et al. (2012) Long-distance dispersal: a framework for hypothesis testing. Trends Ecol Evol 27: 47–56.
39. von der Lippe M, Kowarik I (2007) Long-distance dispersal of plants by vehicles as a driver of plant invasions. Conserv Biol 21: 986–996.
40. Cassey P, Blackburn TM, Jones KE, Lockwood JL (2004) Mistakes in the analysis of exotic species establishment: source pool designation and correlates of introduction success among parrots (Aves: Psittaciformes) of the world. J Biogeogr 31: 277–284.
41. Drake JM, Lodge DM (2004) Global hotspots of biological invasions: evaluating options for ballast-water management. Proc R Soc B 271: 575–580.
42. Lockwood JL, Cassey P, Blackburn T (2005) The role of propagule pressure in explaining species invasions. Trends Ecol Evol 20: 223–228.
43. Dlugosch KM, Parker IM (2008) Founding events in species invasions: genetic variation, adaptive evolution, and the role of multiple introductions. Mol Ecol 17: 431–449.
44. Simberloff D (2009) The role of propagule pressure in biological invasions. Annu Rev Ecol Syst 40: 81–102.
45. Richardson DM, Pyšek P (2008) Fifty years of invasion ecology - the legacy of Charles Elton. Div Distrib 14: 161–168.
46. Pautasso M, Aas G, Queloz V, Holdenrieder O (2013) European ash (Fraxinus excelsior) dieback – a conservation biology challenge. Biol Conserv 158: 37–49.
47. Frankel SJ (2008) Sudden oak death and Phytophthora ramorum in the USA: a management challenge. Australas Plant Path 37: 19–25.
48. Derraik JGB, Phillips S (2010) Online trade poses a threat to biosecurity in New Zealand. Biol Inv 12: 1477–1480.
49. Dehnen-Schmutz K, Touza J, Perrings C, Williamson M (2007) The horticultural trade and ornamental plant invasions in Britain. Conserv Biol 21: 224–231.
50. Lewis T (2008) Smart living: lifestyle media and popular expertise. Vol. 15. New York: Peter Lang Publishing.
51. Snaddon JL, Turner EC, Foster WA (2008) Children's Perceptions of Rainforest biodiversity: Which Animals Have the Lion's Share of Environmental Awareness? PLoS ONE 3(7): e2579. doi:10.1371/journal.pone.0002579
52. Bousé D (2003) False intimacy: close-ups and viewer involvement in wildlife films. Visual Stud 18: 123–132.
53. Żmihorski M, Dziarska-Pałac J, Sparks TH, Tryjanowski P (2013) Ecological correlates of the popularity of birds and butterflies in Internet information resources. Oikos 122: 183–190.

7

Tracking Traders' Understanding of the Market Using e-Communication Data

Serguei Saavedra[1,2,3], **Jordi Duch**[4], **Brian Uzzi**[1,2]*

1 Northwestern Institute on Complex Systems, Northwestern University, Evanston, Illinois, United States of America, **2** Kellogg School of Management, Northwestern University, Evanston, Illinois, United States of America, **3** Northwestern University Clinical and Translational Sciences Institute, Northwestern University, Chicago, Illinois, United States of America, **4** Department of Computer Science and Mathematics, Universitat Rovira i Virgili, Tarragona, Spain

Abstract

Tracking the volume of keywords in Internet searches, message boards, or Tweets has provided an alternative for following or predicting associations between popular interest or disease incidences. Here, we extend that research by examining the role of e-communications among day traders and their collective understanding of the market. Our study introduces a general method that focuses on bundles of words that behave differently from daily communication routines, and uses original data covering the content of instant messages among all day traders at a trading firm over a 40-month period. Analyses show that two word bundles convey traders' understanding of same day market events and potential next day market events. We find that when market volatility is high, traders' communications are dominated by same day events, and when volatility is low, communications are dominated by next day events. We show that the stronger the traders' attention to either same day or next day events, the higher their collective trading performance. We conclude that e-communication among traders is a product of mass collaboration over diverse viewpoints that embodies unique information about their weak or strong understanding of the market.

Editor: Yamir Moreno, University of Zaragoza, Spain

Funding: SS and BU thank the Kellogg School of Management, Northwestern University, the Northwestern Institute on Complex Systems (NICO), and the Army Research Laboratory under Cooperative Agreement W911NF-09-2-0053 for financial support. SS also thanks NUCATS grant UL1RR025741. JD thanks the Spanish Ministry of Science and Technology (FIS2009-13730-C02-02) and the Generalitat de Catalunya (SGR-00838-2009). The funders had no role in study design, data collection and analysis, decision to publish, or preparation of the manuscript.

Competing Interests: The authors have declared that no competing interests exist.

* E-mail: uzzi@northwestern.edu

Introduction

Sir Francis Galton's *vox populi* conjecture [1] that the average estimate of many individuals can exceed individual wit has grown in promise as complex systems become more intricate, interrelated, and immense. Sir Galton's insight laid a foundation for the idea of "collective wisdom" and represents an emerging interdisciplinary study of how collective information can be leveraged to increase our understanding of large-scale social and economic events [2–5]. For example, research embracing the promise of widely available Internet-based data finds that shifts in the volume of keywords in Google searches or Tweets, can detect flu rates, public moods, and consumer demand and prices [6–10]. This research benefits from the existence of preselected, recognizable words that reflect popular interest or sentiment levels–like the name of a movie or an infectious disease. However, a population's understanding of large-scale phenomena emerges in large part through social collaboration, learning and reasoning, not just interest level [2–5,11,12]. Similarly, it has been shown that words derive meaning from the simultaneous association with other words driven by how people characterize and respond to the world around them [13,14]. This suggests that the social dynamics captured by bundles of unique and correlated words can summarize the dynamics of single titles and provide relevant information about a population's understanding of complex systems.

In this paper, we present and test a method for capturing the collective understanding of socioeconomic events using e-communication data by inductively identifying bundles of words that significantly deviate from daily communication routines. The rationale of this method is that non-routinary words, whose daily frequency is not a simple product of the total volume of words, could reveal information external to the communication system [13]. Because the method is not dependent on preselected keywords, it aims to be generalizable. To illustrate our method, we study volatility, a multidimensional construct critical in many complex systems [15]. For instance, asthma attacks, epilepsy, or climate shift display valuable precursors characterized by a slowing or quickening of fluctuations in parameter values [15]. In politics, it relates to legislation, corruption and civil unrest, and in disease control it is linked to new infection rates [4,5,9,16]. In markets, volatility notably affects all investment decisions [17] and scale dynamics including critical transitions such as financial crashes [15,18,19].

In particular, we analyzed the association of traders' person to person communications with their understanding of market volatility. The data we use to identify the collective understanding of the market is distinctive. Unlike past research that has used general public information in Google or Twitter, we draw on the content of instant messages (IMs), an increasingly pervasive form of e-communication [20–22]. Our data includes the full population of more than 3 million IMs sent and received by all the day traders at a typical trading firm from 1/2007-4/2010. IMs represent an excellent source of traders' collective thinking about the market [23,24]. Unlike investors who make money by holding stocks that rise in value over the long term, day traders make money by buying and selling many stocks over a single day with regard to movements of their stock prices. Consequently, day traders face the challenge of continually understanding and deciphering how news is affecting, and will affect, market volatility during the day and the next day, their trading horizon. For example, when a news report states a nuclear reactor may fail the ramifications of that news for the market are unknown at the time of the report. Will oil prices rise and by how much? Will nuclear stocks fall with fears of a meltdown or rise with near term oil shortages? For day traders, the answer to these and other questions are solved in large part through informal consultation with their instant message contacts who are doing likewise with their contact network [23,25]. This communication pattern spreads the IM network of the traders over diverse viewpoints and a broad spectrum of the market (for example, the trader population in our firm trades over 4000 stocks [23]).

Communication of the above type has been shown to effectively capture the collective knowledge of decision makers, while at the same time, canceling out their individual biases [2]. And because communication is costly, it is likely that traders exchange IMs that contain groups of words that efficiently convey their understanding of the market [13]. This social dynamic suggests that as traders use a word bundle more than an alternative bundle, an assimilation of thought averaged over the diverse views of many traders has emerged in such a way that an increase in understanding of the market may be embodied in their communications.

Results

Extraction Method

To extract significant information from traders' IMs, we adapted fluctuation scaling techniques [26,27]. Step one filtered the population of words to those words appearing >1000 times or roughly >1 time daily in order to remove misspellings and to consider commonly used words by the majority of traders [28]. Consistent with universal patterns of human language[29], words

in our filtered IM corpus (over 11 million total words and over 232 thousand unique words) appear approximately twice as often as the next least frequent word (Fig. 1A). Step two classified the population of words in our filtered IM corpus into words that follow either the routinary or external factors of the communication system [27] (Methods). Operationally, words that follow routinary factors have a daily frequency proportional to the total number of daily words (Fig. 1B), suggesting that they are a function of traders' communication routines rather than an exceptional stimulus. Consistent with linguistic research 302 out of 319 English "stop words" (e.g. a, an, for, or, the) [30], which are commonly filtered words in text analysis [28,30], were classified in this category. By contrast, the daily frequency of words following external factors were statistically unrelated to the density of total daily words, suggesting that traders use these words to characterize external stimuli. This subset of words was defined as extracted words in our analysis. A total of 459 words were extracted. Importantly, Figure 2 shows that extracted words can have different temporal dynamics, revealing that each word characterizes a piece of information from the overall communications among traders. This suggests that bundles of words may provide a more general understanding of the market.

Step three found bundles of extracted words that were significantly correlated with each other and weakly correlated with other extracted words based on their daily pairwise frequency. For each pair of extracted words i and j, we calculated the Pearson pairwise correlation $\rho_{ij}(\Delta_{fi},\Delta_{fj})$, where Δ_f is the vector of frequency changes. To appropriately quantify the statistical similarity of each pair of words, we compared the observed daily pairwise correlation to a null model where the word pairs were randomly shuffled. We calculated the expected correlation ρ^* and standard deviation $\sigma(\rho^*)$ from the random model to compute a z-score of the observed relative to the random given by $z_{ij}(\rho_{ij})=(\rho_{ij}-\rho_{ij}^*)/\sigma(\rho_{ij}^*)$. Word bundles were then created using a version [31] of the Extremal Optimization Algorithm [32,33] for community detection in correlation networks. We used words as nodes and the size of z-score between words as edge weights to form the correlation network. The number of bundles is not fixed

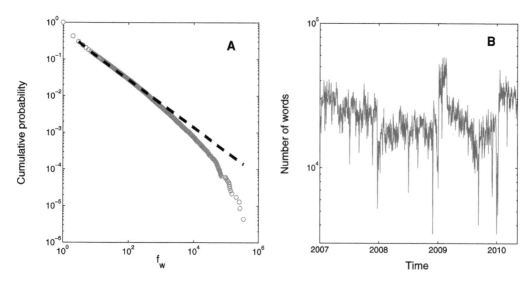

Figure 1. Communication routines. Panel **A** shows that the cumulative frequency on a log-log scale of filtered words f_w (viz. word counts) is approximately distributed following Zipf's law according to a power law $P(f_w) \sim f_w^- 1.88$ (KS test, $p=0.21$). Panel **B** shows the evolution of traders' messaging volume defined as the total daily number of words on a log scale. Note that the daily frequency of words that follow communication routines can be approximated simply by its global frequency and the total number of words in each day.

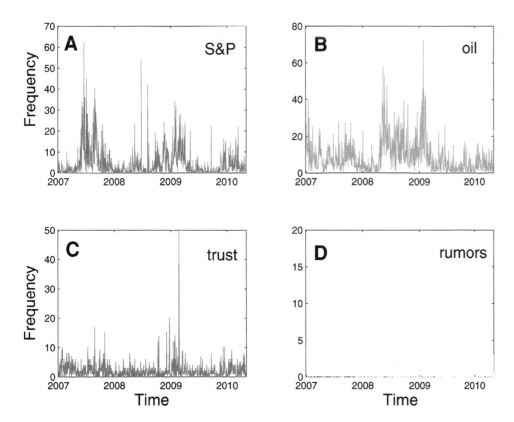

Figure 2. Daily frequency of illustrative extracted words. The figure shows the daily frequency (number of times a word is counted each day) of illustrative extracted words **A** S&P, **B** oil, **C** trust and **D** rumors across the observation period. Note that each word has a unique temporal dynamic characterized by brief periods of intense usage–bursts–preceded by and followed by relatively long periods of low usage.

in advance, bundles of words are formed by maximizing the network's modularity parameter [34]. This method clusters words that are highly correlated between each other and weakly correlated with a different group of words.

As a robustness check on the original partition, we performed a second optimization of the modularity parameter based on the Kernighan-Lin algorithm [34]. This consists in a fine tuning of the clusters of the original partition with a bootstrapping process [31]. Additionally, we obtained the same number of bundles when we applied a simulated annealing approach to maximize the modularity parameter [35]. Moreover, the partition did not change whether we used the entire dataset or split it into datasets of equal size.

Extracted word bundles

Three clusters or word bundles were found. Bundles one and two contained 35% and 45% of our extracted words respectively, and were made up of virtually all English words. Bundle three was made up of principally foreign language words, which suggests a connection to a subset of multilingual traders specific to the population characteristics of this trading company. Bundle one contained extracted words such as negative, lows, cuts, insane, crazy, ugly, banks, oil, weak, interest, s&p. Illustrative examples of bundle two keywords are happy, alert, dollars, excited, bloomberg, reuters, win, trend, china, nyse; while examples of bundle three are prosto, nego, nada, csak, nem. Since there is no a priori reason to expect the resulting grouping of words, any relationship among these words should be treated as a consequence of their own frequency dynamics. Words within a bundle were highly correlated. The proportion of significant correlations (z-score>2) within bundles was 54%, while the proportion between bundles was only 22%. These findings

confirm that word bundles capture information embedded in words that gain meaning through their co-occurrence [13,14].

Collective understanding

To study how traders' communications express their collective understanding of market volatility, we used the daily closing value of market volatility and the daily frequency of word bundles relative to the extracted words. Volatility can be operationalized by the volatility index (VIX) [15,17], which corresponds to the expected future volatility over the next 30 calendar days. The VIX, also known as the "fear" index, gives a good approximation to the overall sentiment of traders by reflecting the price of portfolio insurance, i.e. the higher the level of uncertainty in the market, the higher the VIX. We measured the relative frequency of each word bundle i as $\gamma_i(t) = \frac{\sum_j^c f_j(t)}{\sum_k^W f_k(t)}$, where $f_j(t)$ is the frequency of word j in day t, c is the total number of words in bundle i, and W is the total number of extracted words. To analyze the correlation between word bundles and volatility, we transformed all our variables to their first differences [36], $\Theta_i(t) = \gamma_i(t) - \gamma_i(t-1)$. This process also made all our variables stationary (Methods), a characteristic necessary to analyze time series data [36]. The cross-correlation $\rho(\Delta t)$ is measured with a time lag parameter Δt [7] over the day-to-day movements of each word bundle.

For day traders, same day $\Theta_{VIX}(t)$ and next day $\Theta_{VIX}(t+1)$ volatility are critical to understanding the implications of their trading decisions. Figure 3 shows the time series correlations of day-to-day movements of volatility with day-to-day movements of word bundles. A value of 0 on the x-axis indicates the correlation of same day movements between volatility and the relative frequency of a

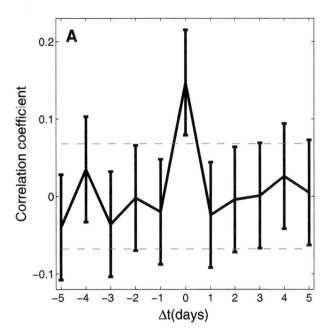
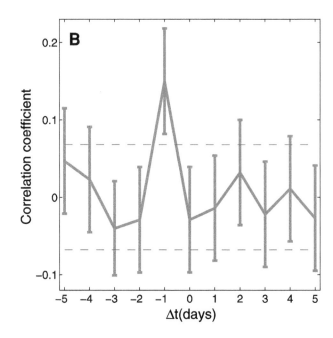

Figure 3. Cross-correlations between market volatility and word bundles. The figure shows the time dependent cross-correlations between day-to-day movements of market volatility given by the daily changes in closing values of VIX [17] at time t, and **A** the day-to-day movements of relative frequency of word bundle one over Δt and **B** word bundle two over Δt. Day-to-day movements are calculated using the first differences. High-low bars indicate the 95% confidence intervals using Fisher's transformation. The red dashed lines indicate the 95% confidence interval for cross-correlations of two independent and identically distributed random variables across the same observation period.

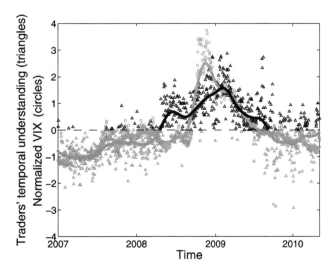

Figure 4. Traders' temporal understanding of market volatility. Triangles show the relative frequency of traders' understanding of same day events (word bundle one) compared to the relative frequency of traders' understanding of next day events (word bundle two) as given by $C(t) = \gamma_1(t) - \gamma_2(t)$ normalized to the z-score using the sample mean and standard deviation. The orange circles show market volatility over time normalized to the z-score using the sample mean and standard deviation calculated over all the data. Orange circles above dashed line represent days of high and low volatility respectively. Black triangles above the dashed line represent days when word bundle one dominated ($z_C(t) > 0$), and green triangles below the dashed line represent days when word bundle two dominated the content of traders' IM communications ($z_C(t) < 0$). These time-series patterns indicate that same day events (word bundle one) systematically dominate traders' understanding on days of high volatility while next day events (word bundle two) systematically dominate on days of low volatility. For visibility purposes, solid lines correspond to the moving average computed using a kernel smoothing regression with a window of one month.

word bundle, and negative or positive values on the x-axis indicate lead and lag correlations for word bundles respectively. Points above or below the dotted horizontal lines are statistically different from chance. We found that word bundle one was significantly ($p < 0.001$) associated with same day movements only (Fig. 3A), suggesting that it captured the collective understanding of same day events $\Theta_{VIX}(t)$. By contrast, word bundle two was significantly ($p < .001$) associated with next day movements only (Fig. 3B), suggesting that it reflects the collective understanding of potential next day events $\Theta_{VIX}(t+1)$. This predictive utility was confirmed with Granger causality tests [36] ($p = 0.031$) according to the equation $\Theta_{VIX}(t+1) = \Theta_{VIX}(t) + \Theta_2(t)$. Word bundle three was unrelated to day-to-day movements of any kind, suggesting that the use of foreign language words in the communications in our sample was related to factors other than volatility. Moreover, we found no association whatsoever between the total number of words (Fig. 1) and volatility.

Second, we found systematic associations between the level of volatility and the degree to which same day events dominate traders' communications–what we called temporal understanding. We defined days of low and high volatility by normalizing VIX to a z-score using its sample mean and standard deviation. Values of $z_{VIX}(t) > 0$ and $z_{VIX}(t) < 0$ were defined as days of high and low volatility respectively [7]. We quantified temporal understanding by the degree to which the relative frequency of word bundle one dominated word bundle two each day $C(t) = \gamma_1(t) - \gamma_2(t)$, and normalized that difference with a z-score computed on the sample mean and standard deviation. Figure 4 indicates that when the level of volatility was high, the word bundle associated with same day events dominated traders' communications ($z_C(t) > 0$). Conversely, when volatility was low, the word bundle associated with next day events dominated traders' communications ($z_C(t) < 0$). The horizontal dashed line is the boundary between the days when one word bundle dominated the other. To guide the eye, the level of temporal understanding changes color to reflect the dominant word bundle. These patterns were confirmed by Fisher's exact test of finding the co-occurrence of these paired events ($p < 10^{-12}$, two-sided, see Methods). This result suggests that the collective understanding updated quickly with changes in market conditions. When traders faced high volatility their communications focused on same day events, which is likely an expression of their attempt to reduce the uncertainty presently in the market. By contrast, when traders faced low volatility, their collective understanding turned to the potential next day events, which has relatively more uncertainty for trading prospects.

These empirical regularities point to possibly new relationships between complex system behavior and communications among the participants in the system. Broadly, like past work that has looked at specific preselected keywords, our bundles of words method appears indicate that only a small fraction of the words are used to communicate the system's behavior. However, we find that the essence of communications is not represented by single keywords but by co-occurring words from which collective meaning is mutually constructed. This suggests that while single words may be useful in certain situations, bundles of related words can capture information different from single keywords. Further, we found that separate bundles of words are related to different dimensions of volatility, most importantly the same day and next day, and high and low, volatility in a system. Finally, the level of collective understanding of same day versus next day events is relative rather than absolute. This suggests that different points of view are simultaneously held by the same population but to different degrees. This raises the interesting and unexpected proposition that the greater the attention to either same day or next day events, the clearer is the collective understanding of the market and vice versa. If this is the case, one would expect that the clearer the understanding of the market, the better their investment decisions, a test we turn to next.

Collective trading performance

Finally, we tested if the level of attention to either same day or next day events was associated with the collective trading performance of our population, predicated on the assumption that the greater the attention in word bundles, the greater the collective understanding of the market. This test is novel for our model and the collective wisdom literature which has not examined whether the attention of a group is correlated with the actual collective performance. To capture these dynamics, we measured collective trading performance $p(t)$ as the percentage of traders that made money at the end of the day t in the firm. We operationalized an attention index as the absolute differ-0ence between the relative frequencies of word bundle one (same day events) and word bundle two (next day events), $A(t) = |\gamma_1(t) - \gamma_2(t)|$. To appropriately compare these time series, we calculated the correlation between the first differences of collective performance and the first differences of collective attention. First differences are operationalized as the difference between the values at time t and the values at time $t-1$, i.e. $\Theta_A(t) = A(t) - A(t-1)$ and $\Theta_p(t) = p(t) - p(t-1)$ for collective attention and collective performance respectively.

We found a significant ($p < 10^{-4}$), positive correlation of 0.19 between the first differences of collective performance $\Theta_p(t)$ and the first differences of collective attention $\theta_A(t)$ (Fig. 5). This positive correlation was supported by the 95% confidence intervals $0.11 - 0.26$ using Fisher's transformation. The statistical significance of this correlation was also confirmed by the lower expected correlation ($0 \pm .037$) between two independent and identically distributed random variables across the same observation period.

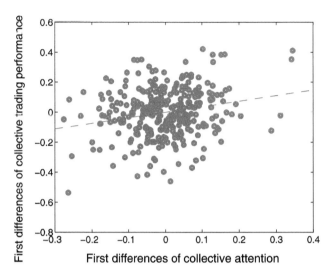

Figure 5. Correlation between collective attention and collective trading performance. The figure shows the relationship between the first differences of collective attention $\Theta_A(t) = A(t) - A(t-1)$ (x-axis) and first differences of collective trading performance $\Theta_p(t) = p(t) - p(t-1)$ (y-axis). We found a significant ($p < 10^{-4}$), positive correlation of 0.19. The red dashed line corresponds to the best linear fit ($p = 0.002$) over all data points and it is used only to guide the eye for the positive correlation.

Figure 5 shows that as the attention in traders' understanding of same day or next day events increased relative to the previous day, their relative collective performance increased on average. Moreover, when the first differences of underlying volatility (VIX), number of traders and collective attention are added into a regression equation to account for the first differences of collective trading performance, the relationship between collective attention and performance holds. This suggests that traders' attention to events, as captured by word bundles, can reveal traders' collective understanding of the market.

Discussion

The conjecture that the average collective information of the many is better than the knowledge of any individual has never been more relevant than today, where large-scale social and economic problems such as financial crises or epidemic outbreaks are necessary to anticipate and prevent. While new widely available e-communication data (IMs, email, blogs, message boards) have presented a new opportunity to apply and test Galton's collective wisdom hypothesis, it has also created new challenges. To date, tests have keyed on single preselected words that reflect the intensity of popular interest but increasingly, these data are a co-mingling of many reactions, events, and activities that participants experience simultaneously. We built on this work by offering a method that inductively garners a population's understanding of external events by moving from single preselected keywords to significant behavioral changes in communication routines. Our methodological framework inductively identifies words different from daily communication routines, making it generalizable to other domains and in domain where keywords are unknown a priori.

Using unique information from more than 3 million IMs sent and received among day traders and their contacts, we showed that just 459 words behave differently from the expected patterns implied by communication routines. Moreover, the 459 words reduced to three word bundles, of which two bundles conveyed traders' understanding of same day and next day market events. When the level of volatility was high, same day events dominated, and when the level of volatility was low the next day events dominated the collective understanding, revealing a link among word bundles, trading horizon and the level of volatility in the market. Importantly, we found that as the level of attention with regard to a specific collective understanding increased, the more the traders appeared to have a clearer understanding of the market, a conclusion supported by their collective trading performance. These results show that non-routinary communication can, in fact, reveal unique information about a populations' understanding of large-scale social and economic dynamics.

Our work also raises the questions about the micro processes at play that lead to an emergence of collective understanding. While we observe the result of those processes in the form of changes in the frequency of word bundles, we know little about how individuals learn from each other, when and what information solidifies in someone's mind the line between supposition and actionable facts, or even what information attracts attention. Along with this information, tracking how the information may propagate through the IM network can also be valuable in studying the micro foundations of collective understanding.

Methods

Ethics Statement

The study meets all Northwestern University Institutional Review Board (IRB) exemption criteria of anonymity, non-interactivity, and 100% archival data. Northwestern University IRB stipulates that data that are (1) archival, (2) do not involve interaction with subjects, and (3) are anonymized are IRB exempt. In our case, all three stipulations were met. The data were 100% archival. The data were 100% archived before we received it. The data were archived according to well known laws that stipulate that all trading data and all electronic communications of every trader be recorded and stored for 7 years and remain accessible for post trading analysis. Under the same ruling, all the data are considered to be wholly the company's assets. Because these reporting factors are a matter of common knowledge among traders, we sort and received verbal confirmation from the company that all their traders were fully aware of and in voluntary compliance with these record keeping and ownership laws. For example, the company confirmed that all traders at the firm were aware of the legal protocols of trading and that the traders know that 100% of their electronic communications and trading are recorded by law. We received written approval from the firm to use their data for research purposes and to publish the results of our findings if the name, location, and other defining characteristics of the firm or its traders were kept confidential in accordance with standard research protocols. Also, Northwestern University IRB stipulates that IRB exempt studies must have no interaction with human subjects and that information must be 100% anonymized. We did not interact with or manipulate human subjects in anyway, all personally identifiable data were 100% anonymized, and all analyses were conducted on data that had been anonymized using randomized IDs in accordance with the protocols set forth by the firm's information technology officer. The ethic committee was not involved because the data were 100% archival, had no human subject interaction, and were 100% anonymized. Research was sponsored by the Army Research Laboratory and was accomplished under Cooperative Agreement Number W911NF-09-2-0053. The views and conclusions contained in this document are those of the authors and should not be interpreted as representing the official policies, either expressed or implied, of the Army Research Laboratory or the U.S. Government. The U.S. Government is authorized to reproduce and distribute reprints for Government purposes notwithstanding any copyright notation here on. The funders had no role in study design, data collection and analysis, decision to publish, or preparation of the manuscript.

Extraction method

We considered extracted words and routinary words, respectively, as words dominated by external and routinary factors of the communication system. For each word i, we calculate the strength of its routinary factor by the ratio $\eta_i = \sigma_i^r / \sigma_i^{ext}$, where σ_i^r and σ_i^{ext} are the standard deviations of the routinary and external factors respectively. Routinary factors are given by $f_i(t)^r = <f_i> \frac{N(t)}{<N>}$, i.e. changes in the overall activity of total number of words in day t are reflected in a proportional fashion on the frequency of word i in day t. Note that $<f_i>$ and $<N>$ are the average frequency of word i and total daily number of words respectively computed over all activity. Thus, external factors are computed by $f_i(t)^{ext} = f_i(t) - f_i(t)^r$, where $f_i(t)$ is the observed frequency of word i in the day t. Typically, $\eta \gg 1$ and $\eta \ll 1$ correspond to frequencies dominated by routinary and external factors respectively [27]. We use a random null hypothesis to appropriately classify words according to their routinary factor strengths. The random null hypothesis is performed by randomly shuffling the daily frequency of each word. For each word i, the random null hypothesis is used to compute the expected ratio $\eta_i^* = \sigma_i^{r*} / \sigma_i^{ext*}$ and standard deviation $\sigma(\eta_i^*)$. If words follow routinary factors, we would expect them to behave significantly different from random fluctuations, i.e. following the observed daily communication routine. However, if they follow external factors, we should observe no difference with the random null hypothesis, i.e. words have no correlation with the observed communication routine. Hence, calculating the z-score $= (\eta_i - \eta_i^*)/\sigma(\eta_i^*)$, we extracted only words that behave similar to random fluctuations, i.e. $-2 < z < 2$. We note that words with $\eta < 0.35$ follow external factors, which we took as our extracted words.

Stationarity

To ensure that all our data sets (once they were first differenced) were stationary, we used three standard approaches. We cleared the Augmented Dickey-Fuller unit-root test at the $p < 10^{-4}$ level, we cleared the Phillips-Perron unit roots test at the $p < 10^{-4}$ level, and had negative $(-0.46 < \phi < -0.15)$ coefficients in all the lagged AR(1) autocorrelation variables.

Fisher's exact test

We test the null hypothesis of no association between the two variables $\delta_C(t)$ and $\delta_{VIX}(t)$ using Fisher's exact test, where $\delta_C(t)$ is defined as a random variable that takes the value of 1 if traders' communications are dominated by same day events (word bundle one) $z_C(t) > 0$ at time t, and the value of 0 otherwise. Similarly, we defined $\delta_{VIX}(t)$ as a random variable that takes the value of 1 if the market is at a state of high volatility $z_{VIX}(t) > 0$ at time t, and the value of 0 otherwise. We have 858 business days in the sample, 255 days under high market volatility (198 happened during the dominance of same day events), and 383 days dominated by same day events in total.

Acknowledgments

We would like to thank Alex Arenas, Jordi Bascompte, Martha de la Vega, Sergio Gómez, Roger Guimerà, Jonathan Haynes, Alejandro Morales

Gallardo, Janet Pierrehumbert, Christopher Rhoads and Olivia Woolley for useful discussions that led to the improvement of this work.

Author Contributions

Conceived and designed the experiments: SS JD BU. Performed the experiments: SS JD. Analyzed the data: SS JD BU. Contributed reagents/materials/analysis tools: BU. Wrote the paper: SS JD BU.

References

1. Galton F (1907) Vox populi. Nature 75: 450.
2. Page SE (2007) The Difference. Princeton University Press.
3. Watts DJ (2007) A twenty-first century science. Nature 445: 489.
4. Lazer D, Pentland A, Adamic L, Aral S, Barabási AL, et al. (2009) Computational social science. Science 323: 721–723.
5. Vespignani A (2009) Predicting the behavior of techno-social systems. Science 325: 425–428.
6. Ginsberg J, Mohebbi MH, Patel RS, Brammer L, Smolinski MS, et al. (2009) Detecting influenza epidemics using search engine query data. Nature 457: 1012–1014.
7. Preis T, Reith D, Stanley HE (2010) Complex dynamics of our economic life on different scales: insights from search engine query data. Phil Trans of the Roy Soc A 368: 5707–5719.
8. Goel S, Hofman JM, Lahaie S, Pennock DM, Watts DJ (2010) Predicting consumer behavior with web search. Proc Natl Acad Sci 107: 17486–17490.
9. O'Connor B, Balasubramanyan R, Routledge BR, Smith NA (2010) From tweets to polls: Linking text sentiment to public opinion time series. Proceedings of the International AAAI Conference on Weblogs and Social Media.
10. Bollen J, Mao H, Zeng XJ (2011) Twitter mood predicts the stock market. J of Computational Science 2: 1–7.
11. Saavedra S, Smith D, Reed-Tsochas F (2010) Cooperation under indirect reciprocity and imitative trust. PLoS One 5: e13475.
12. Bagrow JP, Wang D, Barabasi AL (2011) Collective response of human populations to large-scale emergencies. PLoS One 6: e17680.
13. Pinker S (2008) The Stuff of Thought: Language As a Window Into Human Nature. Harvard Univ. Press.
14. Solé RV, Corominas-Murtra B, Valverde S, Steels L (2010) Language networks: Their structure, function, and evolution. Complexity 15: 20–26.
15. Scheffer M, Bascompte J, Brock WA, Brovkin V, Carpenter SR, et al. (2009) Early-warning signals for critical transitions. Nature 461: 53–59.
16. Diermeier D, Merlo A (2000) Government turnover in parliamentary democracies. Journal of Economic Theory 94: 46–79.
17. Whaley RE (2000) The investor fear gauge. J Portfol Manage 26: 12–17.
18. Poon SH, Granger C (2003) Forecasting volatility in financial markets: A review. J of Economic Literature 41: 478–539.
19. May RM, Levin SA, Sugihara G (2008) Ecology for bankers. Nature 451: 893–895.
20. Harris M, Raviv A (1993) Differences of opinion make a horse race. Review of Financial Studies 6: 473–506.
21. Antweiler W, Frank MZ (2004) Is all that talk just noise? the information content of internet stock message boards. The J of Finance 59: 1259–1294.
22. Hong H, Kubik J, Stein J (2005) Thy neighbor's portfolio: Word-of-mouth effects in the holdings and trades of money managers. The J of Finance 60: 2801–2824.
23. Saavedra S, Hagerty K, Uzzi B (2011) Synchronicity, instant messaging, and performance among financial traders. Proc Natl Acad Sci 108: 5296–5301.
24. Zhao Z, Calderón JP, Xu C, Zhao G, Fenn D, et al. (2010) Effect of social group dynamics on contagion. Phys Rev E 81: 056107.
25. Kirman A (2011) Complex Economics: Individual and collective rationality. New York: Routledge.
26. Zoltán E, Bartos I, Kertész J (2008) Fluctuation scaling in complex systems: Taylor's law and beyond. Advances in Physics 57: 89–142.
27. de Menezes MA, Barabási AL (2004) Separating internal and external dynamics of complex systems. Phys Rev Lett 93: 068701.
28. Altmann EG, Pierrehumbert JB, Motter AE (2009) Beyond word frequency: bursts, lulls, and scaling in the temporal distributions of words. PLoS One 4: e7674.
29. Zipf GK (1949) Human Behaviour and the Principle of Least-Effort. Addison-Wesley.
30. Luhn HP (1960) Keyword-in-context index for technical literature. American Documentation 11: 288–295.
31. Gómez S, Jensen P, Arenas A (2009) Analysis of community structure in networks of correlated data. Phys Rev E 80: 016114.
32. Bak P, Sneppen K (1993) Punctuated equilibrium and criticality in a simple model of evolution. Phys Rev Lett 71: 4083–4086.
33. Duch J, Arenas A (2005) Community detection in complex networks using extremal optimization. Phys Rev E 72: 027104.
34. Newman MEJ (2010) Networks: An Introduction. Oxford University Press.
35. Guimerà R, Nunes Amaral LA (2005) Functional cartography of complex metabolic networks. Nature 433: 895–900.
36. Granger CWJ (1969) Investigating causal relations by econometric models and cross-spectral methods. Econometrica 37: 424–438.

8

The Effect of Online Violent Video Games on Levels of Aggression

Jack Hollingdale[1]*, Tobias Greitemeyer[2]

1 School of Psychology, University of Sussex, Brighton, United Kingdom, **2** Institute of Psychology, University of Innsbruck, Innsbruck, Austria

Abstract

Background: In recent years the video game industry has surpassed both the music and video industries in sales. Currently violent video games are among the most popular video games played by consumers, most specifically First-Person Shooters (FPS). Technological advancements in game play experience including the ability to play online has accounted for this increase in popularity. Previous research, utilising the General Aggression Model (GAM), has identified that violent video games increase levels of aggression. Little is known, however, as to the effect of playing a violent video game online.

Methods/Principal Findings: Participants ($N = 101$) were randomly assigned to one of four experimental conditions; neutral video game—offline, neutral video game—online, violent video game—offline and violent video game—online. Following this they completed questionnaires to assess their attitudes towards the game and engaged in a chilli sauce paradigm to measure behavioural aggression. The results identified that participants who played a violent video game exhibited more aggression than those who played a neutral video game. Furthermore, this main effect was not particularly pronounced when the game was played online.

Conclusions/Significance: These findings suggest that both playing violent video games online and offline compared to playing neutral video games increases aggression.

Editor: Cheryl McCormick, Brock University, Canada

Funding: This research was supported by grant P23809 from the Austrian Science Fund. The funder had no role in study design, data collection and analysis, decision to publish, or preparation of the manuscript.

Competing Interests: The authors have declared that no competing interests exist.

* Email: jack.hollingdale@live.co.uk

Introduction

The video game industry is now the largest entertainment industry in the UK. 2011 industry figures have identified that game sales, including platform and digital, have exceeded both music and video sales [1]. Violent video games have previously been identified to be the most popular video games played by consumers [2]. Research into the effect of violent video games on levels of aggression has led to concerns that they may pose a public health risk [3]. Indeed, cross-sectional studies have found positive correlations between violent video game play and real-life aggression [4–6]. Longitudinal studies showed that habitual violent video game play predicts later aggression even after controlling for initial levels of aggressiveness [7–9]. Finally, experimental studies have revealed that playing violent video games is a causal risk factor for increased aggression [10–12]. It should be noted, however, that there is other research showing no evidence that engagement with violent video games leads to increases in aggression or reductions in prosocial behaviour [13–16], warranting the need for further research in this area. On balance however, evidence from meta-analyses confirm that exposure to violent video games increases aggressive cognitions, aggressive affect and aggressive behaviour, and decreases empathy and prosocial behaviour [17,18].

Much of the research that has provided evidence to indicate the negative effects of violent video games has utilised the General Aggression Model (GAM) [19]. A widely accepted model for understanding media effects, the GAM posits that cognition, affect and arousal mediate an individual's perception of a situation. Thus, in the short term a violent video game may temporarily increase aggression through the activation of one or more of these domains. In the long term aggressive scripts can develop and become more readily available [4]. Therefore the GAM can explain how properties of a video game can affect players' thoughts, feelings, physiological arousal and subsequent behaviour. Technological developments have afforded such games, and subsequent gaming experience, to expand beyond the realms of the console, and computer programmed opponents (offline gaming), and now allow players to engage in video game play with multiple players from all over the world via the internet (online gaming). Schubert, Regenbrecht and Friedmann [20] found that players who interact with other human players experience a heightened sense of being part of the action. Significant differences in physiological arousal and evaluations of game experience, including presence and likability, have also been found when video game opponents are controlled by other humans [21]. In regards to the negative effects, increases in aggressive thoughts and hostile expectations have been found when playing human opponents in a violent video game [22,29]. Further to this, Wei [24] found, from a survey of 312 Chinese adolescents, that those who played violent video games online against human opponents expressed a greater tolerance of violence, a lower empathetic attitude and more aggressive behaviour than those who played against computer opponents. Based on previous studies, engagement with/against human opponents may strengthen gaming experiences and therefore, in accordance with the GAM, heighten their effects on players' thoughts, feelings and behaviour.

As noted above, violent content within violent video games has also been identified to increase levels of aggression. Within specific violent video games, progression through gaming levels achieved by engaging in violence poses an additional risk of increasing levels of aggression. Carnagey and Anderson [25] found that rewarding violence increased in-game violence and that rewards for killing other racing drivers and pedestrians, in the race-car video game *Carmageddon 2*, increased levels of hostile emotion, aggressive thinking and aggressive behaviour. Sherry [26] identified that video games that portray human violence were associated with increases in levels of aggression, potentially due to higher rates of action, and subsequent heightened nonspecific arousal. More specifically, increases in experience of perceived difficulty, enjoyment and action have yielded significant game effects on aggressive thoughts [27]. These findings lend support to the processes involved in the GAM.

One of the most popular violent gaming formats to date is the First Person Shooter (FPS), in which the gamer experiences the action through the eyes of the main protagonist, centred on a projectile weapon. Reports indicate that a specific franchise, utilising the FPS format, *Call of Duty*, a military war game, has broken all previous sales records. *Call of Duty: Modern Warfare 2*, made $550 m (£350 m) in the first five days of sale. This was surpassed by *Call of Duty: Black Ops* and *Call of Duty: Modern Warfare 3*, which made $650 m (£412 m) and $775 m (£490 m) in sales respectively [28]. FPSs have been found to significantly increase hostility and aggression from base line levels [29]. Based on anecdotal evidence much of the success of this franchise has been attributed to features of online game play.

Despite the popularity of the genre, to date, there is a lack of research that has attempted to investigate the effect of playing violent video games, specifically FPSs, online on levels of aggression.

Overview of the present research

In the present research, we examined whether playing a FPS online would exacerbate the negative effects of violent video game play on aggression. Further to this we examined the effect of particular game experiences including perceived difficulty, enjoyment and action, previously identified to be associated with increases in aggressive thoughts [27], on levels of behavioural aggression. To this end, participants played either a violent video game online or offline, or a neutral video game online or offline. Afterwards, aggressive behaviour was assessed. It was expected that playing a violent video game would increase aggression. It was also expected that participants who had played the violent video game online would show the highest levels of aggression (relative to the remaining three experimental conditions) due to the previously identified experiences specific to online game play. Finally, we examined whether these proposed effects would hold when controlling for perceived difficulty, enjoyment and action.

Ethical approval was given by the University of Sussex's School of Life Sciences Research Governance Committee (Ethical Approval Reference: RBJH0510). All relevant data are within the paper and its Supporting Information files.

Method

Within this paper the authors report how we determined our sample size, all data exclusions (if any), all manipulations, and all measures in the study. One hundred and one students (64 men and 37 women; ages range from 18 to 44: $M = 21.38$, $SD = 4.00$) from a UK University participated in the study in exchange for course credits or payment. After being welcomed by the examiner all participants were asked to complete a consent form. Participants were randomly assigned to one of four experimental conditions; 26 participants in a neutral video game offline, 26 participants in a neutral video game online, 23 participants in a violent video game offline and 26 participants in a violent video game online. Participants were advised that they would be undertaking two unrelated marketing surveys that had been combined for the economy of time. The first would ask for their views about a popular video game and the second would involve a marketing survey for a new recipe of hot chilli sauce.

The first task involved playing a video game for thirty minutes [29] either offline or online. In the offline condition participants were allowed to play against computer characters, subject to the video game's narrative. In the online condition participants played against human opponents via the internet, utilising randomly computer selected pre-existing levels, thus reducing the time spent navigating menus. In the online conditions, when appropriate, participants were requested to wait patiently whilst the server selected and loaded following levels. There was no opportunity for players to communicate with other human players via the internet in the online condition. The audio was turned off in all conditions to prevent participants being exposed to other players' attitudes or opinions in the online condition and to promote consistency. The gaming approach and engagement of online opponents was not recorded. All participants were initially introduced to a Playstation 3 computer console. The type of video game (violent and neutral) was identified using their Pan European Game Information (PEGI) ratings. Participants in the neutral video game condition were introduced to *LittleBigPlanet 2*, certificate 7, a game that would normally be rated suitable for all age groups but contains scenes that may be considered frightening for young children [30]. *LittleBigPlanet 2* allows players to create, explore, solve puzzles, and interact with fantasy environments which they can enjoy or share online with other gamers. All participants in the neutral condition played the initial training level and were then allocated to either the offline condition, subject to the game's narrative, or online condition, able to engage freely with the game's online content, for the remainder of the experiment. Participants in the violent video game condition were introduced to *Call of Duty: Modern Warfare*, certificate 18. *Call of Duty: Modern Warfare* is a FPS that sets gamers as soldiers tasked to kill the enemy in various environments. Games with a certificate 18 depict extreme violence including multiple, motiveless killing and violence towards defenceless people that may make the viewer experience a sense of revulsion [30]. All participants were asked to play the initial level, that introduces players to the gaming controls, and then were set up to play offline levels, following the narrative of the game, or online levels, during which the player played against other human operated opponents in free-for-all mode (Death-match). Having played for the allotted time participants were then asked to complete a number of questions about the game they had just played. This survey investigated their attitudes towards the games, including how violent they perceived the content and the

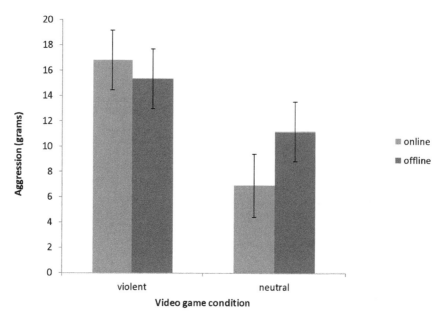

Figure 1. Mean grams of chilli sauce by experimental condition.

graphics to be. Among some filler items, participants indicated how difficult they perceived the game to be (using two items, $\alpha = .72$), to what extent they enjoyed the game (using two items, $\alpha = .79$), and how fast the action of the game was (using one item). All items were assessed on a Likert scale from 1 to 7.

Following this, some affective measures were employed. There were no significant effects on these measures so this is not considered further. Finally, participants completed a marketing survey investigating a new hot chilli sauce recipe. Participants were informed that they were not required to taste the hot chilli sauce but to prepare an amount of chilli sauce for a taste tester. During the instructions they were made aware that the taste tester 'couldn't stand hot chilli sauce' but was taking part due to good payment. They were presented with a hot chilli sauce, depicting three out of three chillies for hotness, a spoon and a plastic receptacle. The amount of chilli sauce was weighed in grams after the participant had left the experiment. The chilli sauce paradigm has been successfully used in previous studies to measure behavioural aggression in the laboratory environment [31]. All participants completed all parts of the experiment with none admitting to knowing the true purpose of the study, therefore all data was included within the study. At the conclusion of the experiment all participants were offered a comprehensive debrief form which included information as to the true purpose of the experiment.

Results

The manipulation check identified that participants in the violent video game condition reported that the violent video game *Call of Duty: Modern Warfare 2* ($M = 4.08$, $SD = 1.29$) depicted a more violent content and more violent graphics compared to the neutral video game *LittleBigPlanet 2* ($M = 1.41$, $SD = 0.89$), $F(1, 97) = 146.97$, $p<.001$, $\eta_p^2 = .60$.

A 2 (type of video game: violent vs. neutral) x 2 (setting: online vs. offline) analysis of variance (ANOVA) on the amount of chili sauce (aggression measure) revealed a significant main effect of type of video game, $F(1, 97) = 8.63$, $p = .004$, $\eta_p^2 = .08$. Participants who had played the violent video game were more

aggressive ($M = 16.12$, $SD = 15.30$) than participants who had played the neutral video game ($M = 9.06$, $SD = 7.65$). The main effect of setting, $F(1, 97) = 0.35$, $p = .558$, $\eta_p^2 = .00$, and the interaction were not significant, $F(1, 97) = 1.44$, $p = .234$, $\eta_p^2 = .02$.

To test our specific prediction that aggressive behaviour, grams of chilli sauce dispensed by participants, would be particularly pronounced after playing a violent video game online, planned contrasts were performed, which are particularly adequate to answer such specific research questions [32,33]. In fact, participants who had played the violent video game online were more aggressive ($M = 16.81$, $SD = 16.57$; contrast weight: 3) compared to participants who had played the violent video game offline ($M = 15.35$, $SD = 14.04$; contrast weight: −1), participants who had played the neutral video game online ($M = 6.92$, $SD = 7.62$; contrast weight: −1), and participants who had played the neutral video game offline ($M = 11.19$, $SD = 7.20$; contrast weight: −1), $t(97) = 2.07$, $p = .041$ (Figure 1). Note, however, that the orthogonal contrast comparing the violent video game offline condition (contrast weight: 2) with the neutral video game online (contrast weight: −1) and the neutral video game offline (contrast weight: −1) condition was also significant, $t(97) = 2.09$, $p = .039$. Finally, the orthogonal contrast comparing the neutral video game online (contrast weight: 1) with the neutral video game offline (contrast weight: −1) condition was not significant, $t(97) = 1.28$, $p = .202$. This pattern of data suggests that both playing violent video games online and offline compared to playing neutral video games increases aggression.

The violent video game ($M = 4.11$, $SD = 1.48$) was perceived as being more difficult than the neutral game ($M = 2.71$, $SD = 1.18$), $F(1, 97) = 27.11$, $p<.001$, $\eta_p^2 = .22$. Participants also enjoyed the violent video game more ($M = 4.81$, $SD = 1.46$) than the neutral game ($M = 3.76$, $SD = 1.38$), $F(1, 97) = 13.34$, $p<.001$, $\eta_p^2 = .12$. The violent video game ($M = 5.00$, $SD = 1.47$) was also perceived as having faster action than the neutral video game ($M = 2.94$, $SD = 1.56$), $F(1, 97) = 46.06$, $p<.001$, $\eta_p^2 = .32$. Note, however, that in a multiple regression the effect of type of video game (violent vs. neutral) was still significant when controlling for these video game ratings, $\beta = .27$, $t(96) = 2.15$, $p = .034$. Moreover, none of the video game ratings received a significant regression weight, all βs < .15, all ts < 1.20, all ps > .202.

Discussion

The present study examined the effect of playing a violent video game online and the impact of game experience including perceptions of difficulty, enjoyment and action on levels of behavioural aggression. Supporting previous research, this study found that playing a violent video game in comparison to a neutral video game significantly increased levels of aggression [3–6]. However, this main effect was not particularly pronounced when the game was played online. That is, both playing the violent video game online and offline relative to playing a neutral video game increased levels of aggression.

It is important to note that the violent and the neutral video game differed in terms of perceived difficulty, enjoyment and action, with the violent game perceived as being more difficult, more enjoyable, and being faster. However, when controlling for these video game properties, there was still a significant influence of type of video game on aggression. To put it differently, the effect that playing the violent relative to the neutral video game increases aggression is *not* due to differences in perceived difficulty, enjoyment and action. It should be noted, however, that controlling for potential confounders within video game research should be viewed with caution [34].

It should be acknowledged that the violent and the neutral video game chosen for this study may differ in properties other than difficulty, pace of action, and enjoyment. For example, the first-person shooter game, even when played offline (alone), contains a great deal of competitive content (competing in shooting battles for survival against other computer-generated characters), whereas the neutral video game contains little to no competitive content. Importantly, previous research has demonstrated an effect of competitive video game content (i.e., competing against other computer-generated characters in a game) on aggressive behavior in the short-term [35] and long-term [36]. Unfortunately, we did not control for competitive content so it may well be that our finding that violent video games increase aggression can be (in part) accounted for by differences in how competitive the game is perceived to be. This is certainly an important endeavor for future investigations.

With the growing popularity and prevalence of online video gaming, more specifically the engagement with violent video games online, and evidence to suggest that playing against human opponents can heighten the gaming experience, we thought it an important endeavor to investigate whether violent video games played online would exacerbate any negative effects on aggression. As expected, online violent video game play relative to the three remaining experimental increased aggression. However, inasmuch as offline violent video game play relative to the neutral video game conditions also significantly increased aggression, we have to conclude that the violent video game affected aggression but that this effect was not further strengthened by playing the game online. Because this is the first study to have examined the effects of online violent video game play on aggression, we hasten to add that more research is needed before the conclusion is warranted that playing online vs. offline has no consequences on the player's social behavior. For instance, future research may address the effects of online violent video game play on behavioural aggression in the long term. Differences in perceived competition when playing video games online and offline should also be explored. Further to this, future research should investigate the properties of violent video games experienced online that impact on players' aggressive cognitions, affect, physiological arousal and behaviour.

Consideration could also be given to potential positive effects of playing prosocial video games online. Previous research has shown that playing a prosocial video game (where the main objective of the game is to benefit video game characters) increases prosocial behaviour [37–39] and empathy [40] and decreases the accessibility of aggressive thoughts [41] and reduces aggressive behaviour [42]. Likewise, playing cooperative team-player (relative to a single-player) video games increases cooperative behaviour and empathy and decreases aggressive cognitions and angry feelings [43–49]. It may well be that prosocial and antisocial outcomes are even more affected by prosocial and cooperative video games when played online.

It is important to acknowledge a limitation in regards to the video games selected in this study. The perspective of the FPS is specific, and the authors are unaware of a neutral video game that utilises the first person perspective. It may be possible, in the future, to identify a non-violent first person perspective video game and thus better match the characteristics of the violent and neutral video games. As a result, *LittleBigPlanet 2* was selected for its low PEGI rating and ease of operating the controls (unrelated to game difficulty). It should also be conceded that the two online conditions differed in that participants competed against human opponents in the first-person shooter game, whereas the neutral video game allowed players to play competitively and cooperatively. This possible confound might have led to increased aggression in the online/violent (relative to the offline/violent) video game condition and decreased aggression in the online/neutral (relative to the offline/neutral) video game condition (that is, an interaction between type of video game and setting). However, we did not find this interaction, but simply a main effect of type of video game. In fact, it is compelling that despite these differences in online/offline shooter games that they did not differ in their effect on aggression.

Further to this some concerns have been raised as to the suitability of the chilli sauce paradigm as an accurate measurement of behavioural aggression within the laboratory environment [50]. In addition the current sample size was relatively small and therefore limits the generalisability of the results. Future research should increase the experimental population and may examine the effects of violent video games online on other measures of aggression.

In conclusion this study has identified that increases in aggression are not more pronounced when playing a violent video game online in comparison to playing a neutral video game online. This is an important finding in relation to the growing online community and popularity of violent video games, specifically FPSs, and the potential for subsequent increases in aggression. We think there should be concern about the harmful effects of playing violent video games but it appears that playing the game online does not further exacerbate these effects.

Supporting Information

File S1   SPSS data file.

Author Contributions

Conceived and designed the experiments: JH TG. Performed the experiments: JH. Analyzed the data: TG. Contributed reagents/materials/analysis tools: JH TG. Wrote the paper: JH TG.

References

1. Entertainment Retailers Association (2012) The voice of entertainment retailing. Available: http://www.eraltd.org/info-stats/overview.aspx. Accessed 2013 Jan 5.

2. Dill KE, Gentile DA, Richter WA, Dill JC (2005) Violence, sex, age and race in popular video games: A content analysis. In Cole E, Henderson-Daniel J, editors. Featuring females: Feminist analyses of media. Washington DC: American Psychological Association. pp. 115–130.

3. Anderson CA, Bushman BJ (2001) Effects of violent video games on aggressive behavior, aggressive cognition, aggressive affect, physiological arousal, and prosocial behavior: A meta-analytic Review of the scientific literature. Psychological Science 12: 353–359.

4. Anderson CA, Dill KE (2000) Video games and aggressive thoughts, feelings, and behavior in the laboratory and life. Journal of Personality and Social Psychology 78: 772–790.

5. DeLisi M, Vaughn MG, Gentile DA, Anderson CA, Shook JJ (2013) Violent video games, delinquency, and youth violence: New evidence. Youth Violence and Juvenile Justice 11: 132–142.

6. Krahé B, Möller I (2004) Playing violent electronic games, hostile attribution style, and aggression related norms in German adolescents. Journal of Adolescence 27: 53–69.

7. Anderson CA, Sakamoto A, Gentile DA, Ihori N, Shibuya A, et al. (2008) Longitudinal effects of violent video games on aggression in Japan and the United States. Pediatrics 122: e1067–e1072.

8. Möller I, Krahé B (2009) Exposure to violent video games and aggression in German adolescents: A longitudinal analysis. Aggressive Behavior 35: 75–89.

9. Willoughby T, Adachi PC, Good M (2012) A longitudinal study of the association between violent video game play and aggression among adolescents. Developmental Psychology 48: 1044–1057.

10. Anderson CA, Carnagey NL (2009) Causal effects of violent sports video games on aggression: Is it competitiveness or violent content? Journal of Experimental Social Psychology 45: 731–739.

11. Greitemeyer T (2014) Intense acts of violence during video game play make daily life aggression appear innocuous: A new mechanism why violent video games increase aggression. Journal of Experimental Social Psychology 50: 52–56.

12. Hollingdale J, Greitemeyer T (2013) The changing face of aggression: The effect of personalized avatars in a violent video game on levels of aggressive behavior. Journal of Applied Social Psychology 43: 1862–1868.

13. Williams D, Skoric M (2005) Internet fantasy violence: A test of aggression in an online game. Communication Monographs 72: 217–233.

14. Elson M, Ferguson CJ (2014) Twenty-five years of research on violence in digital games and aggression: Empirical evidence, perspectives, and a debate gone astray. European Psychologist 19: 33–46.

15. Tear MJ, Nielsen M (2013) Failure to demonstrate that playing violent video games diminishes prosocial behavior. PloS One 8: e68382.

16. Ferguson CJ, Rueda SM (2010) The Hitman study: Violent video game exposure effects on aggressive behavior, hostile feelings and depression. European Psychologist 15: 99–108.

17. Anderson CA, Shibuya A, Ihori N, Swing EL, Bushman BJ, et al. (2010) Violent video game effects on aggression, empathy, and prosocial behavior in Eastern and Western countries. Psychological Bulletin 136: 151–173.

18. Greitemeyer T, Mügge DO (2014) Video games do affect social outcomes: A meta-analytic review of the effects of violent and prosocial video game play. Personality and Social Psychology Bulletin 40: 578–589.

19. Anderson CA, Bushman BJ (2002) Human aggression. Annual Review of Psychology 53: 27–51.

20. Schubert T, Regenbrecht H, Friedmann F (2000, March 27–28)Real and illusory interactions enhance presence in virtual environments. Paper presented at Presence 2000—The Third International Workshop on Presence, Delft University of Technology, Delft, Netherlands.

21. Lim S, Reeves B (2010) Computer agents versus avatars: Responses to interactive game characters controlled by a computer or other player. International Journal of Human-Computer Studies 68: 57–68.

22. Eastin MS (2006) Video game violence and the female game player: Self- and opponent gender effects on presence and aggressive thoughts, Human Communication Research 32: 351–372.

23. Eastin MS, Griffiths RP (2006) Beyond the shooter game. Examining presence and hostile outcomes among male game players, Communication Research 33: 448–466.

24. Wei R (2007) Effects of playing violent video games on Chinese adolescents' pro-violence attitudes, attitudes towards others, and aggressive behavior. Cybersychology & Behaviour 10: 371–380.

25. Carnagey NL, Anderson CA (2005) The effects of reward and punishment in violent video games on aggressive affect, cognition, and behavior. American Psychological Science 16: 882–889.

26. Sherry JL (2001) The effects of violent video games on aggression: A meta-analysis. Human Communication Research 27: 409–431.

27. Anderson CA, Carnagey NL, Flanagan M, Benjamin AJ, Eubanks J, et al. (2004) Violent video games: Specific effects of violent content on aggressive thoughts and behaviour. Advances in Experimental Social Psychology 36: 199–249.

28. British Broadcasting Corporation (BBC) (2011) Call of Duty enjoys record sales despite retail woes. Available: http://www.bbc.co.uk/news/technology-15796585. Accessed 2013 Jan 5.

29. Barlett CP, Harris RJ, Baldassaro R (2007) Longer you play, the more hostile you feel: examination of first person shooter video games and aggression during video game play. Aggressive Behavior 33: 486–497.

30. Pan European Game Information (PEGI) (2013) What do the labels mean? Available: http://www.pegi.info/en/index/id/33/. Accessed 2013 Jan 5.

31. McGregor HA, Lieberman JD, Greenberg J, Soloman S, Arndt J, et al. (1998) Terror management and aggression: Evidence that mortality salience motivates aggression against worldview threatening others. Journal of Personality and Social Psychology 74: 590–605.

32. Rosenthal R, Rosnow RL (1985) Contrast analysis: Focused comparisons in the analysis of variance. Cambridge, United Kingdom: Cambridge University Press.

33. Steiger JH (2004) Beyond the F test: Effect size confidence intervals and tests of close fit in the analysis of variance and contrast analysis. Psychological Methods 9: 164–182.

34. Miller GA, Chapman JP (2001) Misunderstanding analysis of covariance. Journal of Abnormal Psychology 110: 40–48.

35. Adachi PJC, Willoughby T (2011) The effect of video game competition and violence on aggressive behavior: Which characteristic has the greatest influence? Psychology of Violence 1: 259–274.

36. Adachi PJC, Willoughby T (2013) Demolishing the competition: The longitudinal link between competitive video games, competitive gambling, and aggression. Journal of Youth and Adolescence 42: 1090–1104.

37. Greitemeyer T (2011) Effects of prosocial media on social behavior: When and why does media exposure affect helping and aggression? Current Directions in Psychological Science 20: 251–255.

38. Gentile DA, Anderson CA, Yukawa S, Ihori N, Saleem M, et al. (2009) The Effects of Prosocial Video Games on Prosocial Behaviors: International Evidence from Correlational, Experimental, and Longitudinal Studies. Personality and Social Psychology Bulletin 35: 752–763.

39. Greitemeyer T, Osswald S (2010) Effects of prosocial video games on prosocial behavior. Journal of Personality and Social Psychology 98: 211–221.

40. Prot S, Gentile DA, Anderson CA, Suzuki K, Swing E, et al. (2014) Long-term relations between prosocial media use, empathy, and prosocial behavior. Psychological Science 25: 358–368.

41. Greitemeyer T, Osswald S (2009) Prosocial video games reduce aggressive cognitions. Journal of Experimental Social Psychology 45: 896–900.

42. Greitemeyer T, Agthe M, Turner R, Gschwendtner C (2012) Acting prosocially reduces retaliation: Effects of prosocial video games on aggressive behavior. European Journal of Social Psychology 42: 235–242.

43. Eastin MS (2007) The influence of competitive and cooperative play on state hostility. Human Communication Research 33: 450–466.

44. Ewoldsen DR, Eno CA, Okdie BM, Velez JA, Guadagno RE, et al. (2012) Effect of playing violent video games cooperatively or competitively on subsequent cooperative behavior. Cyberpsychology, Behavior, and Social Networking 15: 277–280.

45. Greitemeyer T (2013) Playing video games cooperatively increases empathic concern. Social Psychology 44: 408–413.

46. Greitemeyer T, Cox C (2013) There's no "I" in team: Effects of cooperative video games on cooperative behavior. European Journal of Social Psychology 43: 224–228.

47. Greitemeyer T, Traut-Mattausch E, Osswald S (2012) How to ameliorate negative effects of violent video games on cooperation: Play it cooperatively in a team. Computers in Human Behavior 28: 1465–1470.

48. Schmierbach M (2010) "Killing Spree": Exploring the connection between competitive game play and aggressive cognition. Communication Research 37: 256–274.

49. Velez JA, Mahood C, Ewoldsen DR, Moyer-Gusé E (2014) Ingroup versus outgroup conflict in the context of violent video game play: The effect of cooperation on increased helping and decreased aggression. Communication Research 41: 607–626.

50. Ritter D, Eslea M (2005) Hot sauce, toy guns, and graffiti: A critical account of current laboratory aggression paradigms. Aggressive Behavior 31: 407–419.

9

Heavy Tailed Distributions of Effect Sizes in Systematic Reviews of Complex Interventions

Christopher Burton*

Centre for Population Health Sciences, University of Edinburgh, Edinburgh, United Kingdom

Abstract

Background: Systematic reviews of complex interventions commonly find heterogeneity of effect sizes among similar interventions which cannot be explained. Commentators have suggested that complex interventions should be viewed as interventions in complex systems. We hypothesised that if this is the case, the distribution of effect sizes from complex interventions should be heavy tailed, as in other complex systems. Thus, apparent heterogeneity may be a feature of the complex systems in which such interventions operate.

Methodology/Principal Findings: We specified three levels of complexity and identified systematic reviews which reported effect sizes of healthcare interventions at two of these levels (interventions to change professional practice and personal interventions to help smoking cessation). These were compared with each other and with simulated data representing the lowest level of complexity. Effect size data were rescaled across reviews at each level using log-normal parameters and pooled. Distributions were plotted and fitted against the inverse power law (Pareto) and stretched exponential (Weibull) distributions, heavy tailed distributions which are commonly reported in the literature, using maximum likelihood fitting. The dataset included 155 studies of interventions to change practice and 98 studies of helping smoking cessation. Both distributions showed a heavy tailed distribution which fitted best to the inverse power law for practice interventions (exponent = 3.9, loglikelihood = −35.3) and to the stretched exponential for smoking cessation (loglikelihood = −75.2). Bootstrap sensitivity analysis to adjust for possible publication bias against weak results did not diminish the goodness of fit.

Conclusions/Significance: The distribution of effect sizes from complex interventions includes heavy tails as typically seen in both theoretical and empirical complex systems. This is in keeping with the idea of complex interventions as interventions in complex systems.

Editor: Pedro Antonio Valdes-Sosa, Cuban Neuroscience Center, Cuba

Funding: CB was supported by a Chief Scientist Office Primary Care Research Career Award (www.cso.scot.nhs.uk/). The funders had no role in study design, data collection and analysis, decision to publish, or preparation of the manuscript.

Competing Interests: The author has declared that no competing interests exist.

* E-mail: chris.burton@ed.ac.uk

Introduction

Many interventions in health and social care are complex, in that they involve multiple interacting components [1] and are delivered in differing ways and circumstances [2]. These "complex interventions" contrast with more simple interventions such as a drug given to treat a single condition where most sources of variability can be identified and controlled for, either directly or by randomisation. Reviews of the effects of complex interventions, such as actions to change clinical practice, have shown over many years that effects are commonly small [3] and this has been attributed to various phenomena, most recently the complexity of healthcare systems [4].

The possible link between complex interventions and the science of complex systems [5] has been elaborated by a number of authors [6–9]. They argue that complex interventions typically possess "sensitive" causality in which outcomes depend on multiple steps and interactions [6], although few published studies of complex interventions explicitly describe and model the complexity of the system they are studying [10,11]. Figure 1

outlines three scenarios which display increasing complexity. In the first, the intervention applies to individuals (each with their own personal characteristics) in isolation; in the second the effect of the intervention depends both on the intervention and the environment with which individuals interact. In the third level, the intervention is applied to a healthcare team which then interacts with individuals who are in turn embedded in their own social networks. In the first level, with low complexity, variation within a population can be assumed to be due to statistical chance as each individual is independent. The second level, with moderate complexity can be understood using social cognitive theories such as the Theory of Planned Behaviour [12] which includes both personal elements such as intention and social effects such as norms. The third, high complexity level, extends the previous models by including a range of complex interactions affecting the healthcare system (whether individual, clinical team or whole system) which precede the delivery of care to patients. This extends the personal components of the Theory of Planned Behaviour with group ethos, aims and threats [13–15].

a) low complexity : intervention to change individual patient characteristic

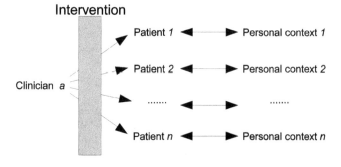

b) moderate complexity: intervention to change individual patient behaviour

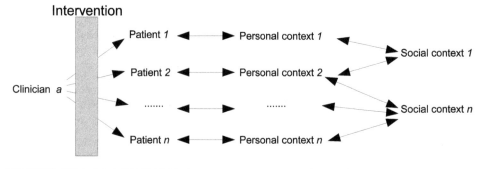

c) high complexity: intervention to change behaviour among groups of clinicians

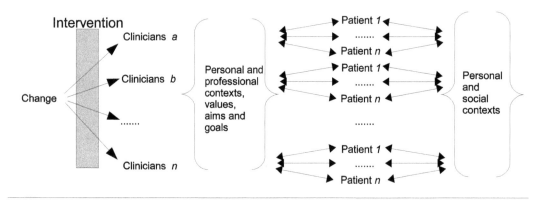

Figure 1. Schematic representation of three levels of complexity in relation to healthcare interventions. (a) shows a simple intervention given to individual and independent patients (for instance administration of a drug). (b) shows a moderately complex intervention – for example advice or support to help smoking cessation – where the treatment is delivered to individual patients but their networks of interaction – some of which may be shared – influence the outcome of the intervention. (c) shows a highly complex intervention – for example interventions to change clinical practice – where the intervention attempts to change the practice in order to deliver individual patient treatment. The effect of the intervention depends on interaction networks at the practice/clinician and at the patient level.

While to date the argument about whether complex interventions should be understood as interventions within complex systems has been largely philosophical, there are testable properties of complex systems [5,16] which should be detectable in the results of complex interventions. One such property is the presence of characteristic heavy-tailed statistical distributions such as the inverse power law [17] and stretched exponential [18]. Such distributions, which appear to be ubiquitous in nature[17,19] and have been found in

healthcare systems [20], are very different from the normal distribution which characterises the distribution of simple effects. In particular, such distributions contain many more small values than a normal distribution, but also a few more extreme values.

We hypothesised that if complex interventions are "interventions in complex systems" [7] the effect sizes of these interventions should show a heavy-tailed distribution typical of those seen in other complex systems.

Methods

Objective

We examined the distribution of effect sizes reported within a series of systematic reviews of complex interventions to change practice. We then compared this with two control distributions: (i) effect sizes from systematic reviews of patient level interventions to stop smoking, which we took to represent moderate complexity as shown in figure 1, and (ii) simulated data representing random variation around a mean effect size.

Selection of studies

In order to test the distribution of effects in complex healthcare systems we sought systematic reviews of interventions which (a) represented changes in systems (for instance the behavior of health care professionals) rather than to a single pathway (for instance a public health measure to add nutritional supplements to food) (b) had a range of possible responses (ranging from ignore, through minor change, to radical revision of a process of care), (c) had causal models with multiple stages in which changes were also likely to lead to trade-offs. The essence of these criteria was that we viewed practitioners as agents within systems with complex causal models and trade-offs between different actions. We chose to study interventions to change practitioner behaviour (either individually or in groups) from reviews published by the Cochrane EPOC collaboration. We selected this source because the process of conducting these reviews identifies and, where possible, quantifies a wide range of biases such that only methodologically robust studies are included.

We reviewed the list of all reviews published by October 2010 to identify those which (a) aimed to change physician behaviour (b) acted remotely from the clinical consultation, (c) included comparisons of at least 10 included studies, and (d) permitted extraction of individual study effect sizes. Criteria (a) and (b) were chosen to reflect the requirements for complexity; criteria (c) and (d) were chosen to permit consistent data reporting and analysis. We identified three reviews: audit and feedback as methods to change physician behaviour [21], educational outreach visiting [22] and continuing education meetings and workshops [23].

Selection of control data

Smoking cessation data were collected from 4 systematic reviews in the Cochrane Database of Systematic Reviews Tobacco Control section. These examined the effect sizes from randomized controlled trials of the following smoking cessation strategies: Nicotine Replacement Therapy [24], physician advice [25], individual behavioural counseling [26] and motivational interviewing [27]. These were chosen to represent moderate complexity because while the treatment was delivered consistently, individual response would be likely to be at least partly socially determined.

Simulation data for independent samples comprised 10,000 points designed to represent a population of risk ratios. As the logarithm of the relative risk ratio is approximately normally distributed, we generated a random lognormal distribution with log-mean and log-standard deviation taken from the log transformed effect sizes for EPOC data.

Extraction of data

For each review we selected all comparisons with more than 10 studies. We then extracted a measure of effect size from each study as follows: for comparisons with dichotomous outcomes, we used the relative risk adjusted for baseline differences. For comparisons reporting continuous outcomes we converted the value reported in the reviews – the proportional change in the intervention group relative to control mean and adjusted for baseline difference – and converted this to a relative risk ratio (relative risk ratio = 1+ adjusted proportional change). Where the aim of an intervention was a reduction in behaviour (e.g. reducing error) the effect was reversed such that in all cases a relative risk ratio greater than one indicated the desired outcome. Within each comparison, these measures were rescaled by transforming the values into natural logarithms, calculating a z score for each study using the log-mean and log-standard deviation for each comparison, then converting the z score back to risk ratios using the overall log-mean and log-standard deviation of the whole population. These data were then pooled so that the analysis was carried out on three datasets: pooled reviews to change practice; pooled reviews of smoking cessation therapy; and simulated data representing a comparable lognormal relative risk ratio population.

Fitting of distributions

We chose to fit the data to two specific distributions, the inverse power law and the stretched exponential. The inverse power law (or Pareto) distribution has historically been associated with the behaviour of complex systems [19] although it has been argued that it may represent a special case, restricted to only a limited range of data, and that the use of an alternative – such as the stretched exponential (or Weibull) distribution, is more appropriate [18]. We considered fitting additional heavy tailed distributions, however given the relatively small numbers of studies in the review we wished to avoid the risks of over-specification and confined the analysis to the two listed above.

The distribution of pooled relative risks was first plotted as a histogram on conventional axes and then as a cumulative distribution on logarithmic axes. Plotting an inverse power law distribution this way would produce a straight line with negative slope equivalent to the power law exponent.

The pooled rescaled effect size distribution was then fitted to both the inverse power law (or Pareto) and stretched exponential (Weibull) distribution using maximum likelihood estimation (with maximization of the tail conditional loglikelihood for the Weibull fitting) as described by Clauset [18]. All distributions were fitted with a lower threshold of 1. Goodness of fit was reported as the log-likelihood and compared between distributions using the non-nested Vuong test. All analyses were carried out using published [18] scripts in R 2.14.

While the estimation of the usefulness of a healthcare intervention requires both size and direction (conventionally expressed as positive effects leading to better outcomes and negative effects to worse), the influence of system complexity on the distribution of effect sizes should be independent of direction. In view of this we used two approaches to deal with negative effects (ie relative risk less <1) prior to fitting distributions: (1) setting a threshold of 1, thereby effectively excluding negative studies; (2) calculating an "absolute" value by inverting all relative risks <1. Analysis was repeated for each of these conditions.

Sensitivity analysis

One possible explanation for a skewed distribution of effect sizes in a systematic review is publication bias [28], whereby unexpectedly strong results are selectively published and, equally importantly, unremarkable weak results are not. Because our model of heavy tailed distributions from complex systems depends on most responses being small, if publication bias existed, small effect studies would tend to be under-reported. We did not attempt to assess whether publication bias was present, rather we considered what effect publication bias – if present – would have on the data. To do this we simulated the effect of publication bias using a bootstrapping procedure. This increased the number of small effect size studies by selectively resampling with replacement from studies in the pooled distribution whose rescaled effect size was below the median value. These resampled studies were added to the original data to increase the size of the dataset by up to 80 points in order to simulate up to one third of all studies being unpublished because of small absolute effects. This bootstrapping procedure was repeated 200 times. The results of this process were plotted to show the effect of adding bootstrapped studies to the original data on the parameters and log-likelihoods of the model fit for the stretched exponential and inverse power law (using the same thresholds as previously).

Ethics

This study comprised a secondary analysis of published data, no ethical permissions were required.

Results

Data from comparisons

There were 55 current systematic reviews in the Cochrane EPOC collection available for inspection at the start of the analysis. 16 of these related to changing practitioner behaviour of which 9 contained more than 10 studies. Four of these related to a range of approaches of addressing specific problems (for instance antibiotic prescribing) while five related to approaches (such as audit and feedback) across problems. Of these, two (audit and feedback [21] and educational outreach visiting [22]) had publicly available detailed data available [29]. Similar tables for a third review [23] were obtained from the authors. These three reviews contained 6 eligible comparisons with more than 10 studies and reported 166 outcomes. For 11 of these there was no measure of change adjusted for baseline and these were discarded leaving 155 outcomes which represented the dataset for this analysis. 72 outcomes were drawn from the review of audit and feedback, 51

from educational outreach visiting and 32 from continuing education meetings. Outcomes were continuous for 31 and dichotomous for 124. Twelve study outcomes appeared in two comparisons, two with continuous and dichotomous measures for the same study and ten appearing in two reviews (for example a study which included audit and feedback with educational outreach visiting could feature in both reviews). There were 54 systematic reviews in the Cochrane Tobacco Addiction Group database from which we identified the four individual reviews with more that 10 studies more comparison [24–27]. The number of outcomes in each comparisons, and a summary of the rescaled effect sizes drawn from the reviews are shown in table 1.

For the changing practice reviews, median relative risk ratio after pooling was 1.17 (before pooling 1.15) with range 0.64 to 8.17. For the smoking reviews, median risk ratio after standardization was 1.42, range 0.47 to 5.62; the simulation data had a median of 1.23 and range 0.23 to 4.65. Twenty seven (17.4%, 95% confidence interval 11.4 to 23.4) risk ratios for the changing practice reviews were less than one, as were 16 (16.3%) for the smoking cessation reviews and 30% of the simulation data points. Histograms of each distribution are shown in figure 2. Figure 3 demonstrates the cumulative density function of the rescaled relative rate ratios for each of the three rescaled distribution on conventional (a) and logarithmic axes (b). These show that both sets of intervention studies possess heavier tails than the log-normal distribution of effect sizes which would be expected by chance. The data for the changing practice interventions appears to fit the inverse power law distribution: of the three sets of data it has the smallest median value and the "heaviest" tail.

Distribution fitting

The results of maximum likelihood fitting of the EPOC and smoking cessation data to both stretched exponential (Weibull) and

Table 1. Characteristics of each comparison included in the analysis. Values represent rescaled effect sizes within each comparison.

Review	Comparison	Continuous or dichotomous	N	Median	Interquartile range	Minimum	Maximum
A. Interventions to change practice							
Audit & Feedback [21]	Audit & Feedback alone	C	13	1.22	1.12 to 1.68	1.05	1.99
	Audit & Feedback alone	D	25	1.07	0.98 to 1.18	0.71	2.16
	Multifaceted including audit & feedback	D	34	1.10	1.03 to 1.36	0.78	18.3
Educational outreach visits [22]	Any intervention including educational outreach visits	C	18	1.22	1.12 to 1.41	1.00	7.17
	Any intervention including educational outreach visits	D	33	1.11	1.07 to 1.35	0.78	4.25
Continuing education meetings & workshops [23]	CME –professional outcomes	C	32	1.32	1.07 to 1.90	1.00	4.57
Combined rescaled data			155	1.16	1.05 to 1.49	0.64	8.17
B. Interventions for smoking cessation							
Nicotine replacement therapy [24]	Any NRT vs placebo/no NRT	D	50	1.34	1.19 to 1.98	0.50	4.33
Counselling [26]	Counselling vs control	D	17	1.56	1.32 to 2.01	0.58	5.5
Physician advice [25]	Minimal intervention	D	17	1.58	1.03 to 2.28	0.95	4.56
Motivational interviewing [27]	Motivational interviewing	D	14	1.62	1.16 to 1.99	0.92	5.28
Combined rescaled data			98	1.47	1.14 to 2.08	0.47	5.62
C. Simulated data		D	10000	1.31	1.02 to 1.69	0.33	4.78

Changing practice interventions

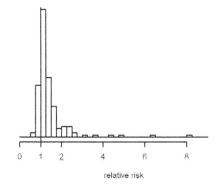

Smoking interventions

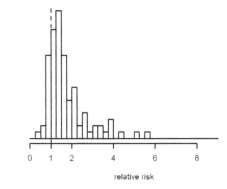

Simulation (lognormal) data

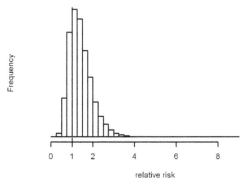

Figure 2. Histograms of pooled effect sizes from three sets of comparisons. (a) shows data from the pooled interventions to change clinical practice (N = 155). (b) shows data from the pooled interventions to help individuals stop smoking (N = 98). (c) shows simulated data from a log-normal distribution with the same log-mean and log-standard deviation as the data in (a).

inverse power law (Pareto) distributions of the data are shown in table 2. This shows good fit for both the values of relative risk above a threshold of 1 and for absolute values, with the EPOC data fitting the inverse power law distribution better and the smoking cessation fitting the stretched exponential.

Sensitivity analysis

The sensitivity analysis showed that resampling with up to 70 additional data points with small effect sizes to simulate publication

bias leading to under-reporting of studies with small results increased rather than diminished goodness of fit, as judged by the log-likelihood, with little change in model parameters (data not shown).

Discussion

We examined the distribution of effect sizes of a range of complex interventions and found heavy tailed distributions typical of those seen in interventions on complex systems. While such distributions are ubiquitous in natural and open systems they have only occasionally been looked for in healthcare [20]; our findings of heavy tails in the effect size distributions of complex interventions support the notion of complex interventions as interventions in complex systems [7].

Strengths and limitations

A key strength of this study is that it uses data collected and processed by the methodologically rigorous Cochrane review group. This markedly reduces the chance that the distribution is due to the inclusion of methodologically weak studies with high risk of bias. Furthermore, we simulated the effect of publication bias against weak results by adding up to 70 resampled studies with small effect sizes and this did not significantly change our findings. However, the number of suitable reviews was modest. While our criteria were relatively restrictive, we chose to limit ourselves to studies which fitted the models of differing levels of complexity.

The study brought together reviews from different aspects of practice, introducing the possibility of differences between comparisons accounting for our findings. We addressed this by rescaling the effect sizes within each comparison before pooling the data, and inspection of summary measures of the comparisons (table 1) suggests that the distributions are broadly similar. While the use of pooled effect sizes in meta-analysis make it possible to compare relatively dissimilar items, they introduce additional potential error. We attempted to reduce this by limiting the analysis to comparisons with 10 or more studies. While the use of relative change values introduced potential bias – studies with smaller baseline values could yield greater relative change for the same absolute change - this was the method used in the Cochrane reviews and so was kept for this analysis.

Twelve studies appeared in two comparisons of changing practice behaviour and six appeared in two comparisons of interventions for stopping smoking. As these resulted in different standardized effect sizes in each comparison we included both instances in the analysis rather than arbitrarily removing one and reducing the sample size. Heavy tailed distributions, such as the inverse power law, typically start at a baseline value of one or zero. Studies with negative effect sizes or fractions of less than one thus present a problem. We took the view that negative effects could arise either through random chance or through interventions leading to change in the unintended direction (so-called unexpected consequences). As the distribution of effects in complex systems relates to the size rather than direction, we deemed it appropriate to take absolute values, however to test for the effects of this we also reported analysis which excluded negative values. Both methods resulted in broadly similar results.

The two distributions tested are not the only heavy tailed distributions and comparable results may have been observed fitting other distributions but we did not test this. As Clauset and Newman [18] argue, the point is less that one specific distribution is correct, rather that a heavy tailed distribution represents a good fit. Our finding that data from the most complex intervention fits best to the inverse power law with the smallest median value and

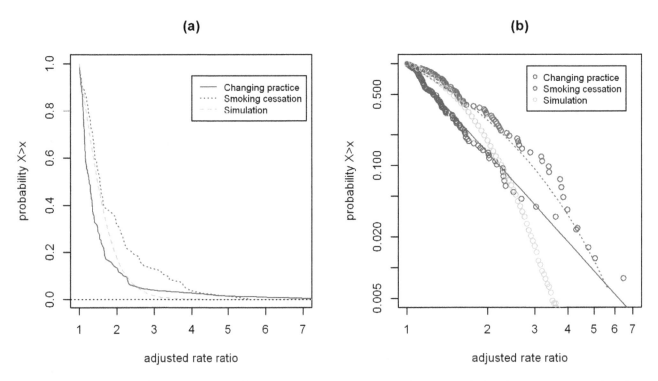

Figure 3. Cumulative distribution of pooled effect sizes. Solid and dashed lines in (b) represent the best fitting inverse power law (changing practice) and stretched exponential (smoking cessation) models identified by maximum likelihood. (a) and (b) show the Log-likelihood of the model fit for inverse power law (a) and stretched exponential (b) distributions. (c) and (d) show the distribution parameters: (c) the exponent of the inverse power law and (d) the shape (solid) and scale (open) of the stretched exponential distribution.

the longest tail, with the moderate complexity intervention fitting a stretched exponential which sits between this and the lognormal distribution of effects which would be expected by chance is in keeping with our model of complexity but requires further testing.

Comparison with other studies

This is the first study to examine the distribution of effect sizes from complex interventions from the perspective of complex systems. Previous theoretical work has argued that this might be expected [6,7,9]. Several authors have argued that the response of theoretical and simulated complex systems to change is inherently unpredictable. These complex systems possess both resilience against change and a capacity to transform in unanticipated ways as local reactions interact with each other and lead to an emergent response. [9] Although heavy-tailed distributions are known to arise in complex systems, the reason for this is not yet clear [30]. Recent work suggests that heavy-tailed distributions may offer an efficient distribution (in information theoretic terms) in respect of members of a group of items, in contrast to a population of individual items [31]. Systems whose group membership follows a heavy tailed distribution may represent an optimal trade-off between robustness and adaptability [32].

Table 2. Results of fitting of data to stretched exponential and inverse power law distributions.

Dataset	Distribution	Approach to negative values	N	Exponent	Shape	Scale	Log likelihood	Tests of difference
EPOC	Inverse Power Law	Exclude values<1	128	3.91			−35.3	Inverse power law better fit than stretched exponential p<0.001
		Absolute values	155	4.31			−16.1	
	Stretched exponential	Exclude values<1	128		0.8	0.46	−42.0	
		Absolute values	155		0.77	0.39	−24.5	
Smoking Cessation	Inverse Power Law	Exclude values<1	82	2.79			−80.2	Stretched exponential better fit than inverse power law (excluding values <1) p<0.001; no difference with absolute values (p=0.77)
		Absolute values	98	3.03			−76.9	
	Stretched exponential	Exclude values<1	82		0.90	0.76	−75.2	
		Absolute values			0.55	0.14	−74.9	

Implications for practice, policy and research

Our findings have implications for the interpretation of intervention studies which go beyond the theoretical importance of considering the complexity involved in so-called complex interventions. These implications relate to the characteristics of the heavy tailed distributions and the inferences which can be made from them.

Each of the reviews included in this analysis reported heterogeneity, in terms of the normal distribution, and none could explain it through meta-regression. Under a heavy-tailed distribution the appearance of a few very large effect sizes is to be expected and the observed values fitted comfortably with this. In practical terms this means that difficult to explain variation may no longer need an explanation, other than that it represents the natural variation of effects seen within a complex system.

There are two additional implication of the heavy tailed distribution for the results of complex interventions. The first arises where policy makers and evaluators seek a grass-roots approach to innovation in multiple sites, with selection of the "best" performer for wider roll-out. This approach runs the real risk of mistaking the random and context-specific effects in a complex system for the inherent merit of the best performing intervention. The second occurs as interventions are reproduced in a range of contexts. As, in a heavy tailed distribution, the vast majority of effects are small, there is the possibility that rolling out apparently successful interventions, may lead to disappointment as smaller effect sizes than originally seen appear more frequently.

Conclusions

The demonstration of heavy tailed distributions of effect sizes from two types of complex interventions is the first empirical evidence to support the argument that complex interventions represent interventions in complex systems.

Author Contributions

Conceived and designed the experiments: CB. Performed the experiments: CB. Analyzed the data: CB. Contributed reagents/materials/analysis tools: CB. Wrote the paper: CB.

References

1. Campbell M, Fitzpatrick R, Haines A, Kinmonth AL, Sandercock P, et al. (2000) Framework for design and evaluation of complex interventions to improve health. BMJ 321(7262): 694–696.
2. Craig P, Dieppe P, Macintyre S, Michie S, Nazareth I, et al. (2008) Developing and evaluating complex interventions: the new Medical Research Council guidance. BMJ 337: a1655.
3. Oxman AD, Thomson MA, Davis DA, Haynes RB (1995) No magic bullets: a systematic review of 102 trials of interventions to improve professional practice. CMAJ 153(10): 1423–1431.
4. Coiera E (2011) Why system inertia makes health reform so difficult. BMJ 342.
5. Rickles D, Hawe P, Shiell A (2007) A simple guide to chaos and complexity. J Epidemiol Community Health 61(11): 933–937.
6. Rickles D (2009) Causality in complex interventions. Med Health Care Philos 12(1): 77–90.
7. Hawe P, Shiell A, Riley T (2009) Theorising interventions as events in systems. Am J Community Psychol 43(3–4): 267–276.
8. Shiell A, Hawe P, Gold L (2008) Complex interventions or complex systems? Implications for health economic evaluation. BMJ 336(7656): 1281–1283.
9. Paley J (2010) The appropriation of complexity theory in health care. J Health Serv Res Policy 15(1): 59–61.
10. Hammond RA (2009) Complex systems modeling for obesity research. Prev Chronic Dis 6(3).
11. Rwashana AS, Williams DW, Neema S (2009) System dynamics approach to immunization healthcare issues in developing countries: a case study of Uganda. Health Informatics Journal 15(2): 95–107.
12. Godin G, Kok G (1996) The theory of planned behavior: a review of its applications to health-related behaviors. Am J Health Promot 11(2): 87–98.
13. Crabtree BF, Nutting PA, Miller WL, McDaniel RR, Stange KC, et al. (2011) Primary care practice transformation is hard work: insights from a 15-year developmental program of research. Med Care 49 Suppl: S28–S35.
14. Miller WL, Crabtree BF, McDaniel R, Stange KC (1998) Understanding change in primary care practice using complexity theory. J Fam Pract 46(5): 369–376.
15. Plsek PE, Greenhalgh T (2001) Complexity science: The challenge of complexity in health care. BMJ 323(7313): 625–628.
16. Newman MEJ (2011) Complex Systems: A Survey. Am J Phys 79: 800–810.
17. West BJ (2006) Where medicine went wrong: rediscovering the path to complexity. Singapore: World Scientific Publishing.
18. Clauset A, Shalizi CR, Newman MEJ (2009) Power-law distributions in empirical data. SIAM Review 51: 661–703.
19. Bak P (1996) How Nature Works: The Science of Self-Organised Criticality. London: Oxford University Press.
20. Love T, Burton C (2005) General practice as a complex system: a novel analysis of consultation data. Fam Pract 22(3): 347–352.
21. Jamtvedt G, Young JM, Kristoffersen DT, O'Brien MA, Oxman AD (2006) Audit and feedback: effects on professional practice and health care outcomes. Cochrane Database Syst Rev (2): CD000259.
22. O'Brien MA, Rogers S, Jamtvedt G, Oxman AD, Odgaard-Jensen J, et al. (2007) Educational outreach visits: effects on professional practice and health care outcomes. Cochrane Database Syst Rev (4): CD000409.
23. Forsetlund L, Bjorndal A, Rashidian A, Jamtvedt G, O'Brien MA, et al. (2009) Continuing education meetings and workshops: effects on professional practice and health care outcomes. Cochrane Database Syst Rev (2): CD003030.
24. Silagy C, Lancaster T, Stead L, Mant D, Fowler G (2004) Nicotine replacement therapy for smoking cessation. Cochrane Database Syst Rev (3): CD000146.
25. Lancaster T, Stead L (2004) Physician advice for smoking cessation. Cochrane Database Syst Rev (4): CD000165.
26. Lancaster T, Stead LF (2005) Individual behavioural counselling for smoking cessation. Cochrane Database Syst Rev (2): CD001292.
27. Lai DT, Cahill K, Qin Y, Tang JL (2010) Motivational interviewing for smoking cessation. Cochrane Database Syst Rev (1): CD006936.
28. Egger M, Dickersin K, Davey Smith G (2001) Problems and limitations in conducting systematic reviews. In: Egger M, Davey Smith G, Altman D, eds. Systematic Reviews in Health Care: meta-analysis in context. London: BMJ Publishing. pp 43–68.
29. Cochrane Effective Practice and Organisation of Care Group (2011) Tables and other information not published in our reviews. Available: http://epoc.cochrane.org/tables.
30. Adamic L (2011) Complex systems: Unzipping Zipf's law. Nature 474(7350): 164–165.
31. Baek S, Bernhardsson S, Minnhagen P (2011) Zipf's law unzipped. New Journal of Physics 13(4): 043004.
32. Carlson JM, Doyle J (2002) Complexity and robustness. Proc Natl Acad Sci U S A 99 Suppl 1: 2538–2545.

10

Anonymous Three-Party Password-Authenticated Key Exchange Scheme for Telecare Medical Information Systems

Qi Xie[1]*, **Bin Hu**[1]*, **Na Dong**[1], **Duncan S. Wong**[2]

1 Hangzhou Key Laboratory of Cryptography and Network Security, Hangzhou Normal University, Hangzhou, China, **2** Department of Computer Science, City University of Hong Kong, Kowloon, Hong Kong, China

Abstract

Telecare Medical Information Systems (TMIS) provide an effective way to enhance the medical process between doctors, nurses and patients. For enhancing the security and privacy of TMIS, it is important while challenging to enhance the TMIS so that a patient and a doctor can perform mutual authentication and session key establishment using a third-party medical server while the privacy of the patient can be ensured. In this paper, we propose an anonymous three-party password-authenticated key exchange (3PAKE) protocol for TMIS. The protocol is based on the efficient elliptic curve cryptosystem. For security, we apply the pi calculus based formal verification tool ProVerif to show that our 3PAKE protocol for TMIS can provide anonymity for patient and doctor while at the same time achieves mutual authentication and session key security. The proposed scheme is secure and efficient, and can be used in TMIS.

Editor: Muhammad Khurram Khan, King Saud University, Kingdom of Saudi Arabia, Saudi Arabia

Funding: This research was supported by the National Natural Science Foundation of China (No. 61070153, URL http://www.nsfc.gov.cn/), the Major State Basic Research Development (973) Program of China (No. 2013CB834205, URL http://www.973.gov.cn/AreaAppl.aspx), and Natural Science Foundation of Zhejiang Province (No. LZ12F02005, URL http://www.zjnsf.gov.cn/). The funders had no role in study design, data collection and analysis, decision to publish, or preparation of the manuscript.

Competing Interests: The authors have declared that no competing interests exist.

* Email: qixie68@126.com (QX); tinrant@163.com (BH)

Introduction

In the traditional medical diagnosis process, a patient goes to a hospital or clinic, and then consults a doctor. With the advancement of computer and network technologies, many countries and regions are establishing telecare medical information systems (TMIS), for making the medical diagnosis process more efficient, reliable and effective. With TMIS, patients can save time and have access to doctors and specialists more easily. Furthermore, patient records can also be exchanged between various hospitals and clinics. The system is also providing enhanced efficiency and effectiveness, especially on doing some basic diagnoses at patients' home [1]. Furthermore, TMIS is also useful for cases where chronic patients are involved. For example, through TMIS, a hypertension patient or a diabetes mellitus patient could exchange his/her daily medical data collected by the patient at home and the medical advice from doctors or nurses directly without requiring the patient to pay a visit to a hospital or a clinic. For emergency patients, such those with angina pectoris, hyperpyretic convulsion and asthma attacks, the TMIS can help exchange the medical records of a patient in concern, for example, between the database of a family doctor and the ICU of a hospital.

In TMIS, patients, doctors and nurses can register onto a trusted medical server (TS) and use passwords to perform authentication or secure channel establishment with the TS. Once a patient needs to consult a doctor, the patient can contact a doctor, and communicate with the doctor through a secure communication channel. For achieving these objectives, anony-

mous three-party password-authenticated key exchange (3PAKE) protocols for TMSI should be addressed. The 3PAKE protocol is to achieve mutual authentication between a patient and a doctor with the aid of the TS, and at the same time, ensure that an adversary does not know the exact identities of both the doctor and the patient. Furthermore, 3PAKE helps establish a secure channel via generating jointly a session key, which is then used for building a secure channel between the patient and the doctor.

In 2007, Lu and Cao [2] proposed an efficient 3PAKE scheme. However, Guo et al. [3], Chung and Ku [4], Phan et al. [5] and Nam et al. [6] later showed that Lu and Cao's scheme is vulnerable to undetectable on-line dictionary attack, off-line password guessing attack, and man-in-the-middle attack, respectively. In 2009, Huang [7] proposed another 3PAKE scheme, which was later shown by Yoon and Yoo [8] that it cannot defend against undetectable password guessing attack and off-line password guessing attack. In 2011, Lou and Huang [9] proposed a new 3PAKE scheme. The scheme is based on Elliptic Curve Cryptosystem (ECC) and is efficient. However, Xie et al. [10] recently showed that Lou and Huang's scheme is vulnerable to off-line password guessing attack and partition attack. Xie et al. also proposed an improved scheme for solving these problems. In 2012, Yang and Cao [11] and Chen et al. [12] also proposed modular exponentiation based and ECC-based 3PAKE schemes, respectively. However, these schemes, when compared with other existing schemes, require heavier computation costs. In 2010, Wang and Zhao [13] proposed a three-party key agreement protocol based on chaotic maps. Later, Yoon and Jeon [14] showed that their scheme is vulnerable to illegal message modification attack, and then proposed an improved one. Unfortunately, both schemes require a reliable third party, which shares a different long-term cryptographic key with each participant, it is inconvenient that each participant should protect the long-term secret key. Furthermore, these schemes are not as efficient as previous 3PAKE schemes. In 2013, Xie et al. [15] proposed the first chaotic maps-based 3PAKE scheme without using timestamp.

In light of all the schemes mentioned above, we notice that none of them can support privacy protection, since anyone can obtain user's identity from the authentication process. As we know, user's privacy protection is very important in some applications, such as telecare medical information systems (TMIS). In 2012, Lai et al. [16] proposed a smart-card-based anonymous 3PAKE using extended chaotic maps. However, Zhao et al. [17] showed that the scheme is vulnerable to the privileged insider attack and the off-line password guessing attack, and proposed an improved one. In 2013, Lee et al. [18] proposed another anonymous 3PAKE scheme using Chebyshev chaotic maps, but their scheme is suffering from the man-in-the-middle attack once after an attacker gets the identity of each participant, which in practice is easy to obtain.

Based on the advantages of elliptic curve cryptosystem (ECC), that is, having shorter secret keys and faster computational speed, it is desirable if an ECC-based anonymous 3PAKE scheme can be built for TMIS. To the best of our knowledge, however, there is no ECC-based anonymous 3PAKE scheme is proposed. In this paper, we propose the first ECC-based anonymous 3PAKE scheme, and show that it is efficient.

The rest of the paper is organized as follows. In Section 2, we propose an anonymous 3PAKE scheme. The security analysis of the scheme is given in Section 3. After that, other security discussions and the performance comparison are described in Sections 4. The paper is concluded in Section 5.

The Proposed Scheme

In this section, we propose an anonymous 3PAKE scheme. Some notations will be used in this paper are defined as follows.

E: an elliptic curve defined over a finite field with large order n.

P: a generator on E with large order n.

$h()$: a secure one-way hash function which maps to an integer.

A: user A, may be a patient.

B: user B, may be a doctor or nurse.

TS: trusted medical sever.

pw_A: user A's password, shared with TS.

pw_B: user B's password, shared with TS.

ID_A, ID_B, ID_{TS}: identities of A, B and TS, respectively.

$(d, F = dP)$: TS's private-public key pair.

$(E_k(), D_k())$: secure symmetric encryption/decryption functions with key k.

The proposed anonymous 3PAKE scheme is described as follows. Algorithm 1 illustrates the proposed scheme.

Step 1: User A randomly chooses t_a, and computes

$$Q_A = t_a P, \ F_A = t_a F = t_a dP = dQ_A, \ V_A = h(pw_A, ID_A, ID_B),$$

$$Z_A = E_{h(F_A)}(ID_A, ID_B, V_A).$$

Then sends $\{Q_A, Z_A\}$ to TS.

Step 2: Upon receiving $\{Q_A, Z_A\}$, the trusted server TS computes $F_A' = dQ_A$, and decrypts Z_A to obtain $\{ID_A, ID_B, V_A\}$, computes $V_A' = h(pw_A, ID_A, ID_B)$ and verifies if $V_A = V_A'$. If not,

terminates. Otherwise, user A is authenticated. Thus, TS knows that user A wants to establish a shared session key and communicate with a user B. TS randomly chooses an integer T_{TS}, computes $Z_{TS} = T_{TS} \oplus h(pw_B, ID_{TS}, ID_B)$, and sends $\{ID_{TS}, Z_{TS}\}$ to B.

Step 3: Upon receiving $\{ID_{TS}, Z_{TS}\}$, user B computes $T_{TS} = Z_{TS} \oplus h(pw_B, ID_{TS}, ID_B)$ and randomly chooses t_b, computes

$$Q_B = t_b P, F_B$$

$$= t_b F, V_B = h(pw_B, ID_{TS}, ID_B, T_{TS}), Z_B = E_{h(F_B)}(ID_B, V_B).$$

Then sends $\{Q_B, Z_B\}$ to TS.

A	TS	B
$Q_A = t_a P$		
$F_A = t_a F$		
$V_A = h(pw_A, ID_A, ID_B)$		
$Z_A = E_{h(F_A)}(ID_A, ID_B, V_A)$		

$$\xrightarrow{\{Q_A, Z_A\}}$$

$$F_A' = dQ_A$$

$$D_{h(F_A')}(Z_A) = \{ID_A, ID_B, V_A\}$$

$$V_A \overset{?}{=} h(pw_A, ID_A, ID_B)$$

$$Z_{TS} = T_{TS} \oplus h(pw_B, ID_{TS}, ID_B)$$

$$\xrightarrow{\{ID_{TS}, Z_{TS}\}}$$

$$T_{TS} = Z_{TS} \oplus h(pw_B, ID_{TS}, ID_B)$$

$$Q_B = t_b P$$

$$F_B = t_b F$$

$$V_B = h(pw_B, ID_{TS}, ID_B, T_{TS})$$

$$Z_B = E_{h(F_B)}(ID_B, V_B)$$

$$\xleftarrow{\{Q_B, Z_B\}}$$

$$F_B' = dQ_B$$

$$D_{h(F_B')}(Z_B) = \{ID_B, V_B\}$$

$$V_B \overset{?}{=} h(pw_B, ID_{TS}, ID_B, T_{TS})$$

$$R_B = E_{h(F_B')}(Q_A, ID_B, ID_A, F_B')$$

$$R_A = E_{h(F_A')}(Q_B, ID_A, ID_B, F_A')$$

$$\xleftarrow{\{R_A\}} \qquad \xrightarrow{\{R_B\}}$$

$$D_{h(F_A)}(R_A) = \{Q_B, ID_A, ID_B, F_A\} \qquad D_{h(F_B)}(R_B) = \{Q_A, ID_B, ID_A, F_B'\}$$

$$F_A' \overset{?}{=} F_A \qquad\qquad F_B' \overset{?}{=} F_B$$

$$sk = h(t_a Q_B, ID_B, ID_A) \qquad sk = h(t_b Q_A, ID_B, ID_A)$$

Session key: $sk = h(t_a t_b P, ID_B, ID_A)$

Algorithm 1 The proposed anonymous 3PAKE scheme

Step 4: Upon receiving $\{Q_B, Z_B\}$, TS computes $F_B' = dQ_B$, and decrypts Z_B to obtain $\{ID_B, V_B\}$. Then TS computes $V_B' = h(pw_B, ID_{TS}, ID_B, T_{TS})$ and verifies if the decrypted V_B is correct or not by $V_B' = V_B$. If not, terminates. Otherwise, user B is authenticated.

TS computes and sends $R_B = E_{h(F_B')}(Q_A, ID_B, ID_A, F_B')$ to B, computes and sends $R_A = E_{h(F_A')}(Q_B, ID_A, ID_B, F_A')$ to A.

Step 5: Upon receiving R_A or R_B from TS, A decrypts R_A and gets $\{Q_B, ID_A, ID_B, F_A'\}$. Then A checks the validity of F_A', and computes $sk = h(t_a Q_B, ID_B, ID_A) = h(t_a t_b P, ID_B, ID_A)$ as the session key. At the same time, B decrypts R_B, and gets $\{Q_A, ID_B, ID_A, F_B'\}$. After checking the validity of F_B', B computes $sk = h(t_b Q_A, ID_B, ID_A) = h(t_b t_a P, ID_B, ID_A)$ as the session key shared with A.

Security Analysis

In this section, we use applied pi calculus [19] based formal verification tool ProVerif [20] to show that the proposed scheme satisfies anonymity, authentication and security. ProVerif is an automatic cryptographic protocol verifier in the formal model and supports automatic and effective security analysis of many cryptographic primitives such as symmetric and asymmetric encryption, digital signature, hash function, Diffie-Hellman key agreements, etc [21].

3.1 Authentication and security

We model the protocol steps according to the message sequences shown in section 2. In particular, public channel ch1 is used for the communication between user A and the trusted medical server TS, and public channel ch2 is used for the communication between user B and TS.

```
(* -------------channel------------------*)
ch1: communication channel between A and TS
ch2: communication channel between B and TS
free ch1: channel.
free ch2: channel.
```

We then define two variables SKA and SKB, which are the session keys calculated by A and B, respectively.

```
(* -------------shared keys --------------------*)
free SKA: bitstring [private].
free SKB: bitstring [private].
```

The constants IDA, IDB and IDTS denote the identities of A, B, and TS, and PWA and PWB denote the passwords of A and B shared with TS, respectively. Let d be TS's secret key, and the constant P is the base point of group E.

```
(*-------------- constants and variables----------------*)
free SKA: bitstring [private].
free SKB: bitstring [private].
const IDA: bitstring.
const IDB: bitstring.
const IDTS: bitstring.
const PWA: bitstring [private].
const PWB: bitstring [private].
const P: bitstring.
free d: bitstring [private].
```

The ProVerif code for non-logical constants and the corresponding equational theory is giving below:

```
(*--------------constructor---------------*)
fun h(bitstring): bitstring. //*hash function
fun senc(bitstring, bitstring): bitstring. //*symmetric encryption
fun xor(bitstring, bitstring): bitstring.
```

```
fun mult(bitstring, bitstring): bitstring.
(*--------------destructors & equations---------------*)
reduc forall x: bitstring, y: bitstring; sdec(senc(x, y), y) = x.
equation forall x: bitstring, y: bitstring; xor(xor(x, y), y) = x.
```

The core message sequences for the proposed scheme are given below. QA, ZA, ZTS, QB, ZB, RA and RB in these messages are computed by corresponding senders before they are transmitted.

```
(*--------------messages--------------*)
Message 1:A→TS: {QA, ZA}
    Message 2:TS→B: {IDTS, ZTS}
Message 3:B→TS: {QB, ZB}
    Message 4:TS→A,B: {RA},{RB}
```

The proposed protocol consists of the parallel execution of three processes: the user A, UserA, the trusted server TrustSever and another user B, UserB. The processes are the core of protocol model, which define the behavior of each participant in applied pi calculus. The process UserA defines the behavior of user A, who computes QA, FA, VA and ZA, and sends message (QA, ZA) through a public channel. After that, user A receives message RA and computes SKA. The process of UserA is modeled as below:

```
(*------------------UserA's process------------------*)
let UserA =
    new ta: bitstring;
    event UserStarted(IDA);
    let QA = mult(ta,P) in
    let FA = mult(d,QA) in
    let VA = h(((PWA,IDA,IDB))) in
    let ZA = senc((((IDA,IDB,VA))),h(FA)) in
    out(ch1,(QA,ZA));
    in (ch1,RA': bitstring);
    let (QB':bitstring,IDA'':bitstring,IDB'':bitstring,FA'':bitstring) =
    sdec(RA',h(FA)) in
        if FA'' = FA then
        let SKA = h(((mult(ta,QB'),IDB,IDA))) in
        0.
```

The process TrustSever defines the behavior of TS during authentication, it computes FA' and ZTS, and sends message (IDTS, ZTS) to UserB through a public channel2 when it receives message (QA, ZA) through a public channel1. After that, TrustSever receives message (QB, ZB), computes RA and RB, and sends RA and RB to UserA and UserB through public channel1 and channel2, respectively. The process of TrustSever is modeled as follows.

```
(*------------------TrustSever's process------------------*)
let TrustSever =
    in(ch1, (QA':bitstring, ZA':bitstring));
    let FA' = mult(d,QA') in
    let (IDA': bitstring,IDB': bitstring,VA': bitstring) = sdec(ZA',
    th(FA')) in
    let VA'' = h(((PWA,IDA',IDB'))) in
    if VA' = VA'' then
    new TTS: bitstring;
    let ZTS = xor(TTS,h(((PWB,IDTS,IDB)))) in
    out (ch2,(IDTS,ZTS));
    in (ch2,(QB': bitstring,ZB': bitstring));
    let FB' = mult(d,QB') in
    let (IDB'': bitstring,VB': bitstring) = sdec(ZB',h(FB')) in
    let VB'' = h((((PWB,IDTS,IDB,TTS)))) in
    if VB' = VB'' then
    let RB = senc(((((QA',IDB,IDA,FB')))),h(FB')) in
    let RA = senc(((((QB',IDA,IDB,FA')))),h(FA')) in
    out(ch1,RA);
    out(ch2,RB).
```

The process UserB defines the behavior of user B during authentication, who computes TTS', QB, FB, VB and ZB, and sends message (QB, ZB) back to TS through a public channe2. After that, user B receives message RB and compute SKB. The process of UserB is modeled as follows:

```
(*-------------------UserB's process-------------------*)
let UserB =
  in(ch2, (IDTS': bitstring, ZTS': bitstring));
  let TTS' = xor(ZTS',h(((PWB,IDTS',IDB)))) in
  new tb: bitstring;
  let QB = mult(tb,P) in
  let FB = mult(d,QB) in
  let VB = h((((PWB,IDTS',IDB,TTS')))) in
  let ZB = senc(((IDB,VB)),h(FB)) in
  out(ch2,(QB,ZB));
  in (ch2,RB': bitstring);
  let (QA':bitstring,IDB'':bitstring,IDA'':bitstring,FB'':bitstring) =
    sdec(RB',h(FB)) in
    if FB'' = FB then
    event UserAuthed(IDA'');
    let SKB = h(((mult(tb,QA'),IDB,IDA))) in
    0.
```

The protocol is modeled as the parallel execution of the above three processes:

```
process !UserA | !TrustSever | !UserB
```

The session key security is formalized by the following two queries for checking by Proverif:

```
(*-------------------query-------------------*)
        query attacker(SKA).
        query attacker(SKB).
```

The Authentication of the protocol was modeled as a correspondence relation between two events: UserStarted and UserAuthed, which are inserted into the processes of UserA and UserB, respectively:

```
        event UserAuthed(bitstring).
        event UserStarted(bitstring).
query id: bitstring; inj-event(UserAuthed(id)) = = > inj-event
(UserStarted(id)).
```

We perform the above process in the latest version 1.85 of ProVerif and the performance results show that (1) the session key in the proposed scheme is secure under Dolev-Yao model; and (2) the authentication property is satisfied.

3.2 Anonymity

In ProVerif, strong anonymity is defined as follows [22].

Let $P = new~\tilde{n}~.(!R_1|\cdots|!R_p)$ be a p-party protocol in its canonical form where $R_i = new~id.new~\tilde{m}.init_i.!(new~s.main_i)$ for any $i \in \{1,...,p\}$. $\forall i \in \{1,...,p\}$, we build the protocol P^{R_i} as:
$P = new~\tilde{n}~.(!R_1|\cdots|!R_p|R_V)$, where $R_V = new~\tilde{m}.init_i\{id_V/id\}.!(new~s.main_i\{id_V/id\})$.

The identity id_V of the agent playing role R_V is a public name, not under any new restriction in P. P is said to preserve strong anonymity of R_i if $P \approx_l P^{R_i}$. Informally, this means that the adversary cannot distinguish a situation where the role R_V with known identity id_V was executed from one in which it was not executed at all [23]. Going back to our proposed protocol, strong anonymity requires a system in which a user (A or B) with publicly known identity IDV executes the protocol to be indistinguishable from a system in which it is not present at all. We formally define user A and user B as follows:

```
let UserA =
  in(kc, xPKTS: bitstring);
  !(new ta: bitstring;
  let QA = mult(ta, P) in
```

```
  let FA = mult(ta, xPKTS) in
  let VA = h((pwa, IDA, IDB)) in
  let ZA = senc(h(FA), (IDA, IDB, VA)) in
  out(c, (QA, ZA));
  in(c, xRA: bitstring)).
let UserB =
  in(kc, xPKTS: bitstring);
  !(new tb: bitstring;
  in(c, (xIDTS: bitstring, xZTS: bitstring));
  let xTTS = sdecr(h(pwb, IDTS, IDB)), xZTS) in
  let QB = mult(tb, P) in
  let FB = mult(tb, xPKTS) in
  let VB = h((pwb, IDTS, IDB, xTTS)) in
  let ZB = senc(h(FB), (IDB, VB)) in
  out(c, (QB, ZB));
  in(c, xRB: bitstring)).
```

And formally define TS as follows:

```
let TS =
  new d:bitstring;
  !(let F = mult(d, P) in out(kc, F))
  |
  !(
  new TTS: bitstring;
  new rand: bitstring;
  in(c, (xQA: bitstring, xZA: bitstring));
  let FA = mult(d, xQA) in
  let (xIDA: bitstring, xIDB: bitstring, xVA: bitstring) =
    sdec(h(FA), xZA) in
  let VA = h((pwa, IDA, IDB)) in
  if VA = xVA then
  let ZTS = sencr(h((pwb, IDTS, IDB)), rand, TTS) in
  out(c, (IDTS, ZTS));
  in(c, (xQB: bitstring, xZB: bitstring));
  let FB = mult(d, xQB) in
  let (xIDB: bitstring, xVB: bitstring) =
    sdec(h(FB), xZB) in
  let VB = h((pwb, IDTS, IDB, TTS)) in
  if VB = xVB then
  let RB = senc(h(FB), (xQA, IDB, IDA, FB)) in
  let RA = senc(h(FA), (xQB, IDA, IDB, FA)) in
  out(c, RB);
  out(c, RA)
  ).
```

For verification, we use randomized symmetric encryption to conceal the random integer T_{TS} instead of using the exclusive-or. The proposed protocol is formally defined as:

```
        process !((UserA) | (UserB) | (TS))
```

Anonymity of users A and B is proved separately as follows. In order to show A's anonymity, the proposed protocol is required to be observational equivalent to the augmented protocol defined as follows:

```
process !((UserA) | (UserB) | (TS)) |
  let IDA = IDV in ((UserA) | (UserB) | (TS))
```

The observational equivalence can be translated into the following ProVerif bi-process:

```
process !((UserA) | (UserB) | (TS)) |
  new ID: bitstring;
  let IDA = choice[ID, IDV] in ((UserA) | (UserB) | (TS))
```

The right hand side of the choice represents a system where a user with public identity IDV can run the protocol. The proposed protocol is simulated using the latest version 1.85 of ProVerif and simulation outcome shows that the scheme achieves the anonymity for user A. The anonymity of user B can be simulated and shown in a similar way.

Security Discussions and Performance Comparison

In this section, we discuss some other aspects related to security, and then evaluate the performance of the scheme.

4.1 Discussions

4.1.1 Offline password guessing attack. Suppose an adversary eavesdrops the communication between A, B and TS, and gets all the transmitted messages $\{\{Q_A,Z_A\},\{ID_{TS},Z_{TS}\}, \{Q_B,Z_B\},R_A,R_B\}$. To launch the off-line password guessing attack, the adversary may choose a trial password pw_A' and compute $V_A'=h(pw_A',ID_A,ID_B)$. Even if the adversary knows $\{ID_A,ID_B\}$, the adversary still cannot compute $E_{h(F_A)}(ID_A,ID_B,V_A')$ and therefore, cannot verify if $Z_A=E_{h(F_A)}(ID_A,ID_B,V_A')$ since the adversary does not know $F_A=t_aF=t_adP$ from $Q_A=t_aP$ or $F=dP$ due to the intractability of the Computational Diffie-Hellman (CDH) problem. Therefore, the adversary cannot verify if his guessed pw_A' is correct or not.

If the adversary guesses B's password pw_B', and computes $T_{TS}'=Z_{TS}\oplus h(pw_B',ID_{TS},ID_B)$, $V_B'=h(pw_B',ID_{TS},ID_B,T_{TS}')$, the adversary still cannot verify if $Z_B=E_{h(F_B)}(ID_B,V_B')$ without knowing F_B. That is, the adversary cannot determine if his guessed pw_B' is correct or not.

Therefore, the proposed scheme can resist off-line password guessing attack. If an adversary launches on-line password guessing attack, TS may detect the attack since it needs to verify the correctness of V_A and V_B.

4.1.2 Perfect forward secrecy. In the proposed scheme, the session key is $sk=h(t_at_bP,ID_B,ID_A)$, where t_a and t_b are nonces chosen by user A and user B, respectively. Even if an adversary can get TS's secret key d, A and B's passwords and identities, the adversary cannot compute the previous established session key due to the intractability of CDH problem.

4.1.3 Replay attack. Suppose that an adversary impersonates A and replays A's message $\{Q_A,Z_A\}$ to TS, the adversary cannot compute $sk=h(t_aQ_B',ID_B,ID_A)$ without knowing t_a. On the other hand, if an adversary impersonates B and replays B's message $\{Q_B,Z_B\}$ to TS, Z_B cannot pass the authentication checking by TS as T_{TS} is a new nonce chosen by TS in each new session. The same reason applies if an adversary replays TS's message $\{ID_{TS},Z_{TS}\},R_A$ and R_B. The replayed message cannot pass the verification performed by A and B, as t_a and t_b are new nonces chosen by A and B, respectively, and $\{F_A,F_B\}$ are refreshed in each new session.

4.1.4 Forgery attack and impersonation. In our scheme, if an adversary attempts to impersonate A (or B, or TS) and sends messages to TS (or B, or A), but these messages cannot pass the verification process of TS (or B, or A) as the adversary does not know the password or secret key d.

4.1.5 Man-in-the-middle attack. If an adversary attempts to launch the man-in-the-middle attack, the adversary has to generate and send the forgery messages to TS and has to pass the verification performed by the TS, before the adversary can obtain the session key shared with A and another session key shared with B. However, it is infeasible as the adversary does not know d or pw_A or pw_B.

4.2 Performance Analysis

Let T, D, H and M be the time for performing a Chebyshev polynomial computation, a symmetric encryption/decryption, a one-way hash function, and a scalar multiplication on elliptic curve, respectively. Li et al. [24] and Li et al. [25] showed that it needs 0.0005 second for completing one hash operation, 0.0087 second for one symmetric encryption/decryption, and 0.063075 second for one elliptic curve scalar multiplication operation, respectively. Kocarev and Lian [26] showed that it needs 0.07 second for a Chebyshev polynomial computation. As we know, these computation costs may vary due to different computational configurations and settings. However, in general, the elliptic curve scalar multiplication operation and the Chebyshev polynomial evaluation are slower than a symmetric key based encryption/decryption or a one-way hash function operation. The performance comparison between the scheme proposed in this paper and three other recently proposed ones [16–18] is given in Table 1.

From Table 1, we can see that all schemes are efficient, but Lai et al.'s scheme is vulnerable to the privileged insider attack and off-line password guessing attack, while Lee et al.'s scheme is vulnerable to man-in-the-middle attack once after the adversary gets to know the identities of at least two users, which in practice, is feasible.

Conclusion

In this paper, we proposed the first anonymous three-party password-authenticated key exchange scheme based on elliptic curve cryptosystem. Anonymity, authentication and security of the proposed scheme are validated using the applied pi calculus based formal verification tool ProVerif. The proposed scheme is secure and efficient, and is suitable for applications in telecare medical information systems.

Author Contributions

Conceived and designed the experiments: QX. Performed the experiments: QX BH. Analyzed the data: BH ND. Contributed reagents/materials/analysis tools: BH ND DSW. Wrote the paper: QX BH DSW. Designed the scheme and wrote the paper: QX DSW. Proved the authentication, security and anonymity of the proposed scheme: BH. Verified the authentication, security and anonymity of the proposed scheme in the latest version 1.85 of ProVerif: ND.

Table 1. Performance comparison.

Schemes	User A	User B	Server	Total	Rounds	Estimated Time (s)
Lai et al. [16]	3T+6H	3T+6H	2T+8H+2D	8T+20H+2D	5	0.5847
Zhao et al. [17]	3T+6H+1D	3T+5H+1D	2T+8H+2D	8T+19H+4D	5	0.6043
Lee et al. [18]	3T+4H	3T +5H	2T +7H	8T +16H	4	0.568
Our scheme	3M+4H+2D	3M+5H+2D	2M+7H+4D	8M+16H+8D	4	0.5822

References

1. Xie Q, Zhang J, Dong N (2013) Robust anonymous authentication scheme for telecare medical information systems. Journal of Medical Systems 37:1–8.
2. Lu RX, Cao ZF (2007) Simple three-party key exchange protocol. Computers and Security 26: 94–97.
3. Guo H, Li ZJ, Mu Y, Zhang XY (2008) Cryptanalysis of simple three-party key exchange protocol. Computers and Security 27:16–21.
4. Chung HR, Ku WC (2008) Three weaknesses in a simple three-party key exchange protocol. Information Sciences 178:220–229.
5. Phan RCW, Yau WC, Goi BM (2008) Cryptanalysis of simple three-party key exchange protocol (S-3PAKE). Information Sciences 178:2849–2856.
6. Nam JY, Paik JY, Kang HK, Kim UM, Won DH (2009) An off-line dictionary attack on a simple three-party key exchange protocol. IEEE Communication Letters 13:205–207.
7. Huang HF (2009) A simple three-party password-based key exchange protocol. International Journal of Communication Systems 22:857–862.
8. Yoon EJ, Yoo KY (2011) Cryptanalysis of a simple three-party password-based key exchange protocol. International Journal of Communication Systems 24:532–542.
9. Lou DC, Huang HF (2011) Efficient three-party password-based key exchange scheme. International Journal of Communication Systems 24: 504–512.
10. Xie Q, Dong N, Tan X, Wong DS, Wang G (2013) Improvement of a Three-Party Password-Based Key Exchange Protocol with Formal Verification. Information Technology And Control 42:231–237.
11. Yang J, Cao T (2012) Provably secure three-party password authenticated key exchange protocol in the standard model. Journal of Systems and Software 855, 340–350.
12. Wu S, Chen K, Pu Q, Zhu Y (2013) Cryptanalysis and enhancements of efficient three-party password-based key exchange scheme. International Journal of Communication Systems 26:674–686.
13. Wang X, Zhao J (2010) An improved key agreement protocol based on chaos. Commun Nonlinear Sci Numer Simulat 15:4052–4057.
14. Yoon E, Jeon I (2011) An efficient and secure Diffie-Hellman key agreement protocol based on Chebyshev chaotic map. Commun Nonlinear Sci Numer Simulat 16:2383–2389.
15. Xie Q, Zhao J, Yu X (2013) Chaotic maps-based three-party password-authenticated key agreement scheme. Nonlinear Dynamics 74:1021–1027.
16. Lai H, Xiao J, Li L, Yang Y (2012) Applying semigroup property of enhanced Chebyshev polynomials to anonymous authentication protocol. Math Probl Eng. doi:10.1155/2012/454823
17. Zhao F, Gong P, Li S, Li M, Li P (2013) Cryptanalysis and improvement of a three-party key agreement protocol using enhanced Chebyshev polynomials. Nonlinear Dyn 74:419–427.
18. Lee C, Li C, Hsu C (2013) A three-party password-based authenticated key exchange protocol with user anonymity using extended chaotic maps. Nonlinear Dyn 73: 125–132.
19. Abadi M, Fournet C (2001) Mobile values, new names, and secure communication. Proceedings of the 28th ACM SIGPLAN-SIGACT symposium on Principles of programming languages, New York, pp.104–115.
20. Abadi M, Blanchet B, Lundh HC (2009) Models and proofs of protocol security: A progress report. 21st International Conference on Computer Aided Verification, Grenoble, France, pp. 35–49.
21. Blanchet B, Cheval V, Allamigeon X, Smyth B. ProVerif: Cryptographic protocol verifier in the formal model. Available: http://prosecco.gforge.inria.fr/personal/bblanche/proverif/. 2013 October 19.
22. Arapinis M, Chothia T, Ritter E, Ryan M (2010) Analysing Unlinkability and Anonymity Using the Applied Pi Calculus. In IEEE Computer Security Foundations Symposium, CSF 2010, pp. 107–121.
23. Arapinis M, Borgaonkar R, Golde N, Mancini L, Redon K, et al. (2012) New privacy issues in mobile telephony: fix and verification. Proceedings of the 2012 ACM conference on Computer and communications security, pp. 205–216.
24. Li CT, Hwang MS, Chu YP (2008) A secure and efficient communication scheme with authenticated key establishment and privacy preserving for vehicular ad hoc networks. Comput Commun 31: 2803–2814.
25. Li W, Wen Q, Su Q, Jin Z (2012) An efficient and secure mobile payment protocol for restricted connectivity scenarios in vehicular ad hoc network. Computer Communications 35:188–195.
26. Kocarev L, Lian S (2011) Chaos-based Cryptography: Theory, Algorithms and Applications. Springer, pp.53–54.

11

Chinese Tobacco Industry Promotional Activity on the Microblog Weibo

Fan Wang[1], Pinpin Zheng[1]*, Dongyun Yang[2], Becky Freeman[3], Hua Fu[1], Simon Chapman[3]

1 Key Laboratory of Public Health Safety, Ministry of Education, School of Public Health, Fudan University, Shanghai, China, 2 School of Statistics and Management, Shanghai University of Finance and Economics, Shanghai, China, 3 School of Public Health, University of Sydney, Sydney, Australia

Abstract

Background: Although China ratified the WHO Framework Convention on Tobacco Control [FCTC] in 2005, the partial ban on tobacco advertising does not cover the internet. Weibo is one of the most important social media channels in China, using a format similar to its global counterpart, Twitter. The Weibo homepage is a platform to present products, brands and corporate culture. There is great potential for the tobacco industry to exploit Weibo to promote products.

Methods: Seven tobacco industry Weibo accounts that each had more than 5000 fans were selected to examine the content of Weibos established by tobacco companies or their advertising agents.

Results: Of the 12073 posts found on the seven accounts, 92.3% (11143) could be classified into six main themes: traditional culture, popular culture, social and business affairs, advertisement, public relations and tobacco culture. Posts under the theme of popular culture accounted for about half of total posts (49%), followed by 'advertisement' and 'tobacco culture' (both at 12%), 'traditional culture' and 'public relations' (both at 11%), and finally 'social and business affairs' (5%). 33% of posts included the words 'cigarette' or 'smoking' and 53% of posts included the tobacco brand name, indicating that tobacco companies carefully construct the topic and content of posts.

Conclusions: Weibo is an important new online marketing tool for the Chinese tobacco industry. Tobacco industry use of Weibo to promote brands and normalize smoking subverts China's ratification of the WHO FCTC. Policy to control tobacco promotion needs reforming to address this widespread circumvention of China's tobacco advertising ban.

Editor: Jean Adams, Newcastle University, United Kingdom

Funding: This study was partly supported by Shanghai Public Health Personnel Training Program (GWHW201203). The funders had no role in study design, data collection and analysis, decision to publish, or preparation of the manuscript. No additional external funding was received for this study.

Competing Interests: The authors have declared that no competing interests exist.

* E-mail: zpinpin@shmu.edu.cn.

Introduction

Guidelines for the implementation of Article 13 of the WHO Framework Convention on Tobacco Control [FCTC] emphasize that a comprehensive ban on tobacco advertising should cover 'any form of commercial communication, recommendation or action with the aim, effect or likely effect of promoting a tobacco product or tobacco use either directly or indirectly' [1]. China ratified the WHO FCTC in 2005. However, the WHO FCTC has not been well implemented in China and tobacco brands continue to be promoted directly and indirectly through a variety of channels, especially via websites [2,3].

The current tobacco provisions of the Advertisement Law of the People's Republic of China prohibit tobacco advertising in movies, radio, television, newspapers, journals, magazines, waiting rooms, cinemas, theatres, conference halls, stadiums, and gyms [4]. Previous research has shown that when governments ban or curtail tobacco advertising in traditional media, the tobacco industry pursues its promotional ambitions through new media [5,6,7,8,9].

Internet promotions present a massive and largely unregulated marketing channel for the tobacco industry with online social media being particularly important. Social media also offer the

tobacco industry a powerful and efficient channel for rapidly countering the denormalising strategies and policies of tobacco control [10]. The tobacco industry has realized that social media are unparalleled new marketing platforms to influence customers, especially youth, and establish positive brand and company images. British American Tobacco employees were shown to be energetically promoting BAT and BAT brands on Facebook [11]. The Camel brand was promoted through interactive activities such as participatory packaging design via a corporate website [7,9].

Weibo is one of China's most important social networking channels. 'Weibo' is the Chinese phonetic translation for 'Micro Blog', and is the Chinese counterpart to Twitter, which is blocked in China. As with Twitter, Weibo users open an account and can then post up to 140-characters. Users can also include web links and emoticons or attach images, music, or video files to each of their posts. Users can either make original posts or re-share content posted by other Weibo users. Weibo posting has become the most popular activity among Chinese internet users [12]. Followers of one's Weibo account are called 'fans'. Fans receive Weibo posts and can choose to further disseminate them to their own Weibo network [13]. Posts on Weibo can also include a 'topic tag' so that users can search for content of interest to them. Weibo commenced operation in August 2009 and grew with phenomenal speed. By the end of June 2013, of 591 million internet users in China, 330 million had Weibo accounts [14], which lead to its most important role in the social media marketing platform [12].

In 2013, the Chinese website (http://www.tobaccochina.com), which is a professional website supported by Chinese tobacco industries with the most authoritative information on available tobacco products [15,16], published an article titled 'How to use Weibo in tobacco marketing' stating (translated from Chinese):

'The open platform of Weibo, is becoming an integral part of a new marketing channel for tobacco industries. As a new communication channel, Weibo significantly reduces the costs of promotion and advertising…. it can break through the current limitation of tobacco advertisement and play an important role in advertisement and promotion….The most popular information or activities of Weibo should be designed to reflect the needs of the consumers, as well as their attitudes and value orientation…. It is helpful to establish the positive image of tobacco industry among the public……Most efforts should be made to figure out most effective strategy in Weibo marketing…' [17]

Up to the time of this study, the tobaccochina website mentioned Weibo marketing strategies more than other avenues due to its leading role in social media [18–20].

To date, there have been no published studies on internet-based tobacco marketing and promotion in China. This study describes and analyzes the thematic content of Weibo posts by Chinese tobacco companies in order to explore how they seek to influence their target audiences. Such studies can provide evidence to inform evaluation of the implementation of the WHO FCTC Article 13 and assist in establishing a more comprehensive policy banning all forms of tobacco advertising.

Method

A thematic content analysis was conducted to assess how tobacco companies promote their products on Weibo [21,22]. Error! Hyperlink reference not valid.We opened a Weibo account with Sina Weibo (www.weibo.com), the most popular micro blog operator in China, with 86.6% of China's Weibo market based on browsing time [23]. Sina Weibo has over 300 million registered users, and is still rapidly growing. It is estimated that there is an average of over 100 million posts per day made via Sina Weibo [24].

To determine which tobacco companies and brands to search for on Weibo, we obtained a list of current tobacco companies and cigarette brands in China from the tobacco marketing website 'smoking happiness' (www.yanyue.cn) [25]. Twenty nine tobacco companies were identified, together selling 98 cigarette brands with thousands of variants.

We then used the names of tobacco companies and cigarette brands as key words in Sina Weibo's search engine to find tobacco companies' Weibo accounts. Weibo accounts that included tobacco content but were operated by private citizens were not included in this study. In total, there were 33 Chinese tobacco company owned Weibo accounts. We ranked these 33 Weibo accounts by their number of fans. In order to make our sample size manageable, we decided to further examine only the top ten most popular tobacco company Weibo accounts, each of these had at least 5000 fans as of 31 December 2012. In addition, for tobacco corporations with more than one Weibo account, only one account would be selected which had a more obvious intention of tobacco marketing.

Of these ten Weibo accounts, three were excluded from the final study sample. One was created by 'Mountain Ali Culture

Communication Corporation' in Taiwan. Although its description includes 'Mountain Ali cigarette', it had made only 147 posts with most describing the scenery of Mountain Ali. We also found two Weibo accounts set up by the Guangdong Tobacco Corporation. After examining posts to both of these accounts, we only selected the one titled as 'Happiness together' which had an obvious emphasis on tobacco advertising and promotion, and included a tobacco logo and brand name on its front page for inclusion in our study. This account had also received formal certification from the Sina Corporation. Weibo users can apply for 'official certification', which confirms that an account is truly operated by the organisation that is claiming to be behind it. This certification is helpful in winning trust from fans and increasing the number of fans. The third account excluded functioned solely as a company enterprise bulletin board for employees. After these three exclusions, seven Weibos related to Chinese tobacco company promotional activity remained in our study.

Code book development

The full text of all posts made by these seven Weibos were downloaded by Rweibo which is a program that provides an interface to the Weibo open platform and allows textual analysis [26]. In total, there were 12,073 posts made by the seven tobacco company Weibos at the data collection date of 31 December 2012. In order to develop a code book for the content analysis of all the posts, a random sample of 5% of all posts (n = 600) was selected. First, two researchers (FW and PPZ) read through each post independently and used one word to describe the main meaning of the post. This produced a list of 70 words. Next, four researchers [FW, PPZ, DYY and HF] held a discussion to group the 70 words by combining the synonyms that were assigned to the 600 posts in to subthemes. A number of the words assigned were significantly overlapping in meaning and intent and a total of 14 subthemes resulted.

Third, the same four researchers combined the 14 subthemes into six main themes and clear definitions were developed and assigned to minimize overlap.

Coding

Coding of all 12,073 downloaded posts was then performed by two trained staff who both independently reviewed all posts. Each post was classified into only one theme. In the case of disagreement between the two coders, a third coder was used to determine the final coding. To assess agreement between the two coders, a Kappa score of 0.89 was calculated which demonstrates that inter-coder reliability was excellent [27]. If the content of the post did not fit any one of the themes, it was coded as 'other' and was not included in the final analysis of this study. To identify what were the most frequently used words in the posts to gain insights into the marketing strategy of the tobacco companies, a word frequency ranking was conducted by Rwordseg. Rwordseg is an R environment open-source Java tool and one of the most accurate Chinese word segmentation tools [28].

Results

Table 1 shows the detailed information of six main themes including traditional culture, popular culture, social and business affairs, advertisement, public relations and tobacco culture. The six themes were then classified into two categories: overt marketing and covert marketing. Overt marketing meant that a tobacco brand or product was being openly promoted, and covert marketing meant that the promotional message was linked to tobacco use, rather than directly mentioning a brand or product.

Table 1. Code book for this study.

Categories	Themes	Definition	Subthemes	Focus of Posts
Covert marketing	Traditional culture	A group ofphilosophies, art and history perspectives which are retrospected from ancestors.	Philosophy	Life philosophy, insights on life, famous quotes
			Literature & art	Serious literature, serious art
			History & geography	Chinese cultural history, cultural geography
	Popular culture	A kind of culture that originates from 'the people' which is also widely favoured or well liked by many people. [32]	Fashion	Clothes, ornaments, pop stars, cosmetics, decoration, entertainment events
			Leisure	Food, drinking, shopping, tourism, sports, healthy life, festivals custom, jokes
			Popular arts	Pop music, movie, TV, book and photography
	Social and business affairs	Including reports of social events and advice for business people.	Current event news	Environment protection, political affairs, economic events, social events
			Business advice	Time management, interpersonal skills, business etiquette
Overt Marketing	Advertisement	The introduction of tobacco brands and products through texts and images.	Tobacco Brand Introduction	Brand history, brand connotation, brand culture, multi-media brand dissemination
			Cigarette advertisement	Tobacco cultivation, leaves, production process, product additives, technique, taste, packaging.
	Public relations	The practice of managing the spread of tobacco information between tobacco industries and customers.	Online marketing	Guessing contests, Repost, lucky draws, favorite product recommendations, crosswords.
			Offline marketing	New products tasting, calls for slogans, club activities (tourism, sports, party, etc.), charity activities, culture contest (poems, photos, singing, etc.)
	Tobacco culture	The ways that tobacco industries associate tobacco products with history, literature and art to normalize smoking behavior in the daily life.	Cigarette use in daily life	Smoking manners, anecdotes related to smoking, celebrity smoking, smoking history and customs, tips for healthy smoking, smoking in classic literature, insights and experiences of smoking.
			Tobacco accessories	Holder, ashtray, lighters, snuff bottles, cigar knives.

Table 1 also illuminates how the original 70 words assigned to the 600 posts were collapsed into the two final categories of six main themes.

Table 2 provides the basic information, such as the number fans, account name and date the account was opened, for the seven tobacco company Weibos. All seven Weibo account names included a tobacco brand. All of the accounts were established after January 2011 when Sina Weibo became the most popular microblog in China. Three of the Weibo accounts were set up by the tobacco companies directly, with the other four being established by marketing agencies. Detailed information about products were published in the posts through text, image and video files: from the growing environment of tobacco plants, the selection method of tobacco leaves, the production process, to the taste, the design of the package, as well as the brands' connotations.

The 'Double happiness fashion' Weibo had the largest number of fans with 252,205, while 'Mountain Tai Club' published the most posts, 3966 as at 31 December 2012. Four Weibos were tagged as being 'Official Weibo', meaning that they had received the formal certification from the Sina Corporation, despite these accounts being used primarily for tobacco product promotion.

Among the 12,073 total posts made by the seven tobacco brands, 11143 posts (92.3%) could be classified into the six main themes shown in Table 3. Word frequency was calculated to provide possible insights into the communication objectives of the companies. Pleasant, attractive words were used to make the content of Weibos more friendly and appealing. For example, 'wonderful', 'life' and 'beautiful' were the most frequently used words in the posts under the theme of 'traditional culture' while among the posts under the 'popular culture' theme, the top three most frequently used words were 'shopping', 'eating' and 'design'. In addition, content of different themes was presented in different ways. Posts under the category of 'overt marketing' included text, images and videos to present information about tobacco products and disseminate news about online and offline activities. Posts under the category of 'covert marketing' included content such as statements about philosophies of life, fashionable lifestyles, leisure and entertainment and social hot topics unrelated to cigarettes. These interesting and fashionable posts included a tobacco brand name as a Weibo topic tag. In all, 'popular culture' was the most frequently used theme, accounting for about half of all posts (49%), followed by 'advertisement' and 'tobacco culture' (both at 12%), 'traditional culture' and public relations' (both at 11%), and 'social and business affairs (5%). Posts under category of 'covert marketing' accounted for 66% of all posts.

Among the seven Weibos selected for this study, the different tobacco companies all linked tobacco use to content that was appealing to youth and young adults (see Table 3). As illustrative examples show in Table 3, Weibo fans were encouraged to strive towards better life under the theme of traditional culture. Tobacco use was connected to living a fashionable, trendy life style via posts containing links to fashion news and content.

Table 2. Basic information from seven most followed Chinese tobacco Weibo accounts, as at 31 December 2012.

Weibo Account Name	Brand Name	Number of Fans	Number of Posts	Account Registrants	Date Launched	Logo
Double Happiness Fashion	Double Happiness	252205	1612	*	2012/5/15	Trademark
Mountain Tai Club#	Mountain Tal	96510	3966	Shandong Mountain Tai Brand Culture Communication Co., Ltd.	2011/5/2	Trademark Commercial
Tongxian Manor#	Tongxian	33020	3050	Xiamen Tongxian Industrial Co., Ltd.	2011/9/15	Trademark Commercial
Zhongnanhai club	Zhongnanhai	25433	1531	Beijing Cigarette Factory	2011/1/11	Trademark Commercial
Happiness together#	Shuangxi	15826	429	Guangdong Shuangxi Culture Communication Co., Ltd.	2012/9/19	Commercial
Real Dragon Club#	Real dragon	11223	787	Guangxi Real Dragon Club Ltd.	2012/3/19	Trademark Commercial
Yuxi 1913	Yuxi	6577	698	**	2012/11/09	Trademark

Tagged as 'Official Weibo.'
*not shown in Weibo. However, the registered address was the same as the Shanghai Tobacco Corporation.
** not shown on Weibo. The content strongly suggests it may have been set up by the advertising agency employed by the Hongta Tobacco Corporation.

Table 4 shows that different tobacco brand Weibos adopted different marketing strategies. For example, the proportion of posts under popular culture accounted for 67% for 'Double Happiness' but only accounted for 10% in 'Real Dragon Club', where public relations accounted for 32% of the total posts.

The results also show that 33% of posts included the word 'cigarette' or 'smoking' and 53% posts included a tobacco brand name either as a topic tag or in the text of the posts. In addition, over 68% of posts had topic tags and 79% were original posts as opposed to re-shared posts.

We also found some posts focused on emotional arousal to encourage smoking such as 'When you are alone in the dark night with no lights, you need a cigarette to light your life' (from Tongxian Manor) and 'Cigarettes mean sincerity, warmth and sharing' (from Mountain Tai Club). Other posts included statements to try to minimize the harms of smoking. For example, advice under the topic tag of 'smoking and health' encouraged tobacco users to do more exercise and use traditional Chinese medicines to reduce the harms of smoking. Also, some posts tried to divert audience attention away from smoking harms to other health risks. The 'Real Dragon Club' shared content under the topic 'environment and health' that included claims that 'air pollution is the most important factor leading to lung cancer, not smoking'.

The strategies adopted by the tobacco companies on Weibo were successful in generating interaction with fans. For example, the 'Zhongnanhai' brand published a post urging the public to participate in the 'Capital Charity Program' which helps teenagers to realize their dreams. This post was re-posted 330 times and commented on by 167 Weibo users.

Discussion

Main findings

This study demonstrates that several Chinese tobacco companies have embraced Weibo to open dialogue and build relations

Table 3. Content analysis of the 11143 Weibo posts which were coded for the six main themes.

Marketing Strategy	Themes Percent Frequency (n)	Word Frequency Percent Ranking (n)	Illustrative Examples
Covert marketing	Traditional culture: 11% (1226)	Wonderful: 1.04% (n = 116); Life: 0.73% (n = 81); Beautiful: 0.38% (n = 42)	# Double Happiness Morning Post# While there is a will, there is a way. (a Chinese traditional proverb traced back to Han Dynasty)
	Popular culture: 49% (5460)	Shopping: 2.25% (n = 251); Eating: 1.80% (n = 201); Design: 1.04% (n = 116)	# Double Happiness creation # Aurora, a new glowing cocktail, can emit light in the dark, and looks like the aurora borealis.
	Social and Business Affairs: 5% (557)	China: 0.56% (n = 62); Job: 0.37% (n = 41); Communicate: 0.31% (n = 35)	# Mountain Tai · Current affairs reviews # To improve the environment of attractions in China, we should improve awareness of civilization.
Overt marketing	Advertisement: 12% (1337)	Cigarette: 7.88% (n = 878); Mountain Tai: 7.23% (n = 806); Tobacco Leaf: 1.15% (n = 128)	Smoke Mountain Tai cigarettes and appreciate the Confucian culture, hospitality and humility.
	Public relations: 11% (1226)	Activities: 4.92% (n = 548); Social gathering: 3.42% (n = 381); Gifts: 1.55% (n = 173)	#Real Dragon: What will you bring home in the Chinese New Year? Repost this and you will have opportunity to get real dragon New Year prizes!
	Tobacco culture: 12% (1337)	Cigarette: 16.0% (n = 1783); Smoking: 8.61% (n = 959); Pipe: 1.12% (n = 125)	# Mountain Tai · Feeling of smoking # Thinking about the early years when cigarettes are rarities. Cigarettes were symbols of the people's identity.

Table 4. Comparison of proportions of the themes in different Weibo (%).

Weibo Name	Traditional culture	Popular Culture	Social and Business Affairs	Advertisement	Public Relations	Tobacco Culture
Double Happiness Fashion	10	67	4	11	7	2
Mountain Tai Club	11	23	6	16	3	41
Tongxian Manor	35	29	6	12	13	5
Zhongnanhai club	0	32	1	8	46	12
Happiness together	5	25	1	8	60	1
Real Dragon Club	0	10	0	26	32	31
Yuxi1913	18	43	12	10	9	8

with target customers by exploiting a major loophole in the current tobacco advertising laws. Given that new media are quickly superseding traditional media as an efficient tool for the dissemination of information and persuasive marketing promotions, this study provides sound evidence that regulation to ban Internet advertising of tobacco in China is urgently needed.

Weibo users are primarily youth and young adults, with 54% of users being under 30 years of age [14].

While our study found that all the tobacco companies linked smoking to youth- friendly content, there were also different marketing strategies adopted according to the particular brand culture and target consumer. For example, Double Happiness, a brand favoured by young people, focused its posts on popular culture. For the 'Mountain Tai Club' Weibo, a brand named after an actual mountain in Shandong Province, homeland of the Chinese philosopher Confucius, nearly half of all posts focused on tobacco culture.

The Weibo posts not only helped to establish a positive image of the tobacco industry, but were also constructed to help normalize smoking behaviors. Tobacco advertisements and promotional content were mixed in with information about food, sports and social events. Positioning tobacco use within these commonplace topics conveys that smoking should be considered a normal part of everyday life. Such tactics could significantly weaken the positive impact of tobacco control policies. In general, the tobacco industry made efforts to normalize tobacco use through both perceptual and rational ways. As shown in this study, some tobacco industry accounts utilized emotional arousal to normalize tobacco use, while other accounts sought to minimize the health effects of smoking. Such descriptions not only potentially weaken knowledge of the harms of tobacco use, but also positively reinforce smoking behavior. Our results confirm that Weibo offers the Chinese tobacco industry an efficient channel to rapidly spread messages about their products and normalize smoking behavior.

Implications for policymakers

With over 300 million users, Weibo is now a major site for discussion of all aspects of contemporary Chinese life [29]. Weibo presents an unparalleled opportunity for the tobacco industry to keep tobacco products in front of current and potential customers without any of the constraints of tobacco advertising legislation. Because new media reflects current social issues and helps establish social norms, monitoring tobacco marketing on new media should be standard practice in tobacco control.

The WHO FCTC also provides impetus for policy makers to take action to end tobacco industry promotions on Weibo. According to the WHO FCTC Article 5.3 implementation guidelines, which focus on the protection of public health policies from tobacco industry interests, signatory countries should require that any product information provided by the tobacco industry be transparent and accurate [30]. Additionally, as per WHO FCTC Article 13, a comprehensive ban on tobacco advertising should include not only traditional media, but also new media platforms including social media.

Also, as internet communication can easily cross borders and influence people from other countries, monitoring will require international cooperation. Countering online tobacco industry marketing through effective social media campaigns is a promising area of tobacco control activity [31].

Limitations

Several potential limitations of this study need to be addressed. First, this study only analyzed 92.3% of the total sample that could be classified into the six main themes. However, the 930 'other' posts may contain material that contradicts or is different to the main results. In addition, though we analyzed both original posts and re-shared posts from the tobacco industry, we did not examine why 21% of posts were re-shared by followers and other users.

Future study

This is a descriptive study which provides information on the Weibo accounts established by the tobacco industry. Further studies could be conducted to assess the possible impact of the posts on both smoking and non-smoking Weibo users. Social media platforms continue to change, evolve and innovate and tobacco control researchers must keep up with emerging technology and communication vehicles. For example, since completing this study, Wechat, a mobile text and voice messaging communication service in China, has gained a huge audience market share and could be another potential source of tobacco marketing exposure.

Conclusion

The Chinese tobacco industry has skillfully employed youth-oriented themes to promote their brands and products and normalize smoking. These promotions expose serious gaps in existing tobacco advertising laws that do not include online media. Given the rapid increase in internet users, more effective measures in accordance with WHO FCTC Article 13 should be adopted to monitor and regulate the online marketing efforts of the tobacco industry.

Provenance and peer review: Not commissioned; externally peer reviewed.

Author Contributions

Conceived and designed the experiments: FW PPZ HF. Performed the experiments: FW PPZ DYY. Analyzed the data: FW PPZ DYY. Contributed reagents/materials/analysis tools: HF SC. Wrote the paper: FW PPZ BF.

References

1. Conference of the Parties (2008) Guidelines for implementation of Article 13 of the WHO Framework Convention on Tobacco Control (Tobacco advertising, promotion and sponsorship). Available: http://www.who.int/fctc/guidelines/article_13.pdf. Accessed 2012 Aug 10.

2. Yang G, Hu A (2010) Tobacco control and the future of China: Joint assessment of tobacco control situation in China. Beijing: Economy Daily Press.

3. Zheng P, Ge X, Qian H, Wang F, Fu H, et al. (2013) 'Zhonghua' tobacco advertisement in Shanghai: a descriptive study. Tobacco control doi: 10.1136/tobaccocontrol-2012-050661.

4. Provision on Tobacco Advertising (1995) Available: http://www.law-lib.com/law/law_view.asp?id=61611. Accessed 2011 Jun 10.

5. Perez DA, Grunseit AC, Rissel C, Kite J, Cotter T, et al. (2012) Tobacco promotion 'below-the-line': exposure among adolescents and young adults in NSW, Australia. BMC public health 12:429.

6. Henriksen L (2012) Comprehensive tobacco marketing restrictions: promotion, packaging, price and place. Tobacco control 21:147–53.

7. Wackowski OA, Lewis MJ, Delnevo CD (2011) Qualitative analysis of Camel Snus' website message board–users' product perceptions, insights and online interactions. Tobacco control 20:e1.

8. World Health Organization. (2013) WHO Report on the Global Tobacco Epidemic, 2013: Enforcing bans on tobacco advertising, promotion and sponsorship. Available: http://www.who.int/tobacco/global_report/2013/en/. Accessed 2013 Jul 10.

9. Freeman B, Chapman S (2009) Open source marketing: Camel cigarette brand marketing in the 'Web 2.0' world. Tobacco control 18:212–7.

10. Freeman B (2012) New media and tobacco control. Tobacco control 21:139–44.

11. Freeman B, Chapman S (2010) British American Tobacco on Facebook: undermining Article 13 of the global World Health Organization Framework Convention on Tobacco Control. Tobacco control 19:e1–9.

12. China Internet labrary and Center for Internet and Society of Zhejiang University. Research Report of Chinese Weibo Develepment (2012–2013). Available: http://wenku.baidu.com/link?url=Wjr9YAYUErv0NJCZ0T3msW2Z5FLDTwlZ87YU8eaJJqNZ0BUt2aDpM-NiI47ZVxP-li0gMM3z2zOMJiii_d-FJIZ8fyFNbU5GjRa0RrYlx72E. Accessed 2014 Feb 17.

13. Introduction of Weibo. Available: http://baike.baidu.com/view/1567099.htm. Accessed 2013 Mar 10.

14. China Internet Network Information Center. The 32st China Internet Development Statistics Report. Available: http://www.cnnic.cn/hlwfzyj/hlwxzbg/hlwtjbg/201307/t20130717_40664.htm. Accessed 2013 Jul 27.

15. Introduction on China tobacco online. Available: http://www.tobaccochina.com. Accessed 2013 Mar 10.

16. He P, Takeuchi T, Yano E (2013) An overview of the China National Tobacco Corporation and State Tobacco Monopoly Administration. Environmental health and preventive medicine 18: 85–90.

17. How to use Weibo in tobacco marketing. Available: http://www.tobaccochina.com/management/market/stratagem/20133/20132278443_556247.shtml. Accessed 2013 Jun 10.

18. Deng Q. An analysis of tobacco Weibo developing path. Available: http://www.tobaccochina.com/management/watch/wu/201311/201311111334_592964.shtml. Accessed 2013 Apr 30.

19. Chen M. The new idea of Weibo markeitng strategy in tobacco brand cultivation. Available: http://www.tobaccochina.com/business/network/information/201211/201211139279_542070.shtml. Accessed 2013 Apr 30.

20. Feng W. Weibo aroused attention on tobacco network marketing. Available: http://www.tobaccochina.com/management/market/stratagem/20133/201332284048_560246.shtml. Accessed 2013 Apr 30.

21. Pope C, Ziebland S, Mays N (2000) Qualitative research in health care. Analysing qualitative data. BMJ 320:114–6.

22. Penney K, Snyder J, Crooks VA, Johnston R (2011) Risk communication and informed consent in the medical tourism industry: a thematic content analysis of Canadian broker websites. BMC medical ethics 12:17.

23. Search Results for sina weibo. Available: http://www.resonancechina.com/page/2/?s=sina+weibo. Accessed 2013 May 2.

24. Sina microblogging registered users exceeded 300 million. Available: http://news.xinhuanet.com/tech/2012-02/29/c_122769084.htm. Accessed 2013 Mar 10.

25. Introduction of Yanyue website. Available: http://www.yanyue.cn. Accessed 2012 Mar 8.

26. Li J. Rweibo: Provides an interface to the Weibo open platform. R package version 0.1–7. Available: http://jliblog.com/app/rweibo. Accessed 2013 May 2.

27. Burla L, Knierim B, Barth J, Liewald K, Duetz M, et al. (2008) From text to codings: intercoder reliability assessment in qualitative content analysis. Nursing research 57:113–7.

28. Content analysis of Sina Weibo. Available: http://www.360doc.com/content/13/0122/13/10942270_261735546.shtml. Accessed 2012 Sep 8.

29. How Weibo is changing China. Available: http://yaleglobal.yale.edu/content/how-weibo-changing-china. Accessed 2013 May 2.

30. Guidelines for implementation of Article 5.3 of the WHO Franmework Convention in Tobacco Control. Available: http://www.who.int/fctc/guidelines/article_5_3.pdf. Accessed 2012 Sep 8.

31. Hefler M, Freeman B, Chapman S (2013) Tobacco control advocacy in the age of social media: using Facebook, Twitter and change. Tob Control 22:210-4. doi: 10.1136/tobaccocontrol-2012-050721.

32. Storey J (2006) Cultural theory and popular culture: an introduction. (5th Edition) Pearson Education. 5–13p.

12

A Protocol for the Secure Linking of Registries for HPV Surveillance

Khaled El Emam[1,2]*, Saeed Samet[1], Jun Hu[3], Liam Peyton[3], Craig Earle[4], Gayatri C. Jayaraman[5,7], Tom Wong[5,8], Murat Kantarcioglu[6], Fida Dankar[1], Aleksander Essex[1]

1 Electronic Health Information Laboratory, Children's Hospital of Eastern Ontario Research Institute, Ottawa, Ontario, Canada, 2 Paediatrics, University of Ottawa, Ottawa, Ontario, Canada, 3 School of Electrical Engineering and Computer Science, University of Ottawa, Ottawa, Ontario, Canada, 4 Institute for Clinical Evaluative Sciences, Toronto, Ontario, Canada, 5 Public Health Agency of Canada, Ottawa, Ontario, Canada, 6 Computer Science, University of Texas at Dallas, Dallas, Texas, United States of America, 7 Department of Epidemiology and Community Medicine, University of Ottawa, Ottawa, Ontario, Canada, 8 Division of Infectious Diseases, University of Ottawa, Ottawa, Ontario, Canada

Abstract

Introduction: In order to monitor the effectiveness of HPV vaccination in Canada the linkage of multiple data registries may be required. These registries may not always be managed by the same organization and, furthermore, privacy legislation or practices may restrict any data linkages of records that can actually be done among registries. The objective of this study was to develop a secure protocol for linking data from different registries and to allow on-going monitoring of HPV vaccine effectiveness.

Methods: A secure linking protocol, using commutative hash functions and secure multi-party computation techniques was developed. This protocol allows for the exact matching of records among registries and the computation of statistics on the linked data while meeting five practical requirements to ensure patient confidentiality and privacy. The statistics considered were: odds ratio and its confidence interval, chi-square test, and relative risk and its confidence interval. Additional statistics on contingency tables, such as other measures of association, can be added using the same principles presented. The computation time performance of this protocol was evaluated.

Results: The protocol has acceptable computation time and scales linearly with the size of the data set and the size of the contingency table. The worse case computation time for up to 100,000 patients returned by each query and a 16 cell contingency table is less than 4 hours for basic statistics, and the best case is under 3 hours.

Discussion: A computationally practical protocol for the secure linking of data from multiple registries has been demonstrated in the context of HPV vaccine initiative impact assessment. The basic protocol can be generalized to the surveillance of other conditions, diseases, or vaccination programs.

Editor: Christos A. Ouzounis, The Centre for Research and Technology, Hellas, Greece

Funding: This work was funded by the Canada Research Chairs program, the Ontario Institute for Cancer Research, a Collaborative Health Research Project grant from the Canadian Institutes of Health Research (CIHR) and the Natural Sciences and Engineering Research Council, an operating grant from CIHR, National Institutes of Health Grant 1R01LM009989, National Science Foundation (NSF) Grant Career-CNS-0845803, and NSF Grants CNS-0964350 and CNS-1016343. The funders had no role in study design, data collection and analysis, decision to publish, or preparation of the manuscript.

Competing Interests: The authors have declared that no competing interests exist.

* E-mail: kelemam@uottawa.ca

Introduction

The human papillomavirus (HPV) is one of the most prevalent sexually transmitted viral infections in the world [1]. Persistent infection with oncogenic high-risk HPV types, in particular 16 and/or 18, accounts for the majority of cervical cancer and is associated with oral, vulvar, vaginal, penile and anal intraepithelial neoplasia and cancer [2]. HPV is also the cause of external genital warts, with over 90% attributable to low-risk HPV types 6 and 11 [2]. HIV co-infected individuals are at greater risk of developing rarer and/or more aggressive forms of cancer such as anal and penile carcinoma as well as genital warts [2].

Since 2007 an effective preventive quadrivalent vaccine has been available in Canada that protects against low risk (non-oncogenic) types 6 and 11, and high risk (oncogenic) types 16 and 18; in 2010 a bivalent second vaccine against types 16 and 18 was approved for use. Currently, publicly funded school-based HPV immunization programs have been implemented for girls in all 13 Canadian jurisdictions. However, program details, such as school grade(s) in which the vaccine is offered and whether or not there is a catch-up program, vary by province/territory. While the vaccine has the potential to substantially reduce costs associated with screening and treatment and to reduce the overall HPV-related disease morbidity/mortality burden, the long-term and population-level effectiveness of this vaccine are not known. HPV surveillance and research are necessary in order to understand the vaccine's impact on population health and to inform policy decisions concerning the allocation of health care resources.

Detailed baseline information on the distribution and determinants of HPV types, variation by geographic location and risk behaviour is not available for all regions in Canada. Noting that vaccine impact on cancer incidence will not be measurable in a vaccinated population for another generation, we need to monitor HPV type distribution, changes in sexual behaviour, and associations with cytological abnormalities (including pre-cancerous lesions), as well as anogenital warts in the short term.

One of the proposed mechanisms to address the short- and long-term objectives to assess the impact of the HPV vaccine introduction is via the linkage of population-based databases (registries) on cancer, cervical screening, health care services, and immunization. Certain jurisdictions, for example, Manitoba, have robust population-based registries; others are in the early stages of developing such systems. Regardless of the maturity of such registry-based systems, data linkages between registries can only be conducted in an environment that is responsive to patient privacy concerns.

Statutes in Canadian jurisdictions permit the reporting of personal health information (PHI) [3] for public health purposes without patient consent. Similarly, the US Health Insurance Portability and Accountability Act (HIPAA) Privacy Rule permits the disclosure of PHI to a public health authority without patient authorization [4–10]. However, in general, the public is more comfortable with their health information being used for secondary purposes if it is de-identified at the earliest opportunity [11–18] and in practice providers and data custodians have been reluctant to disclose identifiable patient information to public health even when permitted by legislation [19–22]. Such reluctance can be overcome if patient consent to disclose the data for public health purposes is sought. However, there is compelling evidence that requiring explicit consent can bias data sets because consenters and non-consenters differ on important demographic and socio-economic characteristics [23–25].

In this paper we present a protocol for the secure linking and surveillance of patient records in different registries where the sharing of identifying patient information is not possible, either because the registries are not set up to allow for such linkages or because the custodians of the registries are not authorized to link data between them due to patient privacy concerns. The proposed protocol will allow a public health unit (PHU) to compute relevant statistics from linked data on an on-going basis while providing strong patient privacy guarantees.

Methods

Motivating Example

While linking data registries when identifiable information about the patients cannot be shared is a general problem, we consider it within the context of an HPV surveillance example to motivate and illustrate our solution. We assume that there are two registries. One registry contains demographic information about the population, and the second registry contains the results of HPV-associated tests. For example, the former can be a large practice, a hospital, or a vital statistics registry. The latter can be at private or public laboratories at the local or provincial level.

As an example, should the PHU wish to investigate the relationship between HPV test results and ethnicity, the relationship can be expressed as a chi-square test, an odds ratio test, or a relative risk. If HPV test results are captured in one registry and ethnicity in another (as is typically the case), any analyses require that the records in the two registries be linked. Table 1 shows the contingency table that we need to construct to investigate the association between ethnicity and the results of an HPV test. The

Table 1. Example of a contingency table for which we want to compute a bivariate relationship.

		Any HPV (R1)	
		−ve	+ve
Ethnicity (R2)	Aboriginal	n_{11}	n_{12}
	White	n_{21}	n_{22}

cells of the table are the counts of patients. We refer to the two registries as R1 (with HPV screening data) and R2 (with ethnicity data). This example can be extended to multiple dimensions without loss of generality, but we will use this simple 2×2 example to discuss previous work in this area and to illustrate our secure linking protocol.

The two registries will not contain exactly the same patients, but there is expected to be an overlap between them. This means that not all patients in R1 will have records in R2 and vice versa.

The two registries hold one or more common linking fields on all of their patients. We assume that these linking fields are direct identifiers, such as a health insurance card number and/or a social insurance number. In practice, multiple fields can be concatenated or encoded to create a single identifier used for linking. Also, note that these direct identifiers do not need to be numeric but can be strings, dates or categorical values. For example, in a Canadian context the date of birth, postal code, and gender uniquely identify approximately 99% of adults living in urban area [26], making that combination of commonly collected demographic information suitable for linking purposes.

For simplicity, and without loss of generality, we will refer to a single linking field in Table 1. By comparing the two registries on the linking field it would be possible to match their records with certainty. Because the linking field is a direct identifier, it can be used to determine the identity of the patients, and would therefore be considered personally identifying information.

Requirements for a Secure Linking Protocol

Based on the practical realities of privacy problems experienced by an actual PHU, we have formulated five requirements for a protocol to link the data in the two registries. We will examine each of these requirements in turn to illustrate the strengths and weaknesses of the various approaches that have been proposed:

- **A1. The PHU cannot collect personal health information from the registries.** The registries cannot disclose identifiable health information to the PHU because of legislative constraints or because they have reservations about privacy.

- **A2. The protocol must not use a trusted third party (TTP).** A TTP would be an entity independent of the registries and the PHU, but would be able to access identifiable information about the patients. While it is possible to use a TTP to link the data from the two registries, there are pragmatic challenges to consider. First, the custodians of both registries need to be able to share the data with the TTP, and this may be challenging if the registries are within different organizations or jurisdictions, and each wants the TTP to be 'housed' within their organization or jurisdiction. For example, if the source registries are in different jurisdictions but cover the same patient population (e.g., provincial and federal) they may not agree on who the TTP should be. Second, the registries may not have the authority to disclose personal information to a third party without patient consent, even if it is for the purpose of linking information and the data remain within the jurisdiction.

- **A3. The two registries must not have to trust each other.** It must not be necessary for the registries linking their data to trust each other. This lack of trust may be driven by security or legal concerns. For example, trust is necessary if the two registries need to share a secret key, in which case each registry must trust the other one will protect the key since a key compromise would endanger the information held by both registries. Furthermore, the registries may not have the authority to share identifiable patient data amongst themselves without patient consent. For example, the two registries may be within two different government departments and there is no legal basis for sharing data between them.

- **A4. No new information can be discovered about patients in any one registry due to the linking exercise.** Any matching protocol must not allow a registry to discover new information about its patients that is gained from the linking with the other registry. It is often the case that a registry is not able to collect new information without consent or additional authorization. This is a common requirement in the privacy-preserving computation literature where parties collaborating in a computation must not learn something new due to their participation [27,28].

- **A5. A security compromise at the site of any party involved in the protocol must not reveal the identity and any sensitive information of any patients.** In addition to the registries that are the data sources for linking, other parties involved in the secure linking protocol should not hold any PHI. This will ensure that if the security of these other parties is compromised that no PHI will be disclosed.

The above requirements have been implicitly acknowledged in the literature in that different protocols have been developed to address subsets of them. In the following review we examine how well these requirements have been met.

Data Linking Architectures and Protocols

Current data linking protocols can be classified into one of the five architectures shown in Figure 1. The simplest architecture is (a), where both registries provide their raw data to the PHU, which then performs the linking. This means that the registries provide the PHU with the linking fields, ethnicity, and the HPV results. This protocol does not meet requirements A1 and A5. For A1, the PHU would get identifiable patient information, and for A5 a security compromise at the PHU would reveal the identity and sensitive information of the patients.

Under architecture (b) in Figure 1, R1 can give the linking fields for all of its patients to R2 to link with its own data. R2 links the data and generates new unique keys for all of the records, which it sends back to R1. Then both registries send their ethnicity and HPV data with the unique keys separately to the PHU, which can re-link the data and create the contingency table in Table 1. However, with this protocol, a registry may discover new information about its patients. For example, R2 may discover which one of its patients has been tested for HPV. This would fail on requirement A4. While the fact of being tested for HPV may not seem like a major breach if testing is common, consider situations where a registry only holds information about those receiving treatment for drug addiction and substance abuse, or individuals who receive social assistance. In such a case knowing that an individual exists in a particular registry could reveal highly

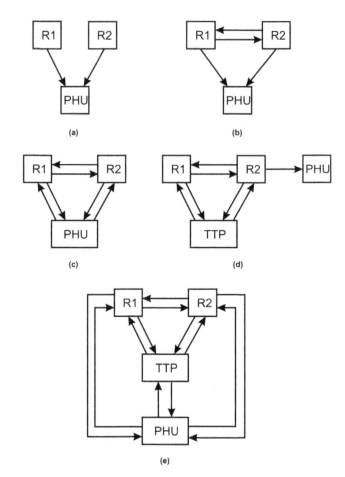

Figure 1. Different architectures in the literature for linking two registries.

sensitive information. Furthermore, this approach does not meet requirement A3. Finally, the PHU could potentially re-identify individuals because when the data is cross-tabulated as in Table 1 there may be small cells in the contingency table. Small cells can allow an adversary to re-identify patients. We examine this situation in more detail below.

Consider Table 2, which covers a known population. The Aboriginal individual who was not HPV positive will know that all of the other Aboriginal individuals in the data set tested positive. In this case an individual in the data can reveal information about all other individuals in the data. Table 3 would allow an external user to know that all Aboriginal individuals in the data set tested positive.

If the data in Table 2 and Table 3 does not represent the whole or a known population, there is still a risk of re-identifying

Table 2. Example of a contingency table for which there is a high identity disclosure risk within the population.

		Any HPV	
		−ve	+ve
Ethnicity	Aboriginal	1	11
	White	50	15

Table 3. Example of a contingency table for which there is a high identity disclosure risk from an external attacker.

		Any HPV	
		−ve	+ve
Ethnicity	Aboriginal	0	5
	White	50	15

Table 5. Example of contingency table that would reveal the contents of the suppressed cells in Table 4.

		Age	
		<20	≥20
Ethnicity	Aboriginal	6	6
	White	50	15

individuals. This would occur, for example, if the data set is a sample. For Table 2, if one can estimate that there was only a single individual in the cell 'Aboriginal and Negative' in the whole population (i.e., can estimate that the sample 'unique' is also a population 'unique'), then the same re-identification risk as for small cells exists. Similarly, for Table 3, if one can determine that there were indeed only five positive Aboriginals in the population then the same re-identification risk exists as for small cells. It is possible to estimate the cell size for the population using sample data [29].

One possible solution is to develop a protocol to suppress the small cells in the contingency table before it is disclosed to the PHU. However, it would not be possible to compute associations on tables with suppressed cells. In addition, by executing additional queries on the data it would be possible to reconstruct the suppressed cells. For example, consider Table 4 which had a small cell suppressed. Now the PHU can execute another query shown in Table 5 that does not have small cells on the same data (assuming a minimal cell size of 5). Because the marginal totals for the ethnicity in the two tables are expected to be the same, it would be possible determine that the value of the suppressed cell in Table 4 was 1. As another example, consider Table 6 which had a small cell suppressed. Another query, shown in Table 7, with gender instead of ethnicity does not have small cells and reveals the marginal totals for the HPV results, which then reveals that the suppressed cell in Table 6 is of size zero. More generally, iterative algorithms can be used to determine the exact value or a narrow value range for suppressed cells if the marginal totals are known [30].

Therefore, as long as multiple tables can be generated it cannot be guaranteed that cell suppression would work. This is a known inference problem in statistical databases [31].

Secure protocols following architecture (b) have been proposed [27,32–38]. These require collaboration among the registries and at the end of their joint computations the contingency table would be shared with the PHU by one or both of the registries. However, they would all be prone to the small cells problem noted above, and the two registries would still need to trust each other since in many of these protocols one of the registries would end up with the contingency table (requirement A3). In addition, some protocols

will only work with three or more registries [34,38], and would therefore not be applicable in the simplest case of two registries.

A slight modification is architecture (c) where the PHU actively participates in the matching and the computations needed rather than being just a recipient of data. One approach is for the two registries to agree on a secret random value and concatenate it to the linking variables, and then hash this concatenated value. The hashed values are then sent to the PHU from each registry [39,40]. The PHU would match the hashed values from the two registries, count the number of matching hashes, and compute the cell values in the contingency table of Table 1. A number of other cryptographic protocols have been developed that are suitable for this architecture [41–45]. These protocols also do not meet the same requirements as the ones following architecture (b) in that they can reveal identifying information to the PHU through small cells and require both registries to trust each other.

Some protocols use a TTP to participate in the linking instead of providing the data to the PHU as illustrated in architecture (d). The TTP would not obtain the contingency table. Instead, the contingency table would be computed from one or both registries and this information would be transmitted to the PHU. One protocol requires the registries to send hashed values to the TTP who then performs the linking [46]. However, this is prone to a dictionary attack, which is when an adversary tries all possible input values until one hashes to the same value. More secure protocols have been proposed [47,48], but these have the same disadvantages as those following architecture (c), as well as requiring a TTP and being vulnerable to collusion between the TTP and one of the registries. Furthermore, if a TTP's security is compromised then this would result in a significant breach affecting both registries.

The final architecture illustrated in panel (e) also requires a TTP. In one deployment of this architecture in Wales, the demographic information is separated from the clinical information, and all of the data sources send the demographic information to a TTP who then performs probabilistic matching of the records on these variables, generates a new unique identifier for each record to allow linking, and sends the unique identifier back to the data sources [49,50]. The data sources then provide the unique identifier with the clinical information to a databank accessed by external parties, such as researchers. In our case the databank

Table 4. Example of contingency table with suppressed cells.

		Any HPV	
		−ve	+ve
Ethnicity	Aboriginal	–	11
	White	50	15

Table 6. Example of contingency table with suppressed cells.

		Any HPV	
		−ve	+ve
Ethnicity	Aboriginal	–	5
	White	50	15

Table 7. Example of contingency table that would reveal the contents of the suppressed cells in Table 6.

		Any HPV	
		−ve	+ve
Gender	Male	25	2
	Female	25	18

would be housed in the PHU. Another protocol that does not use cryptographic techniques utilizes a TTP to run remote sub-queries at the registries and combine and return results back to the PHU [51]. One protocol hashes the linking variables, but also requires that the registries share a secret key [52]. A more secure protocol that utilizes bloom filters has been proposed, which also requires a TTP [53]. A stand alone probabilistic linking technique has been proposed which can be used within this architecture [54]. All of these protocols would not meet requirement A1 because they are vulnerable to the small cells problem that could leak personal information.

Even though various subsets of the requirements have been met in previous research, there have been no protocols developed that address all of the requirements, which is the main contribution of this paper.

Principles and Techniques

As background, we present a set of design elements and building blocks that we integrated into our final protocol.

Using A Semi-Trusted Third Party

In our proposed protocol we use a semi-trusted third party (sTTP). This is a commonly used term to describe a party who would not be able to obtain personal information about the patients, even if it tried to do so. Therefore, there is no risk that patient privacy would be breached, making it unnecessary to fully trust that third party. The only requirement on the sTTP is that they execute the linking protocol faithfully. The utilization of an sTTP in a secure linking protocol would allow us to meet all of the requirements posited earlier. Utilization of an sTTP is a weaker trust requirement than requiring a trusted-third party, who would be able to obtain personal information if it wanted to (hence it needs to be fully trusted). Furthermore, a data breach from an sTTP would not compromise any PHI.

To ensure that the third-party need only be semi-trusted, we propose to compute the statistics that are needed by the PHU directly rather than disclose a contingency table to the PHU. The statistics we will use are the omnibus chi-square test, the odds ratio and its confidence interval, and the relative risk and its confidence interval. The remainder of the paper describes such a protocol while meeting all of the requirements.

Commutative Hash Function

A hash function transforms an input value A to an output value B such that the B value is unique to A and it is not possible to obtain A from B. The input A would typically consist of a message to be hashed and a key. A commutative hash function $H()$ has the additional property that:

$$H(m_1, H(m_2, m_3)) = H(m_2, H(m_1, m_3)) \qquad (1)$$

This means that multiple applications of the hash function in different order will produce the same results. A detailed discussion of a commutative hash function based on the discrete log that is suitable for the problem of matching records from multiple registries is presented in Appendix S1.

Secure Computation

Privacy-preserving computation protocols often utilize Secure Multi-party Computation (SMC) [55,56]. SMC computes the final result in a secure way among multiple parties. Cryptographic and other tools are often used among two or more parties to jointly and securely compute one or more functions using their own private inputs. By using this approach, the final result is the same as that in the corresponding non-secure algorithm, and thus the main trade-off is between security and efficiency. SMC methods have been used previously to define secure disease surveillance protocols [57].

One of the popular encryption techniques used in privacy-preserving methods is homomorphic encryption. In this type of cryptosystem, one operation on the plaintexts will be mapped to another, or even the same, operation on the ciphertexts. For instance, in Paillier [58] encryption, for any two plaintext messages m_1 and m_2 and their encryption $E(m_1)$ and $E(m_2)$, the following equation is satisfied:

$$D\big(E(m_1) \times E(m_2) \mod n^2\big) = m_1 + m_2 \mod n \qquad (2)$$

where n is a product of two large prime numbers, and D is the decryption function. Therefore, in this type of cryptosystem addition of the plaintexts is mapped to multiplication of the corresponding encrypted values. The Paillier cryptosystem also allows a limited form of the product of an encrypted value:

$$D\big(E(m_1)^{m_2} \mod n^2\big) = m_1 \times m_2 \mod n \qquad (3)$$

which allows an encrypted value to be multiplied with a plaintext value to obtain their product.

Another property of Paillier encryption is that it is probabilistic. This means that it uses randomness in its encryption algorithm so that when encrypting the same message several times it will, in general, yield different ciphertexts. This property is important to ensure that an adversary holding a public key would not be able to compare an encrypted message to all possible encrypted counts from zero onwards and determine what the original plaintext value is.

In our protocol we use two sub-protocols based on the Paillier cryptosystem that to perform the intermediate calculations [59]: secure two-party addition and secure two-party multiplication.

Secure two-party addition allows any two parties to jointly add two integers together without either party revealing the value of the individual integer to the other, and without sharing the sum. Each party ends with a partial result (private output values). The two parties, P_1 and P_2, each has her own private integer value, a_1 and a_2 respectively. They obtain their own private output values, b_1 and b_2, such that:

$$a_1 + a_2 = (b_1 \times b_2) \mod n \qquad (4)$$

Secure two-party multiplication allows the two parties to jointly multiply two integers without revealing the values of these integers or the resulting product to each other. For two parties, P_1 and P_2, they compute their own private output values, b_1 and b_2, using their private input values, a_1 and a_2 such that:

$$a_1 \times a_2 = (b_1 + b_2) \bmod n \qquad (5)$$

The Secure Linking Protocol

There are three actors in our protocol as follows:

Registry. The custodians of the data that need to be linked. In our example we assume two registries but this can be easily extended without loss of generality.

Aggregator. The aggregator is a semi-trusted third party who can securely compute the statistics on the contingency table and sends the result back to the PHU. We assume there are two aggregators.

PHU. Defines which data elements are required and receives the final result of the analysis.

The protocol has three phases: (a) request, (b) matching, and (c) analysis.

Request Phase

The protocol is initiated each time an analysis needs to be performed. For example, if the PHU wants to investigate the relationship between HPV test results and ethnicity, then the protocol is initiated. The completion of the protocol results in the production of the desired statistical result. In our example we assume that the PHU wishes to compute the odds ratio on the 2×2 contingency table. If the PHU then wants to investigate another relationship using the same two registries or different registries, say the relationship between HPV vaccination and HPV results, then the protocol would be initiated again.

The PHU then sends four different queries to the registries, one for each row and column in the contingency table. Each query has a unique identifier, Q_k, where the value of k indicates the column or row in the contingency table. For example, the query Q_{1+} is for the Aboriginal patients. Another query, Q_{+2} would be for patients with positive HPV results. This is illustrated in Figure 2. To compute statistics on a 2×2 table, four queries would need to be generated by the PHU with two targeted at each registry.

Upon receiving a query, each registry generates a random number only known to the registry, denoted by R_k. The random number is specific to each query.

Matching Phase

Each registry would respond with a value for each patient matching the query. A registry would select an Aggregator at random to respond to. Let's say that the direct identifier (linking field) for a patient from Registry 1 is denoted by ID_i and the linking field for a patient from Registry 2 is denoted by ID_j. Registry 1 sends the hash value $H(R_{1+}, ID_i)$ to the Aggregator.

In the example in Figure 3, Registry 1 sends this value to Aggregator 1. Aggregator 1 was chosen randomly by the registry and Registry 1 may send the value for the next patient to Aggregator 2. Because this is a hashed value and Aggregator 1 does not know the value of R_{1+}, Aggregator 1 would not be able to determine the ID_i value. Aggregator 1 then forwards that information to Registry 2, which hashes that value and sends it back as $H(R_{+2}, H(R_{1+}, ID_i))$. Aggregator 1 would then store that value.

Registry 2 would also respond with a message for every patient which satisfies the query. In the example of Figure 3, Registry 2 also selects Aggregator 1. By going through the same sequence of messages Aggregator 1 also gets $H(R_{1+}, H(R_{+2}, ID_j))$ for the patient from Registry 2. If the same patient exists in both responses from Registry 1 and Registry 2, then $H(R_{+2}, H(R_{1+}, ID_i)) = H(R_{1+}, H(R_{+2}, ID_j))$ and Aggregator 1 would be able to determine that the same patient appeared in both registries within the cell making up the intersection of the queries. This is illustrated in Table 8. In this case Aggregator 1 matched two patients, and therefore its matched count would be 2.

Because each Registry selects an Aggregator at random, no Aggregator will have a total count for a particular cell. This ensures that neither Aggregator will know with certainty if the cell has a small count. Therefore, Aggregator 1's count of 2 is not a complete count of all Aboriginals with positive HPV results. There are two patients who were not matched by Aggregator 1 and it is not possible for Aggregator 1 to know whether these two patients exist in Aggregator 2's table. Aggregator 2 had 3 patients matched. Therefore, in total we have 5 matched patients. However, the patient with an ID of 2 would not be matched because its values are split between the two Aggregators. The patient with ID number 3 would not be matched because there is no information on the ethnicity of that individual in Registry 2.

Once both registries have sent all of their hashed values to the Aggregators, the Aggregators need to reconcile their lists. Specifically, Registry 1 may have sent its value for a patient to Aggregator 1 and Registry 2 sent its value for the same patient to Aggregator 2. Therefore, it is not possible for either Aggregator to know that the patient exists in that cell. In our example, reconciliation would reveal that the patient with ID 2 is also matched.

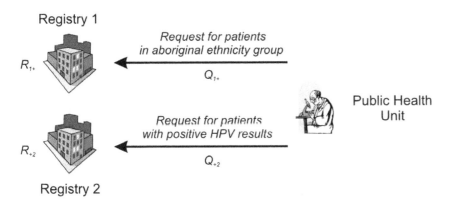

Registry 1

Request for patients in aboriginal ethnicity group

Q_{1+}

R_{1+}

Public Health Unit

Request for patients with positive HPV results

Q_{+2}

R_{+2}

Registry 2

Figure 2. The public health unit sends a query for a particular cell within the desired contingency table.

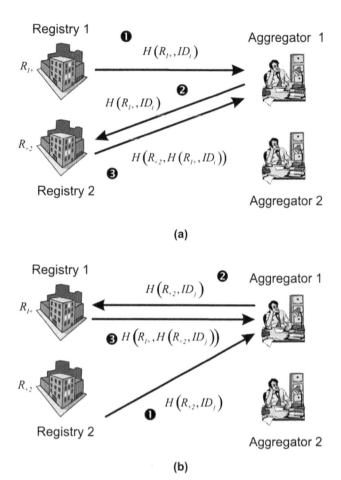

Figure 3. An example showing how a registry responds for a request for counts. A sequence of messages is generated for each patient.

The two Aggregators need to reconcile their lists and compute the final counts for the cell. Aggregator 1 knows that it already has a set of S_1 matching hashes and Aggregator 2 knows that it has a set of S_2 matching hashes. In our example we have $S_1 = \{H(R_{+2}, H(R_{1+}, ID_1)), H(R_{+2}, H(R_{1+}, ID_4))\}$ and $S_2 = \{H(R_{+2}, H(R_{1+}, ID_5)), H(R_{+2}, H(R_{1+}, ID_6)), H(R_{+2}, H(R_{1+}, ID_7))\}$. However, the union of these sets does not give us all of the matching patients.

Define a set of patients from Registry 1 who are not matched in either Aggregator:

$$X = \{x | \{\forall i : H(R_{+2}, H(R_{1+}, ID_i))\} \cap \{S_1 \cup S_2\} = \varnothing\} \quad (6)$$

and similarly from Registry 2:

$$Y = \{y | \{\forall j : H(R_{1+}, H(R_{+2}, ID_j))\} \cap \{S_1 \cup S_2\} = \varnothing\} \quad (7)$$

Consider the notation for the contingency table in Table 9. Let us assume that we are computing the count n_{12}. This consists of two counts, one from each of the aggregators, summed together $n_{1,12} + n_{2,12}$. Below are the steps for computing $n_{1,12}$ and $n_{2,12}$:

1. On all $x_i \times y_j$ pairs, $x_i \in X$ and $y_j \in Y$, the Aggregators run a secure two-party subtraction. At the end of each secure two-party subtraction Aggregator 1 will have a value v_i computed, and Aggregator 2 will have a value w_j computed such that $x_i - y_j = v_i \times w_j \mod n$ (see equation (4)). According to the secure two-party addition protocol, if Aggregator 1 initiates the protocol and $x_i = y_j$, then $v_i = 0$. Otherwise if Aggregator 2 initiates the protocol and $x_i = y_j$, then $w_j = 0$. It does not matter which Aggregator initiates the protocol, but only one should do it to ensure that matches are not double counted. If either of v_i is zero or w_j is zero, then the two values match.

2. Let c_1 be the number of v_i's where $v_i = 0$, and let c_2 be the number of w_j's where $w_j = 0$.

3. Aggregator 1 computes:

$$n_{1,12} = |S_1| + c_1 \quad (8)$$

and Aggregator 2 computes:

$$n_{2,12} = |S_2| + c_2 \quad (9)$$

Note that no single aggregator will know the value of n_{12} at the end of this protocol; it can only be computed by combining the values from both aggregators.

Table 8. Example of the matching performed by Aggregator 1 and Aggregator2 based on the hash values that they receive.

Aggregator 1 Matching Table

Registry 1	Registry 2
$H(R_{+2}, H(R_{1+}, ID_1))$	$H(R_{1+}, H(R_{+2}, ID_1))$
	$H(R_{1+}, H(R_{+2}, ID_2))$
$H(R_{+2}, H(R_{1+}, ID_3))$	
$H(R_{+2}, H(R_{1+}, ID_4))$	$H(R_{1+}, H(R_{+2}, ID_4))$

Aggregator 2 Matching Table

Registry 1	Registry 2
$H(R_{+2}, H(R_{1+}, ID_2))$	
$H(R_{+2}, H(R_{1+}, ID_5))$	$H(R_{1+}, H(R_{+2}, ID_5))$
$H(R_{+2}, H(R_{1+}, ID_6))$	$H(R_{1+}, H(R_{+2}, ID_6))$
$H(R_{+2}, H(R_{1+}, ID_7))$	$H(R_{1+}, H(R_{+2}, ID_7))$

Table 9. Notation for computing statistics.

		Any HPV	
		-ve	+ve
Ethnicity	Aboriginal	$n_{11} = n_{1,11} + n_{2,11}$	$n_{12} = n_{1,12} + n_{2,12}$
	White	$n_{21} = n_{1,21} + n_{2,21}$	$n_{22} = n_{1,22} + n_{2,22}$

Analysis Phase

The Aggregators can now jointly compute the appropriate statistics. As illustrated in Figure 4, the Aggregators then each send partial results of their statistical computations to the PHU, which combines the partial results to obtain the final result.

The count in each cell in the contingency table is split between the two Aggregators. Suppose we have a 2×2 contingency table as in Table 5. Below we go through the steps of calculation for the odds ratio. The computation of other bivariate statistics, such as chi-square, relative risk, and the confidence intervals for the odds ratio and relative risk, are described in Appendix S1.

In Table 9, $n_{1,ij}$ is available to Aggregator 1 and $n_{2,ij}$ is available to Aggregator 2 for every i and j. We can compute the odds ratio as follows:

$$\theta = \frac{n_{11}n_{22}}{n_{12}n_{21}} \tag{10}$$

which can be defined as:

$$\theta = \frac{(n_{1,11}+n_{2,11})(n_{1,22}+n_{2,22})}{(n_{1,12}+n_{2,12})(n_{1,21}+n_{2,21})} \tag{11}$$

To separate the above fraction such that each of the two Aggregators owns her final private values for the odds ratio we will apply secure two-party addition. In the equations below we will not show the "mod n" to simplify the presentation. The steps of the protocol are as follows:

1. Aggregator 1 and Aggregator 2 run secure two-party additions for their following pairs:

$n_{1,11}$ and $n_{2,11}$ such that: $n_{1,11} + n_{2,11} = a_{1,1} \times a_{2,1}$
$n_{1,22}$ and $n_{2,22}$ such that: $n_{1,22} + n_{2,22} = a_{1,2} \times a_{2,2}$
$n_{1,12}$ and $n_{2,12}$ such that: $n_{1,12} + n_{2,12} = a_{1,3} \times a_{2,3}$
$n_{1,21}$ and $n_{2,21}$ such that: $n_{1,21} + n_{2,21} = a_{1,4} \times a_{2,4}$
Therefore, the odds ratio will be converted to:

$$\theta = \frac{(a_{1,1} \times a_{2,1})(a_{1,2} \times a_{2,2})}{(a_{1,3} \times a_{2,3})(a_{1,4} \times a_{2,4})} = \frac{(a_{1,1} \times a_{1,2})}{(a_{1,3} \times a_{1,4})} \times \frac{(a_{2,1} \times a_{2,2})}{(a_{2,3} \times a_{2,4})}$$

2. Aggregator 1 and Aggregator 2 then compute the two fractions $\frac{b_1}{c_1}$ and $\frac{b_2}{c_2}$, respectively, such that:

$$b_1 = a_{1,1} \times a_{1,2} \quad b_2 = a_{2,1} \times a_{2,2}$$

$$c_1 = a_{1,3} \times a_{1,4} \quad c_2 = a_{2,3} \times a_{2,4}$$

3. Aggregator 1 and Aggregator 2 send their private values b_1, b_2, c_1, c_2 to the PHU. The PHU then computes $\theta = \frac{(b_1 \times b_2)}{(c_1 \times c_2)}$.

A summary of the inputs and outputs, including for the statistics described in more detail in Appendix S1, are provided in Table 10.

Empirical Performance Measurement

The challenge with secure computation protocols is that they are slower than non-secure ones. This makes the assessment of performance an important determinant of their practicability. We describe the communication costs in our analysis in Appendix S1. Here we focus on an empirical assessment of computation time.

The objectives of the evaluation were to determine: (a) the time to perform the computations under the different conditions, (b) how the protocol scales as the number of patients returned by the queries increases, and (c) how the protocol scales as the number of cells in the contingency table increases.

We assume that all queries return the same number $N_{..}$ of patients. Let α be the time it takes to perform a single encryption or decryption and let τ be the time it takes to perform a single commutative hash. Table 11 shows the total computation time range (matching and analysis tasks) for each of the statistics based on the detailed analysis in Appendix S1. Matching within the Aggregator is not considered as that computation time would be negligible compared to the computations requiring encryption and decryption. We consider the general case for the number of cells in the contingency table, which is denoted by C in Table 10. By examining Table 11, we would expect that computation time scales linearly with the number of patients and the number of cells.

To evaluate the computation time performance of the protocol we empirically determined the values for τ and α over 100 iterations for random values of the same integer size. The average hash time gave us an estimate for τ. We then encrypted the hashed values and the average encryption time gave us α. Using these two values we could determine the computation time for the implementation of the protocol. The timing was computed on a Windows machine running the XP operating system with an Intel

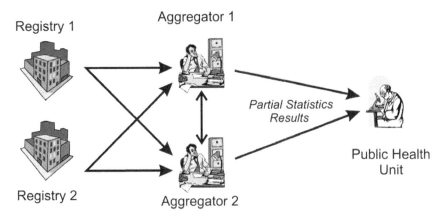

Figure 4. The flow of information between the Aggregators and the PHU.

Table 10. Summary of the inputs and outputs for the building block and analysis protocols.

Protocol	Inputs	Outputs	Equation
Two-party addition	a_1, a_2	b_1, b_2	$b_1 \times b_2$
Two party multiplication	a_1, a_2	b_1, b_2	$b_1 + b_2$
Odds Ratio	$n_{1,11}, n_{2,11}$	b_1, b_2	$\theta = \dfrac{b_1 \times b_2}{c_1 \times c_2}$
	$n_{1,12}, n_{2,12}$	c_1, c_2	
	$n_{1,21}, n_{2,21}$		
	$n_{1,22}, n_{2,22}$		
Chi-square	$n_{1,11}, n_{2,11}$	c_1, c_2	$\chi^2 = \dfrac{c_1 \times c_2}{d_1 \times d_2}$
	$n_{1,12}, n_{2,12}$	d_1, d_2	
	$n_{1,21}, n_{2,21}$		
	$n_{1,22}, n_{2,22}$		
Relative Risk	$n_{1,11}, n_{2,11}$	b_1, b_2	$r = \dfrac{b_1 \times b_2}{c_1 \times c_2}$
	$n_{1,12}, n_{2,12}$	c_1, c_2	
	$n_{1,21}, n_{2,21}$		
	$n_{1,22}, n_{2,22}$		
Confidence Interval for Odds Ratio	$n_{1,11}, n_{2,11}$	i_1, i_2	$CI_{\ln(OR)} = \ln(\theta) \pm z \times \sqrt{\dfrac{i_1 \times i_2}{j_1 \times j_2}}$
	$n_{1,12}, n_{2,12}$	j_1, j_2	
	$n_{1,21}, n_{2,21}$		
	$n_{1,22}, n_{2,22}$		
Confidence Interval for Relative Risk	$n_{1,11}, n_{2,11}$	d_1, d_2	$CI_{\ln(RR)} = \ln(RR) \pm z \times \sqrt{\dfrac{d_1 \times d_2}{g_1 \times g_2}}$
	$n_{1,12}, n_{2,12}$	g_1, g_2	
	$n_{1,21}, n_{2,21}$		
	$n_{1,22}, n_{2,22}$		

Table 11. Summary of the computation time range for each of the statistics.

Statistic	Total Computation Time (max → min)
Chi-square	$2\tau(C \times N..) + 2(\alpha \times C \times N..) + 20(\alpha \times C) \to$ $2\tau(C \times N..) + 20(\alpha \times C)$
Odds Ratio	$2\tau(C \times N..) + 2(\alpha \times C \times N..) + 8(\alpha \times C) \to$ $2\tau(C \times N..) + 8(\alpha \times C)$
Relative Risk	$2\tau(C \times N..) + 2(\alpha \times C \times N..) + 8(\alpha \times C) \to$ $2\tau(C \times N..) + 8(\alpha \times C)$

The computation time is smallest when $m = 100\%$ since that's when all of the matching can be done within the Aggregator. For a contingency table with 4 cells and each query returning 100,000 patients, the total computation is just under one hour. With 16 cells it is just under 4 hours.

The graph in Figure 6 shows how the computation time increases linearly as the number of records returned by a query increases. The graph in Figure 7 shows how the computation time increases linearly as the number of cells increases.

The difference between chi-square and odds ratio and relative risk, and their confidence intervals, is negligible because the total computation time is driven by the matching phase rather than the analysis phase. Thus, the computation time for the two latter ones are almost identical as that for chi-square and are not shown here.

Discussion

Summary

In this paper we have described a secure protocol for linking records from multiple registries that can be used to monitor the effectiveness of the HPV vaccine. We have shown that this protocol is the only one, thus far, that can meet all five requirements that were derived from actual current constraints for sharing patient information. The protocol can provide specific statistics, and is therefore most useful when the statistics to be computed are known in advance. This fits well with the disease surveillance context where the same statistics would need to be computed on an on-going basis.

The performance of this protocol is acceptable even for large data sets. For example, for a 16 cell contingency table where each of the queries returns 100,000 patients and none of the matches can be performed within an Aggregator, the total computation time is less than 4 hours. This is a worse case assumption, but nevertheless would still be acceptable performance for a surveillance application since the data set will not change at a faster rate than 4 hours. It exhibits a linear increase in computation time as the number of records in the data set grows and as the size of the contingency table grows.

Details on issues that would need to be addressed during the deployment of this protocol in practice, such as dealing with small cells and zero-sized cells, are addressed in Appendix S1.

HIPAA and the Common Rule

While our initial deployment of this protocol was intended for a Canadian context, its deployment in the US requires special considerations of current legislation and regulations.

The HIPAA Privacy Rule defines two standards for de-identifying health information (45 CFR 164.514(b)). The first one is called the Safe Harbor standard. Under Safe Harbor any unique identifying number, characteristic, or code must be

dual core CPU running at 2.4 GHz and 2 GB of RAM. The key size used was 1024 bits.

We assume that m hashed values will be matched within an aggregator for all cells. In presenting the results, the value of m is expressed as a percentage of $N..$ and varied from 0% to 100%, with the computation time in seconds calculated each time for a different number of patients. We let the total number of patients returned by each query requested from the two registries be 5,000, 10,000, 50,000, and 100,000. The value of C indicating the number of cells was varied from 4 to 16 in increments of 2.

Results

The average time to perform an encryption using the Paillier cryptosystem is 1.721 ms, and decryption takes 1.882 ms. The secure multiplication and addition take 2.581 ms on average, and the average time to hash a value is 3.07 ms. The performance of the whole protocol was driven by the performance of the matching phase. The matching phase was driven by the size of the data set and the number of cells in the contingency table.

Figure 5 illustrates the computation times for different percentage of matching records within each Aggregator, $m\$$.

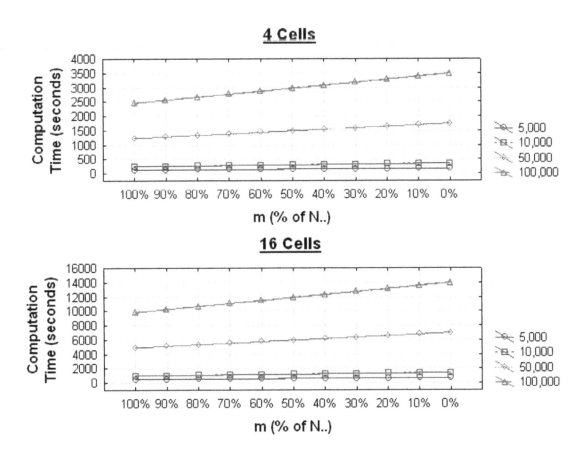

Figure 5. The average computation times for the chi-square test when the total number of records returned by the queries varies from the two registries are 5,000, 10,000, 50,000, and 100,000 for a 4 cell and a 16 cell contingency table.

removed from the data set, otherwise it would be considered personal health information.

In our protocol we used a hash function to perform the matching. If a simple hash function was used then it could be reverse engineered using a dictionary attack. For example, if we are using an individual's social security number and that number is hashed, then an adversary would only need to hash all possible numbers of the same length and compare it to the targeted value until a match is found.

A special type of dictionary attack has also been proposed and utilized to reduce the computation time at the cost of more data storage capacity – the so-called rainbow tables [60]. In this method, a table of hash chains is pre-computed for reversing the hash function by using a reduction function. The chains which create the items in the rainbow table are chains of one way hash functions and reduction functions starting at a certain plaintext, and ending at a certain hashed value. However, only the starting plaintext and ending hashed value are stored in the rainbow table. By comparing against only the stored values a significant reduction in computation can be gained during an attack.

In practice one always adds some randomness to the hash value, as we do in our commutative hash function. This random value is called a "salt" or a "key". This makes the range of possible values that would need to be checked in a dictionary attack, even with a rainbow table, computationally unattainable in any reasonable amount of time.

Is a hashed value with a salt considered a uniquely identifying code under Safe Harbor?

The HIPAA Privacy Rule requires that "The code or other means of record identification is not derived from or related to

information about the individual" *and* that the the covered entity does not use or disclose the code for other purposes or disclose the mechanism for re-identification (45 CFR 164.514(c)). In our protocol we can satisfy the second requirement since the random values used for hashing (the keys) are never shared by the registries. However, a hash value, with or without a salt, is derived from identifiable information and would therefore still be considered personal information under this definition.

The Privacy Rule allows the disclosure of information containing such coded information as a Limited Data Set (45 CFR 164.514(e)). A Limited Data Set would require a data sharing agreement with the data recipient, and the data can only be used for specific purposes: research, public health, or healthcare operations. For users of our protocol, this means that the purpose of the linking and analysis would have to be one of the above. For example, if our protocol is used for public health surveillance or research and a data use agreement is in place between the registries and between the registries and Aggregators, then the requirements for a Limited Data Set would be met.

If our protocol is used for research purposes, then the Common Rule would also apply. Under the Common Rule, which guides IRBs, if the user of the information has no means of getting the key, for example, through an agreement with the other party prohibiting the sharing of keys under any circumstances or through organizational policies prohibiting such an exchange, then this would not be considered human subjects research and would not require an IRB review [61,62]. In our protocol, if each of the registries has a policy against the sharing of the salt values used, then no IRB approval would be required for the linking project, according to the Common Rule, since the hash values

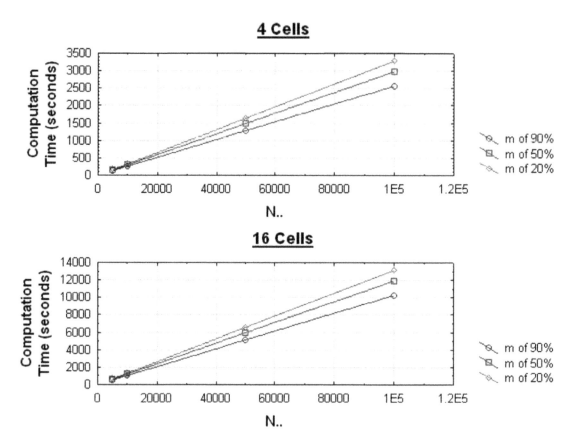

Figure 6. The average computation times for the chi-square test as the proportion of records matching varies for different data set sizes for contingency tables with 4 and 16 cells.

exchanged would not be considered personally identifying information.

This inconsistency between HIPAA and the Common Rule is well documented [63,64].

However, the Privacy Rule does provide a mechanism for an expert with appropriate statistical knowledge to certify that the data exchanged has a very small risk of re-identification (45 CFR 164.514(a)), at which point it would not be considered personal health information [65]. Therefore, should an expert deem that the (salted) hashed value cannot be reversed and that adequate legal mechanisms exist prohibiting the exchange of the salt represent a very small risk of re-identification, then the data exchanges in our protocol would not be considered identifiable.

In other jurisdictions, such precise prescriptions on the interpretability of coded information are absent, making it easier to argue that the exchange of hashed information (with a salt) for the purpose of matching, with prohibitions on the sharing of that random value, would not constitute an exchange of personal health information.

Limitations

Our protocol only allows for deterministic matching of patients in the two registries. Therefore, the linking field value that is hashed needs to be a reliable unique identifier across the registries.

We focused on surveillance where the computed statistics are on a contingency table. Where the variable are continuous and cannot be meaningfully discretized into categorical variables, the approach we present will not be suitable.

Future Work

Extensions of our protocol to allow probabilistic linkage would be expected to result in a higher match rate when there are errors in the variables making up the linking field. For example, the inclusion of names in the set of linking fields would be expected to improve the match rate.

Additional statistics may be added to our protocol to cover more tests that a PHU may wish to use for evaluation of effectiveness or other analytical purposes. We consider two examples of more sophisticated analyses below.

The basic structure of our protocol can also support the computation of population size estimates using a capture-recapture (CR) model. A CR model can estimate the total population of individuals with a particular disease when the registries have an incomplete listing of that population. A secure CR protocol would allow the estimation of population size when the registries are unable to share data. CR models have been used in the biological sciences to estimate the size of animal populations [66,67], and in epidemiology to estimate birth and death rates [68,69], as well as the size of diseased populations [70]. The basic principle is that animals are caught on multiple occasions and marked/identified. Using the information on the number of animals caught/not caught on the multiple occasions, a complete capture history of animal capture is known. Methods have been developed to estimate the total population size from such capture histories. When applied to human populations, the overlap across multiple disease registries is used to mimic recaptures. The matching phase of our protocol can compute the number of overlapping individuals between the two registries. An appropriate

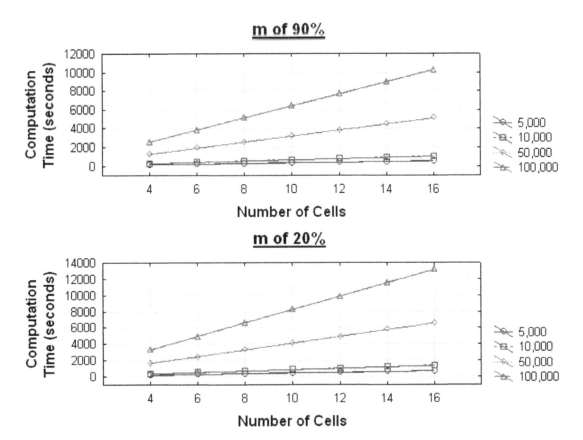

Figure 7. The average computation times for the chi-square test as the number of cells varies for different data set sizes when the proportion of records matching (m) is 90% and 20%.

CR model would then be used to estimate the total population size.

Moving beyond surveillance, multivariate models would need to be constructed to answer questions about whether individuals and populations can be protected against infection and the cervical/anal/oral HPV-associated cancers. They can also be used to better understand HPV vaccine effectiveness through various endpoints [71–73], including changes in type-specific HPV prevalence, changes in lesions (via pap test results/colposcopy results), and over a longer period of time, changes in cervical and other HPV-related cancer rates. However, all these may be somewhat impacted by factors such as SES, ethnicity (in the context of accessing care), age of sexual debut, number of sexual partners, parity, smoking, and other factors. It would therefore be important to control for these factors. Future work would need to take our basic surveillance framework and extend it to allow more general secure multivariate modeling, such as for general linear models.

Supporting Information

Appendix S1 Description of the commutative hashing function, the protocols for computing other statistics, as well as practical considerations when deploying the protocol.

Acknowledgments

We wish to thank Dr. Karim Keshavjee for his feedback on an earlier version of this paper, and the anonymous reviewers for their helpful comments and suggestions.

Author Contributions

Conceived and designed the experiments: KEE SS JH LP CE TW GJ MK FD. Performed the experiments: KEE SS JH. Analyzed the data: KEE SS JH MK FD. Wrote the paper: KEE SS JH LP TW GJ CE MK FD AE.

References

1. Clifford G, Gallus S, Herrero R, Muñoz N, Snijders P, et al. (2005) Worldwide distribution of human papillomavirus types in cytologically normal women in the International Agency for Research on Cancer HPV prevalence surveys: A pooled analysis. Lancet 366: 991–998.

2. Dawar M, Deeks S, Dobson S (2007) Human papillomavirus vaccines launch a new era in cervical cancer prevention. CMAJ 177: 456–461.

3. El Emam K, Fineberg A (2009) Risk Assessment for the Disclosure of Personal Health Information for Public Health Purposes. Public Health Agency of Canada.

4. Sengupta S, Calman N, Hripcsak G (2008) A model for expanded public health reporting in the context of HIPAA. Journal of the American Medical Informatics Association 15: 569–574.

5. Broome C, Horton H, Tress D, Lucido S, Koo D (2003) Statutory basis for public health reporting beyond specific diseases. Journal of Urban Health 80: i14–i22.

6. Wojcik R, Hauenstein L, Sniegoski C, Holtry R (2007) Obtaining the data. In: Lombardo J, Buckeridge D, editors. Disease surveillance: A public health informatics approach. Mississauga: Wiley. 91–142.

7. Centers for Disease Control and Prevention (2003) HIPAA Privacy Rule and Public Health: Guidance from CDC and the U.S. Department of Health and Human Services. Morbidity and Mortality Weekly Report 52. 24 p.

8. Gostin L (2008) Public Health Law. Berkeley: University of California Press.

9. Baker D (2006) Privacy and security in public health: Maintaining the delicate balance between personal privacy and population safety. In: ACSAC '06

Proceedings of the 22nd Annual Computer Security Applications Conference. Washington: IEEE Computer Society. 3–22.

10. Department of Health and Human Services. Disclosures for Emergency Preparedness - A Decision Tool. Available: http://www.hhs.gov/ocr/privacy/hipaa/understanding/special/emergency/decisiontoolintro.html. Accessed 2012 Jan 1.

11. Nass S, Levit L, Gostin L, editors (2009) Beyond the HIPAA Privacy Rule: Enhancing privacy, improving health through research. Washington, DC: National Academies Press.

12. Pullman D (2006) Sorry, you can't have that information: Stakeholder awareness, perceptions and concerns regarding the disclosure and use of personal health information. e-Health 2006 Conference. Victoria, BC, Canada.

13. GPC Alberta (2003) OIPC Stakeholder Survey, 2003: Highlights Report. GPC Research.

14. Willison D, Schwartz L, Abelson J, Charles C, Swinton M, et al. (2007) Alternatives to project-specific consent for access to personal information for health research: What is the opinion of the Canadian public ? Journal of the American Medical Informatics Association 14: 706–712.

15. Nair K, Willison D, Holbrook A, Keshavjee K (2004) Patients' consent preferences regarding the use of their health information for research purposes: A qualitative study. Journal of Health Services Research & Policy 9: 22–27.

16. Kass N, Natowicz M, Hull S, Faden RR, Plantinga L, et al. (2003) The use of medical records in research: what do patients want? Journal of Law, Medicine and Ethics 31: 429–433.

17. Whiddett R, Hunter I, Engelbrecht J, Handy J (2006) Patients' Attitudes Towards Sharing their Health Information. International Journal of Medical Informatics 75: 530–541.

18. Pritts J (2008) The Importance and Value of Protecting the Privacy of Health Information: Roles of HIPAA Privacy Rule and the Common Rule in Health Research. Available: http://www.iom.edu/7/media/Files/Activity%20Files/Research/HIPAAandResearch/PrittsPrivacyFinalDraftweb.ashx. Accessed 2012 Jan 1.

19. El Emam K, Mercer J, Moreau K, Grava-Gubins I, Buckeridge D, et al. (2011) Physician Privacy Concerns when Disclosing Patient Data for Public Health Purposes During a Pandemic Influenza Outbreak. BMC Public Health 11: 454.

20. Birtwhistle R, Keshavjee K, Lambert-Lanning A, Godwin M, Greiver M, et al. (2009) Building a pan-Canadian primary care sentinel surveillance network: Initial development and moving forward. Journal of the American Board of Family Medicine 22: 412–422.

21. Wong T, Mercer J (2009) Rapid Real Time Surveillance and Monitoring of Pandemic Influenza Using Primary Care Electronic Medical Records (EMR). Public Health Agency of Canada.

22. Wong J, Mercer J, Nizar SM, Totten S, El Emam K, et al. (2010) Rapid Real Time Surveillance and Monitoring of Pandemic Influenza Associated Pneumonia & Risk Factors Using Primary Care Electronic Medical Records (EMR). 14th International Congress on Infectious Diseases (ICID). Miami, FL, USA.

23. El Emam K, Dankar F, Issa R, Jonker E, Amyot D, et al. (2009) A Globally Optimal k-Anonymity Method for the De-identification of Health Data Journal of the American Medical Informatics Association 16: 670–682.

24. Kho M, Duffett M, Willison D, Cook D, Brouwers M (2009) Written informed consent and selection bias in observational studies using medical records: systematic review. BMJ 338: b866.

25. El Emam K, Jonker E, Fineberg A (2011) The case for deidentifying personal health information.

26. El Emam K, Buckeridge D, Tamblyn R, Neisa A, Jonker E, et al. (2011) The Re-identification Risk of Canadians from Longitudinal Demographics. BMC Medical Informatics and Decision Making 11: 46.

27. Li Y, Tygar J, Hellerstein J (2005) Private matching. In: D Lee, S Shieh, and J. D Tygar editors. Computer Security in the 21st Century. New York: Springer. 25–50.

28. Lindell Y, Pinkas B (2009) Secure multiparty computation for privacy-preserving data mining. Journal of Privacy and Confidentiality 1: 59–98.

29. Dankar F, El Emam K (2010) A method for evaluating marketer re-identification risk. In: Proceedings of the 2010 EDBT/ICDT Workshops. New York: ACM. Article No. 28.

30. Buzzigoli L, Giusti A (2006) From Marginals to Array Structure with the Shuttle Algorithm. Journal of Symbolic Data Analysis 4: 1–14.

31. Denning DE, Denning PJ, Schwartz MD (1979) The tracker: a threat to statistical database security. ACM Transactions on Database Systems (TODS) 4: 76–96.

32. Yakout M, Atallah M, Elmagarmid A (2009) Efficient private record linkage. Proceedings of the 25th International Conference on Data Engineering. Shanghai, China. 1283–1286.

33. Berman J (2004) Zero-check: A zero-knowledge protocol for reconciling patient identities across institutions. Archives of pathology and laboratory medicine 128: 344–346.

34. Agrawal R, Evmievski A, Srikant R (2003) Information sharing across private databases. In: Proceedings of the 2003 ACM SIGMOD international conference on Management of data. New York: ACM. 86–97.

35. Atallah M, Kerschbaum F, Du W (2003) Secure and private sequence comparisons. In: Proceedings of the 2003 ACM workshop on Privacy in the electronic society. New York: ACM. 39–44.

36. Lu H, He X, Vaidya J, Adam N (2008) Secure construction of contingency tables from distributed data. In: Proceedings of the 22nd annual IFIP WG 11.3

working conference on Data and Applications Security. Berlin: Springer-Verlag. 144–157.

37. Agrawal R, Asonov D, Srikant R (2004) Enabling sovereign information sharing using web services. In: Proceedings of the 2004 ACM SIGMOD international conference on Management of data. New York: ACM. 873–877.

38. Vaidya J, Clifton C (2005) Secure Set Intersection Cardinality with Application to Association Rule Mining. Journal of Computer Security 13: 593–622.

39. Stolba N, Banek M, Tjoa A (2006) The security issue of federated data warehouses in the area of evidence-based medicine. In: The First International Conference on Availability, Reliability and Security. Washington: IEEE Computer Society. 11–22.

40. Swire P (2009) Research Report: Application of IBM Anonymous Resolution to the Health Care Sector.

41. He X, Vaidya J, Shafiq B, Adam N, White T (2010) Privacy Preserving Integration of Health Care Data. International Journal of Computational Models and Algorithms in Medicine 1: 22–36.

42. Eycken v, E, Haustermans K, Buntinx F, Ceuppens A, Weyler JJ, et al. (2000) Evaluation of the encryption procedure and record linkage in the Belgian National Cancer Registry. Archives of public health 58: 281–294.

43. Inan A, Kantarcioglu M, Bertino E, Scannapieco M (2008) A Hybrid Approach to Private Record Linkage. In: Proceedings of the 2008 IEEE 24th International Conference on Data Engineering. Washington: IEEE Computer Society. 496–505.

44. O'Keefe C, Yung M, Gu L, Baxter R (2004) Privacy-preserving data linkage protocols. In: Proceedings of the 2004 ACM workshop on Privacy in the electronic society. New York: ACM. 94–102.

45. He X, Lu H, Vaidya J, Adam N (2011) Secure Construction and Publication of Contingency Tables from Distributed Data. Journal of Computer Security 19: 453–484.

46. Karakasidis A, Verykios V (2009) Privacy preserving record linkage using phonetic codes. In: Proceedings of the 2009 Fourth Balkan Conference in Informatics. Washington: IEEE Computer Society. 101–106.

47. Inan A, Kaya S, Saygin Y, Savacs E, Hintoglu A, et al. (2007) Privacy preserving clustering on horizontally partitioned data. Data and Knowledge Engineering 63: 646–666.

48. Al-Lawati A, Lee D, McDaniel P (2005) Blocking-aware private record linkage. In: Proceedings of the 2nd international workshop on Information quality in Information Systems. New York: ACM. 59–68.

49. Ford D, Jones K, Verplancke J-P, Lyons R, John G, et al. (2009) The SAIL databank: Building a national architecture for e-health research and evaluation. BMC Health Services Research 9: 157.

50. Lyons R, Jones K, John G, Brooks C, Verplancke J-P, et al. (2009) The SAIL databank: Linking multiple health and social care datasets. BMC Medical Informatics and Decision Making 9: 3.

51. Ainsworth J, Crowther P, Buchan I (2009) Federating health systems to enable population level research. In: 22nd IEEE International Symposium on Computer-Based Medical Systems. Washington: IEEE Computer Society. 1–4.

52. Schadow G, Grannis S, McDonald C (2002) Privacy preserving distributed queries for a clinical case research network. Proceedings of the IEEE international conference on Privacy, security and data mining 14: 55–65.

53. Schnell R, Bachteler T, Reiher J (2009) Privacy-preserving record linkage using Bloom filters. BMC Medical Informatics and Decision Making 9: 41.

54. Durham E-A, Xue Y, Kantarcioglu M, Malin B (2010) Private Medical Record Linkage with Approximate Matching. AMIA Annual Symposium Proceedings 2010: 182–186.

55. Lindell Y, Pinkas B (2000) Privacy Preserving Data Mining. The 20th Annual International Cryptology Conference (CRYPTO). Santa Barbara, CA, USA. 36–54.

56. Agrawal R, Srikant R (2000) Privacy-Preserving Data Mining. The ACM Special Interest Group on Management of Data Conference (SIGMOD). Dallas, TX, USA. 439–450.

57. El Emam K, Hu J, Mercer J, Peyton L, Kantarcioglu M, et al. (2011) A Secure Protocol for Protecting the Identity of Providers When Disclosing Data for Disease Surveillance. Journal of the American Medical Informatics Association 18: 212–217.

58. Paillier P (1999) Public-key cryptosystems based on composite degree residuosity classes. In: Proceedings of the 17th international conference on Theory and application of cryptographic techniques. Berlin: Springer-Verlag. 223–238.

59. Samet S, Miri A (2009) Privacy-Preserving Bayesian Network for Horizontally Partitioned Data. The 2009 IEEE International Conference on Information Privacy, Security, Risk and Trust (PASSAT2009). Vancouver, Canada. 9–16.

60. Oechslin P (2003) Making a Faster Cryptanalytic Time-Memory Trade-Off. CRYPTO 2729: 617–630.

61. Department of Health and Human Services (2004) Guidance on Research Involving Coded Private Information or Biological Specimens.

62. Department of Health and Human Services (2008) OHRP - Guidance on Research Involving Coded Private Information or Biological Specimens.

63. Rothstein M (2010) Is Deidentification Sufficient to Protect Health Privacy in Research? American Journal of Bioethics 10: 3–11.

64. Rothstein M (2005) Research privacy under HIPAA and the common rule. Journal of Law, Medicine & Ethics 33: 154–159.

65. National Institutes of Health (2005) Health Services Research and the HIPAA Privacy Rule.

66. Otis D, Burnham K, White G, Anderson D (1978) Statistical Inference from Capture Data on Closed Animal Populations. Wildlife Monographs 62. 1–135.
67. White G, Anderson D, Burnham K, Otis D (1982) Capture-Recapture and Removal Methods for Sampling Closed Populations. Los Alamos National Laboratory. LA-8787-NERP LA-8787-NERP.
68. Chandra Sekar C, Edwards Deming W (1949) On a Method of Estimating Birth and Death Rates and the Extent of Registration. Journal of the American Statistical Association 44: 101–115.
69. Greenfield C (1975) On the Estimation of a Missing Cell in a 2×2 Contingency Table. Journal of the Royal Statistical Society, Series A 138: 51–61.

70. Hook E, Regal R (1995) Capture recapture methods in epidemiology, Methods and limitations. Epidemiologic Reviews 17; 243–264.
71. Medeiros L, Rosa D, da Rosa M, Bozzetti M, Zanini R (2009) Efficacy of human papillomavirus Vaccines: A systematic review. International Journal of Gynecological Cancer 19: 1166–1176.
72. Dillner J, Arbyn M, Unger E, Dillner L (2010) Monitoring of human papillomavirus vaccination. Clinical and Experimental Immunology 163: 17–25.
73. Chang Y, Brewer N, Rinas A, Schmitt K, Smith J (2009) Evaluating the impact of human papillomavirus vaccines. Vaccine 27: 4355–4362.

13

A Watermarking Scheme for High Efficiency Video Coding (HEVC)

Salahuddin Swati[1], Khizar Hayat[1,2]*, Zafar Shahid[1]

1 COMSATS Institute of Information Technology, Abbottabad, Pakistan, **2** College of Arts and Sciences, University of Nizwa, Nizwa, Oman

Abstract

This paper presents a high payload watermarking scheme for High Efficiency Video Coding (HEVC). HEVC is an emerging video compression standard that provides better compression performance as compared to its predecessor, i.e. H.264/AVC. Considering that HEVC may will be used in a variety of applications in the future, the proposed algorithm has a high potential of utilization in applications involving broadcast and hiding of metadata. The watermark is embedded into the Quantized Transform Coefficients (QTCs) during the encoding process. Later, during the decoding process, the embedded message can be detected and extracted completely. The experimental results show that the proposed algorithm does not significantly affect the video quality, nor does it escalate the bitrate.

Editor: Francesco Pappalardo, University of Catania, Italy

Funding: The authors have no support or funding to report.

Competing Interests: The authors have declared that no competing interests exist.

* Email: khizarhayat@ciit.net.pk

Introduction

High Efficiency Video Coding (HEVC) is a relatively new video compression standard, developed by the Joint Collaborative Team on Video Coding (JCT-VC), from ITU-T VCEG and ISO/IEC MPEG [1]. The main goals of HEVC design include increased video resolutions and the exploitation of parallel processing architectures [2]. HEVC is suited for a variety of applications, such as broadcast of high definition (HD) TV signals over satellite, terrestrial transmission systems and cables, video content acquisition and editing systems, security applications, camcorders, Blue-ray discs, Internet and mobile network video and real-time conversational applications that include video conferencing, video chat, and tele-presence systems [3]. One of the downside, of the ever-growing nature of Internet and multimedia technologies, is the high risk associated with the ease of manipulation, tampering and illegal copying of the digital contents, especially the multimedia. The security of digital contents, therefore, constitutes a quintessential aspect of copyright protection in today's multi-media related industries. For this very reason, the integrity, verification and authentication of digital videos form an active research area today [4]. Of special interest is the field of digital watermarking wherein the owner's/consumer's watermark is digitally embedded in the digital content, for protection against unauthorized copying as well as the ownership declaration and contents authorization [5,6].

Digital watermarking of HEVC encoded videos may be a difficult task, because the codec eliminates most of the redundancy that the watermarking process may exploit. Casual embedding of a watermark, thus, may escalate the final video file size or otherwise affect the quality of the video; a carefully conceived embedding strategy is thus needed. Keeping these in view, we intend to propose an HEVC watermarking scheme that would have negligible effect on both the video quality and the final file size.

Our strategy is to embed a watermark, during the encoding process, that can be completely extractable during the decoding process. Normally, a watermark may either be embedded in the spatial domain or the frequency domain. With spatial domain video watermarking, the hidden data may be lost during the quantization step of the underlying video codec. One solution to this problem is to embed the watermark in such a way that it survives the quantization loss. But this may come at the cost of lower imperceptibility. A better solution is to go for the frequency domain and better embed the watermark after the quantization step, i.e. in the quantized transform coefficients (QTCs). In our approach, we adopt this later approach and embed the watermark message in the selected non-zero QTCs of all the frames of the video.

The rest of the paper is organized as follows. For a better comprehension of this article, the first part of Section outlines a brief overview of the state of the art HEVC standard. The second part of the same section provides a brief literature review regarding the watermarking techniques proposed for various video coding standards, in vogue. The proposed watermarking algorithm is outlined in Section 0.2.2, wherein both the embedding and detection processes are described. Section 0.2.2 analyses the experimental results, followed by the concluding remarks in Section 0.2.2.

Previous Work

0.1 An Overview of HEVC

Like its recent predecessors, HEVC is also a hybrid video compression standard based on the Intra/Inter Prediction and a 2D transform. It is an effort to improve upon the existing tools used in H.264. Besides, many new coding tools have been introduced in the HEVC; the most important change being its frame partitioning. Figure 1 illustrates a block diagram of the

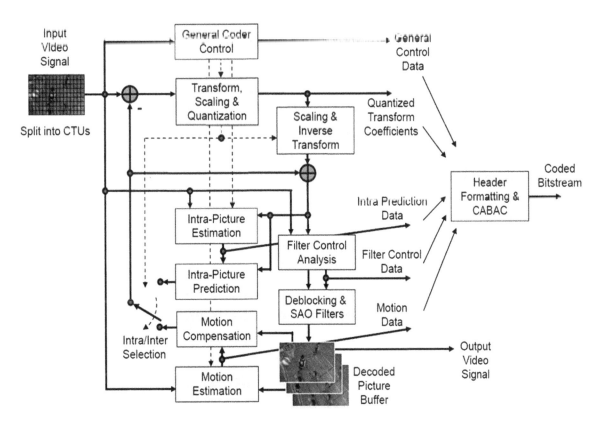

Figure 1. Block Diagram of HEVC [2].

HEVC encoding process. Following are the salient features of HEVC:

1. HEVC introduces the three new concepts of Coding Unit (CU), Prediction Unit (PU) and Transform Unit (TU).

2. The coding pipeline splits each frame into what are called Coding Tree Units (CTU). A CTU has one Coding Tree Block (CTB) covering a $L \times L$ luma block and the corresponding $L/2 \times L/2$ chroma blocks. The size of luma, L, may refer to 64, 32 or 16 samples.

3. A CTB can be partitioned into smaller blocks using a Quad Tree structure. A given CU is a part of CTB and can be divided recursively into 4 CUs and each has an associated division into Prediction Unit (PU) and Transform Unit(TU).

4. PU is created when a prediction method is chosen. The information of the prediction method (Intra/Inter and the related data) is contained in the PU.

5. The Prediction Block can be split using a sampling scheme that may range 64×64 to 4×4 samples.

6. For the intra-prediction in HEVC, 33 angular directions are used.

7. The PU can be sub divided into 2 rectangular or 4 square partitions, in the inter-prediction. For motion compensation, the PU division may be unidirectional or bi-directional.

8. HEVC uses transform coding of the prediction residual in the similar way as its predecessor H.264/AVC. The residual block is split into smaller square transform blocks (TBs).

9. The transform is an approximation of DCT its block sizes can be 32×32, 16×16, 8×8 and 4×4.

10. HEVC also has mode dependent alternative transform. An alternative integer transform derived from discrete sine transform (DST) is applied on each TB of size 4×4. The DST is only applied on luma transform blocks.

11. Transform coefficients in the encoder side are quantized to limit the number of bits. At the start, the quantization level is defined by a quantization parameter (QP) value that controls the uniform-reconstruction quantization (URQ) scheme. To further decrease the bitrate, the QTCs are entropy coded.

12. Only one entropy coding is specified in the HEVC, i.e. the context adaptive binary arithmetic coding (CABAC). The CABAC is used to encode the first coefficients (levels), Golomb-Rice coding to code the next and Exponential-Golomb coding is employed for encoding the last levels.

13. The degradation of frames, which is caused by compression, is restored by applying three kinds of filters namely the sample adaptive offset (SAO), de-blocking and adaptive loop filters (ALF).

14. A new video parameter set (VPS) is also introduced in HEVC.

15. To increase the parallel processing capability, HEVC introduces three new features other than the slices, such as tiles, wavefront parallel processing (WPP) and dependent slices.

It is pertinent to note that H.264 concepts, like the high level syntax and the Network Abstraction layer (NAL), are being retained in HEVC.

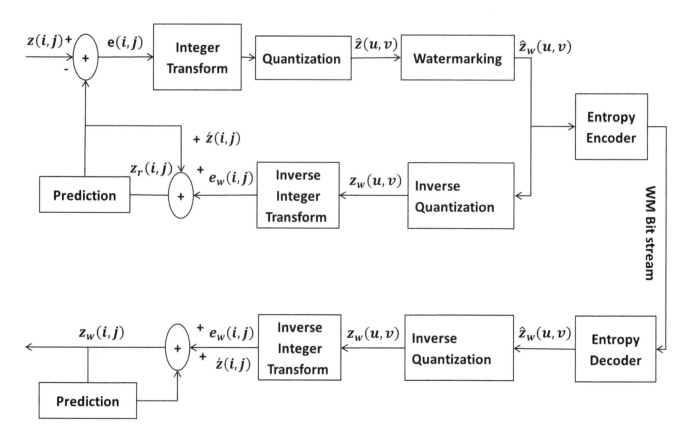

Figure 2. The Proposed Watermarking scheme for HEVC.

0.2 Related literature

While being still in its rudimentary phase, efforts regarding the watermarking of HEVC videos are scarce. The literature is, however, replete with algorithms regarding the watermarking of videos based on H.264 and other coding standards. With H.264, the watermarks are normally embedded into the DCT coefficient from the I- and P-frames [7–13]. Still, there are many methods that rely on the motion vectors (MVs) - rather than the DCT coefficients - for embedding in the compressed video domains and are usually classified as MV-based watermarking schemes [10,14–19]. The embedded watermark may either be detected/extracted from partially decoded video [7,10–12] or from completely decoded video [8,9].

0.2.1 DCT based methods. Zhang et al. [7] propose a robust scheme for H.264/AVC based on the spread spectrum watermarking. In this scheme a 2D-8 bit watermark message (logo) is converted into a binary sequence, and then the watermark message is embedded into the middle frequencies, i.e. the diagonal portion of the corresponding 4X4 DCT block. In another robust method, by Noorkami et al. [8], the watermark is embedded in the QTCs of I-frames. This method requires entropy decoding for embedding the watermark. For handling the visual degradation, the method looks into the human visual model. While using a key dependent algorithm, the message is embedded in a selected subset of the coefficients with reasonable visual watermarking capacity. In [9], the watermarking involves the nonzero quantized AC residuals in the P-frames. The authors have shown that the visual quality of video is not compromised even if all the non-zero

Table 1. Watermark embedding Algorithm.

	Input: QTC $\hat{Z}(i,j)$ and Watermark bit M_b
	Output: Watermarked QTC, $\hat{Z}_w(i,j)$
1.	begin
2.	if $\hat{Z}(i,j) > 1$
3.	then
4.	set $\hat{Z}_w(i,j) \leftarrow (\hat{Z}(i,j) - \hat{Z}(i,j) \bmod 2) + M_b$
5.	replace $\hat{Z}(i,j)$ by $\hat{Z}_w(i,j)$
6.	end if
7.	end

Table 2. Watermark Extraction Algorithm.

	Input: Watermarked QTC, $\hat{Z}_w(i,j)$
	Output: Watermark bit M_b
1.	begin
2.	if $\hat{Z}(i,j) > 1$
3.	then
4.	set $M_b \leftarrow \hat{Z}_w(i,j) \bmod 2$
5.	end if
6.	end

Table 3. Sample video sequences used to evaluate the performance of proposed watermarking scheme.

Videos	Resolution	FPS
PeopleOnStreet	2560 × 1600	30
ParkScene	1920 × 1080	30
Chinaspeed	1024 × 768	30
Vidyo1	1280 × 720	60
BQMall	832 × 480	30–60
RaceHorses	416 × 240	30–60

quantized AC residuals are used to embed the watermark. This scheme may, however, affect the performance of the context adoptive variable length coding (CAVLC), which may in turn increase the bit-rate, due to the presence of many non-zero quantized AC residuals with the value of 1; CAVLC encodes the trailing ones (T1s) separately. In a related method [20] the watermark is embedded in the sign bit of the T1s in CAVLC. The advantage of this technique is that it does not increase the bitrate. The main disadvantage of these schemes is that their payload is very low. Besides, these are not robust to re-encoding with different parameters. The blind scheme of [12] embeds the watermark into the syntactic elements of H.264 compressed bitstream in order to avoid full decoding during both the embedding and extraction. The scheme exploits the 4×4 intra prediction submacroblocks of Luma components from the I-frames. The H.264/AVC fingerprinting technique, in [13], employs the Tardos fingerprinting codes [21] for the underlying spread spectrum robust embedding technique. In [22], a combined watermarking and encryption scheme is presented for H.264/AVC and HEVC. In this scheme, an end to end commutative security system for video distribution is proposed. The authors have investigated the trade off between robust watermarking, encryption scheme security and transcoding possibilities. The watermark is embedded into the DCT coefficient using the quantization index modulation system.

The MPEG-2/4 based Watermarking methods, from the literature, also rely on the DCT coefficients [23–26]. One such method [23] embeds the watermark into the DCT coefficients of the compressed video stream, whereas the watermark detection is performed using the uncompressed video. In one blind scheme [25], the watermark message is embedded in the bit-stream of MPEG-2 without affecting the bit-rate. In [24], the message is embedded into the video by pseudorandomly selecting the macroblocks (MBs) from every luminance block. It selects MBs and QTC pairs, to be modified, and then computes a frequency mask for each selected MB. This is followed by the use of this mask to weigh the watermark amplitude and then modify the selected

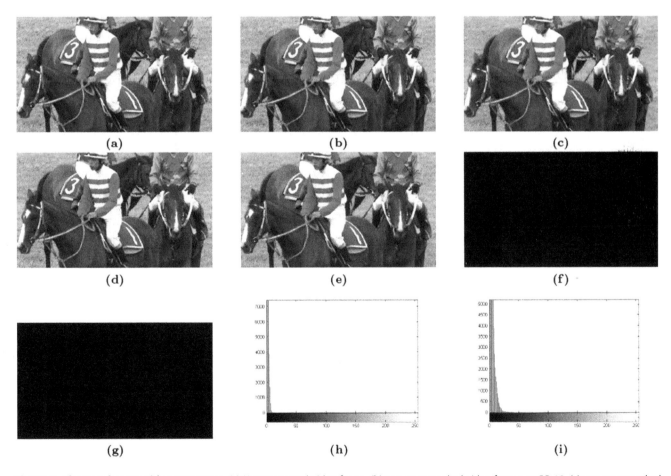

Figure 3. The Racehorses video sequence. (a) Uncompressed video frame, (b) non-watermarked video frames at QP 18, (c) non-watermarked video frames at QP 32, (d) watermarked video frames at QP 18, (e) watermarked video frames at QP 32, (f) the QP 18 difference image (b – d), (g) the QP 32 difference image (c – e), (h) histogram QP 18 difference image (f), and (i) histogram of QP 32 difference image (g).

Table 4. Comparison of PSNR at QP 18 and 32 for watermarked and original video sequences.

QP	Sequences	Y-PSNR		U-PSNR		V-PSNR	
		WM	Orig.	WM	Orig.	WM	Orig.
18	People on Street	45.20	46.28	47.31	47.62	46.93	47.15
	Parkscene	44.02	44.86	45.01	45.68	46.17	46.69
	Chinaspeed	46.26	48.33	47.71	49.38	47.61	49.59
	Vidyo1	46.32	46.81	48.64	48.79	49.41	49.59
	BQmall	43.34	44.87	45.33	45.80	46.51	47.03
	Racehorses	43.42	45.69	44.41	46.06	44.50	46.35
32	People on Street	36.66	36.94	41.37	41.51	41.90	42.02
	Parkscene	35.93	36.06	38.97	39.11	40.28	40.35
	Chinaspeed	36.87	37.87	40.63	41.03	40.05	40.88
	Vidyo1	39.58	39.80	43.89	44.02	44.40	44.57
	BQmall	35.14	35.43	39.20	39.34	40.06	40.15
	Racehorses	34.10	34.39	37.34	37.59	37.64	38.00

middle frequency QTCs to carry the watermark information. The differential energy watermarking (DEW) algorithm [26] is based on the selective discard of high frequency DCT coefficients in the compressed data stream. This real-time method encodes the label bits in the pattern of energy difference between the DCT blocks. The message is embedded bit by bit in a set of an 8×8 DCT blocks from the I-frames of the MPEG compressed video stream.

0.2.2 Motion vector based methods. In MV based watermarking schemes, the watermark is embedded either directly in the video bitstream [14–16,19] or during the video encoding process [10,17,18]. The watermark is usually extracted from partly decoded video. A method, for H.264 video streams [14], hides the copyright information in proper motion vector (MV) component that considers the movement direction in the underlying video. An adaptive threshold, used to select the required MVs, determines the number of bits to be embedded. In [15], the message bits are embedded in the two least significant bit (LSBs) of the larger component from the MVs of H.264 video. The payload of this scheme is very low, however. The technique of [16], for MPEG, hides the copyright information in larger magnitude MVs, especially those with low phase angle change. The scheme is fragile having limited payload. In [17], first the luminance component of P frame is divided into low-texture and high-texture area and then MVs are modified according to the texture of the area. The prediction errors of the matched blocks are calculated again according to the changed MVs. Finally, the new MVs along with new predicted errors are encoded. In one Audio Video Coding Standard (AVS) oriented method, the message embedding is performed by altering the resolution of MVs, from the partition blocks in different MB partitions, during the inter-prediction stage of AVS. The modulation is based on the mapping rules between MV resolution and message bits. The water scrambling scheme of [19] is based on the MPEG compression scheme wherein the MVs are extracted in two ways. In the first, the MVs are extracted from MPEG bitstream using a syntactic analyzer while, in the second, the MVs are directly modified during the MPEG compression.

Beside the DCT based and MV-based strategies, there are approaches, like [27], which embed watermark in H.264 by using the intra-prediction. It is a stream replacement scheme for video watermarking. and changes the H.264 encoded bitstream for watermarking. All such schemes notwithstanding, references regarding the HEVC watermarking are almost non-existent in the literature, mainly due to its early stages of development.

The Proposed Watermarking Scheme for HEVC

The proposed algorithm targets mainly the imperceptibility of the cover and it can be employed in applications where robustness is of secondary importance, e.g. broadcasting and hiding some sort of metadata. For embedding, we are relying on the LSB modification of the QTCs from the HEVC coding pipeline. The watermark is embedded in the coefficients whose values agree to a certain predefined threshold. The value of the threshold is selected on the basis of the size of the watermark, in bits. Figure 2 outlines the proposed watermarking scheme for HEVC. We consider the following points while embedding the message in LSB of QTCs:

- To avoid any significant escalation in the compression efficiency, only the non-zero QTCs are being considered for embedding - otherwise, many zero magnitude coefficient may become non-zero in the embedding process, thereby affecting the zero runlengths.

Table 5. Comparison of Payload and Bitrates at QP 18 and 32 for all video sequences.

Sequences	Payload Kbits/Frame		Frame Size (Kbytes)			
	QP 18	QP 32	QP 18		QP 32	
			WM	Orig.	WM	Orig.
People on Street	327.30	38.84	176.03	163.98	37.72	36.60
Parkscene	204.55	15.47	93.58	88.57	15.51	14.89
Chinaspeed	85.32	17.17	30.72	29.29	10.72	10.29
Vidyo1	28.75	3.51	21.45	19.90	4.05	3.91
BQmall	49.81	5.16	49.20	46.91	11.48	11.11
Racehorses	20.07	1.75	7.65	7.12	2.00	1.92

- The message is embedded should be completely extractable on the decoder side.

The proposed algorithm modifies the LSB of the selected QTCs and embeds one of the watermark bit (M_b) in each QTC. The selection criteria for QTC is based on a threshold value of 1; if the absolute value of QTC is superior to this threshold then a watermark bit is embedded in its LSB, as demonstrated by the algorithm illustrated in Table 1. The watermark embedding function $f()$ has thus two inputs, 1) a subset of QTCs ($\hat{Z}(i,j)$) and 2) the watermark message (M) composed of bits M_b. The watermarked QTCs are denoted by $\hat{Z}_w(i,j)$ and are given by Eq. 4.

$$\hat{Z}_w(i,j) - f(\hat{Z}(i,j), M_b) \qquad (1)$$

The decoding function, $h()$, is blind and needs only the watermarked QTCs - $\hat{Z}_w(i,j)$ - in order to extract the watermark bits M_b as shown in Eq. 2.

$$M_b = h(\hat{Z}_w(i,j)) \qquad (2)$$

The extraction of watermarked bit is illustrated by the algorithm of Table 2.

Experimental Results

The proposed watermarking algorithm had been applied to benchmark video sequences of various resolutions. These video sequences are listed in Table 3, along with their resolutions and frames per second (FPS). The evaluation was based on a sample of 100 frames from each video and involved QP values of 18 and 32 [28].

The presence non-zero coefficients, corresponding to a given frame, is usually attributed to the texture and edges. Being spatial masking parts in the frame, these areas are good candidates for the watermark embedding as far as the conservation of the compression ratio is concerned. The downside, however, may be the ensued negative impact on imperceptibility; In our case, this effect is minimized due to LSB embedding. Peak Signal to Noise Ratio (PSNR) measure has been used to analyze the quality of watermarked video with respect to original video which is given by:

$$PSNR = 10log_{10}\left(\frac{255^2}{MSE}\right) \qquad (3)$$

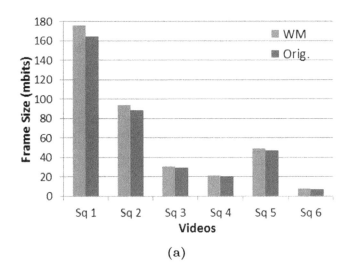

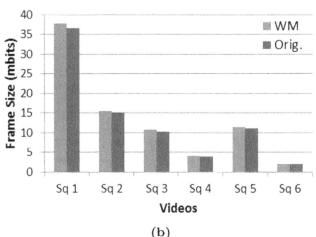

(a)   (b)

Figure 4. Comparison of Bitrates for watermarked and original video sequences. (a) QP 18 and (b) QP 32.

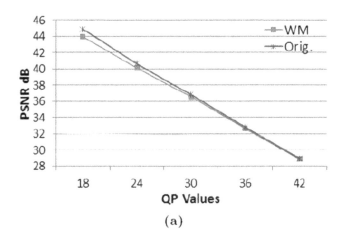

(a)

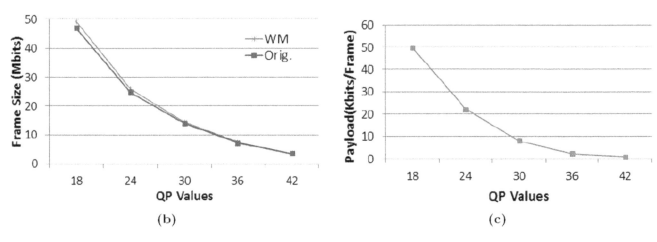

(b)   (c)

Figure 5. Comparison at whole range of QP for BQMall sequence. (a) PSNR, (b) Frame size and (c) Payload.

Where mean square error (MSE) is a measure used to quantify the difference between the initial video frame I and the distorted video frame I'. If the video frame has a size of M x N then:

$$MSE = \frac{1}{MN} \sum_{i=0}^{M-1} \sum_{j=0}^{N-1} (I(i,j) - I'(i,j)) \qquad (4)$$

Table 6. Comparison of PSNR, Frame Size and Payload at different range of QP for watermarked and original BQMall video sequence.

QP	PSNR dB		Frame Size Kbytes		Palyload
	WM	Orig.	WM	Orig.	Kbits/frame
18	43.34	44.87	49.20	46.91	49.81
24	40.13	40.66	25.91	24.71	22.09
30	36.36	36.80	14.36	13.81	7.86
36	32.62	32.76	7.35	7.16	2.26
42	28.91	28.96	3.49	3.41	0.71

Table 4 lists the PSNRs of the HEVC coded Y, U and V components at the two QP values with respect to the corresponding original components. PSNRs of the coded components with watermark (WM) and without watermark (Orig.) are given, for the sake of comparison. It can be readily observed that there is not much of the effect on the quality and the maximum we observe is a degradation of 2.27 dB in case of the luma component of RaceHorses at QP 32; the PSNR of 43.42 dB is still not bad par rapport the original 45.69 dB. Figure 3 shows the visual quality of the selected frames of Racehorse video sequence wherein the part (a) shows the uncompressed video, while parts (b) and (c) illustrate the compressed videos at QP 18 and QP 32, respectively. The images in Figure 3.(d) and (e) are the watermarked versions of Figure 3.(b) and (c), respectively. The excellent imperceptibility offered by our method can be gauged by observing parts (f) to (i) of Figure 3. The first two parts are the difference images, which are almost totally black, i.e. the absolute difference between the corresponding pixels are very close to zero; a fact more effectively observed in the histograms given in the last two parts. Note that the histogram par rapport the QP 32 is more drawn out or dilated, because of the fewer coefficients to modify. Still, the escalation is not enough to compromise the visual quality and the PSNR is still high. The imperceptibility aspect is understandable in the face of the fact that the embedding strategy is LSB based. It can be observed from Table 4 that at QP 18 the average decrease in PSNR, over all video sequences, is around 1.03 dB as against 0.28 dB average decrease at QP 32. As far as effect of QP value on the PSNR is concerned, it can be attributed to the fact that, at smaller QP values, the PSNR is generally high due to the presence a greater number of QTCs suitable for watermarking. With higher QP (read 32) values, however, the PSNR decrease is smaller because of the presence of lesser number of coefficients agreeing to the threshold.

When it comes to payload, it will be higher for lower QP values, for obvious reasons. Table 5 confirms that and one can see that at QP 18, the payload is high as we have large number of coefficients agreeing to the threshold and hence a larger number of watermark bits can be embedded. The corresponding payload decreases manifold at QP 32 but there may still be enough number of coefficients in which watermark bits can be embedded.

The frame size escalation is high at lower QP values, as illustrated in Table 5 that shows the frame size comparison at QP 18 and 32 for the video sequences. The average frame size increase is 6.6% for QP 18 as against 3.9% for QP 32. To be more elaborate, Figure 4 illustrates the change in frame size at QP 18 and 32 for varios video sequences. The reason for the increase in bitrate is that the watermarked coefficients are used for reconstruction through the prediction of future block which increase the energy in the residuals thereby escalating the bitrate.

Table 6 sums up the overall analyses on PSNR, frame size and Payload in the case of BQMall sequence on the basis of a range of QP values. The ensued trends, illustrated in the form of graphs in Figure 5, establish the following facts:

1. Generally, the PSNR decreases with any increase in the QP value, for both original and watermarked videos. For the video in hand the decreasing function is a straight line. Both the watermarked and un-watermarked video behave the same but, at low QP values, their PSNRs are significantly different from each other; still the watermarked video quality is good.

2. The bitrate escalation is not that significant, as it is already an exponential function of the QP value and the watermark is embedded in the LSBs. The escalation at low QP values is more marked, however.

3. The payload decreases exponentially with respect to an increase in QP value. The lower the QP value, higher will be the payload.

Conclusion

We proposed a high payload watermarking algorithm for the emerging video coding standard HEVC. For the sake of imperceptibility, the watermark is embedded into the LSBs of selected non-zero coefficients from the QTC domain. The results show that the proposed scheme has the advantages of imperceptibility, bitrate conservation and high payload. These advantages are, however, highly sensitive to the QP value. The escalations are, however, somewhat marked only when the QP value is low. In future, the robustness of the method needs to be improved and a spread spectrum strategy would be explored for embedding.

Author Contributions

Conceived and designed the experiments: KH ZS. Performed the experiments: SS. Analyzed the data: SS KH ZS. Wrote the paper: SS KH ZS.

References

1. Bross B, Han W, Sullivan GJ, Ohm J, Wiegand T (2012) High efficiency video coding (HEVC) text specification draft 8 document JCTVC-J1003. ITU-T/ISO/IEC Joint Collaborative Team on Video Coding (JCT-VC).
2. Sullivan G, Ohm J, Han W, Wiegand T (2012) Overview of the high efficiency video coding (HEVC) standard. IEEE Transactions on Circuits and Systems for Video Technology 22: 1649–1668.
3. Ayele EA, Dhok SB (2012) Review of proposed high efficiency video coding (HEVC) standard. International Journal of Computer Applications 59: 1–9.
4. Xu D, Wang R, Wang J (2011) A novel watermarking scheme for H.264/AVC video authentication. Signal Processing: Image Communication 26: 267–279.
5. Deshpande N, Archana MR, Manthalkar R (2010) Review of robust video watermarking algorithms. CoRR abs/1004.1770.
6. Cox I, Miller M, Bloom J (2001) Digital watermarking: Principles and practice. Morgan Kaufmann.
7. Zhang J, Ho A, Qiu G, Marziliano P (2007) Robust video watermarking of H.264/AVC. IEEE Transactions on Circuits and Systems II 54: 205–209.
8. Noorkami M, Russell, Mersereau M (2007) A framework for robust watermarking of H.264-encoded video with controllable detection performance. IEEE Transactions on Information Forensics and Security 2: 14–23.
9. Noorkami M, Mersereau R (2008) Digital video watermarking in P-frames with controlled video bit-rate increase. IEEE Transactions on Information Forensics and Security 3: 441–455.
10. Qiu G, Marziliano P, Ho A, He D, Sun Q (2004) A hybrid watermarking scheme for H.264/AVC video. In: Proceedings of the International Conference of Pattern Recognition. volume 4, pp. 865–868. doi:10.1109/ICPR.2004.1333909
11. Shahid Z, Chaumont M, Puech W (2011) Considering the reconstruction loop for data hiding of intra and inter frames of H.264/AVC. Signal, Image and Video Processing 5.
12. Mansouri A, Aznaveh A, Torkamani-Azar F, Kurugollu F (2010) A low complexity video water-marking in H.264 compressed domain. IEEE Transactions on Information Forensics and Security 5: 649–657.
13. Shahid Z, Chaumont M, Puech W (2010) Spread spectrum-based watermarking for tardos code-based fingerprinting for H.264/AVC video. In: IEEE International Conference on Image Processing. pp. 2105–2108. doi:10.1109/ICIP.2010.5652607
14. Mohaghegh N, Fatemi O (2008) H.264 copyright protection with motion vector watermarking. In: Proceedings of the International Conference on Audio, Language and Image Processing. pp. 1384–1389. doi:10.1109/ICALIP.2008.4590217
15. Nguyen C, Tay D, Deng G (2006) A fast watermarking system for H.264/AVC video. In: IEEE Asia Pacific Conference on Circuits and Systems. pp. 81–84. doi:10.1109/APCCAS.2006.342301
16. Zhang J, Li J, Zhang L (2001) Video watermark technique in motion vector. In: Proceedings of the Brazilian Symposium on Computer Graphics and Image Processing. pp. 179–182. doi:10.1109/SIBGRAPI.2001.963053
17. Liu Z, Liang H, Niu X, Yang Y (2004) A robust video watermarking in motion vectors. In: Proceedings of the International Conference on Signal Processing. volume 3, pp. 2358–2361. doi:10.1109/ICOSP.2004.1442254
18. Song X, Su Y, Liu Y, Ji Z (2008) A video watermarking scheme for AVS based on motion vectors. In: Proceedings of the IEEE International Conference on Communication Technology. pp. 738–741. doi:10.1109/ICCT.2008.4716228
19. Bodo Y, Laurent N, Laurent C, Dugelay J (2004) Video waterscrambling: Towards a video protection scheme based on the disturbance of motion vectors. EURASIP J Appl Signal Process 20: 2224 2237.
20. Kim S, Kim S, Hongo Y, Won C (2007) Data hiding on H.264/AVC compressed video. In: Kamel M, Campilho A, editors, Image Analysis and Recognition, Springer Berlin Heidelberg, volume 4633 of Lecture Notes in Computer Science. pp. 698–707.
21. Tardos G (2003) Optimal probabilistic fingerprint codes. In: Proc. 35th Annual ACM Symposium on Theory of Computing (STOC'03), June 9–11, 2003, San Diego, CA, USA. ACM, pp. 116–125.
22. Boho A, Van Wallendael G, Dooms A, De Cock J, Braeckman G, et al. (2013) End-to-end security for video distribution: The combination of encryption, watermarking, and video adaptation. Signal Processing Magazine, IEEE 30: 97–107.
23. Alattar A, Lin E, Celik M (2003) Digital watermarking of low bit-rate advanced simple profile MPEG-4 compressed video. IEEE Transactions on Circuits and Systems for Video Technology 13: 787–800.
24. Barni M, Bartolini F, Checcacci N (2005) Watermarking of MPEG-4 video objects. IEEE Transactions on Multimedia 7: 23–32.
25. Hartung F, Girod B (1998) Watermarking of uncompressed and compressed video. Signal Processing 66: 283–301.
26. Langelaar G, Lagendijk R (2001) Optimal differential energy watermarking of DCT encoded images and video. IEEE Transactions on Image Processing 10: 148–158.
27. Zou D, Jeffrey A, Bloom J (2008) H.264/AVC stream replacement technique for video watermarking. IEEE International Conference on Acoustics, Speech, and Signal Processing, Caesars Palace, Las Vegas, Nevada, USA: 1749 752.
28. Available: ftp://hvc:US88Hula@ftp.tnt.uni-hannover.de/testsequences.

14

Genetic Classification of Populations Using Supervised Learning

Michael Bridges[1], Elizabeth A. Heron[2], Colm O'Dushlaine[2], Ricardo Segurado[2], The International Schizophrenia Consortium (ISC)[¶], Derek Morris[2], Aiden Corvin[2], Michael Gill[2], Carlos Pinto[2]*

1 Astrophysics Group, Cavendish Laboratory, Cambridge, United Kingdom, 2 Neuropsychiatric Genetics Research Group, Department of Psychiatry, Trinity College, Dublin, Ireland

Abstract

There are many instances in genetics in which we wish to determine whether two candidate populations are distinguishable on the basis of their genetic structure. Examples include populations which are geographically separated, case–control studies and quality control (when participants in a study have been genotyped at different laboratories). This latter application is of particular importance in the era of large scale genome wide association studies, when collections of individuals genotyped at different locations are being merged to provide increased power. The traditional method for detecting structure within a population is some form of exploratory technique such as principal components analysis. Such methods, which do not utilise our prior knowledge of the membership of the candidate populations. are termed *unsupervised*. Supervised methods, on the other hand are able to utilise this prior knowledge when it is available. In this paper we demonstrate that in such cases modern supervised approaches are a more appropriate tool for detecting genetic differences between populations. We apply two such methods, (neural networks and support vector machines) to the classification of three populations (two from Scotland and one from Bulgaria). The sensitivity exhibited by both these methods is considerably higher than that attained by principal components analysis and in fact comfortably exceeds a recently conjectured theoretical limit on the sensitivity of unsupervised methods. In particular, our methods can distinguish between the two Scottish populations, where principal components analysis cannot. We suggest, on the basis of our results that a supervised learning approach should be the method of choice when classifying individuals into pre-defined populations, particularly in quality control for large scale genome wide association studies.

Editor: Daniel J. Kliebenstein, University of California, United States of America

Funding: This project has not been directly funded by any agency. The authors employed on research contracts are supported by the Wellcome Trust (http://www.wellcome.ac.uk), Science Foundation Ireland (http://www.sfi.ie), and the UK Science and Technology Research Council (http://www.stfc.ac.uk). The funders had no role in study design, data collection and analysis, decision to publish or preparation of the manuscript.

Competing Interests: The authors have declared that no competing interests exist.

* E-mail: capinto@tcd.ie

¶ Membership of the International Schizophrenia Consortium is provided in the Acknowledgments.

Introduction

The advent of the new large-scale genotyping and sequencing technologies has resulted in unprecedented quantities of data becoming available to the genetics community. Geneticists are now confronted with new and challenging problems in data analysis and interpretation, and novel approaches and techniques will be required to fully exploit these new resources. In view of the fact that other scientific fields have already gone through a similar process of development, it is likely that cross-disciplinary collaborations in data analysis will yield fruitful results in genetics. This paper represents such a collaboration.

We apply machine learning techniques previously used in cosmology to the problem of genetic classification. Such techniques involve the use of automated algorithms to mimic the learning capabilities of animal brains. They have proved extremely useful in the analysis of complex data in many scientific disciplines. There are two basic approaches – *supervised* learning, where the data is pre-classified according to some hypothesis and *unsupervised* learning where the data is unclassified (usually, but not always, because the potential classes are *a priori* unknown). Genetics has, to date, relied mainly on unsupervised methods, such as principal components analysis (PCA), to classify individuals on the basis of their genetic data.

PCA is a standard tool in population genetics, and has been used, for example in a study of 23 European populations [1] and more recently of 25 Indian populations [2]. It is also commonly used in quality control in genetic studies. For example, a dataset destined for a disease association study may be pre-screened using PCA in order to detect and remove population structure so as to minimise noise in the final study. In many of the large scale collaborations now being undertaken it is of interest to determine whether genetic differences exist between groups of controls ascertained from different geographic locations, or genotyped at different laboratories. If the differences are sufficiently small, these groups can be merged to achieve greater power. The aim of this work is to demonstrate and quanmtify the superiority of supervised learning techniques when applied to this problem.

We have adapted two supervised learning algorithms, artificial neural networks (ANN) and support vector machines (SVM) for this purpose. We use sets of control samples genotyped by the International Schizophrenia Consortium (ISC) [3] as our test data. For comparison we also conduct a conventional PCA analysis.

The paper is organised as follows. In the Methods section we briefly discuss the PCA methodology that we use and give a short introduction to ANNs and SVMs. We also include a description of the data used for the analysis. The first part of the Results section presents the PCA analysis and results. The second and third sections describe the ANN and SVM analyses respectively. Finally, the Discussion section contains our interpretation of the analyses and some suggestions for potential applications of the methods.

Methods

We examine three approaches to the problem of genetic classification, given pre–existing candidate populations. More precisely, we wish to determine the confidence with which the individuals in these populations can be distinguished on the basis of their genetic structure. We first consider PCA, the most commonly used unsupervised method. Next, we investigate a sophisticated non–linear supervised classifier, a probabilistic ANN. Lastly we consider a simpler but more limited linear supervised classifier, an SVM.

We would expect the supervised methods to perform better than PCA, since they utilise more information. The aim is to quantify this difference. We therefore adopt a sliding window approach, using genetic windows of different sizes in order to to assess the perfomance of the classifiers given different amounts of genetic data.

According to a recent hypothesis, discussed below, unsupervised methods cannot distinguish between two populations if the amount of data available falls below a certain threshold value. It is therefore of interest to determine whether supervised methods can classify below this limit, and we investigate this question also.

Principal Components Analysis

The PCA technique is well known and commonly used in genetics and we do not describe it in detail here. Briefly, the aim is to determine the direction of maximum variance in the space of data points. The first principal component points in the direction of maximum variance, the second component maximises the remaining variance and so on. Any systematic difference between groups of individuals will manifest itself as a differential clustering when the data points are projected on to these principal components.

We use the smartpca component of the eigensoft (v3.0) software package [4] for our analysis. In addition to the principal components, smartpca produces a biased but asymptotically consistent estimate of Wright's F_{ST} parameter [5]. We use this estimator as our measure of effect size.

The authors of SMARTPCA use a result obtained by [6] and [7], to conjecture the existence of a phase transition (the Baik, Ben Arous, Péché or BBP transition) below which population structure will be undetectable by PCA [4]. They further conjecture that this threshold represents an absolute limit for *any* (presumably unsupervised) classification method. For two populations of equal size, the critical F_{ST} threshold is given by:

$$F_{ST}(crit) = \frac{1}{\sqrt{N_{SNP}S}}$$

where N_{SNP} is the number of single nucleotide polymorphisms (SNPS) and S is the total number of individuals in the dataset.

A measure of statistical significance between any pair of populations is also produced by SMARTPCA. This is obtained by computing the ANOVA F-statistics for the difference in mean values along each principal component. A global statistic is calculated by summing over all components; this statistic follows a χ^2 distribution. We use the associated p-value as our measure of statistical significance.

It is important to point out that we are using the p-value as a quantitative measure. This quantity is more usually used in a hypothesis testing framework, where the decision to accept or reject is made on the basis of some pre-determined threshold. We do not set such a threshold; rather, we use the p-value to detect the onset of the BBP phase transition, when its value drops by many orders of magnitude.

We determine the effectiveness or otherwise of PCA by comparing the estimated value of F_{ST} with the critical value in a sliding window across the chromosome.

Artificial Neural Networks

ANNs are relatively uncommon in genetics and may be unfamiliar to many geneticists. Furthermore the network we employ possesses some novel features particularly relevant to genetic analysis. We therefore give a somewhat more detailed overview in this section.

ANNs are a methodology for computing, based on massive parallelism and redundancy, features also found in animal brains. They consist of a number of interconnected processors each of which processes information and passes it to other processors in the network. Well-designed networks are able to 'learn' from a set of training data and to make predictions when presented with new, possibly incomplete, data. For an introduction to the science of neural networks the reader is directed to [8].

The basic building block of an ANN is the *neuron*. Information is passed as inputs to the neuron, which processes them and produces an output. The output is typically a simple mathematical function of the inputs. The power of the ANN comes from assembling many neurons into a network. The network is able to model very complex behaviour from input to output. We use a three-layer network consisting of a layer of input neurons, a layer of "hidden" neurons and a layer of output neurons. In such an arrangement each neuron is referred to as a node. Figure 1 shows a schematic design for this network with 7 input nodes, 3 hidden nodes and 5 output nodes.

The outputs of the hidden layer and the output layer are related to their inputs as follows:

$$\text{hidden layer}: \quad h_j = g^{(1)}\left(f_j^{(1)}\right); \quad f_j^{(1)} = \sum_l w_{jl}^{(1)} x_l + b_j^{(1)}, \quad (1)$$

$$\text{output layer}: \quad y_i = g^{(2)}\left(f_i^{(2)}\right); \quad f_i^{(2)} = \sum_j w_{ij}^{(2)} h_j + b_i^{(2)}, \quad (2)$$

where the output of the hidden layer h and output layer y are given for each hidden node j and each output node i. The index l runs over all input nodes. The functions $g^{(1)}$ and $g^{(2)}$ are called activation functions. The non-linear nature of $g^{(1)}$ is a key ingredient in constructing a viable and practically useful network. This non-linear function must be bounded, smooth and monotonic; we use $g^{(1)} = \tanh x$. For $g^{(2)}$ we simply use $g^{(2)}(x) = x$. The

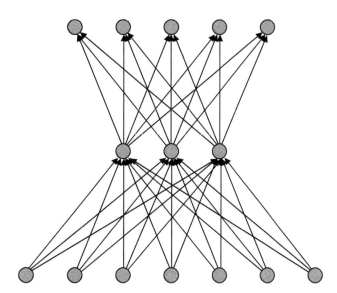

Figure 1. An example of a 3-layer neural network with 7 input nodes, 3 nodes in the hidden layer and 5 output nodes. Each line represents one weight.

layout and number of nodes are collectively termed the *architecture* of the network.

The weights **w** and biases **b** effectively define the network and are the quantities we wish to determine by some *training* algorithm. We denote **w** and **b** collectively by **a**. As these parameters vary during training, a very wide range of non-linear mappings between inputs and outputs is possible. In fact, according to a 'universal approximation theorem' [9], a standard three-layer feed-forward network can approximate any continuous function to *any* degree of accuracy with appropriately chosen activation functions. However a network with a more complex architecture could well train more efficiently.

The use of ANNs in genetics to date has been limited. A comprehensive review is given in [10]. Previous work has focused mainly on investigating the optimum network architecture for specific applications, using a small number of genetic markers. A case-control scenario was considered in [11]. Their networks typically consisted of four input nodes, representing four markers, with two hidden layers incorporating up to three hidden nodes each. The output was the case or control status of the individual. The authors explored a variety of different architectures and assessed the performance of each. In common with other authors such as [12], they noted that the performance of the network was strongly dependent on the choice of architecture. Nevertheless, many authors such as [13] and [14] have successfully used ANNs with pragmatic choice of architecture based on trial and error searching.

A more serious problem is the size of networks that it is possible to train when using traditional back-propagation or quasi-newtonian gradient descent methods. Most such methods are very inefficient in navigating the weight space of a network and can therefore handle only relatively small genetic datasets.

Both these problems are addressed in the MEMSYS package [15] which we use to perform the network training. This package uses a non–deterministic algorithm which allows us to make *statistical* decisions on the appropriate classification. This makes possible the fast efficient training of relatively large network structures on large data sets. Moreover the MemSys package computes a statistic termed the Bayesian evidence (see for example [16] for a review).

The evidence provides a mechanism for selecting the optimum number of nodes in the hidden layer of our three–layer network.

We apply this ANN to our genetic classification problem by associating each input node with the value of a genetic marker from an individual and the output nodes with the probabilities of the individual's membership of each class. As in the case of the PCA analysis we perform the classification in a sliding window across the chromosome.

Support Vector Machines

The ANN described in the previous section is a sophisticated classifier, able to amplify weak signals and to detect non–linear relationships in the data. This feature is potentially of great significance in genetic analysis, since non–linearity is likely to arise due to long-range interactions between genes at different physical locations. It is also of interest to investigate the performance of a more conventional linear supervised classifier on the genetic classification problem. We therefore conduct a parallel analysis with an SVM.

The principle of an SVM is intuitively very simple. The space of data points is partitioned by finding a hyperplane that places as many of the points as possible into their pre-defined class. The SVM algorithm iterates through trial planes, computing the shortest combined distance from the plane to the closest of the data points in each class while simultaneously ensuring all data points of each class remain in the same partition. An example of a two-dimensional feature space partitioned in three different ways is shown in Figure 2.

In the example pictured the plane p3 does not partition the space correctly. The plane p2 produces an adequate classification with all of the data points appropriately divided. However two data points lie very close to the plane and leave little margin for future generalisation to unseen examples. The plane p1 is an

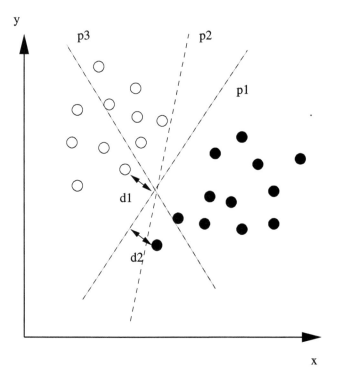

Figure 2. An example of a two-dimensional feature space $x - y$ **for data of known class divided by three hyperplanes p1, p2 and p3.** Clearly p1 divides most efficiently.

optimum partitioning, maximising the combined distance d1 + d2. The function of an SVM is to attempt to identify this optimum partition. In this work we make use of the LIBSVM library of SVM routines [17].

The SVM has the advantage of being simpler to use in practice, but has certain limitations compared with our ANN. Firstly it is a linear classifier and cannot allow for non–linear relationships in the data. Secondly it is deterministic, providing a unique solution for each problem. It is therefore impossible to develop an estimate of the accuracy of the solution–that is, to place confidence limits on the classification. Our ANN, on the other hand, is probabilistic, producing a slightly different solution on each iteration. This

allows us to assess the stability of the solution. Thirdly, the classification is binary–an individual either does, or does not, belong to a particular class. The ANN, in contrast, provides probabilities of class membership for each class.

Data

Our test populations are a subset of the data obtained by the International Schizophrenia Consortium (ISC). The consortium collected genome-wide case–control data from seven sample collection sites across Europe. The final post quality controlled (QC) dataset contained 3322 cases and 3587 controls. The controls from three sites were used for the purposes of this study:

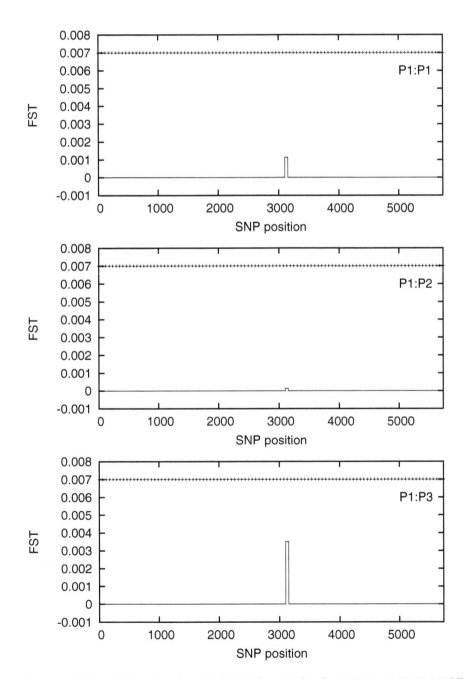

Figure 3. Estimated F_{ST} values for a 50 SNP sliding window for P1:P1 (top), P1:P2 (middle), P1:P3 (bottom). The F_{ST} is essentially zero everywhere except for a small region approximately halfway along the chromosome. The horizontal dotted line is the value of $F_{ST}(crit)$.

- **Aberdeen Site (P1)** A set of 702 controls, consisting of volunteers recruited from general practices in Scotland. These were genotyped on an Affymetrix 5.0 genotyping array.
- **Edinburgh Site (P2)** A set of 287 controls recruited through the South of Scotland Blood Transfusion Service, typed on an Affymetrix 6.0 array.
- **Cardiff Site (P3)** A set of 611 controls recruited from several sources in the two largest cities in Bulgaria, typed on an Affymetrix 6.0 array.

Quality control was performed by the ISC [18]. In addition to the usual genotype and sample QC procedures, attempts were made to resolve technical differences arising from the different genotyping arrays used by the various ISC sites. A multi-dimensional scaling analysis was also performed to detect population stratification and remove outliers from each population.

We start with the cleaned ISC data comprising 739,995 SNPs, all samples having a call rate >0.95 and all SNPs having minor allele frequencies >0.01, with population outlier identifiers removed [18]. For the purposes of this study we examine a linkage-disequilibrium (LD) pruned set of 5739 SNPs ($r^2 < 0.2$) on chromosome 1, selecting only those that were common to both the Affy 5.0 and Affy 6.0 platforms. PLINK v1.06 [19] software was used for this data reduction. The parameters of the three test populations are given in Table S1.

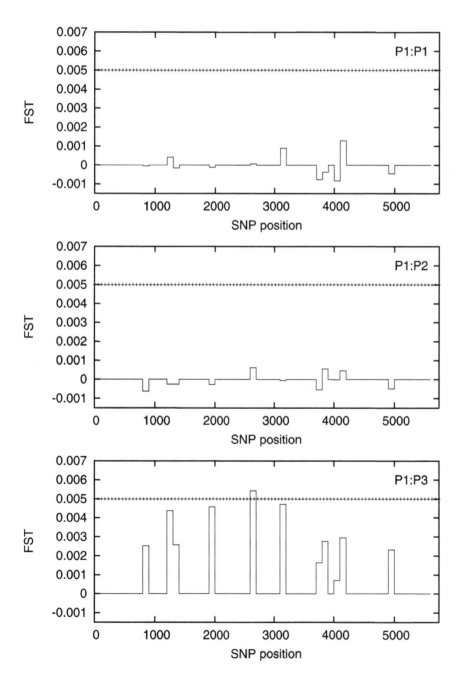

Figure 4. Estimated F_{ST} values for a 100 SNP sliding window for P1:P1 (top), P1:P2 (middle), P1:P3 (bottom). The horizontal dotted line is the value of $F_{ST}(crit)$. Note that although F_{ST} is always non-negative, the estimator may become negative for small values of F_{ST}.

Results

We first perform a principal components analysis (PCA) on the three populations to determine whether the populations can be distinguished using an unsupervised learning approach. We then carry out both ANN and SVM supervised learning classifications on the same three populations.

PCA Classification

We first test for structure *within* each of our three populations. In each case the population is divided into two disjoint subsets. For P1 and P3 each subset consists of 200 samples. In the case of P2, only 287 samples are available in total, so we divide these into two subsets of 140 samples each. We do not remove any residual (post QC) outliers, in order to maximise any signal.

In all three cases we find that the estimated F_{ST} values are vanishingly small, less than 0.0001 even when all 5739 SNPs are used. In no case do the estimated levels of F_{ST} exceed $F_{ST}(crit)$. By comparison a recent study [20] found values ranging as high as 0.023 across Europe. The ANOVA p-values for the three populations P1, P2, and P3 are 0.050, 0.559 and 0.022 respectively. Although two of these p-values fall at or below the conventional threshold of 0.05 this does not in itself imply the ability to detect structure in the absence of a reasonable effect size. The PCA plot for the most significant case ($p = 0.022$) shows that the populations do not separate (Figure S1). We conclude that

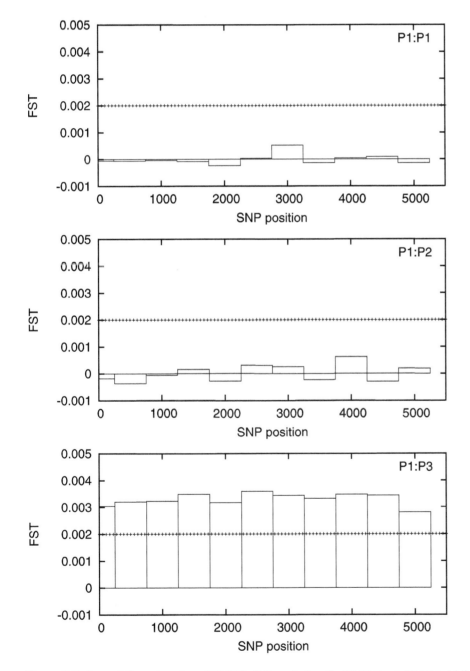

Figure 5. Estimated F_{ST} values for a 500 SNP sliding window for P1:P1 (top), P1:P2 (middle) and P1:P3 (bottom). The horizontal dotted line is the value of $F_{ST}(crit)$.

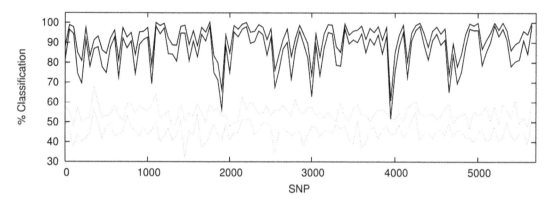

Figure 6. Classification with windows of 50 contiguous, non-overlapping SNPs for P1 against P2 (solid lines) with classification results for a sample of P1 against P1 (dotted lines) shown for comparison. The regions enclosed between the lines illustrate 1σ confidence intervals.

PCA fails to detect structure between the subsets tested in each of our three populations; that is, each population is essentially homogeneous.

We next test for differences between our three populations. We perform a sliding window PCA analysis with non–overlapping windows of length 50, 100 and 500 SNPs. The estimated F_{ST} values are plotted in Figures 3, 4 and 5 with the corresponding critical value shown for comparison.

The estimated F_{ST} is negligible at the 50 SNP level, except for one window about halfway along the chromosome, and even here it does not approach $F_{ST}(crit)$. Some signals are visible for the P1:P3 comparison at the 100 SNP level, but $F_{ST}(crit)$ is exceeded in only one window. At the 500 SNP level the PCA analysis can distinguish between the P1 and P3 populations, with the estimated F_{ST} exceeding $F_{ST}(crit)$ everywhere along the chromosome but the P1:P2 comparison still shows negligible signal. The full results from this analysis are given in Table S2. Sample PCA plots showing the BBP transition given in Figures S2–S4 and S5–S7.

We may summarise the results of our PCA analysis as follows. As expected, no internal structure is detectable within any of the three populations. Moreover, PCA is unable to distinguish the two Scottish populations even when using the full input set of 5739 SNPs. The two Scottish populations can, however, be distinguished from the Bulgarian population, given an input data set of around 500 SNPs, anywhere along the chromosome.

ANN Classification

We next attempt to classify the same data using the ANN. The pre-classified data available is divided into a *training set* used to train the network and a *hold-out set* used to assess the accuracy of the network after training. Since we merely wish to determine whether the ANN is able to classify or not, it is desirable to to maximise the size of the training set while retaining a large enough testing set to ensure statistically meaningful results. In practice we find that a ratio of 80% : 20% to be satisfactory and all the results presented here use this ratio.

As with the PCA analysis we use samples of 200 from each population, except in the P2:P2 case, where we use 140 for each sub-population. We perform multiple repetitions of the network training, drawing a different random starting point (of the weights and biases) on each occasion. In this way we are able to obtain an ensemble of trained classifiers from which we can draw a standard 1σ error on the network classification. For all of the results below we use > 20 repetitions. We present all of our results in terms of % accuracy of classification on the hold-out set, where 100% defines a perfect classifier and 50% is no better than random.

To explore the variation of classification across the chromosome we use an input set of non-overlapping windows each containing 50 SNPs. Figures 6–8 show the classification rate along the chromosome for each population combination. In addition each figure illustrates a reference null classification of two sub-samples

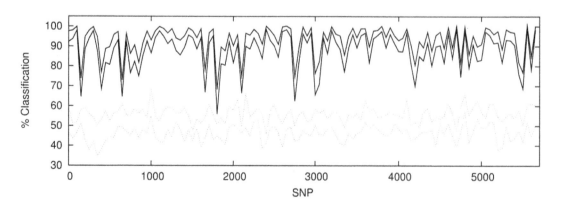

Figure 7. Top panel shows classification with windows of 50 contiguous, non-overlapping SNPs for P1 against P3 (solid lines) with classification results for a sample of P3 against P3 (dotted lines) shown for comparison. The regions enclosed between the lines illustrate 1σ confidence intervals.

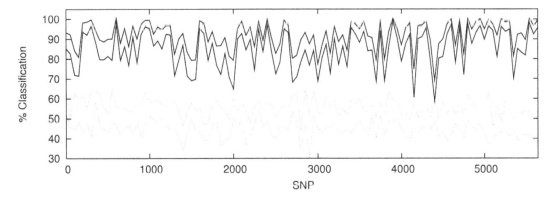

Figure 8. Top panel shows classification with windows of 50 contiguous, non-overlapping SNPs for P2 against P3 (solid lines) with classification results for a sample of P2 against P2 (dotted lines) shown for comparison. The regions enclosed between the lines illustrate 1σ confidence intervals.

from each of the three populations to demonstrate the internal homogeneity of each population.

It is notable that a classification rate of $>80\%$ is achieved across the majority of the chromosome for *both* populations P1:P2 *and* P1:P3. This demonstrates that the network can successfully amplify a much weaker, intra-Scottish population signal to roughly the same level as that obtained for the Scotland-Bulgaria comparison.

We next investigate the variation in performance as the window size is varied. Figure 9 shows results for the classification of P1:P2 with window sizes of 20, 50 and 100 SNPs.

For a window size of 20, one sees considerable structure along the chromosome, with some regions classifying well, and others poorly. As the window size increases, with each window now containing both "good" and "bad" regions, we find that the classification rate converges to the best, rather than the worst rate. This shows that even when the network is presented with a large window that contains a small proportion of informative SNPs it

can successfully filter out the extraneous inputs and produce a classifier with the same level of accuracy as would have been obtained with a reduced set of informative inputs. This feature has many important implications within genetics where data is often noisy or incomplete.

It is common in signal processing to represent the efficiency of a classifier graphically, using a receiver operating characteristic (ROC) curve which plots the true positive rate (TPR) versus the false positive rate (FPR) for increments of the classifier's discrimination threshold. The default threshold is normally 0.5, but variation of this criterion allows classifiers to be tuned to minimise the FPR while simultaneously maximising the TPR. An ideal classifier has a ROC curve that resembles a step-function with a TPR of 1.0 for all values of the threshold, while the ROC curve for a random classifier is a line with slope of unity from a TPR of 0 to 1. Figures 10 and 11 illustrate the ROC curves for the network classifier in two different regimes along the chromosome spectrum. Figure 10 shows the ROC curve of the classifier trained

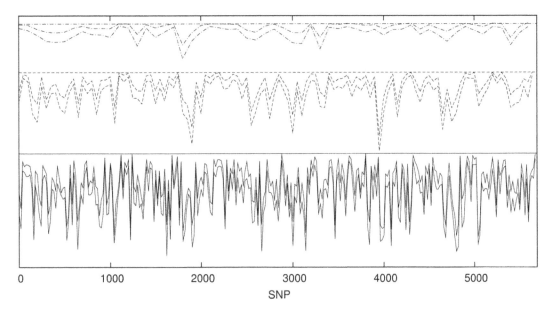

Figure 9. Classification with windows of 100 (dot-dashed), 50 (dashed) and 20 (solid) contiguous, non-overlapping SNPs for P1 against P2. Note that as the window size increases, the accuracy converges to the *most* accurate classification, indicating that the ANN is successfully discarding irrelevant information. For clarity we have added an offset to each spectrum and omitted the ordinate axis, the horizontal lines represent 100% classification in each case.

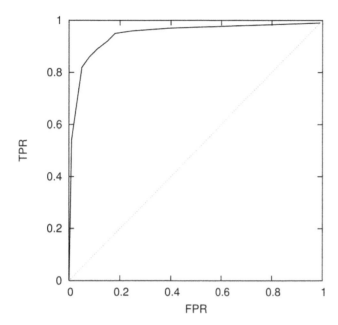

Figure 10. Receiver Operating Characteristic (ROC) curve, that is a plot of true positive rate (TPR) against false positive rate (FPR) of the neural network classifier trained using the first 50 SNPs using P1:P2 (solid curve). A random classifier (dotted curve) is shown for comparison.

using the first 50 SNPs. As is evident from Figures 6–8 this region produces a classifier that is capable of distinguishing the two population groups at the 90% level. The quality of this classifier is then clearly discernible by a ROC curve that approaches a step-function. For comparison we performed the same test on a part of the chromosome spectrum where the classifier was relatively poor, at a SNP window of $1950-2000$. This ROC curve, shown in

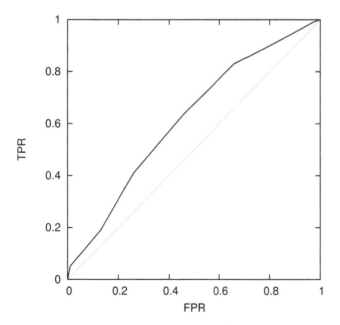

Figure 11. Receiver Operating Characteristic (ROC) curve of the neural network classifier trained using 50 SNPs form 1950 to 2000 also for P1:P2 (solid curve). A random classifier (dotted curve) is shown for comparison.

Figure 11 appears very close to the random classifier line, as would be expected. Along with multiple network realisations computed for each classifier these tests provide a useful way to confirm the stability of the classifiers.

The architecture of our three layer network is determined entirely by the number of nodes in the hidden layer. This number in turn can be estimated from the Bayesian evidence. We find that our results are insensitive to the number of hidden nodes. In fact, reducing the number of hidden nodes from 20 to zero results in negligible degradation in performance, indicating that the signal we detect is essentially linear. It is of course possible to identify such a linear signal using PCA for example, given a signal of sufficient strength, as was demonstrated in the earlier part of this paper. The reason for the increased sensitivity of our ANN here is its utilisation of our prior knowledge of class membership and its efficiency in exploring the space of all *possible* linear (and non-linear) mappings and identifying the choice that maximises the classifier's sensitivity automatically.

In summary, we find that the ANN exhibits considerably greater sensitivity than PCA. In particular, while PCA cannot distinguish between the two Scottish populations, the ANN can do so given fewer than 100 SNPs. Moreover, the ANN can classify on a dataset well below the BBP limit. Furthermore, as we have seen, the ANN can also efficiently eliminate noise. Our results indicate that the signal the ANN is identifying is linear, but nevertheless too weak for PCA to detect.

SVM Classification

In view of the fact that the dominating signal in the data is linear, we would expect the SVM to perform equivalently. We do not repeat the entire analysis here, but simply show the sliding window analysis for the population combination P1 and P2 in Figure 12 (with the equivalent ANN results for comparison in Figure 13). Since the SVM for a given dataset is entirely deterministic it is not possible to generate multiple realisations of the classifier and thus build up 1σ confidence intervals. However it is clear that SVM performs comparably with the ANN on this dataset, locating strikingly similar features in the classification spectrum across the chromosome. It is also of interest to compare the speed of each method. The SVM takes roughly 10 seconds to build a classifier on a 50 SNP window, using a currently standard desktop computer. A single iteration of the ANN takes a roughly equal amount of time, with 1σ limits being generated in a $n_{\text{iterations}}$ multiple of this time.

Discussion

We demonstrate in this paper that supervised learning classification is to be preferred to unsupervised learning in genetics, when we have an *a priori* definition of class membership from some non-genetic source. The classification then serves to determine whether or not the pre-defined populations are *genetically* distinguishable.

Both the techniques investigated in this paper (SVMs and ANNs) significantly outperform PCA on the data presented here. It is noteworthy that the sensitivity of these methods exceeds the conjectured BBP limit on the sensitivity of supervised approaches.

Although ANNs have been previously discussed in the context of genetics, they have yet to come into common use in this field. This is probably due, in part, to the limited number of input nodes that it was possible to handle, and in part to the difficulty of determining the optimal network architecture. Our ANN allows us to handle very large numbers of inputs, an essential feature in many applications in genetics. The problem of deciding on the

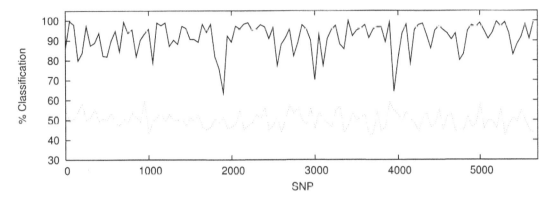

Figure 12. SVM classification with windows of 50 contiguous, non-overlapping SNPs for P1 against P2 (solid lines) with classification results for a sample of P1 against P1 (dotted lines) shown for comparison.

optimal network architecture, much discussed by previous authors, reduces, in the case of a 3-layer network, to deciding on the number of hidden nodes; the MemSys package provides a rigorous method of determining this number.

In the event, we observe a predominantly *linear* signal on this dataset, easily detectable by both SVM and ANN but too weak to be detected by PCA. In a sense, this is be expected, since the SVM and ANN utilise our prior knowledge of class membership to find the optimal linear mapping for classifying the data. In the absence of such prior information, PCA finds the linear mapping that maximises the variance; this is not necessarily the optimal mapping. However the sensitivity of the supervised methods and the small number of SNPs that they need in order to classify efficiently is noteworthy. A further important consequence of this fact is that the SVM and ANN can *localise* the sources of genetic difference along the chromosome and indeed the results of both methods are consistent with each other in this respect.

The linearity of the signal means that the SVM and ANN perform comparably. (The main novelty here is the large number of inputs that our ANN can accept). This linearity is not altogether surprising, since non–linear effects would arise as a result of long–range correlation between loci. The relatively small size of our SNP windows greatly reduces the probability of seeing such correlations. (Short range correlations, which arise from linkage disequilibrium, carry no useful information and were eliminated by LD pruning our data).

When a linear signal is present, both the ANN and the SVM can classify with equal efficiency and we recommend that both be considered for use in genetic classification. The ANN, however, possesses three advantages over the SVM. Firstly the stochastic nature of the classification means that we can place confidence limits on our results. Secondly, the ANN supplies explicit probabilities for the classification of each individual. This provides the potential to "clean" our datasets by removing those individuals who classify with very high (or very low) probability. Thirdly, the ANN is capable of being applied to more general datasets where non–linear signals are significant.

It is noteworthy that the supervised learning methods are able to classify individuals from two populations within Scotland. One would expect sufficient gene flow to occur within this region to homogenise the populations. The differences detected are not necessarily due to ancestry, but may be a consequence of the fact that the two population samples were drawn from different datasets, genotyped on different platforms, at different sites. These differences, whatever their origin, are nevertheless too small to detect using PCA, but in many applications the presence of such differences may be of critical importance.

The behaviour of our ANN in the presence of significant non–linear effects remains to be investigated; one possible target is the common disease common variant (CDCV) model of complex diseases. These are associated with many common genetic variants, each of individually small effect. Interactions between

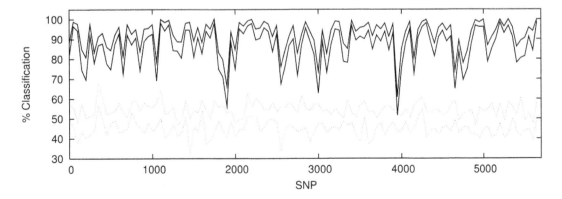

Figure 13. ANN classification with windows of 50 contiguous, non-overlapping SNPs for P1 against P2 (solid lines) with classification results for a sample of P1 against P1 (dotted lines) shown for comparison.

these variants are likely to result in non–linear effects suitable for study with ANNs.

We suggest, on the basis of the evidence presented in this paper, that supervised learning methods have a useful role to play in genetic applications where we are interested in differences between pre–defined groups of individuals. Possible applications include population genetics, case–control studies and quality control for genetic data gathered at different sites or on different platforms.

Additional Information

Software. The LIBSVM library of SVM routines is publicly available [17]. The MEMSYS algorithms can be made available for academic use. We have developed an interface to both the MEMSYS and LIBSVM packages for our specific genetic application and are currently developing it for more general applications. We would be happy to collaborate with interested parties to facilitate this development process.

Supporting Information

Figure S1. Intra- population projection of the P3 population (5739 SNPs, p = 0.022), along the two most significant axes. It is clear that despite the nominally significant p-value, the two sub-populations fail to separate along these axes.

Figure S2. Inter-population projection of the P1 and P2 population along the first most significant set of axes for each value of N. $F_{ST}(crit)$ is never exceeded and the populations do not separate.

Figure S3. Inter-population projection of the P1 and P2 population along the second most significant set of axes for each value of N. $F_{ST}(crit)$ is never exceeded and the populations do not separate.

Figure S4. Inter-population projection of the P1 and P2 population along the third most significant set of axes for each value of N. $F_{ST}(crit)$ is never exceeded and the populations do not separate.

Figure S5. Inter-population projection of the P1 and P3 population along the first most significant set of axes for each value of N. The populations separate as $F_{ST}(crit)$ is exceeded.

Figure S6. Inter-population projection of the P1 and P3 population along the second most significant set of axes for each value of N. The populations separate as $F_{ST}(crit)$ is exceeded.

Figure S7. Inter-population projection of the P1 and P3 population along the third most significant set of axes for each value of N. The populations separate as $F_{ST}(crit)$ is exceeded.

Table S1. Parameters of the reduced dataset used for analysis.

Table S2. PCA results for inter-population tests. P_R and P_C are the reference and comparison datasets, M_R and M_C the respective sample sizes and N the number of SNPs used. $F_{ST}(crit)$ is the value of F_{ST} at which the phase transition is expected. $\hat{F}_{ST}$ is the estimate of the F_{ST} and SE is its standard error. Pval is the ANOVA p-value. The 50 SNP and 500 SNP sets were a contiguous set starting from the 1000th data point along the chromosome. Note the sharp drop in p-value at the BBP transition when $\hat{F}_{ST}$ exceeds $F_{ST}(crit)$.

Acknowledgments

We thank the individuals and families who contributed data to the International Schizophrenia Consortium. We are grateful to the reviewers for their constructive comments. We thank the members of the Statistical Genetics Unit in the Neuropsychiatric Genetics Group for helpful comments and advice at all stages of this work. We acknowledge Anthony Ryan for reviewing and commenting on this manuscript. The authors would like to acknowledge support from the Cambridge Centre for High Performance Computing where this work was carried out, and also to Stuart Rankin for computational assistance. Additionally we acknowledge Steve Gull for useful discussions and for the use of MemSys in this application.

Members of the International Schizophrenia Consortium:

Trinity College Dublin Derek W. Morris, Colm O'Dushlaine, Elaine Kenny, Emma M. Quinn, Michael Gill, Aiden Corvin;

Cardiff University Michael C.O'Donovan, George K. Kirov, Nick J. Craddock, Peter A. Holmans, Nigel M.Williams, Lucy Georgieva, Ivan Nikolov, N. Norton, H. Williams, Draga Toncheva, Vihra Milanova, Michael J. Owen;

Karolinska Institutet/University of North Carolina at Chapel Hill Christina M. Hultman, Paul Lichtenstein, Emma F.Thelander, Patrick Sullivan;

University College London Andrew McQuillin, Khalid Choudhury, Susmita Datta, Jonathan Pimm, Srinivasa Thirumalai, Vinay Puri, Robert Krasucki, Jacob Lawrence, Digby Quested, Nicholas Bass, Hugh Gurling;

University of Aberdeen Caroline Crombie, Gillian Fraser, Soh Leh Kuan, Nicholas Walker, David St Clair;

University of Edinburgh Douglas H. R. Blackwood, Walter J. Muir, Kevin A. McGhee, Ben Pickard, Pat Malloy, Alan W. Maclean, Margaret Van Beck;

Queensland Institute of Medical Research Naomi R. Wray, Peter M. Visscher, Stuart Macgregor;

University of Southern California Michele T. Pato, Helena Medeiros, Frank Middleton, Celia Carvalho, Christopher Morley, AymanFanous, David Conti, James A. Knowles, Carlos Paz Ferreira, AntonioMacedo, M. Helena Azevedo, Carlos N. Pato;

Massachusetts General Hospital Jennifer L. Stone, Douglas M. Ruderfer, Manuel A. R. Ferreira,

Stanley Center for Psychiatric Research and Broad Institute of MIT and Harvard Shaun M. Purcell, Jennifer L. Stone, Kimberly Chambert, Douglas M. Ruderfer, Finny Kuruvilla, Stacey B. Gabriel, Kristin Ardlie, Mark J. Daly, Edward M. Scolnick, Pamela Sklar.

Author Contributions

Conceived and designed the experiments: MB CP. Performed the experiments: MB CP. Analyzed the data: MB EH CTO RS CP. Contributed reagents/materials/analysis tools: MB TISC AC DWM MG. Wrote the paper: MB CP.

References

1. Lao O, Lu T, NothNagel M, Junge O, Freitag-Wolf S, et al. (2008) Correlation Between Genetic and Geographic Structure in Europe. Curr Biol 18: 1241–1248.
2. Reich D, Thangaraj K, Patterson N, Price A, Singh L (2009) Reconstructing Indian Population History. Nature 461: 489–494.
3. International Schizophrenia Consortium website. Available: http://pngu.mgh. harvard.edu/isc. Accessed 2011.
4. Patterson N, Price A, Reich D (2006) Population Structure and Eigenanalysis. PLoS Genetics 2: 2074–2093.

5. Reich D, Kumarasamy T, Patterson N, Price AL, Singh L (2009) Reconstructing Indian Population History. Nature 461: 489–494.
6. Baik J, Ben Arous G, Péché S (2005) Phase Transition of the Largest Eigenvalue for Nonnull Complex Sample Covariance Matrices. Ann Probability 33: 1643–1697.
7. Baik J, Silverstein JW (2006) Eigenvalues of Large Sample Covariance Matrices of Spiked Population Models. J Multivariate Anal 97: 1382–1408.
8. Bailer-Jones C (2001) Automated Data Analysis in Astronomy. New Delhi: Narosa Publishing House. 363 p.
9. Leshno M, Ya Lin V, Pinkus A, Schocken S (1993) Multilayer Feedforward Networks with a Nonpolynomial Activation Function can Approximate Any Function. Neural Networks 6: 861–867.
10. Motsinger-Reif A, Ritchie M (2008) Neural Networks in Genetic Epidemiology; Past, Present and Future. BioData Min 1: 3.
11. Curtis D (2007) Comparison of Artificial Neural Network Analysis with Other Multimarker Methods for Detecting Genetic Association BMC Genet 8: 49.
12. North B, Curtis D, Cassell P, Hitman G, Sham P (2003) Assessing Optimal Neural Network Architecture for Identifying Disease Associated Multi-Marker Genotypes Using a Permutation Test, and Application to Calpain 10 Polymorphisms Associated with Diabetes. Ann Hum Genet 67: 348–356.
13. Seretti A, Smeraldi E (2004) Neural Network Analysis in Pharmacogenetics of Mood Disorders. BMC Med Genet 5: 27.
14. Penco S, Grossi E, Cheng S, Intraligi M, Maurelli G, et al. (2004) Assessment of the Role of Genetic Polymorphism in Venous Thrombosis Through Artificial Neural Networks. Ann Hum Genet 69: 693–706.
15. Gull S, Skilling J (1999) Quantified maximum entropy: MemSys 5 Users' Manual. Royston: Maximum Entropy Data Consultants Ltd.
16. Jaynes E (2003) Probability Theory: The Logic of Science. Cambridge: Cambridge University Press. 727 p.
17. Chang C, Lin C (2001) LIBSVM: A Library for Support Vector Machines LIBSVM. Available: http://www/csie.ntu.edu.tw/cjlin/libsvm. Accessed 2011.
18. The International Schizophrenia Consortium (2009) Common Polygenic Variation Contributes to Risk of Schizophrenia and Bipolar Disorder. Nature 6: 748–52.
19. Purcell S, Neal B, Todd-Brown K, Thomas L, Ferreira Mal (2007) PLINK: A Toolset for Whole-Genome Association and Population-Based Linkage Analysis. Am J Hum Genet 81: 559–575.
20. Nelis M, Esko T, Magi R, Zimprich F, Zimprich A et al (2009) Genetic Structure of Europeans: A View from the North-East. PLoS ONE 4(5): e4572.

15

Do I Have My Attention? Speed of Processing Advantages for the Self-Face Are Not Driven by Automatic Attention Capture

Helen Keyes*, Aleksandra Dlugokencka

Department of Psychology, Anglia Ruskin University, Cambridge, United Kingdom

Abstract

We respond more quickly to our own face than to other faces, but there is debate over whether this is connected to attention-grabbing properties of the self-face. In two experiments, we investigate whether the self-face selectively captures attention, and the attentional conditions under which this might occur. In both experiments, we examined whether different types of face (self, friend, stranger) provide differential levels of distraction when processing self, friend and stranger names. In Experiment 1, an image of a distractor face appeared centrally – inside the focus of attention – behind a target name, with the faces either upright or inverted. In Experiment 2, distractor faces appeared peripherally – outside the focus of attention – in the left or right visual field, or bilaterally. In both experiments, self-name recognition was faster than other name recognition, suggesting a self-referential processing advantage. The presence of the self-face did not cause more distraction in the naming task compared to other types of face, either when presented inside (Experiment 1) or outside (Experiment 2) the focus of attention. Distractor faces had different effects across the two experiments: when presented inside the focus of attention (Experiment 1), self and friend images facilitated self and friend naming, respectively. This was not true for stranger stimuli, suggesting that faces must be robustly represented to facilitate name recognition. When presented outside the focus of attention (Experiment 2), no facilitation occurred. Instead, we report an interesting distraction effect caused by friend faces when processing strangers' names. We interpret this as a "social importance" effect, whereby we may be tuned to pick out and pay attention to familiar friend faces in a crowd. We conclude that any speed of processing advantages observed in the self-face processing literature are not driven by automatic attention capture.

Editor: Alexandra Key, Vanderbilt University, United States of America

Funding: These authors have no support or funding to report.

Competing Interests: The authors have declared that no competing interests exist.

* Email: helen.keyes@anglia.ac.uk

Introduction

We respond more quickly to our own face than to others [1–3], but we are unsure of the mechanism underlying this advantage. One sensible suggestion is that the self-face automatically captures our attention, speeding our reaction to it. However, research investigating whether our own face does selectively grab our attention has produced mixed findings, and studies have suffered from a lack of rigorous control in focus of attention. Here, we report two experiments investigating whether the self-face does indeed selectively capture our attention, and the attentional conditions under which this might be possible.

One of the key questions in attention research revolves around how much information we process from stimuli that we are not directly attending to, and the circumstances in which these unattended stimuli can capture our attention (cf. the Cocktail Party phenomenon; [4,5]). One common way to investigate this question is to present task-irrelevant stimuli and measure their effect on task performance (cf. The Stroop effect; [6]). We can further investigate the phenomenon by measuring the effect of presenting task-irrelevant stimuli both inside and outside the focus of attention, enabling us to define the circumstances in which

different classes of task-irrelevant stimuli selectively capture our attention.

Self-name and attention capture

The idea that self-referential stimuli can selectively capture our attention has largely been studied using the self-name. Several studies show that our own name is processed preferentially, but only when it is task-relevant; our own name does not selectively capture attention when it is irrelevant to the task at hand [7,8]. Conversely, others show that the self-name does have selective attention-capture capacity, even when task-irrelevant: it is more resistant to the attentional blink, inattentional blindness and repetition blindness than other names and words [9–11]. Key to understanding the circumstances in which our own name does automatically capture our attention are studies manipulating the focus of attention.

In an important paper, Gronau and colleagues look at the effects that personally relevant stimuli – self-names – have when presented both inside and outside the focus of attention [12]. Participants were instructed to report the colour of a piece of text, but to ignore the distractor names represented by the text, presented centrally (at the focus of attention; Stroop-like task) or to report the colour of a box presented centrally with distractor names presented peripherally (outside the focus of attention). When presented centrally, the self-name caused significantly more interference on the colour-naming task than other names. However, this effect disappeared when the names were presented peripherally above or below a coloured box, outside the focus of attention. Interestingly, skin conductance responses – taken as a sign of processing a stimulus of personal significance [13] – remained larger for self-names compared to other names for both central and peripheral presentation of the names, suggesting that the peripherally presented stimuli were being processed. It seems that the capacity of our own name to automatically capture our attention exists in a complicated relationship with the focus of attention.

Focus of attention – self-face

Self-referential stimuli may capture attention automatically, but to investigate whether this is due to a truly self-referential effect, Devue and Brédart [14] recommend using self-face stimuli rather than self-name stimuli, as the self-face is unique to each person. Indeed, early evidence suggested that the self-face is more easily detected than recently learned faces [1], but that study suffered from the absence of a familiarity control. There are many reasons to believe that our own face is processed as "special", with evidence of speeded processing [1–3], a widely distributed underlying neural network [15–20] and a stronger feature-based processing approach relative to other faces [3,21–23]. Our own face provides a truly unique stimulus, which appears to receive special treatment in the brain. Considering this special treatment, the self-face is a likely candidate to elicit automatic attention capture. Indeed, there is some evidence of automatic processing of the self-face [24], which in turn might indicate an automatic attention capture mechanism. However, although we may pay particular attention to our own face, it is unclear whether the self-face selectively grabs our attention, or whether it simply holds our attention once attended to (see [25]).

Research on whether our own face automatically captures our attention has produced conflicting results. Brédart and Devue [26] conducted one of the first studies looking at the self-face and attention capture. They showed that our own face causes more distraction than other familiar faces when presented peripherally – ostensibly outside of the focus of attention. The authors presented participants with a pair of vertically aligned word stimuli, presented centrally on a screen. Each word pair comprised a name (either the participant's own name or the name of a familiar classmate) and a letter string. The participant's task was to indicate whose name was present. Flanking these word pairs either to the left or the right, a distractor picture appeared which showed the participant's own face, the face of their classmate or the face of their professor. The authors report that the peripheral presentation of the self-face caused more distraction when identifying a classmate's name than a classmate's face caused when identifying the participant's own name, suggesting that the self-face automatically and selectively captured attention, even when presented outside the focus of attention.

A later paper presented conflicting results. Devue and Brédart [14] showed that the self-face and other highly familiar faces produce a temporary distraction when presented inside the focus of attention (between two target digits), suggesting that these types of face can automatically capture attention. However, these faces did not produce a distraction when presented outside of the focus of attention. Importantly, the faces presented peripherally were presented only briefly (200 ms), unlike the faces in the earlier study

[26], where the stimuli were displayed until the participant responded. Where the stimuli were presented indefinitely, the participant may have had time to shift attention directly towards the distractor faces, bringing them inside the focus of attention. When this factor was adjusted in the later paper [14], self-faces presented peripherally did not selectively capture attention. Further research showed that highly familiar faces (including the self-face) did not reduce inattentional blindness relative to unfamiliar faces, even when presented inside the focus of attention [27]. There remains debate as to whether our own face does selectively capture our attention [26] or whether the self-face is as easily ignored as other familiar [14] and unfamiliar [27] faces. While various methodologies have been employed to investigate this phenomenon, insufficient focus of attention controls may account for many of the reported discrepancies.

Current Study

The current paper addresses previous issues concerning focus of attention in two ways. First, we use a face-word paradigm to present distractor faces directly central to the focus of attention (Experiment 1) and secondly we employ a rigorously controlled hemispheric asymmetry paradigm to examine the effects of distractor faces presented outside the focus of attention (Experiment 2). No studies to date have presented distractor faces centrally behind target names to test the attention capture capacity of face identity on a naming task, and this experiment presents a novel approach to the problem of controlling the focus of attention.

Aims Experiment 1

In Experiment 1, we test whether different types of face cause differential levels of distraction when processing one's own name, a friend's name and a stranger's name, when presented inside the focus of attention. Of additional interest are the properties of a face which are responsible for capturing attention. Highly familiar faces may capture attention because they are "robustly represented" in the brain [1]. These robust representations are likely to rely heavily on configural information [28]. Recent evidence [3] suggests that self-faces may be processed in a qualitatively different way than other highly familiar faces, activating strong configural *and* featural processing. Specifically, while familiar face processing is detrimentally affected by inversion, which disrupts configural processing [29–31], processing speed advantages remain for self-faces when inverted. As such, the comparison of self-faces and other highly familiar faces in an attention capture task which includes upright and inverted faces should tell us much about the relative input of facial configural and featural information which are particularly implicated in attention capture.

If attention-capturing capacity is based largely on configural processing, then differences observed between upright friend and unfamiliar faces should disappear for inverted faces, because configural processing suffers with inversion. For self-faces, any attention-capturing capacity should remain for inverted faces, as we are particularly good at processing the self-face relative to other types of face when configural information is disrupted [3,23]. Alternatively, if the attention-capturing capacity of familiar faces (self, friend) is based on another mechanism, inversion should have the same effect on friend and self-faces.

Aims Experiment 2

In Experiment 2 we investigate how different types of face can attract attention when presented outside of the focus of attention (peripherally). There are a number of reasons why we are particularly interested in following up on previous reports of peripheral self-face attention capture. Firstly, differences in stimulus duration could account for discrepancies in accounts of peripheral self-face attention capture. Stimulus duration control is of importance here; a long stimulus duration potentially allows time for the participant to explicitly shift attention from the name to the face picture, which would elicit a shift in the locus of attention. In this experiment, we employ several measures to rigorously control focus of attention – peripheral stimuli are presented briefly enough to prevent an explicit shift of the focus of attention and a chin rest and participant eye-monitoring techniques are used to ensure that fixation does not shift towards the peripheral stimuli.

A second area of interest involves hemispheric presentation. A previous report of peripheral self-face attention capture found that the presentation location of the distractor face (to the left or right of the target stimulus) did not produce an effect [26]. Considering issues of hemispheric asymmetry in face processing in general (e.g., [32]) and self-face processing in particular (e.g., [16,18]), this is surprising. In the current study, we manipulate hemispheric presentation in a tightly controlled manner. If the attention-grabbing capacity of faces is modulated by visual field presentation, we might expect them to produce more attentional interference when presented in the left visual field (right hemisphere; RH) relative to the right (left hemisphere; LH), as faces are processed preferentially in the RH (e.g., [33]). In addition, considering that self-face processing may activate a more bilateral neural network that other familiar faces [3,15–20], LH interference may be increased for self-face relative to other face distractor trials.

Experiment 1

Method

Participants.   Forty participants (24 female) with a mean age of 26.5 years (SD = 7.8) volunteered to take part in the study. Each participant was paired with a highly familiar same-sex friend whom they had known for at least one year, and whom they saw on a daily or almost daily basis. The majority of the participants were recruited in pairs, where each person served as a friend for the other participant. Data from six participants were discarded due to data coding errors (two participants) or participant error in understanding the instructions (four participants). The remaining 34 participants (21 female) had a mean age of 26.2 years (SD = 8.1).

Ethics Statement.   Written informed consent was obtained from all participants prior to taking part in the study. The consent procedure and all other elements of both experiments detailed in this manuscript received full ethical approval from the Faculty Research Ethics Panel (Science and Technology) at Anglia Ruskin University. The approval number for both experiments is FST/FREP/11/17. The individuals pictured in the figures of this manuscript have given written informed consent (as outlined in PLOS consent form) to publish their images.

Stimuli.   Participants were photographed in similar conditions under controlled lighting. Participants posed with a neutral expression while looking directly at the camera (Nikon D300). Using Adobe Photoshop, images were converted to greyscale and rotated to ensure that the eyes were collinear. An oval vignette (245×320 pixels) was applied to each facial image, ensuring that the jawline and hairline of each face were visible. Images were saved as normal and mirror-reversed copies. The mirror reversed copies of the images served as the "self" stimuli for participants, while the "friend" and "unfamiliar" stimuli were viewed normally (see 34 for evidence that these are the preferred views of self-faces

and other familiar faces). Images were saved in both upright and inverted orientations.

Each participant's set of stimuli comprised images of their own face, a friend's face and a stranger's face overlaid with a name. This name was their own name, their friend's name or the stranger's name. The name was placed centrally in an identical position across each facial image (centre of name at 160 pixels from bottom of image). Where an image of a face was presented in an inverted orientation, the text of the name was presented in upright orientation. Images were checked to ensure that the eyes and mouth were not obscured by text in any of the images (see Figure 1; the individual pictured here has given written informed consent for the use of this image). Images were viewed on a 17 inch screen of a Dell PC. Images subtended a viewing angle of 5.32 by 6.95 degrees when viewed from a distance of approximately 70 cm.

Procedure.   Prior to testing, participants were shown upright versions of all three images (self [mirror-reversed], friend and stranger) without any text across the faces. The names identifying the faces were written on the screen below. Participants were asked to look at the faces for as long as it took for them to be confidently able to name each of the three faces. This was to ensure that participants were able to label the unfamiliar face with a name. This process took between 30–100 s for all participants.

Participants ran ten practice trials followed by a block of test trials. A trial comprised the presentation of a face (self, friend, unfamiliar) in either upright or inverted orientation with a name written across it (participant's own name, friend's name or stranger's name). Participants were required to press a button on the keyboard ("c", "v" or "b") to indicate whether the name presented was their own name, their friend's name or the stranger's name. The order of the buttons allocated to "self",

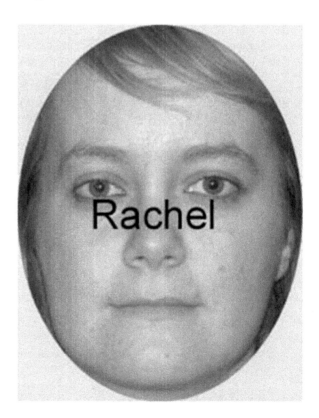

Figure 1. Example of an upright stimulus from Experiment 1.

"friend" and "stranger" was counterbalanced across participants. Stimuli were left on the screen until the participant responded. Each trial was followed by an inter-stimulus interval (ISI) varying between 500 and 1500 ms. Participants were instructed not to attend to the faces, and to respond as quickly and as accurately as possible.

Trials were balanced such that each face type (self, friend, stranger) was paired with each name type (self, friend, stranger) and equal number of times, and these pairings were presented with faces in upright and inverted orientations an equal number of times. Trials were presented in randomised order. The testing block comprised 216 trials (3 face types X 3 name types X 2 face orientations X 12 repetitions each).

Results

Reaction times (RT) for correct responses were analysed. Incorrect responses accounted for 5.2% of the data, and were removed. For each participant, RT's more than two standard deviations away from that participant's mean were removed as outliers [35]; these accounted for 10.3% of trials. Data can be found at http://dx.doi.org/10.6084/m9.figshare.942382 [36].

A 3-way repeated-measures ANOVA was carried out, with factors of Distractor Face (self, friend, stranger), Target Name (self, friend, stranger) and Orientation (upright, inverted), and with RT to correct responses serving as the dependent variable. All post-hoc tests were interpreted using Bonferroni adjustment for multiple comparisons.

Analysis revealed a significant effect of Target Name, $F(2,66) = 10.44$, $p < .001$, $\eta_p^2 = .240$, with a priori follow-up tests showing participants responding significantly faster to their own name than to a friend's name, $t(33) = 4.86$, $p < .05$, $d = .380$, or a stranger's name, $t(33) = 2.56$, $p < .05$, $d = .260$. RT in response to friend and stranger names did not differ, $t(33) = 1.70$, ns, $d = .128$ (see Figure 2).

There was no main effect of Distractor Face, $F(2,66) = 0.09$, ns., $\eta_p^2 = .011$, but this null effect is qualified by a significant interaction between Distractor Face and Target Name, $F(4,132) = 6.84$, $p < .001$, $\eta_p^2 = .172$. Follow-up tests show that when responding to a friend's name, responses were significantly faster when the name was accompanied by the friend's face (Target Name-Distractor Face congruence) relative to the self-face, $t(33) = 2.69$, $p < .017$, $d = .171$, or a stranger's face, $t(33) = 3.44$, $p < .017$, $d = .206$ (Target Name-Distractor Face incongruence), suggesting that the presence of the friend's face facilitated friend name processing. Responses to the friend's name did not differ when accompanied by the self-face compared to the stranger's face, $t(33) = 0.55$, ns, $d = .042$. Alpha is Bonferroni corrected to .017 for three comparisons.

Similarly, when responding to the self-name, responses were significantly faster when the name was accompanied by the self-face (Target Name-Distractor Face congruence) relative to a friend's face, $t(33) = 3.19$, $p < .017$, $d = .289$, or a stranger's face, $t(33) = 2.40$, $p = .022$, $d = .217$ (closely approaching significance at .017; Target Name-Distractor Face incongruence), suggesting that the presence of the self-face facilitated self-name processing. Responses to the self-name did not differ when accompanied by a friend's face or a stranger's face, $t(33) = 0.94$, ns, $d = .063$. Alpha is Bonferroni corrected to .017 for three comparisons.

When responding to the stranger's name, no differences were observed depending on whether the Distractor Face presented was congruent or incongruent to the Target Name (self-face Vs stranger face, $t(33) = 2.14$, ns, $d = .163$; friend face Vs stranger face, $t(33) = 0.70$, ns, $d = .058$; self-face Vs friend face, $t(33) = 1.61$, ns, $d = .108$; alpha is Bonferroni corrected to .017 for three comparisons). Overall, congruent face-name stimuli pairings elicited faster naming responses than incongruent pairings for both Self and Friend pairings, but not for Stranger pairings. See Figure 3 for illustration of these interaction effects.

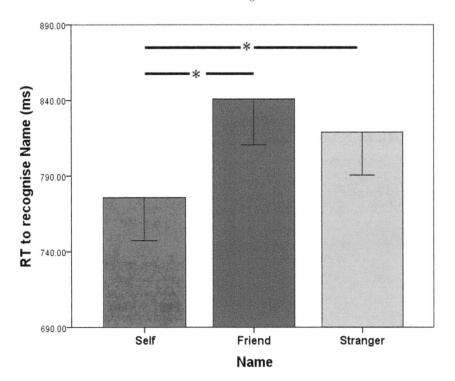

Figure 2. Response times to the self-name, friend's name and stranger's name in Experiment 1. Mean response times to recognise the self-name (red) a friend's name (blue) and a stranger's name (green) in Experiment 1.

A
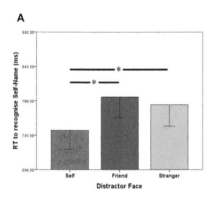

B
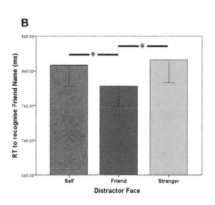

C
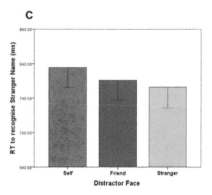

Figure 3. Influence of centrally presented task-irrelevant distractor faces on speed of name recognition. Mean response times to recognise the self-name (panel A) a friend's name (panel B) and a stranger's name (panel C) when the self-face (red), friend face (blue) and stranger face (green) was presented centrally as a distractor (Experiment 1).

There was no effect of Orientation, $F(1,33) = 2.92$, ns, $\eta_p^2 = .081$, nor did Orientation interact with any of the other variables (Orientation by Target Name by Distractor Face: $F(4,132) = 1.48$, ns, $\eta_p^2 = .043$; Orientation by Target Name: $F(2,66) = 1.82$, ns, $\eta_p^2 = .052$; Orientation by Distractor Face: $F(2,66) = 0.08$, ns, $\eta_p^2 = .003$).

Accuracy Analyses. As predicted with a straightforward name-recognition task, there was a ceiling effect for accuracy, with participants correctly identifying whether a name was their own, a friend's or a stranger's at an accuracy rate of 97.56% (SD = 1.81). Here only one minor result reached significance, with participants being slightly less accurate when responding to a stranger's name in the presence of a friend's face (96.81%, SD = 4.82) compared to the stranger's face (98.89%, SD = 2.13), $t(33) = 3.25$, $p < .05$. Considering the obvious ceiling effect in the accuracy data, we do not interpret this effect to be of importance, and do not discuss it further.

Experiment 2

Method

Participants. Thirty-nine participants (23 female) with a mean age of 25.5 years (SD = 6.4) volunteered to take part in the study. Again, each participant was paired with a highly familiar same-sex friend whom they had known for at least one year, and whom they saw on a daily or almost daily basis. Data from one participant were discarded due to data coding errors. The remaining 38 participants (23 female) had a mean age of 25.7 years (SD = 6.4). All participants were right-handed, as assessed by the Oldfield Inventory [37], with a mean laterality quotient of 87.6 (SD = 17.9). Left-handed and ambidextrous individuals were not invited to participate because hemispheric asymmetry in face processing was a variable of interest and the brains of right-handed individuals are considered to be more strongly and conventionally lateralised [38]. Full ethical approval was gained for this study, the details of which are outlined in the Methods section of Experiment 1.

Stimuli. Photographs of participants were collected and edited in a similar manner to Experiment 1. After conversion to greyscale and applying an oval vignette to each face image (370×460 pixels), a set of stimuli were created for each participant comprising images of their own face (mirror-reversed), a friend's face and a stranger's face. These faces were presented to the left (LVF), right (RVF) or both (bilaterally) of a centrally presented name. This name was their own name, their friend's name or the

stranger's name, and was placed in an identical position (225 pixels from the bottom of the image) for each stimulus (see Figure 4; the individual pictured here has given written informed consent for the use of this image). Where images of faces were presented bilaterally, the faces were always identical. Images subtended a viewing angle of 7.76 by 9.80, and the centre of each image was 9.32 degrees to the left or right of the centre of the screen when viewed from a distance of 70 cm. This viewing distance was maintained by the use of a chinrest. To ensure that the face images were presented to each hemisphere (or both) in a controlled manner, the researcher monitored participants' eye movements in real time using a webcam to check that their gaze remained on the centre of the screen at all times.

Procedure. Participants were initially familiarised with their three faces to be used as their stimuli along with their associated names in a similar manner to Experiment 1.

Participants ran ten practice trials followed by two blocks of test trials. One block of testing was completed with the right hand and the other with the left hand; the order of these blocks was counterbalanced across participants. A trial comprised the presentation of a name in the centre of the screen, with the participant's own face, a friend's face or a stranger's face appearing to the left, to the right or on both sides of the name. The name presented was the participant's own name, a friend's name or a stranger's name. The participant's task was to indicate by pressing a button on the keyboard ("c", "v" or "b") who the name belonged to (self, friend, or stranger). The order of the buttons allocated to "self", "friend" and "stranger" was counter-balanced across participants. Each stimulus was presented on screen for 250 ms, followed by an ISI varying between 500 and 1,500 ms. Participants were instructed not to attend to the faces, and to respond as quickly and as accurately as possible.

Trials were balanced such that each face type (self, friend, stranger) was paired with each name type (self, friend, stranger) and equal number of times, and these pairings were presented with faces in the LVF, the RVF and bilaterally an equal number of times. Trials were presented in randomised order. Each testing block comprised 189 trials (3 face types X 3 name types X 3 visual field presentations X 7 repetitions each).

Results

Reaction times (RT) for correct responses were analysed. Incorrect responses accounted for 10.6% of the data, and were removed. For each participant, RT's more than two standard deviations away from that participant's mean were removed as

Figure 4. Example of a bilateral stimulus from Experiment 2.

outliers [35]; these accounted for 14.2% of trials. Data can be found at http://dx.doi.org/10.6084/m9.figshare.942383 [39].

A 3-way repeated-measures ANOVA was carried out, with factors of Distractor Face (self, friend, stranger), Target Name (self, friend, stranger) and Visual Field (LVF, RVF, bilateral), and with RT to correct responses serving as the dependent variable. All post-hoc tests were interpreted using Bonferroni adjustment for multiple comparisons.

Analysis revealed a significant effect of Target Name, $F(2,74) = 13.12$, $p<.001$, $\eta_p^2 = .262$, with a priori follow-up tests showing participants responding significantly faster to their own name than to a friend's name, $t(37) = 4.25$, $p<.05$, $d = .480$, or a stranger's name, $t(37) = 3.29$, $p<.05$, $d = .372$. RT in response to friend and stranger names did not differ, $t(37) = 1.99$, ns, $d = .108$. (see Figure 5).

There was no main effect of Distractor Face, $F(2,74) = 1.71$, ns., $\eta_p^2 = .044$, but this null effect is qualified by a significant interaction between Distractor Face and Target Name,

$F(4,148) = 3.95$, $p<.005$, $\eta_p^2 = .096$. Follow-up tests show that type of Distractor Face did not have any effect when responding to the self-name or a friend's name, but when responding to a stranger's name the presence of a friend's face significantly increased RT relative to both the stranger's face, $t(37) = 3.12$, $p< .017$, $d = .175$, and the self-face, $t(37) = 2.71$, $p<.017$, $d = .135$, suggesting that a peripherally presented friend's face causes more distraction when processing a stranger's name than either the self-face or a stranger's face. There was no difference in effect when responding to a stranger's name in the presence of the self-face or stranger's face, $t(37) = 1.06$, ns, $d = .044$. Alpha is Bonferroni corrected to .017 for three comparisons. See Figure 6 for illustration of the interaction effects.

There was no effect of Visual Field, $F(2,74) = 0.67$, ns., $\eta_p^2 = .018$, nor did Visual Field interact with any of the other variables (Visual Field by Target Name by Distractor Face; $F(8,296) = 0.63$, ns., $\eta_p^2 = .017$; Visual Field by Target Name;

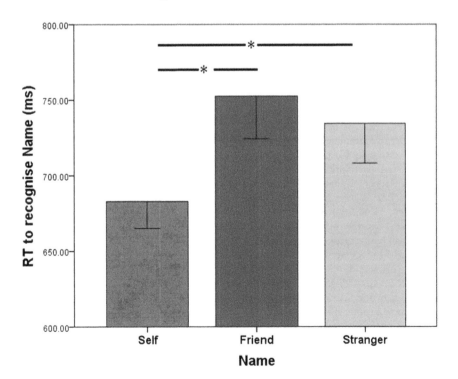

Figure 5. Response times to the self-name, friend's name and stranger's name in Experiment 2. Mean response times to recognise the self-name (red) a friend's name (blue) and a stranger's name (green) in Experiment 2.

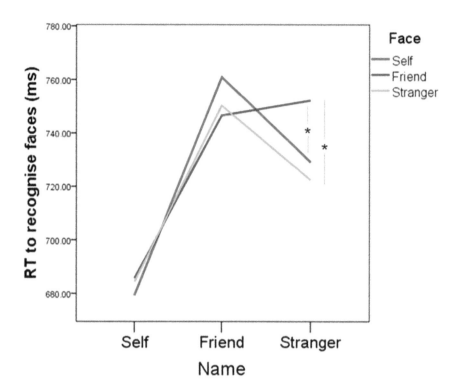

Figure 6. Influence of peripherally presented task-irrelevant distractor faces on speed of name recognition. Mean response times to recognise the self-name, a friend's name and a stranger's name in the peripherally presented presence of the self-face (red line), a friend's face (blue line) and a stranger's face (green line).

$F(4,148) = 0.29$, ns., $\eta_p^2 = .008$; Visual Field by Distractor Face: $F(4,148) = 1.09$, ns., $\eta_p^2 = .029$).

Accuracy Analyses. As expected, there was a ceiling effect for accuracy, with participants correctly identifying whether a name was their own, a friend's or a stranger's at an accuracy rate of 97.18% (SD = 1.82). There were no significant effects for accuracy in Experiment 2.

Cross-Experimental Analyses between Experiments 1 and 2

Examining the data suggested that responses to names were faster in Experiment 2 (when distractor faces were presented peripherally) compared to Experiment 1 (when distractor faces were presented centrally). In order to examine whether the robust self-name RT advantage observed in both experiments differed depending on whether distractor faces were presented centrally or peripherally, additional cross-experimental analyses were carried out, with factors of Experiment (1, 2), Target Name (self, friend, stranger) and Distractor Face (self, friend, stranger).

There was a significant effect of Experiment, with participants responding significantly faster to all types of name in Experiment 2 (distractor presented outside the focus of attention; 723.34 ms, SE = 24.64) compared with Experiment 1 (distractor presented inside the focus of attention; 811.91, SE = 26.05), $F(1, 70) = 6.10$, $p<.05$, $\eta_p^2 = .080$. This suggests a greater interference effect of all types of distractor faces on all types of name when distractors were presented centrally rather than peripherally.

There was no significant interaction effect between Target Name and Experiment or Distractor Face and Experiment, suggesting similar self-name RT advantages across both experiments, regardless of where distractor faces were presented. A significant Target Name by Distractor Face by Experiment interaction mirrored what findings from Experiments 1 and 2

showed separately – for Experiment 1, congruent face-name stimuli pairings elicited faster naming responses than incongruent pairings for both Self and Friend pairings, but not for Stranger pairings and for Experiment 2, congruence did not facilitate naming but rather a friend's face provided more distraction than either the self-face or a stranger's face when responding to a stranger's name.

Discussion

Across two studies, we found that participants responded significantly faster to their own name than to other names. The self-face did not cause more distraction than other faces either when presented centrally or peripherally, suggesting that our own face does not selectively grab our attention when either inside or outside the focus of attention. Instead, we report a facilitation effect of familiar faces on congruent familiar name recognition when those faces are inside the focus of attention, and an interesting distraction effect when friend faces are presented outside the focus of attention.

Self-name processing

A strong finding across both studies was that participants responded significantly faster to their own name than to a friend's or stranger's name. This finding opposes Brédart and Devue's [26] report that the self-name and a classmate's name were identified equally quickly. One possible reason for this discrepancy is that our task was simpler – in the current experiments the participants simply had to identify the name presented, whereas in Brédart and Devue's study [26] the name to be identified was presented in tandem with a letter string. Indeed, when others have used a simple identity decision task, they also report that the self-name elicits faster responses than other familiar names [40]. We interpret our finding as a straightforward self-referential effect, with speeded processing for the self-name due to its importance as a self-referential stimulus. In this way, our finding mirrors previous reports of speeded self-face processing relative to other faces (e.g., [1–3]).

Our own face does not grab our attention

Importantly, the self-face did not cause any more distraction than either a friend's face or a stranger's face, either when presented inside (Experiment 1) or outside (Experiment 2) the focus of attention. We conclude from this that our own face does not automatically or selectively capture our attention. Devue and Brédart [14] argue that the self-face is a better example of a self-referential stimulus than the self-name, as the self-name can be shared with others, whereas the self-face is truly unique to the self. However, the self-name is often used to capture our attention in a real-world setting (i.e. someone may call you by your name to attract your attention), making us particularly sensitive to its presence. The self-face – though an important self-referential stimulus – is not normally used to capture our attention in this way. The self-face may be processed as "special" in several ways – as demonstrated by speeded processing [1–3] and a more bilateral neural representation compared to other faces [15–20] – but it does not appear to have special attention capturing properties. The speeded processing afforded to self-referential stimuli and observed here and elsewhere does not appear to be driven by automatic attention capture.

The findings outlined in this paper are important to theories of self-referential processing because they suggest that not all self-referential stimuli are equal. While it is established that the self-name automatically and selectively captures attention [9–12], our findings show that this is not the case for the self-face. Different types of self-referential stimuli (name, face) may well serve different purposes, particularly in terms of capturing attention. It is both important and interesting to contrast ways in which various types of self-referential stimuli interact with attentional mechanisms and processing speeds. Our findings suggest that in the field of self-referential processing, more focus should be placed on *types* of self-referential stimuli and examining the different purposes preferential processing of these stimuli could serve.

Inside the focus of attention

When presented inside the focus of attention (Experiment 1), task-irrelevant self-face stimuli did not cause more distraction than other types of face. Our findings somewhat contradict Gronau and colleagues [12] in this respect, who showed that centrally presented task-irrelevant self-referential stimuli (the self-name) caused more distraction than other names. In our study, the centrally presented self-faces (and friend's faces) had a very different effect on naming speeds – these highly familiar faces facilitated processing of their associated names. That is, responses to the self-name were faster in the presence of the self-face and responses to a friend's name were faster in the presence of the friend's face. This suggests that the task-irrelevant faces were being processed; they just did not capture attention in a selective way. Indeed, rather than cause distraction, under certain conditions congruent faces facilitated name recognition. Importantly, both the self-face and a friend's face facilitated the processing of their associated names when presented inside the focus of attention, while this was not true for unfamiliar faces. This suggests that the facilitation effect of face presentation on name recognition may occur for all highly familiar faces, and is not self-specific. Tong and Nakayama [1] propose that we develop particularly efficient processing skills for highly familiar, robustly represented faces, and

we consider the facilitated processing for congruent familiar face-name pairs reported here to be evidence of this.

Outside the focus of attention

When faces were presented outside the focus of attention (Experiment 2), an interesting phenomenon emerged. The self-face did not selectively grab attention, as previously reported [26]. Instead, a friend's face selectively captured attention – as demonstrated by significantly increased reaction time to recognise a stranger's name in the presence of a friend's face. We interpret this as a "social importance" effect. In a real-world setting, it would be sensible to be primed to pick out familiar friends' faces outside the focus of attention – for example, in a crowd. This would not be the case for our own face, or a stranger's face. That a friend's face only caused distraction when processing a stranger's name (and not the self-name or a friend's name) supports this interpretation. Both the self-name and a friend's name are socially interesting stimuli to us, and so we invest our attention in them. However, a stranger's name is not an interesting social stimulus, and so our attention can more easily be captured by a socially relevant stimulus – a friend's face.

With several studies – including our own – now demonstrating that the self-face is not more attention-grabbing than other types of face, observing a friend face attention-grabbing effect at peripheral presentation is not wholly surprising. However, cautious interpretation is warranted here as this effect was not predicted in our initial hypotheses. Our interpretation of a "social importance" effect is tentative and warrants a further programme of study, perhaps varying the degree of social importance of the distractor face.

Facilitation versus distraction effects

We report facilitation effects for familiar faces in Experiment 1, when distractor faces were presented inside the focus of attention, but a selective distraction effect for friend faces in Experiment 2, with distractor faces presented outside the focus of attention. We posit that this difference is based on cognitive capacity, which might vary based on the focus of attention.

When distractor faces are presented centrally behind target names, it is likely that there is sufficient capacity to process the distractor faces as well as responding to the target name. Indeed, all types of face (self, friend, stranger) presented inside the focus of attention automatically and non-selectively grabbed attention. This is evidenced by significantly slower response times in the name identification task in in Experiment 1 compared to Experiment 2, where faces were presented outside the focus of attention, and suggests that the presence of faces in general interferes with name identification when those faces are presented inside the focus of attention. That all types of face (self, friend, stranger) capture attention when presented centrally makes the observed differential facilitation effects possible. If we have sufficient cognitive capacity to attend to distractor faces presented inside the focus of attention, the simultaneous presentation of two congruent identity cues – face and name – should lead to speeded processing of the target stimulus. Indeed, this is what was observed in Experiment 1, for robustly represented familiar faces.

Conversely, when distractor faces are presented outside the focus of attention, cognitive capacity during the name identification task may not stretch to easily processing the faces while responding to the target names. In this case, it seems that not all faces have the capacity to grab attention – only a friend's face captured attention, and then only when responding to a socially unimportant stimulus (a stranger's name).

Orientation result

Surprisingly, the orientation of a task-irrelevant face did not have any effect on its ability to facilitate name recognition for robustly represented faces (Experiment 1). This may be because robustly represented faces (self and friend) should contain some view-invariant information [1], allowing them to convey information in both upright and inverted orientations. We were expecting inversion to affect self-face processing to a lesser degree than other familiar face processing [3,23], as self-face processing may be less dependent on configural processing than other familiar face processing [3,21–23]. However, while inversion may affect self-face and other familiar face processing differentially in tasks where the face is attended and task-relevant, it appears that a robustly represented task-irrelevant face's ability to facilitate naming is not affected by inversion. This suggests that whatever information is driving the facilitation effect is not tied to configural processing.

Hemispheric presentation

Similarly, we observed no main effect of hemispheric presentation on the ability of faces to capture attention (Experiment 2). This finding is surprising, considering the dominance of the RH in processing faces (e.g., [33]), but it does support a previous report that the visual field presentation of faces did not affect attention capture [26]. Considering the known hemispheric effects involved in face processing in general and self-face processing in particular, we conclude that task-irrelevant faces presented outside of the focus of attention do not recruit the same processing resources as the task relevant face usually used in studies of hemispheric asymmetry. In this instance, processing the task-irrelevant peripherally presented faces may have been too secondary to the central attentional task for normal hemispheric advantages to be observed. Additionally, the necessity to present the distractor images peripherally led us to choose a large angular distance of 9.32 degrees. While traditional hemispheric effects for face processing can be observed at this angular distance [3], it exceeds the angular distance used in many hemispheric asymmetry studies, and may have lessened any effects of hemispheric presentation. Further study varying angular distance would be useful in informing as to when faces in general can be more fully processed

(providing a facilitation effect) versus when faces can selectively provide a distraction.

Conclusion

We conclude that speed of processing advantages commonly observed for self-faces [1–3] are not driven by automatic attention capture. In two experiments, we demonstrate no distracting effect of the self-face in a name recognition task. Instead, we demonstrate a facilitation effect whereby robustly represented faces (self, friend) speed the processing of familiar names (self and friend, respectively; Experiment 1). This is not true for unfamiliar faces, which do not have robust neural representation. Thus it appears that face-name facilitation is only possible after a robust facial representation has developed. When faces are presented outside of the focus of attention, facilitation no longer occurs. Instead, we observe a significant attention grabbing effect of familiar friend faces when processing strangers' names (Experiment 2). We interpret this as a "social importance" effect, whereby we may be tuned to pick out and pay attention to familiar friend faces in a crowd. Finally, across both experiments the self-name was processed faster than other names, indicating the importance of this self-referential stimulus. It is unlikely that speed of processing advantages for self-face stimuli are tied to their attention-grabbing properties. We propose that any "special" status the self-face holds in the brain may instead be ascribed to a functional uniqueness in terms of how the self-face is processed once attended.

Acknowledgments

We are grateful to Gunay Tacel, a student research assistant, for contributions to participant recruitment and data collection for Experiment 1. Written consent was given by the participants shown in Figures 1 and 4 for the publication of their images.

Author Contributions

Conceived and designed the experiments: HK. Performed the experiments: AD HK. Analyzed the data: HK AD. Contributed to the writing of the manuscript: HK AD.

References

1. Tong F, Nakayama K (1999) Robust representations for faces: Evidence from visual search. J Exp Psychol Hum Percept Perform 25: 1016–1035.
2. Troje NF, Kersten D (1999) Viewpoint-dependent recognition of familiar faces. Perception 28: 483–487.
3. Keyes H, Brady N (2010) Self-face recognition is characterised by faster, more accurate performance, which persists when faces are inverted. Q J Exp Psychol 63: 840–847.
4. Cherry EC (1953) Some experiments on the recognition of speech, with one and two ears. J Acoust Soc Am 25: 975–979.
5. Moray N (1959) Attention in dichotic listening: Affective cues and the influence of instruction. Q J Exp Psychol 11: 56–60.
6. Stroop JR (1935) Studies of interference in serial verbal reactions. J Exp Psychol 18: 643–662.
7. Bundesen C, Kyllinsbaek S, Houmann KJ, Jensen RM (1997) Is visual attention automatically attracted by one's own name? Percept Psychophys 59: 714–720.
8. Harris CR, Pashler HE, Coburn N (2004) High priority affective stimuli and visual search. Q J Exp Psychol 57: 1–31.
9. Shapiro KL, Caldwell J, Sorensen RE (1997) Personal names and the attentional blink: A visual "cocktail party" effect. J Exp Psychol Hum Percept Perform 23: 504–514.
10. Mack A, Rock I (1998) Inattentional blindness. Cambridge, MA: MIT Press.
11. Arnell KM, Shapiro KL, Sorenson RE (1999) Reduced repetition blindness for one's own name. Vis Cogn 6: 609–635.
12. Gronau N, Cohen A, Ben-Shakhar G (2003) Dissociations of personally significant and task-relevant distractors inside and outside the focus of attention: A combined behavioural and psychophysiological study. J Exp Psychol Gen 132: 512–529.

13. Ben-Shakhar G, Elaad E (2002) Effects of questions' repetition and variation on the efficiency of the Guilty Knowledge Test: A reexamination. J Appl Psychol 87: 972–977.
14. Devue C, Brédart S (2008) Attention to self-referential stimuli: Can I ignore my own face? Acta Psychol (Amst) 128: 290–297.
15. Sugiura M, Kawashima R, Nakamura K, Okada K, Kato T, et al. (2000) Passive and active recognition of one's own face. Neuroimage 11: 36–48.
16. Kircher TJ, Senior C, Phillips ML, Rabe-Hesketh S, Benson PJ, et al. (2001) Recognizing one's own face. Cognition 78: B1–15.
17. Turk DJ, Heatherton TF, Macrae CN, Kelley WM, Ganzzaniga MS (2003) Out of contact, out of mind: The distributed nature of the self. Ann N Y Acad Sci 983: 65–78.
18. Sugiura M, Watanabe J, Maeda Y, Matsue Y, Fukuda H, et al. (2005) Cortical mechanisms of visual self-recognition. Neuroimage 24: 143–149.
19. Platek SM, Loughead JW, Gur RC, Busch S, Ruparel K, et al. (2006) Neural substrates for functionally discriminating self-face from personally familiar faces. Hum Brain Mapp 27: 91–98.
20. Keyes H, Brady N, Reilly R, Foxe J (2010) My face or yours? Event-related potential correlates of self-face processing. Brain Cogn 72: 244–254.
21. Brédart S (2003) Recognising the usual orientation of one's own face: The role of asymmetrically located details. Perception 32: 805–811.
22. Greenberg SN, Goshen-Gottstein Y (2009) Not all faces are processed equally: Evidence for featural rather than holistic processing of one's own face in a face-imaging task. J Exp Psychol Learn Mem Cogn 35: 499–508.
23. Keyes H (2012) Categorical perception effects for facial identity in robustly represented familiar and self-faces: The role of featural and configural and featural information. Q J Exp Psychol 65: 760–772.
24. Sui J, Zhu Y, Han S (2006) Self-face recognition in attended and unattended conditions: An event-related brain potential study. Neuroreport 17: 423–427.

25. Devue C, Van der Stigchel S, Brédart S, Theeuwes J (2009) You do not find your own face faster, you just look at it longer. Cognition 111: 114–122.

26. Brédart S, Devue C (2006) The accuracy of memory for faces of personally known individuals. Perception 35: 101–106.

27. Devue C, Laloyaux C, Feyers D, Theeuwes J, Brédart S (2009) Do pictures of faces, and which ones, capture attention in the inattentional-blindness paradigm. Perception 38: 552–568.

28. Buttle H, Raymond JE (2003) High familiarity enhances visual change detection for face stimuli. Percept Psychophys 65: 1296–1306.

29. Caharel S, Fiori N, Bernard C, Lalonde R, Rebaï M (2006) The effects of inversion and eye displacements of familiar and unknown faces on early and late-stage ERPs. Int J Psychophysiol 62: 141–151.

30. Megreya AM, Burton AM (2006) Unfamiliar faces are not faces: Evidence from a matching task. Mem Cognit 34: 865–876.

31. Ramon M, Rossion B (2008) Personally familiar faces and holistic processing. J Vis 8: 886a.

32. Rossion B, Dricot L, Devolder A, Bodart JM, Crommelinck M, et al. (2000) Hemispheric asymmetries for whole-based and part-based face processing in the human fusiform gyrus. J Cogn Neurosci 12: 793–802.

33. Rizzolatti G, Umlita C, Berlucchi G (1971) Opposite superiorities of the right and left cerebral hemispheres in discriminative reaction time to physiognomic and alphabetic material. Brain 94: 431–432.

34. Mita TH, Dermer M, Knight J (1977) Reversed facial images and the mere exposure hypothesis. J Pers Soc Psychol 35: 597–601.

35. Ratcliff R (1993) Methods for dealing with reaction time outliers. Psychol Bull 114: 510–532.

36. Keyes H, Dlugokencka A (2014) Data Experiment 1. Figshare. Available: http://dx.doi.org/10.6084/m9.figshare.942382.

37. Oldfield RC (1971) The assessment and analysis of handedness: The Edinburgh inventory. Neuropsychologia 9: 97–113.

38. Knecht S, Dräger B, Deppe M, Bobe L, Lohmann H, et al. (2000) Handedness and hemispheric language dominance in healthy humans. Brain 123: 2512–2518.

39. Keyes H, Dlugokencka A (2014) Data Experiment 2. Figshare. Available: http://dx.doi.org/10.6084/m9.figshare.942383.

40. Tacikowski P, Nowicka A (2010) Allocation of attention to self-name and self-face: An ERP study. Biol Psychol 84: 318–324.

16

Evaluation of Gene Expression Classification Studies: Factors Associated with Classification Performance

Putri W. Novianti*, Kit C. B. Roes, Marinus J. C. Eijkemans

Biostatistics & Research Support, Julius Center for Health Sciences and Primary Care, University Medical Center Utrecht, Utrecht, The Netherlands

Abstract

Classification methods used in microarray studies for gene expression are diverse in the way they deal with the underlying complexity of the data, as well as in the technique used to build the classification model. The MAQC II study on cancer classification problems has found that performance was affected by factors such as the classification algorithm, cross validation method, number of genes, and gene selection method. In this paper, we study the hypothesis that the disease under study significantly determines which method is optimal, and that additionally sample size, class imbalance, type of medical question (diagnostic, prognostic or treatment response), and microarray platform are potentially influential. A systematic literature review was used to extract the information from 48 published articles on non-cancer microarray classification studies. The impact of the various factors on the reported classification accuracy was analyzed through random-intercept logistic regression. The type of medical question and method of cross validation dominated the explained variation in accuracy among studies, followed by disease category and microarray platform. In total, 42% of the between study variation was explained by all the study specific and problem specific factors that we studied together.

Editor: Jörg D. Hoheisel, Deutsches Krebsforschungszentrum, Germany

Funding: This study was funded by the University Medical Center Utrecht. The funder had no role in study design, data collection and analysis, decision to publish, or preparation of the manuscript.

Competing Interests: The authors have declared that no competing interests exist.

* E-mail: P.W.Novianti-3@umcutrecht.nl

Introduction

Microarray gene expression technology continues to be used to obtain more understanding of the mechanisms of human diseases. The statistical analysis of microarray data may be challenging, with the inherent risk of finding a false positive result due to the high dimensional nature of the data. Common flaws in the three distinctive goals for the statistical analysis of microarray data (e.g. differential expression, class discovery (unsupervised), and class prediction (supervised)) have been found [1]. Inconsistency in the results of microarray analyses within the same dataset unfortunately has also been reported, especially for class prediction [2]. The variability of the reported classification accuracies may be due to the variation in the methods used to build the classification model, e.g. the type of classification model, cross validation and gene selection strategy [3]. Additionally, the performance of a predictive model may also depends on characteristic of the microarray data [4].

Most of the studies evaluating classification performance have concentrated on classification of cancer patients. In general, non-cancer diseases have received low attention in the gene expression literature, maybe because they have more varying levels of complexity than cancers. However, to test the hypothesis that disease complexity influences classification performance, it may be beneficial to use a variety of studies on non-cancerous diseases, instead of cancer studies.

This study focuses on the factors that might be associated with the accuracy of classification models on gene expression datasets, namely the type of disease, the medical question, sample size, the number of genes, the gene selection method, the classification method and cross validation techniques, using published studies outside of the field of cancer. Although it was evaluated differentially, we noticed that there is an overlap of the aforementioned study factors with the observed factors by the MAQC II study [3] that is focused in the field of cancer, i.e. the number of genes, the gene selection method, and the classification method. In the case of non-cancerous diseases, those study factors may also affect the performance of classification method. The results of this study may contribute to understand the dependency of the performance of a classification model on the characteristics of gene expression data as well as the techniques used to build the model.

Materials and Methods

Literature search and data extraction

We searched microarray gene expression studies through PubMed (US National Library of Medicine National Institute of Health) for relevant papers. Applied studies in which the investigator aimed to build supervised models based on microarray gene expression experimental data were primarily of interest. The studies that 1) were published in methodological journals 2) focused on cancer 3) were published before 2005 4) had non-human species as experimental objects 5) were not written in English or 6) were categorized as review papers, were not included. For the details of the search strategy and keywords see Material S1.

The search strategy and selection of studies satisfied the general methods for Cochrane reviews. The following details were

Table 1. Overview of the studied data.

Study	Classification model(s)	Study factor 1	...	Study factor 8	Classfication model accuracy
1	$model_1$				(Nc_1, Nm_{1_1})
2	$model_{2_1}$				(Nc_{2_1}, Nm_{2_1})
3	$model_{3_1}$				(Nc_{3_1}, Nm_{3_1})
4	$model_{4_1}$				(Nc_{4_1}, Nm_{4_1})
5	$model_{5_1}$				(Nc_{5_1}, Nm_{5_1})
6	$model_{6_1}$				(Nc_{6_1}, Nm_{6_1})
7	$model_{7_1}$				(Nc_{7_1}, Nm_{7_1})
7	$model_{7_2}$				(Nc_{7_2}, Nm_{7_2})
7	$model_{7_3}$				(Nc_{7_3}, Nm_{7_3})
7	$model_{7_4}$				(Nc_{7_4}, Nm_{7_4})
...	...	...	...	...	...
45	$model_{45_1}$				(Nc_{45_1}, Nm_{45_1})
46	$model_{46_1}$				(Nc_{46_1}, Nm_{46_1})
47	$model_{47_1}$				(Nc_{47_1}, Nm_{47_1})
48	$model_{48_1}$				(Nc_{48_1}, Nm_{48_1})

$model_{ij}$: Classification model j in study i.
Nc_{ij}: The number of correct classified sample(s) based on the classification model j in study i.
Nm_{ij}: The number of miss-classified sample(s) based on the classification model j in study i.

recorded from each selected study: classification performance, disease type, medical question (diagnosis, prognosis or response-to-treatment), microarray platform (one- or two-color system), total sample size, sample size per group, cross validation technique (single or nested loop cross validation), gene selection technique (filter, wrapper, or embedded), classification method(s), and the number of genes. The selected studies had evaluated the classification models in diverse ways, e.g. accuracy or misclassification error, sensitivity and specificity, positive and negative predictive values, as well as AUC. The accuracy was then used to represent the classification performance, since it is the most commonly used measure by the selected studies and feasible to be produced in some studies when the information about the accuracy lacked.

Sample size was recorded as the sample size in the training set, used to build the model. The degree of class imbalance was measured by dividing the number of samples in the majority class with the total sample size in the training set. Due to the diversity of cross validation methods used, we grouped the cross validation techniques into single and nested cross validation. The studies that used cross validation for both model assessment and model selection were grouped into nested cross validation. Otherwise, it was regarded as single cross validation.

Some classification methods have the ability to automatically handle the curse of dimensionality (p>>n), but others need a gene selection step to reach a lower dimension before applying the classification method. Some of the studies selected genes univariately based on a statistic passing a threshold for selection or the top-K genes to feed the classifier. In other studies, the gene selection method was aimed at finding an optimal set of genes by stepwise iterating between selection and classifier building. Thus, we grouped the gene selection technique based on their interaction with the classifier, namely filter (e.g. univariate selection), wrapper (e.g. stepwise optimization of the selected gene set), and embedded (e.g. penalized likelihood regression). Grouping was also done on the classification method into two categories, depending on their

ability to detect interactions between genes. Genes can be activated independently but also be activated through the activation of other genes. Due to this phenomenon, the classification methods that can automatically model interactions are expected to have better performance than those who cannot, at least in some studies. The methods that could detect the interaction (referred to as "interaction classifiers") in our review were tree-based methods, logistic regression, support vector machines (SVM), k-Nearest Neighbours (kNN), artificial neural networks (ANN), and weighting voting methods. Meanwhile, discriminant analysis, prediction analysis of microarray (PAM), compound covariate predictor, nearest centroid, and LASSO were classified into the group of methods that could not automatically detect interactions (called "non-interaction classifiers").

Among the selected studies, we found 34 different disease types. The diseases were categorized according to SNOMED (http://eagl.unige.ch/SNOCat/) producing 16 categories. Further re-categorization was done to establish etiology-based disease groups. As a result, we obtained 6 disease types: inflammatory disorder, immune disease, degenerative disease, infection, mental disorder and other (i.e. obesity and acute lung injury). See Material S2 for grouping details.

Data analysis

The forty eight selected studies yielded sixty one classification gene expression models. The number of observed classification models is higher than the number of selected studies since some studies had built more than one classification model. We considered the data to be clustered data, where the selected studies act as clusters. Further, in each study, we treated the accuracy as a grouped binomial variable, for which we have the number of samples that are correctly and incorrectly classified. The data structure is visualized in Table 1. The logistic random effect meta-analysis is a natural choice to handle this type of data [5]. The logistic random effects model is the generalization of the

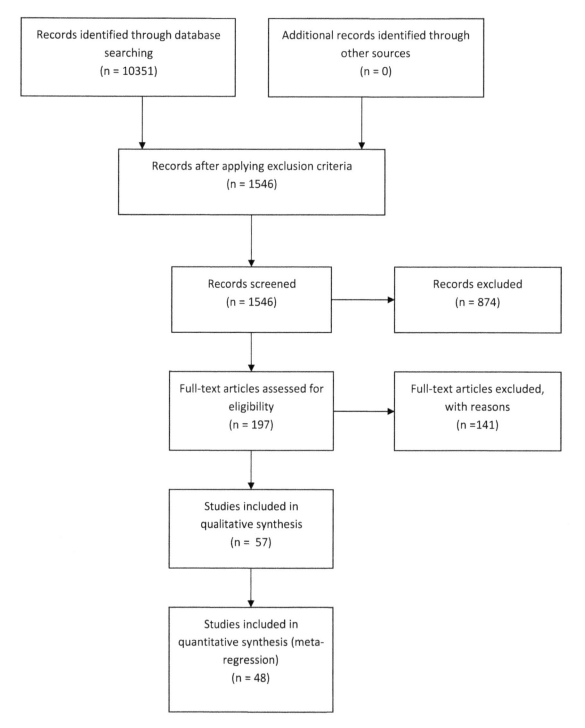

Figure 1. The PRISMA workflow diagram of the literature review search. The diagram represents the process of literature review search. The details for each step can be found in the Material S1.

linear mixed effects model to binomial outcome data using a sigmoid link function

As the accuracy is well known to be biased towards the majority class, the random intercept logistic model was corrected by the class imbalance level, which was always included in the meta-regression model. For the ith study factor, the random effects model is written as

$$log\left(\frac{\pi(x_{jD})}{1-\pi(x_{jD})}\right) = (\beta_0 + \vartheta_{0D}) + \beta_1 class\_imbalance +$$

$$\beta_2 study\_factor_i$$

where $\pi(x_{jD})$ is the probability of a sample j in dataset D to be correctly classified and ϑ_{0D} is the random intercept with respect to

Table 2. Characteristics of 18 fully reviewed studies.

Study characteristics	Number of studies
Year	
2005–2007	15
2008–2010	19
2011–2013	14
Disease Type	
Inflammatory disorder	17
Immune disease	5
Degenerative disease	6
Infection	12
Mental disorder	5
Other	3
Microarray color system	
One-color	35
Two-color	13
Medical question	
Diagnostic	29
Prognostic	6
Response-to-treatment	13
Cross validation	
Single	19
Nested	29
Gene selection	
Filter	13
Wrapper	16
Embedded	19
Classification method *	
Interaction	37
No-interaction	24

*Some studies used more than one classifier.

dataset D, in which $\vartheta_{0D} \tilde{N}(0, \sigma_{0D}^2)$. Multivariable evaluation of study factors was also done by a backward elimination approach. In each backward step, two nested models, with and without a

Table 3. Individual random intercept logistic regression.

Study factor	Df	AIC	P value
Class imbalance level	1	142.3	0.18
Sample size	1	142.9	0.23
Microarray platform (color system)	1	142.8	0.22
Medical question	2	144.1	0.33
Disease type	5	148.3	0.66
Cross validation technique	1	144.0	0.66
Gene selection method	2	144.7	0.45
Classification method	1	144.3	0.90
The number of genes in final model	1	144.3	0.78

particular study factor, were compared by Akaike's information criterion (AIC).

The explained-variation of the model accuracy was then calculated on the log-odds scale using the random effects variance of the study factor. The variation explained by all study factors together was calculated based on the relative difference between the random intercept variances of the null model σ_{null}^2 and the full model σ_{full}^2, divided by σ_{null}^2. The full model is the logistic random intercept model with all study factors as covariates. We also evaluated the explained variation of each factor relative to the full model. The relative contribution in explained variation by the ith factor to the full model was calculated by

$$\frac{\sigma_{model(i)}^2 - \sigma_{full}^2}{\sigma_{null}^2} \qquad (1)$$

where $\sigma_{model(i)}^2$ is the variance of the model based on all factors except the ith factor ($i = 1, 2, \ldots, 8$) and σ_{full}^2 is the variance of the model based on all factors. All analyses have been done in R software (Material S3). The `glmer` function from `lme4` package was used to analyse the data [6].

Table 4. Backward elimination in multiple random intercept logistic regression.

Step	Study factors on the model	Df	AIC+	P value
1	Class imbalance level	1	155.95	0.128
	Sample size	1	153.65	0.928
	Microarray platform (color system)	1	154.85	0.271
	Medical question	2	160.58	0.011
	Disease type *	**5**	**149.10**	**0.629**
	Cross validation technique	1	157.56	0.048
	Gene selection method	2	152.72	0.582
	Classification method	1	153.64	0.950
	The number of genes in final model	1	153.91	0.602
2	Class imbalance level	1	148.52	0.233
	Sample size *	**1**	**147.10**	**0.993**
	Microarray platform (color system)	1	150.62	0.061
	Medical question	2	151.90	0.033
	Cross validation technique	1	150.80	0.054
	Gene selection method	2	148.90	0.149
	Classification method	1	147.18	0.773
	The number of genes in final model	1	147.61	0.476
3	Class imbalance level	1	146.53	0.232
	Microarray platform (color system)	1	149.07	0.046
	Medical question	2	149.90	0.033
	Cross validation technique	1	149.41	0.038
	Gene selection method	2	147.63	0.104
	Classification method *	**1**	**145.19**	**0.766**
	The number of genes in final model	1	145.62	0.473
4	Class imbalance level	1	144.58	0.239
	Microarray platform (color system)	1	147.32	0.042
	Medical question	2	147.99	0.033
	Cross validation technique	1	147.85	0.031
	Gene selection method	2	145.77	0.101
	The number of genes in final model *	**1**	**143.76**	**0.451**
5	Class imbalance level	1	142.76	0.315
	Microarray platform (color system)	1	145.84	0.043
	Medical question	2	145.99	0.044
	Cross validation technique	1	146.02	0.039
	Gene selection method	2	144.08	0.115

+The AIC of multivariable random effect logistic regression model if the corresponding study factor is deleted. The AIC in the full model is 155.7.
*The study factors gave the lowest AIC and was excluded from the model for the next step.

Results

Summary of study characteristics

The automated search strategy yielded over a thousand papers. The first screening was done by examining the title and abstract, and yielded 197 papers to be fully reviewed, which resulted in 57 papers that met all the criteria (last search on September 20, 2013). The PRISMA workflow diagram of the systematic literature review [7] is provided in Figure 1.

For further statistical analyses, we selected the 48 studies [8–55] that mentioned accuracy as their classification performance

measurement. Because some studies had used more than one classification method, the evaluation of factors influencing accuracy was based on 61 classification models. The basic characteristics of the selected studies are described in Table 2.

Within the search period, the number of classification studies that had used microarray technology outside the field of cancer tended to increase with calendar time, and the one color system array (35/48) was mostly used, compare to the two-color system (13/48). We found 34 different diseases, predominantly the inflammatory disorder and infection disease groups, i.e. 17 (35%) and 12 (32%) studies, respectively. The diagnostic problem is the most common medical question addressed by microarray gene expression supervised learning. Classification models were built by either the single (19/48) or the nested (29/48) cross validation technique. The search result shows that there is no clear preference in dimensionality reduction technique among the selected studies. With regards to the classification methods, we notice that SVM (24%) and PAM (21%) are the most commonly used methods. However, when we grouped the classification methods based on their ability to detect interaction between genes, there appeared to be no clear preference for no-interaction or interaction classifiers.

Meta-regression

Table 3 shows the result of individual evaluation for each factor by random effects logistic regression. A model with "class imbalance level" as a fixed effect is considered as the null model. No model with an additional fixed effect is better than the null model. The multivariable model by backward evaluation is summarized in Table 4. We started with the full model which consists of nine study factors. The backward elimination resulted in four study factors that are associated with the performance of a classification method, namely the color system, medical question, cross validation technique, and gene selection method (Table 4). We refer this model as a final meta-regression model. Although the final model would improve without the "class imbalance level" (shown by the lower AIC value if the classification model is excluded from the random effect model), we keep this factor in the logistic model as a correction as stated in the Methods section.

The relative contribution of each study factor to the explained-variation of the full model is shown in Figure 2. The medical question has a large relative explained-variation (25%), followed by cross validation technique (9.2%), disease group (8.0%), microarray color system (2.5%), the number of genes in the final classification model (1.8%), and gene selection technique (1.31%). In total, all study factors together explained 41.9% of the between study variation in the null model.

Discussion

This study was conducted on 48 selected papers that were published between 2005 and 2013 and identified through the PubMed repository. Targeted keywords efficiently selected the relevant papers, among thousands of published microarray classification studies. We aimed to assess the influence of study and method specific determinants of classification model accuracy outside the field of cancer, by analysing eight factors through random effects meta-regression. The accuracy is used as a representation of classification model performance due to the availability of the information in the majority of the selected study. The accuracy is a well-known rough measurement for the performance of a classification model. Especially in highly imbalanced datasets, accuracy may yield overoptimistic results, because a classification model might easily send all samples to the

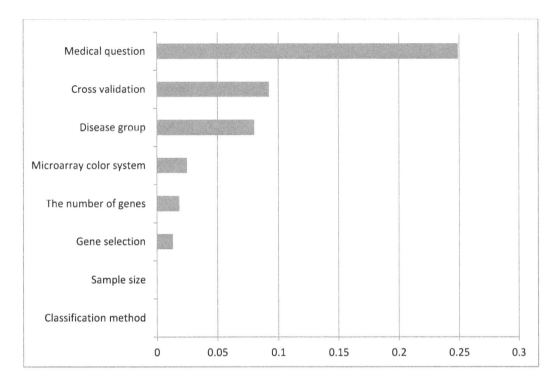

Figure 2. The relative explained-variation of study factors. The x-axis represents the relative explained variation for each study factor, while the y-axis shows the study factors. Table S2 provides more details on the relative explained-variation of each study factor.

majority class. The class imbalance should therefore be taken into account when interpreting the prediction accuracy [1], and a meaningful classification model necessarily should have higher accuracy than the proportion of the majority class. Unfortunately, the classification models in [9,30,35,44] have lower accuracy than their level of class imbalance (Figure S1). Other measurements, such as Mathew's correlation coefficient (MCC), might be less affected by the class imbalance level. However, it was unfeasible to have all information that is necessary to calculate MCC in all selected studies. To deal with the problem of class imbalance when using accuracy, we corrected our random effects models with the

class imbalance level. We then expect that this correction will compensate for the drawback of using accuracy.

The main finding of this study is that four factors were associated with the classification accuracy. The clinical problem (i.e. diagnostic, prognostic or response-to-treatment) had the highest relative contribution to the explained-variation of the full model, which in other terms also had been experienced by the MAQC II consortium study [3]. The MAQC II study defined the difficulty of the classification problem as depending on the endpoint. Further, they found that data using a particular endpoint were easier to be classified than the same data when

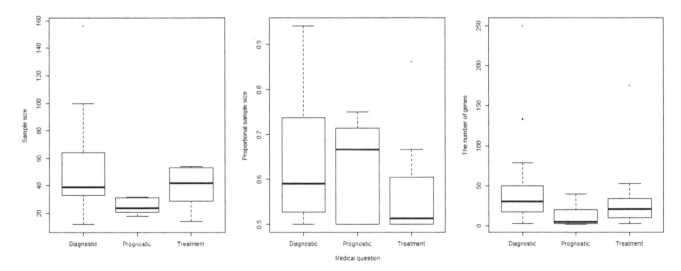

Figure 3. Boxplot of the ''Medical question'' study factor with respect to sample size on training data, proportional sample size (class imbalance level), and the number of genes included in the final classification models.

Table 5. The number of data points (average accuracy) clustered by "medical question" and "cross validation technique".

		Medical question		
		Diagnostic	Prognostic	Response to treatment
Cross validation technique	Single	10 (0.93)	5 (0.90)	13 (0.83)
	Nested	27 (0.87)	2 (0.90)	4 (0.76)

using other endpoints. It shows that the classification performance also depends on the difficulty of the classification problem. In clinical applications, the classification difficulty may also be related to the nature of the medical question: diagnostic, prognostic, or response-to-treatment. In a diagnostic question, the investigator tries to differentiate patients with or without the disease of interest, based on their gene expression. The prediction based on this type of problem should be less complicated than the other two, since the gene expression information is gathered at the time when the disease is already present or not. On the other hand, the response-to-treatment classification predicts an outcome that has to develop over time, based on the gene expression at the start of treatment. The future of a patient is determined by multiple factors, not only on the genomic factors when the information is gathered, but also all events between the information extraction and prediction time. Prognostic classification faces the same issue as response-to-treatment classification, and may be even more difficult. In our study, the classification difficulty is increasing from diagnostic to response-to-treatment. This finding has been experienced previously in Leukaemia [56], where the diagnostic classifier had higher classification performance than prognostic classification. Almost all their diagnostic classifiers had perfect results, while the best model for prognostic questions had only 78% accuracy. The effect of classification difficulty has also been observed by [57], which used the integrated Fisher score to rank the problem difficulty. The number of selected genes did not increase as the classification case became more difficult, which is confirmed by our results (Figure 3). Furthermore, they stated that the gene selection method had a low effect on the classification performance. In our result, the gene selection method was associated with the classification model performance. However, it is also worthy to note that we categorized the gene selection methods based on their interactions with the classifier. Dimensional reduction is often to be done by applying a particular gene selection technique before building a classification model. Some methods, however, have the ability to exclude redundant genes while building the classification model, e.g. PAM and LASSO. Unfortunately, the theoretical advantage of these methods was not used by [28,43,44,48,51,55], making a gene selection step necessary before building the classification model. One reason for this might be because supervised learning and differentially expressed genes analysis were presented in the same paper.

The other important factor that should be considered in building a classification model is the cross-validation technique. It has the second largest of individual explained variability. The variability of classification performance could be due to the diversity of cross validation techniques that were used by investigators. It suggests that more attention shall be put to this factor when we build microarray classification models. Overoptimistic assessment of model performance is the most common flaw in class prediction studies, which causes an upward bias in estimates of prediction accuracy [1,3]. Simple model evaluation is done by dividing the data into a training and a testing set, i.e. build

a model in the training set and test the model into a dataset that is blinded for the training part. The test set should not be involved in any modelling step. An inappropriate approach is to first do the gene selection in the whole dataset and then make the split in training and testing set [1,58], as had been done by [10,18,25,32,43]. In that case, the testing data was partly involved in a model building step through the selection of genes in the model, so that an overoptimistic classifier more likely will be produced. We found 18 studies (40%) that used cross validation for either model assessment or model selection, but not for both. Although our individual evaluation (Table S2 and Figure S2) shows that there is no difference in classification performance of both cross validation techniques, the multivariable final model showed that they do differ. Using cross validation for both model assessment and model selection is definitely to be advised in order to avoid producing an overoptimistic classifier. A framework for building classification models on gene expression data by [59] may be considered as a standard guide.

Another interesting finding in our study is the significant effect of microarray color system on model performance. The one-color microarray platform tends to yield higher accuracy than two-color systems (Figure S3). This result was contradictory with [60] who tested the dependence of the gene expression prediction in neuroblastoma patients on the microarray platform. They concluded that different microarray platforms should be able to yield similar results if the investigators follow the right procedure given by the vendor and they know the nature of those platforms.

Individual evaluation yielded no significant study factors that influenced the class prediction accuracy. A study factor may not be significant in a univariable model, but it may show its effect in a multivariable evaluation, due to the presence of other study factors in the meta-regression model, a mechanism well known as confounding. Hence, we also evaluated the study factors simultaneously by using backward selection. High associations were shown by the medical question and cross validation method (Table 5). The prognostic and response-to-treatment studies tended to use single cross validation method. Nested cross validation is difficult to use in small sample sized data. Hence, they might prefer to use single over nested cross validation. Meanwhile, most of the diagnostic classification studies used nested cross validation, where most of them had relatively large sample size. This explains the confounding in the individual analysis.

Statistical power might be an issue in our study, due to relatively small number of selected studies used for analysis. However, it is also important to note that there are not much published gene expression classification studies outside the cancer field. We found forty eight studies that fulfilled all our requirements (detail search strategy is available in the Supplementary Material). Given the relatively small population of non-cancer published studies, our search yielded a considerable number of studies when it is compared to the literature review studies in the cancer field conducted by [1] (n = 90 studies) and [2] (n = 84 studies). Including cancer studies into our analysis might increase the statistical power and possibly lead to a difference in behaviour of the study factors in cancer and non-cancerous diseases. However, as aforementioned, gene expression studies in the field of cancer have been observed intensively by [1,3,4], particularly in the supervised learning case. Thus, in this study we chose to closely evaluate published classification studies in the microarray gene expression experiment outside the field of cancer. Although we have a relatively small number of studies, our finding in the multivariable evaluation have stable results, in which we found high agreement of the random effect logistic regression model in the jackknife resampling analysis and in the overall analysis (Supplementary Material, Table S3).

This study evaluated eight factors that represent the characteristics of the experiments as well as the gene expression data. The multivariable analysis shows that 42% of the between study variation was explained by these factors, while the other 58% might be explained by un-observed factors, which may include the preprocessing procedures (e.g. batch effect removal, normalization and filtering criteria), the microarray type, and the number of features after the preprocessing steps. We did not include factors such as normalization and batch effect removal due lacking information in the majority of the selected studies. This also rises a recommendation for each published gene expression study to report all steps both in the experiment and in the data analyses, as mentioned by the MIAME (Minimum Information About a Microarray Experiment) guideline [61]. The transparency of study reporting helps to achieve reproducibility of the results and to serve as an input for further research, such as a meta-regression study. The un-reproducibility of result is even more severe when the datasets, in particular the raw dataset, are not publicly available [62]. Among our 48 selected studies, we found only eight studies that had stored both raw and processed datasets; and three studies that stored processed datasets only either in the ArrayExpress or the GEO online repository (last checked on February 4, 2014).

Conclusions

The accuracy of classification models based on gene expression microarray data depends on study specific and problem specific factors. Investigators should pay more attention to these factors when building microarray classification models. The cross validation technique has an important impact in explaining the variability across the studies. Nested cross validation is suggested to be used in any microarray classification study.

Supporting Information

Figure S1 Plot of proportional sample size (the class imbalance level) and the classification model accuracy. The class imbalance level was calculated by dividing the sample size in the majority class by the total sample size in the training data. The diagonal line represents a minimum accuracy that should be achieved by a classification model, based on assigning all subjects to the majority class.

Figure S2 Boxplot of Cross Validation Technique against model accuracy.

Figure S3 Boxplot of microarray platform (color system) against model accuracy.

Table S1 Details of study factors in the selected studies.

Table S2 The variability explained by each modeling factor.

Table S3 Study factors that were included in the multivariable random effect logistic regression models via Jackknife resampling.

Checklist S1 PRISMA checklist.

Material S1 Literature search strategy.

Material S2 Disease classification.

Material S3 R script.

Acknowledgments

Authors would like to thank AI Savitri and G Dalmeijer (Department of Epidemiology, Julius Center for Health Sciences and Primary Care, UMC Utrecht) who helped the Authors in re-classifying the diseases and managing references, respectively.

Author Contributions

Conceived and designed the experiments: KCBR MJCE. Performed the experiments: PWN. Analyzed the data: PWN. Wrote the paper: PWN KCBR MJCE.

References

1. Dupuy A, Simon RM (2007) Critical review of published microarray studies for cancer outcome and guidelines on statistical analysis and reporting. J Natl Cancer Inst 99: 147–157.
2. Coombes KR, Wang J, Baggerly KA (2007) Microarrays: retracing steps. Nat Med 13: 1276–1277.
3. Shi L, Campbell G, Jones WD, Campagne F, Wen Z, et al. (2010) The MicroArray Quality Control (MAQC)-II study of common practices for the development and validation of microarray-based predictive models. Nat Biotechnol 28: 827–838.
4. Ntzani EE, Ioannidis JP (2003) Predictive ability of DNA microarrays for cancer outcomes and correlates: an empirical assessment. Lancet 362: 1439–1444.
5. Stijnen T, Hamza TH, Ozdemir P (2010) Random effects meta-analysis of event outcome in the framework of the generalized linear mixed model with applications in sparse data. Stat Med 29: 3046–3067.
6. Bates D, Maechler M (2009) lme4: Linear mixed-effects models using {S4} classes. {R} package version 0.999375-32.
7. Moher D, Liberati A, Tetzlaff J, Altman DG (2009) Preferred reporting items for systematic reviews and meta-analyses: the PRISMA statement. BMJ 339: b2535.
8. Chen L, Borozan I, Feld J, Sun J, Tannis LL, et al. (2005) Hepatic gene expression discriminates responders and nonresponders in treatment of chronic hepatitis C viral infection. Gastroenterology 128: 1437–1444.
9. Hakonarson H, Bjornsdottir US, Halapi E, Bradfield J, Zink F, et al. (2005) Profiling of genes expressed in peripheral blood mononuclear cells predicts glucocorticoid sensitivity in asthma patients. Proc Natl Acad Sci U S A 102: 14789–14794.
10. Koczan D, Guthke R, Thiesen HJ, Ibrahim SM, Kundt G, et al. (2005) Gene expression profiling of peripheral blood mononuclear leukocytes from psoriasis patients identifies new immune regulatory molecules. Eur J Dermatol 15: 251–257.
11. Moore DF, Li H, Jeffries N, Wright V, Cooper RA, Jr., et al. (2005) Using peripheral blood mononuclear cells to determine a gene expression profile of acute ischemic stroke: a pilot investigation. Circulation 111: 212–221.

12. Ockenhouse CF, Bernstein WB, Wang Z, Vahey MT (2005) Functional genomic relationships in HIV-1 disease revealed by gene-expression profiling of primary human peripheral blood mononuclear cells. J Infect Dis 191: 2064–2074.

13. Tan FK, Hildebrand BA, Lester MS, Stivers DN, Pounds S, et al. (2005) Classification analysis of the transcriptosome of nonlesional cultured dermal fibroblasts from systemic sclerosis patients with early disease. Arthritis Rheum 52: 865–876.

14. Barth AS, Kuner R, Buness A, Ruschhaupt M, Merk S, et al. (2006) Identification of a common gene expression signature in dilated cardiomyopathy across independent microarray studies. J Am Coll Cardiol 48: 1610–1617.

15. Burczynski ME, Peterson RL, Twine NC, Zuberek KA, Brodeur BJ, et al. (2006) Molecular classification of Crohn's disease and ulcerative colitis patients using transcriptional profiles in peripheral blood mononuclear cells. J Mol Diagn 8: 51–61.

16. Pachot A, Lepape A, Vey S, Bienvenu J, Mougin B, et al. (2006) Systemic transcriptional analysis in survivor and non-survivor septic shock patients: a preliminary study. Immunol Lett 106: 63–71.

17. Allantaz F, Chaussabel D, Stichweh D, Bennett L, Allman W, et al. (2007) Blood leukocyte microarrays to diagnose systemic onset juvenile idiopathic arthritis and follow the response to IL-1 blockade. J Exp Med 204: 2131–2144.

18. Kuo CH, Miyazaki D, Nawata N, Tominaga T, Yamasaki A, et al. (2007) Prognosis-determinant candidate genes identified by whole genome scanning in eyes with pterygia. Invest Ophthalmol Vis Sci 48: 3566–3575.

19. Mutch DM, Temanni MR, Henegar C, Combes F, Pelloux V, et al. (2007) Adipose gene expression prior to weight loss can differentiate and weakly predict dietary responders. PLoS One 2: e1344.

20. Tang BM, McLean AS, Dawes IW, Huang SJ, Lin RC (2007) The use of gene-expression profiling to identify candidate genes in human sepsis. Am J Respir Crit Care Med 176: 676–684.

21. Wang Y, Barbacioru CC, Shiffman D, Balasubramanian S, Iakoubova O, et al. (2007) Gene expression signature in peripheral blood detects thoracic aortic aneurysm. PLoS One 2: e1050.

22. Ramilo O, Allman W, Chung W, Mejias A, Ardura M, et al. (2007) Gene expression patterns in blood leukocytes discriminate patients with acute infections. Blood 109: 2066–2077.

23. Aerssens J, Camilleri M, Talloen W, Thielemans L, Gohlmann HW, et al. (2008) Alterations in mucosal immunity identified in the colon of patients with irritable bowel syndrome. Clin Gastroenterol Hepatol 6: 194–205.

24. Cvijanovich N, Shanley TP, Lin R, Allen GL, Thomas NJ, et al. (2008) Validating the genomic signature of pediatric septic shock. Physiol Genomics 34: 127–134.

25. Koczan D, Drynda S, Hecker M, Drynda A, Guthke R, et al. (2008) Molecular discrimination of responders and nonresponders to anti-TNF alpha therapy in rheumatoid arthritis by etanercept. Arthritis Res Ther 10: R50.

26. Vahey MT, Wang Z, Su Z, Nau ME, Krambrink A, et al. (2008) CD4+ T-cell decline after the interruption of antiretroviral therapy in ACTG A5170 is predicted by differential expression of genes in the ras signaling pathway. AIDS Res Hum Retroviruses 24: 1047–1066.

27. Xu H, Tang Y, Liu DZ, Ran R, Ander BP, et al. (2008) Gene expression in peripheral blood differs after cardioembolic compared with large-vessel atherosclerotic stroke: biomarkers for the etiology of ischemic stroke. J Cereb Blood Flow Metab 28: 1320–1328.

28. Arijs I, Li K, Toedter G, Quintens R, Van LL, et al. (2009) Mucosal gene signatures to predict response to infliximab in patients with ulcerative colitis. Gut 58: 1612–1619.

29. Howrylak JA, Dolinay T, Lucht L, Wang Z, Christiani DC, et al. (2009) Discovery of the gene signature for acute lung injury in patients with sepsis. Physiol Genomics 37: 133–139.

30. Julia A, Erra A, Palacio C, Tomas C, Sans X, et al. (2009) An eight-gene blood expression profile predicts the response to infliximab in rheumatoid arthritis. PLoS One 4: e7556.

31. Lin D, Hollander Z, Ng RT, Imai C, Ignaszewski A, et al. (2009) Whole blood genomic biomarkers of acute cardiac allograft rejection. J Heart Lung Transplant 28: 927–935.

32. Nascimento EJ, Braga-Neto U, Calzavara-Silva CE, Gomes AL, Abath FG, et al. (2009) Gene expression profiling during early acute febrile stage of dengue infection can predict the disease outcome. PLoS One 4: e7892.

33. Olsen J, Gerds TA, Seidelin JB, Csillag C, Bjerrum JT, et al. (2009) Diagnosis of ulcerative colitis before onset of inflammation by multivariate modeling of genome-wide gene expression data. Inflamm Bowel Dis 15: 1032–1038.

34. Popper SJ, Watson VE, Shimizu C, Kanegaye JT, Burns JC, et al. (2009) Gene transcript abundance profiles distinguish Kawasaki disease from adenovirus infection. J Infect Dis 200: 657–666.

35. Tanino M, Matoba R, Nakamura S, Kameda H, Amano K, et al. (2009) Prediction of efficacy of anti-TNF biologic agent, infliximab, for rheumatoid arthritis patients using a comprehensive transcriptome analysis of white blood cells. Biochem Biophys Res Commun 387: 261–265.

36. Walter M, Bonin M, Pullman RS, Valente EM, Loi M, et al. (2010) Expression profiling in peripheral blood reveals signature for penetrance in DYT1 dystonia. Neurobiol Dis 38: 192–200.

37. Arijs I, Quintens R, Van LL, Van SK, De HG, et al. (2010) Predictive value of epithelial gene expression profiles for response to infliximab in Crohn's disease. Inflamm Bowel Dis 16: 2090–2098.

38. Fehlbaum-Beurdeley P, Jarrige-Le Prado AC, Pallares D, Carriere J, Guihal C, et al. (2010) Toward an Alzheimer's disease diagnosis via high-resolution blood gene expression. Alzheimers Dement 6: 25–38.

39. Suarez-Farinas M, Shah KR, Haider AS, Krueger JG, Lowes MA (2010) Personalized medicine in psoriasis: developing a genomic classifier to predict histological response to Alefacept. BMC Dermatol 10: 1.

40. Takahashi M, Hayashi H, Watanabe Y, Sawamura K, Fukui N, et al. (2010) Diagnostic classification of schizophrenia by neural network analysis of blood-based gene expression signatures. Schizophr Res 119: 210–218.

41. Woelk CH, Beliakova-Bethell N, Goicoechea M, Zhao Y, Du P, et al. (2010) Gene expression before HAART initiation predicts HIV-infected individuals at risk of poor CD4+ T-cell recovery. AIDS 24: 217–222.

42. Bansard C, Lequerre T, Derambure C, Vittecoq O, Hiron M, et al. (2011) Gene profiling predicts rheumatoid arthritis responsiveness to IL-1Ra (anakinra). Rheumatology (Oxford) 50: 283–292.

43. Kabakchiev B, Turner D, Hyams J, Mack D, Leleiko N, et al. (2010) Gene expression changes associated with resistance to intravenous corticosteroid therapy in children with severe ulcerative colitis. PLoS One 5.

44. Scian MJ, Maluf DG, Archer KJ, Suh JL, Massey D, et al. (2011) Gene expression changes are associated with loss of kidney graft function and interstitial fibrosis and tubular atrophy: diagnosis versus prediction. Transplantation 91: 657–665.

45. Glatt SJ, Tsuang MT, Winn M, Chandler SD, Collins M, et al. (2012) Blood-based gene expression signatures of infants and toddlers with autism. J Am Acad Child Adolesc Psychiatry 51: 934–944.

46. Kong SW, Collins CD, Shimizu-Motohashi Y, Holm IA, Campbell MG, et al. (2012) Characteristics and predictive value of blood transcriptome signature in males with autism spectrum disorders. PLoS One 7: e49475.

47. Maschietto M, Silva AR, Puga RD, Lima L, Pereira CB, et al. (2012) Gene expression of peripheral blood lymphocytes may discriminate patients with schizophrenia from controls. Psychiatry Res 200: 1018–1021.

48. Menke A, Arloth J, Putz B, Weber P, Klengel T, et al. (2012) Dexamethasone stimulated gene expression in peripheral blood is a sensitive marker for glucocorticoid receptor resistance in depressed patients. Neuropsychopharmacology 37: 1455–1464.

49. Murakami Y, Toyoda H, Tanahashi T, Tanaka J, Kumada T, et al. (2012) Comprehensive miRNA expression analysis in peripheral blood can diagnose liver disease. PLoS One 7: e48366.

50. Rahimov F, King OD, Leung DG, Bibat GM, Emerson CP, Jr., et al. (2012) Transcriptional profiling in facioscapulohumeral muscular dystrophy to identify candidate biomarkers. Proc Natl Acad Sci U S A 109: 16234–16239.

51. Rasimas J, Katsounas A, Raza H, Murphy AA, Yang J, et al. (2012) Gene expression profiles predict emergence of psychiatric adverse events in HIV/HCV-coinfected patients on interferon-based HCV therapy. J Acquir Immune Defic Syndr 60: 273–281.

52. Swanson JM, Wood GC, Xu L, Tang LE, Meibohm B, et al. (2012) Developing a gene expression model for predicting ventilator-associated pneumonia in trauma patients: a pilot study. PLoS One 7: e42065.

53. Zhou T, Zhang W, Sweiss NJ, Chen ES, Moller DR, et al. (2012) Peripheral blood gene expression as a novel genomic biomarker in complicated sarcoidosis. PLoS One 7: e44818.

54. Balow JE, Jr., Ryan JG, Chae JJ, Booty MG, Bulua A, et al. (2013) Microarray-based gene expression profiling in patients with cryopyrin-associated periodic syndromes defines a disease-related signature and IL-1-responsive transcripts. Ann Rheum Dis 72: 1064–1070.

55. Lunnon K, Sattlecker M, Furney SJ, Coppola G, Simmons A, et al. (2013) A blood gene expression marker of early Alzheimer's disease. J Alzheimers Dis 33: 737–753.

56. Willenbrock H, Juncker AS, Schmiegelow K, Knudsen S, Ryder LP (2004) Prediction of immunophenotype, treatment response, and relapse in childhood acute lymphoblastic leukemia using DNA microarrays. Leukemia 18: 1270–1277.

57. Popovici V, Chen W, Gallas BG, Hatzis C, Shi W, et al. (2010) Effect of training-sample size and classification difficulty on the accuracy of genomic predictors. Breast Cancer Res 12: R5.

58. Ambroise C, McLachlan GJ (2002) Selection bias in gene extraction on the basis of microarray gene-expression data. Proc Natl Acad Sci U S A 99: 6562–6566.

59. Wessels LF, Reinders MJ, Hart AA, Veenman CJ, Dai H, et al. (2005) A protocol for building and evaluating predictors of disease state based on microarray data. Bioinformatics 21: 3755–3762.

60. Oberthuer A, Juraeva D, Li L, Kahlert Y, Westermann F, et al. (2010) Comparison of performance of one-color and two-color gene-expression analyses in predicting clinical endpoints of neuroblastoma patients. Pharmacogenomics J 10: 258–266.

61. Brazma A, Hingamp P, Quackenbush J, Sherlock G, Spellman P, et al. (2001) Minimum information about a microarray experiment (MIAME)-toward standards for microarray data. Nat Genet 29: 365–371.

62. Ioannidis JP, Allison DB, Ball CA, Coulibaly I, Cui X, et al. (2009) Repeatability of published microarray gene expression analyses. Nat Genet 41: 149–155.

17

Overcoming Catastrophic Interference in Connectionist Networks Using Gram-Schmidt Orthogonalization

Vipin Srivastava[1,2]*, Suchitra Sampath[2], David J. Parker[3]

1 School of Physics, University of Hyderabad, Hyderabad, India, **2** Centre for Neural and Cognitive Sciences, University of Hyderabad, Hyderabad, India, **3** Department of Physiology, Development and Neuroscience, University of Cambridge, Cambridge, United Kingdom

Abstract

Connectionist models of memory storage have been studied for many years, and aim to provide insight into potential mechanisms of memory storage by the brain. A problem faced by these systems is that as the number of items to be stored increases across a finite set of neurons/synapses, the cumulative changes in synaptic weight eventually lead to a sudden and dramatic loss of the stored information (catastrophic interference, CI) as the previous changes in synaptic weight are effectively lost. This effect does not occur in the brain, where information loss is gradual. Various attempts have been made to overcome the effects of CI, but these generally use schemes that impose restrictions on the system or its inputs rather than allowing the system to intrinsically cope with increasing storage demands. We show here that catastrophic interference occurs as a result of interference among patterns that lead to catastrophic effects when the number of patterns stored exceeds a critical limit. However, when Gram-Schmidt orthogonalization is combined with the Hebb-Hopfield model, the model attains the ability to eliminate CI. This approach differs from previous orthogonalisation schemes used in connectionist networks which essentially reflect sparse coding of the input. Here CI is avoided in a network of a fixed size without setting limits on the rate or number of patterns encoded, and without separating encoding and retrieval, thus offering the advantage of allowing associations between incoming and stored patterns. PACS Nos.: 87.10.+e, 87.18.Bb, 87.18.Sn, 87.19.La

Editor: Manabu Sakakibara, Tokai University, Japan

Funding: The Royal Society; The Leverhulme Foundation (UK); National Initiative of Research in Cognitive Science by the Department of Science and Technology, Government of India. The funders had no role in study design, data collection and analysis, decision to publish, or preparation of the manuscript.

Competing Interests: The authors have declared that no competing interests exist.

* Email: vipinsri02@gmail.com

Introduction

Nervous systems have two basic requirements: they must be stable and thus able to generate reliable specific outputs, while at the same time they must be flexible to allow the output to change during development or as a result of experience. This is the "stability-plasticity dilemma" [1], and it is a concern to both neurobiologists who want to understand how nervous systems cope with constantly changing internal and external conditions, and those working on artificial neural networks. While not exclusively related to it, this problem is often considered in relation to memory. The analysis of memory systems has been a major focus of neuroscience research, but there are still many unanswered questions that need to be addressed at both the experimental and theoretical levels. In terms of the stability-plasticity problem, the question is how a system can store new input patterns across shared components without disturbing previously stored information in those components.

One of the first considerations of this problem was highlighted by Bienenstock, Cooper and Munro [2], who suggested that long-term potentiation (LTP), a proposed mechanism for learning and memory [3], could suffer from an inherent instability (the BCM model). They suggested that in systems with a set threshold for plasticity the potentiation of a synapse by a particular input that exceeded the threshold could leave that synapse open to further potentiation when another, non-salient, input was presented (this

has also been referred to as the "ongoing plasticity" problem; see [4]). Due to the initial potentiation of the synapse, non-salient or random inputs caused by a non-stationary environment could exceed the threshold for plasticity, resulting in the potential for run-away cycles of potentiation which would alter the synaptic changes associated with the original memory. This would effectively overwrite the original memory, and in biological systems if left unchecked, excessive activation could also lead to epileptogenic or excitotoxic damage and cell death [5]. The opposite effect could occur with long-term depression, where a synapse is weakened when the input falls below a depression threshold: in this case there could be a positive feedback loop that results in the successive depression of the synapse.

While the exact relationship is not clear, a similar effect may occur in artificial neural networks. When the number of sequentially recorded/stored patterns exceeds a critical value there is a sudden and complete loss of previously stored inputs [6]. This example of retroactive interference is called catastrophic interference (CI) and is caused by the sharing of connections whose weights are changed by the presentation of specific inputs. As more patterns are stored the weights are changed and beyond a critical point new inputs erase the memory of previous inputs. If the memories happen to be overlapping, or correlated, which essentially means that several of their elements are similar (the mathematical meaning is explained in [7], [8]), then a particular synapse may get increasingly more potentiated (or depressed), thus resembling the stability issues addressed in the BCM model. In human memory, although recently stored or retrieved memories are labile (e.g. [9], [10]), it is rare to find a complete disruption or loss of previously acquired information: a relatively small and gradual reduction ("graceful degradation") rather than a large catastrophic loss usually occurs (e.g. [11]; but see [12], [13], [14]). That a catastrophic interference like effect can be shown under some conditions is of interest, as it suggests a basic limitation of storage systems that use a finite (although large) number of components, and further that the brain has presumably evolved a way of avoiding this phenomenon, allowing new information to be stored without disrupting previously stored information (but see [15]). Understanding this capability of the brain and how it can be applied in artificial networks could be of interest to both the psychological/neurobiological and technological communities.

Various strategies have been suggested to overcome the effects of CI. These include the separation of new inputs from those previously stored by using a cascade of synaptic states [16]; separate encoding and storage systems (e.g. hippocampal and neocortical networks; [17]); setting limits on the magnitude or rate of learning [18]); the creation of new storage components through neurogenesis [19]; anti-Hebbian plasticity [20]; reducing the overlap between different patterns by sparse coding or by limiting or "sharpening" the number of units used to encode an input, orthogonal recoding of inputs, or interleaving, refreshing previously stored inputs with the new patterns to be learnt (see [12] for review by French and also Guyon et al. for an orthogonalization like approach that involves pseudoinverse of state matrix). Connectionist architectures use interleaving algorithms that require the network to repeatedly cycle through the patterns to be learned; after the entire set of patterns has been presented many times, the network is expected to converge on an appropriate set of weights for the complete set. The problem of CI has also been addressed by curbing the growth of synaptic efficacy by putting bounds on plasticity (see [4]). This is biologically realistic, as it reflects "soft-bound" plasticity, the difficulty of potentiating synapses that are initially strong [21]. While these approaches can overcome effects in theoretical analyses, they all have limitations in terms of their implementation or their biological relevance [22], [23].

The potential parallels between the stability issues in biological and artificial systems inspire us to study the run-away cycle of potentiation using strategies employed to overcome CI. The BCM model suggested a form of self-organising or homeostatic plasticity that could preserve function within set limits while still offering the possibility of directed plastic changes through a sliding plasticity threshold [24], [25]. This threshold would be increased after LTP (or decreased after long-term depression, LTD) to ensure that the potentiation (or depression) needed to encode relevant changes could occur, but further potentiation would not occur with non-salient or random ongoing inputs, only when the new input exceeded the new plasticity threshold [26], [24]. In this case the plasticity of the synapse would be dependent on the previous activity of the synapse, an example of metaplasticity [27].

The BCM model is an attractive and biologically plausible proposition for introducing bounds on synaptic plasticity that could help to overcome the stability-plasticity dilemma. However, as with most attempts to relate cellular and synaptic effects to network function (e.g. memory), while there is evidence for a shifting plasticity threshold the extent to which a BCM-like effect is involved in human memory has not been established, and the model has not been considered in artificial systems in the context of catastrophic interference. We show that when Gram-Schmidt

orthogonalization is combined with the Hebb-Hopfield model, the model automatically checks the possibility of a run-away potentiation cycle from being set up, and thus attains the ability to eliminate CI.

The model we use is extremely simplified and uses the bare minimum core features of the neural system we wish to study, and its underlying conditions. Consequently it may appear to be far removed from biology. However, it is analytically tractable and is very widely used in theoretical analyses, and it has an inherent property of encoding synapse-like elements that should give the essential science behind the phenomena we are interested in. Also it should generalize to more realistic models, assuming that certain assumptions are met (see Discussion). We believe that the insight we obtain from it may represent real phenomena. Because of the mathematical nature of the model, it is open in that it can, in principle, be generalized indefinitely to include realistic features. At every stage of its generalization (or expansion) to include a new realistic feature, its mathematical tractability has to be ascertained, and in principle the numbers that come out of solving the improved model should be comparable to experimental measurements.

Inherent Bounds on Post-Synaptic Response in Hopfield Model

Outline of the model

For mathematical convenience and in line with most connectionist modeling we will consider a fully connected network in which each neuron is connected to all other neurons, and an information is spread over the entire network and stored as changes in synaptic efficacy that depend on the activities of the pre- and the post-synaptic neurons. The same set of neurons and synapses are involved in storage as well as retrieval of information. A neuron is treated as a binary entity, which assumes values $+1$ and -1 depending on whether it 'fires' or 'does not fire'. An information that comes to be recorded in the network is assumed to trigger 'firing' and 'not firing' activities among the neurons in an asynchronous manner: the neurons exchange signals (i.e. action potentials) which raise or lower the potentials on post-synaptic neurons, and if the net potential on a neuron exceeds its threshold then it fires ($+1$), otherwise it remains quiescent (-1). Thus, an information 'μ' is represented by a vector,

$$\vec{\xi}^{(\mu)} = \{1, -1, -1, 1, \ldots\}, \qquad (1)$$

whose components are a collection of $+1$ and -1 (appearing to be distributed randomly) [28]. The information, represented by a pattern of ± 1's spread over the network, is stored in the synapses according to the following learning rule, originally postulated by Cooper [29] to mimic Hebbian synaptic plasticity:

$$J_{ij} = \frac{1}{N} \sum_{\mu=1}^{p} (\xi_i^{(\mu)} \xi_j^{(\mu)} - \delta_{ij} \xi_i^{(\mu)} \xi_i^{(\mu)}). \qquad (2)$$

J_{ij} is the synaptic efficacy between a pair of neurons i and j, $\xi_i^{(\mu)}$ is the ith component of vector $\vec{\xi}^{(\mu)}$, δ_{ij} is Kronecker delta function ($= 0$ unless $i = j$, when it is 1), N represents the number of neurons in the network, and p is the number of patterns recorded in the network. The right hand side is divided by N to normalise the results so that they become independent of the size of the system, i.e. the number of neurons in the network (note that the length of

$\vec{\xi}^{(\mu)} = (\vec{\xi}^{(\mu)}.\vec{\xi}^{(\mu)})^{1/2} = N^{1/2}$, so by dividing $\vec{\xi}^{(\mu)}$, or equivalently each of its components, by $N^{1/2}$ the length of the vector is normalised to *one* regardless of the size of the system). For simplicity we consider $J_{ij} = J_{ji}$, though the model does not impose this restriction, but $J_{ii} = 0$ is required for mathematical reasons [30]. The δ_{ij} is introduced in the second term on the right hand side to ensure that $J_{ii} = 0$. It is assumed that synaptic efficacy between two neurons depends on the activities of the post- and the pre-synaptic neurons, and following Hebb [31], since the efficacy is expected to be high if both neurons fire and low when one of them is not firing, the J_{ij} is taken as multiplication of ξ_i and ξ_j. This means that if, for example, the postsynaptic neuron fires independently of the presynaptic neuron the synaptic efficacy will be weakened, which has a correlate in spike timing-dependent plasticity in biological systems (e.g. [32]). However, biologically there is no correlate as to how the efficacy of J_{ij} can be increased if both the neurons do not fire, as rule (2) would indicate. This rule is referred to as Hebbian learning in spite of the above discrepancy. In practice, the potentiation predicted when neither neuron fires is often ignored by placing a bound on the synapse [33].

Note that the $i-j$ synapse changes every time a pattern comes to be recorded and the change is added to the changes produced by the previous patterns. Having stored a number of patterns, say p, we should test if they are actually stored in the synapses following the Hebbian prescription in (2). We can present one of the p learnt patterns to the network and check if it can associate with its original version supposedly embedded in the memory store. The presented pattern, say v^{th}, will create local fields on different sites (or neurons) via the synaptic efficacies (or weights) modified in the course of learning p patterns as follows,

$$h_i^{(v)} = \sum_{j=1}^{N}{}' J_{ij}\xi_j^{(v)}. \tag{3}$$

Here i is the post-synaptic neuron, and j are the pre-synaptic neurons with respect to i. The 'prime' on the summation indicates that the sum is over all j's except i so that the inputs from all j sites add up on i and self-connections J_{ii}'s are excluded. The activity or its absence on pre-synaptic neurons j represented by $\xi_j = +1$ and -1 respectively individually influence the neuron i with weights J_{ij}'s, and these influences (which can be positive or negative since the weights as well as ξ_j can be positive as well as negative) add up on the post-synaptic neuron i to produce a net effect, the local potential h_i. This local field (or potential), which is a measure of total post-synaptic potential (PSP) on neuron i can be positive or negative. If its sign matches with the sign of $\xi_i^{(v)}$, and such agreement happens on the majority of neurons (say, more than 97%, a generally accepted level; see [34] and references therein) then the association is considered to be good and the pattern v is considered as recalled, or retrieved.

To elaborate it we will substitute for J_{ij} from eqn.(2). So,

$$h_i^{(v)} = \sum_{j=1}^{N}\left[\frac{1}{N}\sum_{\mu=1}^{p}\left(\xi_i^{(\mu)}\xi_j^{(\mu)} - \delta_{ij}\xi_i^{(\mu)}\xi_i^{(\mu)}\right)\right]\xi_j^{(v)},$$
$$= \frac{1}{N}\sum_{\mu=1}^{p}\xi_i^{(\mu)}\left[\left(\vec{\xi}^{(\mu)}.\vec{\xi}^{(v)}\right) - \xi_i^{(\mu)}\xi_i^{(v)}\right], \tag{4}$$

since $\sum_{j=1}^{N}\xi_j^{(\mu)}\xi_j^{(v)} = \vec{\xi}^{(\mu)}.\vec{\xi}^{(v)}$, the dot-product of two vectors, and δ_{ij} picks out $\xi_i^{(v)}$ from $\sum_{j=1}^{N}\xi_j^{(v)}$ and makes the remaining terms

zero, δ_{ij} also serves the purpose of 'the prime' on $\sum_{j=1}^{N}{}'$, so 'the prime' is dropped in eqn.(4). Isolating the $\mu = v$ component from $\sum_{\mu=1}^{p}$ in the first term on the right hand side, we will get N from $\vec{\xi}^{(v)}.\vec{\xi}^{(v)}$ and will be left with $\xi_i^{(v)}$. Further, $\frac{1}{N}\sum_{\mu=1}^{p}\xi_i^{(\mu)}\xi_i^{(\mu)}$ will give p/N in either case of $\xi_i^{(\mu)}$ being $+1$ or -1. Thus, we find that,

$$h_i^{(v)} = \left(1 - \frac{p}{N}\right)\xi_i^{(v)} + \frac{1}{N}\sum_{\substack{\mu=1 \\ (\mu \neq v)}}^{p}\xi_i^{(\mu)}\left(\vec{\xi}^{(\mu)}.\vec{\xi}^{(v)}\right). \tag{5}$$

This rearrangement has enabled us to isolate $\xi_i^{(v)}$, whose sign is to be compared with that of $h_i^{(v)}$, from a jumble of cross terms involving the test pattern 'v' and all the other patterns in the memory store represented by 'μ'. This is like separating a signal from a jumbled mixture of cross-talks this signal has with a number of other signals. If $\vec{\xi}^{(\mu)}$'s happen to be mutually orthogonal, the cross-talks will vanish and the memories would work perfectly [30].

Analysis of post-synaptic potential

The sign of $h_i^{(v)}$ (or PSP) can become unfavourable (i.e. opposite of $\xi_i^{(v)}$) due to the second term in eqn.(5) (let us call it $\mathcal{A}$). Since the vectors $\vec{\xi}^{(\mu)}$ consist of randomly generated $+1$'s and -1's, each of the p terms in the second term in the right hand side of eqn (5) will take a fractional value, less than 1, with a random sign (+ or −). Thus, for $\xi_i^{(v)} = +1$, $\mathcal{A}$ can take any positive or negative value limited by the values of p and N, but as long as it is greater than $-(1-p/N)$, $h_i^{(v)}$ will match in sign with $\xi_i^{(v)}$. Similarly, for $\xi_i^{(v)} = -1$, $h_i^{(v)}$ will match in sign with $\xi_i^{(v)}$ if $\mathcal{A}$ remains less than $(1-p/N)$. Figure 1 shows the favourable ranges of values of $\mathcal{A}$ in the form of shaded areas. Note that in general $\vec{\xi}^{(\mu)}$'s are not orthogonal to $\vec{\xi}^{(v)}$. So, the dot products $\vec{\xi}^{(\mu)}.\vec{\xi}^{(v)}$ are non-zero. In spite of the signs being randomly + or − the chances of $\mathcal{A}$ growing arbitrarily large, +ve or -ve, become increasingly large with increasing p. This increases the possibility of CI as explained below.

In eqn.(5) the first term on the right hand side is like signal while $\mathcal{A}$ represents noise – note that the first term is obtained by isolating in eqn (4) the relevant component, i.e. i^{th}, of the pattern being retrieved, i.e. the vth vector, while the overlaps of $\vec{\xi}^{(v)}$ with all the remaining vectors in the memory store are clubbed together in the second term; it is these non-zero overlaps that obfuscate the signal and hence act as noise. From the above we see that as long as the noise $\mathcal{A}$ can be bounded by $(p/N-1)$ from below and by $(1-p/N)$ from above, $h_i^{(v)}$ will be confined between $(p/N-1)$ and $(1-p/N)$, and CI will be contained. However, as new patterns come to be recorded, there is no intrinsic mechanism in the Hopfield model to control their overlaps with the patterns already in the store and thereby restrict the noise $\mathcal{A}$ to within the above limits, and thus restrict $h_i^{(v)}$ to within the above favourable limits. Thus, as the number of patterns in the store increases the noise builds up and the likelihood of $h_i^{(v)}$ remaining within favourable limits reduces on more of the neurons (i's) in the system and CI becomes inescapable. These bounds on PSP can slide with the variations in p and N, to make CI more susceptible or less susceptible. If p increases (for a given N) then the bounds shrink and the system becomes more susceptible to CI, which is understandable since the interference among patterns will increase as their number increases. On the other hand the increasing system size (such that

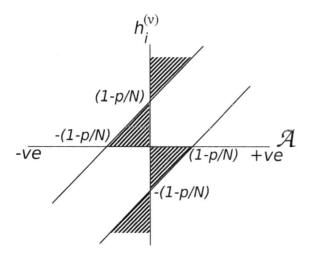

Figure 1. Schematic representation of $h_i^{(v)}$, the post-synaptic potential on an arbitrary site i when one of the learnt patterns, v is presented to check for retrieval, versus $\mathcal{A}$, the noise term in eqn.4. The shaded areas represent the domains where $h_i^{(v)}\xi_i^{(v)}$ will be positive definite. The bounds on $h_i^{(v)}$ slide up and down with variations in p and N enabling, at least in principle, plasticity to control CI to some extent.

$p/N \rightarrow 0$) would widen the gap between the bounds and reduce the chances of CI.

Note that outside the above bounds $\mathcal{A}$ can, in principle, grow to very large positive or negative values, akin to runaway affects in the BCM model (see above). Although indefinitely large positive and negative values of $\mathcal{A}$ will keep $h_i^{(v)}\xi_i^{(v)} > 0$ for $\xi_i^{(v)} = +1$ and $\xi_i^{(v)} = -1$ respectively, the fact is that $\mathcal{A}$ takes positive or negative values in a seemingly uncontrolled and random manner. Therefore, its growth to large values is, in general, detrimental to retrieval (or recall) and leads to CI [34]. This will cause the run-away effect, which will eventually give false (or deceptive) associations with the feature designated by site i.

The uncontrolled growth of $h_i^{(v)}$ on a large number of sites inevitably leads to catastrophic forgetting in the Hopfield model if the ratio p/N exceeds 0.14 (see e.g. [30]). In figure 2 we present the result of a simulation showing how degradation sets in in the quality of retrieval as p/N exceeds 0.14 (details are given in the following section).

A Way Out of Catastrophic Interference

It is our hypothesis that when a stimulus (or vector) $\vec{\xi}$ is presented to the system, the system orthogonalizes it with respect to all the vectors in the memory store and then stores the orthogonalized vector $\vec{\eta}$ rather than the raw vector $\vec{\xi}$ [7]. In real terms this amounts to storing the similarities and differences of the new vector with the old vectors.

Suppose $\vec{\eta}^{(1)}$, $\vec{\eta}^{(2)}$, ..., $\vec{\eta}^{(p)}$ are the orthogonalized versions of $\vec{\xi}^{(1)}$, $\vec{\xi}^{(2)}$, ..., $\vec{\xi}^{(p)}$, and they are stored in the Hebbian manner as,

$$J_{ij}(p) = \sum_{\mu=1}^{p}\left(\hat{\eta}_i^{(\mu)}\hat{\eta}_j^{(\mu)} - \delta_{ij}\hat{\eta}_i^{(\mu)}\hat{\eta}_i^{(\mu)}\right), \qquad (6)$$

where $\{\hat{\eta}_i^{(\mu)}\}$ are the components of $\hat{\vec{\eta}}^{(\mu)}$ obtained by normalising $\vec{\eta}^{(\mu)}$ as $\vec{\eta}^{(\mu)}/|\vec{\eta}^{(\mu)}|$. It is not immediately obvious as to how the brain

would perform the normalization. While there is physiological and behavioural (e.g. psychophysical) evidence for normalization as a canonical neural computation, its role and underlying mechanisms are still an area of intense research [35].

Now a new vector, $\vec{\xi}^{(p+1)}$ comes to be recorded. Some neurons fire and some don't, accordingly they get values $+1$ and -1, and through the above J_{ij}'s, local fields, or PSP's, develop on each neuronal site as,

$$h_i^{(p+1)} = \sum_{j=1}^{N}J_{ij}\xi_j^{(p+1)}; \; for \; i = 1,2,...,N. \qquad (7)$$

As explained above the $h_i^{(p+1)}$'s may or may not match with $\xi_i^{(p+1)}$'s for all values of i, but, in any case, the system would know the difference $(\xi_i^{(p+1)} - h_i^{(p+1)})$ on each neural site. Note that the computation of this difference on each site already amounts to orthogonalization [7], i.e.

$$\vec{\eta}^{(p+1)} = \vec{\xi}^{(p+1)} - \vec{h}^{(p+1)}, \qquad (8)$$

where,

$$\vec{h}^{(p+1)} \equiv \{h_i^{(p+1)}\} = \sum_{\mu=1}^{p}\hat{\vec{\eta}}^{(\mu)}\left(\hat{\vec{\eta}}^{(\mu)}.\vec{\xi}^{(p+1)}\right) - \mathcal{O}\left(\frac{p}{N}\right)\vec{\xi}^{(p+1)}, \quad (9)$$

since $(\hat{\eta}_i^{(\mu)})^2$ is of the order of $1/N$.

The interesting new thing we point out here is that if it so happens that $\vec{\xi}^{(p+1)}$ is already in the memory store, say as the vth vector ($1 \leq v < p$), then $\vec{\xi}^{(v)}$ will not project on to $\vec{\eta}^{(v+1)},...,\vec{\eta}^{(p)}$ [36], and the first $(v-1)$ terms in eqn.(9) will give $(\vec{\xi}^{(v)} - \vec{\eta}^{(v)})$. Then,

$$\vec{h}^{(v)} = \vec{\xi}^{(v)} - \vec{\eta}^{(v)} + \hat{\vec{\eta}}^{(v)}\left(\hat{\vec{\eta}}^{(v)}.\vec{\xi}^{(v)}\right) - \mathcal{O}\left(\frac{p}{N}\right)\vec{\xi}^{(v)} = (1 - \mathcal{O}\left(\frac{p}{N}\right))\vec{\xi}^{(v)} (10)$$

since $\vec{\eta}^{(v)}.\vec{\xi}^{(v)} = \vec{\eta}^{(v)}.\vec{\eta}^{(v)}$. So the presented $\vec{\xi}^{(p+1)}$ will be identified as $\vec{\xi}^{(v)}$, with $\vec{\eta}^{(p+1)}$ on the order of zero. This would imply that $\vec{\xi}^{(p+1)}$ will not be orthogonalized and stored again, no matter how often it is presented. However, if it turns out that $\vec{\xi}^{(p+1)}$ is indeed a new vector, which is not there in the memory store, then $\vec{\eta}^{(p+1)}$ will be computed according to eqn.(8) and will be stored in the synapses following the modified Hebb's learning rule (6). Some clarification is needed here in order to understand how Hebb-Hopfield model with Gram-Schmidt orthogonalization (H-H-G-S) scores over the conventional Hebb-Hopfield (H-H) model.

Let p normalized vectors be stored (for p/N very small, say 0.05) in each of the above two cases, and let a test vector that is similar to (but not exactly the same as) one of the p stored vectors be presented to check if it associates with any of the p stored vectors. In both the cases the test vector will indeed associate with one of those p vectors to which it resembles. This means that in H-H-G-S scheme the p imprinted vectors are stable in the same way as in the H-H scheme, i.e. they have non-zero basins of attraction [30,37], and that the test vector, which falls within the basin of attraction of one of the imprinted vectors, converges to the imprinted vector. Thus the attractor neural network (ANN) character typically attributed to H-H is preserved in H-H-G-S.

To elaborate further we note that two processes are involved in this: (i) 'storage' of information (or vectors) in the synapses through

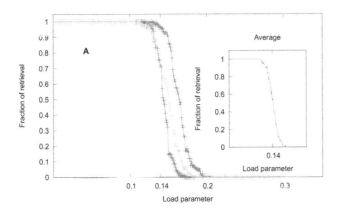
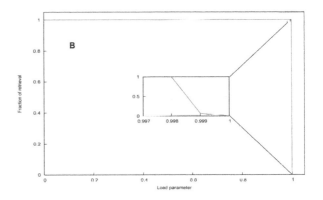

Figure 2. Simulation results for a system of 1000 neurons. (A) Hopfield network showing memory breakdown due to catastrophic interference amongst the stored patterns – the fraction of input patterns that is retrieved drops rapidly around the load parameter, $p/N = 0.14$. The results are shown for three sets of patterns and the inset shows the results averaged over 50 sets of patterns. (B) Hopfield network with Gram-Schmidt orthogonalization of the incoming patterns. All the learnt patterns are retrieved perfectly until $p = N$, when the retrieval fraction drops to zero abruptly. The inset shows magnification very close to the load parameter $= 1$ to highlight the abruptness of the drop. Note that the system does not learn the raw patterns as they are presented but their orthogonalized versions, whereas the retrieval is checked for the raw patterns.

eqns. (2) and (6) respectively in the two cases; and (ii) 'association' of a presented test vector with one of the memorised vectors through prescriptions (3) and (7) respectively. The two processes are invoked independently in H-H in that when a new vector is presented we have to specify whether the process of 'storage' needs to be invoked or whether the vector is meant to be 'associated' with a vector in the memory. If it is instructed to be stored then it will be stored regardless of the extent of its similarity or difference with any of the vectors already in the memory. But in H-H-G-S the two processes are linked.

When a new vector is presented to the H-H-G-S scheme for storage, it has to be first orthogonalized, and as part of orthogonalization it is first subjected to a check, through eqn.(7), whether it 'associates' with any of the stored vectors, and if so, with which one. If it falls within the basin of attraction of one of the stored vectors [30] then it will be associated with that particular vector in the memory store and signs of $\{h_i^{(p+1)}\}$ will coincide with those of the components of that vector. In case the new vector is not similar to any of the stored vectors then $\vec{h}^{(p+1)}$ will be an independent vector that holds the information of the overlaps of the new presented vector with all the stored vectors in a convoluted manner.

The above amounts to half of the orthogonalization process. The process is completed with the comparison (through eqn.(8)) of the new presented vector with $\vec{h}^{(p+1)}$, which may correspond either to one of the stored vectors or to a vector very different from any one of them. The difference calculated by eqn.(8) will be small or large depending on the two situations, but in either case this will tantamount to orthogonalization and the orthogonalized version of the new vector will be 'stored' according to eqn.(6). In case the presented new vector happens to be identical (not just *similar*) to a vector already in the memory store then, as shown in eqn.(10), $\vec{\eta}^{(p+1)}$ will be identically zero.

The H-H-G-S scheme thus appears to be close to reality in which when the brain encounters a new information, before storing it, it knows, in the background of the information already in its memory, that the new information is completely familiar, or completely unfamiliar, or partially familiar. This is accomplished by the first part of orthogonalization represented by eqn.(7), namely 'association'.

The crucial implication in the present context of CI is that orthogonalization diminishes the overlap of any pattern that comes to be recorded with everyone of those that are already in the store and thus suppresses the noise $\mathcal{A}$. The PSPs, $h_i^{(p+1)}$'s on all the sites i, are pinned at $(1 - \mathcal{O}(\frac{p}{N}))\xi_i^{(v)}$. Since $\xi_i^{(v)} = \pm 1$, the PSP's are strictly confined within the range $((\mathcal{O}(\frac{p}{N}) - 1), (1 - \mathcal{O}(\frac{p}{N})))$. Thus, already familiar stimuli are blocked from stimulating the system again and again to cause overloading and a possible runaway potentiation.

In Figure 2 we present results of our simulations showing (a) how the retrieval quality drops rapidly around $p/N = 0.14$ signifying CI, and (b) how Gram-Schmidt orthogonalization overcomes catastrophic interference. We use a system comprising 1000 neurons. Patterns are generated using pseudo-random number generators to assign values $+1$ and -1 to the neurons. The patterns are learnt sequentially and stored by changing the synaptic efficacy J_{ij} and accumulating the changes as in eqn.(2). Soon after a pattern is stored, it is presented back to the network to check if it can be retrieved using the prescription elaborated in eqns.(3–5). Figure 2(A) shows the fraction of retrieval, i.e. the ratio, (no. of retrieved patterns)/(no. of learnt patterns), versus load parameter, which is the ratio of (no. of learnt patterns)/(total number of neurons), i.e. p/N. Around $p/N = 0.14$ the fraction of retrieved patterns dips below 90% quite rapidly and reduces to almost zero around $p/N = 0.17$. The results are shown for three sets of input patters. The inset shows the same plot after averaging over 18 sets of patterns. Figure 2(B) shows the same calculation after invoking Gram-Schmidt orthogonalization on the incoming patterns – an incoming pattern is first orthogonalized with respect to all the stored patterns (using eqn.(8)) and then stored, but the original, or the raw pattern (before orthogonalization) is tested for retrieval. In a system of 1000 neurons all presented patterns are retrieved perfectly until $p = 998$. For $p = 999$ the fraction of retrieved patterns dips abruptly to almost zero, and to exactly zero when $p = 1000$ as amplified in the inset.

Even though by storing orthogonalized patterns the memory capacity appears to rise from $0.14N$ to almost N it is important that we check the stability of the stored memories. As stated above we should do it by computing the basins of attraction for the memories. Using the standard definitions [30,37] we did the simulations for a smaller network of 100 neurons to get an idea as to how the size of basin of attraction changes when we introduce orthogonalization.

To get the right perspective we first did the calculations for the conventional Hopfield model. The network was made to learn 12 randomly generated 100-dimensional patterns (of +1 and −1) according to eqn.(2). The patterns were then picked up one by one and states of certain neurons were switched (from −1 to +1 or vice versa) – starting with switching of state of one neuron chosen randomly – and it was checked if the chosen imprinted pattern, say v^{th}, could be retrieved following the prescription of eqn.(5). If the signs of $\{h_i\}$ did not match with those of the imprinted $\{\xi_i^{(v)}\}$ then $\{h_i\}$ were fed to the right hand side of eqn.(5) as $\{\xi_i\}$ and new $\{h_i\}$ were calculated and their signs were compared with those of the imprinted $\{\xi_i^{(v)}\}$. A maximum of 10 such iterations were tried to check if they led to convergence to the imprinted $\vec{\xi}^{(v)}$. This exercise was repeated for 10 samples generated by picking the 'flipped' neuron from 10 different locations chosen randomly in the array of 100 neurons.

The above procedure was repeated by switching signs of more and more neurons successively until the overlap of the retrieved pattern with the corresponding imprinted pattern fell below 100%. This marked the size of basin of attraction for a particular imprinted pattern.

For the conventional Hopfield model the basin of attraction for 12 imprinted patterns were distributed in a broad range from 26 to 44, with maximum probability for basins of sizes 34 to 37. As the number of imprinted patterns increased beyond 10 certain patterns began to show absence of basin of attraction (i.e. basin of size zero). Beyond 14 memorised patterns the number of patterns with zero basin of attraction increased rapidly.

Orthogonalization improves the situation considerably. We considered the same 12 patterns but stored their orthogonalized versions. The original patterns (before orthogonalization) were considered for retrieval and basins of attraction were computed for them. The sizes of basins ranged between 6 and 45 but were concentrated around 31. From $p = 14$ certain patterns begin to lose basin of attraction (i.e. basin of attraction of size zero) though with very small probability, about 0.0093. The probability increases quite rapidly with p, becoming 0.49 at $p = 24$ and 1.0 when p touches 100. Thus orthogonalization presents an interesting scenario in which in a system of N neurons up to $(N-1)$ patterns are stored and retrieved efficiently, and therefore compete for space for basin of attraction. There are several interesting issues that need close investigation. We are in the process of carrying them out.

Discussion

Many approaches have been used to try and overcome the problems of the actual or predicted loss of stored information in memory systems, both in connectionist networks (catastrophic interference) and in biological systems (e.g. ongoing plasticity, [4]; the stability-plasticity problem, [1]). A system has to be flexible enough to allow salient changes to be encoded continuously while at the same time being stable enough to ensure that stored changes persist. The approach that we show here uses a conventional Hopfield network. It thus makes no claims to be biologically realistic in the sense that it includes details of neuronal or synaptic physiology, but we feel that this simple case allows us to address fundamental issues of the stability-plasticity dilemma. The approach that we use allows the same components to encode and store information. In fact, rather than try and separate stored and new inputs, the input is instead considered in the context of previously stored inputs, which means that only the similarities

and differences of new inputs are encoded while still allowing the full memory of the input to be recalled.

We are able to show the capability of encoding and storing a significantly larger number of sequential inputs than is possible using conventional approaches, and importantly, allowing new inputs to be compared and generalized to those already in the store. This contrasts with the non-overlapping approaches used in connectionist networks in attempts to overcome catastrophic interference (e.g. [38]; see [12]). While separation of input patterns would remove catastrophic interference, it also removes the possibility of generalising and linking together aspects of the stored patterns. This could be a particular problem for learning categories [17]. That a pattern to be stored is compared to those already in the store, without having to impose limits on the rate or extent of the synaptic changes, is a principal advantage of the orthogonalization approach that we show here.

In human memory systems the subject learns on the background of previously stored information rather than isolating the new information from it, or overwriting the previously stored information (see [39]). This feature is an intrinsic component that arises from Gram-Schmidt orthogonalisation rather than having to be imposed from outside. This could allow artificial, and in principle biological systems, to make use of an intrinsic principle of physical systems, ensuring that a system that includes this automatically has this advantage built in. An orthogonalization based neural system acts in a self-organized manner - it compares the new with old, isolates the similarities and differences of the new input with the old, deduces whether the new is unknown or known, and if it is found to be known to it then it refuses to entertain it a second time. In this way it acts as a form of "internal supervisor" [4], determining which synapses have to change to store the new memory while not destroying the changes at synapses that have previously stored information. A stimulus may be presented any number of times but if the input has already been stored then the postsynaptic local field will not change and therefore they will not build up incessantly in the same direction to cause the possible run-away effect, akin to that suggested by the BCM model.

Orthogonalisation has been used previously in attempts to overcome the problems of catastrophic interference in connectionist networks (see, for example, [40]). However, the use of the term orthogonalisation in this context differs to the way that we have used it, where information is represented by a vector and orthogonalization makes the vector of a new information perpendicular to the vectors representing the stored information. Orthogonalized, or mutually perpendicular, vectors do not overlap with each other. This orthogonalization scheme must be distinguished from the 'orthogonalization' approach that is typically used in the learning and memory literature (e.g. [41], [22], [6] and references therein). The latter generally refers to sparse coding of information in the network, i.e., two different pieces of information are stored on two non-overlapping sets of nodes in the network, thus removing the interference effect associated with CI. However, in the scheme presented here the same nodes are used. If patterns of bipolar elements are generated randomly, at the first glance they could be considered orthogonal (i.e., with zero inner product). This would be true in the hypothetical situation of infinite systems (when vectors have an infinite number of components). However, since we are always dealing with finite vectors, inputs of this sort will be only approximately orthogonal, and the inner products will be non-zero. This is not orthogonalization by design, and the non-zero overlaps mean that the signal gets submerged in the noise when $p/N > 0.14$ [42]. The typical/common notion of orthogonal patterns is, thus sparsely coded non-overlapping patterns (see also [43]), and by whatever means it is achieved this can help reduce CI (see [40]). The Gram-Schmidt orthogonalization that we use differs as it forces the network to actively compute and convert a set of vectors into a mutually orthogonal set. In this process the noise arising due to the intrinsic overlap amongst patterns, even though they are generated randomly, is eliminated and the memory capacity increases to $p/N = 1$ from 0.14.

We have examined an artificial system, and the relevance of this effect ideally needs to be shown in an experimental system. While we, and others, believe that the approach can say something relevant to actual systems, this needs to be tested as even in theoretical systems effects differ as the degree of realism changes (see [18]). That there are sliding thresholds for plasticity is known

from experimental analyses (see [27]), but that inputs can be orthogonalised requires certain network arrangements and cellular conditions for its implementation. These include parallel feedforward excitation and feedback inhibition [42], as well as the nature of inputs to single and different dendrites of the same cell, and multiplication in dendrites (see [43]). All of the constraints needed are common network motifs or identified functional properties in biological systems, offering the possibility of testing these predictions experimentally.

Author Contributions

Wrote the paper: VS DJP. Carried out the simulations: SS. Plotted the data: SS.

References

1. Abraham WC, Robins A (2005) Memory retention–the synaptic stability versus plasticity dilemma. Trends Neurosci. Feb;28(2): 73–8.
2. Bienenstock E, Cooper L, Munro P (1982) Theory for the development of neuron selectivity: orientation specificity and binocular interaction in visual cortex. J Neurosci 2: 32–48.
3. Bliss T, Collingridge G (1993) A synaptic model of memory: long-term potentiation in the hippocampus. Nature 361: 31–39.
4. Fusi S, Abbott LF (2007) Limits on the memory storage capacity of bounded synapses. Nat Neurosci. Apr;10(4): 485–93.
5. Fiskum G (2000) Mitochondrial participation in ischemic and traumatic neural cell death. J Neurotrauma 17: 843–855.
6. French R (2003) Catastrophic interference in connectionist networks. Encyclopedia of Cognitive Science 1: 431–435.
7. Srivastava V, Edwards SF (2000) A model of how the brain discriminates and categorises. Physica A 276: 352–358.
8. Srivastava V, Edwards SF (2004) A mathematical model of capacious and efficient memory that survives trauma. Physica A 333: 465–477.
9. Nader K, Schafe G, Doux JL (2000) Fear memories require protein synthesis in the amygdala for reconsolidation after retrieval. Nature 406: 722–726.
10. Ben Mamou C, Gamache K, Nader K (2006) NMDA receptors are critical for unleashing consolidated auditory fear memories. Nature Neuroscience 9(10): 1237–1239.
11. Barnes JM, Underwood BJ (1959) Fate of first-list associations in transfer theory. Journal of Experimental Psychology 58: 97–105.
12. French R (1999) Catastrophic forgetting in connectionist networks. Trends Cogn Sci 3: 128–135; Guyon I, Personnaz L and Dryfus G (1989) Of points and loops. NATO ASI Series, F41, Eckmiller R and Malsburg Ch v d (Eds): 261–269.
13. Ratcliff R (1990). Connectionist Models of Recognition Memory: Constraints Imposed by Learning and Forgetting Functions. Psychological Review, 97: 285–308.
14. Shadmehr R, Brashers-Krug T (1997) Functional stages in the formation of human long-term motor memory. The Journal of Neuroscience, 17 (1): 409–419.
15. Mareschal D, Quinn PC, French RM (2002) Asymmetric interference in 3-to-4 months olds' sequential category learning. Cognitive Science 26: 377–389.
16. Fusi S, Dre PJ, Abbott LF (2005) Cascade models of Synaptically Stored Memories. Neuron 45: 599–611.
17. McClelland JL, McNaughton BL, O'Reilly RC (1995) Why there are complimentary learning systems in the hippocampus and neocortex: insights from successes and failures of connectionist models of learning and memory. Psychological Review, 102 (3): 419–457.
18. Fusi S, Senn W (2006) Eluding oblivion with smart stochastic selection of synaptic updates. Chaos 16: 026112.
19. Kempermann G (2008) The neurogenic reserve hypothesis: what is adult hippocampal neurogenesis good for? Trends Neurosci 31: 163–169.
20. Bogacz R, Brown M (2003) Comparison of computational models of familiarity discrimination in the perirhinal cortex. Hippocampus 13: 494–524.
21. van Rossum M, Shippi M, Barrett A (2012) Soft-bound Synaptic Plasticity Increases Storage Capacity. PLoS Comput Biol 8:e1002836.
22. French R (1997) Selective memory loss in aphasics: An insight from pseudo-recurrent connectionist networks. In: Connectionist Representations. (Bullinaria J, Glasspool D, Houghton G, eds), pp 103–195: Springer.

23. McCloskey M, Cohen N (1989) Catastrophic interference in connectionist networks: the sequential learning problem, in The Psychology of Learning and Motivation (Vol. 24) (Bower, G.H., ed.), pp. 109–164, Academic Press.
24. Bear M (2003) Bidirectional synaptic plasticity: from theory to reality. Phil Trans R Soc Lond B 358: 649–655.
25. Turrigiano G (2007) Homeostatic signaling: the positive side of negative feedback. Current Opinion in Neurobiology 17: 318–324.
26. Bear M (1996) A synaptic basis for memory storage in the cerebral cortex. Proc Natl Acad Sci 93: 13453–13459.
27. Abraham W, Bear M (1996) Metaplasticity: the plasticity of synaptic plasticity. TINS 19: 126–130.
28. Representation of a network state as a vector of +/−1 as opposed to 0/1 has a distinct mathematical advantage. The central one is that the overlap between two states, or vectors, can be represented by the dot (or scalar) product of the two vectors. See [30] for a comparison between these two alternatives, though equivalent, notations for the neural states.
29. Cooper L (1973) A possible organization of animal memory and learning, in Nobel Symposium on Collective Properties of Physical Systems. The Nobel Foundation: Aspensagaerden, Sweden:: 62–84.
30. Amit D (1989) Modeling Brain Function: The world of attractor neural networks. Cambridge University Press; Dayan P and Abbott L F (2001) Theoretical Neuroscience. MIT Press, Cambridge, Massachusetts.
31. Hebb D (1949) The organization of behavior: A neuropsychological theory. Wiley, New York.
32. Bi G-Q, Poo M-M (1998) Synaptic modifications in cultured hippocampal neurons: dependence on spike timing, synaptic strength, and postsynaptic cell type. J Neurosci 18: 10464–10472.
33. Miller K (1996) Synaptic Economics: Competition and Cooperation in Synaptic Plasticity. Neuron 17: 371–374.
34. Srivastava V, Vipin M, Granato E (1998) Recall of Old and Recent Information. Network Comput. Neural Syst. 9: 159–166.
35. Carandini M, Heeger DJ (2012) Normalization as a canonical neural computation. Nature Reviews Neuroscience 13: 51–62.
36. Srivastava V (2000) A unified view of the orthogonalization methods. J Phys A: Math Gen 33(35): 6219–6222.
37. Bar-Yam Y (1997) Dynamics of Complex Systems. Addison-Wesley, Massachusetts.
38. Kruschke JK (1992) ALCOVE: an exemplar-based model of category learning. Psychological Review, 99 (1): 22–44.
39. McRae K, Hetherington PA (1993) Catastrophic interference is eliminated in pretrained networks. In Proceedings of the 15th Annual Conference Sciences Society (Hillsdale NJ: L. Erlbaum), pp. 723–728.
40. Yamaguchi M (2004) Reassessment of catastrophic interference. Neuroreport 25: 2423–2426.
41. Lewandowsky S, Li S-C (1993) Catastrophic interference in neural networks: causes, solutions, and data. In: New Perspectives on Interference and Inhibition in Cognition (Dempster F, Brainerd C, eds), p 329–361: Academic Press.
42. Srivastava V, Parker D, Edwards SF (2008) The nervous system might 'orthogonalize' to discriminate. J Theor Biol 253: 514–517.
43. Marr D (1969) A theory of cerebellar cortex. J Physiol 202: 437–470.

18

Open-Source Syringe Pump Library

Bas Wijnen[1], Emily J. Hunt[1], Gerald C. Anzalone[1], Joshua M. Pearce[1,2]*

1 Department of Materials Science & Engineering, Michigan Technological University, Houghton, Michigan, United States of America, **2** Department of Electrical & Computer Engineering, Michigan Technological University, Houghton, Michigan, United States of America

Abstract

This article explores a new open-source method for developing and manufacturing high-quality scientific equipment suitable for use in virtually any laboratory. A syringe pump was designed using freely available open-source computer aided design (CAD) software and manufactured using an open-source RepRap 3-D printer and readily available parts. The design, bill of materials and assembly instructions are globally available to anyone wishing to use them. Details are provided covering the use of the CAD software and the RepRap 3-D printer. The use of an open-source Rasberry Pi computer as a wireless control device is also illustrated. Performance of the syringe pump was assessed and the methods used for assessment are detailed. The cost of the entire system, including the controller and web-based control interface, is on the order of 5% or less than one would expect to pay for a commercial syringe pump having similar performance. The design should suit the needs of a given research activity requiring a syringe pump including carefully controlled dosing of reagents, pharmaceuticals, and delivery of viscous 3-D printer media among other applications.

Editor: Giorgio F. Gilestro, Imperial College London, United Kingdom

Funding: The authors have no support or funding to report.

Competing Interests: The authors have declared that no competing interests exist.

* Email: pearce@mtu.edu

Introduction

Free and open source (or libre) technological development is a fundamentally new, decentralized, participatory and transparent system to create both software and hardware. It stands in sharp contrast to the closed box, top-down, and secretive standard commercial approach to development [1]. As much of the Internet now relies on free and open-source software (FOSS), open source is becoming the norm in software development [2],[3]. FOSS has been so successful that for many applications it is the defacto standard, with 94% of the World's top 500 supercomputers, 75% of the top 10,000 websites and 98% of enterprises using open-source software [4],[5]. FOSS is computer software made available as source code (open source) that can be used, studied, copied, modified, and redistributed without restriction, or with restrictions that only ensure that further recipients have the same rights under which it was obtained [6]. FOSS is in widespread use in science and engineering and has driven down the cost of numerical simulation in a number of fields ranging from psychotherapy [7] and medicine [8],[9], neural circuit reconstruction [10], genomic sequences annotation [11], education [12],[13], and ecology [14]. In addition, it has been proposed as a solution to the intellectual property tragedy in nanotechnology, which has slowed progress and deployment in the field [15],[16],[17],[18]. Even greater cost reductions for science, however, can be found with the application of open source hardware [19],[20],[21],[22]. The development of open-source hardware has the potential to radically reduce the cost of performing experimental science and put high-quality scientific tools in the hands of everyone from the most prestigious labs to rural clinics in the developing world [19],[22],[23].

This article introduces a low-cost open-source family of syringe pumps. Creation of parametric open-source designs using an open-source computer aided design (CAD) package is described to produce customized syringe pumps for scientific and/or health applications. Details are provided for use of open-source RepRap 3-D printers to fabricate the components. An open-source Rasberry Pi computer used as a wireless control device is also illustrated. The performance of the pumps produced is assessed and the method's advantages, known limitations and potential for radically reducing the cost of doing science are discussed.

Materials and Methods

The low-cost open-source family of syringe pumps are completely customizable allowing both the volume and the motor to scale for specific applications. The bill of materials for the three variations of the syringe pump are shown in Table S1. The user/designer must first determine the size of motor to enable that application. The appropriate motor size can be selected once the required torque is known following [24]. A bigger motor provides more torque, but necessitates larger printed components. A bigger syringe allows more fluid to be pushed out, both per second and in total, but decreases the precision of the device. A simple change to the OpenSCAD script specifying the motor selection defines the dimensions for the printed parts.

OpenSCAD and Open-source 3-D Printing

Open-source and freely available OpenSCAD is script-based, parametric CAD software possessing powerful 3-D modeling capabilities [25]. It is not graphical; models are created by adding and subtracting primitives to produce the desired shape. It

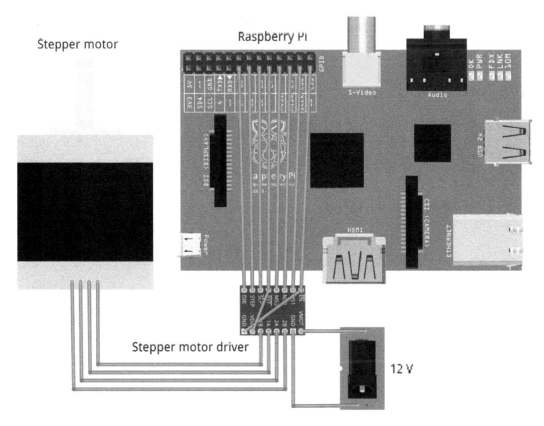

Figure 1. Electronic schematic of Open-Source Syringe Pump.

supports creation and extrusion of polygons and poly lines, so can be used to create very complex shapes. The script language is based upon C++ and only a few methods are required to produce very complex designs, so the learning curve is short, albeit steep for those not possessing programming experience. The scripts are written such that designs are parametric – the design can easily be altered by changing key dimensions. For instance, the syringe pump script can be altered to produce parts fitting different motors simply by specifying which motor to design for. The script written for the syringe pump is available online [26]. Models rendered in OpenSCAD are typically exported as stereolithography (stl) files for the first step in producing a 3-D print using any of the RepRap 3-D printers currently available. Images of syringe pump parts rendered by OpenSCAD and photographs of the printed parts are shown in Figures S1–S10 in File S1.

RepRap printers almost universally require g-code, a human-readable file format specifying the path the print head must follow to produce a physical object from a software model. G-code is produced by software referred to as a "slicer", which, as the name implies, slices an stl model into layers each having the same thickness in the z-direction. Cura was used to slice the syringe pump stl models [27]. Cura is also open-source and freely available.

The parts were printed with RepRap3-D printers. Two different printer designs, a Cartesian [28] and a delta printer [29], were used to produce the parts out of 1.75 mm polylactic acid (PLA) filament. The printer design employed is ultimately irrelevant as both produce shapes using exactly the same method and materials and are different only in the way the print head is moved. Both printers were equipped with hot ends having 0.5 mm nozzles and prints were sliced at a layer height of 0.25 mm and a print speed of

60 mm/s. Parts were printed in plates, that is all of the printed parts needed to assemble a syringe pump were printed in one printer cycle.

RepRap printers typically interface with a host program running on a computer but can also run independently, reading g-code stored on a memory card. The syringe pump was printed using a host computer running ReptierHost [30] another freely available, open-source software written specifically for RepRap and RepRap-like 3-D printers. For detailed instruction on the construction and operation of the printers see [28], [29].

Syringe Pump Control and Interface

The syringe pump is controlled by an open-source Python program developed here [26] running on a Raspberry Pi, which is an ARM based computer running GNU/Linux [31], [32]. The Raspberry Pi is an inexpensive, credit card-sized computer having integrated networking, sound, video, USB host and most importantly, exposed and readily accessible I/O lines. The wiring diagram for the syringe pump controller (Figure 1) utilizes a single Pololu A4988 stepper controller, which controls the stepper motor that drives the syringe pump. The Raspberry Pi is installed with the standard Raspbian operating system [32]. A custom web server is run, which serves a web page via either wired network or wirelessly via a wireless USB adapter attached to the Raspberry Pi's USB port. Any computer on the network can then control the pump through this web page (Figure 2).

Calibration and Performance Assessment Methodology

The pump is calibrated by setting it up with an initial calibration value set to 1 mL/mm. A small arbitrary volume appropriate for the size of syringe used is pushed twice from the

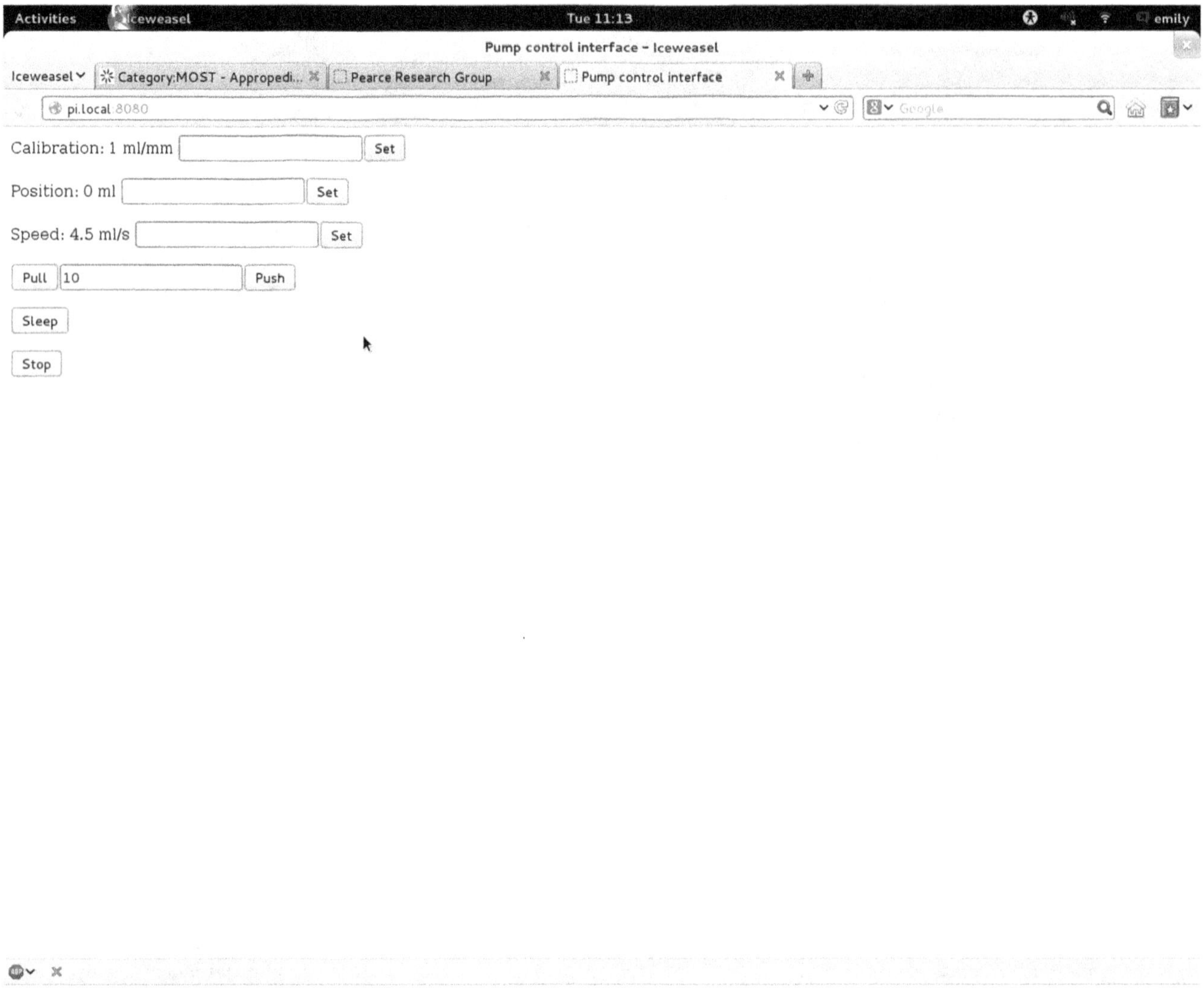

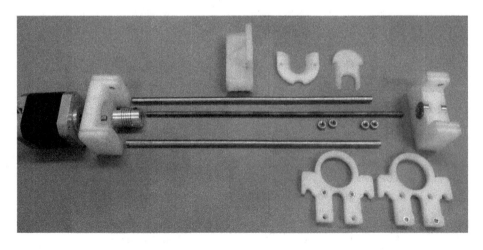

Figure 2. Screenshot of Syringe Pump Web Interface.

Figure 3. Exploded view of Open-Source Syringe Pump.

Figure 4. Digital Photograph of Open-Source Syringe Pump version Nema 11.

syringe and the actual value of the second push is measured. This is done to partially account for drops staying on the end of the syringe. This number is divided by the amount the syringe was told to push out, the resulting number goes into the calibration window. The sequence is repeated three times to ensure correct calibration.

The force produced by the lead-screw actuated design was measured by placing the assembled syringe pump with a steel rod in place of the syringe in a frame along with with a 30 kg-capacity scale. The pump was oriented such that the motor end sat upon the scale and the steel plunger faced upward, pressing against a fixed platform. The pump motor was advanced until it stalled or a component failed and the maximum force produced was read off the scale display.

The pumps' maximum delivery rate is a function of the speed at which the motor stalls. Stall speed was determined by increasing pulse rate to the motor until it stalled and then decreasing to the point where it ran again, establishing the maximum speed and therefore maximum delivery rate.

Precision was tested by repeated delivery of a preset volume (fixed by setting the total number of motor steps) of distilled water onto a Mettler AE100 scale having a readability of 0.1 mg. The relative humidity within the weighing chamber was maintained in a saturated state by placing containers of distilled water in it, permitting it to equilibrate and then ensuring that it was kept well sealed for the duration of the assessment. Performance of both the

NEMA11 and NEMA17 pumps was assessed at different microstepping settings.

Results

Three different pumps were assembled, all of which are relatively easy to construct from the parts shown in exploded view in Figure 3. Assembled pumps are shown in Figures 4, 5 and 6 for the Nema 11, Nema 17 and dual Nema 17 pumps, respectively. The dual version consists of two identically sized pumps connected in parallel to the motor controller (Figure 7). The pumps are driven synchronously at the same rate. The controller has the capacity to drive more than one pump simultaneously if required. If one of the connections from the connector to the pump shown in Figure 7 is reversed then the two pumps will go in opposite directions.

The force developed by the OS syringe pump depends on the motor used. When pushing on an immovable object, the NEMA17 version produced 200 N, and the NEMA11 version produced 93 N. Force did not appear to be affected by the microstepping rate, probably due to the nature of lead-screw actuation that is inefficient at translating force into rotation, particularly with the thread pitch and profile used in this design. The force developed was sufficient to cause damage to some of the printed parts, none of which resulted in impairment and new parts could quickly be printed and replaced.

When calibrated with a 25 mL syringe, the NEMA17 version yielded a maximum delivery rate of 2.1 mL/s and the NEMA11

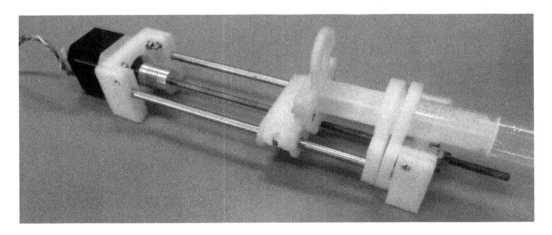

Figure 5. Digital Photograph of Open-Source Syringe Pump version Nema 17.

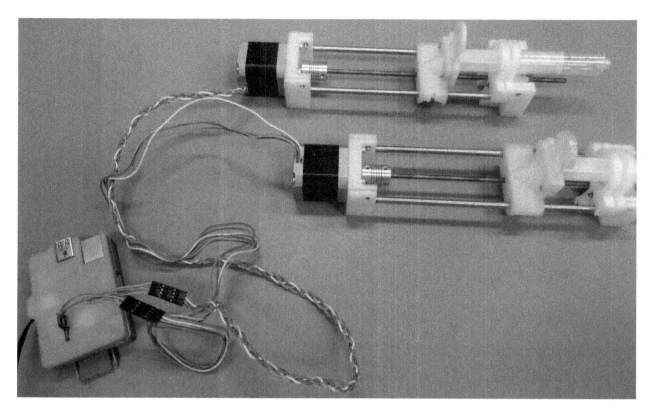

Figure 6. Digital Photograph of Open-Source Syringe Pump version of the Dual Nema 17 Pump.

version yielded 1.4 mL/s when calibrated with 10 mL syringe. Accuracy was +/−1% for the NEMA11 and +/−5% for the NEMA17 measured in 1 mL increments. Precision was found to be relatively insensitive to microstepping for both the NEMA11 and NEMA17 (Table 1). The coefficient of variation when delivering approximately 1 mL of distilled water was about 3% or less regardless of microstepping and it is very likely that precision is actually better than reported as the measurement method was limited to the volume of a single drop (e.g. ∼20 micro Liters). It is unlikely that microstepping need be employed as the

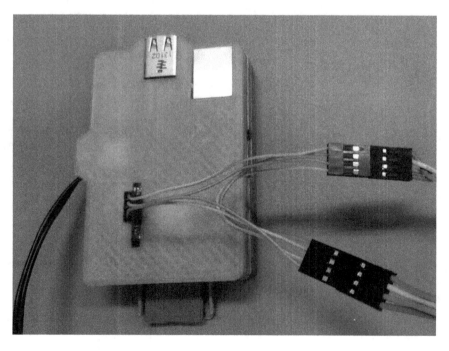

Figure 7. Digital Photograph of the Dual Pump connection.

Table 1. Coefficient of variation as a function of microstepping for NEMA 11 and NEMA 17 open-source syringe pumps

Coefficient of variation			
	Microstepping		
	1	**4**	**16**
NEMA11	1.17%	0.56%	1.55%
NEMA17	3.66%	2.13%	2.26%

200 step/revolution motors coupled with a properly sized syringe should provide virtually any resolution demanded.

It is clear that using open-source methods reduced the cost of the pumps considerably from commercial pumps as summarized in Table 2. The single syringe pumps have a part cost under $100 using hardware from online retailers. This includes the Raspberry Pi controller that permits control of the syringe pump from virtually every web enabled device available. Commercial syringe pumps can cost anywhere from $260 to over $5000 as seen in Table 2.

Overall, using completely open source methods, this pump is economical, user friendly, and accurate. Even considering the approximate $500 price of the RepRap 3-D printer, the value of this approach to design and manufacturing far exceeds that of commercial units, particularly for resource starved laboratories.

Discussion

As has been demonstrated previously, the open-source ecosystem lends itself well to research endeavors, especially with regards to maximizing the value of a research dollar [19],[22],[33],[34]. This is particularly true when designs for desired components, or even designs for similar components to those desired, are made freely available for use and customization [19],[20],[22]. Armed with open-source 3-D printers and hardware, freely available and open-source software and designs, researchers can design and manufacture bespoke apparatus at a small fraction of the price of commercial offerings. The ability to alter and tune designs to produce apparatus that better align with research goals eliminates "making do" with what is available commercially. By way of example, this paper presents an elegantly simple design for a syringe pump that performs admirably and should serve as a good foundation for derivation of better and more useful apparatus for specific research goals.

The simplicity of the design coupled with ready access to its source makes it very easy to customize and construct; even first year students with limited exposure to such activity are able to assemble a complete, working system. The cost of the entire system, including the controller and web-based control interface, is on the order of 5% or less than one would expect to pay for a commercial syringe pump having similar features and performance. The platform is not limited to just use as a syringe pump; it is a relatively high precision linear actuator that can easily be modified for use for positioning, i.e. for stages for microscopy. Similarly it could be used as a head for 3-D printing with viscous media. 3D printing and liquid handling with a syringe pump could be combined as has been done recently by Kitson et al., to produce user-friendly reactionware for chemical synthesis and purification [35]. Using open-source RepRap 3-D printers and the open-source syringe pump developed here chemists not only only have complete control over every aspect of hardware, but can also set up the experiments for a fraction of the cost of commercially available tools.

Incremental improvement of designs in the open-source ecosystem tends to occur organically [22]. It is therefore reasonable to expect that as the population of the interested audience grows, the rate of innovation increases, perhaps at a much greater rate than could be expected in commercial R&D centers. This incremental approach to development not only takes place at a rapid pace, it spreads the cost of development over the entire user/developer community with the currency being predominantly the time spent by the individual developers. Since freely available open-source designs can be made available to the entire globe, even small time investments in development can have significant impact. This is especially important given that the tools developed can be considered appropriate technology and are of particular interest to poorly funded laboratories such as those in undeveloped and developing economies [36]. Development of open-source designs can, from that perspective, be considered a form of philanthropy, although the developer also benefits by the product of his work and the improvements made to it by others [22].

The design presented here is deliberately simple; it is intended to demonstrate the utility and efficiency of the open-source method of development and provide one starting point for derivation of improved designs. There is (by design) ample opportunity for improvement and future work. A syringe pump can be used for a variety of applications requiring carefully controlled dosing of reagents, pharmaceuticals, delivery of viscous 3-D printer media, etc. All of these applications have specific requirements that this endlessly customizable design can be tailored to meet. For instance, microstepping may not be required, making a less expensive motor controller suitable and driving the cost of the syringe pump even lower.

Conclusions

An open-source and freely available design for a simple to build and customize syringe pump has been provided and working pumps have been constructed and evaluated. The design performs well as compared to much costlier commercial models while permitting virtually endless customization and so should suit the needs of a given research activity requiring a syringe pump. Only readily available, open-source hardware and software were used for the design and manufacture of the pumps, further validating application of open-source methodologies for development of research ready laboratory equipment.

Acknowledgments

The authors would like to acknowledge helpful discussions with P. Fraley.

Table 2. Specifications for the open-source syringe pump are shown compared to commercial pumps.

Name	Price	Description	Speed	Force	Other
Most OS Syringe Pump Nema 11	$90.00	Completely customizable, always knows where the syringe is, fits any size syringe, failsafe stop button.	Max: 1.4 mL/s (10 mL syringe)	Max: 93 N	Accuracy: ±1%, Reproducibility: ±0.6%
Most OS Syringe Pump Nema 17	$97.00	Completely customizable, always knows where the syringe is, fits any size syringe, failsafe stop button.	Max: 2.1 mL/s (25 mL syringe)	Max: 200N	Accuracy: ±5%, Reproducibility: ±2.1%
Most OS Dual Syringe Pump Nema 17	$154.00	Completely customizable, holds 2 or more syringes, depending on how many connections desired, always knows where the syringe is, fits any size syringe, failsafe stop button.	Max: 2.1 mL/s (25 mL syringe)	Max: 200N	Accuracy: ±5%, Reproducibility: ±2.1%
NE-300 "Just Infusion" Syringe Pump	$260	Infusion	Max: 0.417 mL/s	–	Up to 60 mL syringes -infusion rate can be changed while pumping, INFUSES ONLY
B.Braun/McGaw BD 360 Syringe Pump	$435	Can be used as primary infusor or can deliver downstream secondary piggyback infusions.	Max: 0.1 mL/s	–	Delivery Time: 10–60 min. in 2.5 min. increments, Accuracy: ±3%
GenieTouch Syringe Pump	$675	The pump always knows how much is left in the syringe and how much the handle can be pushed down. Accuracy is based on carraige position detection, which is +/−0.2 mm.	Max: 3.68 mL/s	Max: 196.13 N	Auto positioning/stalling detection, Multi-directional left or right application
NE-4000 Programmable Double Syringe Pump	$928	Dual pump system allows for continuous infusion or emulsification. Network, control, and monitor up to 100 pumps with one computer.	Max: 2.0 mL/s	Max: 444.82 N (at min speed) or 444.82 N (at max speed)	Dispensing accuracy of +/−1%, Max pumping rate: 6120 mL/hr with a B-D 60 cc syringe, Syringe inside diameter range: 0.100 to 50.00 mm
Advanced Syringe Pump with Computer Control from Med Associates Inc.	$1343.34	The PHM-111EC is controlled by an internal computer so that exact infusion rates can be set. Front panel switches allow for a simple setup, thus avoiding complicated menus or charts.	Max: 0.119 mL/s (depending on the volume of the syringe)	Min: 68.95 kPa Max: 413.685 kPa depending on the syringe)	Controls up to 16 pumps
Fusion Touch 400 Syringe Pump	$1,350	From Chemyx, and can run on select versions of Windows, Mac and Linux.	Max: 0.167 mL/s (10 mL syringe)	Max: 222.41 N	Step Resolution is 0.016 microns, Accuracy ±0.35%, Reproducibility ±0.05%
Fisher Scientific Single Syringe Pump	$1,509	Applications: Calibrating, diluting, dispensing, dosing, emulsifying, fluid transfer, infusions	Max: 0.144 mL/s	–	Dispensing Volume: 10 µL to 60 mL, Auto shut off volume dispense mode
Sono Tek Syringe Pump	$1,800	Accepts up to 2 of the same types of syringes, capacity range from 10 µ to 60 mL. Also has additional valving that can set up the pump to fill the syringe.	Max: 0.5 mL/s	–	Single shot and continuous flow operations
Cole-Parmer Dual Syringe Infusion Pump	$2,606	Dual syringe infusion pump	Max: 2.45 mL/s	Max: 275.79 kPa	Accepts 10 µL to 140 mL syringes, Reproducibility ±0.2% -Accuracy ±0.5%, Power: 115 VAC
Cole-Parmer Continuous Flow Syringe Pump	$3,947	Hold up to four syringes to cycle continuously back and forth in a push-pull action. As two syringes are infusing, two syringes are withdrawing at the same rate.	Max: 1.17 mL/s	Max: 177.93 N	Syringe size: 4–10 uL to 60 mL, Reproducibility: +/−0.1%, Accuracy: +/− <1%
402 Syringe Pump from Gilson Inc.	$5000–5500	Assures accuracy in sample transfer, dilution, reagent addition, mixing and more. Offers speed and reliability for repetitive liquid handling tasks.	Max: 2.0 mL/s	Max: 0.8 MPa(0.1–10-mL syringe) to 0.3 MPa(25-mL syringe)	Reproducibility: 0.8% at 10 µL -Injection Volume: 1.0 µL–25 mL, Accuracy: 98.2% at 10 µL

Supporting Information

File S1 Figures S1–S10: 3-D printable parts for the open-source syringe pump. Figure S1 Carriage STL rendering. Figure S2 Carriage digital image. Figure S3 Clamp STL rendering. Figure S4 Clamp digital image. Figure S5 End idler STL rendering. Figure S6 End idler digital image. Figure S7 End motor STL rendering. Figure S8 End motor digital image. Figure S9 Wedges STL rendering. Figure S10 Wedges digital image.

References

1. Deek FP, McHugh JAM (2007) Open Source: Technology and Policy: Cambridge University Press.
2. Bergquist M, Ljungberg J, Rolandsson B (2011) A Historical Account of the Value of Free and Open Source Software: From Software Commune to Commercial Commons. In: Hissam S, Russo B, de Mendonça Neto M, Kon F, editors. Open Source Systems: Grounding Research Book Series Title: IFIP Advances in Information and Communication Technology 365. Boston: Springer. 196–207.
3. Miller KW, Voas J, Costello T (2010) Free and Open Source Software. IT Professional 12: 14–16. doi: 10.1007/s10530-007-9132-y.
4. 94 Percent of the World's Top 500 Supercomputers Run Linux. Available online: https://www.linux.com/news/enterprise/high-performance/147-high-performance/666669-94-percent-of-the-worlds-top-500-supercomputers-run-linux (accessed on 25 January 2013).
5. Survey: 98 Percent of Enterprises Using Open Source Software, Interrupted–CNET News. Available online: http://news.cnet.com/8301-13846_3-20013258-62.html (accessed on 25 January 2013).
6. The Open Source Definition (Annotated). Available online: http://opensource.org/docs/definition.html (accessed on 25 January 2013).
7. Glynn LH, Hallgren KA, Houck JM, Moyers TB (2012) CACTI: Free, Open-Source Software for the Sequential Coding of Behavioral Interactions. PLoS ONE 7: e39740. doi: 10.1371/journal.pone.0039740.
8. Lang T (2011) Advancing Global Health Research Through Digital Technology and Sharing Data. Science 331: 714–717. doi: 10.1126/science.1199349.
9. Meister S, Plouffe DM, Kuhen KL, Bonamy GMC, Wu T, et al. (2011) Imaging of Plasmodium Liver Stages to Drive Next-Generation Antimalarial Drug Discovery. Science 334: 1372–1377. doi: 10.1126/science.1211936.
10. Cardona A, Saalfeld S, Schindelin J, Arganda-Carreras I, Preibisch S, et al. (2012) TrakEM2 Software for Neural Circuit Reconstruction. PLoS ONE 7: e38011. doi: 10.1371/journal.pone.0038011.
11. Kumar K, Desai V, Cheng L, Khitrov M, Grover D, et al. (2011) AGeS: A Software System for Microbial Genome Sequence Annotation. PLoS ONE 6: e17469. doi: 10.1371/journal.pone.0017469.
12. Christian W, Esquembre F, Barbato L (2011) Open Source Physics. Science 334: 1077–1078. doi: 10.1126/science.1196984.
13. Marzullo TC, Gage GJ (2012) The SpikerBox: A Low Cost, Open-Source BioAmplifier for Increasing Public Participation in Neuroscience Inquiry. PLoS ONE 7: e30837. doi: 10.1371/journal.pone.0030837.
14. Stokstad E (2011) Open-Source Ecology Takes Root Across the World. Science 334: 308–309. doi: 10.1126/science.334.6054.308.
15. Bruns B (2001) Open sourcing nanotechnology research and development: issues and opportunities. Nanotechnology 12: 198–210. doi: 10.5539/jsd.v3n4p17.
16. Mushtaq U, Pearce JM, (2012) Open source appropriate nanotechnology. In Maclurcan D, Radywyl N(Eds). Nanotechnology and global sustainability. 191–213.
17. Pearce JM (2012) Make nanotechnology research open-source, Nature 491: 519–521. doi: 10.1038/491519a.
18. Pearce JM (2013) Open-source nanotechnology: Solutions to a modern intellectual property tragedy, Nano Today, 8(4): 339–341. doi: 10.1016/j.nantod.2013.04.001.
19. Pearce JM (2012) Building Research Equipment with Free, Open-Source Hardware. Science 337: 1303–1304. doi: 10.1126/science.1228183.
20. Zhang C, Anzalone NC, Faria RP, Pearce JM (2013) Open-Source 3D-Printable Optics Equipment. PLoS ONE 8(3): e59840. doi:10.1371/journal.pone.0059840.
21. Anzalone GC, Glover AG, Pearce JM. Open-Source Colorimeter. Sensors. 2013; 13(4): 5338–5346. doi:10.3390/s130405338.
22. Pearce JM (2014) Open-Source Lab: How to Build Your Own Hardware and Reduce Research Costs. Elsevier.
23. Pearce JM, Blair CM, Laciak KJ, Andrews R, Nosrat A, et al. (2010) 3-D Printing of Open Source Appropriate Technologies for Self-Directed Sustainable Development. Journal of Sustainable Development 3: p17. doi: 10.5539/jsd.v3n4p17.
24. NEMA Motor - RepRapWiki (n.d.). Available: http://reprap.org/wiki/NEMA_Motor. Accessed 19 December 2013.
25. OpenSCAD (n.d.). Available: http://openscad.org. Accessed 18 December 2013.
26. mtu-most (2013) Linear-actuator. GitHub.Available: https://github.com/mtu-most/linear-actuator. Accessed 19 December 2013.
27. Cura - User manual | Blog | Ultimaker (n.d.). Available: http://blog.ultimaker.com/cura user manual/. Accessed 19 December 2013.
28. MOST RepRap build (2013). Appropedia: The sustainability wiki Available: http://www.appropedia.org/MOST_HS_RepRap_build Accessed 19 December 2013.
29. Delta Build Overview:MOST (2013) Appropedia: The sustainability wiki Available: http://www.appropedia.org/Delta_Build_Overview:MOST. Accessed 19 December 2013.
30. Repetier Software | The software driving your 3d printer (n.d.). Available: http://www.repetier.com/. Accessed 19 December 2013.
31. Raspberry Pi | An ARM GNU/Linux box for $25. Take a byte! (n.d.). Available: http://www.raspberrypi.org/. Accessed 19 December 2013.
32. FrontPage - Raspbian (n.d.). Available: http://www.raspbian.org/. Accessed 19 December 2013.
33. Woelfle M, Olliaro P, Todd MH (2011) Open science is a research accelerator. Nature Chemistry 3: 745–748. doi: 10.1038/nchem.1149.
34. Nielsen M (2011) Reinventing Discovery: The New Era of Networked Science. Princeton University Press.
35. Kitson PJ, Symes MD, Dragone V, Cronin L. (2013). Combining 3D printing and liquid handling to produce user-friendly reactionware for chemical synthesis and purification. Chemical Science 4(8): 3099–3103.
36. Pearce J (2012) The case for open source appropriate technology. Environment, Development and Sustainability 14: 425–431.

Table S1 Bill of Materials for three examples of the open-source syringe pumps.

Author Contributions

Conceived and designed the experiments: BW GA JP. Performed the experiments: BW EH GA. Analyzed the data: BW EH GA JP. Contributed reagents/materials/analysis tools: GA JP. Contributed to the writing of the manuscript: BW EH GA JP.

19

Active Semi-Supervised Learning Method with Hybrid Deep Belief Networks

Shusen Zhou[1]*, Qingcai Chen[2], Xiaolong Wang[2]

1 School of Information and Electrical Engineering, Ludong University, Yantai, Shandong, China, 2 Shenzhen Graduate School, Harbin Institute of Technology, Shenzhen, Guangdong, China

Abstract

In this paper, we develop a novel semi-supervised learning algorithm called active hybrid deep belief networks (AHD), to address the semi-supervised sentiment classification problem with deep learning. First, we construct the previous several hidden layers using restricted Boltzmann machines (RBM), which can reduce the dimension and abstract the information of the reviews quickly. Second, we construct the following hidden layers using convolutional restricted Boltzmann machines (CRBM), which can abstract the information of reviews effectively. Third, the constructed deep architecture is fine-tuned by gradient-descent based supervised learning with an exponential loss function. Finally, active learning method is combined based on the proposed deep architecture. We did several experiments on five sentiment classification datasets, and show that AHD is competitive with previous semi-supervised learning algorithm. Experiments are also conducted to verify the effectiveness of our proposed method with different number of labeled reviews and unlabeled reviews respectively.

Editor: Catalin Buiu, Politehnica University of Bucharest, Romania

Funding: This work is supported in part by National Natural Science Foundation of China (No. 61300155), and Scientific Research Fund of Ludong University (LY2013004). Shusen Zhou received the funding from Scientific Research Fund of Ludong University. The funders had no role in study design, data collection and analysis, decision to publish, or preparation of the manuscript.

Competing Interests: The authors have declared that no competing interests exist.

* Email: zhoushusen@gmail.com

Introduction

Recently, more and more people write reviews and share opinions on the World Wide Web, which present a wealth of information on products and services [1]. These reviews will not only help other users make better judgements but they are also useful resources for manufacturers of products to keep track and manage customer opinions [2]. However, there are large amounts of reviews for every topic, it is difficult for a user to manually learn the opinions of an interesting topic. Sentiment classification, which aims to classify a text according to the expressed sentimental polarities of opinions such as *'positive'* or *'negative'*, *'thumb up'* or *'thumb down'*, *'favorable'* or *'unfavorable'* [3], can facilitate the investigation of corresponding products or services.

In order to learn a good text classifier, a large number of labeled reviews are often needed for training [4]. However, labeling reviews is often difficult, expensive or time consuming [5]. On the other hand, it is much easier to obtain a large number of unlabeled reviews, such as the growing availability and popularity of online review sites and personal blogs [6]. In recent years, a new approach called semi-supervised learning, which uses large amount of unlabeled data together with labeled data to build better learners [7], has been developed in the machine learning community.

There are several works have been done in semi-supervised learning for sentiment classification, and have get competitive performance [3,8–10]. However, most of the existing semi-supervised learning methods are still far from satisfactory. As shown by several researchers [11,12], deep architecture, which

composed of multiple levels of non-linear operations, is expected to perform well in semi-supervised learning because of its capability of modeling hard artificial intelligent tasks. Deep belief networks (DBN) is a representative deep learning algorithm achieving notable success for text classification, which is a directed belief nets with many hidden layers constructed by restricted Boltzmann machines (RBM), and refined by a gradient-descent based supervised learning [12]. Ranzato and Szummer [13] propose an algorithm to learn text document representations based on semi-supervised auto-encoders that are combined to form a deep network. Zhou et al. [10] propose a novel semi-supervised learning algorithm to address the semi-supervised sentiment classification problem with active learning. Socher et al. [14] introduce a novel machine learning framework based on recursive autoencoders for sentence-level prediction of sentiment label distributions. Socher et al. [15] introduce the recursive neural tensor network for semantic compositionality over a sentiment treebank. The key issue of traditional DBN is the efficiency of RBM training. Convolutional neural networks (CNN), which are specifically designed to deal with the variability of two dimensional shapes, have had great success in machine learning tasks and represent one of the early successes of deep learning [16]. Desjardins and Bengio [17] adapt RBM to operate in a convolutional manner, and show that the convolutional RBM (CRBM) are more efficient than standard RBM.

CRBM has been applied successfully to a wide range of visual and audio recognition tasks [18,19]. Though the success of CRBM in addressing two dimensional issues, there is still no published

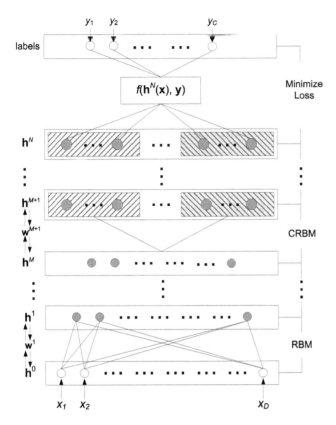

Figure 1. Architecture of HDBN.

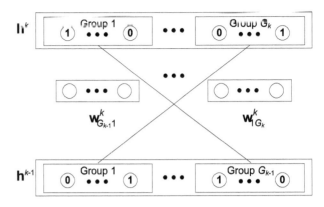

Figure 2. Architecture of CRBM.

research on the using of CRBM in textual information processing. In this paper, we propose a novel semi-supervised learning algorithm called active hybrid deep belief networks (AHD), to address the semi-supervised sentiment classification problem with deep learning. AHD is an active learning method based on deep architecture, which the bottom layers are constructed by RBM, and the upper layers are constructed by CRBM, then the whole constructed deep architecture is fine tuned by a gradient-descent based supervised learning based on an exponential loss function.

Hybrid Deep Belief Networks Method

Problem formulation

The sentiment classification dataset composed of many review documents, each review document composed of a bag of words. To classify these review documents using corpus-based approaches, we need to preprocess them in advance. The preprocess method for these reviews is similar with [9,10]. We tokenize and downcase each review and represent it as a vector of unigrams, using binary weight equal to 1 for terms present in a vector. Moreover, the punctuations, numbers, and words of length one are removed from the vector. Finally, we combine all the words in the dataset, sort the vocabulary by document frequency and remove the top 1.5%, because many of these high document frequency words are stopwords or domain specific general-purpose words.

After preprocess, each review can be represented as a vector of binary weight $\mathbf{x}^i$. If the jth word of the vocabulary is in the ith review, $\mathbf{x}^i_j = 1$; otherwise, $\mathbf{x}^i_j = 0$. Then the dataset can be represented as a matrix:

$$\mathbf{X} = \left[\mathbf{x}^1, \mathbf{x}^2, \ldots, \mathbf{x}^{R+T}\right] = \begin{bmatrix} x_1^1, x_1^2, \ldots, x_1^{R+T} \\ x_2^1, x_2^2, \ldots, x_2^{R+T} \\ \vdots, \vdots, \ldots, \vdots \\ x_D^1, x_D^2, \ldots, x_D^{R+T} \end{bmatrix} \quad (1)$$

where R is the number of training reviews, T is the number of test reviews, D is the number of feature words in the dataset. Every column of $\mathbf{X}$ corresponds to a sample $\mathbf{x}$, which is a representation of a review. A sample that has all features is viewed as a vector in $\mathbb{R}^D$, where the ith coordinate corresponds to the ith feature.

The L labeled reviews are chosen randomly from R training reviews, or chosen actively by active learning, which can be seen as:

$$\mathbf{X}^L = \mathbf{X}^R(\mathbf{S}), \ \mathbf{S} = [s_1, \ldots, s_L], \ 1 \leq s_i \leq R \quad (2)$$

where $\mathbf{S}$ is the index of selected training reviews to be labeled manually.

The L labels correspond to L labeled training reviews is denoted as:

$$\mathbf{Y}^L = \left[\mathbf{y}^1, \mathbf{y}^2, \ldots, \mathbf{y}^L\right] = \begin{bmatrix} y_1^1, y_1^2, \ldots, y_1^L \\ y_2^1, y_2^2, \ldots, y_2^L \\ \vdots, \vdots, \ldots, \vdots \\ y_C^1, y_C^2, \ldots, y_C^L \end{bmatrix} \quad (3)$$

where C is the number of classes. Every column of $\mathbf{Y}$ is a vector in $\mathbb{R}^C$, where the jth coordinate corresponds to the jth class.

$$y_j^i = \begin{cases} 1 & \text{if } \mathbf{x}^i \in j^{\text{th}} \text{ class} \\ -1 & \text{if } \mathbf{x}^i \notin j^{\text{th}} \text{ class} \end{cases} \quad (4)$$

For example, if a review $\mathbf{x}^i$ is positive, $\mathbf{y}^i = [1, -1]'$; otherwise, $\mathbf{y}^i = [-1, 1]'$.

We intend to seek the mapping function $\mathbf{X} \to \mathbf{Y}$ using the L labeled data and all unlabeled data. After training, we can determine $\mathbf{y}$ using the mapping function when a new sample $\mathbf{x}$ comes.

Architecture of HDBN

In this part, we propose a novel semi-supervised learning method HDBN to address the sentiment classification problem. The sentiment datasets have high dimension (about 10,000), and computation complexity of convolutional calculation is relatively high, so we use RBM to reduce the dimension of review with normal calculation firstly. Fig. 1 shows the deep architecture of HDBN, a fully interconnected directed belief nets with one input layer $\mathbf{h}^0$, N hidden layers $\mathbf{h}^1,\mathbf{h}^2,...,\mathbf{h}^N$, and one label layer at the top. The input layer $\mathbf{h}^0$ has D units, equal to the number of features of sample review $\mathbf{x}$. The hidden layer has M layers constructed by RBM and $N-M$ layers constructed by CRBM. The label layer has C units, equal to the number of classes of label vector $\mathbf{y}$. The numbers of hidden layers and the number of units for hidden layers, currently, are pre-defined according to the experience or intuition. The seeking of the mapping function $\mathbf{X}{\rightarrow}\mathbf{Y}$, here, is transformed to the problem of finding the parameter space $\mathbf{W}=\{\mathbf{w}^1,\mathbf{w}^2,...,\mathbf{w}^N\}$ for the deep architecture.

The training of the HDBN can be divided into two stages:

1. HDBN is constructed by greedy layer-wise unsupervised learning using RBMs and CRBMs as building blocks. L labeled data and all unlabeled data are utilized to find the parameter space $\mathbf{W}$ with N layers.

2. HDBN is trained according to the exponential loss function using gradient descent based supervised learning. The parameter space $\mathbf{W}$ is refined using L labeled data.

Unsupervised learning

As show in Fig. 1 , we construct HDBN layer by layer using RBMs and CRBMs, the details of RBM can be seen in [12]. CRBM is introduced below.

The architecture of CRBM can be seen in Fig. 2, which is similar to RBM, a two-layer recurrent neural network in which stochastic binary input groups are connected to stochastic binary output groups using symmetrically weighted connections. The top layer represents a vector of stochastic binary hidden feature $\mathbf{h}^k$ and the bottom layer represents a vector of binary visible data $\mathbf{h}^{k-1}$, $k=M+1,...,N$. The kth layer consists of G_k groups, where each group consists of D_k units, resulting in $G_k \times D_k$ hidden units. The layer $\mathbf{h}^M$ is consist of 1 group and D_M units. $\mathbf{w}^k$ is the symmetric interaction term connecting corresponding groups between data $\mathbf{h}^{k-1}$ and feature $\mathbf{h}^k$. However, comparing with RBM, the weights of CRBM between the hidden and visible groups are shared among all locations [18], and the calculation is operated in a convolutional manner [17].

We define the energy of the state $(\mathbf{h}^{k-1},\mathbf{h}^k)$ as:

$$E(\mathbf{h}^{k-1},\mathbf{h}^k;\theta) = \\ -\sum_{s=1}^{G_{k-1}}\sum_{t=1}^{G_k}(\tilde{w}_{st}^k * h_s^{k-1})\bullet h_t^k - \sum_{s=1}^{G_{k-1}}b_s^k\sum_{u=1}^{D_{k-1}}h_u^{k-1} - \sum_{t=1}^{G_k}c_t^k\sum_{v=1}^{D_k}h_t^k \quad (5)$$

where $\theta=(\mathbf{w},\mathbf{b},\mathbf{c})$ are the model parameters: w_{st}^k is a filter between unit s in the layer $\mathbf{h}^{k-1}$ and unit t in the layer $\mathbf{h}^k$, $k=M+1,...,N$. The dimension of the filter w_{st}^k is equal to $D_{k-1}-D_k+1$. b_s^{k-1} is the sth bias of layer $\mathbf{h}^{k-1}$ and c_t^k is the tth bias of layer $\mathbf{h}^k$. A tilde above an array ($\tilde{w}$) denote flipping the array, $*$ denote valid convolution, and $\bullet$ denote element-wise product followed by summation, i.e., $A\bullet B=trA^TB$ [18].

Gibbs sampler can be performed based on the following conditional distribution.

Table 1. Algorithm of HDBN.

Input:

data $\mathbf{X}$, $\mathbf{Y}^L$

number of training data R; number of test data T;

number of layers N; number of epochs Q;

number of units in every hidden layer $D_1...D_N$;

number of groups in every convolutional hidden layer $G_M...G_N$;

hidden layer $\mathbf{h}^1,...,\mathbf{h}^M$;

convolutional hidden layer $\mathbf{h}^{M+1},...,\mathbf{h}^{N-1}$;

parameter space $\mathbf{W}=\{\mathbf{w}^1,...,\mathbf{w}^N\}$;

biases $\mathbf{b}$, $\mathbf{c}$; momentum ϑ and learning rate η;

Output:

deep architecture with parameter space $\mathbf{W}$

1. Greedy layer-wise unsupervised learning

for $k=1; k<N-1; k++$ **do**

  for $q=1; q\leq Q; q++$ **do**

    for $r=1; r\leq R+T; r++$ **do**

    Calculate the non-linear positive and negative phase:

    if $k\leq M$ **then**

      Normal calculation.

    else

      Convolutional calculation according to Eq. 6 and Eq. 7.

    end if

    Update the weights and biases:

$$w_{st}^k = \vartheta w_{st}^k + \eta\left(\langle h_{s,r}^{k-1}h_{t,r}^k\rangle_{P_0} - \langle h_{s,r}^{k-1}h_{t,r}^k\rangle_{P_1}\right)$$

  end for

  end for

end for

2. Supervised learning based on gradient descent

$$\underset{W}{\arg\min}\ \sum_{i=1}^{L}\sum_{j=1}^{C}\exp\left(-h^N(x_i^i)y_j^i\right)$$

The probability of turning on unit v in group t is a logistic function of the states of $\mathbf{h}^{k-1}$ and w_{st}^k:

$$p\left(h_{t,v}^k=1|\mathbf{h}^{k-1}\right)=\text{sigm}\left(c_t^k+(\sum_s \tilde{w}_{st}^k * h_s^{k-1})_v\right) \quad (6)$$

The probability of turning on unit u in group s is a logistic function of the states of $\mathbf{h}^k$ and w_{st}^k:

$$p\left(h_{s,u}^{k-1}=1|\mathbf{h}^k\right)=\text{sigm}\left(b_s^{k-1}+(\sum_t w_{st}^k \star h_t^k)_u\right) \quad (7)$$

where the logistic function is:

$$\text{sigm}(\eta)=1/(1+e^{-\eta}) \quad (8)$$

A star $\star$ denotes full convolution.

Table 2. Algorithm of AHD.

Input:

data $\mathbf{X}$, $(\mathbf{X}^L, \mathbf{Y}^L)$ (one positive and one negative)

number of training data R

number of iterations I

number of active choosing data for every iteration U

parameter space $\mathbf{W} = \{\mathbf{w}^1, \ldots, \mathbf{w}^N\}$

Output:

deep architecture with parameter space $\mathbf{W}$

for $i = 1; i \leq I; i++$ **do**

    Train HDBN with labeled dataset $\mathbf{X}^L$ and all unlabeled data in $\mathbf{X}$.

    Choose U reviews which near the separating line from train dataset $\mathbf{X}^R$ through Eq. 17.

    Add U reviews into the labeled data set $\mathbf{X}^L$.

end for

Train HDBN with labeled dataset $\mathbf{X}^L$ and all unlabeled data in $\mathbf{X}$.

The convolution computation can extract the information of text effectively based on deep architecture, although it needs more computation time.

Supervised learning

In HDBN, we construct the deep architecture using all labeled reviews with unlabeled reviews by inputting them one by one from layer $\mathbf{h}^0$. The deep architecture is constructed layer by layer from bottom to top, and each time, the parameter space $\mathbf{w}^k$ is trained by the calculated data in the $k-1^{th}$ layer.

According to the $\mathbf{w}^k$ calculated by RBM and CRBM, the layer $\mathbf{h}^k, k = 1, \ldots, M$ can be computed as following when a sample $\mathbf{x}$ inputs from layer $\mathbf{h}^0$:

$$h_t^k(\mathbf{x}) = \text{sigm}\left(c_t^k + \sum_{s=1}^{D_{k-1}} w_{st}^k h_s^{k-1}(\mathbf{x})\right), t = 1, \ldots, D_k \quad (9)$$

When $k = M+1, \ldots, N-1$, the layer $\mathbf{h}^k$ can be represented as:

$$h_t^k(\mathbf{x}) = \text{sigm}\left(c_t^k + \sum_{s=1}^{G_{k-1}} \tilde{w}_{st}^k * h_s^{k-1}(\mathbf{x})\right), t = 1, \ldots, G_k \quad (10)$$

The parameter space $\mathbf{w}^N$ is initialized randomly, just as backpropagation algorithm.

$$h_t^N(\mathbf{x}) = c_t^N + \sum_{s=1}^{G_{N-1} \times D_{N-1}} w_{st}^N h_s^{N-1}(\mathbf{x}), t = 1, \ldots, D_N \quad (11)$$

After greedy layer-wise unsupervised learning, $\mathbf{h}^N(\mathbf{x})$ is the representation of $\mathbf{x}$. Then we use L labeled reviews to refine the parameter space $\mathbf{W}$ for better discriminative ability. This task can be formulated as an optimization problem:

$$\underset{\mathbf{W}}{\arg\min} \quad f\left(h^N(\mathbf{X}^L), \mathbf{Y}^L\right) \quad (12)$$

where

$$f\left(h^N(\mathbf{X}^L), \mathbf{Y}^L\right) = \sum_{i=1}^{L} \sum_{j=1}^{C} T\left(h_j^N(\mathbf{x}^i) y_j^i\right) \quad (13)$$

and the loss function is defined as

$$T(r) = \exp(-r) \quad (14)$$

We use gradient-descent through the whole HDBN to refine the weight space. In the supervised learning stage, the stochastic activities are replaced by deterministic, real valued probabilities.

Classification using HDBN

The training procedure of HDBN is given in Table 1. For the training of HDBN architecture, the parameters are random initialized with normal distribution. All the reviews in the dataset are used to train the HDBN with unsupervised learning. After training, we can determine the label of the new data through:

$$\underset{j}{\arg\max} \, h^N(\mathbf{x}) \quad (15)$$

Active Hybrid Deep Belief Networks Method

AHD description

Given an unlabeled pool $\mathbf{X}^R$ and an initial labeled data set $\mathbf{X}^L$ (one positive, one negative), the AHD architecture $\mathbf{h}^N(\mathbf{x})$ will decide which instance in $\mathbf{X}^R$ to query next. Then the parameters of $\mathbf{h}^N(\mathbf{x})$ are adjusted after new reviews are labeled and inserted into the labeled data set $\mathbf{X}^L$. We choose the reviews that are near the separating hyperplane as the labeled training data.

Table 3. HDBN structure used in experiment.

Dataset	Structure
MOV	100-100-4-2
KIT	50-50-3-2
ELE	50-50-3-2
BOO	50-50-5-2
DVD	50-50-5-2

When HDBN is trained by L labeled data and all unlabeled data, the parameters of deep architecture are adjusted, $\mathbf{h}^N(\mathbf{x})$ is the representation of $\mathbf{x}$. Given an unlabeled pool $\mathbf{X}^R$, the next unlabeled instance to be queried are chosen according to the location of $\mathbf{h}^N(\mathbf{X}^R)$. For review document, there are only 2 classes (*positive* or *negative*), so the dimension of $\mathbf{h}^N(\mathbf{x})$ is 2, the classes separation line is $h_1^N = h_2^N$. The distance between a point $\mathbf{h}^N(\mathbf{x}^i)$ and separation line is:

$$d(\mathbf{x}^i) = |h_1^N(\mathbf{x}^i) - h_2^N(\mathbf{x}^i)| / \sqrt{2} \qquad (16)$$

The selected training reviews to be labeled manually are given by:

$$s = \{j : d(\mathbf{x}^j) = \min(d(\mathbf{X}^R))\} \qquad (17)$$

Classification using AHD

The training procedure of AHD is given in Table 2. The training set $\mathbf{X}^R$ can be seen as an unlabeled pool. We randomly select one positive and one negative reviews in the pool to input as the initial labeled dataset $\mathbf{X}^L$ that are used for supervised learning. The iteration times I and the number of active choosing data U for each iteration can be set manually based on the number of labeled reviews in the experiment.

For each iteration, the HDBN architecture is trained by all the unlabeled reviews and labeled reviews in existence with unsupervised learning and supervised learning firstly. Then U reviews are chosen from the unlabeled pool based on the distance of these review mapping results from the separating line. At last, these U reviews are labeled manually and added to the labeled dataset $\mathbf{X}^L$. For the next iteration, the HDBN architecture can be re-trained by all reviews with unsupervised learning and all labeled reviews

with the new increased labeled dataset $\mathbf{X}^L$. At last, HDBN architecture is retrained by all the reviews with unsupervised learning and existing labeled reviews with supervised learning.

After active training, we can use the Eq. 15 to determine the label of the new data. The purpose of active learning is choose more useful label data to train the deep architecture, which can use fewer label data to train better classifier.

Experiments

Experimental setup

We evaluate the performance of the proposed HDBN and AHD method using five sentiment classification datasets. The first dataset is MOV [20], which is a classical movie review dataset. The other four datasets contain products reviews come from the multi-domain sentiment classification corpus, including books (BOO), DVDs (DVD), electronics (ELE), and kitchen appliances (KIT) [21]. Each dataset contains 1,000 positive and 1,000 negative reviews.

The experimental setup is same as [9] and [10]. We divide the 2,000 reviews into ten equal-sized folds randomly, maintaining balanced class distributions in each fold. Half of the reviews in each fold are random selected as training data and the remaining reviews are used for test. Only the reviews in the training data set are used for the selection of labeled reviews by active learning. All the algorithms are tested with cross-validation.

We compare the classification performance of HDBN with four representative semi-supervised learning methods, i.e., semi-supervised spectral learning (Spectral) [22], transductive SVM (TSVM) [23], deep belief networks (DBN) [12], and personal/impersonal views (PIV) [3]. Spectral learning, TSVM methods are two baseline methods for sentiment classification. DBN [12] is the classical deep learning method proposed recently. PIV [3] is a new sentiment classification method proposed recently.

We also compare the classification performance of AHD with three representative active semi-supervised learning methods, i.e., active learning (Active) [24], mine the easy classify the hard

Table 4. Test accuracy with 100 labeled reviews for semi-supervised learning.

Type	MOV	KIT	ELE	BOO	DVD
Spectral	67.3	63.7	57.7	55.8	56.2
TSVM	68.7	65.5	62.9	58.7	57.3
DBN	71.3	72.6	73.6	64.3	66.7
PIV	–	**78.6**	70.0	60.1	49.5
HDBN	**72.2**	74.8	**73.8**	**66.0**	**70.3**

Table 5. Test accuracy with 100 labeled reviews for active semi-supervised learning.

Type	MOV	KIT	ELE	BOO	DVD
Active	68.9	68.1	63.3	58.6	58.0
MECH	76.2	74.1	70.6	62.1	62.7
ADN	**76.3**	**77.5**	**76.8**	69.0	71.6
AFD	75	77	**76.8**	**70.1**	**73.7**

(MECH) [9], and active deep networks (ADN) [10]. Active learning [24] is a baseline active learning method for sentiment classification. MECH [9] and ADN [10] are two new active learning method for sentiment classification proposed recently.

Performance of HDBN

The HDBN architecture used in all our experiments have 2 normal hidden layer and 1 convolutional hidden layer, every hidden layer has different number of units for different sentiment datasets. The deep structure used in our experiments for different datasets can be seen in Table 3. For example, the HDBN structure used in MOV dataset experiment is 100-100-4-2, which represents the number of units in 2 normal hidden layers are 100, 100 respectively, and in output layer is 2, the number of groups in 1 convolutional hidden layer is 4. The number of unit in input layer is the same as the dimensions of each datasets. For greedy layer-wise unsupervised learning, we train the weights of each layer independently with the fixed number of epochs equal to 30 and the learning rate is set to 0.1. The initial momentum is 0.5 and after 5 epochs, the momentum is set to 0.9. For supervised learning, we run 30 epochs, three times of linear searches are performed in each epoch.

The test accuracies in cross validation for five datasets and five methods with semi-supervised learning are shown in Table 4. The results of previous two methods are reported by [9]. The results of

DBN method are reported by [10]. Li et al. [3] reported the results of PIV method. The result of PIV on MOV dataset is empty, because [3] did not report it. HDBN is the proposed method.

Through Table 4, we can see that HDBN gets most of the best results except on KIT dataset, which is just slight worse than PIV method. However, the preprocess of PIV method is much more complicated than HDBN, and the PIV results on other datasets are much worse than HDBN method. HDBN method is adjusted by DBN, all the experiment results on five datasets for HDBN are better than DBN. This could be contributed by the convolutional computation in HDBN structure, and proves the effectiveness of our proposed method.

Performance of AHD

To evaluate the performance of AHD, we compare its results with several previous active learning methods for sentiment classification. The architectures used in this experiments can be seen in Table 3. We perform active learning for 5 iterations. In each iteration, we select and label 20 of the most uncertain reviews, and then retrain the deep architecture on all of the unlabeled reviews and labeled reviews annotated so far. After 5 iterations, 100 labeled reviews are used for training.

The test accuracies in cross validation for five datasets and four methods with active semi-supervised learning are shown in Table 5. The results of previous two methods are reported by

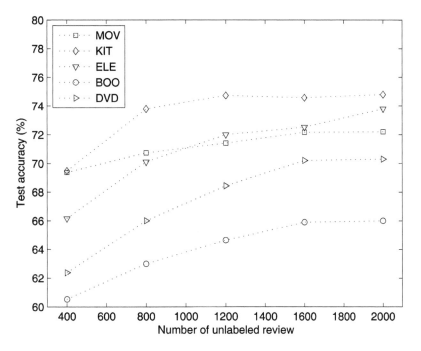

Figure 3. Test accuracy of HDBN with different number of unlabeled reviews on five datasets.

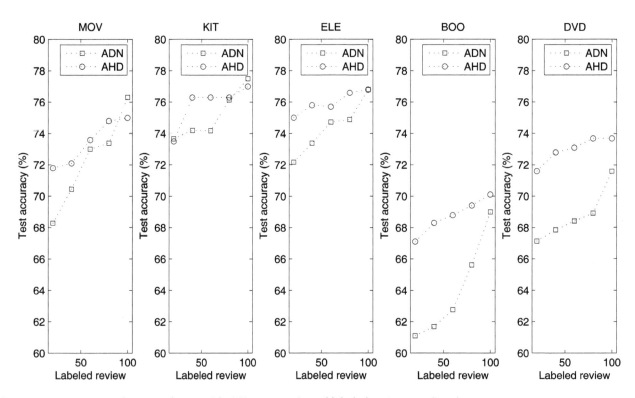

Figure 4. Test accuracy of ADN and AHD with different number of labeled reviews on five datasets.

[9]. The results of ADN method are reported by [10]. AHD is the proposed active learning method in this paper. Through Table 5, we can see that the results of AHD is better than Active and MECH methods, and competitive with ADN method. Because ADN and AHD methods are both deep learning method, these results prove that deep architecture is good for sentiment classification.

Performance with variance of unlabeled data

To verify the contribution of unlabeled reviews for our proposed method, we did several experiments with fewer unlabeled reviews and 100 labeled reviews. We use HDBN method in this part, considering AHD method choose the reviews need to label from an unlabeled pool, it is unfair to compare the performance of AHD when the size of unlabeled pool is different.

The test accuracies of HDBN with different number of unlabeled reviews and 100 labeled reviews on five datasets are shown in Fig. 3. The architectures for HDBN used in this experiment can be seen in Table 3. We can see that the performance of HDBN is much worse when just using 400 unlabeled reviews. However, when using more than 1200 unlabeled reviews, the performance of HDBN is improved obviously. For most of review datasets, the accuracy of HDBN with 1200 unlabeled reviews is close to the accuracy with 1600 and 2000 unlabeled reviews. This proves that HDBN can get competitive performance with just few labeled reviews and appropriate number of unlabeled reviews. Considering the much time needed for training with more unlabeled reviews and less accuracy improved for HDBN method, we suggest using appropriate number of unlabeled reviews in real application.

Performance with variance of labeled data

To verify the contribution of labeled reviews for our proposed method, we did several experiments with different number of

labeled reviews on five datasets. To compare the active learning performance with ADN [10], we use AHD method in this experiment, all the experimental setting are same as ADN. The architectures for AHD used in this experiment can be seen in Table 3.

The test accuracies of ADN and AHD with different number of labeled reviews on five datasets are shown in Fig. 4. We can see that the performance of AHD is better than ADN for most of the experimental setting, although they are both based on the DBN method. This proves that the convolutional computation has better performance than the normal computation in the deep architecture for sentiment classification. We can also see that both ADN and AHD can get high accuracy even with just 20 labeled reviews for training. This proves the effect of deep learning method for semi-supervised learning with very few labeled reviews.

Conclusions

In this paper, we propose a novel semi-supervised learning method, AHD, to address the sentiment classification problem with a small number of labeled reviews. AHD seamlessly incorporate convolutional computation into the DBN architecture, and use CRBM to abstract the review information effectively. One promising property of AHD is that it can effectively use the distribution of large amount of unlabeled data, together with few label information in a unified framework. In particular, AHD can greatly reduce the dimension of reviews through RBM and abstract the information of reviews through the cooperate of RBM and CRBM. Then an exponential loss function is used to refine the constructed deep architecture with few label information. Moreover, it can choose the review to be labeled actively, improve the performance of deep architecture effectively.

Experiments conducted on five sentiment datasets demonstrate that AHD outperforms most of previous methods and is competitive with DBN based method, which demonstrates the performance of deep architecture for sentiment classification. Experiments are also conducted to verify the effectiveness of AHD method with different number of labeled reviews, the results show that AHD can reach very competitive performance with few labeled reviews and large amount of unlabeled reviews. It provides soundness support for the effectiveness of AHD for real applications, where collecting enough unlabeled data is a relatively easy task while it is hard to get enough labeled data.

Author Contributions

Conceived and designed the experiments: SZ QC XW. Performed the experiments: SZ. Analyzed the data: SZ. Contributed reagents/materials/analysis tools: SZ QC. Contributed to the writing of the manuscript: SZ.

References

1. Liu Y, Yu X, Huang X, An A (2010) S-plasa+: Adaptive sentiment analysis with application to sales performance prediction. In: International ACM SIGIR Conference on Research and Development in Information Retrieval. New York, NY, USA: ACM, pp. 873–874.

2. Wei W, Gulla JA (2010) Sentiment learning on product reviews via sentiment ontology tree. In: Annual Meeting of the Association for Computational Linguistics. Stroudsburg, PA, USA: Association for Computational Linguistics. pp. 404–413.

3. Li S, Huang CR, Zhou G, Lee SYM (2010) Employing personal/impersonal views in supervised and semi-supervised sentiment classification. In: Annual Meeting of the Association for Computational Linguistics. Uppsala, Sweden: Association for Computational Linguistics, pp. 414–423.

4. Zhen Y, Yeung DY (2010) Sed: Supervised experimental design and its application to text classification. In: International ACM SIGIR Conference on Research and Development in Information Retrieval. Geneva, Switzerland: ACM, pp. 299–306.

5. Chapelle O, Scholkopf B, Zien A (2006) Semi-Supervised Learning. Cambridge, MA, USA: MIT Press.

6. Pang B, Lee L (2008) Opinion mining and sentiment analysis, volume 2 of *Foundations and Trends in Information Retrieval*.

7. Zhu X (2007) Semi-supervised learning literature survey. Technical report, University of Wisconsin Madison, Madison, WI, USA.

8. Sindhwani V, Melville P (2008) Document-word co-regularization for semi-supervised sentiment analysis. In: International Conference on Data Mining. Pisa, Italy: IEEE, pp. 1025–1030.

9. Dasgupta S, Ng V (2009) Mine the easy, classify the hard: A semi-supervised approach to automatic sentiment classfication. In: Joint Conference of the 47th Annual Meeting of the Association for Computational Linguistics and 4th International Joint Conference on Natural Language Processing of the Asian Federation of Natural Language Processing. Stroudsburg, PA, USA: Association for Computational Linguistics, pp. 701–709.

10. Zhou S, Chen Q, Wang X (2010) Active deep networks for semi-supervised sentiment classification. In: International Conference on Computational Linguistics. pp. 1515–1523.

11. Salakhutdinov R, Hinton GE (2007) Learning a nonlinear embedding by preserving class neighbourhood structure. Journal of Machine Learning Research 2: 412–419.

12. Hinton GE, Osindero S, Teh YW (2006) A fast learning algorithm for deep belief nets. Neural Computation 18: 1527–1554.

13. Ranzato M, Szummer M (2008) Semi-supervised learning of compact document representations with deep networks. In: International Conference on Machine Learning. Helsinki, Finland: ACM, pp. 792–799.

14. Socher R, Pennington J, Huang EH, Ng AY, Manning CD (2011) Semi-supervised recursive autoencoders for predicting sentiment distributions. In: Proceedings of the 2011 Conference on Empirical Methods in Natural Language Processing. Edinburgh, Scotland, UK.: Association for Computational Linguistics, pp. 151–161.

15. Socher R, Perelygin A, Wu J, Chuang J, Manning CD, et al. (2013) Recursive deep models for semantic compositionality over a sentiment treebank. In: Proceedings of the 2013 Conference on Empirical Methods in Natural Language Processing. Seattle, Washington, USA: Association for Computational Linguistics, pp. 1631–1642.

16. Lecun Y, Bottou L, Bengio Y, Haffner P (1998) Gradient-based learning applied to document recognition. Proceedings of the IEEE 86: 2278–2324.

17. Desjardins G, Bengio Y (2008) Empirical evaluation of convolutional rbms for vision. Technical report.

18. Lee H, Grosse R, Ranganath R, Ng A (2009) Convolutional deep belief networks for scalable unsupervised learning of hierarchical representations. In: International Conference on Machine Learning. Montreal, Canada: ACM, pp. 609–616.

19. Lee H, Largman Y, Pham P, Ng A (2009) Unsupervised feature learning for audio classification using convolutional deep belief networks. In: Advances in Neural Information Processing Systems. Vancouver, B.C., Canada: NIPS Foundation, pp. 1096–1103.

20. Pang B, Lee L, Vaithyanathan S (2002) Thumbs up? sentiment classification using machine learning techniques. In: Conference on Empirical Methods in Natural Language Processing. Stroudsburg, PA, USA: Association for Computational Linguistics, pp. 79–86.

21. Blitzer J, Dredze M, Pereira F (2007) Biographies, bollywood, boom-boxes and blenders: Domain adaptation for sentiment classification. In: Annual Meeting of the Association for Computational Linguistics. Prague, Czech Republic: Association for Computational Linguistics, pp. 440–447.

22. Kamvar S, Klein D, Manning C (2003) Spectral learning. In: International Joint Conferences on Artificial Intelligence. Catalonia, Spain: AAAI Press, pp. 561–566.

23. Collobert R, Sinz F, Weston J, Bottou L (2006) Large scale transductive svms. Journal of Machine Learning Research 7: 1687–1712.

24. Tong S, Koller D (2002) Support vector machine active learning with applications to text classification. Journal of Machine Learning Research 2: 45–66.

20

Quantum Attack-Resistent Certificateless Multi-Receiver Signcryption Scheme

Huixian Li[1,2]*, Xubao Chen[1], Liaojun Pang[3], Weisong Shi[2]

1 School of Computer Science and Engineering, Northwestern Polytechnical University, Xi'an, China, **2** Department of Computer Science, Wayne State University, Detroit, Michigan, United States of America, **3** School of Life Sciences and Technology, Xidian University, Xi'an, China

Abstract

The existing certificateless signcryption schemes were designed mainly based on the traditional public key cryptography, in which the security relies on the hard problems, such as factor decomposition and discrete logarithm. However, these problems will be easily solved by the quantum computing. So the existing certificateless signcryption schemes are vulnerable to the quantum attack. Multivariate public key cryptography (MPKC), which can resist the quantum attack, is one of the alternative solutions to guarantee the security of communications in the post-quantum age. Motivated by these concerns, we proposed a new construction of the certificateless multi-receiver signcryption scheme (CLMSC) based on MPKC. The new scheme inherits the security of MPKC, which can withstand the quantum attack. Multivariate quadratic polynomial operations, which have lower computation complexity than bilinear pairing operations, are employed in signcrypting a message for a certain number of receivers in our scheme. Security analysis shows that our scheme is a secure MPKC-based scheme. We proved its security under the hardness of the Multivariate Quadratic (MQ) problem and its unforgeability under the Isomorphism of Polynomials (IP) assumption in the random oracle model. The analysis results show that our scheme also has the security properties of non-repudiation, perfect forward secrecy, perfect backward secrecy and public verifiability. Compared with the existing schemes in terms of computation complexity and ciphertext length, our scheme is more efficient, which makes it suitable for terminals with low computation capacity like smart cards.

Editor: Gerardo Adesso, University of Nottingham, United Kingdom

Funding: This work was supported by Natural Science Foundation of China under Grant Nos. 61103178 and 60803151, and the Research Fund for the Doctoral Program of Higher Education of China under Grant No. 20096102120045. The funders had no role in study design, data collection and analysis, decision to publish, or preparation of the manuscript.

Competing Interests: The authors have declared that no competing interests exist.

* E-mail: lihuixian@nwpu.edu.cn

Introduction

Signcryption is a cryptographic primitive that provides both signature and encryption simultaneously to sensitive information at a lower computation and communication overhead than the traditional signature-then-encryption approach [1]. In terms of the implementation method, there are two kinds of signcryption schemes. One is based on traditional public key infrastructure [2], which causes the costly certificate management problem; the other is based on identity-based public key cryptography [3], which avoids the certificate management, but induces the key escrow problem.

In 2003, Al-Riyami et al. [4] proposed the certificateless cryptosystem (CLC). In their certificateless cryptosystem, a user's secret key is derived from two parts: one is an identity-based secret key generated by Key Generation Center (KGC) and the other is a self-generated secret key. Thus CLC solves the key escrow problem as well as the certificate management problem, and it also reduces the implementation complexity of the cryptosystem. In 2008, Barbosa et al. [5] first proposed the certificateless signcryption scheme (CLSC) based on bilinear pairing operations. However, they did not give the security proof of their scheme. Since then, certificateless signcryption schemes [6–7] have been studied extensively. In 2010, Li et al. proposed another CLSC [8] and proved its security formally. However, these schemes [5–8]

are inefficient in computation because they use the bilinear pairing operation, a quite complex computation. Selvi et al. [9] and Jing et al. [10] constructed an efficient CLSC based on the CDH (Computational Diffie-Hellman) problem without bilinear pairing operations, respectively. At the same time, they proved their schemes' security in the random oracle model. However, their schemes are only single-receiver ones. If there are multiple receivers at the same time, these schemes need to signcrypt the same message for each receiver separately, so they are very inefficient for the multi-receiver scenario. In order to improve the efficiency of signcryption in the multi-receiver setting, Selvi et al. [11] proposed the certificateless multi-receiver signcryption scheme (CLMSC), and this scheme only needs two bilinear pairing operations and $(t+2)$ exponentiation operations (t denotes the number of the receivers) in the signcryption and designcryption phases. However, they found that this scheme cannot resist the forgery attack and then presented an enhanced scheme [12] later. But Miao et al. [13] showed that the enhanced scheme is still insecure against the internal attack and provided a detailed security analysis.

To date, the implementations of almost all certificateless signcryption schemes [5–13] are based on traditional public key cryptosystems, in which the security mainly relies on the hard problems, such as factor decomposition and discrete logarithm. However, in 1994, Shor [14] proposed a polynomial-time quantum algorithm that can successfully factor large integers, which shows that quantum computing has brought a potential challenge to these hard mathematical problems. Once quantum computers is developed successfully, they will pose a fatal threat to the security of almost all certificateless signcryption schemes which are based on public key cryptosystems such as RSA, ElGamal and ECC. So it is more and more urgent to design a certificateless signcryption scheme that can resist quantum attack. Multivariate public key cryptography (MPKC), which can resist quantum attack, is one of the alternative solutions to guarantee the security of communications in the post-quantum age. The security of MPKC is based on the Multivariate Quadratic (MQ) problem and the Isomorphism of Polynomials (IP) problem. Compared with identity-based cryptography, MPKC has lower calculation complexity and is higher in efficiency, which makes MPKC well suitable to implement strongly secure communications for low-end devices. The MPKC-based schemes have been studied widely, and several excellent schemes have been proposed. For example, SFLASH, a signature scheme based on MPKC, has been recommended by the NESSIE European Consortium since 2003 as the best known solution for implementation on low-cost smart cards [15].

Our contribution. Motivated by these concerns, we employ MPKC to construct an efficient quantum attack-resistant certificateless multi-receiver signcryption scheme, which combines the certificateless cryptosystem and MPKC. The new scheme not only has the advantage of the certificateless cryptosystem, which avoids the problem of key management, but also resists quantum attack only with light-weight computation like the multivariate quadratic polynomial operations. In our scheme, multivariate quadratic polynomial operations, which have lower computation complexity than bilinear pairing operations, are employed in signcrypting a message for a certain number of receivers. Therefore, our scheme is more efficient than the existing CLMSC schemes, and it is suitable for mobile terminals with low computing power. Security analysis shows that our scheme is a secure MPKC-based multi-receiver signcryption scheme, and it also has the important security properties such as message confidentiality, unforgeability, non-repudiation, perfect forward secrecy, perfect backward secrecy and public verifiability.

Preliminaries

1 MQ Problem and IP Problem

In this section, we shall briefly recall some basic concepts of MPKC including multivariate polynomial equations, the MQ problem and the IP problem.

Let G be a finite field of prime order p. Let n be the number of variables, namely, x_1, x_2, ..., x_n in the multivariate polynomial equation, g be the number of the multivariate polynomial equations, and d be the degree of the multivariate polynomial equations.

A tuple of multivariate quadratic polynomials consists of a finite ordered set of polynomials of the following form:

$$p_i(x_1,x_2,...,x_n) = \sum_{1 \leq j \leq k \leq n} a_{ijk} x_j x_k + \sum_{j=1}^{n} b_{ij} x_j + c_i \quad (1)$$

where $i = 1, 2, ..., g$, and $x_j, x_k \in G$, and the coefficients $\{a_{ijk}, b_{ij}, c_i\}$ are over G [16]. Then, the MQ problem can be described as follows:

Definition 1. (MQ). Given a tuple $P = (p_1, p_2, ..., p_g)$ of g multivariate quadratic polynomials with n unknowns defined over

G, and the image $y = (p_1(z), p_2(z), ..., p_g(z))$ of an element z randomly chosen from G^n (G^n denotes the nth extension of G), the problem to find an element x of G^n such that $y = (p_1(x), p_2(x), ..., p_g(x))$ is called the MQ problem [16].

Solving a set of randomly chosen quadratic equations with several variables over a finite field is considered as an NP hard problem [17].

Definition 2. (IP). Given P and Q be two public sets of n quadratic equations with n variables over G, if P and Q are isomorphism, then $P = T \circ Q \circ V$ ($\circ$ denotes composition of mappings), where T and V are two invertible affine transformations on $G^n \to G^n$. Finding (T, V) for P, Q such that $P = T \circ Q \circ V$ is called the IP problem [18].

2 Multivariate Public Key Cryptosystem

In a primitive multivariate public key cryptosystem [19], for a user U with identity ID_U, his/her public key is $P_U = T \circ Q \circ V$, and his/her secret key is the 3-tuple $P_U^{-1} = (T, Q, V)$. The encryption operation for a message m is denoted by $\sigma = P_U(m)$ and the corresponding decryption operation for the ciphertext σ is denoted by $m = P_U^{-1}(\sigma)$. For example, Alice wants to send a message m to Bob with identity ID_B. Alice computes the ciphertext $\sigma = P_B(m) = T \circ Q \circ V(m) = T(Q(V(m)))$ with Bob's public key. Bob receives the ciphertext σ from Alice and then decrypts the ciphertext σ by computing $P_B^{-1}(\sigma)$. In a word, Bob computes $\sigma_T = T^{-1}(\sigma)$, $\sigma_Q = Q^{-1}(\sigma_T)$ and $m = V^{-1}(\sigma_Q)$ sequentially. At last, Bob obtains the plaintext message $m = P_B^{-1}(\sigma)$.

3 Framework of CLMSC

A certificateless multi-receiver signcryption scheme consists of five probabilistic polynomial time algorithms, namely Setup, Partial Key Extract, Key Extract, Signcrypt and De-signcrypt. According to the features of MPKC, we improve the existing CLMSC model, that is, KGC produces the common partial public key and partial secret key in the phase of Partial Key Extract.

- **Setup**: This algorithm is run by KGC. It takes as input a security parameter s and returns the public parameters *params*.

- **Partial Key Extract**: This algorithm is run by KGC. KGC first chooses a random number w as the system master key. Then it takes as input w and *params* and returns the common partial public key PP_u and partial secret key PS_u.

- **Key Extract**: This algorithm is run by a user U. It takes as input *params*, PP_u, PS_u and an identity ID_u and returns the full public key PK_u and the full secret key SK_u of the user.

- **Signcrypt**: To securely send a message m to a group of receivers $\{\text{ID}_1, \text{ID}_2, ..., \text{ID}_l\}$, the sender S should run this algorithm to signcrypt it first. It takes as input *params*, a message m, the sender's identity ID_S, the full keys PK_u and SK_u of the sender, and lists of the receiver identities and their public keys, and returns a ciphertext σ.

- **De-signcrypt**: This algorithm takes as input a ciphertext σ, the receiver's identity ID_i, the receiver's full keys PK_i and SK_i, the identity ID_s and the public key PK_s of the sender, and returns either a plaintext m or an error symbol $\perp$.

4 Security Model for CLMSC

Our security model is established based on Selvi et al.'s security model [11]. For a certificateless signcryption scheme, there are two types of attacks corresponding to two types of attackers, namely A_1 and A_2. In the attack of Type 1, A_1 does not have access to the system master key, but he/she has the ability to replace the public key of any user with a value that he/she chooses arbitrarily. A_2 has access to the master key, but he/she cannot change public key of any user.

Definition 3. Confidentiality under the attack of Type 1. A certificateless multi-receiver signcryption scheme is Type-1-CCA2 secure if no probabilistic polynomial-time attacker A has a non-negligible advantage in winning the IND-CLMSC-CCA2-1 game [11].

For A, there are the following constraints. A can not have access to the master key w. No Extract Secret Key query is allowed on any of the challenge identities. No De-signcrypt query is allowed on the challenge ciphertext.

Definition 4. Confidentiality under the attack of Type 2. A certificateless multi-receiver signcryption scheme is Type-2-CCA2 secure if no probabilistic polynomial-time attacker A has a non-negligible advantage in winning the IND-CLMSC-CCA2-2 game [11].

For A, there are the following constraints. No Extract Secret Key query is allowed on any of the challenge identities. No Replace Public Key query is allowed on any of the challenge identities. No De-signcrypt query is allowed on the challenge ciphertext.

Definition 5. Unforgeability under the attack of Type 1. A certificateless multi-receiver signcryption scheme is Type-1-sEUF-CMA-1 secure if no probabilistic polynomial-time attacker A has a non-negligible advantage in winning the EUF-CLMSC-CMA-1 game [11].

For A, there are the following constraints. A can not have access to the master key w. No Extract Secret Key query is allowed on any of the challenge identities.

Definition 6. Confidentiality under the attack of Type 2. A certificateless multi-receiver signcryption scheme is Type-2-sEUF-CMA-2 secure if no probabilistic polynomial-time attacker A has a non-negligible advantage in winning the EUF-CLMSC-CMA-2 game [11].

For A, there are the following constraints. No Extract Secret Key query is allowed on any of the challenge identities. No Replace Public Key query is allowed on any of the challenge identities.

Methods

In order to construct our scheme, we employed the Perturbed Matsumoto-Imai-Plus (PMI+) cryptosystem [20], which can resist the linearization attack, rank attacks, and the differential attack and is much faster than RSA and ECC. The new scheme that we proposed consists of five probabilistic polynomial-time algorithms, namely Setup, Partial Key Extract, Key Extract, Signcrypt and De-signcrypt. We shall give a detailed description of the proposed scheme as follows.

Setup. Given a security parameter s as input, KGC returns a big positive integer q and a small positive integer p. Let G be a finite field of order q and characteristic two, and define two non-collision hash functions $H_1: \{0,1\}^* \times \{0,1\}^* \times G^{n+p} \to G^{n+p}$ and $H_2: \{0,1\}^* \times G^n \times G^{n+p} \to \{0,1\}^{l_m}$, where G^n is the nth extension of G and G^{n+p} is the $(n+p)$th extension of G. The positive integer n is the number of variables in the equation (1) and l_m is the bit length of the message m. Then KGC selects a positive integer g to denote the number of equations. At last, KGC publishes the public parameters *params* denoted by (G,g,n,q,p,H_1,H_2).

Partial Key Extract

1) KGC selects a secure MPKC, which is PMI+ in our scheme. The system public key can be expressed as a typical multivariate quadratic system: $\bar{F}=T \circ F \circ V$ where T is a randomly chosen invertible affine transformation on $G^{n+p} \to G^{n+p}$, V is a randomly chosen invertible affine transformation on $G^n \to G^n$, and F is a public set of $(n+p)$ quadratic equations with n variables over G. The system secret key is (T, F, V). The related parameters refer to [20].

2) KGC randomly chooses T_0 and V_0, where T_0 is a randomly chosen invertible affine transformation on $G^{n+p} \to G^{n+p}$ and V_0 is a randomly chosen invertible affine transformation on $G^n \to G^n$. Then, compute $\bar{F}_0=T_0 \circ \bar{F} \circ V_0$. $\bar{F}_0$ is the system partial public key, and $(T_0 \circ T,F,V \circ V_0)$ is the system partial secret key. It is worth noting that KGC needs to compute the new system partial secret key when some user drops out of the group.

Key Extract. Each user runs this algorithm to compute his/her full public and secret keys. The user U randomly chooses T_u and V_u, where T_u is an invertible affine transformation on $G^{n+p} \to G^{n+p}$ and V_u is an invertible affine transformation on $G^n \to G^n$. Then, compute the public key F_u of user U, that is, $F_u=T_u \circ \bar{F}_0 \circ V_u$, which should be sent to KGC. The secret key of user U is $(T_u \circ T_0 \circ T,F,V \circ V_0 \circ V_u)$.

Signcrypt. Suppose that Alice, whose identity is ID_A, wants to signcrypt a message m to t different receivers denoted by $L=\{ID_1, ID_2, ..., ID_t\}$. Alice performs the following steps:

1) Alice chooses $r \in G^n$ randomly, and computes $X=\bar{F}(r), Y=H_1(m,ID_A,X)$ and $S=F_A^{-1}(Y)$.

2) For all ID_i, $i=1, 2, ..., t$, compute $W_i=F_i(S\|X)$ and $Z=H_2(ID_A,S,X) \oplus m$.

3) Return ciphertext $\sigma=(S,Y,Z,W_1,W_2,...,W_t,L)$.

De-signcrypt. Each receiver ID_i, $i=1, 2, ..., t$, uses his/her secret key to decrypt σ.

1) ID_i extracts his/her corresponding ciphertext information (S, Y, Z, W_i) according to his/her position in L.

2) ID_i computes $Y'=F_A(S)$ and checks whether the equation $Y'=Y$ holds. If it holds, ID_i continues to decrypt σ as follows; otherwise, ID_i outputs $\perp$.

3) ID_i computes $S'\|X'=F_i^{-1}(W_i)$ and $m'=Z \oplus H_2(ID_A,S',X')$.

4) Check whether the equations $S=S'$ and $Y'=H_1(m',ID_A,X')$ hold. If both of them hold, output $m=m'$; otherwise, output $\perp$.

Discussion

1 Correctness Analysis

Theorem 1. The De-signcrypt algorithm is correct.

Proof. Upon receiving a ciphertext σ, each receiver ID_i, $i=1, 2, ..., t$, extracts his/her own corresponding ciphertext information (S, Y, Z, W_i) from σ. According to the Signcrypt algorithm, we have $S=F_A^{-1}(Y)$, so the receiver ID_i can compute $Y'=F_A(F_A^{-1}(Y'))=F_A(S)=Y$. It is worth noting that only the sender, Alice, can generate the correct Y such that $Y'=Y$ because only she knows her secret key F_A^{-1}. The receiver, ID_i, can decrypt the ciphertext by computing $F_i^{-1}(W_i)=F_i^{-1}(F_i(S'\|X'))=S'\|X'$ and $m'=Z \oplus H_2(ID_A,S',X')$. ID_i can judge whether m' is correct by checking whether $S=S'$ and $Y'=H_1(m',ID_A,X')$ hold. Note that only ID_i can obtain $m' = Z \oplus H_2(ID_A, S', X')$correctly because only he/she knows his/her secret key F_i^{-1}. Therefore, the Designcrypt algorithm of our scheme is correct.

2 Security Analysis

2.1 Security of MPKC. In the last twenty years, many MPKC schemes were proposed, and they are mainly based on four basic MPKC schemes including the Matsumoto Imai (MI) cryptosystem, the Hidden Field Equation (HFE) cryptosystem, the Oil Vinegar (OV) cryptosystem and the Stepwise Triangular System [20]. Although most of them have been broken, some variants of the basic MPKC schemes, such as Rainbow and PMI+ [20], have survived known attacks like the linearization equation attack, the rank attack and the differential attack. In 2011, Hashimoto et al. [21] proposed two types of fault attacks which further weaken the security of the MPKC schemes. They detailed the fault attack on the MPKC schemes such as UOV, Rainbow, TTS and HFE, and most of the MPKC schemes were proven insecure. However, the PMI+ cryptosystem is one of the few approved cryptosystems which survived the linearization equation attack, the rank attack, the differential attack and even the fault attacks. PMI+ uses the Plus (+) method of external perturbation to prevent attacks without significantly decreasing the efficiency of the system [20]. So in our work, we used PMI+ which is based on the IP problem to construct our scheme.

Cryptosystems based on the IP problem belong to a major category of MPKC. Faugère et al. [22] gave an upper bound on the theoretical complexity of the "IP-like" problem, and presented a new algorithm to solve the IP problem when S and T are linear mappings. Bouillaguet et al. [23] proposed an improved algorithm combining the linear algebra techniques, together with Gröbner bases and statistical tools. To date, the best algorithm for the IP problem is exponential. For the IP problem used in our scheme, the attacking complexity of the best algorithm will be $O(n^{3.5} \cdot q^{n/2})$ [24], where n is the number of variables and q is the cardinality of the finite field. So the IP problem will be computationally hard if we can choose the parameter properly.

With the knowledge of the most efficient attacks on the IP problem, in order to strengthen the security of our scheme, we suggest that the parameters of our scheme should satisfy the following conditions: the transformations T and V should be affine; the polynomials in P and Q should be homogeneous. In our method, for example, if we choose $n = 16$ and $q = 2^9$, the attacking complexity should be greater than $O(n^{3.5} \cdot q^{n/2}) = 16^{3.5} \cdot (2^9)^{16/2} = 2^{86}$. Usually, it is considered to be a computationally secure MPKC scheme if the attacking complexity is greater than 2^{80} [24]. Therefore, our scheme is a secure MPKC-based scheme.

Although we used PMI+ for the construction of the proposed multi-receiver signcryption scheme, there are still some other multivariate cryptosystems suitable for the construction of our scheme, such as the internally perturbed HFE cryptosystem (IPHFE) [25]. Different from PMI+, IPHFE is build by using the idea of internal perturbation. Vivien et al. [26,27] and Ding et al. [28,29] analyzed the security of IPHFE, and their work showed that IPHFE with appropriate parameters can withstand all known attacks. So IPHFE can be substituted for PMI+ in our construction. Due to space limitations, we do not introduce the detailed realization of the construction based on IPHFE.

2.2 Message Confidentiality. Theorem 2. Confidentiality under the attack of Type 1. In the random oracle model, if an IND-CLMSC-CCA2-1 adversary A has a non-negligible advantage ε against the security of our scheme when performing q_{H_i}queries to random oracles H_i ($i = 1, 2$), q_{ske} Extract Secret Key queries, q_{pke} Extract Public Key queries, q_{pkr} Replace Public Key

queries, q_{sc} Signcrypt queries and q_{dsc} Designcrypt queries, then there exists an algorithm C that can solve the MQ problem with advantage defined as:

$$\varepsilon' > \frac{\varepsilon}{t \cdot q_{sc} + q_{H_1}} (1 - \frac{q_{sc} \cdot (t \cdot q_{sc} + q_{H_2})}{2^{G_2}})(1 - \frac{q_{dsc}}{2^{G_2 - 1}}) \quad (2)$$

where t is the number of receivers in the challenge set and G_2 denotes the bit length of the element over G^n.

Proof. We show how to build an algorithm C that solves the MQ problem with the help of an adversary A. Let C receive a random instance $\{f(x), Y_0 = f(X_0)\}$ of the MQ problem, and the goal of C is to compute X_0. To solve this problem, C acts as A's challenger in the IND-CLMSC-CCA2-1 game.

Setup. C sets $\bar{F} = T \circ F \circ V$ as the system public key, chooses an invertible affine transformation T_0 on $G^{n+p} \to G^{n+p}$, and chooses an invertible affine transformation V_0 on $G^n \to G^n$ randomly. So the system partial secret key is $(T_0 \circ T, F, V \circ V_0)$, and the partial public key is $\bar{F}_0 = T_0 \circ \bar{F} \circ V_0$. C sends the system parameters $(G, g, n, q, p, H_1, H_2)$, the system public key and the system partial secret key to A. Then A outputs a set of target identities, denoted by $L^* = \{ID_1^*, ID_2^*, ..., ID_t^*\}$. To handle A's queries, C maintains a list L_i for each H_i ($i = 1, 2$) query.

Phase1. C simulates A's queries as follows:

H_1 **queries.** A can perform an H_1 query on the input of (m, ID_i, X, L) and then C checks the list L_1. If an entry corresponding to (m, ID_i, X, L) is present in L_1, then C retrieves the hash value h_i from L_1 and returns h_i. Otherwise, it returns a random number $h_i \in G^{n+p}$ and stores the entry $\langle h_i, m, ID_i, X, L, \nabla, \Delta \rangle$ in L_1, where the symbols ∇ and Δ denote the signature information and the encryption information of the message m, respectively.

H_2 **queries.** A can perform an H_2 query on the input of (ID_s, S, X) for ID_i and then C checks the list L_2. If an entry corresponding to ID_i is present in L_2, then C retrieves Z_i from L_2 and returns Z_i. Otherwise, it returns a random number Z_i and stores the entry $(Z_i, ID_s, S, X, ID_i, \Lambda, \Box, \Diamond, b_i = 0)$ in L_2, where the symbols Λ, $\Box$ and $\Diamond$ denote the public key F_i, the secret parameters T_i and V_i, respectively. The bit b_i is a flag bit used to denote whether the public keys have been replaced or not.

Extract Secret Key queries. A can perform an Extract Secret Key query on the input of ID_i. C first checks whether $ID_i = ID_j^* j \in \{1, 2, ..., t\}$ holds. If $ID_i = ID_j^* j \in \{1, 2, ..., t\}$holds, then C aborts the query. Otherwise, C retrieves the entry $(Z_i, ID_s, S, X, ID_i, F_i, T_i, V_i, b_i = 0)$ from L_2. If $b_i = 0$, then C returns the secret key $(T_i \circ T_0 \circ T, F, V \circ V_0 \circ V_i)$; otherwise, the public key of the identity ID_i has been replaced and in this case, C asks A for the new secret parameters (T_i', V_i'), computes the new secret key $(T_i' \circ T_0 \circ T, F, V \circ V_0 \circ V_i')$ and returns it to A.

Extract Public Key queries. A can perform an Extract Public Key query on the input of ID_i and then C checks L_2. If an entry corresponding to ID_i is present in L_2, then C retrieves F_i from L_2 and returns F_i. Otherwise, C chooses $T_i \in_R G^{n+p}, V_i \in_R G^n$, returns the public key $F_i = T_i \circ \bar{F}_0 \circ V_i$ and updates the entry corresponding to ID_i in L_2 with T_i, V_i and F_i.

Replace Public Key queries. When A performs a Replace Public Key query on the input of (ID_i, F_i'), C searches the corresponding entry $(\cdot, ID_i, \cdot)$ in L_2. If the entry is found, then C replaces the public key in the entry corresponding to ID_i in L_2 with F_i' and sets the flag bit b_i to 1. Otherwise, C generates the public key using the Extract Public Key query and then replaces the public key of ID_i with F_i'.

Signcrypt queries. A can perform a Signcrypt query on the input of $(m, ID_s, L = \{ID_{R1}, ID_{R2}, ..., ID_{Rt}\})$. If $ID_s = ID_{Ri}$,

$i \in \{1,2,...,t\}$, or if $ID_s \in L^*$ and at least one $ID_{Ri} \in L^*, i \in \{1,2,...,t\}$, then C aborts the query. Otherwise, C knows the secret key of the sender and performs the computations as the signcryption algorithm to return the ciphertext $\sigma = (S,Y,Z,W_1,W_2,...,W_t,L)$. If $ID_s = ID_j^*, j \in \{1,2,...,t\}$, C does not know the secret key of the sender and in this case, it generates the ciphertext as follows:

First, C retrieves the entry $(\cdot, ID_s, F_s, T_s, V_s, b_s)$ from I_2 and chooses $r \in_R G^n$ and $Z_s \in_R \{0,1\}^{l_m}$. C computes $X = \bar{F}(r)$, extracts $Y = h_s$ by calling the oracle H_1 with the input (m, ID_s, X, L) and computes the signature S. Then, C retrieves the corresponding entry $(\cdot, ID_{Ri}, \cdot, b_{Ri})$ in L_2 and then computes $W_i = F_i(S||X)$ and $Z = Z_s \oplus m$. C updates the corresponding entry in L_1. Note that if $b_i = 1$, then the public key of the receiver has been replaced and in this case, the challenger asks A for (T_i, V_i) and uses it in place of the old value stored in the entry. Finally, add $(Z_s, ID_s, S, X, ID_{Ri}, F_i, T_i, V_i, b_i)$ in L_2 (C fails if H_2 is already defined on any of such entries, but this happens only with probability $\frac{t \cdot q_{sc} + q_{H_2}}{2^{G_2}}$). At last, C sends $\sigma = (S,Y,Z,W_1,W_2,...,W_t,L)$ to A.

Designcrypt queries. When A submits a ciphertext $\sigma = (S,Y,Z,W_1,W_2,...,W_t,L)$, a receiver's identity ID_R and a sender's identity ID_s, C extracts (S, Y, Z, W_i, L) from σ. If $ID_R \notin L^*$, then C knows the secret key of ID_R and hence designcrypts σ using the De-signcrypt Algorithm. Otherwise, C searches all entries $(Y, \cdot, ID_s, \cdot, L, \cdot, Z)$ in L_1, and if no such entries exist, the symbol $\perp$ is returned to indicate that the ciphertext is invalid. Meanwhile, C searches the entry $(Z, ID_s, S, X, ID_s, F_s, T_s, V_s, b_s)$ in L_2, and if it is not found, C rejects the ciphertext σ. If the ciphertext σ passes the above verification, C computes $Y' = F_s(S), S'||X' = F_i^{-1}(W_i)$, and $m' = Z \oplus H_2(ID_s, S', X')$. If $Y' = Y$ and $S' = S$ hold, and (m', X') passes the verification, then C returns m; otherwise, C rejects σ. Note that a valid ciphertext is rejected with probability at most $\frac{q_{dsc}}{2^{G_2 - 1}}$.

Challenge. A outputs two messages m_0 and m_1 together with an arbitrary sender's identity $ID_s \notin L^*$ on which A wishes to be challenged. C selects a bit $b \in_R \{0,1\}$ and sends m_b to the t target identities denoted by $L^* = \{ID_1^*, ID_2^*, ..., ID_t^*\}$. C chooses $X^* \in_R G^{n+p}, S^* \in_R G^n$ and $Z_s \in_R \{0,1\}^{l_m}$, sets $X_0 = X^*||S^*$ and then computes $Y^* = F_s(S^*), W_i^* = F_i(X_0)$ and $Z^* = Z_s \oplus m_b$. Then, C responds with the ciphertext $\sigma^* = \langle Y^*, S^*, Z^*, W_1^*, W_2^*, ..., W_t^*, L^* \rangle$.

Phase2. A performs new queries as in Phase 1. However, A is not allowed to ask Designcrypt queries on σ^* for $ID_i^*, i = 1,2,...,t$.

Guess. At the end of the game, A returns his/her guess result. C ignores the answer to A's guess. According to the above discussion, we know that as long as the simulation of the attacker's environment is perfect, the probability that A asks the value of $W_i = F_i(X^*||S^*)$, $i = 1, 2, ..., t$, by the H_1 oracle is the same as the probability in a real attack. C fetches a random entry $(h_i, m, ID_i, X, L, S, W_i)$ from L_1. With probability $\frac{1}{t \cdot q_{sc} + q_{H_1}}$ (as L_1 contains no more than $t \cdot q_{sc} + q_{H_1}$ elements by our construction), the chosen entry contains the right element $W_i = F_i(X^*||S^*)$. C returns X_0 as a solution to the MQ problem.

Now, we analyze the probability of C's success. Let E be the event that A outputs the correct bit $b^* = b$.

Simulation fails if any of the following events occurs:

E_1: Extract Secret Key query is executed for some chosen challenge identity.

E_2: Both the sender and at least one of receivers belong to the challenge set in some Signcrypt query.

E_3: The H_2 oracle collides in Signcrypt queries.

E_4: C rejects a valid ciphertext in some Designcrypt query.

According to the above discussion, we know that $Pr[E] = \varepsilon$, where E implies that E_1 and E_2 never occur, that is, $\neg E_1 \wedge \neg E_2$. Also, we have $Pr[E_3] \leq \frac{q_{sc} \cdot (t \cdot q_{sc} + q_{H_2})}{2^{G_2}}$ since A conducts a total of q_{sc} Signcrypt queries and there are at most $t \cdot q_{sc} + q_{H_2}$ entries in L_2. $Pr[E_4] \leq \frac{q_{dsc}}{2^{G_2 - 1}}$ represents the probability of rejection of valid ciphertexts.

The event E_5 implies that C chooses the correct entry from L_1 in the Guess Phase. And we know that $Pr[E_5] \leq \frac{1}{t \cdot q_{sc} + q_{H_1}}$. So, the advantage ε' of C is defined as:

$$\varepsilon' = Pr[E \wedge \neg E_1 \wedge \neg E_2 \wedge \neg E_3 \wedge \neg E_4 \wedge E_5] \quad (3)$$

Therefore, we obtain

$$\varepsilon' > \frac{\varepsilon}{t \cdot q_{sc} + q_{H_1}}(1 - \frac{q_{sc} \cdot (t \cdot q_{sc} + q_{H_2})}{2^{G_2}})(1 - \frac{q_{dsc}}{2^{G_2 - 1}}) \quad (4)$$

Theorem 3. Confidentiality under the attack of Type 2. In the random oracle model, if an IND-CLMSC-CCA2-2 adversary A has a non-negligible advantage ε against the security of our scheme when performing q_{H_i} queries to random oracles H_i ($i = 1$, 2), q_{ske} Extract Secret Key queries, q_{pke} Extract Public Key queries, q_{sc} Signcrypt queries and q_{dsc} Designcrypt queries, then there exists an algorithm C that can solve the MQ problem with an advantage ε' defined as:

$$\varepsilon' > \frac{\varepsilon}{t \cdot q_{sc} + q_{H_1}}(1 - \frac{q_{sc} \cdot (t \cdot q_{sc} + q_{H_2})}{2^{G_2}})(1 - \frac{q_{dsc}}{2^{G_2 - 1}}) \quad (5)$$

where t is the number of receivers in the challenge set and G_2 denotes the bit length of the element over G^n.

The attacker has access to the master key, but cannot perform public key replacement under the attack of Type 2. The proof is similar to that of Theorem 2.

2.3 Unforgeability. Theorem 4. Unforgeability under the attack of Type 1. In the random oracle model, if an SUF-CLMSC-CMA-1 adversary A has a non-negligible advantage ε against the security of our scheme when performing q_{H_i} queries to random oracles H_i ($i = 1, 2$), q_{ske} Extract Secret Key queries, q_{pke} Extract Public Key queries, q_{pkr} Replace Public Key queries, q_{sc} Signcrypt queries and q_{ver} Verify queries, then there exists an algorithm C that can solve the IP problem with an advantage ε' defined as:

$$\varepsilon' > \frac{\varepsilon}{t(t \cdot q_{sc} + q_{H_2})}(1 - \frac{q_{sc} \cdot (t \cdot q_{sc} + q_{H_2})}{2^{G_2}})(1 - \frac{q_{dsc}}{2^{G_2 - 1}}). \quad (6)$$

where t is the number of receivers in the challenge set and G_2 denotes the bit length of the element over G^n.

Proof. We show how to build an algorithm C that solves the IP problem with the help of an adversary A. Let C receive a random instance $(F_s = T_s \circ \bar{F}_0 \circ V_s, \bar{F}_0)$ of the IP problem, and the goal of C is to compute (T_s, V_s). To solve this problem, C acts as A's challenger in the SUF-CLMSC-CMA-1 game.

Setup. C sets $\bar{F} = T \circ F \circ V$ as the system public key, and chooses an invertible affine transformation T_0 on $G^{n+p} \to G^{n+p}$ and an invertible affine transformation V_0 on $G^n \to G^n$ randomly.

So the system partial secret key is $(T_0 \circ T, F, V \circ V_0)$, and the partial public key is $\bar{F}_0 = T_0 \circ \bar{F} \circ V_0$. C sends the system parameters $(G, g, n, q, p, H_1, H_2)$, the system public key and the system partial secret key to A. Then A outputs a set of target identities, denoted by $L^* = \{ID_1^*, ID_2^*, ..., ID_t^*\}$. To handle A's queries, C maintains a list L_i for each H_i ($i = 1, 2$) query.

Attack. C simulates A's queries as follows:

H_1 queries. A can perform an H_1 query on the input of (m, ID_i, X, L) and then C checks the list L_1. If an entry corresponding to (m, ID_i, X, L) is present in L_1, then C retrieves h_i from L_1 and returns h_i. Otherwise, it returns a random number $h_i \in G^{n+p}$ and stores the entry $(h_i, m, ID_i, X, L, \nabla, \Delta)$ in L_1, where the symbols ∇ and Δ denote the signature information and the encryption information for message m, respectively.

H_2 queries. A can perform an H_2 query on the input of (ID_s, S, X) for ID_i and then C checks the L_2. If an entry corresponding to ID_i is present in L_2, then C retrieves Z_i from L_2 and returns Z_i. Otherwise, it returns a random number Z_i and stores the entry $(Z_i, ID_s, S, X, ID_i, \Lambda, \square, \Diamond, b_i = 0)$ in L_2, where the symbols Λ, $\square$ and $\Diamond$ denote the public key F_i, the secret parameters T_i and V_i, respectively. The bit b_i is a flag bit used to denote whether the public keys have been replaced or not.

Extract Secret Key queries. A can perform an Extract Secret Key query on the input of ID_i, and C first checks whether $ID_i = ID_j^*$ $j \in \{1, 2, ..., t\}$ holds. If $ID_i = ID_j^*$ $j \in \{1, 2, ..., t\}$ holds, then C aborts the query. Otherwise, C retrieves the entry $(Z_i, ID_s, S, X, ID_i, F_i, T_i, V_i, b_i = 0)$ from L_2. If $b_i = 0$, then C returns the secret key $(T_i \circ T_0 \circ T, F, V \circ V_0 \circ V_i)$. Otherwise, the public key of the identity ID_i has been replaced and in this case, C asks A for the new secret parameters (T_i, V_i), computes the new secret key $(T_i \circ T_0 \circ T, F, V \circ V_0 \circ V_i)$ and returns it to A.

Extract Public Key queries. A can perform an Extract Public Key query on the input of ID_i and then C checks L_2. If an entry corresponding to ID_i is present in L_2, then C retrieves F_i from L_2 and returns F_i. Otherwise C chooses $T_i \in_R G^{n+p}$ and $V_i \in_R G^n$, returns the public key $F_i = T_i \circ \bar{F}_0 \circ V_i$ and updates the entry corresponding to ID_i in L_2 with T_i, V_i and F_i.

Replace Public Key queries. When A performs a Replace Public Key query on the input of (ID_i, F'_i), C searches the corresponding entry $(\cdot, ID_i, \cdot)$ in L_2. If the entry is found, then C replaces the public keys in the entry corresponding to ID_i in L_2 with F'_i and sets the flag bit b_i to 1. Otherwise, C generates the public key using Extract Public Key query and then replaces the public key of ID_i with F'_i.

Signcrypt queries. A can performs a Signcrypt query on the input of $(m, ID_s, L = \{ID_{R1}, ID_{R2}, ..., ID_{Rt}\})$. If $ID_s = ID_{Ri}, i \in \{1, 2, ..., t\}$, or if $ID_s \in L^*$ and at least one $ID_{Ri} \in L^*, i \in \{1, 2, ..., n\}$, then C aborts the query. If $ID_s \neq ID_j^*$ $j \in \{1, 2, ..., t\}$, then C knows the secret key of the sender and performs the computations as the Signcrypt algorithm to return the ciphertext $\sigma = (S, Y, Z, W_1, W_2, ..., W_t, L)$. If $ID_s = ID_j^*$ $j \in \{1, 2, ..., t\}$, C does not know the secret key of the sender and hence it generates the ciphertext as follows:

First, C retrieves the entry $(\cdot, ID_s, F_s, T_s, V_s, b_s)$ from L_2 and chooses $r \in_R G^n$ and $Z_s \in_R \{0, 1\}^{l_m}$. C computes $X = \bar{F}(r)$, extracts $Y = h_s$ by calling the oracle H_1 with the input (m, ID_s, X, L) and computes the signature S. Then, C retrieves the corresponding entry $(\cdot, ID_{Ri}, \cdot, b_{Ri})$ in L_2 and then computes $W_i = F_i(S \| X)$ and $Z = Z_s \oplus m$. C updates the corresponding entry in L_1. Note that if $b_i = 1$, then the public key of the receiver has been replaced and in this case, the challenger asks A for (T_i, V_i) and uses it in place of the old value stored in the entry. Finally, add $(Z_s, ID_s, S, X, ID_{Ri}, F_i, T_i, V_i, b_i)$ in L_2 (C fails if H_2 is already

defined on any of such entries, but this happens only with probability $\frac{t \cdot q_{sc} + q_{H_2}}{2^{G_2}}$). At last, C sends $\sigma = (S, Y, Z, W_1, W_2, ..., W_t, L)$ to A.

Verify queries. When A submits a ciphertext $\sigma = (S, Y, Z, W_1, W_2, ..., W_t, L)$, a receiver's identity ID_R and a sender's identity ID_s, C extracts (S, Y, Z, W_i, L) from σ. If $ID_R \notin L^*$, then C knows the secret key of ID_R and hence designcrypts σ using the De-signcrypt Algorithm. Otherwise, C searches all entries $(Y, \cdot, ID_s, \cdot, L, \cdot, Z)$ in L_1, and if no such entries exist, the symbol $\perp$ is returned to indicate that the ciphertext is invalid. Meanwhile, C searches the entry $(Z_i, ID_s, S, X, ID_s, F_s, T_s, V_s, b_s)$ in L_2, and if it is not found, C rejects the ciphertext σ. If the ciphertext σ passes the above verification, C computes $Y' = F_s(S), S' \| X' = F_i^{-1}(W_i)$ and $m' = Z \oplus H_2(ID_s, S', X')$. If $Y' = Y$ and $S' = S$ hold, and (m', X') passes the verification test, then C accepts σ; otherwise, C rejects σ. Note that a valid ciphertext is rejected with probability at most $\frac{q_{dsc}}{2^{G_2 - 1}}$.

Forge. After a polynomial-bounded number of queries, the adversary A outputs forged ciphertext $\sigma = \langle S, Y, Z, W_1, W_2, ..., W_t, L \rangle$ (a receiver list $L = \{ID_{R1}, ID_{R2}, ..., ID_{Rt}\}$, and at least one $ID_{Ri} \notin L^*$) and the sender's identity $ID_s \in L^*$.

According to the above discussion, we know that as long as the simulation of the attacker's environment is perfect, the probability that A asks the value of (T_s, V_s) by the H_2 oracle is the same as the probability in a real attack. C fetches a random entry $(Z_i, ID_s, S, X, ID_i, F_i, T_i, V_i, b_i)$ from L_2. With probability $\frac{1}{t(t \cdot q_{sc} + q_{H_2})}$ (as L_2 contains no more than $t \cdot q_{sc} + q_{H_2}$ elements by our construction, and C chooses ID_s with probability $1/t$), the chosen entry contains the right element (T_s, V_s). C returns (T_s, V_s) as the solution to the IP problem.

Now, we analyze the probability of C's success. Let E be the event that the forged ciphertext passes verifications.

Simulation fails if any of the following events occurs:

E_1: Extract Secret Key query is executed for some chosen challenge identity.

E_2: Both sender and at least one of receivers belong to the challenge set in some Signcrypt query.

E_3: The H_2 oracle collides in Signcrypt queries.

E_4: C rejects a valid ciphertext in Verify queries.

According to the above discussion, we know that $Pr[E] = \varepsilon$, where E implies that E_1 and E_2 never occur, that is, $\neg E_1 \wedge \neg E_2$. Also, we have $Pr[E_3] \leq \frac{q_{sc} \cdot (t \cdot q_{sc} + q_{H_2})}{2^{G_2}}$, since A conducts a total of q_{sc} Signcrypt queries and there are at most $t \cdot q_{sc} + q_{H_2}$ entries in L_2. $Pr[E_4] \leq \frac{q_{dsc}}{2^{G_2 - 1}}$ represents the probability of rejection of valid ciphertexts.

The event E_5 implies that C chooses the correct entry from L_2 in the last Verify Phase. And we know that $Pr[E_5] \leq \frac{1}{t(t \cdot q_{sc} + q_{H_2})}$. So, the advantage ε' of C is defined as:

$$\varepsilon' = Pr[E \wedge \neg E_1 \wedge \neg E_2 \wedge \neg E_3 \wedge \neg E_4 \wedge E_5] \quad (7)$$

Therefore, we obtain

$$\varepsilon' > \frac{\varepsilon}{t(t \cdot q_{sc} + q_{H_2})}(1 - \frac{q_{sc} \cdot (t \cdot q_{sc} + q_{H_2})}{2^{G_2}})(1 - \frac{q_{dsc}}{2^{G_2 - 1}}) \quad (8)$$

Theorem 5. Unforgeability under the attack of Type 2. In the random oracle model, if an SUF-CLMSC-CMA-2 adversary A has a non-negligible advantage ε against the security of our scheme when performing q_{H_i} queries to random oracles H_i ($i=1, 2$), q_{ske} Extract Secret Key queries, q_{pke} Extract Public Key queries, q_{sc} Signcrypt queries and q_{ver} Verify queries, then there exists an algorithm C that can solve the IP problem with an advantage ε' defined as:

$$\varepsilon' > \frac{\varepsilon}{t(t\cdot q_{sc}+q_{H_2})}(1-\frac{q_{sc}\cdot(t\cdot q_{sc}+q_{H_2})}{2^{G_2}})(1-\frac{q_{dsc}}{2^{G_2-1}}) \quad (9)$$

where t is the number of receivers in the challenge set and G_2 denotes the bit length of the element over G^n.

The attacker has access to the master key, but cannot perform public key replacement under the attack of Type 2. The proof is similar to that of Theorem 4.

2.4 Backward Secrecy. Each time Alice sends a message m to receivers, she chooses $r\in G^n$ randomly as the session key. Even though she sends the same message m, the corresponding ciphertext σ will be different in different sessions. So the new receiver who joins the group later does not have the previous value $X=\bar{F}(r)$ which is computed for the message m, and thus he/she can not obtain the previous message m. Therefore, our scheme is backward secure.

2.5 Forward Secrecy. Forward secrecy means that the members who have quitted the group are not able to know the later session keys. In our scheme, the session key r is randomly chosen in each session. When some member of the group quits the group, the sender will compute the partial key for the rest members again, which guarantees that the members who have quitted the group cannot obtain the plaintext message from the later ciphertext. So our scheme is forward secure.

2.6 Non-repudiation. According to Theorem 4 and Theorem 5, our scheme is unforgeable. Suppose that Alice signcrypts a message m. If others want to repudiate her signature S, they have to solve the MQ problem to get the secret key of Alice, and it is computationally infeasible because the MQ problem is an NP-hard problem. Therefore, only Alice knows her secret key and others can not repudiate her behavior of signcrypting the message m. So our scheme is non-repudiation.

2.7 Public Verifiability. The proposed scheme provides public verifiability of ciphertext source, which is an important requirement in broadcast communications. Any third party can be convinced of the sender of the ciphertext σ by recovering Y' in the second step of the de-signcryption phase and checking whether the equation $Y'=Y$ holds. This is in fact due to the unforgeability of the signature. This verification procedure does not involve the knowledge of messages or the receiver's secret key but only the ciphertext σ. Hence, our scheme supports public verifiability.

3 Performance Comparison

In this section, we shall compare our scheme with the existing schemes [8–10,12] in performance. We mainly consider the computation and communication cost.

The proposed scheme does not involve any bilinear pairing operations, exponentiation operations and multiplications in groups. In the signcryption phase, it needs only two hash operations, ($t+2$) MQ-mapping (it means the mapping operation on the multivariate quadratic equations) operations and one XOR operation, while in the de-signcryption phase, it needs two hash operations, two MQ-mapping operations and one XOR operation. The MQ-mapping operations are linear operations and have

much lower computation complexity than bilinear pairing operations and exponentiation operations. According to the above analysis, the computation complexity of our scheme is $O(t+4)$. The ciphertext of our scheme is $(t+1)G_1+(t+1)G_2+|m|$ bits in length, where t is the number of receivers, G_2 is the bit length of the element over G^n, and G_1 is the bit length of the element over G^{n+p}. Compared with the representative CLMSC scheme [12], the new scheme has lower computation complexity without bilinear pairing operation needed. We also compare our scheme with the naive extension of schemes [8–10] for multi-receiver setting in Table 1, in which par denotes pairing operation, exp denotes exponentiation operation and ciphertext-size denotes the bit length of the ciphertext. The comparisons are summarized in Table 1.

According to the above analyses, the proposed scheme is more efficient than the existing ones, and it is also provably secure in the random oracle model. The proposed scheme is a very useful tool in multicast communication. With the rapid development of wireless networks, it is particularly important to transfer instruction data from the control center to multiple intelligent terminals securely [30]. The control center needs to encrypt the sensitive information to prevent it from being eavesdropped and cracked before sending it to intelligent terminals, while intelligent terminals need to judge whether the received instruction is from the trusted entity. To solve this security problem, we must take both the security requirements and the performance of the intelligent terminals into account, because intelligent terminals are generally characterized by low power consumption, low computing power and narrow communication bandwidth, which make the traditional identity-based scheme not suitable for them. Through the analyses about the security and performance of our scheme, it can be concluded that our scheme can better address these issues and it is in line with the characteristics of intelligent terminals.

Conclusions

As one of the alternative cryptosystems, multivariate public key cryptography can resist quantum attack, and has been researched by scholars extensively. In this paper, we employ multivariate public key cryptography to propose a new construction of the certificateless multi-receiver signcryption scheme, called a quantum attack-resistant certificateless multi-receiver signcryption scheme. The new scheme inherits the security of multi-variable cryptosystems that could resist quantum attack, and it avoids the certificate management and the key escrow problem. We proved its security under the hardness of the MQ problem and its unforgeability under the IP assumption in the random oracle model. In addition, the scheme also has security properties such as forward secrecy, backward secrecy, non-repudiation and public

Table 1. Comparison of our scheme and the existing ones.

scheme	MQ-mapping	par	exp	hash	ciphertext-size
Li et al.'s [8]	0	2	$t+1$	$2t+2$	$2t|l|+t|m|$
Selvi et al.'s [9]	0	0	$5t+7$	$3t+3$	$2t|Z_q|+2|l|+t|m|$
Jing et al.'s [10]	0	0	$3t+2$	$2t+2$	$2t|l|+t|m|$
Selvi et al.'s [12]	0	2	$2t+2$	$t+7$	$(2t+1)|Z_q|+|l|$
Ours	$t+4$	0	0	4	$(t+1)G_1+(t+1)G_2+|m|$

t denotes the number of receivers, $|Z_q|$ denotes the bit length of elements in finite field Z_q, $|l|$ denotes the bit length of elements in group l, $|m|$ denotes the bit length of message m, G_1 denotes the bit length of elements in G^{n+p}, G_2 denotes the bit length of elements in G^n.

verifiability. Analyses show that the proposed scheme is more efficient than the existing ones. Although our scheme is constructed by using PMI+, there are still some other multivariate cryptosystems like IPHFE suitable for our construction. In the future work, we will construct the multi-receiver signcryption scheme by using IPHFE or other better multivariate cryptosystem, and compare the performance of the new scheme with that of the scheme proposed in this paper.

Author Contributions

Analyzed the data: HL XC LP WS. Wrote the paper: HL XC LP WS. Conceived and designed the scheme: HL XC. Proved the security of the scheme: HL XC.

References

1. Zheng Y (1997) Digital signcryption or how to achieve cost (signature & encryption)<<cost (signature)+cost (encryption). In: Proc. 17th Annual International Cryptology Conference on Advances in Cryptology. 165–179.
2. Luo M, Wen Y, Zhao H (2008) A certificate-based signcryption scheme. In: Proc. International Conference on Computer Science and Information Technology. 17–23.
3. Pang LJ, Gao L, Pei QQ, Cui JJ, Wang YM (2013) A new ID-based multi-recipient public-key encryption scheme. Chinese Journal of Electronics 1: 89–92.
4. Al-Riyami SS, Paterson KG (2003) Certificateless public key cryptography. In: Proc. 9th International Conference on the Theory and Application of Cryptology and Information Security (ASIACRYPT 2003). 452–473.
5. Barbosa M, Farshim P (2008) Certificateless signcryption. In: Proc. ACM Symposium on Information, Computer and Communications Security. 369–372.
6. Barreto PSLM, Deusajute AM, Cruz ES, Pereira GCF, Silva RR (2008) Toward efficient certificateless signcryption from (and without) bilinear pairings. http://sbseg2008.inf.ufrgs.br/proceedings/data/pdf/st03_03_artigo.pdf.
7. Li F, Shirase M, Takagi T (2009) Certificateless hybrid signcryption. In: Proc. 5th International Conference on Information Security Practice and Experience. 112–123.
8. Li PC, He MX, Li X, Liu WG (2010) Efficient and provably secure certificateless signcryption from bilinear pairings. Journal of Computational Information Systems 6: 3643–3650.
9. Selvi SSD, Vivek S, Rangan CP (2009) Cryptanalysis of certificateless signcryption schemes and an efficient construction without pairing. In: Proc. 5th international conference on Information security and cryptology (Inscrypt'09). 75–92.
10. Jing XF (2011) Provably secure certificateless signcryption scheme without pairing. In: Proc. International Conference on Electronic and Mechanical Engineering and Information Technology. 4753–4756.
11. Selvi SSD, Vivek SS, Shukla D, Chandrasekaran PR (2008) Efficient and provably secure certificateless multi-receiver signcryption. In: Proc. 2nd International Conference on Provable Security. 52–67.
12. Selvi SSD, Vivek SS, Rangan CP (2009) A note on the certificateless muli-receiver signcryption scheme. IACR Cryptology ePrint Archive. 308–308.
13. Miao SQ, Zhang FT, Zhang L (2010) Cryptanalysis of a certificateless multi-receiver signcryption scheme. In: Proc. International Conference on Multimedia Information Networking and Security. 593–597.
14. Shor PW (1994) Algorithms for quantum computation: discrete logarithms and factoring. In: Proc. 35th Symposium on Foundations of Computer Science. 124–134.
15. Dubois V, Fouque FA, Shamir A, Stern J (2007) Cryptanalysis of the SFLASH signature scheme. In: Proc. 3rd International SKLOIS Conference on Information Security and Cryptology (Inscrypt 2007). 1–4.
16. Billet O, Robshaw MJB, Peyrin T (2007) On building hash functions from multivariate quadratic equations. In: Proc. 12th Australasian conference on Information security and privacy (ACISP'07). 82–95.
17. Patarin J, Goubin L (1997) Trapdoor one-way permutations and multivariate polynomials. In: Proc. first International Conference on Information and Communications Security. 356–368.
18. Patarin J (1996) Hidden fields equations (HFE) and isomorphisms of polynomials (IP): Two new families of asymmetric. In: Proc. International Conference on the Theory and Application of Cryptographic Techniques. 33–48.
19. Bouillaguet C, Faugère JC, Fouque PA, Perret L (2011) Practical cryptanalysis of the identification scheme based on the isomorphism of polynomial with one secret problem. In: Proc.14th International Conference on Practice and Theory in Public Key Cryptography. 473–493.
20. Ding JT, Gower JE (2006) Inoculation multivariate schemes against differential attacks. In: Proc. 9th International Conference on Theory and Practice in Public-Key Cryptography. 290–301.
21. Hashimoto Y, Takagi T, Sakurai K (2012) General fault attacks on multivariate public key cryptosystems. In: Proc. 4th International Workshop on Post-Quantum Cryptography. 1–18.
22. Faugère JC, Perret L (2006) Polynomial equivalence problems: algorithmic and theoretical aspects. In: Proc. 24th Annual International Conference on the Theory and Applications of Cryptographic Techniques. 30–47.
23. Bouillaguet C, Faugère P, Perret L (2009) Differential algorithms for the isomorphism of polynomials problem. http://eprint.iacr.org/2009/583.pdf.
24. Tang SH, Xu LL (2012) Proxy signature scheme based on isomorphisms of polynomials. In: Proc. 6th International Conference on Network and System Security. 113–125.
25. Ding JT, Schmidt D (2005) Cryptanalysis of HFEv and internal perturbation of HFE. In: Proc. 10th International Conference on Practice and Theory in Public-Key Cryptography (PKC 2005). 288–301.
26. Dubois V, Granboulan L, Stern J (2007) Cryptanalysis of HFE with Internal Perturbation. In: Proc. 10th International Conference on Practice and Theory in Public-Key Cryptography (PKC 2007). 249–265.
27. Dubois V, Gama N (2010) The degree of regularity of HFE Systems. In: Proc. 16th International Conference on the Theory and Application of Cryptology and Information Security (ASIACRYPT 2010). 557–576.
28. Ding JT, Hodges TJ (2011) Inverting HFE systems is quasi-polynomial for all fields. In: Proc. 31st Annual International Cryptology Conference on Advances in Cryptology (CRYPTO 2011). 724–742.
29. Ding JT, Kleinjung T (2012) Degree of Regularity of HFE minus. Journal of Math-for-Industry. 2012, Vol 4, 97–104.
30. Pang LJ, Li HX, Pei QQ (2012) Improved multicast key management of Chinese wireless local area network security standard. IET Communications 6: 1126–1130.

21

The Exploration-Exploitation Dilemma: A Multidisciplinary Framework

Oded Berger-Tal[1]*[¤a¤b], Jonathan Nathan[2ⓢ], Ehud Meron[2,3], David Saltz[1]

1 Mitrani Department of Desert Ecology, Jacob Blaustein Institutes for Desert Research, Ben-Gurion University of the Negev, Midreshet Ben-Gurion, Israel, 2 Department of Solar Energy and Environmental Physics, Jacob Blaustein Institutes for Desert Research, Ben-Gurion University of the Negev, Midreshet Ben-Gurion, Israel, 3 Physics Department, Ben-Gurion University of the Negev, Beer Sheva, Israel

Abstract

The trade-off between the need to obtain new knowledge and the need to use that knowledge to improve performance is one of the most basic trade-offs in nature, and optimal performance usually requires some balance between exploratory and exploitative behaviors. Researchers in many disciplines have been searching for the optimal solution to this dilemma. Here we present a novel model in which the exploration strategy itself is dynamic and varies with time in order to optimize a definite goal, such as the acquisition of energy, money, or prestige. Our model produced four very distinct phases: Knowledge establishment, Knowledge accumulation, Knowledge maintenance, and Knowledge exploitation, giving rise to a multidisciplinary framework that applies equally to humans, animals, and organizations. The framework can be used to explain a multitude of phenomena in various disciplines, such as the movement of animals in novel landscapes, the most efficient resource allocation for a start-up company, or the effects of old age on knowledge acquisition in humans.

Editor: Jean Daunizeau, Brain and Spine Institute (ICM), France

Funding: This study was funded by an Israel Science Foundation (ISF) grant 1397/10, and by a seed grant from the Swiss Institute for Dryland Environmental and Energy Research (SIDEER). The funders had no role in study design, data collection and analysis, decision to publish, or preparation of the manuscript.

Competing Interests: The authors have declared that no competing interests exist.

* E-mail: oded.berger.tal@gmail.com

¤a Current address: Department of Ecology and Evolutionary Biology, University of California Los Angeles, Los Angeles, California, United States of America
¤b Current address: Applied Animal Ecology Division, Institute for Conservation Research, San Diego Zoo Global, Escondido, California, United States of America

ⓢ These authors contributed equally to this work.

Introduction

In order to produce high quality science, a scientist needs to be well versed in theory and familiar with other studies in her or his field. However, spending too much time delving into other studies might reduce the time allocated to the scientist's own research, reducing the quality of the research's results. Assuming the scientist wants to maximize his/her contribution to science, how much time should he/she spend on acquiring knowledge vs. putting this knowledge to use?

The trade-off between the exploration of new possibilities and the exploitation of old certainties constitutes one of the most basic dilemmas that both individuals and organizations constantly face at multiple time-scales, and has therefore been investigated by researchers from a variety of fields, including economics [1–3], business management [4,5], psychology [6,7], computer sciences [8] and ecology [9,10]. This dilemma stems from the fact that gathering information and exploiting it are in many cases two mutually exclusive activities. These two activities can be viewed as the two extreme strategies at the ends of a continuous scale. At one end of the continuum, an individual or system that only explores (i.e., obtains information about its environment in order to enhance future performance [11]) will pay the costs of obtaining new information without gaining the benefits of knowledge [2]. On the other end of the continuum, an individual or system that only exploits (i.e., uses existing knowledge only) will lack the

capability to adapt to significant environmental changes and may be trapped in a suboptimal stable equilibrium [2,4]. Thus, optimal behavior usually requires some balance between exploratory and exploitative behaviors [2,9,10].

Most of the studies dealing with the exploration-exploitation tradeoff show optimal solutions that are composed of one or several stationary strategies [12]. These could be a point on the exploration-exploitation continuum representing a division of the subject's resource allocation between exploratory and exploitative behaviors that yields the best long-term rewards under given conditions [13,14], or a point in time in which the subject should switch from a purely explorative strategy to an exploitative one [14,15]. A more realistic approach should consider the strategy itself as a dynamic component that varies with time in order to optimize a definite goal, such as the acquisition of energy, money, or prestige. If we take the scientist from the opening example, it is reasonable to assume that his/her optimal strategy as a graduate student should differ considerably from his/her optimal strategy once he/she received tenure. Therefore, a key question is how will the optimal solution change with time along the different stages of the scientist's career? Only very few studies have explored this optimization problem.

The principles of reinforcement learning (RF) theory, a framework originally used for machine learning that is aimed at facilitating adaptation to an environment based on trial and error [8], were applied in computational biology to construct learning algorithms in which an agent can control the balance between exploration and exploitation in an optimal manner [16–18]. These algorithms are based on a Bayesian modeling approach where the agent's decisions are the product of a weighted average of some prior knowledge regarding the environment and current sampling information [19], and the agent's need to explore is directly based on its perception of the environment, growing whenever the environment changes [16]. This is due to the fact that uncertainty should promote exploration [20] in an attempt to reduce it, and indeed there is evidence that surprising events and changes to the environment promote animals to learn faster [21]. Such algorithms have been tested and found to produce near optimal results in simulations. Moreover, analogical neurophysiologic pathways in the brain of animals and humans have been suggested, highlighting the neurobiological substrates that are related to the regulation of decision-making [17,18,20]. But although RF models are very useful in increasing our understandings of how animals and humans make decisions, they are also very mechanistic in nature and are, in many cases, specifically tailored to solve certain tasks, such as passing through mazes [16], with no attention given to the general motivation and ecological background of the subject. In other words, the abovementioned models have concentrated on the *how* rather than on the *why* of the decision-making process. Furthermore, so far the conclusions of all previous investigations of the exploration-exploitation dilemma are restricted to the discipline in which the study was conducted, and no attempt has been made to create a unifying framework that would be applicable across disciplines.

We present a multidisciplinary general framework of the exploration-exploitation trade-off, motivated by a new mathematical model, in which the balance between exploring new possibilities and exploiting old certainties varies dynamically with time to optimize a predefined goal. In this framework we focus on the optimal exploration-exploitation strategies at different stages of a subject's life-span.

Methods

Our model depicts a subject that can invest in energy acquisition (exploitation) or knowledge acquisition (exploration), according to a strategy that represents the proportion of time the subject invests in knowledge acquisition as a function of time along its lifetime T_{max}. Denoting the subject's energy and knowledge by E and L, respectively, and the time dependent strategy by $u(t)$, the model reads:

$$\frac{dE}{dt} = \frac{f_{max}L}{K_L+L} - m - u(t), \quad \frac{dE}{dt} = \frac{f_{max}L}{K_L+L} - m - u(t)$$

According to this model, energy E is gained as a saturating function of the existing knowledge L, with the half saturation constant k_L, so that an increase in knowledge yields a smaller increase in energy gain when existing knowledge is higher. The constant k_L can also represent spatial unpredictability – a low value of k_L reflects a homogeneous environment in which a low amount of exploration is all the subject requires in order to gain benefits from it, while a high value of k_L represent a heterogeneous environment. Energy is lost due to maintenance costs at a constant rate m, and also due to knowledge acquisition at a rate proportional to the strategy $u(t)$. Knowledge gain is proportional to $u(t)$, with efficiency α, and knowledge loss due to maintenance costs is proportional to the existing amount of knowledge with a rate m_L. A high value of m_L (i.e., a high rate of knowledge loss or "forgetting") can represent low temporal predictability in the

environment or, alternatively, the subject's limited ability to retain stored knowledge. To obtain physically feasible results, we must also add constraints requiring that energy will not become lower than some minimal level needed for survival (E_{min}), and also enforcing positive values of knowledge throughout the simulation:

$$E(t) \geq E_{min}$$

$$L(t) \geq 0$$

We also require the strategy $u(t)$ to be limited by the following constraints: Energy expenditure for exploration, per unit time, cannot have a negative value and should be smaller than the maximal energy acquisition rate f_{max}.

$$0 \leq u(t) \leq f_{max}$$

Table 1 lists the different parameters used in the model, the range of values which we investigated for each parameter, their units, their meaning, and the initial conditions and constraints of the model.

Each strategy, $u(t)$, correspond uniquely to a value of energy at the end of life, $E_i(T_{max})$.

We define the optimal strategy $u^*(t)$ to be the strategy that maximizes the amount of energy at the end of the subject's life-span, T_{max}. This does not mean that the subject ends its life with stores of wasted energy, since this energy is presumably used during its life-span to produce offspring, increase the subject's material wealth, etc. In order to find such optimal strategy one can transform the optimization problem above to a set of differential equations. The rules to make this transformation were formalized by Lev Pontryagin and Richard Bellman, and are now widely known as Optimal Control Theory [22]. The differential equations obtained by this method are often quite complicated to solve analytically and may require the use of numerical solution methods. In this work we use an optimization problem solving code for MATLAB (version 7.6.0, MathWorks, Natick, Massachusetts) called *"General Pseudospectral Optimization Software (GPOPS)"* *available freely online* [23]. This code transforms the model, constraints, and optimization criteria using the optimal control scheme into a set of partial differential equations, and proceeds to solve these equations using a numerical pseudospectral method. The solution yields the optimal strategy $u^*(t)$ that corresponds to the maximal energy gain during lifetime. We used this method iteratively to explore how changing model parameters affect the optimal strategy.

As in all models, we make several simplifying assumptions in the construction of this model. We assume that all parameters remain constant throughout a subject's life-span, as well as the value of information. We also assume that the rate of learning is reduced with the accumulation of knowledge. We believe that while these assumptions imply that the model may not apply to some specific cases, they also keep the model general enough to be applicative across disciplines.

Table 1. The different parameters that were used in the model and the range of parameter values we investigated (A), and the parameters that were used in solving the optimization problem (B).

A. Model Parameters

Parameter name	Values	Units	Meaning
f_{max}	[0.5–10]	E/t	Maximal energy consumption rate
k_L	[0.001–10]	L	Efficiency of foraging: The level of knowledge that will yield half of the maximal consumption rate.
m	0.02	E/t	Maintenance cost of living
α	[0.5–10]	L/E	Efficiency of learning: Knowledge gain per unit energy.
m_L	[0.01–1]	1/t	Knowledge maintenance cost (temporal predictability)
T_{max}	[5–100]	T	Life duration

B. Optimization problem parameters

Parameter name	Values	Units	Meaning
$E(t=0)$	5.5	E	Initial energy
$L(t=0)$	0	L	Initial knowledge
E_{min}	5	E	Minimal energy for survival
L_{min}	0	L	Minimal knowledge
U_{min}	0	E/t	Minimal investment in learning
U_{max}	1	E/t	Maximal investment in learning

Results and Discussion

The model results were very robust, and remarkably produced only four distinct phases that emerged in a fixed order regardless of the parameter values that were assigned. The phases differed in the subject's relation to knowledge (Fig. 1) and can be defined as: 1. Knowledge establishment. 2. Knowledge accumulation. 3. Knowledge maintenance. 4. Knowledge exploitation. Each of these phases relates to a different stage in the life-span of the decision making subject, be it a foraging animal, a human or a company. The framework is relevant across disciplines and can be used to explain a multitude of phenomena and allow for better informed decision making.

The Four Knowledge Phases

Knowledge Establishment

In order to exploit any resource, even in the most inefficient manner, the exploiting entity must have some knowledge of its environment. At the very least, knowledge of the existence of a resource and how to reach it are needed. The more is known about alternative resources, ways of obtaining them and various aspects of the environment, the more efficient the exploitation of resources will be. Thus, *knowledge establishment* is an obligatory phase when entering unfamiliar territory, such as for a dispersing or translocated animal, or an emerging company.

During this phase the subject devotes all of its resources to exploration (Fig. 1). Since the subject does not exploit any resources, it relies solely on its internal reserves (i.e., the energy state of an exploring animal or investors' funds in an emerging company). Consequently, the length of this phase is mainly determined by the subject's initial state. A subject that is in a relatively good state can afford to extend this phase considerably, thus improving its future prospects.

It is important to note that both humans and animals frequently use inherited knowledge (that was passed to them genetically or through culture transmission) when entering an unfamiliar territory, and thus may act upon some prior expectations based on that knowledge. If this knowledge is reliable, these individuals may skip this phase entirely and start their life from the knowledge accumulation phase. However, inherited knowledge may sometimes hinder the utilization of resources [24], such as in the case of rapidly changing environments, in which case individuals may be left with diminished resources for the establishment phase.

This phase is commonly apparent in technological ventures where in the early stages of a development project, an exploratory search should be undertaken in an attempt to discover something new, as well as to form exploration alliances [5,25]. In the context of animals, this phase exists in dispersing individuals that have reached unfamiliar territories. It is usually very short, and thus there is very little empirical work investigating it in the wild. However, we do know that captive animals that are introduced to new environments exhibit specific behaviors aimed at exploring their new environment [26,27]. The rapid integration of high resolution GPS collars into wildlife reintroductions [28] promises exciting advances in this field, as we now have the means to investigate the movement behavior of animals that are released to novel environments to better understand the knowledge establishment phase.

Knowledge Accumulation

This phase is what most literature dealing with the exploration-exploitation trade-off refers to as the exploration stage. During this phase the subject focuses on obtaining new information while exploiting resources from existing knowledge at a low rate aimed only at keeping the subject at some minimal pre-defined state. Thus, the subject is sacrificing its short-term benefits in order to obtain long-term rewards. As this phase progresses the rate of obtaining new information increases slowly because with the accumulation of knowledge, the exploitation of existing resources becomes more efficient and the subject needs to devote less time and energy to reach its minimum pre-defined state, and can

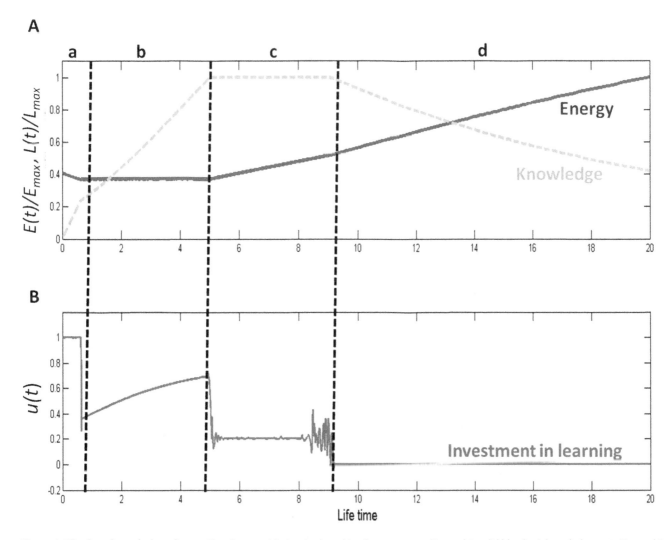

Figure 1. The four knowledge phases. The change with time in the subject's energy state (E; panel A, solid blue line), knowledge state (L; panel A, dashed green line), and its optimal proportion of time devoted to knowledge acquisition ($u^*(t)$; panel B, solid red line). The vertical dashed lines make a distinction between the four life-phases with regards to the exploration-exploitation dilemma: *a.* Knowledge establishment. *b.* Knowledge accumulation. *c.* Knowledge maintenance. *d.* Knowledge exploitation. The parameters used to generate this example are: $f_{max} = 1$, $k_L = 1$, $m_L = 0.08$, *alpha* = 1 and $T_{max} = 20$.

therefore allocate more time and energy for further exploration (Fig. 1).

Since exploratory behavior is such a fundamental behavior in both humans and animals [29], there have been many attempts to describe and characterize the behavior of individuals in novel environments. Some of the more in-depth studies of exploratory behavior have been done on rodents, but even within these studies, exploratory behavior varies according to the species and context. Laboratory mice introduced to a novel arena, showed exploratory behavior of increasing complexity, first examining their nest's surroundings, then progressively the walls around the arena and only later venturing to the center of the arena [29]. A similar behavior was performed by fat sand rats, *Psammomys obesus*, under lit conditions, but in the dark the rats performed looping behavior, in which travel paths tangle into loops [26]. Outside the laboratory, brown rats, *Rattus norvegicus*, released into the wild, exhibited random walk patterns, increasing in perimeter with time and mediated by central place foraging behavior [30]. Whatever the exploration method is, in all of these cases the behavior of the animals is clearly primarily aimed at increasing their knowledge

about their surroundings and not at the acquisition of resources. Thus, all of these different exploration mechanisms ultimately represent the same phase – *knowledge accumulation*.

The subject's time horizon (T_{max}) is an important factor determining the length of this phase. Because there is a temporal gap between paying the short-term costs of accumulating knowledge (i.e., exploring) and reaping the benefits of information, subjects with short life-spans should invest less in accumulating knowledge, since for them the benefits of knowing more are greatly reduced. Indeed, numerous studies on humans and animals report that as the relevant time horizon decreases, so does the tendency of the subject to explore [9,18,31]. A limited time horizon can stem from the time left available for a specific task [32] or the age of the subject [33]. Increasing the time-span of a learning subject will lengthen the *knowledge accumulation* period, but only up to a certain value. Because of cognitive or physiological constraints, as well as environmental stochasticity (that in most cases cannot be fully predicted), there is a limit to the benefits of exploration. Thus, eventually the exploring subject reaches a point in which additional exploration does not improve its future prospects and

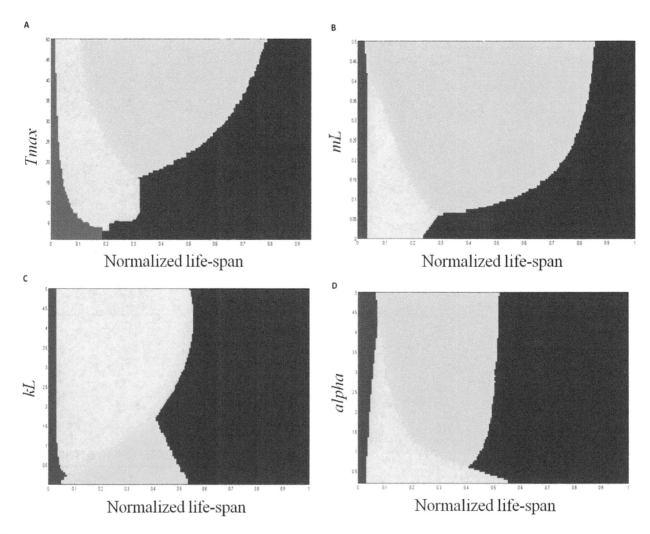

Figure 2. The optimal knowledge phases as a function of age and environment. The four optimal knowledge phases (dark blue - knowledge establishment, light blue - knowledge accumulation, orange - knowledge maintenance, red - knowledge exploitation) as a function of the subject 'age' (i.e., its position on its life-span trajectory, normalized here to a scale of 0–1), and different parameter values: (A) T_{max} - length of life-span. (B) m_L - rate of knowledge loss. (C) k_L - learning half saturation constant representing the environmental spatial predictability. (D) *alpha* - learning efficiency. In all simulations, the values of all parameters not tested (e.g., for plate A - all parameters but T_{max}) are as described for figure 1.

this phase becomes constant (decreasing the relative weight of this phase as the subject's life-span increases, Fig. 2a).

The environment's temporal unpredictability (m_L), which can reflect either external conditions that change with time (such as a highly fluid market environment), or the subject's own cognitive abilities and liabilities (such as memory capacity or decay), will also determine the length of the knowledge accumulation period. The more unpredictable the environment is, the harder it is to make predictions about the future state of the environment, which lowers the value of exploration (Fig. 2b). This result is supported by both theoretical models of learning in stochastic environments and empirical studies with humans [20,34,35].

As the spatial unpredictability (k_L) of the environment decreases (i.e., as the environment becomes more homogeneous) the need for exploration is reduced, and in extremely predictable conditions the knowledge gained during the *knowledge establishment* period is sufficient for optimal exploitation, eliminating the *knowledge accumulation* phase (Fig. 2c). Lastly, the learning efficiency *(α)* of the subject will determine the length of the *knowledge accumulation* period. An extremely efficient learner already accumulates enough

knowledge during the knowledge establishment period, and can skip the accumulation stage altogether. In contrast, for an inefficient learner the accumulation period is greatly extended to allow for the accumulation of sufficient information for optimal exploitation of resources at a later stage (Fig. 2d).

Knowledge Maintenance

In this phase the subject focuses on the utilization of resources while maintaining its knowledge at a constant optimal level. i.e., learning is only used to replace lost information or update existing knowledge. The leveling of the knowledge curve (Fig. 1) represents an optimal level of knowledge. Obtaining additional knowledge is too costly (because of the saturating shape of the energy gain function) when weighted against the benefits of knowledge and the rate of knowledge loss (m_L).

For animals foraging in heterogeneous landscapes with renewable resources, trap-lining, defined as repeated visitation to a series of resource patches in a predictable order, is usually the most beneficial foraging strategy [36], and has been reported for a wide variety of species [37–39]. Trap-lining foragers utilize resources based on existing knowledge, but since the environment is constantly changing, some method of updating the forager's information regarding its environment is needed for it to avoid getting 'stuck' in an inefficient foraging route. Indeed, several cognitive mechanisms for updating trap-lines have been suggested [10,36]. One suggested mechanism that can control both this phase as well as the *knowledge accumulation* phase is the adding of a (usually positive) bias to the subject's estimation of its environment when it encounters a novel environment (or alternatively, the adding of stochastic variability to its estimate). This idea originates from the field of RL and machine learning [8,40], but has lately been expanded to explain animal behavior [10,41]. A positively biased estimation of the environment encourages exploration by motivating the subject to keep looking for better rewards. As the subject explores, it constantly updates it estimate of the environment reducing its initial bias. Thus, the longer it explores, the more realistic this estimation will become, until eventually the subject will cease exploration and move into the knowledge maintenance phase. The same mechanism will also ensure that the subject maintains its knowledge in the maintenance phase. Either that stochastic error in the subject's learning mechanism will keep him exploring to some degree throughout this phase, or alternatively, in the case of an initially biased estimation, whenever the subject encounters a lower than usual reward, as a result of some degradation in the quality of the familiar environment, it will again possess an estimate that is higher than the rewards it acquires, which will send him exploring for a better alternative.

In business management, during the *knowledge maintenance* phase, knowledge regarding existing products is used and maintained, but new lines of products are not pursued [2,14]. The maintenance of knowledge is essential to effectively manage the inevitable errors and changes that are associated with knowledge storage bases, and is therefore considered an essential element of knowledge management [42].

Just as in the *knowledge accumulation* phase, a short time horizon will reduce the length of the *knowledge maintenance* phase, or even eliminate it altogether (Fig. 2a). When the subject's time-span is very short, it will be sub-optimal to spend any time learning new information, even if only to maintain the subject's current knowledge. However, unlike the *knowledge accumulation* phase, as the time-span of the subject expands so does the amount of time devoted to *knowledge maintenance*. During this phase the subject reaps the rewards of past explorations, and thus the longer this period lasts, the more the subject gains.

This phase is strongly affected by the environment's temporal unpredictability. In an environment that is predictable (as a result of stable conditions and low memory decay of the subject) this phase diminishes as the knowledge that was acquired earlier does not need maintaining and the subject should focus only on exploiting it. On the other hand, in a very fluid (and hence, unpredictable) environment, this phase replaces the *knowledge accumulation* phase simply because there is no point in accumulating knowledge for future use in a constantly changing environment and the subject should focus on continuous learning while exploiting resources (Fig. 2b). The learning efficiency of the subject produces a similar trend - when it is very low, there is no use in trying to maintain knowledge, since the benefits of investing only partial efforts in learning are close to nil. In this case the subject should concentrate only on the exploitation of knowledge once its *knowledge accumulation* phase is over. When the learning efficiency is especially high the amount of resources devoted to learning during this phase can be maintained at a very low level, and it can replace much of the *knowledge accumulation* phase (Fig. 2d).

Knowledge Exploitation

This phase arrives towards the end of a subject's life-span, and is characterized by a learning investment of 0. As the end approaches, it is sub-optimal to continue investing in gaining new information and the subject should invest its time only in exploiting the knowledge it had already accumulated, temporarily increasing its intake rate of resources (Fig. 1). It is worthwhile to note that in most cases a subject will have no prior information on its expected life-span. However, there are usually detectable cues that can inform the subject it is approaching the end of its life.

We do not presume to suggest a mechanistic explanation to the effects of old age on learning performance. However, from an evolutionary perspective, our framework corresponds to several of the main paradigms of the psychology of human aging. It is common knowledge that the processing of information and memory in humans decay in old age [43]. Moreover, in respect to reading, older subjects show a substantial decline in their working memory, but an increase in their use of prior knowledge [44]. Three processing styles have been identified in relation to age [45]: The 'youthful' style focuses on learning, intense data gathering and bottom-up processing. The 'mature' style balances the use of relevant knowledge and information seeking, and the 'old' style relies on top-down processing, making use of existing knowledge. This notion that aging is accompanied by an increase in top-down processes pervades recent literature on language in old age [46,47].

Another popular theory that supports our framework is the Socioemotional Selectivity Theory [31,48,49]. The theory proposes two primary motivations for social interactions: emotion regulation and knowledge acquisition. The perceived time-span of an individual determines the relative importance of these motivational objectives. A long time-horizon tends to be related to knowledge acquisition goals, while a limited time-horizon tends to be related to emotion regulation goals. Because of their limited future time extension, older adults are assumed to be less motivated to acquire knowledge. The theory has received empirical support in a variety of studies [50,51]. While this can also be explained by the biological fact that the cognitive abilities in humans decay in older people, empirical evidence demonstrates that young people with a limited time horizon (such as terminally ill patients) show similar tendencies to forgo knowledge acquisition [51,52].

It is interesting to note that for very short T_{max} only two phases emerge - knowledge acquisition and knowledge exploitation. Animals with very short life-spans are usually also very small (as they do not have the time to invest in a large body). Small size and a short life-span may promote a more homogeneous environment in space and time (e.g., the animal only lives through one season and forages in a single habitat), which means that there is no need to maintain the knowledge and once enough knowledge is acquired, the animal can immediately switch to the exploitation of resources with no further investment in learning. As lifetime increases, animals need to deal with a more complex environment (more seasons, more habitats), and thus knowledge accumulation and maintenance stages are added to their life-time strategy.

Conclusions

We provide a unifying framework of the exploration-exploitation trade-off, a trade-off prevalent in many disciplines and situations. It is important to note that the timeline presented in our model is restricted to monotonic linear time changes (e.g. lifetime of a human; lifetime of an economical project). However, the model could be easily extended to account for non-linear time-frames. For example, a major change to the environment (e.g., a flood that changes the entire topography, or an economical crisis that changes the entire economical landscape) can force a subject to revert from the *knowledge maintenance* or even the *knowledge exploitation* phases back to the *knowledge accumulation* or *knowledge establishment* phases. Similarly, there can be cases in which the entire sequence of 4 phases can occur multiple times within a subject's life-span, such as in the case of animals that disperse to new areas several times during their lifetime. In such cases, the length of each sequence can change with time and 'dispersal experience', i.e., the explorative phases of an animal dispersing for the first time may be considerably longer than for an animal dispersing to an unfamiliar area for the fifth time in its life.

Our framework demonstrates that the optimal solution to the exploration - exploitation trade-off depends on the life-stage of the subject as well as on the environmental conditions, and that the same strategies can be used by a variety of subjects - animals, humans and organizations alike. This fact points to the universality of the exploration-exploitation dilemma and the strategies aimed at solving it. Thus, the proposed framework can improve our understanding and consequently, our decision making in a multitude of disciplines.

Acknowledgments

O. B-T. is supported by the Adams Fellowship Program of the Israel Academy of Sciences and Humanities. This is publication number 828 of the Mitrani Department of Desert Ecology.

Author Contributions

Conceived and designed the experiments: OBT JN EM DS. Performed the experiments: OBT JN. Analyzed the data: OBT JN. Contributed reagents/materials/analysis tools: JN EM. Wrote the paper: OBT.

References

1. Schumpeter JA (1934) The theory of economic development. Cambridge: Harvard University Press.
2. March JG (1991) Exploration and exploitation in organizational learning. Organ Sci 2: 71–87.
3. Azoulay-Schwartz R, Kraus S, Wilkenfeld J (2004) Exploitation vs. exploration: choosing a supplier in an environment of incomplete information. Decis Support Syst 38: 1–18.
4. Uotila J, Maula M, Keil T, Zahra SA (2009) Exploration, exploitation, and financial performance: analysis of S&P 500 corporations. Strat Mgmt J 30: 221–231.
5. Molina-Castillo F-J, Jimenez-Jimenez D, Munuera-Aleman J-L (2011) Product competence exploitation and exploration strategies: the impact on new product performance through quality and innovativeness. Ind Market Manag 40: 1172–1182.
6. Daw ND, O'Doherty JP, Dayan P, Seymour B, Dolan RJ (2006) Cortical substrates for exploratory decisions in humans. Nature 441: 876–879.
7. Cohen JD, McClure SM, Yu AJ (2007) Should I stay or should I go? How the human brain manages the trade-off between exploitation and exploration. Phil Trans R Soc B 362: 933–942.
8. Sutton RS, Barto AG (1998) Reinforcement learning: an introduction. Cambridge: MIT Press.
9. Eliassen S, Jorgensen C, Mangel M, Giske J (2007) Exploration or exploitation: life expectancy changes the value of learning in foraging strategies. Oikos 116: 513–523.
10. Berger-Tal O, Avgar T (2012) The glass is half full: Overestimating the quality of a novel environment is advantageous. PLoS ONE 7: e34578.
11. Mettke-Hofmann C, Winkler H, Leisler B (2002) The significance of ecological factors for exploration and neophobia in parrots. Ethology 108: 249–272.
12. Gittins JC (1979) Bandit processes and dynamic allocation indices. J R Stat Soc B 41: 148–177.
13. Benner MJ, Tushman ML (2003) Exploitation, exploration, and process management: the productivity dilemma revisited. Acad Manage Rev 28: 238–256.
14. Gupta AK, Smith KG, Shalley CE (2006) The interplay between exploration and exploitation. Acad Manage J 49: 693–706.
15. Burgelman RA (2002) Strategy as a vector and the inertia of coevolutionary lock-in. Admin Sci Quart 47: 325–357.
16. Ishii S, Yoshida W, Yoshimoto J (2002) Control of exploitation-exploration meta-parameter in reinforcement learning. Neural Networks 15: 665–687.
17. Schweighofer N, Doya K (2003) Meta-learning in reinforcement learning. Neural Networks 16: 5–9.
18. Khamassi M, Enel P, Dominey PF, Procyk E (2012) Medial prefrontal cortex and the adaptive regulation of reinforcement learning parameters. Prog Brain Res 202: 441–464.
19. Jacobs RA, Kruschke JK (2011) Bayesian learning theory applied to human cognition. Wiley Interdiscip Rev Cogn Sci 2: 8–21.
20. Doya K (2008) Modulators of decision making. Nat Neurosci 11: 410–416.
21. Courville AC, Daw ND, Touretzky DS (2006) Bayesian theories of conditioning in a changing world. Trends Cogn Sci 10: 294–300.
22. Kirk DE (2004) Optimal control theory. Mineola: Dover Publications.
23. Rao AV, Benson DA, Darby C, Patterson MA, Francolin C, et al. (2010) Algorithm 902: GPOPS, a MATLAB software for solving multiple-phase optimal control problems using the gauss pseudospectral method. ACM T Math Software 37: 1–39.
24. Giraldeau L-A, Valone TJ, Templeton JJ (2002) Potential disadvantages of using socially acquired information. Phil. Trans. R. Soc. Lond. B 357: 1559–1566.
25. Rothaermel FT, Leeds DL (2004) Exploration and exploitation alliances in biotechnology: a system of new product development. Strat Mgmt J 25: 201–221.
26. Avni R, Eilam D (2008) On the border: perimeter patrolling as a transitional exploratory phase in a diurnal rodent, the fat sand rat (*Psammomys obesus*). Anim Cogn 11: 311–318.
27. Fryxell JM, Hazell M, Borger L, Dalziel BD, Haydon DT, et al. (2008) Multiple movement modes by large herbivores at multiple spatiotemporal scales. P Natl Acad Sci USA 105: 19114–19119.
28. Cagnacci F, Boitani L, Powell RA, Boyce MS (2010) Animal ecology meets GPS-based radiotelemetry: a perfect storm of opportunities and challenges. Phil Trans R Soc B 365: 2157–2162.
29. Fonio E, Benjamini Y, Golani I (2009) Freedom of movement and the stability of its unfolding in free exploration of mice. Proc Natl Acad Sci USA 106: 21335–21340.
30. Russel JC, McMorland AJC, MacKay JWB (2010) Exploratory behaviour of colonizing rats in novel environments. Anim Behav 79: 159–164.
31. Carstensen LL, Isaacowitz D, Charles ST (1999) Taking time seriously: a theory of socioemotional selectivity. Am Psychol 54: 165–181.
32. Krebs JR, Kacelnik A, Taylor P (1978) Tests of optimal sampling by foraging great tits. Nature 275: 27–31.
33. Wajnberg E, Bernhard P, Hamelin F, Boivin G (2006) Optimal patch time allocation for time-limited foragers. Behav Ecol Sociobiol 60: 1–10.
34. Eliassen S, Jorgensen C, Mangel M, Giske J (2009) Quantifying the adaptive value of learning in foraging behavior. Am Nat 174: 478–489.
35. Greville WJ, Buehner MJ (2010) Temporal predictability facilitates causal learning. J Exp Psychol Gen 139: 756–771.
36. Ohashi K, Thomson JD (2005) Efficient harvesting of renewing resources. Behav Ecol 16: 592–605.
37. Watts DP (1998) Long-term habitat use by mountain gorillas (*Gorilla gorilla beringei*). 2. Reuse of foraging areas in relation to resource abundance, quality, and depletion. Int J Primatol 19: 681–702.
38. Comba L (1999) Patch use by bumblebees (*Hymenoptera Apidae*): temperature, wind, flower density and traplining. Ethol Ecol Evol 11: 243–264.
39. Garrison JSE, Gass CL (1999) Response of a traplining hummingbird to changes in nectar availability. Behav Ecol 10: 714–725.
40. Gullapalli V (1990) A stochastic reinforcement learning algorithm for learning real-valued functions. Neural Networks 3: 671–692.
41. McNamara JM, Trimmer PC, Eriksson A, Marshall JAR, Houston AI (2011) Environmental variability can select for optimism or pessimism. Ecol Lett 14: 48–62.
42. Nevo D, Furneaux B, Wand Y (2008) Towards an evaluation framework for knowledge management systems. Inf Technol Manage 9: 233–249.
43. Birren JE, Schaie KW eds (2006) Handbook of the psychology of aging. Amsterdam: Elsevier.
44. Meyer BJF, Pollard CK (2006) Applied learning and aging: a closer look at reading. In: Birren JE, Schaie KW eds. Handbook of the psychology of aging. Amsterdam: Elsevier. 233–261.
45. Sinnott JD (1989) A model for solution of ill-structured problems: implications for everyday and abstract problem solving. In: Sinnott JD ed. Everyday problem solving: theory and applications. Westport: Praeger. 72–99.
46. Thornton R, Light LL (2006) Language comprehension and production in normal aging. In: Birren JE, Schaie KW eds. Handbook of the psychology of aging. Amsterdam: Elsevier. 262–288.
47. Burke DM, MacKay DG, James LE (2000) Theoretical approaches to language and aging. In: Perfect T., Maylor, E. eds. Models of cognitive aging. New York: Oxford University Press. 204–237.

48. Carstensen LL (1993) Motivation for social contact across the life span: a theory of socioemotional selectivity. Nebr Sym Motiv 40: 209–254.

49. Carstensen LL (1998) A life-span approach to social motivation. In: Heckhausen J, Dweck, C eds. Motivation and self- regulation across the life span. Cambridge: Cambridge University Press. 341–364.

50. Carstensen LL, Fung HH, Charles ST (2003) Socioemotional selectivity theory and the regulation of emotion in the second half of life. Motiv Emotion 27: 103–123.

51. Riediger M, Li S-C, Lindenberger U (2006) Selection, optimization, and compensation as developmental mechanisms of adaptive resource allocation: review and preview. In: Birren JE, Schaie KW eds. Handbook of the psychology of aging. Amsterdam: Elsevier. 289–314.

52. Fung HH, Carstensen LL, Lutz AM (1999) Influence of time on social preference: implications for life-span development. Psychol Aging 14: 595–604.

22

An Efficient and Provable Secure Revocable Identity-Based Encryption Scheme

Changji Wang[1,2]*, **Yuan Li**[1,2], **Xiaonan Xia**[1,2], **Kangjia Zheng**[1,2]

1 School of Information Science and Technology, Sun Yat-sen University, Guangzhou, China, **2** Guangdong Province Information Security Key Laboratory, Sun Yat-sen University, Guangzhou, China

Abstract

Revocation functionality is necessary and crucial to identity-based cryptosystems. Revocable identity-based encryption (RIBE) has attracted a lot of attention in recent years, many RIBE schemes have been proposed in the literature but shown to be either insecure or inefficient. In this paper, we propose a new scalable RIBE scheme with decryption key exposure resilience by combining Lewko and Waters' identity-based encryption scheme and complete subtree method, and prove our RIBE scheme to be semantically secure using dual system encryption methodology. Compared to existing scalable and semantically secure RIBE schemes, our proposed RIBE scheme is more efficient in term of ciphertext size, public parameters size and decryption cost at price of a little looser security reduction. To the best of our knowledge, this is the first construction of scalable and semantically secure RIBE scheme with constant size public system parameters.

Editor: Cheng-Yi Xia, Tianjin University of Technology, China

Funding: This paper is jointly supported by the National Natural Science Foundation of China (Grant No. 61173189) and Guangdong Province Information Security Key Laboratory Project. The funders had no role in study design, data collection and analysis, decision to publish, or preparation of the manuscript.

Competing Interests: The authors have declared that no competing interests exist.

* Email: isswchj@mail.sysu.edu.cn

Introduction

Shamir [1] first introduced the concept of identity-based public key cryptography (ID-PKC) where a public key can be an arbitrary string such as an email address or a telephone number, while the corresponding private key can only be generated by a private key generator (PKG) who has the knowledge of the master secret. The first secure and practical identity-based encryption (IBE) scheme was proposed by Boneh and Franklin [2] from bilinear pairings, which is proved to be semantically secure against adaptive chosen ciphertext attack (IND-ID-CCA) under the Decisional Bilinear Diffie-Hellman (DBDH) assumption in the random oracle model.

Boneh and Franklin's work spurred a great deal of research on IBE. One important research direction is to construct provably secure IBE schemes in the standard model, because random oracle model only provides heuristic security [3]. Canetti, Halevi, and Katz [4] defined a weaker security notion for IBE, known as selective-ID model, in which the adversary commits ahead of time to the identity that it intends to attack. Boneh and Boyen [5] proposed two efficient IBE schemes that are secure in the selective-ID model without random oracle. The first IBE construction (BB1-IBE) is based on the DBDH assumption, while the second IBE construction (BB2-IBE) is based on a non-standard Decision Bilinear Diffie-Hellman Inversion (DBDHI) assumption. Waters [6] improved BB1-IBE scheme and proposed an efficient IBE scheme which is proved to be semantically secure without random oracles under the DBDH assumption in adaptive-ID model. Gentry [7] presented an IBE scheme with short public parameters which is proved to be semantically secure without random oracles

under a non-static assumption in adaptive-ID model. Waters [8] introduced a new technique called dual system encryption and proposed an IBE scheme that is proved to be semantically secure without random oracle under standard (static) assumption in adaptive-ID model. Recently, Lewko and Waters [9] gave a new dual system encryption realization of IBE from composite order bilinear groups, which is proved to be semantically secure without random oracle under the subgroup decision assumption in adaptive-ID model.

Another important research direction is to construct IBE schemes with efficient revocation. Suppose that Alice has left the organization or her private key is compromised or stolen by an adversary in some scenarios [10]. On the one hand, Alice will be withdrawn from the right of accessing the information with respect to her public key. On the other hand, Alice's private key will be revoked to prevent the adversary with her compromised private key to access confidential data encrypted under her public key. Thus, revocation functionality is necessary and crucial to public-key cryptosystems. In the public key infrastructure setting, numerous solutions have been proposed, such as periodic publication mechanisms (e.g. certificate revocation list) and online query mechanisms (e.g. online certificate status protocol). In the ID-PKC setting, however, key revocation is non-trivial. This is because a user's identity is itself a public key, thus one can not simply change her public key, as this changes her identity as well. An ideal revocation method for IBE is that a sender can generates a ciphertext as the same as that of IBE without worrying about the revocation of a receiver and only the receiver needs to check the revocation of his private key to decrypt the ciphertext.

Revocable IBE (RIBE) has attracted a lot of attention in recent years, many RIBE schemes have been proposed [9,11–15]. Boneh and Franklin [2] proposed a trivial method to achieve revocation functionality for IBE (BF-RIBE for short) by representing an identity as ID‖T where ID is the real identity and T is a current time. Since new decryption keys are needed to be issued by the PKG for each time period, this introduces huge overheads for PKG that are linearly increased in the number of users and a secure channel is needed between PKG and users to transmit updated private key. Thus, BF-RIBE is not scalable.

Boldyreva et al. [11] proposed the first scalable RIBE scheme (BGK-RIBE for short) by combining Sahai and Waters' fuzzy IBE scheme [16] and Naor et al.'s complete subtree method [17], where the PKG's overhead increases logarithmically (instead of linearly) in the number of users. The idea of BGK-RIBE scheme consists in assigning users to the leaves of a complete binary tree. Each user is provided by PKG with a set of private keys sk_{ID} corresponding to his/her identity ID for each node on the path from his/her associated leaf to the root of the tree via a secure channel as in IBE scheme. PKG broadcasts key updates ku_T in each time period T for a set $\mathbf{Y}$ of nodes that contains no ancestors of revoked users and exactly one ancestor of any non-revoked one (as illustrated in Figure 1 where the nodes of $\mathbf{Y}$ are the squares). Then, a user assigned to leaf η is able to form an effective decryption key $dk_{ID,T}$ for period T if the set $\mathbf{Y}$ contains a node on the path from the root to η. By doing so, every update of the revocation list $\mathbf{RL}$ only requires PKG to perform logarithmic work in the overall number of users and no secure channel is required between PKG and users. The size of users' private keys also logarithmically depends on the maximal number of users.

Another idea of BGK-RIBE scheme consists in applying fuzzy IBE primitive. In fuzzy IBE systems, identities are regarded as sets of descriptive attributes instead of a single identity string in IBE systems, and a user with private key for the attribute set $\bar{\omega}$ is able to decrypt a ciphertext encrypted for an attribute set $\bar{\omega}'$ if and only if $\bar{\omega}$ and $\bar{\omega}'$ have an overlap of at least d attributes. The BGK-RIBE scheme uses a special kind of fuzzy IBE where ciphertexts are encrypted using the receiver's identity and the period number as "attributes". The decryption key of the receiver has to match both attributes to decrypt the ciphertext. For each node on the path from the root to its assigned leaf, the user is given a key attribute that is generated using a new polynomial with degree 1 for which the constant term is always the master secret. The same polynomials are used, for each node, to generate key updates. To

compute a decryption key for period T, each user thus needs to combine two key attributes associated with the same node of the tree. Since there is no adaptive-ID secure fuzzy IBE scheme in the literature, BGK-RIBE scheme [11] is only proved to be secure in selective-ID model.

Later, Libert and Vergnaud [12] proposed the first adaptive-ID secure scalable RIBE scheme (LV-RIBE for short) based on same idea as BGK-RIBE scheme, but, instead of using fuzzy IBE scheme, they applied the idea of two-level hierarchial IBE scheme (HIBE for short). They use adaptive-ID secure Libert and Vergnaud's black-box accountable authority IBE scheme [18] in the first level to handle user's long term private keys (associated with identities), and use selective-ID secure Boneh and Boyen's BB1-IBE scheme [5] in the second level to handle decryption keys (associate with time periods). Seo and Emura [13] refined the security model of RIBE by considering the decryption key exposure attacks, and proposed a scalable RIBE scheme (SE-RIBE for short) with decryption key exposure resistance based on same idea as LV-RIBE scheme. Seo and Emura use adaptive-ID secure Waters IBE scheme [6] in the first level to handle user's long term private keys, and use selective-ID secure BB1-IBE scheme [5] in the second level to handle decryption keys. Recently, Park et al. [14] proposed a scalable RIBE scheme with shorter private key and update key by using multilinear maps, but the size of the public parameters is dependent to the number of users. Lee et al. [15] presented a new technique for RIBE that uses the subset difference method instead of using the complete subtree method to improve the size of update keys.

Existing adaptive-ID secure scalable RIBE constructions are built on combining two-level HIBE schemes and complete subtree method, and proved security with partition strategy in which the space of identities is partitioned into the set of identities for which a valid secret key can be simulated and those for which a valid challenge ciphertext can be simulated.

In this paper, we propose an efficient adaptive-ID secure scalable RIBE scheme by combineing two-level Lewko and Waters HIBE scheme [9] and complete subtree method. To prove security for our RIBE scheme in adaptive-ID model, we adopt Waters dual system encryption methodology [8]. However, we can not use dual system encryption methodology directly to prove the security of RIBE schemes. This is because an adversary in RIBE schemes can issue private key query for the challenge identity ID* as long as ID* has been revoked before the challenge time T*, while an adversary in IBE schemes can not issue private key query for the

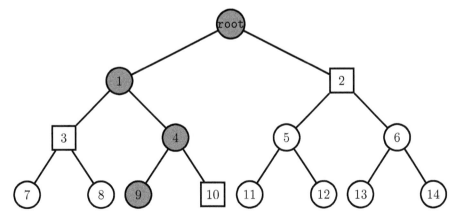

Figure 1. Example of KUNode Algorithm. Assume that the user associated with node 9 is revoked. As figure illustrated, user assigned to leaf node 7 has subkeys of node 7, 3, 1 and root. In time period T, only user assigned to leaf node 9 is revoked, the square nodes are update nodes set outputted by the KUNode algorithm, it's obvious that this set does not contain any node on the path from node 9 to root node.

challenge identity ID^*. Furthermore, as stated in Seo and Emura [13], an adversary in a scalable RIBE scheme with decryption key exposure resistance may obtain not a private key sk_{ID*} but a decryption key $dk_{ID*,T}$, and ID^* can still be alive in the system in the challenge time period $T^* \neq T$.

To make dual system encryption methodology work properly, we need to make sure that all decryption keys, including those generated by the adversary, are semi-functional in the last step. It is not a trivial job to accomplish this transformation directly. To circumvent this issue, our approach is to design semi-functional private key and semi-functional update key, and generate a semi-functional decryption key from a semi-functional private key or a semi-functional update key.

During registration, PKG assigns a user with identity ID to a leaf node η of a complete binary tree, and issues the private key sk_{ID} for identity ID which is composed by a set of subkeys $sk_{ID,\theta} = \{(K_1, K_2, K_3)\}_{\theta \in Path(\eta)}$, wherein each subkey is associated with a node on $Path(\eta)$. At time period T, PKG broadcasts the update key ku_T which is composed by a set of subkeys $ku_{T,\theta} = \{(U_1, U_2, U_3)\}_{\theta \in Y}$, wherein each subkey is associated with a node in Y. An intuitive way to make all decryption keys be semi-functional in the last step is to transform all subkeys of all private keys or all subkeys of update keys from normal form into semi-functional form. However, similar to the security proof in Lewko and Waters' IBE scheme [9], the adversary cannot issue private key query for identities which are equal to the challenge identity ID^* modulo p_2, and cannot issue update key query for time periods which are equal to the challenge time T^* modulo p_2, namely all subkeys of these private keys and all subkeys of these update keys can not be transformed. On the one hand, if we transform either all subkeys of the corresponding private key sk_{ID} satisfying $ID \neq ID^* \bmod p_2$ or all subkeys of the corresponding update key ku_T satisfying $T \neq T^* \bmod p_2$ from normal form into semi-functional form independently, the resulting decryption keys $dk_{ID,T}$ may not be semi-functional. On the other hand, if we transform all subkeys of the corresponding update key ku_T from normal form into semi-functional form, this will result in security degradation $O(r \log(N/r))$ when $r \leq N/2$, and security degradation about $O(N-r)$ when $r > N/2$, where N is the number of users and r is the number of revoked users.

To solve the problem of security degradation, we take advantage of the special structure of complete subtree method. We do not need to transform all subkeys of sk_{ID} that satisfy $ID \neq ID^* \bmod p_2$ and all subkeys of ku_T that satisfy $T \neq T^* \bmod p_2$ from normal form into semi-functional form, we just need to transform subkeys of above sk_{ID} that satisfy $\theta \in Path(\eta) \land \theta \notin Path(\eta^*)$, and subkeys of above ku_T that satisfy and $\theta' \in Y \land \theta' \in Path(\eta^*)$ from norm form into semi-functional form, where η and η^* are leaf nodes of binary tree that assigned to ID and ID^*, respectively. Thus, security degradation is reduced to $O(1)$ per transformation of a update key.

Compared to existing adaptive-ID secure scalable RIBE schemes, our RIBE scheme is more efficient in term of ciphertext size, public parameters size and decryption cost at price of a little looser security reduction. To the best of our knowledge, this is the first construction of scalable semantically secure RIBE scheme with constant size public system parameters. Table 1 shows a comparison between our RIBE scheme and existing RIBE schemes.

The rest of the paper is organized as follows. In Section 2, we introduce some preliminary works necessary for our constructions, such as bilinear group generator and complexity assumptions. In Section 3, we give formal syntax and security definitions of RIBE. In Section 4, we describe our RIBE construction. In Section 5, we

Table 1. Comparison among RIBE schemes.

RIBE schemes	Security model	Complexity assumption	Scalability	DKE resistance	CT size	Dec. cost	Mpk size
BF-RIBE [2]	Adaptive RO	DBDH	No	Yes	$|G|+|P|$	t_e	$3|G|$
BGK-RIBE [11]	Selective RO	DBDH	Yes	No	$3|G|+|P|$	$4t_e$	$6|G|$
LV-RIBE [12]	Adaptive Standard	DBDH	Yes	No	$3|G|+2|P|$	$3t_e$	$(n+6)|G|$
SE-RIBE [13]	Adaptive Standard	DBDH	Yes	Yes	$3|G|+|P|$	$3t_e$	$(n+6)|G|$
Our RIBE	Adaptive Standard	SGD	Yes	Yes	$2|G|+|P|$	$2t_e$	$4|G|+|G_T|$

$|G|$ and $|G_T|$ are the sizes of groups G and G_T, respectively. $|P|$ is the size of plaintext space, and n is the size of identity space. t_e is the cost for performing a bilinear pairing $\hat{e}(G,G) \rightarrow G_T$. Selective (Adaptive, respectively) is a selective-identity security model (adaptive-identity security model, respectively). RO (Standard, respectively) is a random oracle model (standard model, respectively). DBDH is Decisional Bilinear Diffie-Hellman assumption, and SGD is Subgroup Decision assumption. DKE is decryption key exposure.

prove our RIBE construction are IND-RID-CPA secure. Finally, we conclude the paper in Section 6.

Preliminaries

Bilinear group generator and complexity assumptions

Definition 1. (Bilinear Group Generator) *A bilinear group generator $\mathcal{G}$ is an algorithm that takes as input a security parameter κ and outputs a bilinear group $(n, \mathbf{G}, \mathbf{G}_T, \hat{e})$, where $\mathbf{G}$ and $\mathbf{G}_T$ are cyclic groups of order n, and $\hat{e}: \mathbf{G} \times \mathbf{G} \rightarrow \mathbf{G}_T$ is a bilinear map with the following properties:*

- *Bilinearity: For all $g, h \in \mathbf{G}$ and $a, b \in \mathbf{Z}_n$, we have $\hat{e}(g^a, h^b) = \hat{e}(g, h)^{ab}$.*
- *Non-degeneracy: There is an element $g \in \mathbf{G}$ such that $\hat{e}(g,g)$ has order n in $\mathbf{G}_T$.*
- *Computability: There is an efficient algorithm to compute $\hat{e}(g_1, g_2)$ for all $g_1, g_2 \in \mathbf{G}$.*

Denote $\mathcal{G}(1^\kappa) \rightarrow (n = p, \mathbf{G}, \mathbf{G}_T, \hat{e})$ a prime order bilinear groups generator, where p is a prime. We call $\mathcal{G}(1^\kappa) \rightarrow (n = p_1 p_2 p_3, \mathbf{G}, \mathbf{G}_T, \hat{e})$ a composite order bilinear groups generator, where p_1, p_2 and p_3 are distinct primes. The subgroups of order p_1, p_2 and p_3 in $\mathbf{G}$ are denoted by $\mathbf{G}_{p_1}$, $\mathbf{G}_{p_2}$ and $\mathbf{G}_{p_3}$, respectively. Note that when $h_i \in \mathbf{G}_{p_i}$ and $h_j \in \mathbf{G}_{p_j}$ for $i \neq j$, we have $\hat{e}(h_i, h_j)$ is the identity element in $\mathbf{G}_T$.

Definition 2. (Decision Bilinear Diffie-Hellman Assumption) *Given a prime order bilinear group $(p, \mathbf{G}, \mathbf{G}_T, \hat{e})$ generated by $\mathcal{G}(1^\kappa)$, we define the following two distributions:*

$$\mathcal{D}_0(\kappa) = \left(g, g^a, g^b, g^c, \hat{e}(g,g)^{abc} \right) \text{ and } \mathcal{D}_1(\kappa) = \left(g, g^a, g^b, g^c, \hat{e}(g,g)^z \right)$$

where $g \xleftarrow{\$} \mathbf{G}$ and $a, b, c, z \xleftarrow{\$} \mathbf{Z}_p$. The DBDH problem in the prime order bilinear group $(p, \mathbf{G}, \mathbf{G}_T, \hat{e})$ is to decide a bit b from given $\mathcal{D}_b$, where $b \xleftarrow{\$} \{0,1\}$. The advantage of an algorithm $\mathcal{A}$ in solving the DBDH problem in the prime order bilinear group $(p, \mathbf{G}, \mathbf{G}_T, \hat{e})$ is defined by

$$Adv_{\mathcal{G},\mathcal{A}}^{DBDH}(\kappa) = |\Pr[\mathcal{A}(\mathcal{D}_0(\kappa)) \rightarrow 1] - \Pr[\mathcal{A}(\mathcal{D}_1(\kappa)) \rightarrow 1]|$$

We say that the DBDH assumption holds in the prime order bilinear group $(p, \mathbf{G}, \mathbf{G}_T, \hat{e})$ if no probabilistic polynomial time (PPT) algorithm has a non-negligible advantage in solving the DBDH problem in the prime order bilinear group $(p, \mathbf{G}, \mathbf{G}_T, \hat{e})$.

Assumption 1. (Subgroup decision problem for 3 primes) *Given a composite order bilinear group generator $\mathcal{G}(1^\kappa)$, we define the following two distributions:*

$$\mathbb{G} = (n = p_1 p_2 p_3, \mathbf{G}, \mathbf{G}_T, \hat{e}) \xleftarrow{\$} \mathcal{G}(1^\kappa), g \xleftarrow{\$} \mathbf{G}_{p_1}, X_3 \xleftarrow{\$} \mathbf{G}_{p_3},$$

$$D = (\mathbb{G}, g, X_3), L_1 \xleftarrow{\$} \mathbf{G}_{p_1 p_2}, L_2 \xleftarrow{\$} \mathbf{G}_{p_1}.$$

We define the advantage of an algorithm $\mathcal{A}$ in breaking the subgroup decision assumption 1 to be:

$$Adv1_{\mathcal{G},\mathcal{A}}(\kappa) = |\Pr[\mathcal{A}(D, L_1) = 1] - \Pr[\mathcal{A}(D, L_2) = 1]|.$$

We note that L_1 can be written (uniquely) as the product of an element of $\mathbf{G}_{p_1}$ and an element of $\mathbf{G}_{p_2}$. We refer to these elements as the "$\mathbf{G}_{p_1}$ part of L_1" and the "$\mathbf{G}_{p_2}$ part of L_1" respectively.

Definition 3. *We say that $\mathcal{G}$ satisfies the subgroup decision Assumption 1 if $Adv1_{\mathcal{G},\mathcal{A}}(\kappa)$ is a negligible function of κ for any polynomial time algorithm $\mathcal{A}$.*

Assumption 2. (Subgroup decision problem for 3 primes) *Given a composite order bilinear group generator $\mathcal{G}(1^\kappa)$, we define the following two distributions:*

$$\mathbb{G} = (n = p_1 p_2 p_3, \mathbf{G}, \mathbf{G}_T, \hat{e}) \xleftarrow{\$} \mathcal{G}(1^\kappa), g, X_1 \xleftarrow{\$} \mathbf{G}_{p_1}, X_2, Y_2$$

$$\xleftarrow{\$} \mathbf{G}_{p_2}, X_3, Y_3 \xleftarrow{\$} \mathbf{G}_{p_3},$$

$$D = (\mathbb{G}, g, X_1 X_2, X_3, Y_2 Y_3), L_1 \xleftarrow{\$} \mathbf{G}, L_2 \xleftarrow{\$} \mathbf{G}_{p_1 p_3},$$

We define the advantage of an algorithm $\mathcal{A}$ in breaking the subgroup decision assumption 2 to be:

$$Adv2_{\mathcal{G},\mathcal{A}}(\kappa) = |Pr[\mathcal{A}(D, L_1) = 1] - Pr[\mathcal{A}(D, L_2) = 1]|.$$

Definition 4. *We say that $\mathcal{G}$ satisfies the subgroup decision Assumption 2 if $Adv2_{\mathcal{G},\mathcal{A}}(\kappa)$ is a negligible function of κ for any polynomial time algorithm $\mathcal{A}$.*

Assumption 3. (Subgroup decision problem for 3 primes) *Given a composite order bilinear group generator $\mathcal{G}(1^\kappa)$, we define the following two distributions:*

$$\mathbb{G} = (n = p_1 p_2 p_3, \mathbf{G}, \mathbf{G}_T, \hat{e}) \xleftarrow{\$} \mathcal{G}(1^\kappa), \alpha, s \xleftarrow{\$} \mathbf{Z}_n,$$

$$g \xleftarrow{\$} \mathbf{G}_{p_1}, X_2, Y_2, Z_2 \xleftarrow{\$} \mathbf{G}_{p_2}, X_3 \xleftarrow{\$} \mathbf{G}_{p_3},$$

$$D = (\mathbb{G}, g, g^\alpha X_2, X_3, g^s Y_2, Z_2), L_1 = \hat{e}(g,g)^{\alpha s}, L_2 \xleftarrow{\$} \mathbf{G}_T.$$

We define the advantage of an algorithm $\mathcal{A}$ in breaking the subgroup decision assumption 3 to be:

$$Adv3_{\mathcal{G},\mathcal{A}}(\kappa) = |\Pr[\mathcal{A}(D, L_1) = 1] - \Pr[\mathcal{A}(D, L_2) = 1]|.$$

Definition 5. *We say that $\mathcal{G}$ satisfies the subgroup decision Assumption 3 if $Adv3_{\mathcal{G},\mathcal{A}}(\kappa)$ is a negligible function of κ for any polynomial time algorithm $\mathcal{A}$.*

KUNode Algorithm

The KUNode algorithm was proposed by Boldyreva et al. [11] to achieve efficient revocation for IBE schemes. In the description hereafter, we employ similar notations as in [11]. Denote the root node of the tree $\mathbb{T}$ by root. If η is a leaf node, we denote the set of nodes on the path from η to root by $\text{Path}(\eta)$. If η is a non-leaf node, we denote the left and right child of η by η_L and η_R, respectively.

At each time period, KUNode algorithm determines the smallest subset $\mathbf{Y} \subset \mathbb{T}$ of nodes that contains an ancestor of all leaves corresponding to non-revoked users. This minimal set precisely contains nodes for which key updates have to be publicized in such a way that only non-revoked users will be able to generate the appropriate decryption key for the matching period. To identify the set $\mathbf{Y}$, KUNode algorithm takes as input a binary tree $\mathbb{T}$, revocation list $\mathbf{RL}$ and a period number T. If a user (assigned to η) is revoked on time T, then $(\eta,T) \in \mathbf{RL}$. KUNode algorithm first marks all ancestors of users that were revoked by time T as revoked nodes. Then, it inserts in $\mathbf{Y}$ the non-revoked children of revoked nodes. The description of $\text{KUNode}(\mathbb{T},\mathbf{RL},T)$ is given in Table 2 Algorithm 2.

The example illustrated in Figure 1 can be used to help the reader understand the $\text{KUNode}(\mathbb{T},\mathbf{RL},T)$ algorithm. Assume that a user associated with node x_9 is revoked, then $\mathbf{X}=\text{Path}(x_9)=\{x_9,x_4,x_1,\text{root}=x_0\}$ and $\mathbf{Y}=\{x_2,x_3,x_{10}\}$. Intuitively, all users, except the user associated with noed x_9, have a node $x \in \mathbf{Y}$ that is contained in the set of nodes on the path from their assigned node to root, whereas $\mathbf{Y} \cap \text{Path}(x_9) = \emptyset$.

When a user joins the system, PKG assigns a leaf node η of a complete binary tree to the user, and issues a set of keys, wherein each key is associated with a node on $\text{Path}(\eta)$. At time period T, PKG broadcasts key updates for a set $\text{KUNode}(\mathbb{T},\mathbf{RL},T)$. Then, only non-revoked users have at least one key corresponding to a node in $\text{KUNode}(\mathbb{T},\mathbf{RL},T)$ and are able to generate decryption keys on time T.

Dual System Encryption

Dual system encryption is a proof methodology first introduced by Waters [8], which opens up a new way to prove adaptive

Table 2. Algorithm 2: KUNode Algorithm $\text{KUNode}(\mathbb{T},\mathbf{RL},T)$.

$\mathbf{X},\mathbf{Y} \leftarrow \emptyset$.

$\forall (\eta_i,T_i) \in \mathbf{RL}$

if $T_i \leq T$ **then**

　Add $\text{Path}(\eta_i)$ to $\mathbf{X}$

end if

$\forall x \in \mathbf{X}$

if $x_L \notin \mathbf{X}$ **then**

　Add x_L to $\mathbf{Y}$

end if

if $x_R \notin \mathbf{X}$ **then**

　Add x_R to $\mathbf{Y}$

end if

if $\mathbf{Y} = \emptyset$ **then**

　Add root to $\mathbf{Y}$

end if

Return $\mathbf{Y}$

---

security under simple assumptions for IBE and related encryption systems.

In a dual system encryption system, both ciphertexts and private keys can take on one of two indistinguishable forms [9]. A private key or ciphertext is normal if they are generated from the system's key generation or encryption algorithm. Semi-functional ciphertexts and private keys are not used in the real system, they are only used in the security proof. A normal private key can decrypt normal or semi-functional ciphertexts, and a normal ciphertext can be decrypted by normal or semi-functional private keys. However, decryption will fail with high probability if one attempts to decrypt a semi-functional ciphertext with a semi-functional private key.

Unlike previous proof technique called partitioning strategy which partitions the identity space into two parts, dual system encryption defines a sequence of games and proves their indistinguishability with the real game. The first game is the real security game in which the challenge ciphertext and private keys are normal. In the next game, the ciphertext is switched from normal to semi-functional, while all the private keys are normal. For an adversary that makes q private key requests, games 1 through q follow. In game k, the first k private keys are semi-functional while the remaining private keys are normal. In game q, all the private keys and the challenge ciphertext given to the adversary are semi-functional. Hence none of the given private keys are useful for decrypting the challenge ciphertext. At this point, At this point proving security becomes relatively easy since the reduction algorithm does not need to present any normal private keys to the adversary and all semi-functional private keys are useless for decrypting a semi-functional ciphertext.

Syntax and Security Definitions of RIBE

In this section, we recall the syntax and security model of RIBE as defined in [13]. Unlike the syntax definition in [13], we define the decryption key generation algorithm as probabilistic rather than deterministic. A RIBE scheme can be defined by the following seven polynomial-time algorithms:

Setup The stateful setup algorithm is run by the PKG, which takes a security parameter κ and a maximal number of users N as input, it outputs the public parameter mpk, the master secret key msk, the initial revocation list $\mathbf{RL} = \emptyset$, and a state ST. We assume that the message space $\mathbf{M}$ and the identity space $\mathbf{I}$, the time space $\mathbf{T}$, and the ciphertext space $\mathbf{CT}$ are contained in mpk.

Extract The stateful private key extract algorithm is run by the PKG, which takes mpk, msk, an identity $\text{ID} \in \mathbf{I}$, a state ST as input, it outputs a secret key sk_{ID} associated with ID and an updated state ST.

KeyUpdate The key update generation algorithm is run by the PKG, which takes mpk, msk, the key update time $T \in \mathbf{T}$, the current revocation list $\mathbf{RL}$, and ST as input, it outputs the key update ku_T.

DKeyGen The probabilistic decryption key generation algorithm is run by a user, which takes mpk, sk_{ID}, and ku_T as input, it outputs a decryption key $dk_{\text{ID},T}$ to be used during period T or a special symbol $\perp$ indicating that ID was revoked.

Encrypt The probabilistic encryption algorithm is run by a sender, which takes mpk, $\text{ID} \in \mathbf{I}$, $T \in \mathbf{T}$, and a message $m \in \mathbf{M}$ as input, it outputs a ciphertext c.

Decrypt The deterministic decryption algorithm is run by the receiver, which takes mpk, $dk_{\text{ID},T}$, and c as input, it outputs m or $\perp$ if C is an invalid ciphertext.

Revoke The stateful revocation algorithm is run by the PKG, which takes an identity to be revoked $\text{ID} \in \mathbf{I}$, a revocation time

$T \in \mathbf{T}$, the current revocation list $\mathbf{RL}$, and a state ST as input, it outputs an updated $\mathbf{RL}$ by adding ID as a revoked user at time T.

We have a basic consistency requirement that for any $(mpk, msk) \leftarrow \mathbf{Setup}(1^\kappa, N)$, $m \in \mathbf{M}$, all possible state ST, and a revocation list $\mathbf{RL}$, if $ID \in \mathbf{I}$ is not revoked before or at time $T \in \mathbf{T}$, then for $(sk_{ID}, ST) \leftarrow \mathbf{Extract}(mpk, msk, ID, ST)$, $ku_T \leftarrow \mathbf{KeyUpdate}(mpk, msk, T, \mathbf{RL}, ST)$, and $dk_{ID,T} \leftarrow \mathbf{DKeyGen}(mpk, sk_{ID}, ku_T)$, the following equation holds.

$$\mathbf{Decrypt}(mpk, dk_{ID,T}, \mathbf{Encrypt}(mpk, ID, T, m)) = m$$

The property of indistinguishability under adaptively chosen identity and chosen plaintext attack (IND-ID-CPA) is considered a basic requirement for provably secure IBE schemes. For RIBE scheme, we define indistinguishability under adaptively chosen revocable identity and chosen plaintext attack (IND-RID-CPA) by the following game between an adversary and a challenger. Note that the security model captures realistic threats including decryption key exposure [13].

Definition 6. *Let Π be a RIBE scheme, we say that Π is IND-RID-CPA secure if any PPT adversary $\mathcal{A}$ has negligible advantage in this following experiment:*

$$\mathrm{Exp}_{\Pi,\mathcal{A}}^{IND-RID-CPA}(1^\kappa, N)$$

$$(mpk, msk, \mathbf{RL}, st) \leftarrow \mathbf{Setup}(1^\kappa, N),$$

$$(m_0, m_1, ID^*, T^*, ST) \leftarrow \mathcal{A}^{\mathcal{O}}(Find, mpk) \text{ such that } |m_0| = |m_1|.$$

$$b \xleftarrow{\$} \{0,1\}, c^* \leftarrow \mathbf{Encrypt}(mpk, ID^*, T^*, m_b),$$

$$b' \leftarrow \mathcal{A}^{\mathcal{O}}(Guess, c^*, ST),$$

return 1 if $b' = b$ and 0 otherwise.

The adversary $\mathcal{A}$'s advantage is defined as follows.

$$Adv_{\Pi,\mathcal{A}}^{IND-RID-CPA}(\kappa, N) = |\Pr[\mathrm{Exp}_{\Pi,\mathcal{A}}^{IND-RID-CPA}(1^\kappa, N) = 1] - \frac{1}{2}|.$$

In the above experiment, $\mathcal{O}$ is a set of oracles defined as follows.

- **Extract Oracle**: For $ID \in \mathbf{I}$, it runs **Extract**$(mpk, msk, ID, ST) \rightarrow (sk_{ID}, ST)$, then returns sk_{ID} and update state ST.
- **KeyUpdate Oracle**: For $T \in \mathbf{T}$, it runs **KeyUpdate**$(mpk, msk, T, \mathbf{RL}, ST) \rightarrow ku_T$, then returns ku_T.
- **Revoke Oracle**: For $ID \in \mathbf{I}$ and $T \in \mathbf{T}$, it runs **Revoke**$(mpk, ID, T, \mathbf{RL}, ST) \rightarrow \mathbf{RL}$, then returns the updated revocation list $\mathbf{RL}$.

- **DKeyGen Oracle**: For $ID \in \mathbf{I}$ and $T \in \mathbf{T}$, it runs **Extract** $(mpk, msk, ID, ST) \rightarrow sk_{ID}$ and **DKeyGen**$(mpk, sk_{ID}, ku_T) \rightarrow dk_{ID,T}$, then returns $dk_{ID,T}$.

The adversary $\mathcal{A}$ is allowed to query above oracles with the following restrictions:

- **KeyUpdate Oracle** and **Revoke Oracle** can be queried on time which is greater than or equal to the time of all previous queries, i.e. the adversary is allowed to query only in non-decreasing order of time.
- **Revoke Oracle** cannot be queried on time T if **KeyUpdate Oracle** was queried on T.
- If **Extract**(ID^*) was queried, then **Revoke**(ID^*, T) must be queried for $T \leq T^*$.
- **DKeyGen Oracle** cannot be queried on time T before **KeyUpdate Oracle** was queried on T.
- **KeyGen**(ID^*, T^*) cannot be queried.

This definition naturally extends to the chosen ciphertext scenario where the adversary is further granted access to a **Decrypt Oracle** that, on input of a ciphertext c and a pair (ID,T), it returns $m \in \mathbf{M}$ or $\bot$ by running **Decrypt**$(mpk, dk_{ID,T}, c)$. Of course, **Decrypt Oracle** cannot be queried on the ciphertext c^* for the pair (ID^*, T^*).

Our Construction

In this section, we propose an efficient and provable secure RIBE scheme by exploiting Lewko and Waters IBE scheme [9] and KUNode algorithm.

Setup The PKG runs composite order bilinear group generator $\mathcal{G}(1^\kappa) \rightarrow (n = p_1 p_2 p_3, \mathbf{G}, \mathbf{G}_T, \hat{e})$, chooses $g, u_1, u_2, h \xleftarrow{\$} \mathbf{G}_{p_1}$ and $\alpha \xleftarrow{\$} \mathbf{Z}_n$. The PKG publishes the public system parameters as follows.

$$mpk = \{n, g, u_1, h, u_2, \hat{e}(g,g)^\alpha\}.$$

The master secret keys are α and a generator of $\mathbf{G}_{p_3}$.

Extract The PKG chooses an unassigned leaf η from $\mathbb{T}$ at random, and stores ID in the node η. For each node $\theta \in \mathrm{Path}(\eta)$, PKG performs as follows.

- Recall g_θ if it was defined. Otherwise, $g_\theta \xleftarrow{\$} \mathbf{G}_{p_1}$ and store $(g_\theta, \tilde{g}_\theta = g^\alpha / g_\theta)$ in the node θ.
- Choose $r_\theta \xleftarrow{\$} \mathbf{Z}_n$ and $R_3, R'_3, R''_3 \xleftarrow{\$} \mathbf{G}_{p_3}$ at random. Note that we can get a random elements of $\mathbf{G}_{p_3}$ by taking a generator of $\mathbf{G}_{p_3}$ and raising it to random exponents modulo n.
- Compute $(K_1, K_2, K_3) = (g^{r_\theta} R_3, u_2^{r_\theta} R'_3, g_\theta (u_1^{ID} h)^{r_\theta} R''_3)$.
- Return $sk_{ID} = \{(K_1, K_2, K_3)\}_{\theta \in \mathrm{Path}(\eta)}$.

KeyUpdate The PKG parses $ST = \mathbb{T}$, and performs the following steps for each node $\theta \in \mathrm{KUNode}(\mathbb{T}, \mathbf{RL}, T)$.

- Retrieve $\tilde{g}_\theta$ (note that $\tilde{g}_\theta$ is always pre-defined in the **Extract** algorithm).
- Choose $s_\theta \xleftarrow{\$} \mathbf{Z}_n$ and $Q_3, Q'_3, Q''_3 \xleftarrow{\$} \mathbf{G}_{p_3}$.
- Compute $(U_1, U_2, U_3) = (g^{s_\theta} Q_3, u_1^{s_\theta} Q'_3, \tilde{g}_\theta (u_2^T h)^{s_\theta} Q''_3)$.
- Return $ku_T = \{(U_1, U_2, U_3)\}_{\theta \in \mathrm{KUNode}(\mathbb{T}, \mathbf{RL}, T)}$.

DKeyGen User parses $sk_{ID} = \{(\theta, D_1, D_2, D_3)\}_{\theta \in \mathbf{J}_1}$ and $ku_T = \{(\theta, U_1, U_2, U_3)\}_{\theta \in \mathbf{J}_2}$. If $\mathbf{J}_1 \cap \mathbf{J}_2 = \emptyset$, then outputs error symbol $\perp$. Otherwise, user chooses $\theta \in \mathbf{J}_1 \cap \mathbf{J}_2$ and $r \xleftarrow{\$} \mathbf{Z}_n$ and outputs

$$dk_{ID,T} = (D_1, D_2) = (K_1 U_1 g^r, K_2^T U_2^{ID} K_3 U_3 (u_1^{ID} u_2^T h)^r)$$

Encrypt A sender chooses a random integer $t \xleftarrow{\$} \mathbf{Z}_n$ and outputs

$$C_0 = M\hat{e}(g,g)^{\alpha t}, C_1 = (u_1^{ID} u_2^T h)^t, C_2 = g^t.$$

Decrypt The receiver parses $C = (C_0, C_1, C_2)$ and $dk_{ID,T} = (D_1, D_2)$ and outputs

$$C_0 \frac{\hat{e}(D_2, C_2)}{\hat{e}(D_1, C_1)}$$

Revoke Let η be the leaf node associated with ID. The PKG updates the revocation list by $\mathbf{RL} \leftarrow \mathbf{RL} \cup \{(\eta, T)\}$ and returns the updated revocation list.

The correctness of our RIBE construction can be verified as follow.

$$\frac{\hat{e}(D_2, C_2)}{\hat{e}(D_1, C_1)} = \frac{\hat{e}(K_2^T U_2^{ID} K_3 U_3 (u_1^{ID} u_2^T h)^r, g^t)}{\hat{e}(K_1 U_1 g^r, (u_1^{ID} u_2^T h)^t)}$$

$$= \frac{\hat{e}(g_\theta \tilde{g}_\theta (u_1^{ID} u_2^T h)^{r_\theta + s_\theta + r} R_3'' Q_3'' Q_3'^{ID} R_3'^T, g^t)}{\hat{e}(g^{r_\theta + s_\theta + r} R_3 Q_3, (u_1^{ID} u_2^T h)^t)}$$

$$= \hat{e}(g_\theta \tilde{g}_\theta, g^t)$$

$$= \hat{e}(g,g)^{\alpha t}$$

Security Proofs

To prove the security of our RIBE scheme, we first define three additional structures: semi-functional ciphertexts, semi-functional private keys and semi-functional update keys. For the semi-functional type, we let g_2 denote a fixed generator of the subgroup $\mathbf{G}_{p_2}$.

- **Semi-functional Ciphertext**: A normal ciphertext $C' = (C_0', C_1', C_2')$ is first generated by the encryption algorithm. It then chooses $x, z_c \xleftarrow{\$} \mathbf{Z}_n$ and sets:

$$C_0 = C_0', C_1 = C_1' g_2^{x z_c}, C_2 = C_2' g_2^x.$$

- The semi-functional ciphertext is $C = (C_0, C_1, C_2)$.

- **Semi-functional Private Key**: A normal private key $sk_{ID}' = \{(K_1', K_2', K_3')\}_{\theta \in \text{Path}(\eta)}$ is generated by the private key generation algorithm for an identity ID. It then chooses $\gamma, z_k, z_k' \xleftarrow{\$} \mathbf{Z}_n$ and sets:

$$K_1 = K_1' g_2^\gamma, K_2 = K_2' g_2^{z_k' k \gamma}, K_3 = K_3' g_2^{\gamma z_k}.$$

- The semi-functional private key is $sk_{ID} = \{(K_1, K_2, K_3)\}_{\theta \in \text{Path}(\eta)}$.

- **Semi-functional Update Key**: A normal update key $ku_T' = \{(U_1', U_2', U_3')\}_{\theta \in \text{KUNode}(\mathbb{T}, \mathbf{RL}, T)}$ is generated by the update key generation algorithm. It then chooses $\lambda, z_u, z_u' \xleftarrow{\$} \mathbf{Z}_n$ and sets:

$$U_1 = U_1' g_2^\lambda, U_2 = U_2' g_2^{z_u' u \lambda}, U_3 = U_3' g_2^{\lambda z_u}.$$

- The semi-functional update key is $ku_T = \{(U_1, U_2, U_3)\}_{\theta \in \text{KUNode}(\mathbb{T}, \mathbf{RL}, T)}$.

- **Semi-functional Decryption Key**: A normal decryption key $dk_{ID,T}' = (D_1', D_2')$ is generated by the decryption key generation algorithm. It then chooses $\rho, z_d \xleftarrow{\$} \mathbf{Z}_n$ and sets:

$$D_1 = D_1' g_2^\rho, D_2 = D_2' g_2^{z_d \rho}.$$

- The semi-functional decryption key is $dk_{ID,T} = (D_1, D_2)$.

Note that when a semi-functional decryption key is used to decrypt a semi-functional ciphertext, the decryption algorithm will compute the blinding factor multiplied by the additional term $\hat{e}(g_2, g_2)^{x\rho(z_d - z_c)}$. If $z_d = z_c$, decryption will still work. In this case, the decryption key is nominally semi-functional. In our proof, normal decryption keys are generated by normal subkeys of private keys and normal subkeys of update keys, while semi-functional decryption keys are generated by semi-functional subkeys of private keys and normal subkeys of update key, or normal subkeys of private keys and semi-functional subkeys of update keys.

There are two types of adversaries in simulation. Type-I adversary issues private key queries on the challenge identity ID^*, but the challenge identity should be revoked before the challenge time T^*; Type-II adversary will never issue private key queries on the challenge identity. Obviously, if a RIBE scheme is secure against Type-I adversary, it is definitely secure against Type-II adversary. For this reason, we only consider Type-I adversary in the following security proofs.

Denote by q_{sk} and q_{ku} the number of private key queries for non-challenge identities and update key queries for non-challenge time issued by an adversary, respectively. Denote by ℓ the maximum node number a private key involves, and those nodes are not on the path from the root node to the challenge node η^*.

We give our proof as a sequence of games, which are defined in the order as follows.

- $Game_A$: The actual RIBE security game, where all private keys, update keys, decryption keys and the challenge ciphertext are normal.
- $Game_R$: The restricted game, is the actual security game except that adversary can not issue private key queries for $ID = ID^* \bmod p_2$ and update key queries for $T = T^* \bmod p_2$. Note that adversary can issue private key queries for $ID = ID^* \bmod n$, but ID^* should be revoked before T^*.
- $Game_{i,j}^{sk}$: The restricted security game where the challenge ciphertext, all ℓ subkeys of first $i-1$ private keys and all first j subkeys $sk_{ID,\theta}$ of the i-th private key sk_{ID} are semi-functional, while all subkeys of the rest private keys and all subkeys of update keys are normal. Here $0 \leq j \leq \ell$, $1 \leq i \leq q_{sk}$ and $\theta \notin Path(\eta^*)$.
- $Game_k^{ku}$: The restricted security game where the challenge ciphertext, all ℓ subkeys of all private keys, and subkeys $ku_{T,\theta}$ of the first k update key ku_T are semi-functional, while the rest subkeys of q_{sk} private key and the rest subkeys of q_{sk} update keys are normal. Here $\theta \in Path(\eta^*)$. It is obvious that $Game_{q_{sk},\ell}^{sk} = Game_0^{ku}$.
- $Game_F$: The final game, is the same as security game $Game_{q_{ku}}^{ku}$ except that the challenge ciphertext is a semi-functional encryption of a random message.

Next, we prove the indistinguishability of those games by following lemmas.

Lemma 1. *Suppose there exists an algorithm A such that $Adv_A^{Game_A} - Adv_A^{Game_R} = \epsilon$, then we can build an algorithm B with advantage $\frac{\epsilon}{2}$ in breaking Assumption 2.*

Proof. Given $g, X_1 X_2, X_3, Y_2 Y_3$, algorithm B can simulate $Game_A$ with A. Assume that A produces identities ID and ID^* such that $ID \neq ID^* \bmod n$ and p_2 divides $ID - ID^*$ with probability ϵ (If A fails to do this, B simply guesses at random). B uses these identities to produce a nontrivial factor of n by computing $a = \gcd(ID - ID^*, n)$. Set $b = \frac{n}{a}$, and consider the following three cases:

- Case 1 one of a,b is p_1, and the other is $p_2 p_3$
- Case 2 one of a,b is p_2, and the other is $p_1 p_3$
- Case 3 one of a,b is p_3, and the other is $p_1 p_2$

B can determine if Case 1 has occurred by testing if either of $(Y_2 Y_3)^a$ or $(Y_2 Y_3)^b$ is the identity element. If this happens, we will suppose that $a = p_1$ and $b = p_2 p_3$ without loss of generality. B can then learn whether T has a $\mathbf{G}_{p_2}$ component or not by testing if $\hat{e}(T^a, X_1 X_2)$ is the identity element. If it is not, then T has a $\mathbf{G}_{p_2}$ component.

B can determine if Case 2 has occurred by testing if either of $(X_1 X_2)^a$ or $(X_1 X_2)^b$ is the identity element. Assuming that B has already ruled out Case 1 and neither of them is the identity element, then Case 2 has occurred. B can learn which of a,b is equal to $p_1 p_3$ by testing which of g^a, g^b is the identity. Without loss of generality, we assume that $a = p_2$ and $b = p_1 p_3$. Then, B can learn whether T has a $\mathbf{G}_{p_2}$ component or not by testing if T^b is the identity element. If it is not, then T has a $\mathbf{G}_{p_2}$ component.

B can determine that Case 3 has occurred when the tests for both Cases 1 and Case 2 fail. It can learn which of a,b is equal to p_3 by testing which of X_3^a, X_3^b is the identity. Without loss of generality, we assume that $a = p_3$. B can learn whether T has a $\mathbf{G}_{p_2}$ component or not by testing whether $\hat{e}(T^a, Y_2 Y_3)$ is the identity. If it is not, then $\mathbf{G}_{p_2}$ has a $\mathbf{G}_{p_2}$ component.

This completes the proof. $\qquad\square$

Lemma 2. *Suppose there exists an algorithm A such that $Adv_A^{Game_R} - Adv_A^{Game_{0,0}^{sk}} = \epsilon$, then we can build an algorithm B with advantage ϵ in breaking Assumption 1.*

Proof. B first receives g, X_3, L, then simulates $Game_R$ or $Game_0$ with A. B chooses $\alpha, a_1, b, a_2 \xleftarrow{\$} Z_n$, sets public parameters as $g = g$, $u_1 = g^{a_1}$, $u_2 = g^{a_2}$, $h = g^b$, and sends the public parameters to A.

- When B is asked to provide a update key with time period T. For each node $\theta \in KUNode(\mathbb{T}, \mathbf{RL}, T)$, B performs the following steps.

  — Retrieve $\tilde{g}_\theta$ (Note that $\tilde{g}_\theta$ is always pre-defined in the **Extract** algorithm).
  — Choose $s_\theta, t_\theta, t'_\theta, t''_\theta \xleftarrow{\$} Z_n$.
  — Compute $(U_1, U_2, U_3) = (g^{s_\theta} X_3^{t_\theta}, u_1^{s_\theta} X_3^{t'_\theta}, \tilde{g}_\theta (u_2^T h)^{s_\theta} X_3^{t''_\theta})$.
  — Return $ku_T = \{(U_1, U_2, U_3)\}_{\theta \in KUNode(\mathbb{T}, \mathbf{RL}, T)}$.

- When B is asked for a private key with identity ID. For each node $\theta \in Path(\eta)$ where η is the leaf node assigned to ID, B performs the following steps.

  — Recall g_θ if it was defined. Otherwise, $g_\theta \xleftarrow{\$} \mathbf{G}_{p_1}$ (We can do this by by taking the generator of $\mathbf{G}_{p_1}$, g, and raising it to random exponents modulo n) and store $(g_\theta, \tilde{g}_\theta = g^\alpha / g_\theta)$ in the node θ.
  — Choose $r_\theta, y_\theta, y'_\theta, y''_\theta \xleftarrow{\$} Z_n$.
  — Compute $(K_1, K_2, K_3) = (g^{r_\theta} X_3^{y_\theta}, u_2^{r_\theta} X_3^{y'_\theta}, g_\theta (u_1^{ID} h)^{r_\theta} X_3^{y''_\theta})$.
  — Return $sk_{ID} = \{(K_1, K_2, K_3)\}_{\theta \in Path(\eta)}$.

- When B is asked for a decryption key with identity ID and time period T, then B successively runs the **Extract** algorithm, **KeyUpdate** algorithm and **DKeyGen** algorithm.

A sends B two message, M_0 and M_1, and a challenge identity, ID^*, challenge time period, T^*. B chooses $\beta \in \{0,1\}$ randomly. The ciphertext is formed as follows.

$$C_0 = M_\beta \hat{e}(L,g)^\alpha, \quad C_1 = L^{z_c}, \quad C_2 = L.$$

This implicitly sets g^s equal to the $\mathbf{G}_{p_1}$ part of L. If $L \in G_{p_1 p_2}$, then this is a semi-functional ciphertext with $z_c = a_1 ID^* + a_2 T^* + b$. We note that the value of z_c modulo p_2 is not correlated with the values of a and b modulo p_1, so z_c is properly distributed. If $L \in \mathbf{G}_{p_1}$, this is a normal ciphertext. Hence, simulator B can use the output of A to distinguish between these possibilities for L.

This completes the proof. $\qquad\square$

Lemma 3. *Suppose there exists an algorithm A such that $Adv_A^{Game_{k,k'-1}^{sk}} - Adv_A^{Game_{k,k'}^{sk}} = \epsilon$, then we can build an algorithm B with advantage ϵ in breaking Assumption 2.*

Proof. $\mathcal{B}$ first receives $g, X_1 X_2, X_3, Y_2 Y_3, L$, and picks $\alpha, a_1, b, a_2 \xleftarrow{\$} \mathbf{Z}_n$, then $\mathcal{B}$ sets the public parameters as $g = g$, $u_1 = g^{a_1}$, $h = g^b$, $u_2 = g^{a_2}$, $\hat{e}(g,g)^\alpha$ and sends the public parameters to $\mathcal{A}$.

- When $\mathcal{A}$ issues the i-th private key query for all subkeys corresponding to the challenge identity, or subkeys that associated with nodes are not on the path from the node associated with challenge identity to the root node, $\mathcal{B}$ generates normal private keys by calling the normal private key generation algorithm. Otherwise, $\mathcal{B}$ generate the j-th subkey, associated with those ℓ subkeys, of the i-th private key as follows.

  1. For $i < k \vee (i = k \wedge j \leq k')$ and $\theta \in \text{Path}(\eta)$

     — Recall g_θ if it was defined. Otherwise, $g_\theta \xleftarrow{\$} \mathbf{G}_{p_1}$ and store $(g_\theta, \tilde{g}_\theta = g^\alpha / g_\theta)$ in the node θ.
     — Choose $r_\theta, y_\theta, y_\theta', y_\theta'' \xleftarrow{\$} \mathbf{Z}_n$ randomly.
     — Compute $(K_1, K_2, K_3) = (g^{r_\theta}(Y_2 Y_3)^{y_\theta}, u_2^{r_\theta}(Y_2 Y_3)^{y_\theta'},$ $g_\theta(u_1^{\text{ID}} h)^{r_\theta}(Y_2 Y_3)^{y_\theta''})$.
     — Return $sk_{\text{ID}} = \{(K_1, K_2, K_3)\}_{\theta \in \text{Path}(\eta)}$.

  2. For $i = k \wedge j = k'$ and $\theta \in \text{Path}(\eta)$,

     — Recall g_θ if it was defined. Otherwise, $g_\theta \xleftarrow{\$} \mathbf{G}_{p_1}$ and store $(g_\theta, \tilde{g}_\theta = g^\alpha / g_\theta)$ in the node θ.
     — Choose $w, w' \xleftarrow{\$} \mathbf{Z}_n$ randomly.
     — Compute $(K_1, K_2, K_3) = (L, L^{a_2} X_3^{w'}, g_\theta L^{z_k} X_3^w)$.
     — Return $sk_{\text{ID}} = \{(K_1, K_2, K_3)\}_{\theta \in \text{Path}(\eta)}$.

  3. For $i > k \vee (i = k \wedge j > k')$, $\mathcal{B}$ generates normal private keys by calling the normal private key generation algorithm.

- When $\mathcal{A}$ issues a update key query with time period T, then $\mathcal{B}$ generates normal update keys by calling the normal update key generation algorithm.
- When $\mathcal{A}$ issues a a decryption key query with identity ID and time period T, then $\mathcal{B}$ successively runs the **Extract** algorithm, **KeyUpdate** algorithm, and **DKeyGen** algorithm.

At some point $\mathcal{A}$ sends two messages, M_0 and M_1, a challenge identity ID^*, and a challenge time period T^* to $\mathcal{B}$. $\mathcal{B}$ sets $\beta \in \{0,1\}$ randomly. The challenge ciphertext is formed as follows.

$$C_0 = M_\beta \hat{e}(X_1 X_2, g)^\alpha, \quad C_1 = (X_1 X_2)^{z_c}, C_2 = X_1 X_2.$$

We note that this sets $g^s = X_1$ and $z_c = a_1 \text{ID}^* + a_2 \text{T}^* + b$. Since $f(\text{ID}, \text{T}) = a_1 \text{ID} + a_2 \text{T} + b$ is a pairwise independent function modulo p_2, as long as $\text{ID} \neq \text{ID}^* \bmod p_2$ and $\text{T} \neq \text{T}^* \bmod p_2$, z_k and z_c will seem randomly distributed to $\mathcal{A}$.

If $L \in \mathbf{G}_{p_1 p_3}$, then $\mathcal{B}$ has properly simulated $\text{Game}_{k,k'-1}^{\text{sk}}$. If $L \in \mathbf{G}$, then $\mathcal{B}$ has properly simulated $\text{Game}_{k,k'}^{\text{sk}}$. Hence, $\mathcal{B}$ can use the output of $\mathcal{A}$ to distinguish between these possibilities for L.

This completes the proof. $\qquad\square$

Lemma 4. *Suppose there exists an algorithm $\mathcal{A}$ such that $Adv_\mathcal{A}^{\text{Game}_{k,\ell}^{\text{sk}}} - Adv_\mathcal{A}^{\text{Game}_{k+1,0}^{\text{sk}}} = \epsilon$, then we can build an algorithm $\mathcal{B}$ with advantage ϵ in breaking Assumption 2.*

Proof. This proof is analogous to the proof of lemma 3. $\qquad\square$

Lemma 5. *Suppose there exists an algorithm $\mathcal{A}$ such that $Adv_\mathcal{A}^{\text{Game}_{k-1}^{\text{ku}}} - Adv_\mathcal{A}^{\text{Game}_k^{\text{ku}}}$, then we can build an algorithm $\mathcal{B}$ with advantage ϵ in breaking Assumption 2.*

Proof. $\mathcal{B}$ first receives $g, X_1 X_2, X_3, Y_2 Y_3, L$, and picks $\alpha, a_1, b, a_2 \xleftarrow{\$} \mathbf{Z}_n$, then $\mathcal{B}$ sets the public parameters as $g = g$, $u_1 = g^{a_1}$, $h = g^b$, $u_2 = g^{a_2}$, $\hat{e}(g,g)^\alpha$ and sends the public parameters to $\mathcal{A}$.

- When $\mathcal{A}$ issues private key query for the challenge identity or subkeys that associated with nodes are not on the path from the node associated with challenge identity to the root node, $\mathcal{B}$ generates normal private keys by calling the normal private key generation algorithm. Otherwise, for each node $\theta \in \text{Path}(\eta)$, $\mathcal{B}$ performs as follows.

  — Recall g_θ if it was defined. Otherwise, $g_\theta \xleftarrow{\$} \mathbf{G}_{p_1}$ and store $(g_\theta, \tilde{g}_\theta = g^\alpha / g_\theta)$ in the node θ.
  — Choose $r_\theta, y_\theta, y_\theta', y_\theta'' \xleftarrow{\$} \mathbf{Z}_n$ randomly.
  — Compute $(K_1, K_2, K_3) = (g^{r_\theta}(Y_2 Y_3)^{y_\theta}, u_2^{r_\theta}(Y_2 Y_3)^{y_\theta'},$ $g_\theta(u_1^{\text{ID}} h)^{r_\theta}(Y_2 Y_3)^{y_\theta''})$.
  — Return $sk_{\text{ID}} = \{(K_1, K_2, K_3)\}_{\theta \in \text{Path}(\eta)}$.

- When $\mathcal{A}$ issues the update key query for the challenge time period, $\mathcal{B}$ generates normal update keys by calling the normal update key generation algorithm. Otherwise, $\mathcal{B}$ performs as follows.

  1. For $i < k$. When $\theta \in \text{KUNode}(\mathbb{T}, \mathbf{RL}, \text{T}) \wedge \theta \notin \text{Path}(\eta^*)$, $\mathcal{B}$ calls the normal update key generation algorithm. When $\theta \in \text{KUNode}(\mathbb{T}, \mathbf{RL}, \text{T}) \wedge \theta \in \text{Path}(\eta^*)$, $\mathcal{B}$ acts as follow. Note that there is only one node that satisfies this condition in each update node set.

     — Retrieve $\tilde{g}_\theta$.
     — Choose $s_\theta, t_\theta, t_\theta', t_\theta'' \xleftarrow{\$} \mathbf{Z}_n$.
     — Compute $(U_1, U_2, U_3) = (g^{s_\theta}(Y_2 Y_3)^{t_\theta}, u_1^{s_\theta}(Y_2 Y_3)^{t_\theta'},$ $\tilde{g}_\theta(u_2^{\text{T}} h)^{s_\theta}(Y_2 Y_3)^{t_\theta''})$.
     — Return $ku_{\text{T}} = \{(U_1, U_2, U_3)\}_{\theta \in \text{KUNode}(\mathbb{T}, \mathbf{RL}, \text{T})}$.

  2. For $i = k$. When $\theta \in \text{KUNode}(\mathbb{T}, \mathbf{RL}, \text{T}) \wedge \theta \notin \text{Path}(\eta^*)$, $\mathcal{B}$ generates normal update keys by calling the normal update key generation algorithm. When $\theta \in \text{Path}(\eta^*)$, $\mathcal{B}$ performs as follows.

     — Retrieve $\tilde{g}_\theta$.
     — Choose $s_\theta, w_\theta, w_\theta' \xleftarrow{\$} \mathbf{Z}_n$.
     — Compute $(U_1, U_2, U_3) = (L, L^{a_1} X_3^{w_\theta'}, \tilde{g}_\theta L^{z_u}(X_3)^{w_\theta})$.
     — Return $ku_{\text{T}} = \{(U_1, U_2, U_3)\}_{\theta \in \text{KUNode}(\mathbb{T}, \mathbf{RL}, \text{T})}$.

     — Here we note that $z_u = a_2 \text{T} + b$ and $\text{T} \neq \text{T}^*$, therefore both $z_u = a_2 \text{T} + b$ and $z_c = a_1 \text{ID}^* + a_2 \text{T}^* + b$ seem random in adversary's view. If $\text{T} = \text{T}^*$, namely we transform update key with time period T^*, then we can not ensure that $z_u = a_2 \text{T}^* + b$ and $z_c = a_1 \text{ID}^* + a_2 \text{T}^* + b$ seem random in adversary's view.

  3. For $i > k$. When $\theta \in \text{KUNode}(\mathbb{T}, \mathbf{RL}, \text{T})$, $\mathcal{B}$ generates normal update keys by calling the normal update key generation algorithm.

- When $\mathcal{B}$ is asked for a decryption key with identity ID and time period T, $\mathcal{B}$ successively runs the **Extract** algorithm, **KeyUpdate** algorithm and **DKeyGen** algorithm.

At some point $\mathcal{A}$ sends two messages, M_0 and M_1, a challenge identity ID^*, and a challenge time period T^* to $\mathcal{B}$. $\mathcal{B}$ sets $\beta \in \{0,1\}$ randomly. The challenge ciphertext is formed as follows.

$$C_0 = M_\beta \hat{e}(X_1 X_2, g)^\alpha, \; C_1 = (X_1 X_2)^{zc}, \; C_2 = X_1 X_2.$$

If $L \in \mathbf{G}_{p_1 p_3}$, then $\mathcal{B}$ has properly simulated Game'_{k-1}. If $L \in \mathbf{G}$, then $\mathcal{B}$ has properly simulated Game'_k. Hence, $\mathcal{B}$ can use the output of $\mathcal{A}$ to distinguish between these possibilities for L.

This completes the proof.

$\square$

Lemma 6. *Suppose there exists an algorithm $\mathcal{A}$ such that $Adv_\mathcal{A}^{\text{Game}^{ku}_{q_{ku}}} - Adv_\mathcal{A}^{\text{Game}_F}$, then we can build an algorithm $\mathcal{B}$ with advantage ϵ in breaking Assumption 3.*

Proof. $\mathcal{B}$ first receives $g, g^\alpha X_2, X_3, g^s Y_2, Z_2, L$, chooses $a, b, a', b' \xleftarrow{\$} \mathbf{Z}_n$, then $\mathcal{B}$ sets the public parameters as $g = g$, $u_1 = g^{a_1}$, $h = g^b$, $u_2 = g^{a_2}$, $\hat{e}(g,g)^\alpha = \hat{e}(g^\alpha X_2, g)$ and sends the public parameters to $\mathcal{A}$.

- When $\mathcal{A}$ issues private key queries with the challenge identity or nodes on the path from challenge identity node to root node, $\mathcal{B}$ generates normal private keys by calling the normal private key generation algorithm. Otherwise, for each node $\theta \in \text{Path}(\eta)$, $\mathcal{B}$ performs as follows.

  — Recall g_θ if it was defined. Otherwise, $g_\theta \xleftarrow{\emptyset} \mathbf{G}_{p_1}$ and store $(g_\theta, \tilde{g}_\theta = 1/g_\theta)$ in the node θ.
  — Choose $r_\theta, z_\theta, z'_\theta, z''_\theta, y_\theta, y'_\theta, y''_\theta \xleftarrow{\$} \mathbf{Z}_n$ randomly.
  — Compute $(K_1, K_2, K_3) = (g^{r_\theta} Z_2^{z_\theta} X_3^{y_\theta}, u_2^{r_\theta} Z_2^{z_\theta} X_3^{y_\theta},$
    $g^\alpha X_2 g_\theta (u_1^{ID} h)^{r_\theta} Z_2^{z''_\theta} X_3^{y''_\theta})$.
  — Return $sk_{ID} = \{(K_1, K_2, K_3)\}_{\theta \in \text{Path}(\eta)}$.

- When $\mathcal{A}$ issues update key query with the challenge time period, $\mathcal{B}$ generates normal update keys by calling the normal update key generation algorithm. Otherwise, $\mathcal{B}$ performs as follows.

  — If $\theta \notin \text{Path}(\eta^*)$, $\mathcal{B}$ generates normal update keys by calling the normal update key generation algorithm.
  — If $\theta \in \text{Path}(\eta^*)$, $\mathcal{B}$ performs the following steps. Note that there is only one such node in each time period T.

    * Retrieve $\tilde{g}_\theta$ (note that $\tilde{g}_\theta$ is always pre-defined in the **Extract** algorithm).
    * Choose $s_\theta, v_\theta, v'_\theta, v''_\theta, w_\theta, w'_\theta, w''_\theta \xleftarrow{\$} \mathbf{Z}_n$.
    * Compute $(U_1, U_2, U_3) = (g^{s_\theta} Z_2^{v_\theta} X_3^{w_\theta}, u_1^{s_\theta} Z_2^{v'_\theta} X_3^{w'_\theta},$
      $g^\alpha X_2 \tilde{g}_\theta (u_2^T h)^{s_\theta} Z_2^{v''_\theta} X_3^{w''_\theta})$.
    * Return $ku_T = \{(U_1, U_2, U_3)\}_{\theta \in \text{KUNode}(\mathbb{T}, \mathbf{RL}, T)}$.

- When $\mathcal{A}$ issues decryption key query with identity ID and time period T, $\mathcal{B}$ successively runs the **Extract** algorithm, **KeyUpdate** algorithm and **DKeyGen** algorithm.

At some point $\mathcal{A}$ sends two messages, M_0 and M_1, a challenge identity ID^*, and a challenge time period T^* to $\mathcal{B}$. $\mathcal{B}$ sets $\beta \in \{0,1\}$ randomly. The challenge ciphertext is formed as follows.

$$C_0 = M_\beta L, \; C_1 = (g^s Y_2)^{zc}, \; C_2 = g^s Y_2.$$

Here $z_c = a_1 ID^* + u_2 T^* + b$. We note that the value of z_c only matters modulo p_2, whereas $u_1 = g^{a_1}$, $u_2 = g^{a_2}$ and $h = g^b$ are elements of $\mathbf{G}_{p_1}$, so when a_1, a_2 and b modulo n are chosen randomly modulo n, there is no correlation between the values of a_1, a_2 and b modulo p_1 and the value $z_c = a_1 ID^* + a_2 T^* + b \bmod p_2$.

If $L = \hat{e}(g,g)^{\alpha s}$, then this is a properly distributed semi-functional ciphertext with message M_β. If L is a random element of $\mathbf{G}_T$, then this is a semi-functional ciphertext with a random message. Hence, $\mathcal{B}$ can use the output of $\mathcal{A}$ to distinguish between these possibilities for L.

This completes the proof.

$\square$

Theroem 1. *If above lemmas hold, then our RIBE scheme is adaptively secure under assumption 1, 2 and 3. More precisely, for any adversary $\mathcal{A}$ that makes at most q_1 private key queries, q_2 update key queries against our RIBE scheme, we have*

$$Adv_\mathcal{A}^{\text{RIBE}} \leq \frac{1}{2} q_1 q_2 (q_1 Adv_{\mathcal{G},\mathcal{A}}^{SGD2}(\kappa) \log N_{max} + q_2 Adv_{\mathcal{G},\mathcal{A}}^{SGD2}(\kappa) + Adv_{\mathcal{G},\mathcal{A}}^{SGD3}(\kappa))$$

Proof. If above assumptions hold, then we have shown by the previous lemmas that the real security game is indistinguishable from $\text{Game}_{\text{Final}}$, in which the value of β is information-theoretically hidden from the adversary. Hence the adversary can attain no advantage in breaking our RIBE scheme.

This completes the proof.

Conclusion

In this paper, we presented a scalable RIBE scheme with decryption key exposure resilience in the composite order group setting by combining Lewko and Waters' IBE scheme and complete subtree method, and proved our proposed RIBE scheme to be adaptive-ID secure by employing the recent dual system encryption methodology. Compared to existing adaptive-ID secure LV-RIBE scheme and SE-RIBE scheme, our proposed RIBE construction is more efficient in term of ciphertext size, public parameters size and decryption cost at price of a little looser security reduction. In our future work, we will focus on constructing an adaptive-ID secure RIBE scheme with decryption key exposure resilience in the prime order group setting and devising an adaptive-ID secure RIBE scheme that can resist decryption key exposure attack with a tighter reduction.

Acknowledgments

The authors would like to thank the anonymous reviewers of this paper for his/her objective comments and helpful suggestions while at the same time helping us to improve the English spelling and grammar throughout the manuscript.

Author Contributions

Conceived and designed the experiments: CW YL. Performed the experiments: CW YL XX KZ. Analyzed the data: CW YL. Contributed

reagents/materials/analysis tools: CW YL XX KZ. Wrote the paper: CW YL. Constructed the scheme: CW YL XX KZ. Proved the security of scheme: CW YL.

References

1. Shamir A (1985) Identity-based cryptosystems and signature schemes. In: Advances in Cryptology- CRYPTO 84. California, USA: Springer Berlin Heidelberg, volume 196 of Lecture Notes in Computer Science, pp. 47–53.
2. Boneh D, Franklin M (2001) Identity-based encryption from the weil pairing. In: Advances in Cryptology - CRYPTO 2001. California, USA: Springer Berlin Heidelberg, volume 2139 of Lecture Notes in Computer Science, pp. 213–229.
3. Canetti R, Goldreich O, Halevi S (2004) The random oracle methodology, revisited. Journal of the ACM 51: 557–594.
4. Canetti R, Halevi S, Katz J (2004) Chosen-ciphertext security from identity-based encryption. In: Advances in Cryptology - EUROCRYPT 2004. Interlaken, Switzerland: Springer Berlin Heidelberg, volume 3027 of Lecture Notes in Computer Science, pp. 207–222.
5. Boneh D, Boyen X (2004) Efficient selective-id secure identity-based encryption without random oracles. In: Advances in Cryptology - EUROCRYPT 2004. Interlaken, Switzerland: Springer Berlin Heidelberg, volume 3027 of Lecture Notes in Computer Science, pp. 223–238.
6. Waters B (2005) Efficient identity-based encryption without random oracles. In: Advances in Cryptology - EUROCRYPT 2005. Aarhus, Denmark: Springer Berlin Heidelberg, volume 3494 of Lecture Notes in Computer Science, pp. 114–127.
7. Gentry C (2006) Practical identity-based encryption without random oracles. In: Advances in Cryptology - EUROCRYPT 2006. St. Petersburg, Russia: Springer Berlin Heidelberg, volume 4004 of Lecture Notes in Computer Science, pp. 445–464.
8. Waters B (2009) Dual system encryption: Realizing fully secure ibe and hibe under simple assumptions. In: Advances in Cryptology - CRYPTO 2009. California, USA: Springer Berlin Heidelberg, volume 5677 of Lecture Notes in Computer Science, pp. 619–636.
9. Lewko A, Waters B (2010) New techniques for dual system encryption and fully secure hibe with short ciphertexts. In: Theory of Cryptography - TCC 2010.

Zurich, Switzerland: Springer Berlin Heidelberg, volume 5978 of Lecture Notes in Computer Science, pp. 455–479.
10. Zhang Y, Wang L, Zhang Y, Li X (2012) Toward a temporal network analysis of interactive wifiusers. Europhysics Letters 98: 68002.
11. Boldyreva A, Goyal V, Kumar V (2008) Identity-based encryption with efficient revocation. In: Proceedings of the 15th ACM Conference on Computer and Communications Security. Virginia, USA: ACM, CCS 2008, pp. 417–426.
12. Libert B, Vergnaud D (2009) Adaptive-id secure revocable identity-based encryption. In: Topics in Cryptology - CT-RSA 2009. California, USA: Springer Berlin Heidelberg, volume 5473 of Lecture Notes in Computer Science, pp. 1–15.
13. Seo J, Emura K (2013) Revocable identity-based encryption revisited: Security model and construction. In: Public Key Cryptography - PKC 2013. Nara, Japan: Springer Berlin Heidelberg, volume 7778 of Lecture Notes in Computer Science, pp. 2161–234.
14. Park S, Lee K, Lee D (2013). New constructions of revocable identity-based encryption from multilinear maps. Cryptology ePrint Archive. Report 2013/880.
15. Lee K, Lee D, Park J (2014). Efficient revocable identity-based encryption via subset difference methods. Cryptology ePrint Archive. Report 2014/132.
16. Sahai A, Waters B (2005) Fuzzy identity based encryption. In: Advances in Cryptology - EUROCRYPT 2005. Aarhus, Denmark: Springer Berlin Heidelberg, volume 3494 of Lecture Notes in Computer Science, pp. 457–473.
17. Naor D, Naor M, Lotspiech J (2001) Revocation and tracing schemes for stateless receivers. In: Advances in Cryptology - CRYPTO 2001. California, USA: Springer Berlin Heidelberg, volume 2139 of Lecture Notes in Computer Science, pp. 41–62.
18. Libert B, Vergnaud D (2009) Towards black-box accountable authority ibe with short ciphertexts and private keys. In: Public Key Cryptography - PKC 2009. California, USA: Springer Berlin Heidelberg, volume 5443 of Lecture Notes in Computer Science, pp. 235–255.

23

Efficient Unrestricted Identity-Based Aggregate Signature Scheme

Yumin Yuan[1]*, **Qian Zhan[2]**, **Hua Huang[3]**

1 School of Applied Mathematics, Xiamen University of Technology, Xiamen, China, **2** University of Science and Technology Beijing, Beijing, China, **3** University of Xiamen, Xiamen, China

Abstract

An aggregate signature scheme allows anyone to compress multiple individual signatures from various users into a single compact signature. The main objective of such a scheme is to reduce the costs on storage, communication and computation. However, among existing aggregate signature schemes in the identity-based setting, some of them fail to achieve constant-length aggregate signature or require a large amount of pairing operations which grows linearly with the number of signers, while others have some limitations on the aggregated signatures. The main challenge in building efficient aggregate signature scheme is to compress signatures into a compact, constant-length signature without any restriction. To address the above drawbacks, by using the bilinear pairings, we propose an efficient unrestricted identity-based aggregate signature. Our scheme achieves both full aggregation and constant pairing computation. We prove that our scheme has existential unforgeability under the computational Diffie-Hellman assumption.

Editor: Francesco Pappalardo, University of Catania, Italy

Funding: The authors have no support or funding to report.

Competing Interests: The authors have declared that no competing interests exist.

* Email: yuanymp@163.com

Introduction

An aggregate signature [1] is a useful primitive that allows anyone to compress n individual signatures, say $\sigma_1, \ldots, \sigma_n$ where σ_i is a signature from user with identity ID_i on message m_i for $1 \leq i \leq n$, into a single (shorter) signature even if these signatures are on the same message or are produced by the same signer. The main goal in the design of such protocols is to reduce the costs on storage, communication and computation. Informally, the length of the aggregate signature should be constant, independent of the number of messages and signers. The resulting signature can convince a verifier that the user ID_i indeed signed the corresponding message m_i for all $i{:}1 \leq i \leq n$. This primitive is useful in many real-world applications (which involve multiple signatures on multiple messages generated by multiple users) especially in environments with low-band-width communication, low-storage and low computability. Typical applications for such schemes are Wireless sensor networks (WSNs) since WSNs are resource constraint: limited power supply, bandwidth for communication, memory space [2]. For example, in an environment monitoring network, the sensors record measurements from the environment, sign its data and send them to a monitoring center. The center aggregates these data and the signatures to save storage [3]. Aggregate signature scheme can also be applied to vehicular communications [4], many-to-one authentication [5], electronic transactions [6] and cloud computing [7] to enhance the efficiency of verification and reduce the communication over-head.

Boneh, Gentry, Lynn and Shacham [1] first defined of aggregate signature and presented a concrete aggregate signature which was constructed under traditional public key cryptography (PKC). In traditional PKC, a digital signature provides the authenticity of a signed message with respect to a public key, while the authenticity of the public key with respect to a signer is contained in a certificate provided by a certificate authority (CA). Whenever a verifier wants to verify a signature, he has first to verify the corresponding certificate. Therefore, aggregate signature working under traditional PKC requires heavy management, communication and computation cost to achieve authenticity of all signers' public keys, making the scheme both space and time inefficient, especially when the number of signers is large. To reduce this burden, Shamir [8] proposed the concept of identity-based public key cryptography (IB-PKC). The IB-PKC requires a trusted third party, typically called a "Private Key Generator" (PKG) which serves a similar role to the CA in a PKC system, to generate system parameters and user's private key. In an identity-based cryptosystem, only the PKG has a traditional public key, and the public key of each user is derived directly from his identity information, such as his email address. The direct derivation of users' public keys in these infrastructures eliminates the need for the certificate and some of the problem associated with them. In an identity-based signature (IBS) scheme, to generate valid signatures of a signer with the identity ID, one needs to know the private key of ID, while verifier can directly use the signer's identity ID and the PKG's public key to verify signatures. This advantage of identity-based aggregate signature (IBAS) becomes more compelling when we consider multiple signers. In this setting, when all signers have their secret keys issued by the same private key generator (PKG), the verifier needs only one traditional public key (of the PKG) to verify multiple identity-based signatures on multiple messages.

To shorten the length of signatures and to avoid the authentication of the public keys, Cheon et al. [9] presented the first identity-based aggregate signature (IBAS) scheme. To date several IBAS schemes have been proposed [9–20]. However, some of them have additional restrictions conditions on aggregation step. The schemes [10,11] do not support simultaneous aggregation, which only allow each signer to aggregate his signature to a previously aggregated signature in turn. The scheme [12] requires that all signers participating in aggregation have to agree upon a common random string which was never used by any of the signers. Secure use of the scheme [12] is restricted to the aggregation of signatures from distinct signers. The scheme [13] requires interactive communication between signers to generate an aggregate signature, and hence increases the communication complexity.

Among existing unrestricted aggregate signature schemes (which enable any user to freely aggregate multiple signatures) in the identity-based setting [9,14–20], all but one of them [9,14–19] are able to achieve only partial aggregation and not full aggregation, i.e., the length of the resulting aggregate signature grows with the number of aggregated individual signatures, which departs from the main goals of aggregate signatures. Obviously, such schemes are impractical for some wireless network scenarios. Only the scheme in [20] achieves constant-length aggregate signature. But this scheme requires a large number of pairing operations in which the number of pairing operations in the aggregate signature verification algorithm is proportional to the number of aggregated individual signatures.

In this paper, we construct an efficient IBAS scheme without any restriction. The proposed protocol is based on bilinear pairings. The new scheme simultaneously achieves constant-length aggregate signature and constant pairing operations during signature verification, and is shown to be existentially unforgeable against adaptive chosen message attacks under the computational Diffie-Hellman assumption in the random oracle model.

Preliminaries

In this section, we review the basic concept of bilinear pairings and the complexity assumption on which our scheme relies.

2.1 Bilinear pairings

Let G_1 be a cyclic additive group of prime order q and G_2 be a cyclic multiplicative group of the same order. A map $e : G_1 \times G_1 \rightarrow G_2$ is called a bilinear pairing if it satisfies the following properties:

1. Bilinear: $e(aP,bQ)=e(P,Q)^{ab}$ for all $P,Q\in G_1$ and all $a,b\in Z_q$.
2. Non-degeneracy: There exist $P,Q\in G_1$ such that $e(P,Q)\neq 1$.
3. Computable: There is an efficient algorithm to compute $e(P,Q)$ for any $P,Q\in G_1$.

2.2 Related complexity assumption

Definition 1. A function $: N \rightarrow R$ is said to be negligible if, for every positive polynomial $poly(\cdot)$ there exists an integer $K>0$ such that for all $k>K$ it holds.

$$(k) < \frac{1}{poly(k)}$$

Otherwise, we call non-negligible.

Definition 2. Let G be a group of prime order $q\geq 2^k$ where k is a security parameter. Computational Diffie-Hellman (CDH)

Problem is that given three elements $P,aP,bP\in G$ for unknown randomly chosen $a,b\in Z_q$, compute abP.

Let $\mathcal{A}$ be a probabilistic polynomial-time algorithm. The advantage of $\mathcal{A}$ in solving the CDH problem in group G is defined to be.

$$Adv_{\mathcal{A}}^{CDH} = \Pr[\mathcal{A}(P,aP,bP)=abP]$$

where the probability is taken over the uniformly and independently chosen instance with a given security parameter k and over the random choices of $\mathcal{A}$.

The CDH assumption states that for every probabilistic polynomial-time algorithm $\mathcal{A}$, $Adv_{\mathcal{A}}^{CDH}$ is negligible.

Definitions and Security Models

We first review the definition and the formal security model for IBS schemes. Then we describe the definition and the formal security model for IBAS schemes.

3.1 Formal model of identity-based signature schemes

3.1.1 Definition of identity-based signature schemes. An identity-based signature (IBS) scheme is a tuple of probabilistic polynomial-time algorithms (**Setup**, **Extract**, **Sign**, **Verify**). The description of each algorithm is as follows.

- **Setup**. This algorithm is run by a private key generator (PKG). It takes a security parameter k as input and outputs a master key msk and a list of system parameters $params$. The system parameters will be publicly known while the master key will be known to the PKG only.
- **Extract**. This algorithm takes a user's identity ID_i, a system parameters $params$ and a master key msk as input, and outputs the user's private key D_i. Usually, this algorithm is run by the PKG. The PKG sends D_i to the user ID_i through a secure channel.
- **Sign**. This algorithm takes a system parameters $params$, a message m_i, an identity ID_i and corresponding private key D_i as input, and outputs an individual signature σ_i on the message m_i for the user with identity ID_i. This algorithm is executed by the user ID_i.
- **Verify**. This algorithm takes a system parameters $params$, an identity ID_i, a message m_i and an individual signature σ_i as input, and outputs 1 or 0 for valid or invalid, respectively.

3.1.2 Security requirements for identity-based signature schemes. We review the usual security model of IBS [17,21] which is an extension of the usual notion of existential unforgeability under chosen-message attacks [22]. The security model mainly captures the following two attacks:

1. Adaptive chosen message attack: It allows an adversary to ask the signer to sign any message of its choice in an adaptive way, it can adapt its queries according to previous answers;
2. Adaptive chosen identity attack: It allows the adversary to forge a signature with respect to an identity chosen by the adversary.

Finally, the adversary could not provide a new message-signature pair with non-negligible advantage. The security for an IBS scheme is defined via the following game.

Game I (Unforgeability of IBS). This game is performed between a challenger $\mathcal{C}$ and an adversary $\mathcal{A}$ with respect to scheme (**Setup**, **Extract**, **Sign**, **Verify**), which captures the attacking scenario where a dishonest user who is allowed to have access to the signing oracle for any desired messages and identities, but he is not able to obtain victim's private key, and wants to create a new valid signature.

Setup. Taking a security parameter k as input, the challenger $\mathcal{C}$ runs the Setup algorithm to obtain a master secret key msk and system parameters $params$. Then $\mathcal{C}$ sends $params$ to the adversary $\mathcal{A}$, but keeps msk secret.

Queries. $\mathcal{A}$ makes a polynomially bounded number of the following queries in an adaptive manner.

- *Extraction queries.* Given an identity ID_i, the challenger returns the private key D_i corresponding to ID_i.
- *Signature queries.* Given an identity ID_i and a message m_i, $\mathcal{C}$ returns an individual signature σ_i on m_i with respect to ID_i.

Forgery. Eventually, $\mathcal{A}$ outputs an identity-based signature σ^* on a message m^* for an identity ID^*. We say that $\mathcal{A}$ wins Game I, iff.

(1) σ^* is a valid signature on message m^* under identity ID^*.
(2) ID^* has never been queried during the Extraction queries. And (ID^*, m^*) has never been queried during the Signature queries.

The advantage of $\mathcal{A}$ is defined as the probability that it wins in Game I.

Definition 3. An IBS scheme is said to satisfy the property of existential unforgeability against adaptive chosen-message attack and adaptive chosen-identity attack (EUF-IBS-CMA) if there is no probabilistic polynomial-time adversary $\mathcal{A}$ with non-negligible advantage in Game I.

3.2 Formal model of identity-based aggregate signature schemes

3.2.1 Definition of identity-based signature aggregate signature schemes. An IBAS scheme involves a PKG, an aggregating multiset of n users and an aggregate signature generator. It allows the generator to compress any n individual signatures along with a multiset of n message-identity pairs, which include on the same message from the same signer, into a single signature. An IBAS scheme is a tuple (**Setup, Extract, Sign, Verify, Agg, AggVerify**) based on the IBS scheme (**Setup, Extract, Sign, Verify**) by six polynomial-time algorithms with the following functionality:

- **Setup, Extract, Sign, Verify.** These algorithms are the same as those in the IBS scheme in Section 3.1.1.
- **Agg.** This algorithm is run by an aggregate signature generator and allows the generator to compress multiple individual signatures into an aggregate signature. It takes a system parameters $params$, n signatures $(\sigma_1, \ldots, \sigma_n)$ with each signature σ_i under an identity ID_i on a message m_i as input, and outputs an aggregate signature σ_{Agg} for the multiset of message-identity pairs $\{(m_1, \text{ID}_1), \ldots, (m_n, \text{ID}_n)\}$.
- **AggVerify.** This algorithm takes an aggregate signature σ_{Agg}, a multiset of n message-identity pairs $\{(m_1, \text{ID}_1), \ldots, (m_n, \text{ID}_n)\}$ as input, and outputs 1 if the aggregate signature is valid, or 0 otherwise.

3.2.2 Security requirements for identity-based aggregate signature schemes. An IBAS scheme should be secure against traditional existential forgery under adaptive chosen-message attack and adaptive chosen-identity attack. An unforgeability of IBAS is defined via the following unforgeability game which is performed between a challenger and an adversary. The adver-

sary's goal is the existential forgery of an aggregate signature. Informally, it should be computationally infeasible for any adversary to produce a forgery. We formalize the security model as follows.

Game II (Unforgeability of IBAS). This game is performed between a challenger $\mathcal{C}$ and an adversary $\mathcal{A}$ with respect to scheme (**Setup, Extract, Sign, Verify, Agg, AggVerify**), which captures the attacking scenario where a dishonest user who is allowed to have access to the signing oracle for any desired messages and identities, wants to create a forgery without knowing the private keys of all the signers.

Setup. Taking a security parameter k as input, the challenger $\mathcal{C}$ runs the Setup algorithm to obtain a master secret key msk and system parameters $params$. Then $\mathcal{C}$ sends $params$ to the adversary $\mathcal{A}$, but keeps msk secret.

Queries. $\mathcal{A}$ makes a polynomially bounded number of the following queries in an adaptive manner.

- *Extraction queries.* Given an identity ID_i, the challenger returns the private key D_i corresponding to ID_i.
- *Signature queries.* Given an identity ID_i and a message m_i, $\mathcal{C}$ returns a signature σ_i.

Forgery. Eventually, $\mathcal{A}$ outputs a multiset of n message-identity pairs $\{(m_1^*, \text{ID}_1^*), \ldots, (m_n^*, \text{ID}_n^*)\}$ and an aggregate signature σ_{Agg}^*. We say that $\mathcal{A}$ wins the game, iff.

(1) σ_{Agg}^* is a valid aggregate signature on message-identity pairs $\{(m_1^*, \text{ID}_1^*), \ldots, (m_n^*, \text{ID}_n^*)\}$, i.e., AggVerify$(params, \sigma_{\text{Agg}}^*, \{(m_1^*, \text{ID}_1^*), \ldots, (m_n^*, \text{ID}_n^*)\}) = 1$.
(2) At least one of the identities, without loss of generality, say $\text{ID}_i^* \in I_{\text{ID}}^* = (\text{ID}_1^*, \ldots, \text{ID}_n^*)$ has never been queried during the Extraction queries. And (ID^*, m^*) has never been queried during the Signature queries.

The advantage of $\mathcal{A}$ is defined as the probability that it wins in Game II.

Definition 4. An IBAS scheme is said to satisfy the property of existential unforgeability against adaptive chosen-message attack and an adaptive chosen-identity attack (EUF-IBAS-CMA) if there is no probabilistic polynomial-time adversary $\mathcal{A}$ with non-negligible advantage in Game II.

A New Identity-Based Signature Scheme

In this section, we propose a provably secure identity-based signature scheme which can be used to construct an unrestricted IBAS scheme.

4.1 Proposed basic identity-based signature scheme

The proposed IBS scheme consists of the following four concrete algorithms:

- **Setup.** Given a security parameter k, the private key generator (PKG) chooses a prime q, a cyclic additive group G_1 and a cyclic multiplicative group G_2 of prime order q, a random generator P in G_1, an admissible pairing $e: G_1 \times G_1 \to G_2$, and two cryptographic hash functions $H_1: \{0,1\}^* \to G_1$ and $H_2: \{0,1\}^* \to Z_q^*$. It also randomly chooses $s_1, s_2 \in Z_q^*$, sets the master key $msk = (s_1, s_2)$, and computes $P_1 = s_1 P$ and $P_2 = s_2 P$. Finally, it broadcasts the system parameters, $params = (q, G_1, G_2, e, P, P_1, P_2, H_1, H_2)$.

- **Extract.** For a given identity ID_i, the PKG computes $Q_i = H_1(ID_i)$ and sets this user's private key D_i to be $(s_1Q_i, s_2Q_i) = (D_{i,1}, D_{i,2})$.

- **Sign.** To sign a message m_i with private key D_i, the signer with ID_i chooses $r_i \in Z_q^*$ and computes $U_i = r_iP$, $h_i = H_2(m_i, ID_i)$, $V_i = h_iD_{i,1} + r_iP_1$ and $W_i = D_{i,2} + r_iP_2$. The signature on m_i is $\sigma_i = (U_i, V_i, W_i)$.

- **Verify.** Upon receipt of an individual signature $\sigma_i = (U_i, V_i, W_i)$, the verifier computes $Q_i = H_1(ID_i)$ and $h_i = H_2(m_i, ID_i)$, and checks $e(V_i, P) = e(h_iQ_i + U_i, P_2)$ and $e(W_i, P) = e(Q_i + U_i, P_2)$. If both the equations hold, then the individual signature $\sigma_i = (U_i, V_i, W_i)$ is valid.

4.2 Security proof of the IBS scheme

The following theorem shows that in the random oracle model, our IBS scheme is existentially unforgeable against adaptive chosen-message attack and adaptive chosen-identity attack under the assumption that CDH problem in G_1 is intractable. Concretely, we show that if a probabilistic polynomial-time bounded adversary exists who can break our IBS scheme with non-negligible probability , we will be able to solve the computational Diffie-Hellman problem with non-negligible probability ', which contradicts the CDH assumption.

Theorem 1. In the random oracle model, if there exists a polynomial-time adversary $\mathcal{A}$ who has an advantage in forging a signature of our IBS scheme in an attack modeled by Game I of Section 3.12 within a time at most t, after asking at most q_{H_i} times H_i ($i = 1, 2$) queries, q_E times Extraction queries and q_S times Signature queries, then the CDH problem in G_1 can be solved within time.

$$t' < 2(t + t_M(q_{H_1} + 2q_E + 4q_S)) + t_M + 2t_I$$

and with probability

$$\epsilon' \geq \frac{1}{(e(q_E+1))^2 q_{H_2}}(\epsilon - \frac{1}{q})^2 - \frac{1}{q}$$

where e is the base of the natural logarithm, t_M is the time of computing a scalar multiplication in G_1, and t_I is the time of computing an inversion in Z_q^*.

Proof. Using a similar proof technique in [17,23,24], we are going to construct a probabilistic polynomial-time algorithm $\mathcal{C}$ to solve the CDH problem by using the adversary $\mathcal{A}$ who can break our IBS scheme. Suppose that $\mathcal{C}$ is given an random instance of the CDH problem $(P, aP, bP) \in G_1^3$ for some unknown $a, b \in Z_q^*$. The task of $\mathcal{C}$ is to compute abP. $\mathcal{C}$ plays the role of $\mathcal{A}$'s challenger in Game I and interacts with $\mathcal{A}$ as follows:

Setup. $\mathcal{C}$ simulates the Setup algorithm as follows:

1. Choose a random value $s \in Z_q^*$ and sets $P_1 = aP$, $P_2 = sP$, where $a \in Z_q$ is unknown to $\mathcal{C}$.

2. Choose a cyclic group G_2 of prime order q, a bilinear map $e : G_1 \times G_1 \to G_2$.

3. Choose two hash functions H_1 and H_2 as random oracle.

4. Send the system parameters $params = (q, G_1, G_2, e, P, P_1, P_2, H_1, H_2)$ to $\mathcal{A}$.

Query. Proceeding adaptively, $\mathcal{A}$ is allowed to query the random oracles H_1, H_2, Extraction oracle and Signature oracle in

a polynomial number of times. $\mathcal{C}$ simulates these oracles for $\mathcal{A}$ as follows:

H_1 queries. At any time, $\mathcal{A}$ can issue an H_1 query on an identity. To avoid collision and consistently respond to H_1 queries, $\mathcal{C}$ maintains a list L_{H_1} of tuples (ID, t, c, Q) which stores his responses to such queries. This list is initially empty. When querying the oracle H_1 on ID, $\mathcal{C}$ responds as follows:

1. If the query ID already appears on L_{H_1} in a tuple $(ID, t, c, Q), \mathcal{C}$ responds to $\mathcal{A}$ with $H_1(ID) = Q$.

2. Otherwise, $\mathcal{C}$ picks a random coin $c \in \{0, 1\}$ with $Pr[c = 0] = \delta$.

   - If $c = 0$, then $\mathcal{C}$ randomly chooses $t \in Z_q^*$ and computes $Q = t(bP)$.

   - If $c = 1$, then $\mathcal{C}$ randomly chooses $t \in Z_q^*$ and computes $Q = tP$.

$\mathcal{C}$ adds the tuple (ID, t, c, Q) to the L_{H_1} and responds to $\mathcal{A}$ with $H_1(ID) = Q$.

H_2 queries. To respond to H_2 queries, $\mathcal{C}$ maintains a list L_{H_2} of tuples (ID, m, h), which is initially empty. When querying the oracle H_2 on (ID, m), $\mathcal{C}$ responds as follows:

1. If the query (ID, m) already appears on L_{H_2} in a tuple (ID, m, h), $\mathcal{C}$ responds to $\mathcal{A}$ with $H_2(m, ID) = h$.

2. Otherwise, $\mathcal{C}$ randomly chooses $h \in Z_q^*$, adds the tuple (ID, m, h) to L_{H_2} and responds to $\mathcal{A}$ with $H_2(m, ID) = h$.

Extraction queries. When $\mathcal{A}$ queries the private key corresponding to ID, $\mathcal{C}$ first finds the corresponding tuple (ID, t, c, Q) from the L_{H_1}.

1. If $c = 0$, $\mathcal{C}$ fails and aborts the simulation.

2. Otherwise, $\mathcal{C}$ computes $D_1 = tP_1$ and $D_2 = tP_2$, and responds to $\mathcal{A}$ with $D = (D_1, D_2)$.

Signature queries. When $\mathcal{A}$ makes a Signature query on m for ID, $\mathcal{C}$ randomly chooses $r \in Z_q^*$ and computes $U = (rP - hQ)$, $V = rP_1$. Then, $\mathcal{C}$ computes $W = s(Q + U)$ and responds to $\mathcal{A}$ with signature $\sigma = (U, V, W)$.

Forgery. Eventually, $\mathcal{A}$ outputs a forged signature $\sigma^* = (U^*, V^*, W^*)$ on a message m^* for an identity ID^*. $\mathcal{C}$ finds the corresponding tuple (ID^*, t^*, c^*, Q^*) from the L_{H_1}. If $c^* \neq 0$, $\mathcal{C}$ fails and aborts. Otherwise, by applying the forking lemma [25], after replaying $\mathcal{A}$ with the same random tape but different choices of oracle H_2, $\mathcal{C}$ can get two valid signatures $(m^*, ID^*, h^*, \sigma^* = (U^*, V^*, W^*))$ and $(m^*, ID^*, h'^*, \sigma'^* = (U^*, V'^*, W^*))$ such that $h^* \neq h'^*$. Now, since both forgeries are valid, we have

$$e(V^*, P) = e(h^*Q^* + U^*, P_1)$$

$$e(V'^*, P) = e(h'^*Q^* + U^*, P_1)$$

Combining the above two equations, we have

$$e(V^* - V'^*, P) = e((h^* - h'^*)Q^*, P_1)$$

Note that $P_1 = aP$ and $H_1(ID^*) = Q^* = t^*(bP)$ since $c^* = 0$. We have

$$e(V^* - V'^*, P) = e((h^* - h'^*) \cdot t^* bP, aP)$$

$$= e((h^* - h'^*)t^* abP, P)$$

which implies

$$V^* - V'^* = (h^* - h'^*)t^* abP$$

Consequently, $\mathcal{C}$ could solve the CDH by computing

$$abP = (h^* - h'^*)^{-1} t^* - 1(V^* - V'^*)$$

Probability analysis. It remains to evaluate the probability $'$ that $\mathcal{C}$ solves the given instance of CDH. First, we analyze the events needed for $\mathcal{C}$ to succeed before the rewinding.

- E_1: $\mathcal{C}$ does not abort as a result of any of $\mathcal{A}$'s Extraction query.
- E_2: $\mathcal{A}$ generates a valid and nontrivial aggregate signature forgery σ^*_{Agg} for $\{(m^*_1, \mathrm{ID}^*_1), \cdots, (m^*_n, \mathrm{ID}^*_n)\}$.
- E_3: Event E_2 occurs and $c^*_1 = 0$, $c^*_j = 1$ for $2 \le j \le n$, where for each i, c^*_i is the c-component of the tuple containing ID_i on the L_{H_1}.

$\mathcal{C}$ succeeds before the rewinding if all of these events occur. The probability $\epsilon = \Pr[E_1 \wedge E_2 \wedge E_3]$ is decomposed as

$$\Pr[E_1 \wedge E_2 \wedge E_3] = \Pr[E_1] \Pr[E_2 | E_1] \Pr[E_3 | E_1 \wedge E_2]$$

The following claims give a lower bound for each of these terms.

Claim 1. The probability that algorithm $\mathcal{C}$ does not abort as a result of $\mathcal{A}$'s Extraction query is at least $(1-\delta)^{q_E}$. Hence we have $\Pr[E_1] = (1-\delta)^{q_E}$.

Proof. Since $\mathcal{A}$ makes at most q_E queries to the Extraction oracle and $\Pr[c=1] = (1-\delta)$, the probability that algorithm $\mathcal{C}$ does not abort as a result of $\mathcal{A}$'s Extraction queries is at least $(1-\delta)^{q_E}$.

Claim 2. If $\mathcal{C}$ does not abort as a result of $\mathcal{A}$'s Extraction query, then $\mathcal{A}$'s view is identical to its view in the real attack. Hence, $\Pr[E_2 | E_1] \ge -1/q$.

Proof. Since the probability that $\mathcal{A}$ generates a valid and nontrivial signature for (m^*, ID^*) without asking H_2 oracle in advance is less than $1/q$, the probability that $\mathcal{A}$ outputs a valid forgery σ^* after querying $H_2(m^*, \mathrm{ID}^*)$ is at least $-1/q$.

Claim 3. The probability that $\mathcal{C}$ does not abort after $\mathcal{A}$ outputs a valid and nontrivial forgery is at least δ. Hence, $\Pr[E_3 | E_1 \wedge E_2] \ge \delta$.

Proof. After $\mathcal{A}$ outputs a valid and nontrivial forgery, algorithm $\mathcal{C}$ does not abort if and only if $c^* = 0$. Since $\Pr[c^* = 0] = \delta$, the probability that $\mathcal{C}$ does not abort is at least δ.

Combining all of the above results, the probability $\epsilon = \Pr[E_1 \wedge E_2 \wedge E_3]$ is at least

$$(1-\delta)^{q_E} \delta \cdot (-\frac{1}{q})$$

Therefore, in the first run of $\mathcal{A}$, $\mathcal{C}$ does not abort with probability.

$$\epsilon \ge (1-\delta)^{q_E} \delta \cdot (-\frac{1}{q})$$

According to the general forking lemma [25], the probability that $\mathcal{C}$ obtains two successful forgeries of $\mathcal{A}$ and does not abort is

$$\epsilon' > \epsilon(\frac{\epsilon}{q_{H_2}} - \frac{1}{q})$$

where $\epsilon = \Pr[E_1 \wedge E_2 \wedge E_3]$. When $\delta = 1/(q_E + 1)$, $(1-\delta)^{q_E}\delta$ is maximized at

$$(1 - \frac{1}{q_E + 1})^{q_E} \frac{1}{q_E + 1}$$

$$\ge \frac{1}{e} \cdot \frac{1}{q_E + 1}.$$

Therefore, the probability of solving the CDH problem is

$$\epsilon' \ge \frac{1}{(e(q_E + 1))^2 q_{H_2}} (\epsilon - \frac{1}{q})^2 - \frac{1}{q}$$

which is non-negligible if is non-negligible.

Algorithm $\mathcal{C}$'s running time is roughly the same as $\mathcal{A}$'s running time plus the time it takes to respond to hash queries, Extraction queries and Signature queries, and the time to transform $\mathcal{A}$'s final forgery into the CDH solution. The H_1 query requires a scalar multiplication. The Extraction query requires two scalar multiplications. The Signature query requires 4 scalar multiplications and the output phase requires a scalar multiplication and two inversions. Hence, the total running time is at most $2(t + t_M(q_{H_1} + 2q_E + 4q_S)) + t_M + 2t_I$.

A New Identity-Based Aggregate Signature Scheme

5.1 Proposed identity-based aggregate signature scheme

Now, we construct an IBAS scheme using our basic IBS scheme constructed in the previous section.

- **Setup, Extract, Sign, Verify.** These algorithms are the same as those in our proposed IBS scheme.
- **Agg.** Begin with n signatures $(\sigma_1, \ldots, \sigma_n)$ along with n message-identity pairs $\{(m_1, \mathrm{ID}_1), \cdots, (m_n, \mathrm{ID}_n)\}$ where $\sigma_i = (U_i, V_i, W_i)$ is the individual signature on message m_i for identity $\mathrm{ID}_i, i = 1, \ldots, n$. The aggregate signature generator computes $U = \sum_{i=1}^{n} U_i$, $V = \sum_{i=1}^{n} V_i$ and $W = \sum_{i=1}^{n} W_i$, and outputs $\sigma_{Agg} = (U, V, W)$ as an aggregate signature for message-identity pairs $\{(m_1, \mathrm{ID}_1), \cdots, (m_n, \mathrm{ID}_n)\}$.
- **AggVerify.** To verify the validity of an aggregate signature $\sigma_{Agg} = (U, V, W)$ for message-identity pairs $\{(m_1, \mathrm{ID}_1), \cdots, (m_n, \mathrm{ID}_n)\}$, the verifier computes $Q_i = H_1(\mathrm{ID}_i)$, $h_i = H_2(m_i, \mathrm{ID}_i)$, for $i = 1, \ldots, n$, and checks.

$$e(V,P)=e(\sum_{i=1}^{n}h_iQ_i+U,P_1)$$

and

$$e(W,P)-e(\sum_{i=1}^{n}Q_i+U,P_2)$$

If both the equations hold, then the aggregate signature σ_{Agg} is valid.

5. 2 Security proof of the IBAS scheme

In this subsection, we are going to prove the security of our identity based aggregate signature scheme. The proof outline is as follows.

We assume on the contrary that our IBAS scheme is not EUF-IBAS-CMA secure. That is, assume there exists a polynomial time bounded adversary $\mathcal{A}$ who can forge a signature in IBAS under the adaptive chosen message and chosen identity attacks. The proof's goal is to show that under this assumption, our IBS scheme is not EUF-IBS-CMA secure.

Theorem 2. If there exists an adversary $\mathcal{A}$ who has an advantage in forging an aggregate signature of our IBAS scheme in the chosen aggregate modeled by Game II within a time at most t, after asking at most q_{H_i} times H_i $(i=1,2)$ queries, q_E times Extraction queries, q_S times Signature queries and at most N signers, then there exists an algorithm which in forging a signature of our IBS scheme in an attack modeled wins Game I within time.

$$t'<t+t_M(q_{H_1}+2q_E+4q_S+2N)$$

and with advantage

$$\epsilon'>\frac{\epsilon}{(q_E+N)e}$$

where e and t_M denote the same quantities as in Theorem 1.

Proof. Here we follow the idea from [17,26,27]. Suppose that $\mathcal{A}$ is a forger who breaks the IBAS scheme. By using $\mathcal{A}$, we will construct an algorithm $\mathcal{C}$ which outputs a forgery of our IBS scheme. Algorithm $\mathcal{C}$ performs the following simulation by interacting with the adversary $\mathcal{A}$.

Setup. It is the same as that described in the proof of Theorem 1.

H_1 queries. To respond to H_1 queries, $\mathcal{C}$ maintains a list L_{H_1} of tuples (ID, t, c, Q), which is initially empty. When $\mathcal{A}$ queries the oracle H_1 on ID, $\mathcal{C}$ responds as follows:

1. If the query ID already appears on the L_{H_1} in a tuple (ID, t, c, Q), $\mathcal{C}$ responds with $H_1(ID)=Q$.
2. Otherwise, $\mathcal{C}$ picks a random coin $c\in\{0,1\}$ with $\Pr[c=0]=\delta$.

- If $c=0$ then $\mathcal{C}$ chooses $t\in Z_q^*$ and computes $Q=t(bP)$.
- If $c=1$ then $\mathcal{C}$ chooses $t\in Z_q^*$ and computes $Q=tP$.

$\mathcal{C}$ adds the tuple (ID, t, c, Q) to the L_{H_1} and responds to $\mathcal{A}$ with $H_1(ID)=Q$.

H_2 queries, Extraction queries, Signature queries. When $\mathcal{A}$ make H_2 queries, Extraction queries, Signature queries, $\mathcal{C}$ responds as those defined in the proof of Theorem 1.

Forgery. Eventually, $\mathcal{A}$ outputs an aggregate signature $\sigma_{Agg}^*=(U^*,V^*,W^*)$ together with $\{(m_1^*,ID_1^*),\cdots,(m_n^*,ID_n^*)\}$.

$\mathcal{C}$ recovers the corresponding tuples $(ID_i^*,t_i^*,c_i^*,Q_i^*)$ from the L_{H_1} and the corresponding tuples (ID_i^*,m_i^*,h_i^*) from the L_{H_2} for all i, $1\leq i\leq n$.

It requires that there exists $k\in\{1,\ldots,n\}$ such that $c_j^*=1$ for $j=1,\ldots,n, j\neq k$, $c_k^*=0$ (without loss of generality, we let $k=1$), $\mathcal{A}$ has not made a query Signature oracle on (ID_1^*,m_1^*) and AggVerify$(params, \sigma_{Agg}^*,\{(m_1^*,ID_1^*),\ldots,(m_n^*,ID_n^*)\})=1$. Therefore, the aggregate signature $\sigma_{Agg}^*=(U^*,V^*,W^*)$ should satisfy the aggregate verification equations.

$$e(V^*,P)=e(\sum_{i=1}^{n}h_i^*Q_i^*+U^*,P_1)$$

$$e(W^*,P)=e(\sum_{i=1}^{n}Q_i^*+U^*,P_2)$$

$\mathcal{C}$ sets $V_j^*=t_j^*h_j^*P_1$ and $W_j^*=sQ_j^*$. Obviously (V_j^*,W_j^*) satisfy the equations $e(V_j^*,P)=e(h_j^*Q_j^*,P_1)$ and $e(W_j^*,P)=e(Q_j^*,P_2)$ for $2\leq j\leq n$. Then, $\mathcal{C}$ constructs as $(V^*-\sum_{j=2}^{n}V_j^*)$ and W'^* as $W^*-\sum_{j=2}^{n}W_j^*$. $\sigma'^*=(U^*,V'^*,W'^*)$ is a valid individual signature on m_1^* for ID_1^* since it satisfies the verification equations as follows:

$$e(V'^*,P)=e(h_1^*Q_1^*+U^*,P_1)$$

$$e(W'^*,P)=e(Q_1^*+U^*,P_2)$$

Finally, $\mathcal{C}$ outputs σ'^* as a forgery of the IBS scheme.

Probability analysis. Similar to the analysis in **Theorem 1**, we analyze three events needed for $\mathcal{C}$ to succeed.

- E_1: $\mathcal{C}$ does not abort as a result of any of $\mathcal{A}$'s Extraction query.
- E_2: $\mathcal{A}$ generates a valid and nontrivial aggregate signature forgery σ_{Agg}^* for $\{(m_1^*,ID_1^*),\cdots,(m_n^*,ID_n^*)\}$.
- E_3: Event E_2 occurs and $c_1^*=0$, $c_j^*=1$ for $2\leq j\leq n$, where for each i, c_i^* is the c-component of the tuple containing ID_i on the L_{H_1}.

$\mathcal{C}$ succeeds if all of these events happen. The probability $\Pr[E_1\wedge E_2\wedge E_3]$ is the same as in Theorem 1

Claim 1. The probability that $\mathcal{C}$ does not abort as a result of $\mathcal{A}$'s Extraction query is at least $(1-\delta)^{q_E}$. Hence, $\Pr[E_1]\geq(1-\delta)^{q_E}$.

Claim 2. If $\mathcal{C}$ does not abort as a result of $\mathcal{A}$'s Extraction query and Signature queries, then $\mathcal{A}$'s view is identical to its view in the real attack. Hence, $'>\frac{}{(q_E+N)e}$.

Claim 3. The probability that $\mathcal{C}$ does not abort after $\mathcal{A}$ outputs a valid and nontrivial forgery is at least $(1-\delta)^{N-1}\cdot\delta$.

Proof. Algorithm $\mathcal{C}$ will abort unless $\mathcal{A}$ generates a forgery such that $c_1^*=0$ and $c_j^*=1$ for $2\leq j\leq n$. Thus, $c_1^*=0$ occurs with probability δ. And the probability that $c_j^* = 1$, for $2 \le j \le n$, is at least $(1-\delta)^{N-1}$. Therefore

$$\Pr[E_3|E_1 \wedge E_2] \ge (1-\delta)^{N-1} \cdot \delta.$$

Combining all of the above results, the advantage $'$ that $\mathcal{C}$ produces the correct answer is at least $\delta(1-\delta)^{q_E}(1-\delta)^{N-1} = \delta(1-\delta)^{q_E+N-1}$ which is maximized at $\delta = 1/(q_E+N)$. Therefore, the advantage $'$ is

$$' \ge (1 - \frac{1}{q_E+N})^{q_E+N-1} \frac{1}{q_E+N}$$

$$' \ge (1 - \frac{1}{q_E+N})^{q_E+N-1} \frac{1}{q_E+N}$$

as required.

With Theorems 1 and 2, we can get the conclusion that the proposed IBAS scheme is secure against adaptively chosen-message and chosen-identity attacks under the hardness assumption of CDH problem in the random oracle model.

5.3 Performance analysis

Computation cost and aggregate signature size are two important parameters affecting the efficiency of an IBAS scheme. In this section, we compare our scheme with the existing unrestricted identity-based aggregate signature schemes [9,14–17,19,20] from the aspects of aggregate signature size and computation cost in signature phase and aggregate signature verify phase, respectively. Detailed comparisons are summarized in Table 1. Here we only consider the costly operations (i.e., pairing operation, MapToPoint hash operation and multiplication operation in G_1) and omit the computational efforts which can be pre-computed. We use notations as follows:

- pair: the time for performing a pairing operation.
- mul_{G_1}: the time for performing a scalar multiplication in group G_1.
- mtp: the time for performing a map-to-point hash operation.
- $|G_1|$: the length of element in group G_1.
- $|m|$: the length of the message m.
- $|ID|$: the length of the identity ID.
- t: the number of distinct signers.
- n: the number of aggregated signatures.

From Table 1, we can see that the aggregate signature length of both of the scheme in [20] and our scheme is the same as that of a single individual signature regardless of the number n of signatures while that of the other schemes is directly proportional to either the number n of signatures or the number t of signers.

We also can observe that although the aggregate signature size overhead of Hohenberger et al.'s scheme [20] is better than that of ours (which is the shortest among the protocols under comparison), their scheme is less efficient in signing and aggregate verifying, which requires $O(|m|)$ pairing operations to generate a signature and $O(n(|m|+|ID|))$ pairing operations to verify an aggregate signature. Our IBAS scheme requires no pairing operations for the signer and only four pairing operations for the verifier. As the pairing computation is the most time consuming in pairing-based cryptosystems [28], the computation overhead in our scheme is much faster than that in the scheme [20]. Therefore, the proposed scheme is more practical.

Conclusions

In this paper, we proposed a new identity-based signature scheme that is provably secure in the random oracle model under the CDH assumption. We constructed an identity-based aggregate signature scheme using our IBS as the base signature scheme. The proposed IBAS enjoys significant advantages: aggregation is very general in that it allows for the aggregation of any multiple signatures from various users on various messages into a single compact signature; the aggregation operation does not require any restricted; AS meets the merit of signatures in ID-PKC which is free from the public key certificate management burden. The most important point is the compared with previous unrestricted IBAS schemes, our proposed scheme is the first IBAS scheme which satisfies both constant length aggregate signature and constant pairing operations. The security analysis has been provided and shown that the proposed schemes are secure against adaptive chosen-message attack and chosen-identity attack in the random oracle model. These features render our IBAS scheme an efficient solution to reduce bandwidth and storage, and are especially attractive for mobile devices like sensors, cell phones and PDAs where communication is more power-expensive than computation and contributes significantly to reducing battery life. Moreover, our scheme can adaptively work as a multi-signature scheme or a proxy signature scheme or a sequential aggregate scheme without any modifications.

Table 1. Comparisons of computation cost and aggregate signature size.

Scheme	Sign Time	AggVerify Time	Aggregate Signature Size
Cheon et al. [9]	1 mul_{G_1}	$(t+1) \text{ pair} + t \text{ mul}_{G_1}$	$(n+1)|G_1|$
Xu et al. [14]	$1 \text{ mul}_{G_1} + 1 \text{ mtp}$	$(n+2) \text{ pair} + n \text{ mtp}$	$(n+1)|G_1|$
Herranz [15]	$1 \text{ mul}_{G_1} + 1 \text{ mtp}$	$(t+1) \text{ pair} + t \text{ mul}_{G_1} + n \text{ mtp}$	$(t+1)|G_1|$
Kar [16]	1 mul_{G_1}	$2 \text{ pair} + t \text{ mul}_{G_1}$	$(2n+1)|G_1|$
Shim [17]	1 mul_{G_1}	$2 \text{ pair} + n \text{ mul}_{G_1}$	$(n+1)|G_1|$
Kang [19]	1 mul_{G_1}	$3 \text{ pair} + t \text{ mul}_{G_1}$	$(n+1)|G_1|$
Hohenberger et al. [20]	$|m| \text{ pair}$	$(n(|m|+|ID|-1)+1) \text{ pair}$	$1 |G_1|$
Our scheme	1 mul_{G_1}	$4 \text{ pair} + t \text{ mul}_{G_1}$	$3|G_1|$

Acknowledgments

The authors would like to thank anonymous reviewers for their constructive suggestions.

References

1. Boneh D, Gentry C, Shacham H, Lynn B (2003) Aggregate and verifiably encrypted signatures from bilinear maps. In: Proc. Advances in Cryptology – EUROCRYPT 2003, Springer LNCS 2656, 416–432.

2. Niu S, Wang C, Yu Z, Cao S (2013) Lossy data aggregation integrity scheme in wireless sensor networks. Computers and Electrical Engineering 39(6):1726–1735.

3. Bellare M, Namprempre C, Neven G (2007) Unrestricted Aggregate Signatures. In: Proc. 34th International Colloquium on Automata, Languages and Programming (ICALP 2007), Springer LNCS 4596, 411–422.

4. Liu JK, Yuen TH, Au MH, Susilo W (2014) Improvements on an authentication scheme for vehicular sensor networks. Expert Systems with Applications 41(5): 2559–2564.

5. Zhang L, Qin B, Wu Q, Zhang F (2010) Efficient many-to-one authentication with certificateless aggregate signatures. Computer Networks 54(14): 2482–2491.

6. Shao Z (2008) Fair exchange protocol of signatures based on aggregate signatures. Computer Communications 31: 1961–1969.

7. Wei L, Zhu H, Cao Z, Dong X, Jia W, et al. (2014) Security and privacy for storage and computation in cloud computing. Information Sciences 258: 371–386.

8. Shamir A (1984) Identity-based cryptosystem and signature scheme. In: Proc. Proceedings of CRYPTO '84 on Advances in Cryptology, Springer LNCS 196, 47–53.

9. Cheon JH, Kim Y, Yoon HJ (2004) A new ID-based signature with batch verification. Cryptology ePrint Archive. Available: http://eprint.iacr.org/2004/131.pdf.

10. Dou B, Chen CH, Zhang H, Xu C (2012) Identity-based sequential aggregate signature scheme based on RSA. International journal of innovative computing information and control 8(9): 6401–6413.

11. Tsai JL, Lo NW, Wu TC (2013) New Identity-Based Sequential Aggregate Signature Scheme from RSA. In: Proc. 2013 International Symposium on Biometrics and Security Technologies. 136–140.

12. Gentry C, Ramzan Z (2006) Identity-based aggregate signature. In: Proc. 9th International Conference on Theory and Practice of Public-Key Cryptography (PKC 2006), Springer LNCS 3958, 257–273.

13. Bagherzandi A, Jarecki S (2010) Identity-based aggregate and multisignature schemes based on RSA. In: Proc. 13th International Conference on Practice and Theory in Public Key Cryptography (PKC 2010), Springer LNCS 6056, 480–498.

14. Xu J, Zhang Z, Feng D (2005) ID-based aggregate signatures from bilinear pairings. In: Proc. 4th International Conference on Cryptology and Network Security (CANS 2005), Springer LNCS 3810,110–119.

15. Herranz J (2006) Deterministic identity-based signatures for partial aggregation. The Computer Journal 49(3): 322–330.

16. Kar J (2012) Provably secure identity-based aggregate signature scheme. In: Proc. 2012 International Conference on Cyber-Enabled Distributed Computing and Knowledge Discover. 137–142.

17. Shim KA (2010) An ID-based aggregate signature scheme with constant pairing computations. The Journal of Systems and Software 83(10): 1873–1880.

18. Selvi SSD, Vivek SS, Shriram J, Rangan CP (2010) Efficient and provably secure identity based aggregate signature schemes with partial and full aggregation. Cryptology ePrint Archive, Available: http://eprint. iacr.org/2010/461.pdf.

19. Kang B (2012) On the security of some aggregate signature schemes. Journal of Applied Mathematics 2012: Article ID 416137.

20. Hohenberger S, Sahai A, Waters B (2013) Full Domain Hash from (Leveled) Multilinear Maps and Identity-Based Aggregate Signatures. In: Proc. 33rd Annual International Cryptology Conference on Advances in Cryptology (CRYPTO 2013), Springer LNCS 8042, 494–512.

21. Cha JC, Cheon JH (2003) An identity-based signature from gap Diffie-Hellman groups. In: Proc. 6th International Workshop on Theory and Practice in Public Key Cryptography (PKC 2003), Springer LNCS 2567, 18–30.

22. Goldwasser S, Micali S, Riverst R (1988) A digital signature scheme secure against adaptive chosen message attacks. SIAM Journal of Computing 17(2): 281–308.

23. Tian H, Chen X, Zhang F, Wei B, Jiang Z, et al. (2013) A non-delegatable strong designated verifier signature in ID-based setting for mobile environment. Mathematical and Computer Modelling 58 (5–6): 1289–1300.

24. He D, Chen Y, Chen J (2013) An efficient certificateless proxy signature scheme without pairing. Mathematical and Computer Modelling 57: 2510–2518.

25. Bellare M, Neven G (2006) Multi-signatures in the plain public-key model and a general forking lemma. In: Proc. Proceedings of the 13th ACM conference on Computer and communications security. 390–399.

26. Xiong H, Guan Z, Chen Z, Li F (2013) An efficient certificateless aggregate signature with constant pairing computations. Information Sciences 219: 225–235.

27. Tu H, He D, Huang B (2014) Reattack of a certificateless aggregate signature scheme with constant pairing computations. The Scientific World Journal 2014: Article ID 343715.

28. He D, Chen J, Hu J (2011) An ID-based proxy signature scheme without bilinear pairings. Annalas of Telecomunications 66: 657–662.

Author Contributions

Contributed reagents/materials/analysis tools: YY QZ. Conceived and designed the experiments: YY QZ. Analyzed the data: YY QZ HH. Wrote the paper: YY QZ HH. Proved the security of the scheme: YY QZ.

24

An Image Encryption Algorithm Utilizing Julia Sets and Hilbert Curves

Yuanyuan Sun[1]*, Lina Chen[2], Rudan Xu[1], Ruiqing Kong[1]

1 College of Computer Science and Technology, Dalian University of Technology, Dalian, China, **2** National Astronomical Observatories, Chinese Academy of Sciences, Beijing, China

Abstract

Image encryption is an important and effective technique to protect image security. In this paper, a novel image encryption algorithm combining Julia sets and Hilbert curves is proposed. The algorithm utilizes Julia sets' parameters to generate a random sequence as the initial keys and gets the final encryption keys by scrambling the initial keys through the Hilbert curve. The final cipher image is obtained by modulo arithmetic and diffuse operation. In this method, it needs only a few parameters for the key generation, which greatly reduces the storage space. Moreover, because of the Julia sets' properties, such as infiniteness and chaotic characteristics, the keys have high sensitivity even to a tiny perturbation. The experimental results indicate that the algorithm has large key space, good statistical property, high sensitivity for the keys, and effective resistance to the chosen-plaintext attack.

Editor: Helmut Ahammer, Medical University of Graz, Austria

Funding: This research is supported by the National Natural Science Foundation of China (No. 61103147, 61075018, 61070098, http://www.nsfc.gov.cn), the National Key Project of Science and Technology of China (No. 2011ZX05039-003-4, http://www.most.gov.cn) and the Fundamental Research Funds for the Central Universities (No. DUT12JB06, http://www.dlut.edu.cn). The funders had no role in study design, data collection and analysis, decision to publish, or preparation of the manuscript.

Competing Interests: The authors have declared that no competing interests exist.

* E-mail: syuan@dlut.edu.cn

Introduction

With the increasingly wide reach of the Internet, communications via Internet are getting more frequent. Due to a large number of threats against communications security, information protection has become an important issue. Especially because digital images contain so much information, security for images is a widespread concern. Nowadays, image encryption has been a focus in the research of information security.

Most conventional encryption algorithms put the emphasis on text data or binary data. Therefore, they have highly computational complexity. Because the digital images have special coding structures and large amounts of data, the conventional encryption algorithm may change the original data format in the image encryption. So, among the popular applications of multimedia, research on image encryption has both theoretical and practical significance.

Currently, there are various kinds of image encryption techniques, including image-scrambling-based techniques, data-processing-based techniques, key-based encryption techniques, etc. Some algorithms are based on certain transformation rules. For instance, Shyu used random grids to accomplish the encryption of secret gray-scale and color images [1]. Some algorithms are proposed according to the characteristics of the image itself, such as Yuen's proposal of a chaos based joint image compression and encryption algorithm using discrete cosine transformation (DCT) and Secure Hash Algorithm-1 (SHA-1) [2]. Combining the encryption with other data processing technologies, Hermassi introduced a new scheme based on joint compression and encryption using the Huffman code [3]. Among the algorithms

utilizing the keys, there has been a great deal of research in chaotic cryptography. For example, Chen produced a key through 3D chaotic cat maps and operated a pixel value with XOR to get the cipher image [4].

In the fractal research field, image encryptions are also explored. Using the fractal set directly as the key is the common method. Kumar proposed a method of encrypting a Mandelbrot set with the RSA method and Elliptical curve [5]. Liu studied a novel fractal cryptographic algorithm based on a fractal model and fractal dimension [6]. Rozouvan encrypted an image with the transformed Mandelbrot set [7]. Lock compressed the original picture for matrix multiplication with the fractal image [8]. Sun used a Mandelbrot set and the Hilbert transformation to generate the random key [9]. Lin encrypted an image by assembling the fractal image additional method and the binary encoding method [10]. Tong proposed an image encryption scheme based on 3D baker with dynamical compound chaotic sequence cipher generator [11].

At the same time, a great deal of analysis has been performed on the image encryption algorithms based on fractal sets or chaos sets. Yuen made a cryptanalysis on secure fractal image coding based on fractal parameter encryption [12]. For some shortcomings in encryption algorithms, Li et al. made the optimal quantitative cryptanalysis of permutation-only multimedia ciphers against plaintext attacks [13] [14].

Many conventional fractal-based encryption methods are combined with fractal coding compression or treat the fractal image as a host image to hide some information, e.g., keys. For the former, fractal coding operation itself may bring the time consumption. This will result in reducing efficiency of the algorithm. For the latter, usually the key length is invariant, which is not flexible and may have some restrictions in the encryption. To meet these challenges, we propose a novel image encryption algorithm. The algorithm uses several parameters to generate the keys with the same size as the plain images and has a good efficiency in the encryption. Firstly, we generate a Julia set and scramble it with the Hilbert curve in bit-level, and then make the scrambled Julia set modulo with the plain image. Finally, the cipher image is obtained by diffusion process. The Julia set is a classical set in fractal theory and can be calculated by several parameters iteratively. For this property, the key is much easier to store and transmit. What's more, the Julia set has the infiniteness and the chaotic features, so tiny changes of the parameters will lead to dramatic changes of the cipher image. In addition, the diffusion process guarantees that if one pixel value changes, then all the pixels will change, which makes the algorithm resist the chosen plaintext attack effectively.

The Algorithm

1 Julia Set

According to the Escape Time Algorithm, a generalized Julia set can be constructed in the complex plane by the mapping function $f(z)=z^m+c,(m\in R,c\in C)$. Studies have shown that the Julia set $J(f)$ is a closure of the repelling periodic points in the polynomial f [15]. The Julia set has sophisticated structures, infinity feature, and self-similarity. When an area of a Julia set border is enlarged, it is still a Julia-like image. What is more, a Julia set has an important feature that f is chaotic on the border of Julia set, that is, f has sensitive dependence relation to the initial conditions [15]. An arbitrary small perturbation can cause drastic changes in the iterated sequence of f. Therefore, we choose the border of the Julia image in the algorithm.

2 Hilbert Scrambling

The two-dimensional Hilbert curves are drawn as follows: divide a square into four squares and start the curve from the southwest corner of the center square to the northwest corner; then go to the northeast center, and finally go to the southeast corner. This is one iteration for a Hilbert curve. If we repeat the above process, we can get a curve that fills the whole square. Considering that the Hilbert curve can fill the square and has been

proven to be a continuous closed curve, we utilize the curve to scramble the Julia image.

It is known that the RGB color model is commonly used for representing and displaying the images on the computer screen. The pixel value in each layer can be represented by eight binary bits. Figure 1 displays the scrambling process, where the odd bits are calculated with the forward pixel along the Hilbert curve and the even bits are calculated with the backward pixel along the curve simultaneously. In Figure 1, the values in R layer of pixels A, B, and C are denoted by $(a_7\,a_6\,a_5\,a_4\,a_3\,a_2\,a_1\,a_0)$, $(b_7\,b_6\,b_5\,b_4\,b_3\,b_2\,b_1\,b_0)$ and $(c_7\,c_6\,c_5\,c_4\,c_3\,c_2\,c_1\,c_0)$ respectively. The odd bits of A are calculated through an AND operation with B, and the even bits are obtained in the same way with C, then the pixel value in R layer of A is reset. The scrambling process is recyclable along the Hilbert curve. Equation (1) shows the scramble function.

$$a_i=\begin{cases} b_i\&a_i, i=1,3,5,7 \\ c_i\&a_i, i=0,2,4,6 \end{cases} \tag{1}$$

Taking R channel for example, the current pixel value of A is 182, 10110110 in binary. B is the forward pixel along the Hilbert curve with the value 154, 10011010 in binary. C is the backward pixel along the curve with the value 62, 00111110 in binary. Applying Equation (1), we can get the new value of A. Its odd bits are $1\times0\times0\times1\times$ and even bits are $\times0\times1\times1\times0$. So the final pixel value of A changes to 150 in decimal after scrambling. Figure 2 shows the pseudocode.

3 Encryption and Diffusion

The final keys are obtained after the Julia set is scrambled by Hilbert curve. Using Equation (2), we encrypt the plain image with the final keys and get a temporary cipher image.

$$e'_{ij}=(e_{ij}+d_{ij}) \bmod l \tag{2}$$

where e_{ij} is the pixel value of (i,j) coordinate in the plain image, e'_{ij} is the pixel value after encryption, and d_{ij} is the pixel value in the final keys. Because the image in the experiments is 256-color, the value of l is 256.

The diffusion algorithm is also an important image encryption process. Based on a single pixel unit having three layers R, G, and

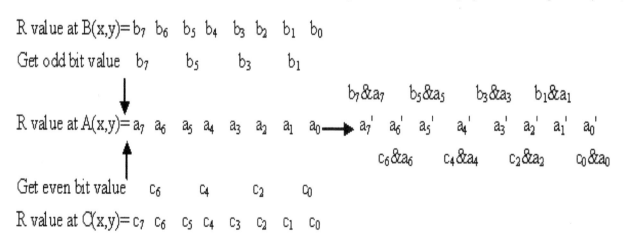

Figure 1. The scrambling process. It is assumed that A, B and C are coordinates in the image, and their pixel values of the R-layer are denoted by $(a_7\,a_6\,a_5\,a_4\,a_3\,a_2\,a_1\,a_0)$, $(b_7\,b_6\,b_5\,b_4\,b_3\,b_2\,b_1\,b_0)$ and $(c_7\,c_6\,c_5\,c_4\,c_3\,c_2\,c_1\,c_0)$ respectively. a_0 is obtain from the AND operation between a_0 and c_0. Other values are in the same way.

```
COLORREF* GetHilbertedJulia(int* step, COLORREF * julia)
{
        int s,fs,bs; // s : current pixel step in Hilbert curve; fs : forward pixel step in the curve ;bs: backward pixel step in the curve
        int k=0;
        COLORREF backcolor=0; // the backward pixel along the Hilbert curve
        COLORREF frontcolor=0;  // the forward pixel along the Hilbert curve
        COLORREF origncolor=0;// the current pixel  before scrambled
        COLORREF* pHilbertJulia // the pixels after scrambled
        for(i=0; i<WIDTH; i++)
        {
                for(j=0; j<HEIGHT; j++)
                {
                        origncolor=julia[j*WIDTH+i]; // the current pixel after scrambled

                        s=hil_s_from_xy(i,j,n); //the step of current pixel in Hilbert curve
                        fs=s+forward step; // the step of forward pixel
                        if(fs>65536)
                                fs=fs%65536;

                        POINT pos=hil_xy_from_s(fs,n,i,j);  // translating the forward pixel Hilbert curve step to coordinate
                        frontcolor=julia[pos.y*WIDTH+pos.x];

                        //ADD operation between the current pixel and the forward pixel in odd bits
                        pHilbertJulia[k] =(origncolor & 170) & ( frontcolor & 170);

                        bs=s-backward step; // the step of forward pixel
                        if(bs<0)
                                bs=bs+65536;

                        pos=hil_xy_from_s(bs,n,i,j);  // translating the backward pixel Hilbert curve step to coordinate
                        backcolor=julia[pos.y*WIDTH+pos.x];

                        //ADD operation between the current pixel and the backward pixel in even bits
                        pHilbertJulia[k]|=(origncolor &85)&( backcolor &85);

                        k++;
                }
        }
        return pHilbertJulia;
}
```

Figure 2. Hilbert scrambling pseudocode.

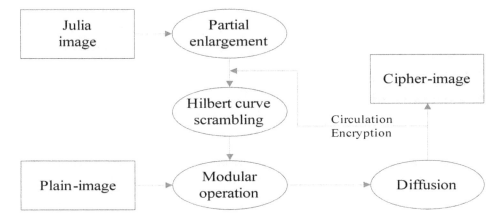

Figure 3. Encryption process. The encryption process can be recycled in the circulation encryption for a better effect. The final encrypted image is the cipher image.

```
COLORREF* GetJulia(double m,double p,double q, double xmin, double xmax, double ymin, double ymax)
{
        int k;   //current iteration times
        double xk,yk,r; // current position of the coordinate and the current radius
        double M=4.0; //radius of the escape
        int exit=0;
        int kmax =100; //max iteration times
        COLORREF* pJuliaCipher=new COLORREF[width*height]; // Julia set

        for(x=0; x<WIDTH; x++)
                for(y=0; y<HEIGHT; y++)
                {
                        currentPoint=GetCurrentPoint(x,y); //record current point
                        k=0;
                        exit=0;
                        while(!exit)
                        {
                                r=GetRadius(currentPoint);  //current radius
                                if(r>M)
                                {
                                        //If current radius is bigger than M, this point is a escape point, choosing a color and recording it
                                        pJuliaCipher[y*height+x]=Cor[c];
                                }
                                else if(k==kmax-1)
                                {
                                        // If the point is not a escape point, record it balck
                                        pJuliaCipher[y*height+x]=BLACK;
                                        exit=1;
                                }
                                nextPoint=currentPoint;
                                k++
                        }
                }
                return pJuliaCipher;
}
```

Figure 4. Julia set generation pseudocode.

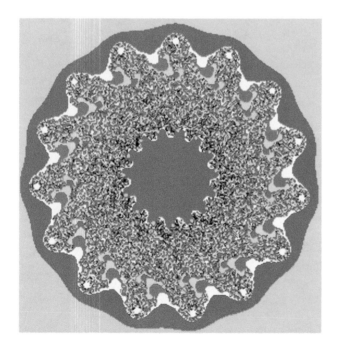

Figure 5. Julia set. The Julia set maps from the complex plane with the ranges from −2 to 2 in X-coordinate and Y-coordinate to the screen with the size of 256×256. The formula is $f(z) = z^m + c$, in which the $m = 15$, and $c = 0.5 - 0.7i$.

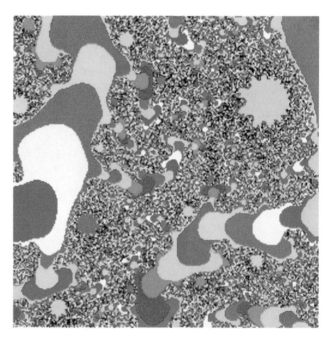

Figure 6. Partial image. This image is partial enlarged one from the Figure 4, and the enlarged area is −0.466866–0.426705 of X-axis, and −0.603235–0.563074 of Y-axis.

Figure 7. Plain image. The plain image has the same size with the Figure 6.

Figure 9. Correct decryption image.

B, we propose a diffusion method. To ensure each pixel in the image can be affected in the diffusion process, the method diffuses the temporary cipher image in horizontal direction firstly, then in vertical direction. Equation (3) shows the diffusion function,

$$q_i = (p_i + p_{i+1} + q_{i-1}) \bmod l \tag{3}$$

where q_i and q_{i-1} are the pixel values in the cipher image, p_i and

p_{i+1} are the pixel values in the temporary cipher image. For each layer in the diffusion process, the last pixel value is assigned to the initial value for the next layer iteration, that is $q_{N2} = q_0$. There are no specific values of q_0 in the cipher image and p_{i+1} in the

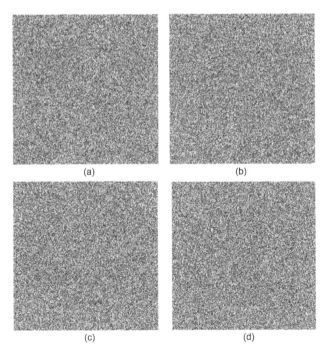

Figure 10. Cipher image with the wrong key and decrypted images. (a) shows the cipher image with the value of m changed to 15.000000000000001. (b) is the corresponding decrypted image. (c) is the decrypted image with the value of scrambling key 5001 instead of 5000, which has obvious differences from the Lena image in Figure 9. (d) is the decrypted image with the diffusion key p_{i+1} changed from 42 to 41 and the value of q_{i-1} remains 100.

Figure 8. Cipher image. The encryption image is obtained through the scrambling process and the diffusion process.

Table 1. Different ratio between Lena image and encrypting Lena image with a certain key changed.

	Rate of change in R-Layer	Rate of changes in G-Layer	Rate of changes in B-Layer
key value–m(15 changed to 15.000000000000001)	99.612%	99.612%	99.632%
key value–forward scrambling key(5000 changed to 5001)	99.167%	99.249%	99.196%
key value–qi-1 of R-Layer(80 changed to 81)	99.608%	99.619%	99.622%

temporary cipher image; therefore they are the keys in the diffusion process.

4 Decryption

As the proposed algorithm is a symmetric algorithm, the decryption process is the reverse order of the encryption, noting that the iteration order is reversed correspondingly.

The diffusion process starts from the first pixel in the temporary cipher image, with directions from left to right and top to bottom. So, for the inverse diffusion process, it starts from the last pixel in the cipher image, with the directions from bottom to top and right to left. The equation is as follows:

$$p_i = (q_i - p_{i+1} - q_{i-1}) \bmod l \tag{4}$$

For the module operation decryption, the order is also reversed and the equation is as follows:

$$e_{ij} = (e'_{ij} - d_{ij}) \bmod l \tag{5}$$

The Encryption System

Suppose the initial image is of the size $M \times N$. The whole encryption process is as follows:

(1) Generate a Julia image by Escape Time Algorithm, select a Julia-like set at the boundary of the Julia set, and then enlarge it to the size of $M \times N$;
(2) Scramble the Julia-like image by the Hilbert curve to a key image;
(3) Encrypt the plain image by the modulo operation with the key image;

(4) Diffuse the temporary cipher image;
(5) Repeat step (2) - (4) if needed;

An encryption flow diagram of the system is shown in Figure 3. The details of Escape Time Algorithm are as follows:

(1) For complex mapping $f(z) = z^m + c, (m \in R, c \in C)$, c is a complex constant, L is the escape radius and T is the maximum escape time. z is a point in the mapping region of the size $M \times N$. Denote $counter[M][N]$ as the two-dimensional array with the initial value 0.
(2) For z, its coordinate on the screen is $(i,j), i,j \in 2N, 0 \leq i \leq M, 0 \leq j \leq N$,
(3) If $|f^T(z)| < L$, then $counter[i][j] = T$ or if $|f^k(z)| < L$, $|f^l(z)| \geq R, 1 \leq k \leq l, l \leq T$, then $counter[i][j] = l$.
(4) Repeat step (2) and (3) until all points in the mapping region are covered.
(5) The color of the point$(i,j)$is marked according to $counter[i][j]$.

The pseudocode of the algorithm is shown in Figure 4.

Experiment Results and Security Analysis

1 Simulation Results

We use the Miscellaneous [16] as our database, which consists of 16 color images and 28 monochrome images. All the experiments were conducted on a Core(TM) i5(2.40 GHz) PC. The mapping function of Julia set is $f(z) = z^m + c$ ($m \in R$, $c = p + q \times i, p, q \in R$). In our experiments, $m = 15$, $c = 0.5 - 0.7i$. The Julia set is shown in Figure 5. The area of -0.466866 to -0.426705 of X-axis and -0.603235 to -0.563074 of Y-axis in Figure 5 is selected to map to a Julia-like set, as shown in Figure 6.

In our experiments, the whole algorithm runs in one iteration. There are two keys in the Hilbert scrambling process, forward step and backward step. They are assigned as 5000 and 9000

Table 2. The NPCR values for encrypting Lena image.

	Change pixel-value in plain image	NPCR in R-Layer	NPCR in G-Layer	NPCR in B-Layer
(195,112,76) in (0,0)	(196,112,76)	100%	100%	100%
	(195,111,76)	100%	100%	100%
	(195,112,75)	100%	100%	100%
(186,139,124) in (100,150)	(185,139,124)	99.451%	100%	100%
	(185,138,124)	99.976%	100%	100%
	(186,139,125)	100%	100%	99.451%
(69,39,37) in (255,255)	(68,39,37)	100%	100%	100%
	(69,40,37)	100%	100%	100%
	(69,39,36)	100%	100%	100%

Table 3. The UACI values for encrypting Lena Image.

	Change pixel-value in plain image	UACI in R-Layer	UACI in G-Layer	UACI in B-Layer
(195,112,76) in (0,0)	(196,112,76)	33.46%	33.45%	33.52%
	(195,111,76)	32.16%	33.5%	33.33%
	(195,112,75)	33.45%	32.45%	33.58%
(186,139,124) in (100,150)	(185,139,124)	33.58%	33.71%	33.41%
	(185,138,124)	33.45%	33.28%	33.5%
	(186,139,125)	33.47%	33.56%	33.60%
(69,39,37) in (255,255)	(68,39,37)	33.41%	33.32%	33.46%
	(69,40,37)	33.6%	32.8%	33.5%
	(69,39,36)	33.4%	33.6%	32.8%

respectively. As discussed in Section 3 in the algorithm part, the diffusion process needs only two keys. One is q_0 in R layer of the horizontal direction, and the other is p_{N^2+1} in B layer of the vertical direction. Experimental results show that the images with size of 256×256 cost less than 610 ms for the whole encryption process, in which the Julia set generation costs about 550 ms and the Hilbert scrambling process costs about 15 ms. The experiments produce a satisfying result. In fact, once the Julia set is generated, the scrambling, encryption and diffusion process can be accomplished in a flash. Figure 7 shows the plain image, Figure 8 shows the corresponding cipher image and Figure 9 shows the correct decryption result.

2 Key Space

The keys in the algorithm consist of the parameters of the Julia set, forward step and backward step along the Hilbert curve, and two diffusion keys. The Julia keys are the mapping parameters m, p, and q $(c = p+qi)$ and the area X_{max}, X_{min}, Y_{max}, Y_{min} (four parameters represent an image area, such as the X-axis scope ranges from X_{min} to X_{max}). There are a total of seven keys. They are stored in double data type; the required memory space for one parameter is eight bytes, i.e. 64 bits. The keys for scrambling a Hilbert curve and the keys for diffusion are both in integer data type, with values ranging from 0 to 65535 and 0 to 255 respectively. Therefore, they need 16 bits and 8 bits for storage respectively. As all the above mentioned, the size of the key space is larger than $2^{64 \times 7} \times 2^{16 \times 2 \times k} \times 2^{8 \times 2 \times k} = 2^{448+48k}$, in which k denotes the iterations times (k = 1, 2, 3......).

3 Key-sensitive Analysis

The whole encryption process includes three sub-processes. They are Julia set generation, Hilbert scrambling, and diffusion process. If the key values change, the corresponding cipher image or decrypted images will be of great difference.

In the decryption, if any key value of the Julia image is changed, the cipher image cannot be decrypted correctly. Taking the key m for example, we change the value of m from 15 to 15.000000000000001. Figure 10(a) shows the cipher image when m value is changed. Comparing the right cipher image (Figure 8) and the wrong cipher image (Figure 10(a)), there are 99.620%, 99.591%, and 99.624% difference in R, G, and B layers, respectively. Figure 10(b) shows the decrypted image by the wrong key. It can be seen that the decrypted image in Figure 10(b) has obvious difference from the plain image in Figure 9, which illustrates the algorithm has a high sensitivity for tiny changes of the initial value m.

The scrambling by the Hilbert curve is in bit-level. The keys in this process include a forward scrambling key and a backward scrambling key ranging from 0 to 65535. Figure 10(c) shows the decrypted image with the forward scrambling key 5001 instead of 5000, which has great differences from the Lena image in Figure 9.

The diffusion keys are q_0 for R layer in horizontal direction diffusion and p_{N^2+1} for B layer in vertical direction diffusion. In the experiment, the value of p_{N^2+1} is changed from 42 to 41 and the value of q_0 remains 100. Decrypting the cipher image in Figure 8, we get the wrong decrypted image shown in Figure 10 (d).

Table 1 shows the different ratio between two decrypted images in R, G, and B layers, respectively. The correct cipher image and the wrong cipher image have great differences when a key value is changed slightly, that means the correct decryption will happen only when all keys are correct. So it is easy to conclude that the keys have a high-sensitivity.

4 Plain image Sensitivity Analysis

Generally speaking, a chosen-plaintext attack is an attack model in which the attacker obtains the right to use the encryption system, makes a minor change of the plaintext and examines the changes of the ciphertext. The purpose of the attack is to gain some further information to reduce the security of the encryption

Table 4. The entropy of the ciphertext.

Cipher image	Entropy in R-layer	Entropy in G-layer	Entropy in B-layer	Average entropy
Lena	7.99728	7.99746	7.99716	7.99730
Baboon	7.99693	7.99695	7.99706	7.99698
pepper	7.99604	7.99457	7.99610	7.99567

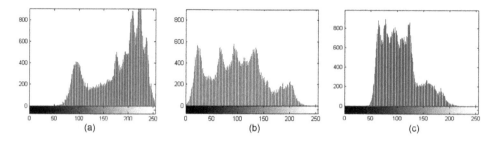

Figure 11. (a), (b), (c) are the R, G, B channel distributions of Lena image, respectively.

scheme. In the worst case, the attack could reveal the scheme's secret keys. If a minor change in the plaintext could cause large changes in the ciphertext, then the aggressive behaviors may be meaningless.

The common standards to test plain image sensitivity are NPCR (the number of pixels change rate) and UACI (unified average changing intensity) [17]. Usually, the plaintext sensitivity will be better if the NPCR value is larger. The formulas are shown in Equation (6) and Equation (7).

$$\text{NPCR} = \frac{1}{W \times H} \sum_{i=1, j=1}^{W, H} D(i, j) \times 100\% \qquad (6)$$

$$\text{UACI} = \frac{1}{W \times H} \sum_{i=1, j=1}^{W, H} \frac{|C_1(i, j) - C_2(i, j)|}{255} \times 100\% \qquad (7)$$

where C_1 and C_2 are the encrypted images, and their corresponding plaintexts have only a one-bit difference in the same pixel before encrypted. The $C_1(i,j)$ and $C_2(i,j)$ are the pixel value at grid (i,j) in C_1 and C_2, respectively. And W and H are the width and height of the images. If $C_1(i,j) = = C_2(i,j)$ then $D(i,j) = 1$; otherwise, $D(i,j) = 0$. Therefore NPCR is to measure the percentage of the different pixels between two images. And the UACI is to test the average intensity of differences.

Table 2 and Table 3 show the plain image sensitivity. We calculate NPCR and UACI values for each pixel LSB (Least Significant Bit) changed in the R channel of the Lena image, Baboon image and Pepper image. Their average NPCR are all about 99.6% and their average UACI are 33.4877%, 33.4175%, and 33.4743%, respectively. Some NPCR and UACI are listed in Table 2 and Table 3.

The experimental results show that the sensitivity of the plain image is significant. When any pixel bit is changed in one layer, it can influence almost all the pixel values of the cipher image. In this case, the cipher image cannot be decrypted correctly. It is noted

that such experimental effects partially owes to the diffusion process in the algorithm. From the above experimental results, we can draw the conclusion that the encryption algorithm can resist chosen plaintext attacks effectively.

5 Information Entropy Analysis

It is widely known that the entropy $H(g)$ of a message source g can be calculated in Equation (8) [17].

$$H(g) = \sum_{i=1}^{N \times N} P(g_i) \log_2 \frac{1}{P(g_i)} bits \qquad (8)$$

Where $N \times N$ is the amount of the information, $P(g_i)$ is the occurrence probability of the g_i value in all of values. The logarithmic function is to represent the entropy in bit form. If the source sends 2^8 symbols (containing g_i) with equal probability, i.e., $G = \{g_1, g_2, g_3, \ldots\ldots g_{2^8}\}$, then the entropy value should be equal to 8. In this case, it is a truly random source. So, the entropy value of an encrypted image should be up to 8.

Table 4 lists the entropy value of the cipher image, which is close to the ideal standard value. It is a clear proof that the encryption system has a good randomness, which indicates it can resist the entropy attack.

6 Statistical Analysis

The plain image histograms are shown in Figure 11(a) to Figure 11(c) and cipher image histograms are shown in Figure 12(a) to Figure 12(c), in which the X-ordinate represents the gray-level value and the Y-ordinate represents the occurrence frequency for each gray-level value. The experimental results indicate that each layer's gray value distribution of the cipher image tends toward equilibrium. These figures demonstrate a uniform distribution of pixel color values for the three image channels, which proves the success of the algorithm in randomizing the output.

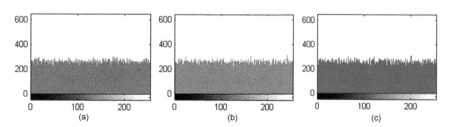

Figure 12. (a), (b), (c) are the R, G, B channel distributions of encrypting Lena image, respectively.

Table 5. The encrypting Lena image result of sp800–22 test suit for encrypting Lena image.

Statistical test	P-value	Result
Frequency	0.936447	SUCCESS
Block Frequency (m = 128)	0.584900	SUCCESS
Cusum-Forward	0.372175	SUCCESS
Cusum-Reverse	0.427874	SUCCESS
Runs	0.602041	SUCCESS
Long Runs of Ones	0.731317	SUCCESS
Rank	0.030824	SUCCESS
Spectral DFT	0.712291	SUCCESS
NonOverlapping Templates (m = 9,B = 000000001)	0.292611	SUCCESS
Overlapping Templates (m = 9)	0.919983	SUCCESS
Universal	0.819843	SUCCESS
Approximate Entropy (m = 10)	0.946813	SUCCESS
Random Excursions (x = +1)	0.882358	SUCCESS
Random Excursions Variant (x = −1)	0.538752	SUCCESS
Linear Complexity (M = 500)	0.278069	SUCCESS
Serial	0.960519	SUCCESS
	0.934595	SUCCESS

7 Randomness Test

Table 5 shows that our encrypting Lena image passes the sp800–22 test suite. It proves once again that the cipher image has a good randomness.

Conclusions

In this study, we have proposed an encryption algorithm combining the classical Julia set and the Hilbert curve. In the algorithm, the Julia set is scrambled in bit-level by the Hilbert curve to enhance the key sensitivity. The diffusion operation is implemented to resist the chosen plaintext attack. Through the analysis of the experimental results, we obtained the following conclusions:

(1) The abundant Julia-like images are the copies of a Julia set and can be generated by a few parameters, which greatly reduces the key store space. The chaotic characteristic of the boundaries in the Julia image gives the key extreme sensitivity to the slight parameter changes, improving the security of the encryption algorithm greatly. In our experiments, the key sensitivity achieves 10^{-15}.

(2) The diffusion process has a good effect in the pixel spread, and provides much large key space, has a high sensitivity to the plain image and keys, and especially enhances the resistance against chosen plaintext attack.

(3) The entropy value of the cipher image achieves an ideal value, illustrating that the encryption system not only has a good randomness but also can resist the entropy attack. The statistical analysis shows that the distributions of the cipher image are uniform, also indicating the success of the algorithm in randomizing the output. In addition, the randomness test passes the sp800-22 test suite, proving the randomness of the cipher image on another side.

For future work, we will consider choosing better Julia set keys and other methods to improve the algorithm for the key conversion.

Author Contributions

Conceived and designed the experiments: YYS. Performed the experiments: LNC. Analyzed the data: RDX. Contributed reagents/materials/analysis tools: RQK. Wrote the paper: YYS RDX.

References

1. Shyu SJ (2007) Image encryption by random grids. Pattern Recognition 40: 1014–1031.
2. Yuen CH, Wong KW (2011)A chaos-based joint image compression and encryption scheme using DCT and SHA-1. Applied Soft Computing 11: 5092–5098.
3. Hermassi J, Rhouma R, Belghith S (2010) Joint compression and encryption using chaotically mutated Huffman trees. Communications in Nonlinear Science and Numerical Simulation 15: 2987–2999.
4. Chen GR, Mao YB, Chui CK (2004) A symmetric image encryption scheme based on 3D chaotic cat maps. Chaos, Solitons & Fractals 21: 749–761.
5. Kumar S (2006) Public key cryptographic system using Mandelbrot sets. Military Communications Conference in Washington DC, 1–5.
6. Liu WT, Sun WS (2008) Application of Fractal theory in cryptographic algorithm. Journal of China Acadamy of Electronics and Information Technology.3: 580–585. (In Chinese).
7. Rozouvan V (2009) Modulo image encryption with fractal keys. Optics and Lasers in Engineering, 47: 1–6.
8. Lock AJJ, Loh CH, Juhari SH, Samsudin A (2010) Compression-encryption based on fractal geometric. Second International Conference on Computer Research and Development. 213–217.
9. Sun YY, Kong RQ, Wang XY, Bi LC (2010) An Image Encryption Algorithm Utilizing Mandelbrot Set. International Workshop on Chaos-Fractal Theories and Applications. 170–173.
10. Lin KT, Yeh SL (2012) Encrypting image by assembling the fractal-image addition method and the binary encoding method. Optics Communications 285: 2335–2342.
11. Tong XJ, Cui MG (2009) Image encryption scheme based on 3D baker with dynamical compound chaotic sequence cipher generator. Signal processing 89: 480–491.
12. Yuen CH, Wong KW (2012) Cryptanalysis on secure fractal image coding based on fractal parameter encryption. Fractals 20: 41–51.
13. Li CQ, Lo KT (2011) Optimal quantitative cryptanalysis of permutation-only multimedia ciphers against plaintext attacks. Signal processing 4: 949–954.
14. Li CQ, Zhang LY, Ou R, Wong KW, Shu S (2012) Breaking a novel colour image encryption algorithm based on chaos. Nonlinear Dynamics 70: 2383–2388.
15. Falconer KJ (2003) Fractal: Mathematical Foundations and Applications (Second Edition). Chichester: Wiley.
16. http://sipi.usc.edu/database/database.php?volume = misc.
17. Chen GR, Mao YB, Chui CK (2004) A symmetric image encryption scheme based on 3D chaotic cat maps. Chaos, Solitons & Fractals 21: 749–761.

25

Anger Is More Influential than Joy: Sentiment Correlation in Weibo

Rui Fan[1], Jichang Zhao[2], Yan Chen[1], Ke Xu[1]*

1 State Key Laboratory of Software Development Environment, Beihang University, Beijing, P. R. China, 2 School of Economics and Management, Beihang University, Beijing, P. R. China

Abstract

Recent years have witnessed the tremendous growth of the online social media. In China, Weibo, a Twitter-like service, has attracted more than 500 million users in less than five years. Connected by online social ties, different users might share similar affective states. We find that the correlation of anger among users is significantly higher than that of joy. While the correlation of sadness is surprisingly low. Moreover, there is a stronger sentiment correlation between a pair of users if they share more interactions. And users with larger number of friends possess more significant sentiment correlation with their neighborhoods. Our findings could provide insights for modeling sentiment influence and propagation in online social networks.

Editor: Rodrigo Huerta-Quintanilla, Cinvestav-Merida, Mexico

Funding: This work was supported by 863 Program (grant no. 2012AA011005), SKLSDE (grant no. SKLSDE-2013ZX-06), and Research Fund for the Doctoral Program of Higher Education of China (grant no. 20111102110019). Jichang Zhao was partially supported by the Fundamental Research Funds for the Central Universities (grant nos. YWF-14-RSC-109 and YWF-14-JGXY-001). The funders had no role in study design, data collection and analysis, decision to publish, or preparation of the manuscript.

Competing Interests: The authors have declared that no competing interests exist.

* Email: kexu@nlsde.buaa.edu.cn

Introduction

From the view of conventional social theory, *homophily* leads to connections in social networks, as the saying "Birds of a feather flock together" states [1]. Even in the online social network, more and more evidence indicates that the users with similar properties would be connected in the future with high probabilities [2,3]. It is clear that *homophily* could affect user behavior both online and offline [4,5], while the records in online social networks are relatively easier to be tracked and collected. Moreover, the continuous growth of the online social media attracts a vast number of internet users and produces many huge social networks. Twitter(www.twitter.com), a microblogging website launched in 2006, has over 300 million active users, with over 500 million microblog posts, known as tweets, being posted everyday. In China, Weibo(www.weibo.com), a Twitter-like service launched in 2009, has accumulated more than 500 million registered users in less than five years. Every day there will be more than 100 million Chinese tweets published. The high-dimension content generated by millions of global users is a "big data" window [6] to investigate the online social networks. That is to say, these large-scale online social networks provide an unprecedented opportunity for the study of human behavior.

Beyond typical demographic features such as ages, races, hometowns, common friends and interests, *homophily* also includes psychological states, like loneliness and happiness [1,4,7]. Previous studies also show that the computer-mediated emotional communication is similar to the traditional face-to-face communication, which means there is no evident indication that human communication in online social media is less emotional or less personally [8]. Each user in the online social network could be a

social sensor and the huge amount of tweets convey complicated signals about the users and the real-world events, among which the sentiments are an essential part. Therefore, emotion states of the users play a key role in understanding the user behaviors in social networks, whether from an individual or group perspective [9–11]. Meanwhile, users' mood states are significantly affected by the real-world events [12], which could be employed to predict the stock market [13] or to detect the abnormal event [14]. Recent study [4] shows that happiness is assortative in Twitter network and [6] finds that the average happiness scores are positively correlated between the Twitter users connected by one, two or three social ties. An interesting phenomenon of emotion synchronization is also unraveled in [15]. While in these studies, the human emotion is simplified to two classes of positive and negative or just a score of general happiness, neglecting the detailed aspects of human sentiment, especially the negative emotion. Because of oversimplification of the emotion classification, it is hard for the previous literature to disclose the different correlations of different sentiments and then make comparisons. However, the negative emotions, like anger, sadness or disgust, are more applicable in real world scenarios such as abnormal event detection or emergency tracking [14]. In [5], the authors also find that negative emotion could boost user activity in BBC forum. In fact, figuring out the correlation of these emotions might shed light on understanding why people participate in the diffusion of abnormal event in the network and how the large-scale collective behavior could form across the entire network. On the other hand, the investigation of how the local structure affects the emotion correlation is not systematically performed yet, while which is essential to studying the mechanism of sentiment influence and contagion.

Aiming at filling these vital gaps, we divide the sentiment of an individual into four categories, including *anger, joy, sadness* and *disgust*, and investigate the emotion correlation between connected users in the interaction network obtained from Weibo. Out of our expectation, it is found that *anger* has a stronger correlation between different users than that of *joy*, while *sadness*'s correlation is trivial. Further analysis demonstrates that *anger* in Weibo is related with the real-world events about food security, government bribery or demolition scandal, which are always the hot trends in Internet of China. Moreover, node degree, node clustering and tie strength all could positively boost the emotion correlation in online social networks, especially for the mood of *anger*. Finally, we make our data set in this paper publicly available to the research community.

Materials and Methods

Weibo Dataset

As pointed out in [4], the following relationship in Twitter-like social networks does not stand for the social interaction, while if two users reply, retweet or mention each other in their tweets for certain times, the online social tie between them is sufficient to present an alternative means of deriving a conventional social network [6]. Starting from several influential seeds (like the users verified by Weibo), we adapt a typical Breadth-First-Search strategy to crawl tweets from Weibo through its open APIs. For each user we get, we first save all its tweets into the database and then add its followers (users that follow it) into the candidate queue for further explorations. Finally from December 2010 to February 2011, we accumulated around 70 million tweets posted by 278,654 users. While here we only construct an interaction network from the tweets posted during April 2010 to September 2010, where interaction means the number that two users retweet or mention each other is larger than a threshold T. From around 26 million tweets posted during the period we select and 140,000 users we crawled, an undirected but weighted graph $G(V,E,T)$ is constructed, in which V is the set of users (the ones without links are omitted), E represents the set of interactive links among V, and T is the minimum number of interactions on each link. For each link in E, its weight is the sum of retweeting or mentioning times between its two ends in the specified time period. Specifically, to exclude occasional users that are not truly involved in the Weibo social network, we only reserve those active users in our interaction network that posted more than one tweet every two days on average over the six months. And to guarantee the validity of users' social interaction, if the number of two users retweet or mention each other is less than T, we would omit the connection between them. As shown in Figure 1, by tuning T we can obtain networks of different scales. Generally we set $T=30$ and then the interaction network G contains 9,868 nodes and 19,517 links. We also make our entire dataset publicly available(http://www.datatang.com/data/44650, http://goo.gl/iXzoXm). Note that here we collect tweets from Weibo through its open APIs(http://open.weibo.com) under the authority granted by Weibo and we have also anonymized user IDs and names in the published data set to protect users' privacy.

Emotion classification

The content in online social media like Twitter or Weibo is mainly recorded in the form of short text. Many approaches have been presented to mine sentiment from these texts in recent years. One of them is the lexicon based method, in which the sentiment of a tweet is determined by counting the number of sentimental words, i.e., positive terms and negative terms. For example, Dodds

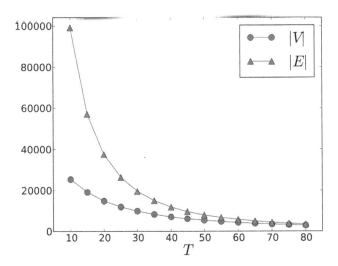

Figure 1. The number of nodes or edges varies for different interaction threshold T. In the following part of the present work, we set $T=30$ to extract a large enough network with convincing interaction strength.

and Danforth measured the happiness of songs, blogs and presidents [16]. They also employed Amazon Mechanical Turk to score over 10,000 unique English words on an integer scale from 1 to 9, where 1 represents sadness and 9 represents happiness [9]. Golder and Macy collected 509 million English tweets from 2.4 million users in Twitter, then measured the positive and negative affects using Linguistic Inquiry and Word Count(LIWC) (http://www.liwc.net). While another one is the machine learning based solution, in which different features are considered to perform the task of classification, including terms, smileys, emoticons and etc. The first step was taken by Pang et al. in [17], they treated the sentiment classification of movie reviews simply as a text categorization task and investigated several typical classification algorithms. According to the experimental results, machine learning based classifiers outperform the baseline method based on human words list [18–20]. Different from most work which just categorized the emotion into negative and positive, our previous work [14] divided the sentiment into four classes, then presented a framework based on emoticons without manually-labelled training tweets and achieved a convincing precision. Because of the ability of multi-emotions classification, we employ this framework in the present paper.

A vast number of training samples is necessary for handing the extremely short text in social media. To avoid intensive labor, we use emoticon to label tweets into different emotions. It has been found that both smiley and emoticon are strongly related with typical sentiment words and could be convincing indicators of different emotions [21]. They help the users to express their moods when post the tweet [22]. Tossell et al. also confirm that emoticon usage is contextual [23]. Hence, we could treat these emoticons as sentiment labels of the tweets. In fact, it is a kind of crowdsourcing, i.e., the users label the tweet with emoticons to express their emotions themselves [14]. In the labeling stage, first we manually label the emotion of the emoticon. We select the most popular 95 emoticons and several students are working separately to label their emotions. Their judgements are based on the image of the emoticon and around 50 frequent words occurring together with the emoticon. Finally we find that most of the emoticons are labelled by four sentiments, including *anger, joy, disgust* and *sadness*. For other emotions like *fear* or *surprise*, we do not find enough votes. So we split the emotion into these four classes. In fact it is also sort of consistent with the traditional Chinese culture that the human emotion are mainly constituted by four elements, including pleasure, anger, sorrow and joy.

From around 70 million tweets, 3.5 million tweets with valid emoticons are extracted and labeled. Using this data set as a training corpus C_{tr}, a simple but fast Bayesian classifier is built in the second stage to mine the sentiment of the tweets without emoticons, which are about 95% in Weibo. Be specific, for each tweet t in C_{tr}, we converts it into a sequence of words $\{w_i\}$, where w_i is a word and i is its position in t. From the labeled tweets, we could obtain the word w_i's prior probability of belonging to the sentiment category m is $P(w_i\|m) = \dfrac{n^m(w_i)+1}{\sum_q (n^m(w_q)+1)}$, where $m = 1,2,3$ or 4, $n^m(w_i)$ is the times that w_i appears in all the tweets in the category m and *Laplace smoothing* is used to avoid the problem of zero probability. Then for an unlabeled tweet t with word sequence $\{w_i\}$, its category could be obtained as $m^*(t) = arg\max_m P(m)\Pi_i P(w_i\|m)$, where $P(m)$ is the prior probability of m. The averaged precision of this classifier is 64.3% and particularly the large amount of tweets we employ in the experiment can guarantee its accuracy further. For example, in the applications like *MoodLens*(http://gana.nlsde.buaa.edu.cn/hourly_happy/moodlens.html) and *Sentiment Search*(http://xinqings.nlsde.buaa.edu.cn/), it can be used to detect abnormal events effectively in real-time tracking. Moreover, the mechanism of incremental learning in this classifier can tackle the problems like sentiment drift of terms [9] or emergence of new features [14].

Based on this framework, we demonstrate a sampled snapshot of the interaction network with $T = 30$. As shown in Figure 2b, in which each user is colored by its emotion. We can roughly find that closely connected nodes generally share the same color, indicating emotion correlations in Weibo network. Besides, different colors show different clusterings. For example, the color of red, which represents *anger*, shows more evident clustering. These preliminary findings inspire us that different emotions might have different correlations and a deep investigation is indeed necessary.

Emotion correlation

Emotion correlation is a metric to quantify the strength of sentiment similarity between connected users. For a fixed T, we first extract an interaction network G and all the tweets posted by the nodes in G. Then by employing the classifier established in the former section, the tweets for each user are divided into four categories, in which f_1, f_2, f_3 and f_4 represent the fraction of angry, joyful, sad and disgusting tweets, respectively. Hence we can use emotion vector $e_i(f_1^i, f_2^i, f_3^i, f_4^i)$ to denote user i's sentiment status. Based on this, we define the pairwise sentiment correlation as follows. Given a certain hop distance h, we collect all user pairs with distance h from G. For one of the four emotions $m(m = 1,2,3,4)$ and a user pair (j,q), we put the source user j's f_m^j into a sequence S_m, and the target user q's f_m^q to another sequence T_m. Then the pairwise correlation could be calculated by Pearson correlation as

$$C_p^m = \frac{1}{l-1}\sum_{i=1}^l \left(\frac{S_i - \langle S_m \rangle}{\sigma_{S_m}}\right)\left(\frac{T_i - \langle T_m \rangle}{\sigma_{T_m}}\right),$$

where $\langle S_m \rangle = \frac{1}{l}\sum_{i=1}^l S_i$ is the mean, $\sigma_{S_m} = \sqrt{\frac{1}{l-1}\sum_{i=1}^l (S_i - \langle S_m \rangle)^2}$ is the standard deviation and l is the

length of S_m or T_m. Or it can also be obtained from Spearman correlation as

$$C_s^m = 1 - \frac{6\sum_{i=1}^l d_i^2}{l(l^2-1)},$$

where d_i is the rank difference between S_i in S_m and T_i in T_m. Intuitively larger C_p^m and C_s^m both suggest a more positive correlation for sentiment m. In order to investigate fluctuations in the sentiment correlation, we also use the approach of *bootstrap* [24] to perform the error analysis. For instance, given two emotion sequences of length $x > 1$, denoted as $S_m = \{s_1, s_2, ..., s_x\}$ and $T_m = \{t_1, t_2, ..., t_x\}$, we do not calculate their correlation directly. Contrarily, we first uniformly sample x integer indexes from the range of $[1,x]$ with replacement and then put them into an index sequence defined as $R_m = \{r_1, r_2, ..., r_x\}$. Through traversing each index $r_i \in R_m$, we can construct two new lists by putting s_{r_i} into S_m' and t_{r_i} into T_m', respectively. Obviously after this we can generate two sampled sequences $S_m' = \{s_1', s_2', ..., s_x'\}$ and $T_m' = \{t_1', t_2', ..., t_x'\}$. Finally for each round of index-sampling we can obtain a correlation value between S_m' and T_m', and through $z = 1000$ times of repetitions we would obtain an averaged correlation and a standard deviation (the error) for m. Apparently lower errors stand for more significant correlations. Note that in the rest of the paper, averaged correlation would be presented as correlation if there is no conflict in the context.

Based on the dataset and classifier, interaction networks could be built and tweets of each user in the network would be emotionally labelled. Using the definition of correlations, we can then present the comparison of emotion correlations and the impact of local structures in the following section.

Results

First we compare the correlation of different emotions based on the graph of $T = 30$, which ensures enough number of ties and users, and at the same time guarantees relatively strong social tie strength. As shown in Figure 3, both Pearson correlation and Spearman correlation indicate that different sentiments have different correlations and *anger* has a surprisingly higher correlation than other emotions. In addition, the standard deviations of all sentiments' correlations are extremely small, which indicates that the sentiment correlation in online social networks is indeed significant and only shows trivial fluctuations. Although the previous studies [4,6] show that happiness is assortative in online social networks, but Figure 3 further demonstrates that the correlation of *anger* is much stronger than that of happiness, especially as $h < 3$. While for *sadness* and *disgust*, they both have an unexpected low correlation even for small h. For instance, the correlation of *sadness* is less than 0.15 as $h = 1$. The results are also consistent with the previous findings that strength of the emotion correlation decreases as h grows, especially after $h > 6$ [6]. In fact, as $h > 3$, the emotion correlation becomes weak for all the sentiments, which means that the correlation of the sentiment in the social network is limited significantly by the social distance. For example, for strong assortative emotions like *anger* and *joy*, their correlations just fluctuate around 0 as $h > 3$.

In order to test the above correlation further, we also shuffle S_m and T_m randomly for sentiment m and recalculate its correlation. As shown in Figure 4, for the shuffled emotion sequence, there is no correlation existing for all the sentiments. It indicates that the former correlation we get is truly significant and for random pairs of users in the social network, there is no *emotion homophily*. It

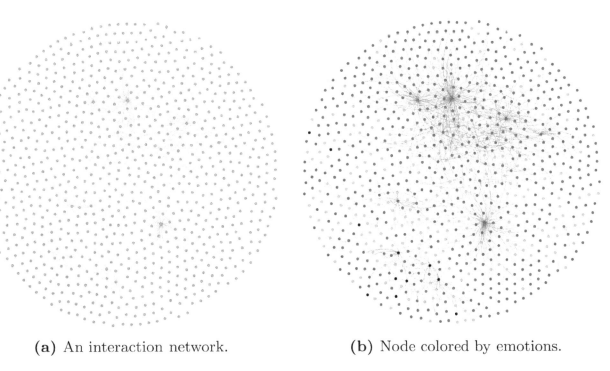

(a) An interaction network.   (b) Node colored by emotions.

Figure 2. (Color online) The giant connected cluster of a network sample with $T = 30$. (a) is the network structure, in which each node stands for a user and the link between two users represents the interaction between them. Based on this topology, we color each node by its emotion, i.e., the sentiment with the maximum tweets published by this node in the sampling period. In (b), the red stands for *anger*, the green represents *joy*, the blue stands for *sadness* and the black represents *disgust*. The regions of same color indicate that closely connected nodes share the same sentiment.

further justifies that through social ties, closely connected friends indeed share similar affective states.

Investigating to what extent the local structure, like tie strength, node degree and node clustering, could affect the emotion correlation and its error is of importance for modeling sentiment influence and propagation in future work. As shown in Figure 5, we first disclose how the interaction threshold T affects the sentiment correlations. As discussed in Section *Weibo Dataset*,

larger T produces smaller networks but with closer social relations and more frequent online interactions. It is also intuitive that frequent interactions in online social networks are positively related with strong social ties and convincing social bonds. Because of this, we can see in Figure 5 that for all the four emotions, their correlations inside two hops continue a steady increasing trend with T's growth. Particularly for *anger*, its Pearson correlation could rise to around 0.5. For weakly correlated emotions like

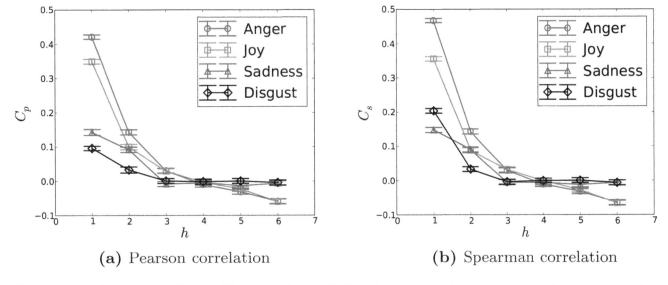

(a) Pearson correlation   (b) Spearman correlation

Figure 3. Correlations with error-bar for different emotions as the hop distance varies. Large h means a pair of users are far away from each other in the social network we build. Here $T = 30$ is fixed.

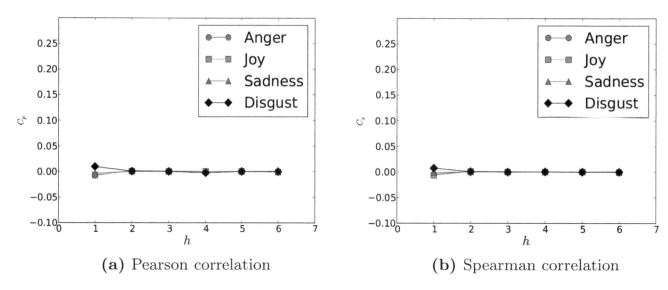

(a) Pearson correlation

(b) Spearman correlation

Figure 4. The emotion sequence is randomly shuffled to test the correlation significance.

sadness and *disgust*, although the correlation shows a slow growth for $h=1$ and $h=2$, while the maximum value of the correlation is still lower than 0.25. As $h=3$, the increment of the sentiment correlation is trivial, especially for *sadness* and *disgust*. It illustrates that the primary factor of controlling the emotion correlation is still the social distance and the social tie strength just functions for close neighbors in the scope of two hops. Note that as T grows, the size of the network is reduced and the length of emotion sequences would be shortened accordingly, which might import more noise and produce larger errors. As can be seen in Figure 5, errors of correlations grow with T, especially as $h=1$. Secondly, we check the effect of users' degrees to the sentiment correlation. Given a random node i with degree k, we have a sequence of the number of tweets with sentiment m for its friends, which is denoted as $\{\eta_m^j\}_i$ and η_m^j is the number of tweets with emotion m posted by an arbitrary neighbor j. Then the number of tweets with emotion m posted by i's neighborhood is $\sum_j \eta_m^j$. Ultimately the sentiment vector for i's neighborhood could be defined as e_i^{nei}

$(\frac{\sum_j \eta_1^j}{\sum_m \sum_j \eta_m^j}, \frac{\sum_j \eta_2^j}{\sum_m \sum_j \eta_m^j}, \frac{\sum_j \eta_3^j}{\sum_m \sum_j \eta_m^j}, \frac{\sum_j \eta_4^j}{\sum_m \sum_j \eta_m^j})$. Through add-

ing f_m^i into S_m and $\frac{\sum_j \eta_m^j}{\sum_m \sum_j \eta_m^j}$ into T_m, we could get the

correlation of sentiment m for the users with degree k. As can be seen in Figure 6a, the sentiment correlation grows with k, especially for *anger* and *joy*, which illustrates that nodes with higher degrees in online social networks possess stronger emotion correlation with their neighborhoods. That is to say, having more friends in the social media indicates more significant sentimental correlation with the neighborhood. Specifically, the correlation of *anger* and *joy* are almost same for very small degrees, but later *anger* shows a significant jump for large degrees and enlarges the gap as compared to *joy*. As k raises to 30, the correlation of *anger* grows almost to 0.85. While the correlation of *sadness* and *disgust* do not demonstrate an obvious increasing trend and just fluctuate around 0.2 or even lower. Similarly, here errors also grow with increasing k, because nodes with large degrees only occupy a little fraction in the online social network [25], which would reduce the length of the emotion sequence and import noise, especially for *sadness* and *disgust* as shown in Figure 6a. However, *anger*'s

correlation is still significantly higher than that of *joy* as $k>15$. It is also worthy emphasizing that because the network size is small and we only have the maximum degree around 30, which is far below the Dunbar's Number [25,26]. We suspect that the correlation might stop rising if the degree is larger than Dunbar's Number. Thirdly, we investigate the impact of the clustering of a node i, which is defined as $\frac{2|E_i|}{k_i(k_i-1)}$, where E_i is the set of ties among i's friends and k_i is the degree of i. For $k_i=1$, we set i's clustering to zero. Then similar to the case of degree, we could get the correlation variation as clustering grows for different emotions. As shown in Figure 6b, correlations of *anger* and *joy* grow very slowly with the clustering, while *disgust* and *sadness* just demonstrate fluctuations without obvious increment. The correlation of *anger* is still stronger than that of *joy*. However, different from the case of degree, even the correlations of *anger* and *joy* fluctuate as the clustering rises. While with respect to the error, it again shows a rising trend with the growth of clustering, since nodes with highly clustered neighborhoods take a trivial fraction in the social network [25]. Generally the above observations indicate that for *anger* and *joy*, the emotion correlation between a node and its neighborhood would be a little bit stronger as its neighbors are more closely clustered. The results of Spearman correlation are similar and not reported here.

To sum up, different emotions have different correlations in the social media. Compared to other sentiments, *anger* has the most positive correlation. Local structures can affect the sentiment correlation in near neighborhoods, from which we can learn that tie strength, node degree and node clustering could enhance the sentiment correlation, especially for *anger* and *joy*, and their contributions to *sadness* and *disgust* are greatly limited.

Discussion

Users with similar demographics have high probabilities to get connected in both online and offline social networks. Recent studies reveal that even the psychological states like happiness are assortative, which means the happiness or well-being is strongly correlated between connected users in online social media like Twitter. Considering the oversimplification of the sentiment classification in the previous literature, we divide the emotion

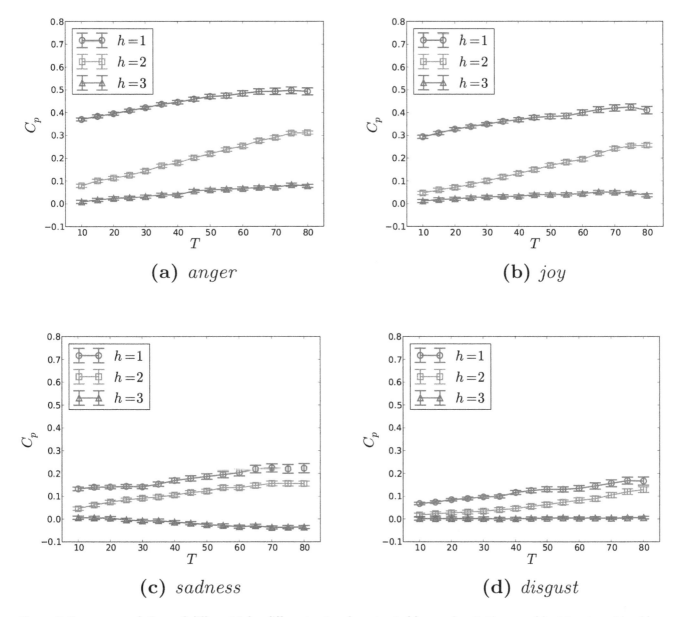

Figure 5. Pearson correlations of different h for different networks extracted by varying T. The case of $h > 3$ is not considered here because of the weak sentiment correlation found in Figure 3.

into four categories and discuss their different correlations in details based on the tweets collected from Weibo of China, and the dataset has been publicly available to research community. Our results show that *anger* is more significantly correlated than other emotions like *joy*. While out of our expectation, the correlation of *sadness* is low.

We try to unravel the underlying reason of why *anger* has a surprisingly high correlation but the correlation of *sadness* is weak from the view of keywords the corresponding tweets present. For a certain emotion m, we collect all the retweeted tweets(usually contain phrase like "@" or "retweet") with this sentiment in a specified time period to combine into a long text document. Focusing only on retweeted tweets could help reduce the impact of external media and just consider the contagion from the social ties in Weibo. Several typical techniques are employed to mine the keywords or topic phrases from the documents [27], which are reported in Figure 7. Based on the keywords or topics we find, the

real-world events or social issues could be summarized to understand the sentiment correlation in detail.

With respect to *anger*, we find two kinds of social events are apt to trigger the angry mood of users in Weibo. First one is the domestic social problems like food security, government bribery and demolition for resettlement. The "shrimp washing powder" which results in muscle degeneration and the self-burning event in Fenggang Yihuang County of Jiangxi province represent this category. These events reflect that people living in China are dissatisfied about some aspects of the current society and this type of event can spread quickly as the users want to show their sympathy to the victims by retweeting tweets and criticizing the criminals or the government. Frequently appearing phrases like "government", "bribery", "demolition" and so on are strongly related with these events. The second type is about the diplomatic issues, such as the conflict between China and foreign countries. For instances, in August 2010, United States and South Korea

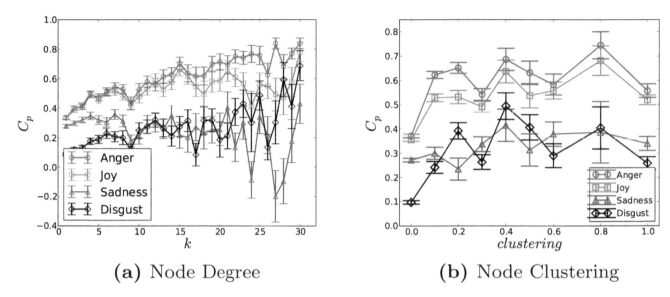

(a) Node Degree **(b)** Node Clustering

Figure 6. Here T is fixed to 10 to reduce the data sparsity. Because the network is relatively small, the largest degree we get is only 30. Therefore, the results in Figure 6a just demonstrate that when the degree is small, how the sentiments' correlations vary with node degrees. While regarding to Figure 6b, the linear bin is used to get emotion sequences for nodes with clusterings within the same bin.

held a drill on the Yellow Sea, which locates in the east of China. In September 2010, the ship collision of China and Japan also made users in Weibo extremely rageful. Actually, these events could arouse patriotism and stimulate the angry mood. Keywords like "Diaoyu Island", "ship collision" and "Philippines" show the popularity of these events at that time. To sum up, Weibo is a convenient and ubiquitously channel for Chinese to share their concern about the continuous social problems and diplomatic issues. Pushed by the real-world events, these users tend to retweet tweets, express their anger and hope to get resonance from neighborhoods in online social networks. While regarding to *sadness*, we find its strength of correlation is strongly affected by the real-world natural disasters like earthquake, as shown in Figure 7(right). Because the natural disaster happens occasionally and then the averaged correlation of the sadness is very low and the strength of its correlation might be highly fluctuated.

With the continuous growth, online social media in China like Weibo have been becoming the primary channel of information

exchange. In Weibo, the messages do not only deliver the factual information but also propagate the users' opinions about the social event or individual affairs. Real-world society issues are easy to get attention from the public and people tend to express their feelings towards these issues through posting and retweeting tweets in online social media. Through keywords and topics mining in retweeted angry tweets, we find the public opinion towards social problems and diplomatic issues are always angry and this extreme mental status also possesses the strongest correlation between connected users in Weibo. We conjecture that *anger* plays a non-ignorable role in massive propagations of the negative news about the society, which are always hot trends in today's Internet of China. This might be the origin of large scale online collective behavior in Weibo about society problems such as food security and demolition for resettlement in recent years. It is also consistent with a finding that good news never goes beyond the gate while bad news spread far and wide by ancient Chinese people more than one thousand years ago [28]. It should also be mentioned that

Figure 7. The example Chinese keywords extracted for *anger*(left) and *sadness*(right), respectively. The top 20 keywords are also translated into English, which could be found through http://goo.gl/tl4q45.

the study of this paper has received great attention from many media like MIT Technology Review, CNN, BBC and the Washington Post (just to name a few of them) after a preprint of this paper was posted on the Internet [29]. It is widely believed that similar results might also exist in the social media of other countries. In the future work we would investigate the role of emotion in the information diffusion and comprehensively understand how different sentiments function in the formation of the public opinion or the massive collective behavior. Meanwhile, our findings could inspire the modeling of emotion contagion, like different emotions might diffuse with diverse strengths, local structures such as tie strengths, degrees and clusterings might affect the spread and the emotion might only function between individuals with social distance no more than three hops. Another interesting direction is to study how to make the social media more neutral by introducing some new mechanisms, e.g. delaying the post of an angry tweet can give people additional time for consideration and so might be of use for reducing the number of angry tweets.

Acknowledgments

The authors would like to thank the anonymous reviewers for their valuable suggestions, which improve this paper greatly.

Author Contributions

Performed the experiments: RF JZ YC. Analyzed the data: RF JZ YC. Wrote the paper: JZ KX. Designed the experiments: JZ RF KX. Prepared the figures: RF JZ YC.

References

1. Miller M, Lynn SL, James CM (2001) Birds of a feather: Homophily in social networks. Annual Review of Sociology 27: 415–444.
2. Mislove A, Marcon M, Gummadi KP, Druschel P, Bhattacharjee B (2007) Measurement and analysis of online social networks. In: the 7th ACM SIGCOMM conference on Internet measurement. IMC '07, pp. 29–42.
3. Liben-Nowell D, Kleinberg J (2003) The link prediction problem for social networks. In: the twelfth international conference on Information and knowledge management. CIKM '03, pp. 556–559.
4. Bollen J, Gonçalves B, Ruan G, Mao H (2011) Happiness is assortative in online social networks. Artif Life 17: 237–251.
5. Chmiel A, Sobkowicz P, Sienkiewicz J, Paltoglou G, Buckley K, et al. (2011) Negative emotions boost user activity at BBC forum. Physica A: Statistical Mechanics and its Applications 390: 2936–2944.
6. Bliss CA, Kloumann IM, Harris KD, Danforth CM, Dodds PS (2012) Twitter reciprocal reply networks exhibit assortativity with respect to happiness. Journal of Computational Science 3: 388–397.
7. Traud AL, Kelsic ED, Mucha PJ, Porter MA (2008) Comparing community structure to characteristics in online collegiate social networks. ArXiv e-prints, arXiv:0809.0690.
8. Derks D, Fischer AH, Bos AE (2008) The role of emotion in computer-mediated communication: A review. Computers in Human Behavior 24: 766–785.
9. Dodds PS, Harris KD, Kloumann IM, Bliss CA, Danforth CM (2011) Temporal patterns of happiness and information in a global social network: Hedonometrics and twitter. PLoS ONE 6: e26752.
10. Golder SA, Macy MW (2011) Diurnal and seasonal mood vary with work, sleep, and day length across diverse cultures. Science 333: 1878–1881.
11. Marchetti-Bowick M, Chambers N (2012) Learning for microblogs with distant supervision: Political forecasting with twitter. In: 13th EACL. pp. 603–612.
12. Bollen J, Pepe A, Mao H (2011) Modeling public mood and emotion: Twitter sentiment and socio-economic phenomena. In: Fifth ICWSM.
13. Bollen J, Mao H, Zeng X (2011) Twitter mood predicts the stock market. Journal of Computational Science 2: 1–8.
14. Zhao J, Dong L, Wu J, Xu K (2012) Moodlens: an emoticon-based sentiment analysis system for Chinese tweets. In: KDD '12. pp. 1528–1531.
15. Xiong X, Zhou G, Huang Y, Haiyong C, Xu K (2013) Dynamic evolution of collective emotions in social networks: a case study of sina weibo. Science China Information Sciences 56: 1–18.
16. Dodds PS, Danforth CM (2010) Measuring the happiness of large-scale written expression: Songs, blogs, and presidents. Journal of Happiness Studies 11: 441–456.
17. Pang B, Lee L, Vaithyanathan S (2002) Thumbs up?: sentiment classification using machine learning techniques. In: EMNLP. pp. 79–86.
18. Parikh R, Movassate M (2009) Sentiment analysis of user-generated twitter updates using various classification techniques. Technical report.
19. Read J (2005) Using emoticons to reduce dependency in machine learning techniques for sentiment classification. In: ACLstudent. pp. 43–48.
20. Go A, Bhayani R, Huang L (2011) Twitter sentiment classification using distant supervision. Technical report, Stanford Digital Library Technologies Project.
21. Liu B (2010) Sentiment analysis and subjectivity. In: Handbook of Natural Language Processing, Second Edition. Taylor and Francis Group, Boca.
22. Aoki S, Uchida O (2011) A method for automatically generating the emotional vectors of emoticons using weblog articles. In: Proceedings of the 10th WSEAS international conference on Applied computer and applied computational science. ACACOS'11, pp. 132–136.
23. Tossell CC, Kortum P, Shepard C, Barg-Walkow LH, Rahmati A, et al. (2012) A longitudinal study of emoticon use in text messaging from smartphones. Computers in Human Behavior 28: 659–663.
24. Shalizi C (2010) The bootstrap. American Scientist 98: 186–190.
25. Zhao J, Wu J, Liu G, Xu K, Chen G (2010) Being rational or aggressive? A revisit to Dunbar's Number in online social networks. ArXiv e-prints, arXiv: 1011.1547.
26. Dunbar R (1998) Grooming, Gossip, and the Evolution of Language. Harvard University Press, Cambridge, MA.
27. Li C, Sun A, Datta A (2012) Twevent: Segment-based event detection from tweets. In: Proceedings of the 21st ACM International Conference on Information and Knowledge Management. CIKM '12, pp. 155–164.
28. Sun GX (2012) Tang and Five Dynasties. Bei meng suo yan. A book of short stories from the Tang and Five Dynasties.
29. Fan R, Zhao J, Chen Y, Xu K (2013) Anger is more influential than joy: Sentiment correlation in Weibo. ArXiv e-prints, arXiv: 1309.2402.

26

Binary DNA Nanostructures for Data Encryption

Ken Halvorsen[1,2], Wesley P. Wong[1,2]*

1 Immune Disease Institute/Program in Cellular and Molecular Medicine, Harvard Medical School and Children's Hospital Boston, Boston, Massachusetts, United States of America, **2** Department of Biological Chemistry and Molecular Pharmacology, Harvard Medical School, Boston, Massachusetts, United States of America

Abstract

We present a simple and secure system for encrypting and decrypting information using DNA self-assembly. Binary data is encoded in the geometry of DNA nanostructures with two distinct conformations. Removing or leaving out a single component reduces these structures to an encrypted solution of ssDNA, whereas adding back this missing "decryption key" causes the spontaneous formation of the message through self-assembly, enabling rapid read out via gel electrophoresis. Applications include authentication, secure messaging, and barcoding.

Editor: Meni Wanunu, Northeastern University, United States of America

Funding: This work was supported by IDI startup funds. The funders had no role in study design, data collection and analysis, decision to publish, or preparation of the manuscript. URL of IDI: http://www.idi.harvard.edu/.

Competing Interests: KH and WW have submitted a patent application on the technique presented in this paper.

* E-mail: wong@idi.harvard.edu

Introduction

As the blueprint for all living things, DNA has a remarkable ability to robustly store and relay information. Two salient features of DNA make this possible: its modular construction from four distinct bases (A, C, G, T) whose sequence determines the genetic code, and the specific base pairing between complementary bases that enables hybridization into a double-stranded complex. These features of DNA have been exploited to perform computations and process information [1–6], including the hiding and encryption of secret messages [7–10]. Not only has DNA formed a foundation for the field of biomolecular computing, but the robustness of DNA-base pairing has also led to its use as a *programmable* structural material to construct objects with nanoscale features [11]. Recently, the accessibility and versatility of DNA nanotechnology has been remarkably increased with an approach referred to as DNA origami [12]. With a carefully designed collection of oligonucleotides, DNA can self-assemble into 2D and 3D shapes of stunning complexity [12–14], some of which incorporate sensing and actuation [15,16]. Combining the concepts of DNA as an information processing molecule and as a structural material, we have developed a simple and powerful approach for encoding and encrypting information.

In previous work, we used DNA origami methods to construct a nanoscale mechanical switch [17], which we used to study the force-dependence of molecular interactions at the single-molecule level. This switch could be in one of two states, looped or unlooped, and we observed that these conformational differences were clearly resolvable in an agarose gel (Figure 1a). Thus, while other schemes for representing binary data using DNA have been presented [8,18,19], here we focus on using the geometric conformation of DNA nanostructures to encode binary values, due to the ease of both encoding and decoding information using this approach. We have made three distinct realizations of this concept, as demonstrated in Figure 1. These nanoscale structures can switch between two distinct states, acting as a "mechanical bit" to enable the storage and processing of information

(analogous to mechanical relays in the earliest digital computers). These mechanical bits can be prepared in either state (0 or 1), and transitions between these states could be controlled using chemical or physical means (e.g. by changing the presence or absence of a critical molecular component, by varying the temperature, by interactions with light [20], or by applying mechanical force [17,21]). Importantly, the state of these bits can be read out in minutes using gel electrophoresis, or faster using single-molecule imaging and manipulation techniques, and multiple bits can be represented with different lengths of DNA to facilitate multiplexed information processing and readout.

Each mechanical bit is formed via DNA self-assembly, and can be encrypted by omitting a critical component of its structure (e.g. a key single-stranded DNA molecule) that reduces it to an unstructured mixture of oligonucleotides. Messages encrypted as a collection of such bits are difficult to decipher since the 0 bits and 1 bits are nearly indistinguishable mixtures of oligonucleotides that are identical in all but sequence. On the other hand, decryption with a key is very easy–simply adding the missing component triggers the self-assembly of these nanoscale mechanical bits into their unencrypted forms. The separation of each mechanical bit into two parts or two "keys" forms an asymmetric encryption system. This system has the "public key" property if the key is distributed physically, since one key cannot be readily determined from the other without knowledge of the sequence. Furthermore, suitable countermeasures, such as adding "distractor" oligos to the physical encryption key to obscure information, can make the decryption sequence difficult to obtain.

As an example, let us consider how Alice could send an encrypted message to Bob (Figure 2) using the linear binary switch shown in Figure 1C. Suppose she would like to send a three bit message, such as "101". First, Bob must generate the appropriate DNA encryption and decryption keys for each bit. To distinguish between bits, he chooses each to be a different DNA length, (e.g 20 bases, 30 bases and 40 bases), and then generates 3 equal length oligos for each bit (A, A', and B), two of which are complementary and hybridize together (A and A') and one of which is inert (B) (see

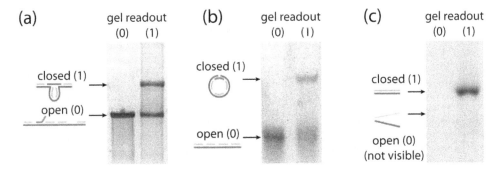

Figure 1. DNA as a binary switch. The conformations of two-state DNA nanostructures can represent bits through open or closed states, representing 0 and 1 respectively. We demonstrate this concept with three different implementations: a) a self-assembled construct with an addressable loop closure as described previously [17], b) a switchable circular/linear construct, and c) a double-stranded/single-stranded segment.

Materials and Methods for details on oligo design). Then Bob makes vials of A and B for each bit available, which represent the 1 and 0 values, respectively, while keeping the vials of oligo A' private. Together, the vials of A and B oligos form the *encryption key*, which can be used by anyone to encrypt a message. To send a message to Bob, Alice would mix either A (for a 1) or B (for a 0) for each bit into a single vial and send this mixture to Bob over a public channel. At this point, only Bob can decrypt the message by mixing in the private *decryption key* (the set of A' oligos) and running a gel–even Alice has no way to decrypt her own message once it's been made.

Results and Discussion

We experimentally demonstrated this encryption scheme for an 8-bit encoding by using 8 different lengths of DNA strands to represent the individual bits. We encoded a plaintext message using an 8-bit binary ASCII encoding with the 8th bit as an even parity bit, and encrypted the message into an ordered sequence of DNA mixtures, one for each letter. These mixtures were then decrypted by mixing them with the private key oligos and read out by immediately running an agarose gel. Reading each gel lane from top to bottom, the decrypted message "Hello world" becomes unambiguously clear (Figure 3).

One of the most intriguing aspects of encrypting messages with DNA as described is the difficulty for an interceptor or attacker to decrypt it. At a minimum, decryption attempts require possession of the physical message as well as technical skill, laboratory equipment, and time. Since the message is encrypted physically, the transmission of data can be well controlled, and even copying

the encrypted message poses a significant technical challenge. Unlike encryption schemes that rely on mathematical algorithms, our biochemical based encryption is not directly vulnerable to increasing computational power. With physical decryption, the number of decryption attempts is limited by the availability of physical material comprising the message, which is depleted with each attempt. In fact, the message could theoretically be reduced to enable only a single decryption attempt.

Attempts to crack the message without the decryption key would be difficult, especially for an attacker limited to the same resources as the intended recipient (i.e. electrophoresis and mixing equipment). For example, a naïve brute force attack to find the decryption key would require the physical generation and testing of an astronomical number of possible keys, with 4^N distinct possibilities, or 10^{155} for our simple 8-bit encoding scheme (and an approximately 1 in 10^{63} chance of guessing a decryption key if we allow for 25% mismatched bases [8,22]). However, aside from the correct decryption key, there could also exist a pseudo key or set of pseudo keys that could allow an attacker to distinguish between individual mixtures, providing a toehold for unauthorized decryption using language statistics on a large set of messages. Additionally, if the attacker has access to more sophisticated approaches, including sequencing techniques, DNA profiling with microarrays, or the ability to make libraries of oligos to test multiple keys at a time, then the security will be reduced. Fortunately, many of these approaches can be impeded by implementing the appropriate countermeasures, as described below. In addition, it is interesting to note that many of the potential ways to crack the code may involve significant technical

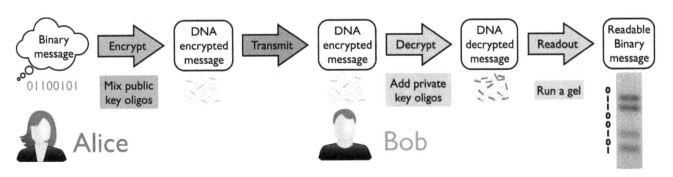

Figure 2. Conceptualization of DNA encryption and decryption. Alice prepares her message by mixing together oligos that correspond to either a binary 0 or 1 for each bit. This mixture is sent to Bob through a public channel, who decrypts the message by adding the DNA decryption key. This causes the message to self-assemble, enabling rapid read out by gel electrophoresis.

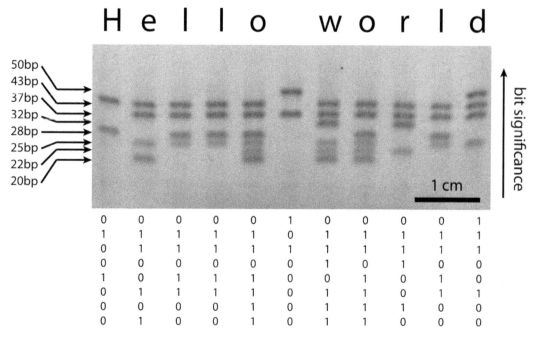

Figure 3. Decoding a binary message on a gel. Each lane of the gel contains a mixture of oligonucleotides which together form an 11 byte binary ASCII message which reads "Hello world". The bit strings are read from top to bottom with the most significant bit being the largest DNA segment. Presence of a band indicates a binary 1, while absence of a band indicates a binary 0. All lanes have the same amount of DNA present, but only the double stranded pieces dye.

expertise, expensive laboratory equipment, or time consuming processes, giving rise to a large asymmetry in effort compared to encrypting and decrypting the message with the proper keys.

To maximize encryption security, a variety of countermeasures can be used that comprise a two pronged approach: 1) limiting access to physical information about the message (e.g. the oligo sequences), and 2) making this physical information difficult to decipher. One simple countermeasure is to limit the physical amount of material comprising the message, as mentioned above. Additionally, we can impede chemical analysis by modifying the ends of the oligos to prevent the chemical conjugation required for some sequencing and profiling techniques. One important countermeasure against unauthorized decryption that falls into both categories is the addition of noise by mixing "distractor strands" into the physical message (described in detail elsewhere [8,23]). Adding oligonucleotides with a similar length and composition as the message strands but with different sequences increases the time and effort required to obtain the sequences of the oligonucleotides within the encrypted mixture, which is already a challenge due to their short lengths [24–26]. Also, distractor strands make deciphering the message more difficult since the true message can be obscured by noise designed to like the signal, or vice versa [23]. For a public key system, special care should be taken in designing the distractor strands to ensure that the two values for each bit are difficult to distinguish using a pseudo key or other biochemical techniques (e.g. mass spectrometry). For a private key system, distractor strands can be very effective at deterring statistical analysis, as each occurrence of a given letter could be mixed with a different set of distractor strands. In fact, false messages could be encoded into the mixture with distractor strands that represent "false encryption keys", and the attacker would have little way to identify the true message without knowing the specific decryption key sequence. Alternatively, to make the signal look more like the noise, DNA structures

could be pre-encrypted with standard computer encryption algorithms. Furthermore, cracking the code becomes increasingly challenging the more distractor strands are added, and the more bits per message are encoded.

While our demonstration showed 1 byte (8 bits) of data storage per mixture (and per gel lane), the amount of data stored and read out could be readily increased. If DNA lengths were optimized to be evenly spaced on the gel, a resolution of 1 mm would give 10 bits/cm of gel length, corresponding to roughly 8 bytes of data for a single short gel lane, 10–20 bytes for longer gels, and up to 125 bytes ($\sim$1000 bits) for more elaborate sequencing gels with base pair resolution [27]. Expanding to a few bytes could enable the transmission of entire words or short messages in a single mixture, especially if a more efficient character encoding scheme were used (e.g. the 5 bit Baudot code), or a word-based encoding scheme (e.g. 10 bytes could encode eight words of a 1000 word vocabulary). In addition, data density could be dramatically increased by combining multiple messages within a single mixture, with each message associated with a different decryption key. We note that these approaches will improve security by making statistical analysis of the message difficult.

In summary, we have developed a novel technique for encoding binary information in two-state DNA nanostructures, for encrypting and decrypting this information using self-assembly, and for rapidly reading this information back out with gel electrophoresis. As the state of such nanostructures can be used to report molecular events (such as the rupture of intermolecular bonds [17]), additional applications of this work beyond information security include the characterization of molecular interactions with a multiplexed gel readout. More directly, this approach provides a relatively simple and inexpensive way to send secure, and potentially hidden, messages over a public channel. Unlike similar DNA encryption methods that require specialized laboratory work (e.g. PCR, sequencing, cloning) that can take hours to days [7–10], our technique enables encrypting and decrypting messages in just minutes, requiring as little as disposable droppers and a no-prep bufferless (even handheld) gel system (e.g. Invitrogen E-gel systems). This convenience and simplicity also opens the technology to other applications such as authentication and barcoding. For example, increasing storage capacity to 40 bits would enable storage of the ubiquitous 12 digit Universal Product Code (UPC). Several methods have been demonstrated for storing printed DNA on paper [28,29], which combined with our quick readout method could enable a new level of security in product identification. In fact, tagging with DNA inks has recently found commercial use (DNA Technologies, Halifax, Canada) in anti-counterfeiting efforts for a variety of products including sports memorabilia, artwork, pharmaceuticals, and luxury goods. As previously proposed, DNA barcodes may also find use in labeling of liquids such as paint and oil, or possibly even food [8]. As another example, it could provide a simple and inexpensive way for pharmaceutical companies to discretely label drugs with production or expiration information, even at the level of edible encrypted barcodes on individual tablets. This is particularly timely in light of recently introduced government mandates (e.g. California E-Pedigree Law) to serialize pharmaceuticals and to ultimately "track and trace" them, since our method offers a way to identify and authenticate drugs, reducing theft and counterfeiting. One could also envision personal identification cards (e.g. driver's license, passports) being printed with DNA markers on them as an additional prevention against fraud or identity theft, or even using one's own genomic DNA as an authentication key.

Materials and Methods

We designed and purchased oligos (Bioneer, Inc.) to represent 8 different bits, which would be about evenly spaced on a 4%

agarose gel. The lengths we chose were 20 nt, 22 nt, 25 nt, 28 nt, 32 nt, 37 nt, 43 nt, and 50 nt. For each length, 3 oligos were purchased: a randomly generated sequence, it's complementary strand, and a random set with arbitrary bases. We denote these as set A, A', and B respectively.

To encode messages, we first converted our plain text message "Hello world" into binary code using 8 bit ASCII character encoding with the 8th bit as an even parity bit for error checking. Since we have 8 bits total, each letter was prepared using a mixture of A and B oligos to represent the 0 s and 1 s. As an example, the "H" in "Hello world" has an 8 bit binary representation of 01001000. The least significant bit is encoded in the smallest (20 nt) oligo, which we will denote oligo 1. To encode the "H", we mix oligos 4 and 7 from set A with oligos 1, 2, 3, 5, 6, and 8 from set B.

For decoding, the encoded message mixtures were individually mixed with the entire set A' of oligos in a buffer solution (1 × Buffer 4, New England Biolabs) and loaded into a gel (within minutes). We ran an automated precast 4% agarose gel (E-gel, Invitrogen) containing a proprietary dye (with characteristics remarkably similar to Sybr gold) for 15 minutes and took a picture immediately after. The binary representation of each gel lane could be read directly from top to bottom.

Acknowledgments

The authors would like to thank Daniel Cheng, Ted Feldman, Darren Yang, and Mounir Koussa for helpful discussions.

Author Contributions

Conceived and designed the experiments: KH WW. Performed the experiments: KH. Analyzed the data: KH WW. Wrote the paper: KH WW.

References

1. Adleman L (1994) Molecular computation of solutions to combinatorial problems. Science 266: 1021–1024.
2. Lipton R (1995) DNA solution of hard computational problems. Science 268: 542–545.
3. Guarnieri F, Fliss M, Bancroft C (1996) Making DNA add. Science 273: 220–223.
4. Ouyang Q, Kaplan P, Liu S, Libchaber A (1997) DNA solution of the maximal clique problem. Science 278: 446–449.
5. Braich R, Chelyapov N, Johnson C, Rothemund P, Adleman L (2002) Solution of a 20-variable 3-sat problem on a DNA computer. Science 296: 499–502.
6. Qian L, Winfree E (2011) Scaling up digital circuit computation with DNA strand displacement cascades. Science 332: 1196.
7. Clelland C, Risca V, Bancroft C (1999) Hiding messages in DNA microdots. Nature 399: 533–534.
8. Leier A, Richter C, Banzhaf W, Rauhe H (2000) Cryptography with DNA binary strands. Biosystems 57: 13–22.
9. Tanaka K, Okamoto A, Saito I (2005) Public-key system using DNA as a one-way function for key distribution. Biosystems 81: 25–29.
10. Cui G, Qin L, Wang Y, Zhang X (2008) An encryption scheme using DNA technology. Bio-Inspired Computing: Theories and Applications, 2008 : 37–42.
11. Seeman N (2007) An overview of structural DNA nanotechnology. Molecular biotechnology 37: 246–257.
12. Rothemund P (2006) Folding DNA to create nanoscale shapes and patterns. Nature 440: 297–302.
13. Yin P, Hariadi R, Sahu S, Choi H, Park S, et al. (2008) Programming DNA tube circumferences. Science 321: 824–826.
14. Douglas S, Dietz H, Liedl T, Högberg B, Graf F, et al. (2009) Self-assembly of DNA into nanoscale three-dimensional shapes. Nature 459: 414–418.
15. Andersen E, Dong M, Nielsen M, Jahn K, Subramani R, et al. (2009) Self-assembly of a nanoscale DNA box with a controllable lid. Nature 459: 73–76.
16. Douglas S, Bachelet I, Church G (2012) A logic-gated nanorobot for targeted transport of molecular payloads. Science 335: 831–834.
17. Halvorsen K, Schaak D, Wong W (2011) Nanoengineering a single-molecule mechanical switch using DNA self-assembly. Nanotechnology 22: 494005.
18. Roweis S, Winfree E, Burgoyne R, Chelyapov N, Goodman M, et al. (1998) A sticker-based model for DNA computation. Journal of Computational Biology 5: 615–629.
19. Yan H, LaBean T, Feng L, Reif J (2003) Directed nucleation assembly of DNA tile complexes by barcode-patterned lattices. Proceedings of the National Academy of Sciences 100: 8103.
20. Schäfer C, Eckel R, Ros R, Mattay J, Anselmetti D (2007) Photochemical single-molecule affinity switch. Journal of the American Chemical Society 129: 1488–1489.
21. Quek S, Kamenetska M, Steigerwald M, Choi H, Louie S, et al. (2009) Mechanically controlled binary conductance switching of a single-molecule junction. Nature Nanotechnology 4: 230–234.
22. Lee I, Dombkowski A, Athey B (2004) Guidelines for incorporating non-perfectly matched oligonucleotides into target-specific hybridization probes for a DNA microarray. Nucleic acids research 32: 681–690.
23. Gehani A, LaBean T, Reif J (2004) DNA-based cryptography. Aspects of Molecular Computing : 34–50.
24. Oberacher H, Mayr B, Huber C (2004) Automated de novo sequencing of nucleic acids by liquid chromatography-tandem mass spectrometry. Journal of the American Society for Mass Spectrometry 15: 32–42.
25. Oberacher H, Pitterl F (2009) On the use of esi-qqtof-ms/ms for the comparative sequencing of nucleic acids. Biopolymers 91: 401–409.
26. Farand J, Gosselin F (2009) De novo sequence determination of modified oligonucleotides. Analytical chemistry 81: 3723–3730.
27. França L, Carrilho E, Kist T (2002) A review of DNA sequencing techniques. Quarterly reviews of biophysics 35: 169–200.
28. Kawai J, Hayashizaki Y (2003) DNA book. Genome research 13: 1488–1495.
29. Hashiyada M (2004) Development of biometric DNA ink for authentication security. The Tohoku Journal of Experimental Medicine 204: 109–117.

27

Dimensionality of Social Networks Using Motifs and Eigenvalues

Anthony Bonato[1]*, **David F. Gleich**[2]*, **Myunghwan Kim**[3], **Dieter Mitsche**[4], **Paweł Prałat**[1], **Yanhua Tian**[5], **Stephen J. Young**[6]

1 Department of Mathematics, Ryerson University, Toronto, Ontario, Canada, 2 Computer Science Department, Purdue University, West Lafayette, Indiana, United States of America, 3 Electrical Engineering Department, Stanford University, Stanford, California, United States of America, 4 Laboratoire J.A. Dieudonné, Université de Nice Sophia-Antipolis, Nice, France, 5 Department of Mathematics and Statistics, York University, Toronto, Ontario, Canada, 6 Mathematics Department, University of Louisville, Louisville, Kentucky, United States of America

Abstract

We consider the dimensionality of social networks, and develop experiments aimed at predicting that dimension. We find that a social network model with nodes and links sampled from an m-dimensional metric space with power-law distributed influence regions best fits samples from real-world networks when m scales logarithmically with the number of nodes of the network. This supports a logarithmic dimension hypothesis, and we provide evidence with two different social networks, Facebook and LinkedIn. Further, we employ two different methods for confirming the hypothesis: the first uses the distribution of motif counts, and the second exploits the eigenvalue distribution.

Editor: Satoru Hayasaka, Wake Forest School of Medicine, United States of America

Funding: NSERC DG grants; NSF CAREER award CCF-1149756; MITACS for hosting the authors' research team at the Advances in Network Analysis and its Applications Workshop held at the University of British Colombia in July 2012. The funders had no role in study design, data collection and analysis, decision to publish, or preparation of the manuscript.

Competing Interests: The authors have declared that no competing interests exist.

* Email: abonato@ryerson.ca (AB); dgleich@purdue.edu (DFG)

Introduction

Empirical studies of on-line social networks as undirected graphs suggest these graphs have several intrinsic properties: highly skewed or even power-law degree distributions [1,2], large local clustering [3], constant [3] or even shrinking diameter with network size [4], densification [4], and localized information flow bottlenecks [5,6]. These are challenging properties to capture in concise models of social network connections and growth [7–9], and many models only possess them in certain parameter regimes. One model that captures these properties *asymptotically* is the geometric protean model (GEO-P) [10]. It differs from other network models [1,4,11,12] because all links in geometric protean networks arise based on an underlying metric space. This metric space mirrors a construction in the social sciences called *Blau space* [13]. In Blau space, agents in the social network correspond to points in a metric space, and the relative position of nodes follows the principle of *homophily* [14]: nodes with similar socio-demographics are closer together in the space.

In order to accurately capture the observed properties of social networks—in particular, constant or shrinking diameters—the dimension of the underlying metric space in the GEO-P model must grow logarithmically with the number of nodes. The logarithmically scaled dimension is a property that occurs frequently with network models that incorporate geometry, such as in multiplicative attribute graphs [7] and random Apollonian

networks [15]. Because of its prevalence in these models, the logarithmic relationship between the dimension of the metric space and the number of nodes has been called the *logarithmic dimension hypothesis* [10]. This hypothesis generalizes previous analysis which shows that individuals in a social network can be identified with relatively little information. For instance, Sweeney found that 87% of the U.S. population had reported attributes that likely made them unique using only zip code, gender and date of birth, and concluded that few attributes were needed to uniquely identity a person in the U.S. population [16]. Here, we find evidence of the log-dimension property in real world social networks.

We emphasize that the present paper is the first study that we are aware of which attempts to quantify the dimensionality of social networks and Blau space. While we do not claim to prove conclusively the logarithmic dimension hypothesis for such networks, our experiments, such as those of [16], suggest a much smaller dimension in contrast to the overall size of the networks. Interestingly, speculation on the low dimensionality of social networks arose independently from theoretical analysis of mathematical models of social networks in [7,10,15].

Our findings provide evidence for dimensional properties underlying social networks that have a number of potential applications in future studies. First, the dimensional properties could be used for further classification and characterization of different types of networks. Second, many NP-hard optimization problems related to graph properties and community detection are polynomial time solvable in a low dimensional metric space, and thus, our findings suggest new techniques to explore for understanding why we may expect to solve these problems in social networks. Finally, if techniques to find these dimensions emerge, we should be able to create powerful new methods to harness the insight they offer into the network structure.

MGEO-P

The particular network model we study is a simple variation on the GEO-P model that we name the memoryless geometric protean model (MGEO-P), since it enables us to approximate a GEO-P network without using a costly sampling procedure. Both GEO-P and the MGEO-P model depends on five parameters described in Table 1.

The nodes and edges of the network arise from the following process. Initially the network is empty. At each of n steps, a new node v arrives and is assigned both a random position q_v in $\mathbb{R}^m$ within the unit-hypercube $[0,1]^m$ and a random rank r_v from those unused ranks remaining in the set 1 to n. The influence radius of any node is computed based on the formula:

$$I(r) = \frac{1}{2}(r^{-\alpha}n^{-\beta})^{1/m}.$$

With probability p, the node v forms an undirected connection to any preexisting node u where $\mathcal{D}(v,u) \leq I(r_v)$, where the distances are computed with respect to the following metric:

$$\mathcal{D}(v,u) = \min\{\|q_v - q_u - z\|_\infty : z \in \{-1,0,1\}^m\},$$

and where $\|\cdot\|_\infty$ is the infinity-norm. We note that this implies that the geometric space is symmetric in any point as the metric "wraps" around like on a torus. The volume of space influenced by the node is $r_v^{-\alpha}n^{-\beta}$. Then the next node arrives and repeats the process until all n nodes have been placed. In the MGEO-P model, the process ends here, whereas in the GEO-P model, the network then removes the least-recently added node, and inserts a new node following the same procedure. This iterative replacement process continues until it reaches it reaches a random point.

Figure 1 illustrates two features of the model. First, after a few steps, only a few nodes exist and even a large influence region will only produce a few links. Second, when the number of steps approaches n, a large influence region will produce many links. The idea behind the model is a simple abstraction of the growth of an on-line social network. When the network is first growing (few steps), even influential members will only know a few other members who have also joined. But after the network has been around for a while (many steps), influential members will begin with many friends.

We formally prove that the MGEO-P model has the following properties. Let $\alpha \in (0,1)$, $\beta \in (0,1-\alpha)$, $p \in (0,1]$ and m be positive integer. The following statements hold with probability tending to 1 as n tends to ∞. See the MGEO-P section of File S1 for the proofs. We actually show these results hold with extremely high probability, which is a stronger notion that implies probability tending to 1.

1. Let v be a node of $\mathbf{MGEO-P}(n,m,\alpha,\beta,p)$ with rank R that arrived at step t. Then

$$\deg(v) = \left(\frac{i-1}{n-1}\frac{p}{1-\alpha}n^{1-\alpha-\beta} + (n-i)pR^{-\alpha}n^{-\beta}\right) \cdot \left(1 + \mathcal{O}\left(\sqrt{\frac{\log^2(n)}{n^{1-\alpha-\beta}}}\right)\right)$$

This result implies that the degree distribution follows a powerlaw with exponent $\eta = 1 + \frac{1}{\alpha}$.

2. The average degree of node of $\mathbf{MGEO-P}(n,m,\alpha,\beta,p)$ is

$$\rho = \frac{p}{1-\alpha}n^{1-\alpha-\beta}\left(1 + \mathcal{O}\left(\sqrt{\frac{\log^2(n)}{n^{1-\alpha-\beta}}}\right)\right).$$

3. The diameter of $\mathbf{MGEO-P}(n,m,\alpha,\beta,p)$ is $n^{\Theta\left(\frac{1}{m}\right)}$.

This last property suggests that, ignoring constants, for a network with n nodes and diameter D, the expected dimension based on the MGEO-P model is

$$m \approx \frac{\log n}{\log D}.$$

Thus, like some network models that incorporate geometry [7,15], in the MGEO-P model, the dimension m must scale logarithmically in order for the diameter to remain constant as n increases.

Experimental Design and Graph Summaries

Both graph motifs and spectral densities are numeric summaries of a graph that abstract the details of a network into a small set of values that are independent of the particular nodes of a network. These summaries have the property that isomorphic graphs have the same values, and we will use these summaries to determine the dimension of the metric space that best matches Facebook and LinkedIn networks as illustrated in Figure 2. Graph motifs, graphlets, or graph moments are the frequency or abundance of specific small subgraphs in a large network. We study undirected, connected subgraphs up to four nodes as our graph motifs (with the exception of the number of edges, or two-node motifs, as the networks are created to preserve this count). This is a set of 8 graphs shown in at the bottom of Figure 2 along with the single two node graph of an edge. The spectral density of a graph is the statistical distribution of eigenvalues of the normalized Laplacian matrix as indicated in the upper right of that figure. These eigenvalues indicate and summarize many network properties including the behavior of a uniform random walk, the number of connected components, an approximate connectivity measure,

Table 1. The parameters of the MGEO-P model.

n	the total number of nodes
m	the dimension of the metric space
$0 < \alpha < 1$	the attachment strength parameter
$0 < \beta < 1 - \alpha$	the density parameter
$0 < p \leq 1$	the connection probability

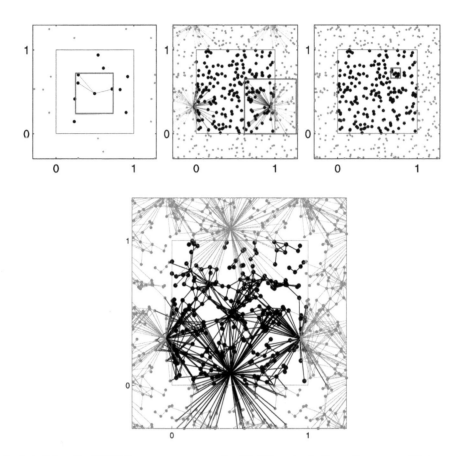

Figure 1. An example describing the MGEO-P process on a graph with 250 nodes in the unit square with torus metric, where $\alpha = 0.9$ and $\beta = 0.04$ and $p = 1$. Each figure shows the graph "replicated" in grey on all sides in order to illustrate the torus metric. Links are drawn to the closest replicated neighbor. The blue square indicates the region $[0,1]^2$. *Top row (left to right)* The MGEO-P process begins with relatively few nodes, and thus, nodes must have large influence radii (red squares) to link anywhere. As more nodes arrive, large radii result in many connections, modeling influential users, and small radii result in a few connections, modeling standard users. *Bottom row* Illustrates the final constructed graph.

and many other features [17,18]. Thus, the spectral density of the normalized Laplacian is a particularly helpful characterization that captures many such separate network properties.

We study dimensional scaling in social networks by comparing samples of the MGEO-P networks of varying dimensions with samples of social network data from Facebook and LinkedIn. We pay particular attention to the relationship between the number of nodes n of the network and the dimension m of the best fit MGEO-P network. In order to determine what underlying dimension for MGEO-P best fits a given graph, we employ two distinct methods. For one experiment, we use features known as graph motifs, graphlets, or graph moments in concert with a support vector machine (SVM) classifier. This approach has been used successfully to determine the best generative mechanism of a network [19] and to select parameters of a complicated network models to fit real-world data [9,20]. In a second experiment, we use spectral densities of the normalized Laplacian matrix of a graph and a Kullback-Leibler divergence (KL divergence) similarity measurement, which has been used to match protein networks between species [21,22]. We find evidence of the logarithmic dimension hypothesis in both cases.

The data

Facebook distributed 100 samples of social networks from universities within the United States measured as of September 2005 [23], which range in size from 700 nodes to 42,000 nodes.

We call these networks the Facebook samples. The LinkedIn samples were created from the LinkedIn connection network together with the creation time of each connection from May 2003 to October 2006. To perform our experiments on networks of different size, we build 71 snapshots of the LinkedIn network at various timestamps. We then extracted a dense subset of their graph at various time points that is representative of active users; we used the 5-core of the network for this purpose [24]. The k-core of a network is a maximum size subset of vertices such that all vertices have degree k. See Figure 3 and the full statistics tables of File S1 for additional properties of these networks. In both networks, the number of edges per node grows at essentially the same rate.

Results

The results of our dimensional fitting for graphlets are shown in Figure 4 and the results of the fitting using spectral densities are in Figure 5. For both datasets and both types of statistics, the best-fit dimension scales logarithmically with the number of nodes and closely tracks a simple model prediction based on the diameter D of the network (the model curve plots $m = \log(n)/\log(D)$). These experiments corroborate the logarithmic dimension hypothesis; although the precise fits differ as shown in Table 2.

The most important feature of these results is that both methodologies show similar scaling in how the dimensionality

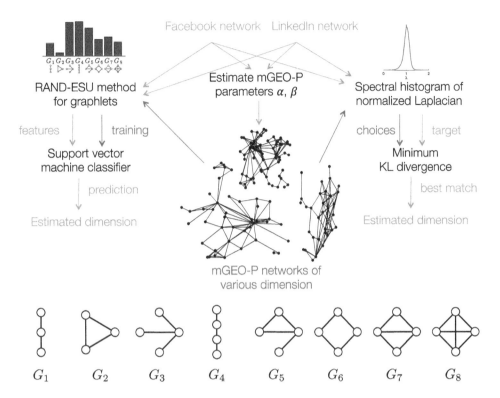

Figure 2. At left and center, we have the steps involved in fitting via graphlets; at right and center, we have the steps involved in fitting via spectral histogram. Throughout, red lines denote the flow of features for the MGEO-P networks whereas blue lines denote flow of features for the original networks. At the bottom, we show an enlarged representation of the 8 graphlets we use.

scales with network size. There are minor differences between the precise predicted dimensions–for instance, the spectral density approach predicts slightly higher dimensions for Facebook than does the graphlet approach–but the results agree to a reasonable degree with the dimension predicted by the model: $\log(n)/\log(D)$. Also, the confidence bounds are small around the chosen dimension.

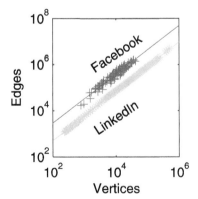

Figure 3. The scale of the network data involved in our study varies over three orders of magnitude. We see similar scaling for both types of networks, but with slightly different offsets. For Facebook, $\log_{10}(\text{edges}) = 1.06 \log_{10}(\text{nodes}) + 1.35$ with $R^2 = 0.945$; for LinkedIn $\log_{10}(\text{edges}) = 1.07 \log_{10}(\text{nodes}) + 0.56$ with $R^2 > 0.999$. The regularity in the LinkedIn sizes is due to our construction of those networks.

Sensitivity and robustness

We investigate the sensitivity of the graphlet results in two settings. If we reduce the training set size of the SVM classifier by using a random subset of 20% of the input training data and then rerun the training and classification procedure 50 times, then we find a distribution over dimensions that we report as a box-plot, shown in Figure 4. In File S1, we further study perturbation results that argue against these results occurring due to chance. In particular, we find that these dimensions are robust to moderate changes to the network structure (Figure S2 in File S1) and we find that our methodology does not predict useful dimensions of Erdös-Rényi random graphs or random graphs with the same degree distribution (Figure 1 in File S1). We do not report a precise *p*-value as there are no widely accepted null-models for network data. We study the sensitivity of the spectral densities that look for matches that are within 105% of the true minimum divergence. This defines a dimension interval around each match that is small for all of our examples.

Discussion

There is a growing body of evidence that argues for some type of geometric structure in social and information networks. An important study in this direction views networks as samples of geometric graphs within a hyperbolic space [25–27]. Recent work has further shown that hyperbolic embeddings reproduce shortest path metrics in real-world networks [28]. In both MGEO-P and hyperbolic random geometric networks, highly skewed or power-law degree distributions are imposed–either directly as in MGEO-P, or implicitly as in the hyperbolic space scaling. These results further support hidden metric structures in networks by empirically confirming a prediction about the dimension of the metric

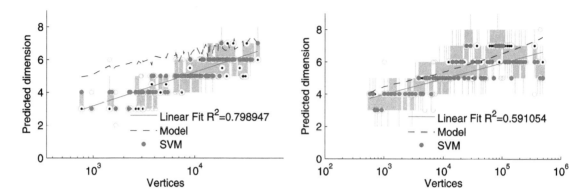

Figure 4. Facebook dimension at left, LinkedIn dimension at right. Each red dot (SVM) is the predicted dimension computed via graphlet features and a support vector machine classifier. For the Facebook data, we find that $m = 2.06 \log(n)/\log(10) - 3.00$. For the LinkedIn data, we find that $m = 0.7333 \log(n)/\log(10) + 1$. And these are plotted as the red linear fit line. Our theoretical model predicts a dimension of $log(n)/log(D)$ and we plot this as the dashed line. In each figure, we show the variance in the fitted dimension as a box-plot. We estimate the variance by using only 20% of the original training data and repeating over 50 trials. There are only a few outliers for small dimensions.

space made by one particular model. The importance of this finding is that it provides new insight into how the metric space must behave as the network grows. Previous studies assume a fixed dimension metric structure and our results indicate that a variable dimension may be more appropriate. In practice, estimating the dimensions of these networks could be useful for anomaly detection in the network and characterizing new types of network data.

Note that these results do not conclusively argue that MGEO-P is a **perfectly accurate** model for social networks; there are meaningful differences between the spectral histograms from MGEO-P and real social networks, see Figure 6. There are also similar differences in the graphlet counts. Our results support a **different** hypothesis. The closest MGEO-P network to a given social network has a metric space whose dimension scales logarithmically with the number of nodes. In File S1 (Sensitivity studies section), we have determined that this property is not due to either the edge density or the degree distribution; thus, our findings appears to reflect a new intrinsic property of social networks.

This finding suggests a number of opportunities for designing social network models with metric spaces that evolve in time. We believe that such models offer the opportunity to identify new

properties of social network based on emergent properties of the models. One question to address is how the metric space and connection radius change, if at all, as the network grows. Answering this question would provide insight into the value of additional users of a network. Additionally, our results suggest that many network models that assume a fixed dimension should be reevaluated.

Materials and Methods

Powerlaw fitting

To determine the powerlaw exponent η, we use the Clauset-Shalizi-Newman power-law exponent estimator [29] as implemented by Tamás Nepusz [30].

Diameters

The MGEO-P model of a network predicts that the dimension m should approximate $\log(n)/\log(D)$, where D is the diamater. However, as D is sensitive to outliers we use the 99% effective diameter computed via an asymptotically accurate approximation scheme [31] as implemented in the SNAP library on 2011-12-31. The effective diameter of all Facebook networks ranges between 3.5 and 4.6, with a mean of 4.1. For the LinkedIn data, the

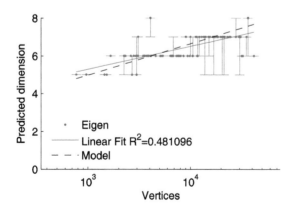
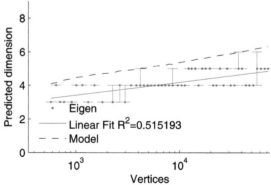

Figure 5. Facebook data at left, LinkedIn data at right. Each blue point (Eigen) is the dimension of the MGEO-P sample with the minimum KL-divergence between the graph and the MGEO-P sample. We also show any other other dimensions within 5% of this divergence value. The dimensions shift modestly higher for Facebook and remain almost unchanged for LinkedIn. Both still are closely correlated with the theoretical prediction based on the model based on $\log(n)/\log(D)$ (dashed line). The linear fits to the predicted dimensions is plotted as the red linear fit line.

Table 2. Dimension scaling for Facebook and LinkedIn.

Data	Dimension fit	Coefficients		95% Confidence	
	$a \log(n)/\log(10)+b$	a	b	a	b
Facebook	Graphlet	2.06	−3.00	(1.851, 2.264)	(−3.821, −2.182)
	Spectral density	1.21	1.65	(0.9782, 1.446)	(0.7272, 2.578)
LinkedIn	Graphlet	0.98	1.01	(0.786, 1.178)	(0.1591, 1.87)
	Spectral density	0.77	1.1	(0.56, 0.99)	(0.23, 1.95)

The specific dimensional scaling lines fit to the data in Figures 4 and 5 illustrate the growth of the network is logarithmic in the number of nodes.

effective diameter ranges between 4.3 and 5.9, with a mean of 5.4. In both networks, larger graphs have bigger effective diameters, although the differences are slight and the full data is available in the File S1, Full statistics tables.

Graphlets

To compute graphlets, we employ the rand-esu sampling algorithm [32] as implemented in the igraph library [33]. This algorithm approximates the count of each subgraph via a stochastic search, which then depends on the probability of continuing to search. Thus, if the probability is near 1 then the scores are nearly exact, but very expensive to compute, and small probabilities truncate the search early to produces fast estimates. The value we use is $10/n$. We use log-transformed output from this procedure in order to capture the dynamic range of the resulting values.

Spectral densities

We approximate the spectral density via a 201-bin histogram of the eigenvalues of the normalized Laplacian, which all fall between 0 and 2. (The choice of 201 was based on prior experiences with the spectral histograms of networks.) To compute eigenvalues of a network, we employ the recently developed ScaLAPACK routine using the MRRR algorithm [34–36].

SVM

We used a multi-class support-vector machine (SVM) based classification tool from Weka [37] to predict the relationship between the graphlets and the dimension. We considered

alternatives, such as alternating decision trees and logistic regression; however, we settled on the SVM approach as it has the most flexible classification boundary to fit the highly nonlinear relationships between graphlet counts and dimensions.

Setting MGEO-P Parameters

Consider a graph $G=(V,E)$ that we wish to compare to an MGEO-P sample. The MGEO-P model depends on four parameters: n, m, α, and β. The choice of n is straightforward as we use the number of nodes of the original graph. Both α and β can be chosen independently of the dimension m. Specifically, both α and β determine the average degree of the network and the exponent of the power law in the degree distribution, up to lower-order terms, as shown by property 1 and property 2. By computing just these two simple statistics of a network–the exponent of the power law and the average degree–we can invert these relationships and choose these parameters. Let η be the power-law exponent and ρ be the average degree. Then:

$$\alpha+\beta=1-\log(\rho)/\log(n) \quad \text{and} \quad \alpha=\frac{1}{\eta-1}.$$

In order to derive this simple expression, we make the simplifying assumption that p does not go to zero too quickly, for example $p=n^{-o(1)}$, in which case: $\log(\rho)=(1-\alpha-\beta)\log(n)+o(1)$ follows from the expression for the average degree of a MGEO-P network. We use the following treatment of the probability p in order to maximize the clustering coefficient of the network. We first generate

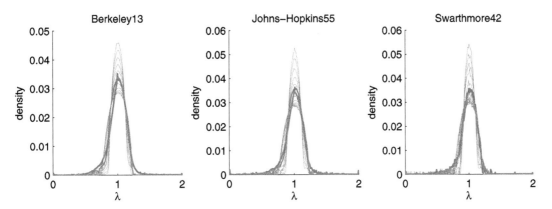

Figure 6. For three of the Facebook networks, we show the eigenvalue histogram in red, the eigenvalue histogram from the best fit MGEO-P network in blue, and the eigenvalue histograms for samples from the other dimensions in grey. The MGEO-P model correctly captures the peak of the distribution around 1, but fails to completely capture the tail between 1 and 2. Thus, we see meaningful difference between these profiles and hence, do not suggest that MGEO-P captures all of the properties of real-world social networks.

an MGEO-P network with $p=1$. Then suppose that the original network had $E=n\rho/2$ edges, we continue by randomly deleting edges until the output has exactly the same number of edges as the input network. This step can be interpreted as using the value of p necessary to get the same edge count as the original graph. In the case where there are insufficient edges, we leave the output from the MGEO-P generator untouched. This process effectively chooses p as large as possible, which gives us the largest local clustering.

Acknowledgments

We acknowledge Jure Leskovec for allowing us to access the LinkedIn dataset.

Supporting Information

File S1 This supporting document contains the following components of our analysis. (i) Formal proofs of the MGEO-P properties. (ii) Full statistical information about each of the Facebook and LinkedIn networks including the graphlet counts. (iii) Figure S1: Predicted dimensions of random graphs with the same degree distribution. (iv) Figure S2: The change in predicted dimension found by perturbing the graph structure. (v) A discussion of the sensitivity results about the predicted dimension.

Author Contributions

Conceived and designed the experiments: AB DG. Performed the experiments: DG MK YT. Analyzed the data: DG MK. Contributed to the writing of the manuscript: DG AB PP SY PP. Contributed theory: DM PP SY.

References

1. Barabási AL, Albert R (1999) Emergence of scaling in random networks. Science 286: 509–512.
2. Faloutsos M, Faloutsos P, Faloutsos C (1999) On power-law relationships of the internet topology. SIGCOMM Comput Commun Rev 29: 251–262.
3. Watts DJ, Strogatz SH (1998) Collective dynamics of "small-world" networks. Nature 393: 440–442.
4. Leskovec J, Kleinberg J, Faloutsos C (2007) Graph evolution: Densification and shrinking diameters. ACM Trans Knowl Discov Data 1: 1–41.
5. Estrada E (2006) Spectral scaling and good expansion properties in complex networks. EPL (Europhysics Letters) 73: 649.
6. Leskovec J, Lang KJ, Dasgupta A, Mahoney MW (2009) Community structure in large networks: Natural cluster sizes and the absence of large well-defined clusters. Internet Mathematics 6: 29–123.
7. Kim M, Leskovec J (2012) Multiplicative attribute graph model of real-world networks. Internet Mathematics 8: 113–160.
8. Kolda TG, Pinar A, Plantenga T, Seshadhri C (2013) A scalable generative graph model with community structure. arXiv cs.SI: 1302.6636.
9. Gleich DF, Owen AB (2012) Moment based estimation of stochastic Kronecker graph parameters. Internet Mathematics 8: 232–256.
10. Bonato A, Janssen J, Prałat P (2012) Geometric protean graphs. Internet Mathematics 8: 2–28.
11. Kumar R, Raghavan P, Rajagopalan S, Sivakumar D, Tomkins A, et al. (2000) Stochastic models for the web graph. In: Proceedings of the 41st Annual Symposium on Foundations of Computer Science. IEEE Computer Society, FOCS '00, pp. 57–65. URL 10.1109/SFCS.2000.892065.
12. Leskovec J, Chakrabarti D, Kleinberg J, Faloutsos C, Ghahramani Z (2010) Kronecker graphs: An approach to modeling networks. Journal of Machine Learning Research 11: 985–1042.
13. McPherson JM, Ranger-Moore JR (1991) Evolution on a dancing landscape: Organizations and networks in dynamic Blau space. Social Forces 70: 19–42.
14. McPherson M, Smith-Lovin L, Cook JM (2001) Birds of a feather: Homophily in social networks. Annual Review of Sociology 27: 415–444.
15. Zhang Z, Comellas F, Fertin G, Rong L (2006) High-dimensional Apollonian networks. Journal of Physics A: Mathematical and General 39: 1811.
16. Sweeney L (2000) Uniqueness of simple demographics in the U.S. population. Technical Report LIDAPWP4, Carnegie Mellon University.
17. Chung FRL (1992) Spectral Graph Theory. American Mathematical Society.
18. Banerjee A, Jost J (2009) Graph spectra as a systematic tool in computational biology. Discrete Applied Mathematics 157: 2425–2431.
19. Memišević V, Milenković T, Pržulj N (2010) An integrative approach to modeling biological networks. Journal of Integrative Bioinformatics 7: 120.
20. Moreno SI, Neville J, Kirshner S (2013) Learning mixed Kronecker product graph models with simulated method of moments. In: Proceedings of the 19th ACM SIGKDD International Conference on Knowledge Discovery and Data Mining. ACM, KDD '13, pp.1052–1060. doi: 10.1145/2487575.2487675.
21. Patro R, Kingsford C (2012) Global network alignment using multiscale spectral signatures. Bioinformatics 28: 3105–3114.
22. Banerjee A (2012) Structural distance and evolutionary relationship of networks. Biosystems 107: 186–196.
23. Traud AL, Mucha PJ, Porter MA (2011) Social structure of Facebook networks. arXiv cs.SI: 1102.2166.
24. Seidman SB (1983) Network structure and minimum degree. Social Networks 5: 269–287.
25. Krioukov D, Papadopoulos F, Kitsak M, Vahdat A, Boguñá M (2010) Hyperbolic geometry of complex networks. Phys Rev E 82: 036106.
26. Krioukov D, Kitsak M, Sinkovits RS, Rideout D, Meyer D, et al. (2012) Network cosmology. Sci Rep 2: 2012/11/16/online.
27. Krioukov D, Ostilli M (2013) Duality between equilibrium and growing networks. Phys Rev E 88: 022808.
28. Zhao X, Sala A, Zheng H, Zhao B (2011) Efficient shortest paths on massive social graphs. In: Proceedings of the 7th International Conference on Collaborative Computing: Networking, Applications and Worksharing. CollaborateCom, pp.77–86.
29. Clauset A, Shalizi CR, Newman MEJ (2009) Power-law distributions in empirical data. SIAM Review 51: 661–703.
30. Nepusz T (2012). plfit software. https://github.com/ntamas/plfit. Accessed 2012.
31. Palmer CR, Gibbons PB, Faloutsos C (2002) ANF: A fast and scalable tool for data mining in massive graphs. In: Proceedings of the Eighth ACM SIGKDD International Conference on Knowledge Discovery and Data Mining. ACM, KDD '02, pp.81–90. doi:10.1145/775047.775059.
32. Wernicke S (2006) Efficient detection of network motifs. Computational Biology and Bioinformatics, IEEE/ACM Transactions on 3: 347–359.
33. Csardi G, Nepusz T (2006) The igraph software package for complex network research. InterJournal Complex Systems: 1695.
34. Dhillon IS (1997) A new $O(n^2)$ algorithm for the symmetric tridiagonal eigenvalue/eigenvector problem. Ph.D. thesis, University of California, Berkeley.
35. Dhillon IS, Parlett BN, Vömel C (2006) The design and implementation of the MRRR algorithm. ACM Trans Math Softw 32: 533–560.
36. Vömel C (2010) ScaLAPACK's MRRR algorithm. ACM Trans Math Softw 37: 1:1–1:35.
37. Witten IH, Frank E (2005) Data Mining: Practical machine learning tools and techniques. Morgan Kaufmann.

Permissions

The contributors of this book come from diverse backgrounds, making this book a truly international effort. This book will bring forth new frontiers with its revolutionizing research information and detailed analysis of the nascent developments around the world.

We would like to thank all the contributing authors for lending their expertise to make the book truly unique. They have played a crucial role in the development of this book. Without their invaluable contributions this book wouldn't have been possible. They have made vital efforts to compile up to date information on the varied aspects of this subject to make this book a valuable addition to the collection of many professionals and students.

This book was conceptualized with the vision of imparting up-to-date information and advanced data in this field. To ensure the same, a matchless editorial board was set up. Every individual on the board went through rigorous rounds of assessment to prove their worth. After which they invested a large part of their time researching and compiling the most relevant data for our readers.

The editorial board has been involved in producing this book since its inception. They have spent rigorous hours researching and exploring the diverse topics which have resulted in the successful publishing of this book. They have passed on their knowledge of decades through this book. To expedite this challenging task, the publisher supported the team at every step. A small team of assistant editors was also appointed to further simplify the editing procedure and attain best results for the readers.

Apart from the editorial board, the designing team has also invested a significant amount of their time in understanding the subject and creating the most relevant covers. They scrutinized every image to scout for the most suitable representation of the subject and create an appropriate cover for the book.

The publishing team has been an ardent support to the editorial, designing and production team. Their endless efforts to recruit the best for this project, has resulted in the accomplishment of this book. They are a veteran in the field of academics and their pool of knowledge is as vast as their experience in printing. Their expertise and guidance has proved useful at every step. Their uncompromising quality standards have made this book an exceptional effort. Their encouragement from time to time has been an inspiration for everyone.

The publisher and the editorial board hope that this book will prove to be a valuable piece of knowledge for researchers, students, practitioners and scholars across the globe.

List of Contributors

Chuanqi Xie, Qiaonan Wang and Yong He
College of Biosystems Engineering and Food Science, Zhejiang University, Hangzhou, China

Michele Tumminello
Department of Social and Decision Sciences, Carnegie Mellon University, Pittsburgh, Pennsylvania, United States of America
Dipartimento di Fisica, Università di Palermo, Palermo, Italy

Salvatore Miccichè and Rosario N. Mantegna
Dipartimento di Fisica, Università di Palermo, Palermo, Italy

Fabrizio Lillo
Dipartimento di Fisica, Università di Palermo, Palermo, Italy
Santa Fe Institute, Santa Fe, New Mexico, United States of America
Scuola Normale Superiore di Pisa, Pisa, Italy

Jyrki Piilo
Department of Physics and Astronomy, Turku Centre for Quantum Physics, University of Turku, Turun yliopisto, Finland

Zoltan Gingl and Robert Mingesz
Department of Technical Informatics, University of Szeged, Szeged, Hungary

Kimberly N. Gajewski
Response Directorate, Federal Emergency Management Agency, Washington, DC, United States of America

Amy E. Peterson, Rohit A. Chitale and Jean-Paul Chretien
Division of Integrated Biosurveillance, Armed Forces Health Surveillance Center, Silver Spring, MD, United States of America

Julie A. Pavlin and Kevin L. Russell
Headquarters, Armed Forces Health Surveillance Center, Silver Spring, MD, United States of America

Stefan Woltmann, Philip C. Stouffer, Christine M. Bergeon Burns and Sabrina S. Taylor
School of Renewable Natural Resources, Louisiana State University AgCenter, Baton Rouge, Louisiana, 70803, United States of America

Mark S. Woodrey
Mississippi State University - Coastal Research and Extension Center, Grand Bay National Estuarine Research Reserve, Moss Point, Mississippi, 39562, United States of America

Mollie F. Cashner
Department of Biology, Austin Peay State University, Clarksville, Tennessee, 37040, United States of America

Magdalena Lenda, Karolina Kuszewska and Michał Woyciechowski
Institute of Environmental Sciences, Jagiellonian University, Krakow, Poland

Piotr Skórka
Institute of Zoology, Poznan University of Life Sciences, Poznan, Poland

Johannes M. H. Knops
School of Biological Sciences, University of Nebraska, Lincoln, Nebraska, United States of America

Dawid Moroń
Institute of Systematics and Evolution of Animals, Polish Academy of Sciences, Kraków, Poland

William J. Sutherland
Conservation Science Group, Department of Zoology, University of Cambridge, Cambridge, United Kingdom

Serguei Saavedra
Northwestern Institute on Complex Systems, Northwestern University, Evanston, Illinois, United States of America
Kellogg School of Management, Northwestern University, Evanston, Illinois, United States of America
Northwestern University Clinical and Translational Sciences Institute, Northwestern University, Chicago, Illinois, United States of America

Jordi Duch
Department of Computer Science and Mathematics, Universitat Rovira i Virgili, Tarragona, Spain

Brian Uzzi
Northwestern Institute on Complex Systems, Northwestern University, Evanston, Illinois, United States of America
Kellogg School of Management, Northwestern University, Evanston, Illinois, United States of America

Jack Hollingdale
School of Psychology, University of Sussex, Brighton, United Kingdom

Tobias Greitemeyer
Institute of Psychology, University of Innsbruck, Innsbruck, Austria

Christopher Burton
Centre for Population Health Sciences, University of Edinburgh, Edinburgh, United Kingdom

Qi Xie, Bin Hu and Na Dong
Hangzhou Key Laboratory of Cryptography and Network Security, Hangzhou Normal University, Hangzhou, China

Duncan S. Wong
Department of Computer Science, City University of Hong Kong, Kowloon, Hong Kong, China

Fan Wang, Pinpin Zheng and Hua Fu
Key Laboratory of Public Health Safety, Ministry of Education, School of Public Health, Fudan University, Shanghai, China

Dongyun Yang
School of Statistics and Management, Shanghai University of Finance and Economics, Shanghai, China

Becky Freeman and Simon Chapman
School of Public Health, University of Sydney, Sydney, Australia

Khaled El Emam
Electronic Health Information Laboratory, Children's Hospital of Eastern Ontario Research Institute, Ottawa, Ontario, Canada
Paediatrics, University of Ottawa, Ottawa, Ontario, Canada

Saeed Samet, Fida Dankar and Aleksander Essex
Electronic Health Information Laboratory, Children's Hospital of Eastern Ontario Research Institute, Ottawa, Ontario, Canada

Jun Hu and Liam Peyton
School of Electrical Engineering and Computer Science, University of Ottawa, Ottawa, Ontario, Canada

Craig Earle
Institute for Clinical Evaluative Sciences, Toronto, Ontario, Canada

Gayatri C. Jayaraman
Public Health Agency of Canada, Ottawa, Ontario, Canada
Department of Epidemiology and Community Medicine, University of Ottawa, Ottawa, Ontario, Canada

Murat Kantarcioglu
Computer Science, University of Texas at Dallas, Dallas, Texas, United States of America

Tom Wong
Public Health Agency of Canada, Ottawa, Ontario, Canada
Division of Infectious Diseases, University of Ottawa, Ottawa, Ontario, Canada

Salahuddin Swati and Zafar Shahid
COMSATS Institute of Information Technology, Abbottabad, Pakistan

Khizar Hayat
College of Arts and Sciences, University of Nizwa, Nizwa, Oman

Michael Bridges
Astrophysics Group, Cavendish Laboratory, Cambridge, United Kingdom

Elizabeth A. Heron, Colm O'Dushlaine, Ricardo Segurado, Derek Morris, Aiden Corvin, Michael Gill and Carlos Pinto
Neuropsychiatric Genetics Research Group, Department of Psychiatry, Trinity College, Dublin, Ireland

Helen Keyes and Aleksandra Dlugokencka
Department of Psychology, Anglia Ruskin University, Cambridge, United Kingdom

Putri W. Novianti, Kit C. B. Roes and Marinus J. C. Eijkemans
Biostatistics & Research Support, Julius Center for Health Sciences and Primary Care, University Medical Center Utrecht, Utrecht, The Netherlands

Vipin Srivastava
School of Physics, University of Hyderabad, Hyderabad, India
Centre for Neural and Cognitive Sciences, University of Hyderabad, Hyderabad, India

Suchitra Sampath
Centre for Neural and Cognitive Sciences, University of Hyderabad, Hyderabad, India

David J. Parker
Department of Physiology, Development and Neuroscience, University of Cambridge, Cambridge, United Kingdom

Shusen Zhou
School of Information and Electrical Engineering, Ludong University, Yantai, Shandong, China

Qingcai Chen and Xiaolong Wang
Shenzhen Graduate School, Harbin Institute of Technology, Shenzhen, Guangdong, China

Xubao Chen
School of Computer Science and Engineering, Northwestern Polytechnical University, Xi'an, China

Liaojun Pang
School of Life Sciences and Technology, Xidian University, Xi'an, China

Weisong Shi
Department of Computer Science, Wayne State University, Detroit, Michigan, United States of America

Huixian Li
School of Computer Science and Engineering, Northwestern Polytechnical University, Xi'an, China
Department of Computer Science, Wayne State University, Detroit, Michigan, United States of America

Oded Berger-Tal and David Saltz
Mitrani Department of Desert Ecology, Jacob Blaustein Institutes for Desert Research, Ben-Gurion University of the Negev, Midreshet Ben-Gurion, Israel

Jonathan Nathan
Department of Solar Energy and Environmental Physics, Jacob Blaustein Institutes for Desert Research, Ben-Gurion University of the Negev, Midreshet Ben-Gurion, Israel

Ehud Meron
Department of Solar Energy and Environmental Physics, Jacob Blaustein Institutes for Desert Research, Ben-Gurion University of the Negev, Midreshet Ben-Gurion, Israel
Physics Department, Ben-Gurion University of the Negev, Beer Sheva, Israel

Changji Wang, Yuan Li, Xiaonan Xia and Kangjia Zheng
School of Information Science and Technology, Sun Yat-sen University, Guangzhou, China
Guangdong Province Information Security Key Laboratory, Sun Yat-sen University, Guangzhou, China

Yumin Yuan
School of Applied Mathematics, Xiamen University of Technology, Xiamen, China

Qian Zhan
University of Science and Technology Beijing, Beijing, China,

Hua Huang
University of Xiamen, Xiamen, China

Yuanyuan Sun, Rudan Xu and Ruiqing Kong
College of Computer Science and Technology, Dalian University of Technology, Dalian, China

Lina Chen
National Astronomical Observatories, Chinese Academy of Sciences, Beijing, China

Rui Fan, Yan Chen and Ke Xu
State Key Laboratory of Software Development Environment, Beihang University, Beijing, P. R. China

Jichang Zhao
School of Economics and Management, Beihang University, Beijing, P. R. China

Ken Halvorsen and Wesley P. Wong
Immune Disease Institute/Program in Cellular and Molecular Medicine, Harvard Medical School and Children's Hospital Boston, Boston, Massachusetts, United States of America
Department of Biological Chemistry and Molecular Pharmacology, Harvard Medical School, Boston, Massachusetts, United States of America

Anthony Bonato and Paweł Prałat
Department of Mathematics, Ryerson University, Toronto, Ontario, Canada

David F. Gleich
Computer Science Department, Purdue University, West Lafayette, Indiana, United States of America

Myunghwan Kim
Electrical Engineering Department, Stanford University, Stanford, California, United States of America

Dieter Mitsche
Laboratoire J.A. Dieudonné, Université de Nice Sophia-Antipolis, Nice, France

Yanhua Tian
Department of Mathematics and Statistics, York University, Toronto, Ontario, Canada

Index